Canon Law in the Anglican Communion

CANON LAW IN THE ANGLICAN COMMUNION

A Worldwide Perspective

NORMAN DOE

Senior Lecturer
Cardiff Law School
University of Wales

CLARENDON PRESS · OXFORD
1998

Oxford University Press, Great Clarendon Street, Oxford OX2 6DP
Oxford New York
Athens Auckland Bangkok Bogota Buenos Aires
Calcutta Cape Town Chennai Dar es Salaam
Delhi Florence Hong Kong Istanbul Karachi
Kuala Lumpur Madras Madrid Melbourne Mexico City
Mumbai Nairobi Paris São Paolo Singapore
Taipei Tokyo Toronto Warsaw
and associated companies in
Berlin Ibadan

Oxford is a registered trade mark of Oxford University Press

Published in the United States
by Oxford University Press Inc., New York

British Library Cataloguing in Publication Data
Data available

Library of Congress Cataloging in Publication Data
Doe, Norman.
Canon law in the Anglican communion: a worldwide perspective/
Norman Doe.
p. cm.
Includes bibliographical references and index.
1. Canon law—Anglican communion. I. Title.
262.9'83—dc21 98–12335
ISBN 0–19–826782–7

1 3 5 7 9 10 8 6 4 2

Typeset by Hope Services (Abingdon) Ltd.
Printed in Great Britain
on acid-free paper by
Bookcraft Ltd., Midsomer Norton, Somerset

Contents

Preface

The Anglican Communion still awaits a definitive treatment of the canon law of its member churches. Unlike the Roman Catholic Church, which has its Code of Canon Law 1983 containing 'universal law' applicable to the Latin Church throughout the world, the Anglican Communion has neither a central legislative body competent to legislate for all member churches nor, consequently, a body of globally binding law. Each church in the Communion is autonomous, with its own constitution, its own *corpus* of canons and other regulatory instruments. This book is an attempt to describe comparatively the legal systems of individual churches within the Anglican Communion, their similarities and their differences, and one of its central questions is whether it is possible to speak of 'Anglican canon law', a family of identifiable principles shared by all churches. The book has grown from discussions with students studying for the LL M in Canon Law, set up at the Cardiff Law School in 1991 as a collaborative venture with St Michael's Theological College, Llandaff. A persistent issue for those involved with the course, an issue which needless to say is of considerably wider interest and significance, has been whether for Anglicans 'communion' is characterized by a common legal tradition. The absence of a rudimentary text treating this subject directly has been a cause of frustration for many, and to the students on the course, for their tolerance with the process of experimentation, I owe an enormous debt of gratitude.

For the academic session 1996–97, the Cardiff Law School kindly gave me study leave to work on this project. A generous grant from the Isla Johnston Trust, managed by the Representative Body of my own church, the Church in Wales, enabled me to study at various libraries outside Cardiff. Two special privileges came to me during the year. I am extremely grateful to the President and Fellows of Magdalen College, Oxford, who elected me an honorary member of the senior common room for the academic year, particularly to Dr David Ibbetson, a law fellow at the college, who, along with his colleagues, made my stay there such a memorable, pleasurable and stimulating experience. Moreover, whilst I still have a great fondness for Magdalene College, Cambridge, where my doctoral studies covered a little of the work of the medieval canonists, it is to Magdalen College, Oxford, that the graduates of the Cardiff LL M owe thanks for hosting their annual reunion, organized by the Revd. John Masding, a former demi at the college. I am equally grateful, for a visiting fellowship during the Hilary Term 1997, to the governors of Pusey House, Oxford, where many happy hours were spent in the magnificent library, and in the convivial company of the Principal, the Revd. Philip Ursell, the Chapter, the Revd. William Davage, Priest Librarian and Custodian of the Library, and the Revd. Kenneth Macnab, Priest Librarian and Archivist, as well as the many students of the university for whom the House and its Chapel are home at Oxford. Indeed, it was at Pusey House in January 1980 that I met the Revd. Wayne Hankey, an essay by whom later provoked this search for a fundamental Anglican canon law; it was at that meeting, incidentally, that I first drank a cup of Earl Grey tea. The opportunity afforded by both Magdalen and Pusey, to experiment with occasional papers on law and religion was invaluable, and to Dr Frank Robson and the Revd. John Rees, Chairman and Treasurer respectively of the Ecclesiastical Law Society and based at Oxford, I owe much for their suggestions and encouragement.

The process of gathering in materials from the churches of the Anglican Communion was time-consuming but enjoyable, and I should very much like to record my thanks to David McIntyre, Secretary General of the Church in Wales, for his advice concerning the harvesting of these. Very many provincial officers and bishops of the member churches of the Communion responded generously to my request for materials, and without their kind assistance, this book would not have been possible: the Ven. James Boyles (Toronto), Revd. John Cobb (Chile), Bernard Georges, (Seychelles), Bishop Sergio Carranza-Gomez (Mexico), Revd. Richard Chance (Botswana), Susan Edward (Juba), John Govier (Brazil), Revd. Dr Bruce Kaye, Mark Pickhaver and Mr Justice Peter Young (Australia), Martin Gardham (Papua New Guinea), Francis Helminski (Minnesota), George Koshy (Madras), Dr V. S. Lall (New Delhi), Floyd Lalwet and Revd. Rex Rayes (Philippines), Bishop Carlos Lozano (Madrid), Rt Revd. Ghais Malik and Barbara Pegen (Cairo), Peter Mang'ati (Tanzania), David Meredith (Dublin), David Bindon and R. A. I. Nairn (New Zealand), Revd. Canon Donald Nickerson (New York), Most Revd. Livingstone Nkoyoyo (Uganda), Franco Sciortino (Venezuela), Revd. Telmo Silva (Portugal), Rt. Revd. John Tan (Singapore), Anne McGavin and R. Whiteman (Edinburgh), and Revd. Nathaniel Uematsu (Tokyo). Deirdre Martin, and the staff at the Anglican Communion Office at Lambeth, provided invaluable help with the documents located there. For translations from Swahili, I thank Katarina Juma, from Portuguese, Anna Phillips, and from Japanese, Michelle Gooden. I have endeavoured to describe the law, contained in those documents made available to me, as it stood in June 1997. Any errors in the exposition are my responsibility entirely.

The word processor rendered the production of the typescript relatively painless, but special thanks are due to Linda Mackleworth, and to Val Simpson, at the Cardiff Law School, for their patience and help. For their unfailing, cheerful inspiration and assistance with the subject itself, I should also like to thank the Revd. Irving Hamer, from my own church of St. Edward's, Cardiff, Susan Mansell, and the tireless and constructive criticism given by Mark Hill and Brian Hanson, two of the United Kingdom's leading ecclesiastical lawyers. Similarly, I wish to thank the staff at Oxford University Press, especially Mr Christopher Rycroft, commissioning editor at the Press, for his commitment to the project, as well as to his predecessor Richard Hart to whom I first suggested the study. Finally, I should like to thank for their kindness and constant support my family: my mother, father, and brother, my parents-in-law, and above all my wife Heather and our children Rachel, Elizabeth and Edward.

C.N.D.
Cardiff,
13 October 1997

Abbreviations

Complete references to the legal texts of individual churches are to be found in the Bibliography. For the purposes of footnotes, normally the abbreviations listed below are used, unless the context is not obvious in which case, for the sake of clarity, the full title is given. Resolutions of the Lambeth Conference are to be found in E. Coleman (ed.), *Resolutions of the Twelve Lambeth Conferences 1867–1988* (Toronto, 1992).

ACC	Anglican Consultative Council
Acts of Convocation	A. F. Smethurst, H. R. Wilson and H. Riley (eds.), *Acts of the Convocations of Canterbury and York* (London, 1961)
AR	Thirty-Nine Articles of Religion (1562, confirmed 1571)
Art.	Article
Australia	Anglican Church of Australia
BCP	Book of Common Prayer
Bermuda	Anglican Church of Bermuda
Brazil	Episcopal Anglican Church of Brazil
Burundi	Church of the Province of Burundi
CA	Court of Appeal
Can(s)	Canon(s)
Canada	Anglican Church of Canada
Central Africa	Church of the Province of Central Africa
Chile	Anglican Church of Chile
Const.	Constitution
Cuba	Episcopal Church of Cuba
ECUSA	Protestant Episcopal Church in the United States of America
England	Church of England
Evans & Wright	G. R. Evans and J. R. Wright. (eds.), *The Anglican Tradition: A Handbook of Sources* (London, 1991)
GS	General Synod
Halsbury	Halsbury, *Laws of England*, Volume 14, *Ecclesiastical Law* (4th edn., London, 1975)
H Ct	High Court
HL	House of Lords
Indian Ocean	Church of the Province of the Indian Ocean
Ireland	Church of Ireland
Japan	Holy Catholic Church in Japan (Nippon Sei Ko Kai)
Jerusalem	Episcopal Church in Jerusalem and the Middle East

Kenya	Church of the Province of Kenya
Korea	Anglican Church of Korea
LC	Lambeth Conference
LFCE	N. Doe, *The Legal Framework of the Church of England*: *A Critical Study in a Comparative Context* (Oxford, 1996)
Marshall	P. V. Marshall, *Prayer Book Parallels*: *Anglican Liturgy in America*, 2 Volumes (New York, 1989)
Melanesia	Church of the Province of Melanesia
Mexico	Anglican Church of Mexico
New Zealand	Anglican Church in Aotearoa, New Zealand and Polynesia
Nigeria	Church of the Province of Nigeria
North India	United Church of North India
Papua New Guinea	Anglican Church of (the Province of) Papua New Guinea
Phillimore	R. Phillimore, *The Ecclesiastical Law of the Church of England*, 2 Volumes (2nd edn., London, 1895)
Philippines	Episcopal Church in the (Province of the) Philippines
Portugal	Lusitanian Church (Portuguese Episcopal Church)
Puerto Rico	Episcopal Church of Puerto Rico
Res.	Resolution
Rwanda	Church of the Province of Rwanda
Scotland	Scottish Episcopal Church
SO	Standing Order
South East Asia	Church of the Province of South East Asia
South India	United Church of South India
Southern Africa	Church of the Province of Southern Africa
Southern Cone	Anglican Church of the Southern Cone of America
Spain	Spanish Reformed Episcopal Church
Sudan	Church of the Province of the Sudan
Sykes & Booty	S. Sykes and J. Booty (eds.), *The Study of Anglicanism* (London, 1988)
Tanzania	Church of the Province of Tanzania
Uganda	Church of the Province of Uganda
Venezuela	Extra-Provincial Diocese of Venezuela
Wales	Church in Wales
West Africa	Church of the Province of West Africa
West Indies	Church of the Province of the West Indies
Zaire	Church of the Province of Zaire

Table of Secular Legislation

In the following Table, unless its origin is obvious from the title of the enactment, the state in which the legislation was enacted is indicated in brackets after each entry. In the case of statutes enacted by the United Kingdom parliament for application to Anglican churches in the British Isles, the church to which it applies is indicated.

Table of Cases

Introduction

The Reverend Wayne Hankey wrote in an essay in 1988:

the diversity of the canon law and the attitudes toward it in the various Anglican Churches is overwhelming . . . Strict legal uniformity is not to be expected in the Anglican Communion, nor can it be found. But there are common legal traditions and patterns. The Communion has a unity in fundamental canon law, although it cannot be doubted that this unity is at risk.[1]

The function of this book is to explore these challenging propositions. At present no book exists which contains a comparative study of the contemporary legal systems of churches in the Anglican Communion. However, important studies have been carried out this century, to draw together common legal ideas and principles, by Henry Lowther Clarke (Archbishop of Melbourne) in 1924,[2] by G. W. O. Addleshaw and, with others, J. W. G. Wand in 1948,[3] and by the American lawyer Spencer Ervin, who in the 1960s embarked on an ambitious but regrettably unfinished survey of the legal systems of individual churches.[4] Indeed, the subject is one upon which some scholars are engaged currently, notably Phillip Thomas.[5] By way of contrast, in a small handful of churches lawyers are beginning to produce a literature on the particular laws of their churches. In the United Kingdom, recent years have witnessed a series of books on

---

[1] W. Hankey, 'Canon law', in S. W. Sykes and J. Booty (eds.), *The Study of Anglicanism* (London, 1988), 200 at 206, 213.

[2] H. L. Clarke, *Constitutional Church Government in the Dominions beyond the Seas and in other parts of the Anglican Communion* (London, 1924); this treats the churches separately: there is little detailed comparative discussion of legal subjects as between churches.

[3] G. W. O. Addleshaw, 'The law and constitutions of the church overseas', in E. R. Morgan and R. Lloyd, *The Mission of the Anglican Communion* (London, 1948); J. W. C. Wand (ed.), *The Anglican Communion: A Survey* (Oxford, 1948): like Clarke (n. 2), this treats churches separately.

[4] S. Ervin, *Some Deficiencies in the Canon Law of the American Episcopal Church* (New York, 1961); *An Introduction to Anglican Polity* (Pennsylvania, 1964); *The Polity of the Church of Ireland* (Pennsylvania, 1964); *The Polity of the Church of the Province of South Africa* (Pennsylvania, 1965); *The Political and Ecclesiastical History of the Anglican Church in Canada* (Pennsylvania, 1967); and *The Development of the Synodical System in the Anglican Church of Canada* (Pennsylvania, 1969).

[5] See e.g. P. Thomas, 'A family affair: the pattern of constitutional authority in the Anglican Communion', in S. W. Sykes (ed.), *Authority in the Anglican Communion* (Toronto, 1987), 119.

the law of the Church of England, in the form of both commentaries,[6] and practical handbooks,[7] or on specific aspects of it.[8] A similar trend may be found in some other churches, in the USA,[9] in Ireland,[10] and in Australia,[11] for example, but most Anglican churches are not well-served by expositions of their particular laws.

This volume aims to provide an analysis of the modern constitutions, canons and other forms of regulatory instrument of churches in the worldwide Anglican Communion. It seeks both to describe the law, the similarities and the differences between individual ecclesiastical legal systems, and the ecclesiastical jurisprudence underlying it. In particular it examines whether there is such a phenomenon as 'Anglican canon law'. The study opens with a discussion of the legal position of churches under the secular laws of the states in which they exist, the forms of regulation employed by churches, and the processes by which they are made. After a description of the institutional organization of individual national, regional and provincial churches, including arrangements for the resolution of ecclesiastical conflict, the study moves to an analysis of laws on ministry: the ministry of primates, metropolitans (or archbishops), diocesan bishops and other episcopal offices; the ministry of priests and deacons; and the ministry of the laity and lay office-holders in the church. Law on ministry is followed by a discussion of how churches regulate the subjects of doctrine and public worship, and the study explores basic rules about the administration of the rites of the church: baptism, confirmation, holy communion, marriage, divorce and re-marriage, confession and funerals. The penultimate chapter deals with perhaps the most detailed body of law possessed by churches, that of property, and the study ends with a discussion of legal relations between Anglican churches and of ecumenical law on their relations with other Christian churches. This presentation, of a practical description of the subject within its jurisprudential setting, is intended to make the studies accessible and of use and interest both to the practitioners of church law in the individual churches of the Communion, and to members of other churches seeking to understand the institutional and legal organization of Anglican churches. The studies contain little

---

[6] M. Hill, *Ecclesiastical Law* (London, 1995), and T. Briden and B. Hanson (eds.), *Moore's Introduction to English Canon Law* (3rd edn., London, 1992).

[7] L. Leeder, *Ecclesiastical Law Handbook* (London, 1997).

[8] R. D. H. Bursell, *Liturgy, Order and the Law* (Oxford, 1996).

[9] E. A. White and J. A. Dykman (ed.), *Annotated Constitution and Canons of the Episcopal Church in the USA* (2nd edn., New York, 1954) (Supplement, 1991).

[10] J. L. B. Deane, *The Church of Ireland Handbook* (Dublin, 1982); see also A. Ford, J. McGuire and K. Ine (eds.), *As By Law Established: The Church of Ireland Since the Reformation* (Dublin, 1995).

[11] J. Davis, *Australian Anglicans and their Constitution* (1993); B. Kaye, *A Church without Walls: Being Anglican in Australia* (1995).

theological and historical material, and this for many may be an unforgivable defect – theology and history are treated only when this is necessary to elucidate the meaning of actual church law.[12]

The Anglican Communion, a fellowship of churches in communion with the See of Canterbury, is composed of thirty-seven self-governing churches, each organized as a national,[13] regional,[14] or provincial church,[15] and includes extra-provincial dioceses,[16] and united churches;[17] special relations of communion exist between the Communion members themselves and other Christian churches.[18] For the purposes of the analysis of individual legal systems, sometimes churches may be placed in natural groups existing as such as a result of their historical origins and associations. There are similarities between the legal systems of Anglican churches in the British Isles, commonly deriving rules from the legal order of the Church of England.[19] The laws of the Anglican church in the

[12] See Gerald Bray's distinguished and comprehensive study, *The Historic Anglican Canons: 1529–1947* (Woodbridge, 1998): the existence of this volume now enables, for the first time, a meaningful study of the historical pedigree of actual rules found in contemporary canonical systems.

[13] The Church of England; the Protestant Episcopal Church in the United States of America; the Anglican Church of Australia; the Episcopal Church of Brazil; the Church of Ceylon (Sri Lanka); the Holy Catholic Church in Japan (*Nippon Sei Ko Kai*); the Anglican Church of Mexico; the Anglican Church of Papua New Guinea; the Philippine Episcopal Church; the Anglican Church of Korea; the Scottish Episcopal Church; the Church in Wales; and the Anglican Church of Zaire; see Ch. 1 for qualifications to this categorization.

[14] The Church of Ireland; the Anglican Church of Canada; the Church of the Province of the Indian Ocean; the Episcopal Church in Jerusalem and the Middle East; the Church of the Province of South East Asia; the Anglican Church of the Southern Cone of America; and the Church of the Province of the West Indies.

[15] The Church of the Province of Aotearoa, New Zealand and Polynesia; the Church of the Province of Burundi; the Church of the Province of Central Africa; the Church of the Province of Kenya; the Church of the Province of Melanesia; the Church of the Province of Myanmar; the Church of the Province of Nigeria; the Church of the Province of Rwanda; the Church of the Province of South Africa; the Church of the Province of the Sudan; the Church of the Province of Tanzania; and the Church of the Province of Uganda.

[16] The Anglican Church of Bermuda; the Episcopal Church of Cuba; the Falkland Islands; the Lusitanian Church (the Portuguese Episcopal Church); and the Spanish Reformed Episcopal Church.

[17] The United Church of North India; the United Church of South India; the United Church of Bangladesh; the United Church of Pakistan.

[18] For example, other churches in communion with the Church of England are: the Old Catholic Churches (in Austria, Croatia, the former Czechoslovakia, Germany, the Netherlands, and Poland), the Philippine Independent Church, and the Mar Thoma Church; churches in a special relationship with the Church of England are: the Nordic and Baltic Lutheran Churches and the Evangelical Church in Germany: see Ch. 12.

[19] The Church of England was established by a series of secular parliamentary statutes in the sixteenth century; the legal union in 1801 between the Church of England and the Church of Ireland (forming the United Church of England and Ireland) was dissolved by parliamentary statute of 1869; the Church of England in the four Welsh

Philippines and some of those in Latin America are,[20] broadly, derivative of the substantive law of ECUSA, the Protestant Episcopal Church in the United States of America. The laws of most of the African churches, organized as provincial churches,[21] resemble closely the law of the church in the Province of Southern Africa. Melanesian canon law has been influenced, at least in part, by the canon law of the church in Aotearoa, New Zealand and Polynesia.[22] Within these groupings, therefore, it is not surprising to find similarities in the substantive law. But the laws of some churches do not easily fall into groups: the canon law of the church in the West Indies contains direct parallels with the law of both ECUSA and of the church in Southern Africa.[23] Indeed, in Australia it is difficult to speak of a canon law applicable throughout the provincially organized national church: canons of the General Synod concerning order and good government are operative in the dioceses only when adopted by ordinance of the diocesan synods; and yet, in many areas there are direct points of contact between these 'provisional' national canons and those currently operative in the Church of England.[24]

The studies in this volume seek to elucidate the laws of individual churches located in a number of obvious formal documents. An attempt has been made to gather from each church the following sources: the constitution; the canons; samples of diocesan law; liturgical rubrics found in the service books; informal administrative rules, or 'quasi-legislation', contained in 'guidelines' and other such policy documents; samples of

dioceses was disestablished by parliamentary statute of 1914 in 1920; the Scottish Episcopal Church was disestablished in 1689.

[20] The Episcopal Church of the Philippines, founded in 1901, became a province autonomous from ECUSA in 1990; the Church in Japan was founded as a result of missionary work in 1859 by, amongst others, the American Episcopal Church, the Church of England and the Church in Canada. The Anglican Church of the Southern Cone of America became a province in 1983, a result of the Archbishop of Canterbury relinquishing metropolitical jurisdiction in 1974 for the dioceses of, *inter alia*, Chile, Bolivia and Peru.

[21] The Province of West Africa was inaugurated in 1951 and that of Central Africa in 1955; the Province of Uganda, Rwanda and Burundi was inaugurated in 1961 and in 1980 these became independent provinces; in 1969, the Province of East Africa was divided into the Provinces of Kenya and of Tanzania; the Province of Nigeria was formed by a division of the Province of West Africa in 1979; the Province of Zaire was formed as a result of discussions in 1992.

[22] In 1861 the church in New Zealand founded the missionary diocese of Melanesia which, in 1975, became an independent province.

[23] The Province of the West Indies was formed in 1883; its diocese of Venezuela joined the IXth Province of ECUSA in 1982.

[24] The first General Synod was convened in Australia in 1872 and from 1854 various secular parliamentary statutes of state legislatures have constituted the Church of England in those states as a voluntary organization culminating in the enactment of the church's current constitution in 1962; the Australian church's diocese of Papua New Guinea became an autonomous province in 1977.

judicial decisions of church courts and tribunals; secular state law, in the form of legislation and judicial decisions, applicable to Anglican churches; and secondary literature. The attempt has proved successful in relation to most churches, but not all.[25] Whilst the vast majority of churches possess a formal written constitution, some do not;[26] thirty-seven constitutions have been examined.[27] Some churches do not have a body of canons,[28] but the canons of twenty-nine national, regional or provincial churches have been studied. The laws or other forms of regulation of twenty dioceses, from twelve churches, are included in the study and reference is made to the liturgical books of sixteen churches. The evidence from decisions of church courts is weakest: this was available in only half a dozen churches, notably England, Ireland, and ECUSA; in several churches, replies indicated that church courts simply do not sit. A little information is contained on the secular law of twenty-one churches. Equally, an attempt has been made both to cover the law of all churches in the Anglican Communion and to produce parity of treatment as between churches. Consequently, when a subject is treated in the formal law of a church, descriptions of the law are contained in the text, along with evidence for the existence of a general principle of fundamental Anglican canon law, and the evidence for all propositions is provided in the footnotes, which carry references to formal legal texts. Sometimes, however, when a particular arrangement is found in the law of only one or a small number of churches, discussion in the text is devoted exclusively to the law of the particular church in question. From these sources an attempt is made to describe uniformity, diversity, whether churches follow the state, and whether or not churches employ a minimalist approach to ecclesiastical regulation.

A paragraph may be devoted here to terminology used in these studies. Throughout the book the expression 'canon law' is used to signify the collection of rules, found in a diversity of sources of formal law and other regulatory instruments of a particular church, designed to fulfil the purposes for which that church exists in the public sphere of its internal life: governmental, ministerial, pastoral, doctrinal, liturgical, ritual and proprietorial. By way of contrast, for the purposes of this study, the

---

[25] I have been unsuccessful in obtaining legal texts concerning the Church of Ceylon (Sri Lanka), and the Church of the Province of Myanmar. The Holy Catholic Church in China (*Chung Hua Sheng Hui*) is not included in this study: for this see e.g. T. Lambert, *The Resurrection of the Chinese Church* (London, 1991).

[26] For the established Church of England, the constitution is dispersed in a complex of parliamentary statutes, measures and canons of the General Synod, and in judicial decisions of the church and state courts; the Scottish Episcopal Church has no formal written 'constitution': this is found in its Code of Canons.

[27] See e.g. Rwanda, Draft Constitution 1996.

[28] See e.g. North India and South India: these have *Constitutions* only; for a full list of constitutions, canons and other documents studied, see the Bibliography.

understanding of 'Anglican canon law' is rather different. Its meaning is, needless to say, rather more diffuse. It is that *corpus* of principles, deduced from the substantive and procedural law of individual churches, shared by the majority of member churches of the Anglican Communion. The construction of such a concept is not easy, and a majoritarian approach is notoriously susceptible to criticism. On the positive side, with respect to many areas of ecclesiastical life, churches share a common legal treatment of particular subjects and problems. When the laws of the vast majority of churches contain the same rule on a given subject, and similarity is expressed either through the same linguistic formula or through the substantive content or purpose of a rule, for practical purposes from this it may be understood that a principle of Anglican canon law emerges. When a bare majority of churches shares a rule, assumptions about the existence of a general principle are more problematic. Resolutions of the Lambeth Conference are important in this regard. Frequently these are implemented by member churches of the Communion, and their terms are incorporated, either expressly or impliedly, in the actual law of individual churches. Sometimes, however, this is not the case. On the negative side, often the laws of the vast majority of churches, or of a bare majority, are silent on a subject. A small number of churches may deal with a subject, but most do not. Obviously, this is the most problematic situation for the search for general principles. On the one hand, of course, the absence of shared or common laws on a subject may mean that there are no general principles of Anglican canon law on that subject. On the other hand, however, the general principle is rooted in the silence of the law: that most churches do not require X or forbid Y or permit Z. In these circumstances it is possible only to conclude that, in relation to a given subject, A group of churches shares X principle, B group shares Y principle, and in C group the laws are silent. Whilst this book presents the evidence, or lack of it, for the existence of general principles of Anglican canon law, the studies in it proceed on the assumption that criteria to determine their existence may be formulated by reference to shared institutions, rules, procedures and jurisprudence.

The Lambeth Conference meets in the summer of 1998, and, on the practical level, it is hoped that this book may provide material to assist in the quest for a distinct Anglican identity, at least from a legal perspective. After all, law may legitimately be considered a fruitful indication of the way in which any church, as with any society, views itself. Indeed, the current renewal of interest in church law, with the establishment world-wide of societies devoted to its study, in the United Kingdom and Ireland, in Canada, and in the near future in the USA,[29] generates for law a higher

---

[29] The British Isles has the Ecclesiastical Law Society and Canada its Church Law Association of Canada; Francis Helminski (Minnesota) is currently working on the establishment of an Ecclesiastical Law Society in the USA.

profile today. The legal systems of churches are changing rapidly and, when a church proposes the introduction of new law, or when there is a particular legal problem or gap in existing law, the studies here may provide guidance as to how fellow churches in the Anglican Communion deal with subjects and problems. On the level of ecclesiology, it is also hoped that the studies might provide an introduction to the world of comparative canon law, and the terms and nature of ecclesiastical order and justice in Anglicanism.

1
Churches, States and Laws

Churches in the Anglican Communion have clearly defined ideas, expressed in juridic form, about their nature and purpose. Living as they do in the wider legal environment, the relationship between these churches and the secular states in which they exist gives rise to particular questions about the legal position of churches in civil law and the status of their internal systems of rules. Within the church, competence to legislate is distributed to synodical institutions in which both the episcopate and the clergy and laity of the church are represented. As a basic principle, the exercise of legislative power is confined to national, provincial or diocesan assemblies: it is not usually enjoyed at the lowest levels of the church. This chapter concentrates on the main bodies of formal church legislation: fundamental declarations and principles, national and provincial constitutions and canons, diocesan law and delegated legislation, as well as the increasingly extensive use of ecclesiastical quasi-legislation, informal administrative rules. Some churches possess all of these sources, others do not.

CANONICAL DEFINITIONS OF THE CHURCH

Resolutions of Lambeth Conferences, which broadly enjoy a recommendatory rather than a binding force in individual churches in the Communion, provide a reasonable starting point from which to analyse canonical concepts about the nature and governance of Anglican churches. The nature of the Anglican Communion itself, of individual churches within it, and of legal and extra-legal relations between them, is summed up in four basic ideas: 'the true constitution of the Catholic Church involves the principle of the autonomy of particular Churches based upon a common faith and order'; within the Communion churches 'uphold and propagate the Catholic and Apostolic faith and order as they are generally set forth in the Book of Common Prayer' authorized in each church; they are 'particular or national' churches and, as such, 'promote within each of their territories a national expression of Christian faith, life and worship'; and these churches are bound together 'not by a central legislative and executive authority, but by a mutual loyalty sustained through the common counsel of the bishops in conference'.[1]

[1] LC 1930, Ress. 48, 49; see also Thirty-Nine Articles, Art. 19: the church 'is a

First, looking to the actual laws of churches, the Lambeth distinction between national and particular churches is a useful generalization. According to their individual constitutional documents churches within the Communion fall into five broad categories: national, provincial, regional, extra-provincial or united.[2] National churches are those in which the church's territorial boundaries correspond to those of the secular state in which they exist: they may be organized on the basis of a group of provinces (such in the USA),[3] or on the basis of a single province which corresponds to a single secular state (such as Sudan);[4] alternatively a province (as in Wales) or provinces (as in England) may correspond to secular jurisdictional divisions within a state.[5] Regional churches are those operating territorially over a number of secular states: such churches may be organized as a single province (such as in the West Indies), or more (as in Ireland),[6] or as non-provincial (such as the Episcopal Church in Jerusalem and the Middle East).[7] Extra-provincial churches are those organized on the basis of a diocese which is not part of a province: some are

congregation of faithful men, in which the pure Word of God is preached, and the sacraments duly administered according to Christ's ordinance'; for the relationship between churches of the Communion, see Ch. 12.

[2] For historical material on these distinctions, see generally H. L. Clarke, *Constitutional Church Government* (London, 1924), 1–14; J. W. G. Wand, *The Anglican Communion* (Oxford, 1948), 1–21; G. F. S. Gray, *The Anglican Communion* (London, 1958); W. Hankey, 'Canon law', in S. Sykes and J. Booty (eds.), *The Study of Anglicanism* (London, 1988), 200. For the institutional organization of churches, see Ch. 2.

[3] ECUSA, Const. Preamble: it is the Protestant Episcopal Church 'in the United States of America'; see P. M. Dawley, *The Episcopal Church and its Work* (Revised edn., New York, 1961) esp. Pt. 1.

[4] Sudan, Const. Art. I(a): 'By "Province" is meant the Episcopal Church of the Sudan . . . in the Republic of the Sudan'; Papua New Guinea, Const. Preamble: it is a 'National Church within the Anglican Communion'; Tanzania, Const. II.3(a): the Province exists within 'the boundaries of the united Government of Tanzania'; Korea, Const. I.1: 'The Anglican Church of Korea is a Province of three dioceses exercising jurisdiction over the whole of the Korean peninsula and its adjacent islands'.

[5] England, the Provinces of Canterbury and York extend beyond England: York includes the Isle of Man (see K. F. W. Gumbley, 'Church legislation in the Isle of Man', *Ecclesiastical Law Journal*, 3 (15) (1994), 240) and Canterbury the Channel Islands (Channel Islands (Church Legislation) Measure 1931, s. 1); the Diocese of Europe is treated for some purposes 'as if the Diocese were in the province of Canterbury' (Diocese in Europe Measure 1980, s. 6); Wales, Welsh Church Act 1914, Preamble: see n. 38.

[6] Southern Cone, Const. Art. 2: the province covers, *inter alia*, the Republics of Argentina, Paraguay and Peru; Melanesia, Const. Art. 3: the area of the Province of Melanesia comprises the Solomon Islands, the Republic of Vanuatu and the Territory of New Caledonia.

[7] The Episcopal Church of Jerusalem and the Middle East is not classed as a 'province' in the preamble of its constitution, but the term is used in later Articles; correspondence included in the document, from the Secretary General of the Anglican Consultative Council (20/6/78), describes the church as 'an autonomous Anglican Province'; see also P. Osterbye, *The Church in Israel* (Lund, Sweden, 1970), 180.

under the jurisdiction of the Archbishop of Canterbury (such as Bermuda or Ceylon) or of another church (such as Costa Rica or Puerto Rico which are associated with the Episcopal Church in the USA).[8] United churches are those founded as the result of constitutional union between Anglican churches and other Christian churches (such as in South India).[9]

Secondly, the laws of actual churches mirror the general understanding of the Lambeth resolution about the theological nature of individual churches. Perhaps the fullest legal definition appears in the constitution of ECUSA, the Protestant Episcopal Church in the United States of America: the church is 'a constituent member of the Anglican Communion, a Fellowship within the One, Holy, Catholic, and Apostolic Church, of those duly constituted Dioceses, Provinces, and regional Churches in communion with the See of Canterbury, upholding and propagating the historic Faith and Order as set forth in the Book of Common Prayer'.[10] Most legal definitions are narrower, restricted to the statement that the church is 'part of the one, holy, catholic and apostolic church'.[11] Only the law of the church in New Zealand presents a definition of these characteristics.[12] Occasionally the church is described legally as 'a reformed and Protestant Church' as well as being part of the catholic and apostolic church.[13] The law of many churches contains no definition of the church, beyond state-

---

[8] Costa Rica is under the jurisdiction of the House of Bishops of Province IX of ECUSA and Puerto Rico under that of the President Bishop and Synod of Province IX; Cuba is under the jurisdiction of a Metropolitan Council for Cuba. The Lusitanian Church of Portugal and the Spanish Reformed Episcopal Church are under the metropolitical authority of the Archbishop of Canterbury in his capacity as the focus of unity of the Anglican Communion. The extra-provincial diocese of Hong Kong has currently a Commission considering the establishment of a Province.

[9] South India, Const. I: the church is 'constituted by the union of the . . . Church Councils of the South India United Church, the South India Province of the Methodist Church . . . and the dioceses . . . in the [Anglican] Church of India, Burma and Ceylon'; see also North India, Const. II.I.I.2; see generally C. J. Grimes, *Towards an Indian Church* (London, 1946).

[10] ECUSA, Const. Preamble; for the same formula, see West Africa, Const. Preamble (a); for a similar formula, see Canada, Declaration of Principles, Solemn Declaration 1; Melanesia, Cans. A.1.A: the church is 'God's family, his people and the Body of Christ'.

[11] Korea, Const. Preface: the church 'is part of the one, holy, catholic and apostolic Church, the Body of Christ'; Scotland, Can. 1.1; Mexico, Const. Preamble; Japan, General Principles; Central Africa, Fundamental Declarations, 1; compare England, Can. A1: the church 'belongs to the true and apostolic Church of Christ'.

[12] New Zealand, Const. Preamble: 'the Church is the body of which Christ is the head'; 'the Church (a) is One because it is one body, under one head, Jesus Christ; (b) is Holy because the Holy Spirit dwells in its members and guides it in mission; (c) is Catholic because it seeks to proclaim the whole faith to all people to the end of time and (d) is Apostolic because it presents the faith of the apostles and is sent to carry Christ's mission to all the world'.

[13] Ireland, Const. Preamble and Declaration, I.3.

ments of this sort, but rather identifies it by reference to its doctrine and worship.[14]

The third feature of the Lambeth definition, the concept of autonomy, does not commonly appear in explicit form, though arguably the existence of a constitution may of itself be conceived as an explicit declaration of autonomy. The laws of only a few national and provincial churches claim for these churches a right to independence and self-government.[15] Rather, the concept of autonomy is implicit, particularly in constitutional statements, presented in historical form, which describe the process by which individual churches have been founded – in cases, that is, of churches being created as a direct result of a legislative act by a mother church.[16] By way of contrast, the laws of extra-provincial dioceses incorporate provisions enabling the exercise of metropolitical authority by the Archbishop of Canterbury.[17]

Lastly, laws of churches spell out the purposes for which those churches exist in more elaborate fashion than ideas appearing in the Lambeth resolution. Whilst many confine purposes exclusively to purely spiritual matters,[18] some laws include reference to what may be described as the temporal mission of the church.[19] In this context, the practice of listing political activity to promote justice in the world is remarkably common.[20]

[14] Australia, Const. I.I.1; South East Asia, Const. Fundamental Declarations, 1; Tanzania, Const. III; this is the most common approach: see Ch. 7.

[15] See e.g. South East Asia, Const. Fundamental Declarations, 5: 'the Province is a fully autonomous part of the Anglican Communion'; Burundi, Const. Art. 3: 'the right to accept modifications in its . . . internal regulations'; North India, Const. I.IV.4: 'The Church of North India shall be an autonomous Church and free from any control, legal or otherwise, of any Church or Society external to itself'; Korea, Const. Preface: 'in a spirit of self-reliance, self-support and self-sustainment, the Anglican Church of Korea becomes independent and promulgates this new Constitution and Canons'.

[16] See e.g. Philippines, Const. Preamble: 'the Church . . . shall be one Household of Faith, bound together by the common tradition of doctrine, discipline and worship . . . received from the Episcopal Church in the United States of America'; this was to be after a process towards 'the ultimate establishment of an autonomous Church Province in the Philippines'.

[17] See Chs. 4 and 12.

[18] South East Asia, Const. Preamble: '[t]o give glory to God through united and common witness and proclamation of the Gospel of our Lord Jesus Christ'; to 'strengthen and further the Church's fellowship and partnership'; and 'to make disciples of all nations'; see also Sudan, Const. Preamble; Ireland, Const. Preamble, I.3: 'to minister the doctrine and sacraments and discipline of Christ'; for a similar provision see Canada, Declaration of Fundamental Principles, Solemn Declaration, 1.

[19] See e.g. North India, Const. II.I.II: the church must proclaim the gospel and undertake service 'which may include educational, medical, social, agricultural and other service'.

[20] See e.g. Philippines, Const. Art. I.1; Cans. I.2.2(d): one of the functions of the Provincial Synod's Commission on Social Concerns and Development is 'to study the nature and root causes of poverty and underdevelopment in the country and review the participation of the Church in the development process'; for regulations seeking to

The constitution of the church in New Zealand is highly programmatic, presenting probably the most comprehensive statement embracing all of these ideas – the mission of the church includes: 'proclaiming the Gospel of Jesus Christ'; teaching, baptizing and nurturing believers within eucharistic communities; responding to human needs by loving service; seeking 'to transform unjust structures of society, caring for God's creation, and establishing the values of the Kingdom'; the church must advance its mission, safeguard and develop its doctrine and order its affairs.[21]

SECULAR LAW, CHURCHES AND THEIR LAWS

The internal law of a church may spell out its relationship with the state in which it exists: but this is rare and claims to ecclesiastical autonomy are usually stated succinctly and dogmatically.[22] In most states the fundamental relationship of autonomy of a church from the state, based on the principle of freedom and equality of religions,[23] is to be found in secular written constitutions, the terms of which are judicially enforceable.[24] It is not the purpose of this study to analyse this large and complex subject upon which a specialist and abundant literature already exists.[25] This section describes in outline the variety of church-state models which treat directly the legal position of individual churches and the secular legal status of their internal rules. Its purpose is threefold: to suggest that Anglican churches fall into four basic legal categories – established, quasi-established, disestablished and non-established; to analyse the almost global principle that, with regard to the last three categories, secular courts

limit the political activities of clergy, see Social Concerns Resolutions and Statements of the Philippine Episcopal Church (1962–88) (published by the National Commission of Social Justice and Human Rights, 1988) esp. Res. 10 1980; see also Venezuela, Const. II: the church is to contribute to the 'moral and spiritual' welfare of society.

[21] New Zealand, Const. Preamble.

[22] See e.g. North India, Const. I.IV.2: it 'shall of right be free in all spiritual matters from the direction or interposition of any civil government' (spiritual matters are listed as including worship, membership, spiritual office, confession of and instruction in the faith, and church polity); see M. E. Gibbs, *The Anglican Church in India 1600–1970* (Delhi, 1972), 396f.

[23] For the legal meanings of 'religion' see W. Sadurski, 'On legal definitions of "religion"', *Australia Law Journal*, 63 (1989), 834; for European concepts, see the studies in *The Legal Status of Religious Minorities in the Countries of the European Union*, Proceedings of the European Consortium for Church-State Research (Milan, 1994); see also n. 25.

[24] Throughout the studies in this book, where appropriate reference is made to secular cases decided under constitutional provisions on religion.

[25] See e.g. the excellent and exhaustive J. D. van der Vyver and J. Witte (eds.), *Religious Human Rights in Global Perspective*, 2 vols. (The Hague, 1996) and W. Sadurski (ed.), *Law and Religion* (Aldershot, 1992).

treat the internal laws of churches as terms of a consensual compact between their members; and to analyse instances where it has been necessary for the secular courts to determine the possible continuing applicability of English ecclesiastical law.

Established and Quasi-Established Churches

Doctrines of establishment are notoriously difficult to construct. Judicial definitions of establishment, throughout the world, are broadly agreed that establishment involves: action by a state 'to grant legal status, recognition or protection' to a church; 'to confer on a religion or religious body the position of a state religion or a state church'; 'to support a church in the observance of its ordinances and doctrines'; and 'to found or set up a new church or religion'; full establishment may involve duties on the state and the citizen to maintain the established church as well as legal preference to the exclusion of other religious communities.[26] No Anglican church is fully established, and several states forbid the establishment of any church.[27] The canon law of the Church of England describes the church as 'established according to the laws of this realm under the Queen's Majesty': whilst there is no 'Establishment Act' as such, the institutional English church has been formed at least in part by a series of legislative acts of the civil power; the terms or incidents of establishment include the principle that the monarch is 'the highest power under God in the kingdom, and has supreme authority of all persons in all causes, as well ecclesiastical as civil'; the sovereign must join in communion with the church and undertake to maintain and uphold it; the monarch appoints persons to episcopal office (with some bishops having membership of the House of Lords); and the power of the church to enact some forms of legislation, which must be submitted to parliament for approval, is conferred by statute.[28] In so far as the law of the church is treated as part of the

[26] *AG (Victoria) ex rel Black v Commonwealth* (1981) 146 CLR 559 (H Ct Australia); relying on *General Assembly of the Free Church of Scotland v Lord Overtoun* [1904] AC 515 (HL); see also M. H. Ogilvie, 'What is a church by law established', *Osgoode Hall Law Journal*, 28 (1990), 179.

[27] See e.g. Paraguay, Const. Art. 24: 'No confession shall have official status'; Ireland, Const. Art. 44.2: 'The State guarantees not to endow any religion'; for the USA, see L. Tribe, *American Constitutional Law* (2nd edn., Mineola, New York, 1988), Ch. 14 and T. J. Gunn, *A Standard for Repair: The Establishment Clause, Equality and Natural Rights* (New York, 1992); for Australia, see P. J. Hanks, *Constitutional Law in Australia* (London, 1991), 13, 14, 429–33; compare, for the absence of an 'anti-establishment clause', Canada: see G-A. Beaudoin and E. Meades (eds.), *The Canadian Charter of Rights and Freedoms* (3rd edn., Ontario, 1995), Ch. 4.

[28] See e.g. C. F. Garbett, *Church and State in England* (London, 1950); for the Henrician Reformation legislation effecting the exclusion of Roman jurisdiction, see G. R. Elton, *The Tudor Constitution: Documents and Commentary* (2nd edn., Cambridge, 1982); see below for the process of law-making in the church.

ecclesiastical law of the secular English legal system, conferring public law rights and duties, the possibility for judicial intervention to ensure compliance is considerable.[29]

Though the following churches are not established in the English manner, they may be classified broadly as quasi-established in the sense that: whilst having the status of contractual societies, there are close legal links between the church and state; the authority of internal church law rests at least in part upon the existence of secular legislation; and secular legislation expressly and directly regulates some of the temporal affairs of the church. In Canada, in Nova Scotia, New Brunswick and Prince Edward Island, the Anglican church enjoys certain statutory privileges over other churches; secular law requires judicial enforcement of contractual terms of the church's canonical system involving civil law rights, particularly in matters of property.[30] In Australia the church is classified under secular law as a voluntary association – but its system of government and law rests in a fundamental way upon secular legislation. As in the other states,[31] in New South Wales, according to recent judicial *dicta*, '[t]he Constitution of the Anglican Church . . . came into existence formally on the enactment of the Church of England in Australia Constitution Act 1961'; the church's constitution is embodied in a schedule to the 1961 statute and, therefore, 'to an extent the Act of 1961 has given statutory force' to its rules, but it is not the case that 'the Act intended that those rules should have the force of a statute'.[32] Whilst in Australian states church law is not 'state law', the possibility for judicial intervention to ensure compliance with statutorily recognized internal rules is high.[33] In New Zealand, several parliamentary statutes 'declare and define the

---

[29] See L. Leeder, *Ecclesiastical Law Handbook* (London, 1997), Ch. 2: whilst the church itself is not a corporation and its sometimes described as a quasi-corporation; certainly, some authorities within it have the status of corporations: see Ch. 12.

[30] (N.S.) 32 Geo. II, c.5 (1758); (N.B.) 26 Geo. III, c.4 (1786) and *Doe d. St George's Church v Congle* (1870) 13 N.B.R. 96 (S.C.); (P.E.I.) 43 Geo. III, c.6 (1802); compare *Johnson v Glen* (1879) 26 Gr. 162 (Ch): Anglican canons requiring consultation by a bishop with churchwardens prior to appointment of a rector were enforced under contract law; and *Dunnet v Forneri* (1877) 25 Gr. 199 (Ontario H Ct): the court declined jurisdiction to restrain an Anglican minister from refusing Holy Communion; see generally M. H. Oglivie, 'Canadian civil court intervention in the exercise of ecclesiastical jurisdiction', *Studia Canonica*, 31 (1997), 49; see also generally, by the same author, *Religious Institutions and the Law in Canada* (Toronto, 1996).

[31] *Canon Law in Australia*, Report of the Canon Law Commission (Alexandria, NSW, undated but probably c. 1977), Chs. 9, 10; for historical material see R. Border, *Church and State in Australia: 1788–1872* (London, 1962).

[32] *Scandrett v Dowling* [1992] 27 NSWLR 483 at 489 *per* Mahoney JA; see also the Anglican Church of Australia Act 1976 (NSW) which forbids the use of names relating to the church unless authorized by canon.

[33] *Ex p The Rev George King* (1861) 2 Legge 1307; for the principle that the church is not established, see e.g. *Wylde v AG* (1948) 78 CLR 224.

Powers of the General Synod of the Church of the Province of New Zealand', they govern the alteration of the formularies of the church, and they regulate its trust property, its missionary dioceses and its clergy pensions funds; the church exists as a consensual society and the secular courts may intervene to effect compliance by the church with its own internal law and with state law applicable to the church.[34]

Disestablished Churches

Several Anglican churches world-wide were established prior to the enactment of secular legislation severing links between the local church and the state in which it existed.[35] There is a high degree of consistency between secular disestablishment enactments, in terms of both substance and form. The Irish Church Act 1869 seems to have provided a standard model – it was enacted by parliament 'to put an end to the Establishment of the Church of Ireland'. Under the statute the church 'shall cease to be established by law' and its legal union with the Church of England, effected by the Act of Union of Ireland with Great Britain in 1800, was dissolved. The statute declares that 'nothing in any Act, or custom shall prevent the bishops, clergy and laity . . . from . . . framing constitutions and regulations for the general management and good government' of the church. It provided that 'the ecclesiastical law of Ireland . . . shall cease to exist as law' but that it, along with 'the present articles, doctrines, rites, rules, discipline, and ordinances' of the church, 'subject to such (if any) modification or alteration' subsequently made, 'shall be deemed to be binding on the members . . . as if such members had mutually contracted and agreed to abide by and observe the same'. These forms of regulation are 'capable of being enforced in the temporal courts in relation to any property' of the church. Ecclesiastical courts and jurisdiction were abolished as was royal appointment of bishops.[36] Under modern Irish law the church exists as a voluntary association.[37] The Irish Church Act set the

---

[34] Church of England Empowering Act 1928 (as amended); Anglican Church Trusts Act 1981; New Zealand Anglican Church Pension Fund Act 1972; Church of England (Missionary Dioceses) Act 1955; see also St. John's College Trusts Act 1972; for historical material see W. P. Morrell, *The Anglican Church in New Zealand* (Dunedin, 1973).

[35] See generally the material cited in n. 2.

[36] Irish Church Act 1869, Preamble and esp. ss. 19–22; for the church's status as a voluntary association, see *State (Colquhoun) v D'Arcy* [1936] IR 641: 'The status of a church not established by law is . . . [that] of a voluntary association the membership of which subscribe or assent to certain rules and regulations'; see generally K. B. Nowlan, 'Disestablishment 1800–1869', in M. Harley (ed.), *Irish Anglicanism 1869–1969* (Dublin, 1970), 1–22.

[37] J. Casey, 'Church and state in Ireland', in G. Robbers (ed.), *State and Church in the European Union* (Baden-Baden, 1996), 147; G. W. Hogan, 'Law and religion: church–state relations in Ireland', *American Journal of Comparative Law*, 47 (1987), 35.

pattern for subsequent secular disestablishment legislation in Wales,[38] the West Indies,[39] and India.[40]

Non-Established Churches

Most Anglican churches fall into this category.[41] Whilst secular written constitutions purport to confer religious freedom and equality upon these (see above), by virtue of their very nature there is little or no formal state legislation dealing expressly with individual non-established churches. Needless to say, this is particularly the case in states whose secular constitutions provide for a non-Anglican 'established' church, such as those in Central and South America.[42] Generally they exist as voluntary associations and, for the purposes of holding and administering property, many states require their registration,[43] or the registration of bodies within

[38] Welsh Church Act 1914: an Act 'to terminate the establishment of the Church of England in Wales and Monmouthshire and to make provision in respect of the Temporalities thereof' (preamble); see esp. ss. 3 and 13 for provisions equivalent to those in the Irish Church Act.

[39] See e.g. Church of England in Bermuda Act 1975, ss. 1, 3, 4, 8; Barbados, Anglican Church Act 1969, ss. 3, 4, 24; Laws of Dominica 1961, Ordinance 1878, ss. 2, 4; Jamaica, Church of England Disestablishment Law 1938; and Grenada, Church of England Disestablishment Act 1959.

[40] Indian Church Act 1927: 'An Act to make provision incidental to and consequential on the dissolution of the legal union between the Church of England and the Church' in India; legislation of the Church Assembly of the Church of England (the Indian Church Measure 1927, ss. 2, 3) effected termination of '[t]he ecclesiastical law of the Church of England, so far as it exists in India' and the principle that pre-dissolution rules bound as if agreed to by the church's members; see generally, C. J. Grimes, *Towards an Indian Church* (London, 1946), 275, 396ff.

[41] See e.g. Southern Africa, Const. Preamble: this church is 'not by laws established' but is an 'unestablished Church'; see e.g. B. Johanson, *Church and State in South Africa* (Johannesburg, 1973).

[42] See e.g. Argentina, Const. Art. 2: 'The federal government supports the Roman Catholic Apostolic Religion'; Bolivia, Const. Art. 3: 'The State recognizes and supports the Roman Catholic Apostolic Religion . . . The relationship with the Catholic Church will be governed by concordats between the Bolivian State and the Holy See'; Costa Rica, Const. Art. 75: 'The Roman Catholic, Apostolic religion is that of the state, which contributes to its support, without preventing the free exercise in the Republic of other religions'; Paraguay, Const. Art. 24: 'the relationship of the State with the Catholic Church is based on independence, cooperation and autonomy'.

[43] See e.g. Panama, Const. Art. 35: 'Religious associations have legal capacity and order, and administer their properties within the limits established by the law in the same way as other juridical persons'; Mexico, Const. Art. 27: 'Religious associations . . . are constituted in accordance with article 130 and its implementing law'; Cuba, Const. Art. 75: 'The law regulates the State's relations with religious institutions'; Rwanda, Decree of 1888 and Edict of 1962: recognition by the Ministry of Justice arises if the religious association is non-profit-making, has not less than three members, a body of statutes, defined objects and a fixed place of organization; for historical material on church and state in Africa see A. Hastings, *The Church in Africa: 1450–1950* (Oxford,

them.[44] In South African secular law, a church is a juridic person having rights and duties of its own as distinct from those of its members: it can own property, enter legal transactions, sue and be sued. Depending on the internal organization of a church, legal personality may be conferred on either the church as a denomination, a particular congregation of the church, or both. A church's capacity to create rules for its own internal life is recognized by state law and these have force as rules and regulations of a voluntary association.[45] A similar system operates in the USA.[46] The fact that non-established churches are subject to the general law of the land is occasionally expressed in internal church law; for example, the constitution of the Diocese of Europe provides: 'The chaplaincies and archdeaconries shall conform to the domestic law of the country or countries within which they are situated and shall accept or maintain the measures necessary for them to act as juridical persons within the jurisdiction of those countries'.[47]

The Doctrine of Consensual Compact

As has been seen, whilst in England ecclesiastical law is treated as part of the law of the land, quasi-established and non-established churches are classified under secular law as voluntary associations. Consequently, their internal rules have under secular law the status of terms of a contract, enforceable in the civil courts as a matter of private law. With regard to the disestablished churches in Wales, Ireland and the West Indies, for example, the consensual compact is imposed by secular legislation. With

1994), 540ff. and H. B. Hansen, *Mission, Church and State in a Colonial Setting: Uganda* (London, 1984), 344ff.; A. Omoyajawo, *The Anglican Church in Nigeria: 1842–1992* (Lagos, 1994); Philippines, Const. Art. IX.1: 'The Church of this Province shall be registered as a "religious society" under Philippine laws . . . as a non-profit, non-stock entity and shall be considered as comprehending all persons who are baptized members thereof'; see also Chile, Cans. A.1 ; Brazil, Const. XVI; for Nigeria, *Ex p the Cherubim and Seraphim Society* (1960) LLR 129.

[44] In Canada secular Acts of 1921, 1951 and 1956 incorporate the General Synod; see generally M. H. Ogilvie, *Religious Institutions and the Law in Canada* (Toronto, 1996).

[45] J. D. van der Vyver, 'Religion', in W. A. Joubert and T. J. Scott (eds.), *The Law of South Africa* (Durban/Pretoria, 1986), vol. 23, 175–202; for the system applicable to the Spanish Episcopal Reformed Church, see I. C. Iban, 'State and church in Spain', in G. Robbers (ed.), *State and Church in the European Union* (Baden-Baden, 1996), 93.

[46] When a constitution is adopted by a religious society it is binding on the members unless contrary to law or public policy; the constitution is the embodiment of the terms of the compact by which the unincorporated voluntary association was formed: *Rock Zion Baptist Church v Johnson*, App, 47, So 2d 397 (La).

[47] Diocese of Europe, Const. 25; see also e.g. ECUSA, Cans. I.14; Melanesia, Cans. E.16 (Education Act 1978 of the Solomon Islands); Papua New Guinea, Anglican Church of Papua New Guinea Property Trust Act 1993; for historical material, see C. W. Forman, *The Island Churches of the South Pacific* (New York, 1982).

respect to non-established churches the doctrine is essentially judge-made, or it rests on the civil codes of those jurisdictions where such exist. Sometimes churches expressly refer to consensual compact as the basis of their internal systems of government and law.[48] The doctrine was developed in a series of cases from the 1860s dealing with the position of the colonial Anglican dioceses in South Africa: 'The Church of England, in places where there is no Church established by law, is in the same situation with any other religious body – in no better, but in no worse position: and the members may adopt, as the members of any other communion may adopt, rules for enforcing discipline within their body which will be binding on those who expressly or by implication have assented to them'.[49] The doctrine was refined by the English House of Lords in *Forbes v Eden* (1867), a case dealing with the Scottish Episcopal Church: according to Lord Colonsay 'A Court of Law will not interfere with the rules of a voluntary association unless to protect some civil right or interest which is said to be infringed by their operation'; Lord Cranworth's approach was narrower: '[s]ave for the due disposal and administration of property, there is no authority in the Courts of England or Scotland to take cognizance of the rules of a voluntary association entered into merely for the regulation of its own affairs'.[50]

These *dicta* have been consistently relied upon in several secular jurisdictions: in some cases the courts intervene only where a strict property issue is involved; in others where a (wider) civil right is involved, and in some these restrictions seem to have been relaxed. In one Canadian case the court held: 'All religious organizations are here considered as voluntary associations; the law recognizes their existence, and protects them in their enjoyment of property, but unless civil rights are in question it does not interfere with their organization or with questions of religious faith'.[51] In the Australian case of *Scandrett v Dowling* (1992) it was decided that, in the absence of ecclesiastical jurisdiction in the secular courts over 'purely spiritual matters', '[t]he binding effect of the "voluntary consensual compact" . . . must have come from the shared faith of the members of the

---

[48] South India, Const. XI(a): 'The Constitution of the Synod of the Church of South India is a contract between the Church and each member and members (whether collectively or individually) and the provisions therein shall be binding on all such members concerned'; Australia, Const. XII.71; Southern Africa, Const. Preamble: 'it is expedient that the members of a Church, not by law established, should . . . formally set forth the terms of the compact under which it is associated'.

[49] *Long v Bishop of Cape Town* (1863) 1 Moo NS 411; 15 ER 756 (PC) at 461–2 *per* Lord Kingsdown; see also *In re Bishop of Natal* (1865) III Moo NS 115; 16 ER 43; and *Bishop of Natal v Gladstone* (1866) LR 3 Eq 1; see generally, A. Ive, *The Church of England in South Africa: A Study of Its History, Principles and Status* (Capetown, 1966).

[50] (1867) LR 1 Sc & Div 568.

[51] *Dunnet v Forneri* (1877) 25 Gr. 199 (Ont. H Ct).

Church, or . . . their baptism in Christ', from 'a willingness to be bound to it because of shared faith . . . in *foro conscientiae*': '[i]ts binding effect does not come from the availability of the secular sanctions of State courts of law'. In *Scandrett* the court also observed: '[t]he availability of these latter sanctions when spiritual matters become mixed with property matters is an incident of the consensual compact or contract'. This means that 'where property is involved the consensual compact or contract is given the same effect, in relation to property matters, as if it were a common law contract, but does not in any way alter the primary basis of that compact or contract'.[52] The doctrine has been applied in Ireland,[53] the United Kingdom and New Zealand,[54] the West Indies,[55] South Africa,[56] and the USA.[57] A fundamental consequence of this doctrine is that internal church rules are inferior to secular law in cases of inconsistency.[58] In turn, challenges to the validity of internal church law, on both substantive and procedural grounds, may be entertained by secular courts.[59]

[52] [1992] 27 NSWLR 483 (CA NSW); see also *Ex p Hay* (1897) 18 LR (NSW) 206; *McQueen v Frackelton* (1909) 8 CLR 673; *AG v Wylde* (1948) 48 SR 366 and *Gent v Robin* (1958) SASR 328.

[53] Ireland: *State (Colquhoun) v D'Arcy* [1936] IR 641: church members 'bind themselves to conform to certain laws and principles, the obligation to such conformity and observance resting wholly in the mutual contract of the members, enforceable only as a matter of contract by the ordinary tribunals of the land when brought within their cognizance and not enforceable under any independent coercive jurisdiction'.

[54] Wales: *Powell v Representative Body of the Church in Wales* [1957] 1 All ER 400; see also *Davies v Presbyterian Church of Wales* [1986] 1 WLR 323; for New Zealand, see *Baldwin v Pascoe* (1889) 7 NZLR 759.

[55] West Indies: *Trustees of the Church of God in the Bahamas v Davies* (1965) [1965–70] 2 Law Reports of the Bahamas, 31.

[56] South Africa: see e.g. *Motaung v Mukubela* [1975(1)] 1 SALR 619.

[57] USA: *Carter v Papineau*, 222 Mass. 464, 111 N.E.: ECUSA has 'a body of canons or ecclesiastical law of its own, by which the plaintiff upon baptism and confirmation agreed to be bound, and under which her rights of worship must be determined'; *Fiske v Beaty*, 120 Misc. 1, 198 N.Y.S. 358: New York Supreme Court held that ECUSA canons are binding when not in conflict with state laws; see also n. 46.

[58] Australia, NSW, Anglican Church Act 1976, s. 3: 'Any canon or rule made under . . . the said Constitution which contravenes any law or statute in force for the time being in the said State shall to the extent of such contravention be incapable of having any force or effect'; Canada, *Re Incorporated Synod of the Diocese of Toronto and HEC Hotels Ltd* (1987) 44 DLR (4th) 161, 61 OR (2d) 737 (Ont. CA): a private incorporation Act takes precedence over a public general statute in relation to the specific church for which the private Act was made.

[59] England: *R v Ecclesiastical Committee of Both Houses of Parliament, ex p Church Society* (1994) 6 Admin LR 670 (CA): the court assumed jurisdiction to inquire into the validity of a synodical measure; once enacted, however, it would enjoy the same effect as a parliamentary statute: see LFCE, 59; compare Australia: *Baker v Gough* [1963] NSWR 1345.

The Applicability of Pre-Existing Canonical Systems

One question which has been fairly well settled is whether upon legal severance of a local church from the Church of England or from another
mother Anglican church – by disestablishment, dissolution or the establishment of a new province or diocese – the pre-existing canonical system
survives and continues.[60] With respect to some non-established churches,
formal law occasionally treats this expressly.[61] As to disestablished
churches, and a small group of non-established churches, the question is
whether prior English ecclesiastical law survives. In Wales, Ireland and
the West Indies, as we have seen, the matter is settled by secular legislation: prior English law continues until and unless altered by the church.[62]
For other churches, the secular courts have settled the matter. It has been
decided by its Supreme Court that ecclesiastical law, as part of the common law of England, applies in Barbados.[63] In ECUSA, English ecclesiastical law continues for some purposes only, but in Australia, the secular
courts have decided that it does not generally apply.[64] Indeed, the
Australian church itself has made canonical provision for the subject.[65] In
the Diocese of Europe, 'so far as the local law of any state or country shall
permit, Canons and other Ecclesiastical Law of the Church of England
shall, as far as applicable, apply in the diocese'; it does so subject to 'such
modifications or exceptions as, on the submission of the Diocesan Bishop
after consultation with the diocesan synod, are deemed appropriate by the

---

[60] See Ch. 3 for the limited applicability of doctrines of binding judicial precedent.

[61] Philippines, Const. I.5: 'Where and when the Constitution and canons of the new
Province are silent . . . the provisions of the old Constitution and Canons shall prevail,
except as local circumstances may prevent, until the same shall be altered and enacted
by the Provincial Synod'; Sudan, Const. Art. 7: 'The laws and regulations of the
"Constitution of the Diocese of the Sudan" which were in force before the inauguration
of the Province shall, so far as they are not inconsistent with any provisions of [this]
Constitution . . . remain in force . . . until repealed or amended'; Burundi, Const. Art. 20.

[62] See nn. 36–9.

[63] *Blades and Another v Jaggard and Others* [1961] 4 WIR 207.

[64] USA: *Town of Pawlet v Clark* 13 U.S. (9 Cranch) 292; for an early discussion see M.
Hoffman, *A Treatise on the Law of the Protestant Episcopal Church in the United States* (New
York, 1850), 64; for Australia, *Ex p The Rev George King* (1861) 2 Legge 1307; see also *R v
Inhabitants of Brampton* (1808) 10 East 282; 103 ER 782: 'For I may suppose in the absence
of any evidence to the contrary that the Law of England Ecclesiastical and Civil was recognized by subjects of England in a place occupied by the King's troops, who would
impliedly carry that law with them'.

[65] Australia, Const. XII.71.2: 'The law of the Church of England including the law
relating to faith ritual ceremonial or discipline applicable and in force in the several dioceses . . . at the date upon which this Constitution takes effect shall apply to and be in
force in such dioceses of this Church unless and until the same be varied'; see also
Southern Africa, Const. Preamble for the idea that new laws shall be made 'according
to the . . . Laws and Usages of the Church of England so far as such Laws and Usages
are applicable to an unestablished Church in South Africa'.

Archbishop of Canterbury acting with the concurrence of the Vicar-General of the Province'; their determination is conclusive.[66]

THE FORMS AND EFFECTS OF REGULATION

Anglican churches employ a very complex and sometimes bewildering set of technical terms to signify the sources of ecclesiastical regulation. In some they are defined, in others this is not the case.[67] For some churches *ecclesiastical law* is law created by the state applicable to the church, but in England it embraces both church-made and state-made law.[68] All churches have a *constitution*, a body of primary or fundamental law: in all but two of the thirty-seven self-governing churches of the Communion the constitution is contained in a single written document; this is sometimes accompanied by a separate document containing *fundamental declarations* or *fundamental principles*.[69] The expression *canon law* is sometimes defined as that binding domestic law which is made by the church for itself; occasionally it is collected in *codes*.[70] Other species of law are, broadly, inferior

[66] Diocese of Europe, Const. 22.

[67] Australia, Can. 18 1992: 'a law . . . shall be read as including a reference to a rule relating to discipline, a principle, a practice or a tradition of the Church of England'; Sudan, Const. Art. 1(b): '"Law" is any resolution adopted by General Synod which is intended to have mandatory effect'.

[68] England: *AG v Dean and Chapter of Ripon Cathedral* [1945] Ch 238: ecclesiastical law is 'the law relating to any matter concerning the Church of England administered and enforced in any court', ecclesiastical or temporal, and 'law administered by ecclesiastical courts and persons'; *Mackonochie v Lord Penzance* (1881) 6 App Cas 424 at 446: 'ecclesiastical law is not a foreign law. It is part of the general law of England'; compare, for Wales, T. G. Watkin, 'Vestiges of establishment', *Ecclesiastical Law Journal*, 2 (7) (1990), 110 at 111: here it is defined as law made by the state for the church; compare New Zealand, Cans. A.II.3: clergy undertake to be 'obedient to the ecclesiastical laws' in force in the diocese.

[69] See the next section and Ireland, Const. Preamble and Declaration IV, which describes it as an 'episcopal constitution'; for Fundamental Declarations and Principles see e.g. Canada, Australia, South East Asia, North India, South India, Southern Africa and Central Africa. By way of contrast, the 'constitution' of the church in England is dispersed amongst a host of legal sources (including parliamentary statutes, and measures and canons of the General Synod); in Scotland, similarly, there is no single document entitled 'the constitution': rules about the government of the church are located in its Code of Canons.

[70] Central Africa and Southern Africa Const. Definitions: 'By "Canon" is and shall be meant any measure passed by Synod which is intended to have mandatory effect and to be part of the permanent corpus of Ecclesiastical Law of this Province'; Papua New Guinea, Diocese of Port Moresby, Can. 2(2): 'The Canons of the Diocese shall consist of the more constant governing rules of the Diocese but may be changed from time to time'; Melanesia, Cans. D.4.A: 'Canon is the name given to a Church law'; Scotland has a Code of Canons, and New Zealand a constitution and a code of canons; for the notion of 'canons' as implementary instruments, to execute the constitution, see Southern

and made as the result of delegated powers. These include: Acts,[71] by-laws,[72] rules and regulations,[73] ordinances,[74] resolutions,[75] decrees,[76] and liturgical rubrics found in service books.[77] As is discussed in the next section, these various expressions may be used to designate laws operating at national, regional, provincial or diocesan levels which, in turn, produce a hierarchy of sources. Alongside these species of formal laws exist less formal and sometimes unwritten sources: customs or traditions,[78] the decisions of church courts,[79] the 'principles of canon law',[80] and for a small number of churches, the English Canons Ecclesiastical 1603,[81] or pre-

Africa, Const. XXII and Can. 1.12: this refers to itself as 'the code of Canons'; for 'canonical norms', see Chile, Cans. H.3: these have to be renewed at every triennial Diocesan Synod.

[71] Southern Africa, Standing Rules, 3(i): '"Act" shall mean a regulation adopted by [the Provincial] Synod which is intended to have a mandatory effect and to require any person or persons, as of obligation, to perform or abstain from performing any action or actions'; see the next section for Acts of the Provincial Synod.

[72] Papua New Guinea, Diocese of Port Moresby, Const. and Canons 1996, Can. 2: 'The By-Laws of the Diocese shall consist of the everyday procedures of the Diocese'.

[73] Wales, Const. I.1.1: the constitution consists *inter alia* of 'all rules and regulations made from time to time by or under the authority or with the consent of the Governing Body'; Australia, Can. 6 1985: the bishop may make 'regulations' governing admission of children to holy communion.

[74] Australia, Const. XII.74: '"Ordinance" includes any act canon constitution statute legislative measure or provision of a provincial or diocesan synod'.

[75] Sudan, Art. 6; Scotland, Cans. 52.22; compare Central Africa, Const. Definitions: 'resolution' is 'any expression of the judgment or opinion of the Synod, which is intended to have an appreciative, hortatory or advisory and not a mandatory effect'; Southern Africa, Standing Resolutions, 3(xiii).

[76] Wales, Const. IV.35.

[77] See Ch. 8.

[78] Scotland, Can. 1.1: episcopal consecration takes place in accordance with 'the law and custom of the ancient Church'; South East Asia, Const. Preamble: that dioceses are associated as a province is 'in accordance with the accepted traditions and usages of the Anglican Communion'; see also Sudan, Const. Preamble, where the same is treated as 'in accordance with ancient laws and usages of the Catholic Church'; Canada, *Book of Alternative Services* (1985), 184: 'For the rest of the service local custom may be established and followed'; Southern Africa, *Prayer Book* (1989), 115: the peace is given 'according to local custom'; New Zealand, *Prayer Book* (1989), 517: 'In accordance with Anglican tradition there shall be no celebration of the Eucharist unless at least one other person is present'.

[79] See Ch. 3.

[80] For 'the general principles of canon law', see West Indies, Const. Art. 6.2; Southern Africa, Can. 50; Central Africa, Can. 32.1; see also New Zealand, Const. Preamble, 12: the 'principles of partnership'.

[81] Australia, Can. 11 1992, 4: this lists canons of 1603 which have 'no operation or effect in a diocese which adopts this canon'; but a right is reserved to a diocese to adopt them if it so wishes; for England, see Hill, *Ecclesiastical Law*, Ch. 1; for Wales, see G. K. Cameron, 'The Church in Wales, the Canons of 1604 and the doctrine of custom', LL M dissertation, University of Wales, Cardiff, 1997.

Reformation Roman Catholic canon law.[82] In addition, and this is increasingly the case, alongside laws properly so called, churches are regulated by quasi-legislation, informal administrative rules designed to supplement the formal law: 'directions', 'guidelines', 'codes of practice' or 'policy documents';[83] sometimes these are treated as having binding effect, but more often they are merely recommendatory.[84] Resolutions of the Lambeth Conference are ordinarily treated as being of recommendatory rather than binding effect in local churches.[85]

Various devices are employed by churches to ensure the binding effect of church laws and the rights and duties distributed by them, devices which may be applied to clergy, lay officers or the lay members generally: overriding principles containing general statements that the law of the church is binding;[86] declarations, promises or oaths by which an undertaking is made to assent to or conform to the law of the church or the decisions of its tribunals;[87] provisions requiring compliance with executive directions (typified with the doctrine of canonical obedience).[88] This means that, unlike in England where the canons do not bind the

[82] Australia, Can. 11 1992, 3(1): 'all canon law of the Church of England made prior to the Canons of 1603 . . . shall have no operation or effect in a diocese' unless adopted by that diocese.

[83] For 'guidelines', see ECUSA, Cans. I.1.14: made by General Convention; III.3.1: made by the bishop; New Zealand, Cans. B.V.6: the parish must have 'proper regard for such guidelines as may be laid down . . . by the Archives Committee'; Papua New Guinea, Diocese of Port Moresby, Can. 2(4): 'The Bishop's Guidelines will outline basic doctrine and procedures concerning the teaching of the faith and the administration of the sacraments. They will support the worship pattern, discipline and policies of the Provincial and Diocesan Constitutions, Canons and/or By-laws'; see also n. 75.

[84] Papua New Guinea, Diocese of Port Moresby, Can. 10(3): 'All clergy . . . are subject to lawful obedience to the . . . Bishop's Guidelines'; ECUSA, Cans. IV.1.1: it is an ecclesiastical offence to violate episcopal 'Pastoral Directions'. For the idea that quasi-legislation may operate *contra legem*, in which case it is unlawful, *secundum legem*, where it is designed to implement law, and *praeter legem*, where the law is silent and it supplements law, see N. Doe, 'The use and legality of ecclesiastical quasi-legislation: *imperium* or *dominium*?', unpublished paper, 8 March 1996.

[85] See Ch. 12.

[86] Wales, Const. I.2: 'The Constitution shall be binding on all office-holders in the Church in Wales, all clerics and deaconesses . . . and all persons whose names are entered on the electoral roll of any parish in Wales'; Australia, Const. XII.70: 'This Constitution and all canons and rules passed and made thereunder shall be binding on the bishops, clergy and laity as members of this Church'.

[87] Scotland, Can. 58, App. Nos. 1A and 12: 'I . . . promise . . . I will give all due obedience to the Code of Canons . . . to the decisions and judgments of the tribunals . . . and decisions of ecclesiastical authorities in all questions falling under their spiritual jurisdiction'; Wales, Const. VII.66: all clergy at ordination and appointment must declare and undertake 'to be bound by the Constitution . . . and to accept, submit to and carry out any sentence or judgment' passed by a bishop or church court; for lay members see ibid., VI.3; New Zealand, Cans. A.I, A.II.3; Burundi, Const. Art. 5.

[88] For canonical obedience see Ch. 5 and for judicial enforcement of church law see Ch. 3.

non-office-holding laity,[89] in most churches the canons do bind the laity.[90] An analysis of the subjects treated by law provides some indication, if not a general theory, of Anglican concepts about the purposes of ecclesiastical regulation.[91] Many constitutions are in line with recent guidance issued by the Anglican Consultative Council as to the subjects with which constitutions ought to deal.[92] At the same time, however, there is little consistency as between churches concerning the subject-matter of canons.[93] Finally, in canonical theory it is sometimes assumed that all ecclesiastical regulation serves the purpose of fulfilling divine law. But this is a concept which has largely been left undeveloped in Anglican jurisprudence: only occasionally is it the case that formal laws make reference to such a notion.[94] In this context, devices enabling the relaxation of laws in times of urgent necessity sometimes surface in formal law.[95] This is particularly so with the con-

---

[89] See *Middleton v Crofts* (1736) 2 Atkins 650: canons bind the laity only if declaratory of ancient usage and law; this was approved in *Bishop of Exeter v Marshall* (1868) LR 3 HL 17.

[90] See Ch. 3 for the jurisdiction of church courts and Ch. 6 generally.

[91] Anglican jurisprudence is summed up neatly in Diocese of Europe, Const. Bishop's Introduction: 'the Church, like any other organization, needs its structures, and agreed ways of working . . . [t]he laws, canons and regulations of the church are not the heart of the christian life', but 'the church may and should have rules to facilitate its task of mission and pastoral care, both in its own internal life and in the image it presents to the world at large. These rules must never be allowed to substitute for the christian life, but they are intended to serve the christian life'; for an appearance of the idea in actual law, see e.g. Ireland, Const. I.28: laws are 'necessary for the order, good government and efficiency' of the church.

[92] ACC – 4, 1979, Ontario: Guidelines for Provincial Constitutions: Pt. 1: preamble and fundamental declarations; Pt. 2: metropolitical authority and bishops, provincial assembly, liturgy, discipline, property, definitions, amendment; Pt. 3: rules of order and procedure; see e.g. Uganda, South East Asia, Sudan.

[93] Compare the three different approaches of Ireland (Const. IX contains the canons of the church which deal only with church services), Philippines (where, in addition to the constitution, the canons deal with institutional organization and administration, ministry, discipline, worship, and the enactment of canonical legislation) and Scotland (where, in the absence of a separate 'constitution' the Code of Canons covers all aspects of church life).

[94] For constitutional duties placed on national and provincial assemblies to legislate in conformity with 'the standards of faith and order', which function in some churches as the 'ultimate rule' (or 'norm') of church life, see e.g. Jerusalem, Const. Art. 4(i); see generally Ch. 7; for its appearance in secular judicial decisions see *Mwase and Blackman Church of God (Tongaland) v Church of Central Africa (Presbyterian) Sanca Division* (1935) 1 African Law Reports 45: the court is not to be guided by 'the law of scriptures' which 'is chiefly to be found in the Old Testament and . . . forms no part of the native law'; for a rejection of divine law in a secular case in which a cleric of the Church of England sought to rely on it as a defence to a charge of criminal damage, see *Blake v DPP* (1992), in M. Hill, *Ecclesiastical Law* (London, 1995), 13; compare *Kachasu v AG* (1967) Zambian Law Journal 44.

[95] For a discussion of the non-applicability of desuetude, see *Canon Law in Australia* (n. 31), Ch. 11 and R. Bursell, 'What is the place of custom in English canon law?', *Ecclesiastical Law Journal*, 1(4) (1989), 12.

cept of dispensation: whilst it is occasionally presumed to be a general power vested in bishops by virtue of their office,[96] more often the assumption is made that dispensatory powers exist only when they are conferred expressly by the law.[97]

THE PROCESS OF LAW-MAKING

As has already been indicated, law-making power may be derived from a variety of sources and it may exist in a number of forms: it may be explicitly conferred upon ecclesiastical assemblies by means of internal church constitutions;[98] an explicit conferral may be accompanied by a justification for the scheme in question;[99] it may be implicit;[100] the function may be cast as a duty rather than as a power;[101] and legislative competence may be

[96] See *Dispensation in Practice and Theory with special reference to Anglican Churches* (London, 1942); see also *Canon Law in Australia* (n. 31), 57: 'It would appear that a Bishop may dispense in the following cases: 1. If the breach of positive law is a very small thing; 2. In cases of frequent occurrence; 3. In extraordinary and pressing cases for the church is mother not mistress; 4. Where it is doubtful whether any dispensation is needed at all; 5. By custom; and 6. In cases where the Canon Law so provides'.

[97] Southern Africa, Const. XII: this allows the Synod of Bishops to legislate, in order to give effect to the constitution, by waiving compliance with procedures in urgent necessity with subsequent ratification by the Provincial Synod; Wales, Const. VI.2: members of churches not in communion may be admitted on the electoral roll by 'the written dispensation of the Diocesan Bishop'; for England, see LFCE, 51.

[98] Sudan, Const. Art. 3: the General Synod is 'the legislative body of this Province'; Rwanda, Draft Const. 1996, Art. 16: the Provincial Synod 'establishes the canons of the Church for the Province'; Australia, Const. II.5: the Church has 'plenary authority and power to make canons, ordinances and rules for the order and government of the Church'. Similar schemes operate with diocesan law: see e.g. Sudan, Const. Art. 1(k): the Diocesan Synod is 'the legislative body of each Diocese' and West Africa, Diocese of Gambia and Guinea, Constitution 1982, Art. 4: 'The Synod may from time to time make, amend and revoke rules, regulations and standing orders'.

[99] Southern Africa, Const. Art. II and Preliminary Resolutions 1870, V: '[t]he Provincial Synod of this Church . . . shall be the Legislative body of the Church of this Province', 'in order that the counsel of Lay Members of the Church may be had with regard to all such Rules or Canons, and that the consent of the Laity of the Church may be obtained to the same through their representatives'; consequently, 'no Rules for the government of the entire Church should be enacted without the consent, express or implied, of the whole body of the Church'; ibid. Art. XXII: the Provincial Synod has full power and authority 'to make, from time to time, such Canons, Rules, Regulations, and Bye-Laws for giving effect to the provisions of this Constitution, as to the said Provincial Synod shall seem fit'.

[100] See e.g. Tanzania, Const. IV.14(b): the Provincial Synod has 'the final authority regarding all spiritual matters in the Province'; for the many other examples of this formula, see Ch. 2.

[101] Melanesia, Const. Art. 7.A: the General Synod 'shall make laws for the province and has final authority in matters of spiritual discipline in the Church of this Province'.

conferred by the state,[102] recognized expressly by state law,[103] or, in some former British colonies, by royal licence.[104] This section examines laws governing the process of enacting the main forms of ecclesiastical legislation. Very many churches have Commissions specifically charged with the responsibility of considering and recommending constitutional and canonical development within the church.[105] Special provisions apply to legislation dealing with doctrine and liturgy and these are discussed in Chapters 7 and 8.

Fundamental Declarations and Principles

For those few churches which operate a system of Fundamental Declarations (or Fundamental Principles), either incorporated into the constitution or existing as a separate document, additions or alterations to these may be effected only by compliance with a series of stringent procedural rules. Three approaches are employed. First, Fundamental Declarations or Principles may be altered only in accordance with those procedures applicable to constitutional amendment (which are discussed in the next section) to which special procedures are added: in Korea, '[n]o alteration to [the] Fundamental Declaration may be made unless the proposed amendment [has] been approved according to procedures laid down for amending the Constitution and Canons'. In addition, the proposal must have been sent 'to all the Metropolitans of the Anglican Communion and an assurance received from them that the proposed amendment is not contrary to the terms of the Communion between the Anglican Church of Korea and the Churches of which they are Metropolitans'.[106]

Secondly, and more commonly, churches employ special provisions enabling additions or alterations to Fundamental Declarations and

[102] England: Church of England Assembly (Powers) Act 1919; New Zealand: Church of England Empowering Act 1928; Australia: Const. Art. XII.69: 'Subject to all necessary parliamentary enactments this Constitution shall apply to every diocese of the Church . . . which assents to the Constitution'.

[103] Wales: Welsh Church Act 1914; Ireland: Irish Church Act 1869; Bermuda: Church of England in Bermuda Act 1975; Barbados: Anglican Church Act 1969. For joint ecclesiastical and state recognition see the Church of England's Indian Church Measure 1927 and the parliamentary Indian Church Act 1927.

[104] New Zealand, Const. A.3: if 'a Licence be granted by the Crown to this Branch of the Church of England to frame new and modify existing rules . . . with the view of meeting the peculiar circumstances of this Colony and native people, it shall be lawful for this Branch of the said Church to avail itself of that liberty'.

[105] See e.g. Australia, General Synod Commissions Cans. 1969–92, 14; West Indies, Const. Art. 3.5; ECUSA, Cans. I.1.2; Canada, Province of Rupert's Land, Can. VII; North India, Const. II.IV.XVI.5; Philippines, Const. X.1. These sometimes assist with the interpretation of church law: see Ch. 3.

[106] Korea, Fundamental Declaration on Faith and Rites.

Principles which are distinct from procedures normally employed for ordinary constitutional amendment. In the Church of the Province of Central Africa the Fundamental Declarations may be altered by the Provincial Synod only if the Episcopal Synod, a Diocesan Synod, the Provincial Standing Committee, or a duly constituted provincial or diocesan board, has by resolution proposed such alteration – and notice of the alteration must be given to the Archbishop at least six months before the opening of the Provincial Synod. Alterations come into effect two months after their promulgation, or upon a date determined by the Provincial Synod. No alteration to the Fundamental Declarations may be made unless the proposed amendment, after having been provisionally approved by the Provincial Synod, has been approved by the synod of each diocese in the province. It must, in addition, be confirmed by the Provincial Synod by a two-thirds majority of those present, and subsequently be endorsed by the Archbishop of Canterbury as not affecting the terms of Communion between the church, the Church of England, and the rest of the Anglican Communion.[107] Stricter majority rules are employed in the church in South India. Any proposal for an alteration or addition to the church's Governing Principles must be brought before the General Synod by a resolution passed by one or more Diocesan Councils. The proposal must be passed by the Synod 'in substantially the same terms by not less than two-thirds of the Diocesan Councils'. If it is accepted by these, it must be brought again before the Synod and passed 'in substantially the same terms by a three-quarters majority'.[108]

Procedures are more complex in national churches with a provincial structure. Canadian law allows the amendment of the church's Declaration of Principles, which deal with the composition and jurisdiction of the General Synod and contain a set of Fundamental Principles about provincial government and disciplinary proceedings. A change in the Declaration of Principles may be considered only when a majority of each order (of bishops, clergy and laity) is present at a session of the General Synod. To take effect a two-thirds majority is required in each order at two successive sessions having first been referred for consideration to all diocesan and provincial synods following first approval by the General Synod. No change in the Declaration of Principles can be made without the consent of all provincial synods; however, if a vote on the proposed amendment has not taken place in any provincial synod prior to the next regular session of the General Synod, such provincial synod is deemed to have approved the amendment. Any proposed amendment to the Declaration of Principles which has been defeated by a vote of the

---

[107] Central Africa, Fundamental Declarations, VII and Can. 33.1–2.
[108] South India, Const. XIV.1.

General Synod may be introduced again at any subsequent session of the General Synod.[109]

Thirdly, and by way of contrast, in three notable cases the law prohibits any alteration of Fundamental Declarations or Principles – this is because they are treated as statements of historical fact about the nature of the church and its doctrine. The Australian church operates a system of absolute entrenchment concerning its Fundamental Declarations and the prohibition itself.[110] In Canada, '[t]he Solemn Declaration of the Declaration of Principles, while continuing to be part of the Declaration of Principles, belongs in a particular historic context and therefore cannot be altered or amended'.[111] Similarly, the constitution of the church in New Zealand states with respect to its Fundamental Provisions that 'it shall not be within the power of the General Synod, or of any Diocesan synod, to alter, revoke, add to, or diminish any of the same'.[112] In these churches, therefore, the law is fundamental in the sense that it is unalterable – it imposes a complete substantive fetter on the church's legislative competence.

National and Provincial Constitutions

Churches treat amendment of their constitutions by means of either a permissive or a prohibitive jurisprudence.[113] Most law dealing with constitutional development is procedural. Laws do not generally contain express substantive limitations on the exercise of legislative powers. Rather, limitations are implicit: competence to effect constitutional reform is restricted to those subjects falling within the jurisdiction of national or provincial assemblies.[114] In terms of procedure, there is a remarkable degree of uni-

---

[109] Canada, Declaration of Principles, 11.

[110] Australia, Const. XI.66: this applies to Const. I, Fundamental Declarations, 1–3 (the church is part of the One Holy Catholic and Apostolic Church of Christ; it receives the canonical scriptures; and it will 'ever obey the commands of Christ'); XI.66 itself is also absolutely entrenched.

[111] Canada, Declaration of Principles, 11(a)(i).

[112] New Zealand, Const. A.6.

[113] Compare, on the one hand, e.g. West Indies, Const. Art. 3.3: '[t]he Provincial Synod shall be the legislative body of the Church in the Province of the West Indies, and shall have full power and authority to amend or repeal the Constitution'; North India, Const. II.VII: 'A proposal for amendments and alterations in this Constitution . . . may be brought before Synod' in accordance with the prescribed procedures; and, on the other hand, Southern Africa, Can. 49.1: 'No Article of the Constitution . . . shall be liable to alteration, amendment, or repeal, and no new Article of the Constitution . . . shall be added at any future Provincial Synod' without compliance with the required procedures. The latter is the more common practice: see e.g. Uganda, Const. Art. 19: 'This Constitution shall not be amended except in accordance with the following procedures'.

[114] For the subject-matter jurisdictions of national and provincial synods, see Ch. 2; and for provisional or contingency arrangements in laws by which occasionally

formity as between churches, with differences being of detail rather than of principle.[115] Most churches employ a system of *proposal* on notice, *adoption* by the provincial or national assembly, *reference* to the dioceses (for either consultation or consent), subsequent *confirmation* by the national or provincial assembly and finally *promulgation*. A very few churches, on the other hand, employ a system of three readings in the central legislature (without reference to the dioceses) followed by promulgation.[116] For the sake of convenience, these may be classified respectively as the Referral Model and the Westminster Model.

The Referral Model The first stage, concerning the introduction of proposed constitutional innovation or amendment, is the giving of notice, usually to the metropolitan or archbishop; periods vary but six months prior to the sitting of the provincial or national assembly is the norm.[117] The law of some churches refines the notice procedure by imposing a duty to give reasons for the proposed development.[118] Generally, the right to propose legislation, or to give notice, is confined to specified ecclesiastical authorities or persons: in some churches rights to propose are widely enjoyed, in others a more restrictive approach is used. The church in South East Asia requires a resolution of the House of Bishops, the Provincial Synod itself, a Diocesan Synod, the Provincial Standing Committee, or a duly constituted provincial or diocesan board.[119] In some churches the right to propose is confined to the central legislature or its members.[120] In others, the law would seem to confine the right to propose constitutional amendments to diocesan assemblies.[121]

churches prescribe that their legislatures are subordinate to the authority of a General Synod of the Anglican Communion (were such an institution to exist), see Ch. 12.

[115] For an imaginative critique of constitutional reform, and suggestions for the use of ecclesiastical referenda in the Church in Wales, see T. G. Watkin, 'Consensus and the constitution', *Ecclesiastical Law Journal* 3(15) (1994), 232.

[116] Dioceses are involved for theological reasons, but the entertainment of legislation at successive sessions of national or provincial assemblies also has to do with the timing of their sittings, which in some churches may be every three or more years; see Ch. 2.

[117] The shortest period found, two months' notice to the President and to the dioceses, is in Jerusalem and the Middle East, Const. Art. 17(i); it is twelve months in North India, Const. II.IV.XVI.5.2.

[118] South East Asia, Const. Art. 19(b).

[119] South East Asia, Const. Art. 19(a); see also Nigeria, Const. Art. XIX.

[120] Uganda, Const. Art. 19(1); Melanesia, Const. Art. 7.D; Jerusalem and Middle East, Const. Art. 17(i); Papua New Guinea, Const. Art. 19: a simple majority of the Provincial Council may propose; New Zealand, Const. G.4; ECUSA, Const. Art. I.1; Cans. I.2.4(a)(5): either of the two Houses of General Convention 'may originate and propose legislation' and the Presiding Bishop has a special duty to recommend legislation; Diocese of Europe, Const. 48(b): members of the Church of England's General Synod may propose.

[121] North India, Const. II.VII.2: 'One or more of the Diocesan Council/Councils may send a proposal for amendment to the Constitution'; and ibid. II.IV.IV.29: the Synod

The second part of the legislative process is ratification or adoption by the provincial or national assembly.[122] Rules governing this stage are designed to enable a full debate on the proposed legislation. As a matter of general ecclesiastical practice, at this stage the proposed legislation must obtain the assent of a majority of the members present and voting, the orders or houses of the assembly voting either together or separately with a majority required in each; voting separately is sometimes mandatory and sometimes optional at the instigation of a prescribed number of assembly members.[123] The formal laws of a small number of churches require ratification by special majorities, usually two-thirds.[124]

The third stage is referral to the dioceses. Two significant variations appear in formal laws: one requires the diocesan assemblies simply to be consulted about the proposed change,[125] and the other requires the consent of diocesan assemblies before the proposal may proceed. In those churches employing the consent model, practices vary. A small number of laws require a special majority of dioceses to assent to the change.[126] A

'shall receive and examine all amendments to the Constitution . . . proposed by Diocesan Councils or by any other body or organisation of the Church entitled to do so'; South India, Const. XIV.2: proposals 'must be brought before the Synod by a resolution passed by one or more Diocesan Councils of the Church'; Southern Cone, Const. Art. 6.1; Jerusalem and the Middle East, Const. Art. 9: Diocesan Synods or the Standing Committee of the Central Synod may recommend.

[122] Burundi, Const. Art. 19.1; Zaire, Const. Art. 23; Sudan, Const. Art. 63; New Zealand, Cans. C.I.1 and 2.1.

[123] For mandatory separate voting, see South East Asia, Const. Art. 19(b); Korea, Const. p.49. For optional separate voting, see e.g. Melanesia, Const. Art. 7.D.

[124] Southern Cone, Const. Art. 6.2: 'The proposed change must be accepted as a proposal by a ⅔ vote of the provincial Synod'; for voting by orders see e.g. Philippines, Const. X.1 and Sudan, Const. Art. 17(ii). In North India, Const. II.VII.1 and South India, Const. XIV.2 the proposal may be ratified finally at this stage by a two-thirds majority of the synod before submission to the dioceses.

[125] South East Asia, Const. Art. 19(b)(i); Rwanda, Draft Const. 1996: this requires 'formal notification of the proposed amendments to all Diocesan Synods'; Philippines, Const X.1: referral for 'consideration'; South East Asia, Const. Art. 19(b): 'for their consideration'; ECUSA, Const. Art. XII: the proposal must be 'made known' to Diocesan Conventions; North India, Const. II.VII.3: '[t]he Synod Secretariat shall forward proposals for amendment to the Constitution as finally approved by the Executive Committee to all Diocesan Councils. The Dioceses or their Executive Committees within a period of six months from the date of receipt of proposals shall send comments or amendments to the President'; the Law and Procedures Committee 'shall then formulate the amendments in their final form for presentation to the Synod'.

[126] South India, Const. XIV.2(iii): 'The resolution so passed must be ratified by not less than two-thirds of the Diocesan Councils of the Church'. The position in Australia is complex: Const. Art. II.5: 'this church has plenary authority and power to make canons . . . for the order and good government of the Church, and to administer the affairs thereof'; Const. Art. XI.67: bills to alter the constitution must be passed, depending on the subject involved, by: a two-thirds majority of each house and they must be assented to by a majority of all the dioceses of which at least two must be metropolitical sees; a majority of the members of each house and three-quarters of Diocesan

larger number of laws require the agreement of all Diocesan Synods in order for the proposal to proceed directly to the fourth stage.[127] One church specifies that a simple majority only is needed.[128] Occasionally laws are framed somewhat vaguely requiring simply 'the agreement' of Diocesan Synods.[129] Others employ a mixture of both special and full majorities depending which sections of the constitution are to be affected.[130]

The fourth stage of final confirmation is of two types. If on referral to the diocesan assemblies the proposed constitutional change is rejected, the laws of a small number of churches forbid final confirmation without additional debate in the provincial or national assembly and further referral back to the dioceses for approval.[131] The law of one church expressly provides that silence of a diocesan assembly will be deemed to constitute its consent to the proposed change.[132] Some churches allow final confirmation, even in cases of rejection by diocesan assemblies, provided a special majority vote supports this.[133] Ordinarily, in the event of acceptance by the dioceses, confirmation may then take place; sometimes laws do not

Synods including all metropolitan sees; or by adoption in the dioceses; Const. VII.41: the constitution of a province must be altered in accordance with the terms of that province's constitution or with the consent of all that province's dioceses and must be ratified by a canon of the General Synod; for a general discussion, see *Canon Law in Australia*, Canon Law Commission, Alexandria, NSW (undated but probably c. 1977), Ch. 12.

[127] Papua New Guinea, Const. Art. 19; Melanesia, Const. Art. 20; Uganda, Const. Art. 19(3),(6); Burundi, Const. Art. 19; Zaire, Const. Art. 23; Southern Cone, Const. Art. 6.3–4.

[128] New Zealand, Const. G.4.

[129] Sudan, Const. Art. 63: reference 'for their agreement'; West Africa, Const. Art. 15: for their 'approval'; see also Jerusalem and the Middle East, Const. Art. 17(i).

[130] Tanzania, Const, IV.22: changes to Parts 4–6, 12, 15–17, 20 and 22 require approval by all the dioceses, and changes to Parts 3, 9, 10, 11, 14, 18, 19 and 21 require assent of two-thirds of the dioceses.

[131] Melanesia, Const. Art. 20: if any Diocesan Synod does not agree, the Executive Committee must refer the matter to the next meeting of the General Synod which must reconsider the change 'bearing in mind the opinions of the Diocesan Synods, and then if desired submit a new draft to the Diocesan Synods for their agreement'; see also Burundi, Const. Art. 19.6–9; and Sudan, Const. Art. 63.

[132] Papua New Guinea, Const. Art. 19: if no decision is reported by any synod 'it will be assumed that that Diocese is in agreement with the change'.

[133] Papua New Guinea, Const. Art. 19: the Provincial Council may pass a rejected proposal if three-quarters of its total members agree; Uganda, Const. Art. 19(7)–(12): a draft rejected by the dioceses must be reconsidered by the Provincial Assembly; the reformulated draft must be circulated to the Diocesan Synods; '[w]here not all the Diocesan Synods are agreed', on this second referral, 'the draft shall be discussed by the Provincial Assembly and passed if there is a two-thirds majority of the total membership of the full Assembly'.

make express provision for special majorities at this stage,[134] but most do.[135] This fourth stage is followed by publication or promulgation and, after prescribed periods which vary from church to church, the constitutional amendment becomes effective.[136]

The Westminster Model   Several churches, notably those in the British Isles and in Southern Africa and Central Africa, employ a style of constitutional amendment which approximates to that of the Westminster parliament, based on readings of an amending draft or bill.[137] The distinguishing feature is the absence of reference to diocesan assemblies: constitutional reform may take place without submission of proposals to the dioceses for either consultation or consent.[138] No special provisions are applicable to the amendment of the dispersed constitution of the Church of England: contained as it is in both an Act of Parliament and in a Measure of the General Synod, the constitution may be altered by means of parliamentary statute or synodical measure. To be operative, measures must receive both parliamentary approval and royal assent. Before submission to parlia-

---

[134] Uganda, Const. Art. 19(6): 'If the draft has been approved by all Diocesan Synods the Provincial Assembly may by decision bring the amendment into force'; Sudan, Const. Art. 64; for simple majorities see North India, Const. II.VII.4; Jerusalem, Const. Art. 17(ii); Philippines, Const. Art. X.1: approval is by a majority of each order.

[135] ECUSA, Const. Art. XII: after referral to Diocesan Conventions the proposal may be 'adopted by the General Convention at its next succeeding regular meeting by a majority of all Bishops' and by an affirmative vote in each order in the House of Deputies by a majority of the dioceses entitled to representation there; for two-thirds majorities, see: Brazil, Const. XVI; South East Asia, Const. Art. 19(b)(iii): two-thirds majority in each order voting separately; see also Zaire, Const. Art. 23; Burundi, Const. Art. 19; South India, Const. XIV.2; Rwanda, Draft Const. 1996, Art. 52; Korea, Const. p.49. For an exceptional rule, see Southern Cone, Const. Art. 6.4: 'ratification will be sought from the Anglican Consultative Council'.

[136] Korea, Const. p.49: 'promulgation' is by the Primate; Uganda, Const. Art. 19(12): after signing by the Archbishop it comes into effect. For publication see e.g. ECUSA, Cans. V.1.5(b); Melanesia, Cans. D.4. For immediate effect, see North India, Const. II.VII.4 and Sudan, Const. Art. 64; for effect three months after enactment, see Philippines, Const. X.4.

[137] See also Canada, in which the law makes no general provision for reference to the dioceses: Declaration of Principles, 11(b): 'The Constitution of the General Synod may be amended by a two-thirds majority of each Order voting at a session of the General Synod, except that any section of the Constitution which has its origin in the Declaration of Principles must be consistent with the principles concerned'; Constitution of General Synod, IV, deals with procedure and practice. For provincial constitutional reform by a two-thirds majority vote by separate orders, see the Province of Rupert's Land, Const. 1994, 8.

[138] The point is sometimes made that reference to the dioceses is not necessary in view of the frequency of assembly meetings and the representation of dioceses on the assembly (see Ch. 2). Amendment of the Scottish Episcopal Church's Code of Canons, which incorporates constitutional material, is discussed below in the section on Provincial Canons.

ment, where it is considered initially by the Ecclesiastical Committee of both Houses of Parliament, the proposed measure must be processed within the General Synod in accordance with its constitution and Standing Orders. Ordinarily, a synod member moves General Synod to instruct its Standing Committee to introduce the proposed legislation; it is circulated to members, a Steering Committee is appointed and 'general approval' may be given by synod. The draft proceeds to the revision committee stage (which reports with amendments and recommendations including advice to withdraw). At revision stage, the draft is considered by synod clause by clause and then undergoes final drafting. Final approval is carried on a motion on division by houses (of bishops, clergy and laity) by simple majority vote. Once enacted measures have the same authority of an Act of Parliament. The dioceses are not directly involved.[139]

In the Church of Ireland, 'chapters' of the Constitution may be altered by a 'statute' which must be introduced as a 'bill'. Leave to introduce, by a member of the General Synod, is given by resolution of the full synod. There is a formal first reading, a second reading at which debate on the principles of the bill occurs, and then the bill is considered by a committee of the whole synod at which each clause is discussed and voted on separately with amendments proposed. After report to the synod a day is fixed for the third reading. A vote by orders may be required at the instigation of ten members of either order of the synod's two houses of bishops and of representatives. The whole process may be completed at one synod session.[140] Much the same pattern is adopted in the Church in Wales. The Governing Body may 'add to, alter, amend or abrogate any of the provisions of the Constitution' in accordance with 'bill procedure': after circulation to its members the bill has three readings – at the first there is no debate, at the second debate ensues on the principles and a vote is taken; after consideration by committee, the bill receives a third reading at which it must be passed by a two-thirds majority of the members of each of the three orders, bishops, clergy and laity.[141]

In Southern Africa and in Central Africa, additions, alterations or repeals of Articles of the Constitution are permitted if 'it shall have been resolved at one Session of the Provincial Synod that the alteration,

---

[139] England, Church of England Assembly (Powers) Act 1919; Synodical Government Measure 1969, esp. Sched. 2: this contains the constitution of General Synod; see generally M. Hill, *Ecclesiastical Law* (London, 1995), Ch. 2; see Chs. 7 and 8 below for doctrinal and liturgical legislation.

[140] Ireland, Const. I.25; see B. McHenry, 'The General Synod of the Church of Ireland', *Ecclesiastical Law Journal*, 3(14) (1994), 192.

[141] Wales, Const. II.36–44: the bill is promulgated by the President as a canon; accelerated bill procedure is permitted by II.38; see generally, T. G. Watkin, 'Disestablishment, self-determination and the constitutional development of the Church in Wales', in N. Doe (ed.), *Essays in Canon Law* (Cardiff, 1992), 25 at 44.

amendment, or repeal of such Article is desirable, and such alteration, amendment, or repeal be agreed to at the Session of the Provincial Synod next ensuing'. Notice must be given of proposed additions, alterations or repeals of the constitution together with a statement of the reasons for the change. The notice must be communicated by the Metropolitan to all diocesan bishops 'for the information' of those who represent the several dioceses in the provincial assembly. The right to propose change is vested in the House of Bishops, the Provincial Synod itself, a Diocesan Synod, the Provincial Standing Committee, or a duly constituted Provincial or Diocesan Board. Every enactment of the Provincial Synod must receive the assent of a majority of the members present at a duly constituted session of the said synod; 'if voting by orders be required, then a majority of each order shall be necessary'.[142]

National and Provincial Canons

As a matter of ecclesiastical practice, in Anglican churches the constitution provides a procedure for the making of canons. In most churches constitutional amendment itself is effected by means of the enactment of a canon. Therefore, procedures for constitutional amendment (described in the previous section) apply *mutatis mutandis* to the making of canons.[143] In some churches, however, where constitutional amendment is not effected by the enactment of a canon, a special procedure exists for the canon-making. Consequently, this section explores a selection of largely idiosyncratic arrangements about the creation of canons, provisions which appear in the law of a relatively small number of churches. First, express reference to substantive limitations upon canon-making powers of national and

---

[142] Southern Africa, Const. Arts. VII, XXIII, Can. 49.1–2 (for detailed procedures see the Standing Rules of the Provincial Synod, esp. 42–47); a 'Motion of a Controversial Nature' is 'a motion which is deemed likely to be a cause of serious division within the body of the Church at large, or is likely to cause grave problems of conscience to members of the Church'; these, ruled as such by the President, must be passed by a two-thirds majority with a vote by orders if demanded. Central Africa has an identical set of provisions: Const. Art. 26 and Can. 33; see also Southern Africa, Const. Art. XII: the Synod of Bishops may waive compliance with procedures for constitutional amendment in times of urgent necessity; for a modest parallel, see Wales, Const. II.35: this allows constitutional amendment by means of a 'resolution' of the Governing Body until its next ordinary meeting.

[143] For the application of the same procedures regulating constitutional amendment to canon-making see: Papua New Guinea, Const. Art. 19; Melanesia, Const. Art 7; Cans. D.4: canons are made by 'bills' passed by General Synod and proposals must be forwarded 'to any Body which may be affected by such proposals'; Wales, Const. II.34–44; Ireland, Const. I.25; West Africa, Can. 18: formal notice must be proposed by the Provincial Synod, or any of its individual members, or any Diocesan Synod; canons take immediate effect on approval; South East Asia, Const. Art. 19; Korea, Const. p.49; Mexico, Can. 48; Brazil, Can. I.1, 2.

provincial assemblies is rare. In this regard, English church law is exceptional. In England, canons are generally treated as an inferior species of
internal church law. General Synod enjoys the sole power to make canons
'for the Church of England as a whole' – that is, for both the Province of
Canterbury and that of York – a power formerly exercised by the
Convocations of Canterbury and York. As to process, the same procedure
within General Synod as applies to the making of Measures (see above)
also applies to canon-making. One significant difference, however, is that
canons do not have to be approved by parliament: on completion of the
procedure within General Synod, the draft canon is submitted to the
monarch for licence and assent; it is then promulgated. Moreover, unlike
Measures (which may repeal parliamentary statutes), canons do not enjoy
the same authority as Acts of Parliament; they may do so only if a parent
Measure provides for this. The fundamental substantive limitation is that:
'[n]o Canons are to be made or put in execution . . . which are contrary or
repugnant to the Royal prerogative or the customs, laws or statutes of the
realm'.[144] According to a secular court decision in England, '[i]f there is
anything in the canons inconsistent with the statute law the Canons are so
far invalid and of no force or effect'.[145]

Secondly, the laws of some churches allow for the direct participation of
diocesan assemblies in the process of making national or provincial
canons. Two practices are employed: proposed canons must be referred to
dioceses either for consultation only or for consent or adoption.[146] The
Scottish Episcopal Church possesses a well-developed body of law which
gives expression to the idea of consultation. The Scottish General Synod
has power, by a simple majority of the members of each of its three houses,
'to propose alterations to the Canons . . . including modification or abro-
gation of or addition to any Canon or part thereof and the enactment of
new Canons'. However, no development may take effect until confirmed
by a two-thirds majority of the members of each house present and voting
at a subsequent meeting of the General Synod. This is to be held 'after
an interval of time sufficient to give Diocesan Synods opportunity of

[144] Synodical Government Measure 1969, s. 1; as with constitutional amendment,
substantive limits on canon-making powers of churches are implicit within the jurisdictional boundaries of national and provincial assemblies, particularly when law
expressly defines the relationship between the central assembly and a diocesan assembly; typically, for example, a National or Provincial Synod is unable to make law on the
powers of a Diocesan Synod without the consent of that synod (see e.g. Australia,
Const. VIII.52); for these problems see Ch. 2.

[145] *R v Dibdin* [1910] P 57 at 120 *per* Fletcher Moulton LJ; see also e.g. Melanesia,
Const. Art. 21: canons which conflict with or adversely affect any trusts set up for the
benefit of the church shall 'automatically be void and of no effect'.

[146] This is the case, of course, when constitutional amendment is effected by means
of canons in those churches which employ the Referral Model (described in the previous section); see n. 143.

considering the proposed alteration'; the period must not exceed fifteen months after proposal. Prior to confirmation, the General Synod 'shall consider any opinions received from the Diocesan Synods'. An alteration confirmed may incorporate amendments made at that meeting provided: (a) the amendment is not (in the judgement of the President) 'irrelevant to, beyond the scope of or inconsistent with the general subject-matter and purport of the alteration' as submitted to diocesan synods for their consideration; and (b) it is passed by a two-thirds majority of each house. If, in the President's view, the amendment does not 'substantially reflect' an opinion communicated to General Synod by a Diocesan Synod, or if it is 'not merely a verbal or drafting amendment', it cannot be moved unless due notice is given or the President grants leave to dispense with due notice. Following promulgation the canon takes effect forty days after confirmation.[147]

The concept of adoption operates in a developed form in the unique case of Australia, where some canons made by the national General Synod are operative in the dioceses only if they are adopted by the enactment of an ordinance of the Diocesan Synod. If General Synod declares that the provisions of a canon not involving ritual, ceremonial or discipline affect 'the order and good government of the Church within, or the church trust property of a diocese, such canon shall not come into force in any diocese unless and until the diocese by ordinance adopts the said canon'. In the event that the General Synod does not so declare, the Diocesan Synod may declare its opinion and notify the President that the canon affects the order and good government of the church or church trust property within the diocese. Whether this opinion is correct is determined by the Standing Committee of General Synod in an advice to the President: if the view is taken that the opinion of the Diocesan Synod is correct, the canon does not come into force until adopted by the diocese; if the opposite view is taken, the matter is submitted to a tribunal for determination. Any canon adopted may subsequently be 'excluded' by diocesan ordinance. This set of provisions does not apply, 'and shall be deemed never to have applied', to a canon to alter the constitution. Special provisions apply to canons imposing financial liabilities on dioceses.[148]

A third idea, found in the laws of a small number of churches in which canon-making is distinguished from constitutional amendment, places emphasis on the implementary nature of canons and their communication to the church at large. In Southern Africa, the Provincial Synod has 'full

---

[147] Scotland, Can. 52.17–18; Res. 9: Diocesan Synods 'should observe' the guidelines contained in its Appendix. For a wide-ranging study of this and related subjects, see Anne McGavin, 'The distribution of legislative power within the Scottish Episcopal Church', LL M dissertation, University of Wales, Cardiff, 1997.

[148] Australia, Const. V.30; for finance see Ch. 11.

power and authority' to make canons 'for giving effect to the provisions of [the] Constitution' and, from time to time, to alter, amend or repeal these.[149] However, 'no . . . Canon . . . shall be regarded as a Law of the Church of this Province, but such as shall have received the concurrent assent of all orders of the church' represented at the Provincial Synod.[150] Consequently, no canon may be altered, amended or repealed, and no new canon may be added, unless formal notice is given to the Metropolitan at least five months before the day for the opening of the Provincial Synod. Notice must be accompanied by a statement of the reasons for the change and it must be communicated by the Metropolitan to all diocesan bishops not less than three months before the synod's meeting 'for the information of those who shall represent their several Dioceses at that Synod'. The right to propose canonical change is vested in a more extensive range of ecclesiastical authorities than the right to propose constitutional change: no formal notice may be received unless it proceeds from a resolution of the House of Bishops, the Provincial Synod, the Provincial Standing Committee, a Committee or Commission of the Provincial Synod, or a Diocesan Synod, Council, Board, Committee or Commission, or is accompanied by a declaration signed by a diocesan bishop or three diocesan representatives to the Provincial Synod. It is competent for the Provincial Synod to amend, modify, or adopt in part, the wording of any formal notice of any new canon, or the wording of a proposed change to an existing canon. It is empowered to reject any such wording in whole or in part and, further, to substitute new wording, 'so long as no new subject matter is introduced of which five months' notice has not been given'. All canons come into force two months from the date of their authentication and promulgation.[151] A copy of the canons of the Provincial Synod must be sent, by a synod committee, to each diocesan bishop 'for the information of Diocesan Synod' and, in turn, each diocesan bishop must notify, 'in such manner as he shall see fit, to all the congregations in his Diocese, the alterations that have been made in the code of Canons'.[152] There seems to be no express provision in the law of the church in Southern Africa stating that provincial canons must be consistent with the provincial constitution.

Finally, in yet another small group of churches, the law makes express provision for the use of special majority procedures for the enactment of canons not involving constitutional amendment. In ECUSA, no new canon may be enacted, nor any existing canon amended or repealed, except by

[149] Southern Africa, Const. Art. XXII.
[150] Southern Africa, Preliminary Resolutions 1870, Res. VI.
[151] Southern Africa, Can. 49.1, 3–5.
[152] Southern Africa, Can. 1.11–12; for the same provisions see Central Africa, Cans. 1.8, 33; Nigeria, Const. XIX.

concurrent resolution of the two Houses of the General Convention. The resolutions may be introduced in either house and must be referred in each house to its Committee on Canons for consideration, report and recommendation before adoption by that house. However, in either house the requirement of reference may be dispensed with by a three-quarters vote of the members present. Whenever a canon is enacted, amended or repealed by two or more independent enactments at the same General Convention, the separate enactments must be considered as one enactment containing all the amendments, enactments or repeals to the extent that the changes made in separate amendments or enactments are not in conflict with each other. Furthermore, when a canon which repeals another canon is itself repealed, the earlier canon is not thereby revived without express words to that effect; that is, repeals of repealing canons are not re-enactments of the original canon. The Committee on Canons of each house must appoint two of its members to certify any changes in the canons and these are then published in the Journal of the General Convention.[153]

Diocesan Law

With the exception of a very small minority, notably the Church of England,[154] the laws of most churches in the Anglican Communion confer powers upon diocesan assemblies to create law for the diocese. Two forms of diocesan law are commonplace: constitutions and canons or other instruments (variously styled as regulations, ordinances, resolutions, decrees or acts). Legal arrangements display a high degree of consistency as between churches in terms of general principles. Indeed, the existence of law at this level of the church may be thought to generate a fundamental theological assumption about the nature of the diocese as a basic ecclesiastical unit.[155] The legislative competence of diocesan assemblies is

---

[153] ECUSA, Cans. V.1; for the doctrine of non-revival, see also New Zealand, Cans. C.III.4: 'statutes' may repeal or amend 'canons'; Philippines, Const. V.2: provincial canons may be altered or new canons added by a vote of two-thirds majority of the voting members present in the provincial assembly; Canada, Declaration of Fundamental Principles, 11(c): special provisions apply to national liturgical and doctrinal canons, but 'All other canons may be approved or amended by a two-thirds majority of the Order of Bishops, and of the Orders of Clergy and Laity voting together'; Province of Rupert's Land, Const. 1994, 8: the Provincial Synod may make canons by a two-thirds majority of each order voting separately at one session with confirmation by the same majorities at a subsequent session.

[154] England, Synodical Government Measure 1969, s. 4(2): legislative power is not included in the functions of the diocesan synod, though they are empowered to 'make provision' for matters in relation to the diocese. The constitution of the Southern Cone makes no mention of diocesan law.

[155] LC 1988, Res. 72.

conferred by national or provincial constitutions, and sometimes by canons. It is in relation to diocesan law that substantive limits are most conspicuous.

Diocesan Constitutions   Several churches impose a duty on the diocesan assembly to create a constitution for its diocese. The Ugandan provisions are typical of African churches: '[t]he [Diocesan] Synod shall make a Constitution for the government and administration of the Diocese, provided that a constitution of a Diocese shall be approved by the Provincial Assembly'; moreover, '[w]here there is any conflict between the Diocesan Constitution and the provisions of this Constitution, the Provincial Constitution shall prevail, at any rate to the extent of the inconsistency'.[156] Some churches require special majorities for the amendment of diocesan constitutions. In Australia, diocesan constitutions must be consistent with the national constitution. They may be altered by an ordinance of the diocesan synod only in accordance with their own terms. Amendments to diocesan constitutions must, by national canon, be passed by a majority of two-thirds of the members of each House (of clergy and laity) voting separately at the same sitting of the synod. The amendment must then be confirmed by resolution in like manner within three years at a subsequent sitting of that or a later synod – and it must be assented to by the bishop.[157] Occasionally the laws of churches confer upon the bishop an express power to veto amendments to diocesan constitutions, but this may be overridden by invoking special procedures.[158]

[156] Uganda, Const. Art. 14(a)–(b); see also Tanzania, Const. IV.18; Burundi, Const. Art. 7; Zaire, Const. Art. 7; West Africa, Diocese of Gambia and Guinea, Const. 1982, Art. 24; see also Papua New Guinea, Const. Art. 16: each Diocesan Synod must 'enact a Constitution for the government and administration of the Diocese'; it must be formally approved by the Provincial Council; in cases of conflict between the diocesan constitution and the provincial constitution the latter prevails; see e.g. Diocese of Port Moresby, Const. 1996, 3; Scotland, Can. 58: 'In the event of inconsistency as between the terms of the Canons and the Constitutions of any . . . diocese, the terms of the Canons shall supersede the provision of the Constitution'.

[157] Australia, Const. Art. VIII.47; Can. 3 1995: this canon is operative only on adoption by dioceses; see also Jerusalem, Const. Art. 10: a two-thirds majority is required and the alteration 'must be accepted by the Central Synod as consistent with the provisions of this Constitution'; Diocese of Europe, Const. 48: draft schemes of amendments must be approved by not less than two-thirds of the Diocesan Synod and laid by the bishop before General Synod for approval.

[158] ECUSA, Diocese of Western New York, Const. Art. VIII.1 and 2: after presentation and approval by a majority of both orders voting separately, it is presented at the next following Annual Convention for adoption which, similarly, must be by majority of both orders voting separately; the amendment must then be assented to by the bishop; reasons for a refusal to assent must be communicated in writing to the Annual Convention; if the bishop refuses, the amendment will nevertheless be effective 'if it be again adopted by a two-thirds vote of both Orders voting separately'; see also Diocese of Mississippi, Const. Art. XIV.

Diocesan Canons and Other Forms of Legislative Instrument   The laws of most churches prescribe procedures for the making of diocesan *canons*.[159] It is also usually the case that laws require these and other forms of legislation to conform to national or provincial law: arrangements in Australia,[160] and Canada,[161] are typical, though the express requirement of conformity to secular law, appearing in the laws of some American dioceses, is not: in the Diocese of Western New York diocesan canons are amended by the Diocesan Convention by either: (a) a majority vote of both clergy and lay members voting separately at two successive conventions; or (b) by a two-thirds vote of both voting separately at one convention; they are subject 'at all times' to the national constitution and canons and – and this is an untypical provision – 'the laws of the State of New York'.[162] The laws of several churches include a special episcopal power of veto over diocesan legislation: two slightly contrasting approaches are used in Ireland and Southern Africa.

In Ireland, every *act* of a Diocesan Synod must be assented to by the presiding bishop (or a commissary of the bishop) and a majority of the clergy and synodsmen present and voting conjointly, or by a majority of the members of each order present and voting by orders. If a majority of the clergy and synodsmen assent, the bishop may take a reasonable time, not exceeding one month, to consider whether or not to assent. If the president dissents from the other two orders, all action must be suspended until the next annual meeting. If the proposed act is re-affirmed by two-thirds of each of the other orders, and the president still dissents, it must be submitted to the General Synod the decision of which is final; this is subject to the proviso that where any proposed act has been affirmed by a majority of each order, it is competent for the president to refer the question to the next session of the General Synod for decision. Every Diocesan Synod may also make 'regulations as to the temporalities of the Church', 'not being

[159] Sudan, Const. Arts. 1.k and 3; New Zealand, Const. D, E and F; Melanesia, Diocese of Temotu, Can. 4 (bill procedure); Chile, Can. H.3.

[160] Australia, Const. Art. VIII.51; Art. XII.74(1): the Diocesan Synod may make ordinances for the order and good government of the diocese in accordance with powers conferred by the diocesan constitution; Const. V.30: unless a national canon of the General Synod deals with the order and good government of the church in a diocese, in which case it may be adopted by the Diocesan Synod, 'any ordinance of any diocesan synod inconsistent with the canon shall to the extent of the inconsistency have no effect' (see e.g. Diocese of Sydney, *The 7th Handbook*, 4.6 for the procedure for creating ordinances).

[161] Canada, Province of Rupert's Land, Const. 1994, 1.10: 'No regulation of a Diocesan Synod shall have force in any Diocese if it is contrary to or in conflict with an enactment of the Provincial Synod'; North India, Const. II.III.IX.37: rules and by-laws of diocesan councils for the functioning of the diocese and for discipline must be approved by the central Synod's Executive Committee; see also New Zealand, Can. B.II.

[162] ECUSA, Diocese of Western New York, Cans. 21–22.

repugnant to any law of the Church or to any regulation of the General Synod', or to any trusts, 'as the synod may deem necessary for the welfare of the Church in such diocese'. If 'any act of the diocesan synod be varied, repealed, or superseded by the General Synod, and shall be re-enacted by the diocesan synod . . . such act shall not come into operation until it shall have received the assent of the General Synod'.[163]

Whereas in Ireland the bishop's veto over diocesan legislation is subject to review by the General Synod, representative of bishops, clergy and laity, a rather different system operates in Southern Africa – here review is reserved to an episcopal assembly. 'All Acts and Resolutions' passed by a Diocesan Synod shall be reviewed and, if he sees fit, promulgated either by the diocesan bishop or, in cases of absence or incapacity, by the metropolitan. The diocesan bishop possesses 'the right of veto upon all Acts and Resolutions of the Synod of his Diocese'. If the bishop dissents from any Act or Resolution which is passed with a majority of less than two-thirds, 'such Act or Resolution shall be void and of no effect'. However, if the instrument is passed by a majority of two-thirds or more, the bishop must express his intention of exercising the veto or the possibility of doing so. Then separate votes of the synod's two houses, of clergy and laity, must be taken on the Act or Resolution. If passed by majorities of not less than two-thirds in each house, and the instrument is still vetoed by the bishop, an appeal against the bishop's decision to the Metropolitan and diocesan bishops sitting in synod is obligatory. If these override the diocesan bishop's veto, the diocesan bishop must promulgate the Act or Resolution in the diocese without delay. Furthermore, 'no regulation of any Diocesan Synod shall have force in any Diocese of this province, if it be contrary to, or in conflict with, any enactment of the Provincial Synod' – and 'any act of a Diocesan Synod shall be liable to be reviewed by the Provincial Synod'. Rules on ecclesiastical discipline must ordinarily be made by the Provincial Synod, but if a Diocesan Synod legislates on the matter, its instrument has force until the next session of the Provincial Synod, unless, that is, it is already contrary to rules of the Provincial Synod.[164]

CONCLUSIONS

One function of particular church law is to define the nature of the church in question. Anglican laws do so in the most general of terms treating individual churches as branches of the one, holy, catholic and apostolic

---

[163] Ireland, Const II.I.28–33; see e.g. United Dioceses of Cork, Cloyne and Ross, Rules and Regulations 1989, Ch. 1, ss. 2.

[164] Southern Africa, Const. Art. VIII, IX; XI; Cans. 9,10; see also Central Africa, Can. 10.

church. Whilst they exist ecclesiastically as national, provincial, regional or united churches, or as extra-provincial dioceses, for the purposes of secular law, Anglican churches may be classified as established or quasi-established, disestablished or non-established. In the vast majority of states, secular law contains a developed jurisprudence in the doctrine of consensual compact, under which churches exist as voluntary associations, their rules enforceable in the secular courts when property matters or those concerning civil rights are involved. Forms of internal ecclesiastical regulation are multiple: most are binding on church members, by means of a voluntary undertaking, to facilitate and to order the mission of the church. Canons of all churches should not be contrary to the law of the state, or else they may lose their authority in the wider legal environment. Legislative powers are distributed in all churches to assemblies operating at national, regional or provincial level, and in the vast majority to diocesan assemblies also. Most laws governing the law-making process are procedural: special procedures must be followed for the amendment of national and provincial constitutions and canons to which diocesan legislation must conform.

2

The Institutional Organization of Churches

The assertion is often made, in Anglican constitutional thought, that the church is episcopally led and synodically governed. Certainly, one of the achievements of Anglican canon law is the extent to which it enables the participation of the laity in ecclesiastical government. The principle of representation enables the laity to share directly, together with the episcopate and clergy, in decision-making at all levels of the church. The involvement of the laity is not, however, confined to the synods and other assemblies of the church, from the national, regional or provincial level down to the lowest ecclesiastical unit, the parish or pastorate. Recent years have witnessed a marked increase in the number of commissions, committees and other bodies which carry out the administrative tasks of ecclesiastical assemblies: in these too the laity is active. This chapter examines the organization of churches in terms of their institutions: the national, regional and provincial assemblies, diocesan assemblies, and assemblies operating within the various divisions of the diocese, as well as those administrative bodies accountable to the representative assemblies. It concentrates on their composition, functions and jurisdiction, the transaction of their business and their relations one with another. The doctrine of the separation of powers is implicit in Anglican laws dealing with the institutional organization of churches: laws delineate precisely the functions, responsibilities and powers appropriate to institutions operating at the different levels of each church.

NATIONAL AND REGIONAL ASSEMBLIES

Successive resolutions of the Lambeth Conference have addressed directly the need for structures which facilitate the full participation of the laity in the government of Anglican churches.[1] For national and regional churches the central organ of government is the national or regional assembly,

---

[1] LC 1920, Res. 14: 'every branch of the Anglican Communion should develop the constitutional government of the Church and should make a fuller use of the capacities of its members for service'; for representative synods, see LC 1867, Ress. 4, 5, 8, 10; LC 1897, Res. 24; LC 1920, Res. 43; LC 1930, Res. 53.

styled variously as the General Synod,[2] General Convention,[3] or Synod.[4] The composition and functions of these assemblies are carefully defined by national or regional church law, as is their relationship with the provinces, those ecclesiastical sub-divisions of national or regional churches under the authority of a metropolitan.[5] Frequently, arrangements operating at the level of the diocese mirror those operating at national, regional or provincial level.

The central assembly of most national or regional churches is composed of three Houses or orders – bishops, clergy and laity – but in some it is bicameral.[6] The House of Bishops consists of the primate, metropolitans, and all diocesan bishops,[7] and it is often the case that other bishops, having the status of coadjutors, suffragans or assistants, are either represented in the assembly, or else are *ex officio* members.[8] The House of Clergy is composed of representatives of the clergy from each of the dioceses of the church; sometimes these are elected in accordance with rules made at the diocesan level,[9] and sometimes the rules governing election are to be found in national or regional laws.[10] The right to be elected is most commonly conferred upon both priests and deacons.[11] In several churches,

[2] England, Synodical Government Measure 1969, s. 2; for the concept of a 'national church', see LC 1930, Res. 52: 'Saving always the moral and spiritual independence of the divine society, the Conference approves the association of dioceses or provinces in the larger unit of a "national Church", with or without the formal recognition of the civil government, as serving to give spiritual expression to the distinctive genius of races and peoples, and thus to bring more effectually under the influence of Christ's religion both the process of government and the habit of society'; see also LC 1878, Res. 1; LC 1908, Res. 8.

[3] ECUSA, Const. Art. I.1.

[4] North India, Const. II.IV; the 'National Assembly' of the Province of Korea is considered in the next section.

[5] See n. 42 and Ch. 4.

[6] ECUSA, Const. Art. I.2–4: the General Convention has two Houses: the House of Bishops and the House of Deputies, composed of deputies of the clergy and of the laity (with not more than four from each class representing each diocese); Ireland, Const. I.2: the General Synod is composed of a House of Bishops and a House of Representatives composed of members elected from the clergy and laity of each diocese by the clerical and lay members of the Diocesan Synod; elections take place every three years.

[7] Australia, Const. IV.16; Scotland, Can. 52.3.

[8] England, Can. H3: nine representatives are elected by and from the suffragan bishops of each province; see also ECUSA, Const. Art. I.2–4: coadjutor, suffragans and retired bishops are all entitled to vote; Japan, Can. VI: suffragans are members but have no vote; see also Canada, Declaration of Principles, 3(b) and South India, Const. IX.2.

[9] Australia, Const. IV.17; ECUSA, Const. Art. I.2–4; Canada, Declaration of Principles, 3(c): clergy are elected by Diocesan Synods according to their own rules; South India, Const. IX.4.

[10] Scotland, Can. 52.5: clerical members are elected from the clerical membership of Diocesan Synods.

[11] Australia, Const. IV.17; ECUSA, Const. I.2–4; Cans. I.1.4 (until 1982 deacons were not permitted to serve); Chile, Cans. C.10; compare North India, Const. II.II.IV.III: presbyters only serve.

non-diocesan bishops may be elected to the House of Clergy.[12] The House of Laity is composed of representatives of the laity of each diocese: again, national or diocesan law provides for the timing of elections,[13] and the right to be elected is reserved normally to adult communicant members of the church,[14] resident in the diocese.[15] Special constituencies of clergy and laity may also be represented, typically chaplains to the armed forces, members of religious communities and youth.[16] Laws usually provide that in instances of dispute as to whether a person is qualified, the matter must be decided by the national or regional assembly itself.[17] A standard legal provision is that irregularities in elections will not invalidate the proceedings of the assembly.[18]

Invariably, the president of the assembly is the primate,[19] and sessions must be held at times prescribed by law: these vary; sometimes annually,[20] or at intervals not exceeding two years,[21] three years,[22] or four years.[23] Commonly the primate is empowered to convene an extraordinary meeting of the assembly, and may be required to do so on the requisition of: prescribed majorities in each of the houses of the assembly,[24] a majority of the bishops, or the assembly's Standing Committee.[25] Notice of meetings

[12] See e.g. Australia, Const. IV.17.

[13] Scotland, Can. 52.5: lay members are elected from the lay membership of Diocesan Synods; Canada, Declaration of Principles, 3(d): members of the order of laity, who must be communicant lay members of the church are elected by Diocesan Synods according to their own rules (3(f) sets out the apportionment in terms of numbers as between the dioceses); South India, Const. IX.2, 5.

[14] ECUSA, Cans. I.1(4): they must be 'in good standing'; Scotland, Can. 52.5: members must be 18 years or more and confirmed communicants; Ireland, Const. I.8; Japan, Can. VIII, Art. 75.

[15] Australia, Const. IV.17.

[16] See e.g. Canada, Declaration of Principles, 3(g) and (h): representatives of the Armed Forces and of youth (aged 16–26); South India, Const. IX.2.

[17] Australia, Const. IV.18; for resolution by the Standing Committee until the General Synod determines the matter, see Scotland, Can. 52.11.

[18] Scotland, Can. 52.12: this is the case unless the General Synod considers the irregularity to be 'of such a character to make it unjust or unfair' to transact business until the irregularity is corrected.

[19] Australia, Const. IV.20; Canada, Declaration of Principles, 4; Japan, Can. VIII, Art. 72.

[20] Scotland, Can. 52.1; Ireland, Const. I.14.

[21] ECUSA, Const. Art. I.7; South India, Const. IX.20.

[22] Canada, Const. of General Synod, I.2(a). [23] Australia, Const. IV.23.

[24] Ireland, Const. I.15: the Archbishop of Armagh may call a meeting 'at his own discretion' or on a written application of one third of any order of General Synod; Canada, Const. IV.23: half the House of Bishops or a third of the members of either of the other houses may requisition.

[25] ECUSA, Cans. I.1.3(a): the Presiding Bishop convenes but a majority of bishops may requisition; Scotland, Can. 52.1: the College of Bishops may requisition; Canada, Const. of General Synod, I.2(b): it may be convened at any time by the primate or by direction of the Council of General Synod or on the requisition of any five diocesan bishops; South India, Const. IX: special meetings may be called by the Executive Committee.

is required as is circulation of the agenda.[26] Laws contain detailed provisions on voting,[27] and the norm is for houses to vote together,[28] unless a prescribed number of assembly members request separate voting by houses or orders.[29] Ordinarily sessions are in public but a right is reserved to the assembly to sit in private at its discretion.[30] Between sessions, the business of the assembly is transacted by a Standing or Executive Committee, being under a general duty to carry out the decisions and policies of the assembly to which it is responsible and to which it must submit periodic reports – the composition and functions of the committee are carefully prescribed by national or regional law.[31] A wide variety of tasks is also assigned to the assembly's other advisory and recommendatory committees, commissions, boards and councils, composed of both assembly members and others, which are responsible to the assembly for the fulfilment of their designated functions.[32] Titles of such subordinate bodies vary, but typically they exist to deal with matters of ministry, mission, education, liturgy and doctrine.[33]

[26] See e.g. Scotland, Can. 52.2; Canada, Const. of General Synod, I.4.

[27] See e.g. Ireland, Const. I.21: no motion is carried unless a majority of the bishops support it and a majority of clerical and lay representatives voting conjointly or by orders; if the bishops are not in favour, but at the next session two-thirds of clerical and lay representatives voting jointly or by orders support it, the motion is carried unless negatived by two-thirds of the House of Bishops (who must give reasons).

[28] ECUSA, Const. I.5; Scotland, Can. 52.3: normally General Synod is to meet as one body but at the request of a majority of any house may meet in separate houses.

[29] Ireland, Const. I.23: the House of Representatives must vote together unless 10 require a vote by orders; see also Canada, Declaration of Principles, 5; Australia, Const. IV.15.

[30] See e.g. Canada, Const. of General Synod, IV.24.

[31] ECUSA, Cans. I.4(1): the Executive Council is obliged 'to carry out the program and policies adopted by the [General] Convention' and has a special responsibility for the missionary, educational and social work of the church; it is accountable to the General Convention to which it must submit a full report on its work; the Presiding Bishop is chair and president, and other members include bishops, clergy and lay persons elected by the Convention and various *ex officio* members; see also Japan, Can. VIII, Art. 83; Brazil, Cans. I.2; Mexico, Cans. I.1; Chile, Cans. C.11; North India, Const. II.IV.X.

[32] ECUSA, Cans. I.1.2: the General Convention is empowered to establish Standing Commissions (to study and recommend on major subjects of continuing concern) and Joint Commissions (to study and recommend on specific matters of concern during a single interval between two regular meetings of the Convention); canons must prescribe composition (which may include non-members of the Convention); every commission is convened by a bishop and the Presiding Bishop is an *ex officio* member; Canada, Const. of General Synod: VII.35: the Executive Council is responsible for 'overall strategic planning and visioning within the mandate of the General Synod'; it must consider and report on any matter referred to it by General Synod and co-ordinate the work of Synod's boards and commissions; for Standing Committees see also Scotland, Digest of Resolutions, 19.1; Ireland, Standing Orders of General Synod, 1–15; South India, Const. IX.28–29.

[33] ECUSA, Cans. I.1,2 and 13: the General Convention has Standing Commissions on Small Communities, the Constitution and Canons, Ecumenical Relations, Health,

Whilst there is a consistency in practice as between national and regional churches with respect to the jurisdiction and functions of central church assemblies, laws do not generally devote a separate title to the subject; instead they recognize a general authority in the central assembly.[34] Jurisdictional boundaries and functions are scattered amongst laws dealing with discrete topics. However, for the purposes of law-making,[35] policy-making and administration,[36] these central assemblies have jurisdiction over and discharge functions concerning, typically: membership of the church,[37] relations (particularly union) with other churches,[38] controlling the funds of the church,[39] and considering matters concerning the church and expressing an opinion on any other matters of religious or public interest.[40] Untypically, the church in Canada deals under a separate title with 'the jurisdiction' of the General Synod: it has 'authority and jurisdiction in all matters affecting in any way the general interest and well-being of the whole Church'; in particular: its own constitution and organization; the national character, constitution, integrity and autonomy of the whole church; relations between the church and other religious bodies in Canada and in the Anglican Communion; the creation and constitution of new provinces; the election, retirement and resignation of the

Human Affairs, Metropolitan Areas, Peace with Justice, the Structure of the Church, World Mission, Stewardship and Development, Evangelism, and a Commission on Aids; Scotland, Digest of Resolutions, 19.2ff: the Faith and Order Board (which must appoint committees on Doctrine, Inter-Church Relations, Liturgy and the canons), the Mission Board, and the Administration Board (which appoints, *inter alia*, the Finance Committee, the Property Committee and the Pensions Committee); Ireland, Const. I.III.32; Australia, Const. VI.35 and Cans. 1969–92: the commissions deal with Liturgy, International Affairs, Social Responsibilities, Doctrine, Canon Law, Mission and Ecumenism, and Ministry and Training; Canada, Const. of General Synod, VIII: Faith, Worship and Ministry Committee, Partners in Mission Committee, Eco-Justice Committee, and the Financial Management and Development Committee; see also South India, Const. IX.18–27.

[34] See e.g. Ireland, Const. Preamble, Declaration IV: the General Synod 'shall have chief legislative power . . . and such administrative power as may be necessary for the Church and consistent with its episcopal constitution'; South India, Const. IX.13: 'The Synod is the supreme governing and legislative body of the Church of South India, and the final authority in all matters pertaining to the Church'; North India, Const. II.IV.IV.38: the Synod 'shall do all acts and things which it considers necessary for the spiritual health, temporal well-being and administrative efficiency of the Church'.

[35] See Ch. 1.

[36] For the process of adjudication by the courts of central assemblies, see Ch. 3; the following provision seems to be unique: Scotland, Can. 52.16: 'The General Synod shall have no judicial power, either primary or on appeal'; compare e.g. North India, Const. II.IV.IV.37: the Synod may suspend or dissolve any Diocesan Council 'with a view to restore order, unity, fellowship and normal functioning of the Diocese'.

[37] North India, Const. II.IV.IV.34.

[38] North India, Const. II.IV.IV.35; South India, Const. IX.15; see Ch. 12.

[39] Scotland, Can. 52, Digest of Resolutions, 1; see Ch. 11.

[40] England, Synodical Government Measure 1969, s. 2(1).

Primate; 'structural uniformity in relation to the episcopal prerogative of licensing clergy'; ecclesiastical discipline and disciplinary proceedings.[41]

PROVINCIAL ASSEMBLIES

A province is, broadly, an ecclesiastical territory consisting of a group of dioceses organized under the jurisdiction of a metropolitan (usually styled archbishop) and governed by a provincial assembly (usually styled the Provincial Synod or Council).[42] As was seen in Chapter 1, national and regional churches may be divided into provinces but in most cases the province constitutes the whole territory of the church. Indeed, in line with resolutions of the Lambeth Conference, commonly laws recognize that it is in accordance with 'the ancient laws and usages of the Holy, Catholic Church' that 'dioceses be associated in Provinces'.[43] Laws of a handful of both national and provincial churches deal with the creation of new provinces.[44] As a general principle, the establishment of a province is in the keeping of the central assembly which must not act without the consent of any diocese forming part of the proposed province.[45] The same applies to mergers with other provinces.[46] The mutual consent of both the provincial assembly and the diocese is also necessary for the transfer of a

[41] Canada, Declaration of Principles, 6, 7A.

[42] ACC – 4, 1979, B: a province is 'a self-governing Church composed of several dioceses operating under a common Constitution and having one supreme legislative body'; see e.g. Uganda, Const. Preamble: 'Dioceses should be associated in Provinces presided over by an Archbishop . . . for the furtherance of fellowship, comity and mutual support among them'; Sudan, Const. Art. 1: the province is 'a combination under the Archbishop and a General Synod of the several Dioceses in the Republic of the Sudan'; Southern Africa, Const. Art. XXIV.2: the 'Province of Southern Africa' is 'a combination under Metropolitical and Synodical Authority . . . of the several Dioceses'; see also Canada, Declaration of Principles, 9: 'Ecclesiastical Province' means 'any group of dioceses under the jurisdiction of a provincial synod'.

[43] LC 1878, Res. 2: dioceses should 'associate themselves into a province or provinces, in accordance with the ancient laws and usages of the Catholic Church'; this is repeated in Indian Ocean, Const. Preamble; Sudan, Const. Preamble; and Uganda, Const. Preamble.

[44] LC 1920, Res. 43: 'In the opinion of the Conference four is the minimum number of dioceses suitable to form a province. No number should be considered too great to form a province, so long as the bishops and other representatives of the diocese are able conveniently to meet for mutual consultation and for the transaction of provincial business'; see also LC 1930, Res. 53.

[45] ECUSA, Const. Art. VII: 'Dioceses may be united into Provinces in such manner, under such conditions, and with such powers, as shall be provided by Canon of the General Convention, Provided always, that no Diocese shall be included in a Province without its own consent'; see also Papua New Guinea, Const. Art. 1: the Provincial Council is empowered to divide the province to form two or more new provinces; Canada, Declaration of Principles, 6(e).

[46] New Zealand, Const. C8; Burundi, Const. Art. 1.

diocese to another province.[47] The constitution of one church expressly provides that 'the release of a constituent diocese . . . shall not be unreasonably withheld if sought' by the Provincial Assembly.[48] Some churches require the association of at least four dioceses for the creation of a new province.[49]

Composition and Proceedings

In terms of institutional organization, provincial assemblies follow much the same pattern as applies to national or regional assemblies. Most provincial assemblies consist of three houses or orders, bishops, clergy and laity, though some are bicameral.[50] The House or Order of Bishops may consist exclusively of the metropolitan and diocesan bishops,[51] or else of these and coadjutor, suffragan and assistant bishops.[52] The other houses or orders are composed of representatives of the diocesan clergy and laity. The House or Order of Clergy is composed of priests and deacons elected by the clerical members of the diocesan assembly in accordance either with national or provincial law,[53] or with diocesan law.[54] Similarly, the House or Order of Laity is composed of adult communicant members of the church elected, under national, provincial or diocesan law, by the lay members of the diocesan assembly.[55] The number of members

[47] Papua New Guinea, Const. Art. 1: a diocese may leave the province provided the Provincial Council is satisfied that the reasons are adequate and the diocese will remain in fellowship with the Anglican Communion or with a church in communion with it; ECUSA, Cans. I.9.2: this governs transfer.

[48] Uganda, Const. Art. 6(c).

[49] Australia, Const. VII.37: both the General Synod (by canon) and the synod of the diocese concerned must consent; this implements LC 1920, Res. 43: see n. 44.

[50] ECUSA, Cans. I.9: the House of Bishops and the House of Deputies of the Provincial Synod; Diocese of Western New York, Can. 5: the Diocesan Council elects 4 clergy and 4 lay people (who must be adult communicants of good standing) to the Provincial Synod.

[51] Wales, Const. II.2: the Order of Bishops consists of the archbishop and all diocesan bishops; II.4: all other bishops 'residing and assisting' are members of the Order of Clergy; see also Indian Ocean, Const. Art. 7; Papua New Guinea, Const. Art. 6; South East Asia, Const. Art. 7; Korea, Const. Ch. I, Art. 28.

[52] Central Africa, Const. Art. 7(a); Melanesia, Const. Art. 7; see also Rwanda, Draft Const. Art. 26 and Burundi, Const. Art. 6: coadjutor bishops have no vote; Nigeria, Const. Ch. XI.

[53] Papua New Guinea, Const. Art. 6: 1 clerical member from each diocese; South East Asia, Const. Art. VII(b)(ii): 3 clergy elected by each diocese; Wales, Const. II.5; Melanesia, Const. Art. 7; Indian Ocean, Const. Art. 7; Tanzania, Const. IV.15; Central Africa, Const. Art. 7(b).

[54] Southern Africa, Can. 1.3; Uganda, Const. 5(h); see n. 56.

[55] Wales, Const. II.6: 30 are elected for each diocese by the lay members of the Diocesan Conference; they must be 18 or over; for 18 as the required age, see also Southern Africa, Const. VI; Indian Ocean, Const. Art. 7; Melanesia, Const. Art. 7; compare Tanzania, Const. IV.17: 19 years; South East Asia, Const. Art. 7(b), Central Africa,

is organized on the basis of apportionment as between the dioceses, and some laws provide for equal numbers of clerical and lay representatives,[56] and others for greater lay representation.[57] Membership of clerical and lay houses is usually held for a term of years, ceasing with a fresh election or the attainment of a fixed age.[58] Laws commonly allow for representation of special constituencies including chaplains to the armed forces, schools, prisons and hospitals, and youth,[59] as well as for the co-option of members.[60] Laws often provide that the failure or neglect on the part of any diocese to send representatives, or the failure of these to attend, does not invalidate the proceedings or enactments of the provincial assembly, which in any event enjoy the same force and effect in that diocese as if its representatives were present.[61] Only occasionally do formal laws expressly empower the provincial assembly to remove members.[62]

Ordinarily the president of the provincial assembly is the metropolitan upon whom a duty is placed to convene the assembly at those times pre-

Const. Art. 7(c); see also Uganda, Const. Art. 5(i): members must be communicants who have attained 21 years of age.

[56] West Indies, Const. Art. 3: 2 clergy and 2 lay representatives are to be elected from each diocese in accordance with rules made by the Diocesan Synod; compare West Africa, Can. III.2: 3 clerical and 3 lay representatives must be 'elected . . . in such manner as the Diocesan Constitution and Canons or the Diocesan Synod may determine'; the same rule is found in Rwanda, Draft Const. Art. 15; Kenya, Can. XI: each house consists of 4 clerical and 4 lay members from each diocese elected by the diocese in accordance with its constitution; Korea, Const. Ch. 4, Art. 20: the National Synod has 10 clerical and 10 lay members elected by each diocesan synod; Tanzania, Const. IV. IV.16 and VI, Order 1: the number is to be determined by the diocese.

[57] New Zealand, Const. C.4: each diocese is entitled to be represented by 3 clergy and 4 laity; for the same rule see South East Asia, Const. Art. 7(b).

[58] New Zealand, Cans. B.I.1.1.9: 2 years (and Const. C2: 'A fresh General Election shall take place before each biennial meeting of the General Synod'); Wales, Const. II.12,15: office is held for 3 years and membership ceases at 75; South East Asia, Const. Art. VII(b): 'no person who has attained the age of 65 years shall be a member of the Provincial Synod'; Papua New Guinea, Const. Art. 6: 4 years; Jerusalem, Const. Art. 6(ii): 5 years; see also Korea, Const. Art. 23.

[59] Southern Africa, Can. 12(b): youth; Zaire, Const. Art. 5: this requires representatives of youth (18–25 years) and of women's organizations; Burundi, Const. Art. 6: representatives from the Theological Centre; Melanesia, Const. Art. 7: 1 representative of religious communities, 1 of the Mothers' Union and 1 (aged 17–25) representing the youth.

[60] Wales, Const. II.5, 6; for *ex officio* membership of provincial officers, see e.g. Melanesia, Const. Art. 7; Rwanda, Draft Const. Art. 15: representatives of theological college staff, students, the provincial secretary, senior staff of the provincial secretariat and the provincial chancellor act as 'consultants'; South East Asia, Const. Art. 7(b): the provincial chancellor and registrar are *ex officio* members but have no voting rights.

[61] See e.g. Southern Africa, Const. Art. VI; Central Africa, Const. Art. 9; South East Asia, Const. Art. VII(k); Uganda, Const. Art. 5(j).

[62] See e.g. Wales, Const. II.56: the Governing Body is empowered to make rules enabling it 'to remove any member of the Governing Body . . . for sufficient reason' and the assembly is the final judge 'of what constitutes a sufficient reason'.

scribed by law; these vary, from annual meetings,[63] to meetings every two,[64] three.[65] or, more rarely, four years.[66] The metropolitan is also empowered to call meetings at his discretion,[67] and is obliged to do so on the requisition of prescribed persons or bodies; sometimes the right to requisition is reserved to the bishops alone,[68] but more often the right is more widely distributed, to bishops or prescribed majorities of clerical or lay members of the assembly,[69] or a fixed number of these,[70] or to the assembly's Standing Committee.[71] Notice of the meeting must be given, and the periods required vary as between churches as do times for circulation of the agenda,[72] and to transact its business prescribed rules about quorum must be satisfied.[73] Sometimes, the law requires the session to open with a liturgical celebration of the eucharist.[74] Ordinarily, the houses of the assembly must sit together for the transaction of business and for debate, and decisions are arrived at by a simple majority unless the law provides

[63] Wales, Const. II.20: at least one ordinary meeting *per annum* (in practice it meets twice yearly); Papua New Guinea, Const. Art. 6; South East Asia, Const. Art. VII(g): 'There shall be a meeting of the Provincial Synod biennially'.

[64] Sudan, Const. Art. 6(iii); Uganda, Const. Art. 5(d); Rwanda, Draft Const. 1996, Art. 17; Korea, Const. Art. 24; New Zealand, Cans. B.II.2.1.

[65] Southern Cone, Can. 5; Southern Africa, Can. 1.1; West Africa, Const. Art. XIII.5; Tanzania, Const. IV.14; Melanesia, Const. Art. III.4.

[66] Indian Ocean, Const. Art. 6; Zaire, Const. Art. 6.

[67] West Africa, Const. Art. XII.6: no provision is made for any other form of extraordinary session.

[68] A majority of bishops may requisition in Southern Africa, Const. IV and Central Africa, Const. Art. 8(b).

[69] South East Asia, Const. Art. VII(h): half the bishops or half the clerical members or half the lay members may requisition; Uganda, Const. Art. 5(e): one-third of the assembly members or two-thirds of any house; Korea, Const. Art. 25: all the members of the Bishops' Conference or two-thirds of the members of the National Executive Committee, two-thirds of delegates to National Synod; see also Tanzania, Const. Art. IV.14; and Philippines, Const. Art. III.4.

[70] West Indies, Can. 1.2: 5 bishops, or 7 clerical or 7 lay members of the Provincial Synod; Papua New Guinea, Const. Art. 6: 10 members.

[71] Indian Ocean, Const. Art. 6: the Standing Committee; Southern Cone, Can. 5.1: the Executive Council or when at least half the Provincial Synod's members 'so desire'.

[72] South East Asia, Const. Art. VII(j): 2 months' notice; Southern Africa, Can. 1.1: 7 months' notice; West Indies, Can. 1.4: 3 months' notice; with the agenda circulated at least 4 weeks in advance of the meeting; West Africa, Const. Art. XIII.5: notice of at least 3 months and the agenda must be circulated at least 1 month before the session; Tanzania, Const. Art. IV.14.

[73] For a quorum constituted by a simple majority of members, see Southern Cone, Can. 5.3.2; Korea, Const. Art. 30; and Philippines, Const. Art. III.5; compare South East Asia, Const. Art. VII(i): 3 diocesan bishops and one half of the members of each house of clergy and of laity; West Indies, Can. 1.4: the president plus 5 bishops, 8 clerical and 8 lay representatives constitutes a quorum; Papua New Guinea, Const. Art. 6: quorum is at least three-fifths of each house; Uganda, Const. Art. 5(g)–(i): two-thirds of the bishops and one-half of each other house are required.

[74] See e.g. West Africa, Const. Art. XIII.11.

otherwise.[75] It is usually the case that the houses or orders must vote together, but if any member, before any motion is put, requests a vote by houses, the request must be granted provided there is support from a pre-scribed number of assembly members.[76] It is not often the case that formal law requires proceedings to be open to the public, but those laws which deal with the matter reserve to the assembly a discretion to exclude.[77] Normally, in national churches, these arrangements are governed by provincial law.[78]

Functions: Subject-Matter Jurisdiction

In terms of form, it is usually the constitution of a church which, under a separate title, deals with the jurisdiction of provincial assemblies, whether the church comprises a single province or, in the case of national or regional churches, several provinces. The jurisdictional laws of each church are either positive, listing subjects over which the assembly has competence, or negative, listing matters over which it has no competence. In provincial churches the assembly has jurisdiction over the whole church, being a single province, and in national or regional churches com-posed of several provinces, jurisdiction is confined to the individual province. Generally, with respect to the former, subject-matter jurisdiction covers the spiritual,[79] governmental,[80] liturgical,[81] proprietorial,[82] and ministerial life of the provincial church.[83] Typically, therefore, to the

[75] West Africa, Const. Art. XIII.8; Southern Cone, Can. 5.3.4; Uganda, Const. Art. 5(f); Zaire, Const. Art. 6; Philippines, Const. Art. III.6; West Indies, Can. 1.8: the houses may meet and deliberate either separately or together as the members of each house may by majority decide, 'but all matters debated shall be decided by the three Houses voting separately'; an affirmative vote of a simple majority of the three houses is necessary for the adoption of any resolution, unless the law provides otherwise.

[76] West Africa, Const. Art. XIII.10; Uganda, Const. Art. 5(f)(iii): 3 bishops or 10 mem-bers; Central Africa, Const. Art. 8: 'a vote by Houses may be required by any member'; West Africa, Const. Art. XIII.8: a majority of any house may require 'opportunity for separate deliberation, [and] such opportunity shall be given as soon as practicable'; Burundi, Const. Art. 6: 3 bishops or 10 clergy or 10 lay members may require it; Southern Cone Can. 5.3.4: this does not specify numbers.

[77] Southern Africa, Can. 1.13.

[78] See e.g. Australia, Const. VII.42; ECUSA, Can. I.9.

[79] West Africa, Const. Art. XXIII.3: 'The Provincial Synod has the final authority in matters concerning the spiritual discipline of the Church'; see also Zaire, Const. 6.

[80] Papua New Guinea, Const. Art. 6: the Provincial Council is 'the final governing body of the Church and, subject to certain exceptions as defined in this Constitution . . . on all matters affecting the life, order and canonical discipline of this Church'; for much the same provision, see Philippines, Const. Art. III.1 and Rwanda, Draft Const. 1996, Art. 27.

[81] See Chs. 7 and 8.

[82] Southern Africa, Const. Art. XVI; Papua New Guinea, Const. Art. 18; see generally Ch. 11.   [83] Southern Africa, Const. Art. XI.

provincial assembly belongs *inter alia* responsibility for regulating the appointment of bishops,[84] ecclesiastical discipline, the establishment of courts and ecclesiastical offences,[85] and the appointment and functions of provincial officers.[86] It is the provincial assembly that acts in the name of the church,[87] particularly in its dealings with agencies of world-wide bodies and other Christian churches,[88] and with fellow member churches of the Anglican Communion.[89] In short, alongside its law-making functions (discussed in Chapter 1), the provincial assembly is involved with a host of administrative matters. In national or regional churches, though, jurisdictional law is different: the law defines the respective competences of the national or regional assembly and of the provincial assembly.[90]

Examples of positive jurisdictional law, law which is by nature power-conferring, are to be found in Uganda and Canada. A comparison of these two churches illustrates the all-embracing authority of the assembly of a provincial church, and the more limited competence of provincial assemblies in a national church composed of several provinces. According to the constitution of the Provincial Church of Uganda, the Provincial Assembly has 'responsibility for the overall direction of the Church . . . to formulate broad, basic policies . . . and the right to require the Constituent Dioceses to ensure the smooth implementation of these policies'. Furthermore, the assembly may perform such 'other functions as may be consistent with the spirit and intent of this Constitution'. The assembly is competent to legislate on church courts and ecclesiastical discipline, and on the standards and procedures necessary for ordination. It may establish schemes for the retirement of clergy and the terms and conditions of service for church employees. In the area of ritual, the assembly is competent to regulate 'the procedures, qualifications and requirements for Marriage, Baptism and Confirmation . . . Divorce and Nullity of Marriage'. With respect to property it may regulate the consecration of land, buildings and articles, and it may establish and regulate trusts, colleges, foundations, and other institutions for the general benefit of the work of the church. In short, the Ugandan provincial assembly is competent to regulate any matter of

---

[84] Wales, Const. II.33.   [85] West Indies, Const. Art. 3.8.

[86] See Ch. 6.

[87] Papua New Guinea, Const. Art. 7; Uganda, Const. Art. 6(a): the Provincial Assembly has 'supreme authority to speak and act in the name of this Church'.

[88] Philippines, Const. Art. VIII.2; Korea, Const. Art. 21: functions include evangelism.

[89] Rwanda, Draft Const. 1996, Art. 27.

[90] ECUSA, Cans. I.9: the functions of provincial synods include the enactment of provincial ordinances, the election of judges of the Provincial Court of Review, the adoption of a budget for the province, and consideration of any issue submitted to them by General Convention; England, Can. H1(2): the clerical provincial Convocations of Canterbury and York have no legislative functions (see LFCE, 72).

'common interest to the province'.[91] By way of contrast, in Canada, positive jurisdictional law seeks to strike a balance between the respective competences of the national assembly, the General Synod, and the assemblies of the provinces. Under the law of the national church, whilst the General Synod has jurisdiction over 'all matters affecting . . . the whole Church', Provincial Synods have 'authority and jurisdiction' in all matters affecting the general interests and well-being of the church in the province. They may regulate the constitution and organization of the synod itself; this is not a function of General Synod. They may fix the boundaries of the province, with the consent of the General Synod and that of any other province or diocese thereby affected. Whereas General Synod regulates the office of Primate, Provincial Synods are empowered to regulate the election, consecration and resignation of bishops, and to define the 'authority, powers and duties' of the metropolitan. The establishment of a Provincial Court of Appeal is the responsibility of the assembly, but the General Synod has ultimate authority over the substantive law on ecclesiastical discipline. The assembly is competent to authorize special forms of prayers, services and ceremonies for use in the province, so long as no provision has already been made by the General Synod. The Provincial Synod is also empowered to govern relations between the province and civil authorities, to administer funds and to establish provincial branches of organizations of the General Synod.[92]

Negative jurisdictional law, power-limiting rules imposing constraints on the competence of provincial assemblies, reflects doctrines of the separation of powers. Separation ideas appear in a number of forms: for example, some rules forbid interference by a provincial assembly in the decision-making of ecclesiastical courts;[93] others reserve the resolution of doctrinal controversies to an episcopal assembly rather than to the provincial assembly;[94] and occasionally laws forbid the assembly to usurp functions inherent to metropolitical or episcopal office.[95] The concept of separation is most evident in jurisdictional laws dealing with the legal relationship of a province to the diocese. This is a subject which has been

---

[91] Uganda, Const. Art. 6.   [92] Canada, Declaration of Principles, 7.

[93] See e.g. West Indies, Const. Art. 3.4: the Provincial Synod may determine matters 'concerning the common life of the Church . . . save and except . . . such matters as lie within the jurisdiction of the Ecclesiastical Courts . . . such matters affecting the general administration of the Province as, in the opinion of the President, the House of Bishops should debate and determine . . . and such matters as be within the rights and powers of a Diocesan Synod to determine for itself'.

[94] See Chs. 7 and 8.

[95] Wales, Const. II.32: no proceedings of the Governing Body 'shall interfere with the exercise by the Archbishop of the powers and functions inherent in the Office of Metropolitan, nor with the exercise by the Diocesan Bishop of the powers and functions inherent in the Episcopal Office'.

treated by the Lambeth Conference: 'the Provincial Synod should deal with the questions of common interest to the whole province, and with those that affect the Communion of the Dioceses with one another, and with the rest of the Church, whilst the Diocesan Synods should be free to dispose of matters of local interest and to manage the affairs of the Dioceses'.[96] It is a general principle of Anglican canon law that, unless a power is clearly reserved by law, the provincial assembly is not competent to interfere with the internal affairs of a diocese or to usurp the jurisdiction of a diocesan assembly. The Lambeth provision itself has been incorporated verbatim in the laws of a small number of churches,[97] and in several it has been the subject of refinement and elaboration,[98] most interestingly in the church in West Africa whose laws are echoed in South East Asia. The Provincial Synod must deal with matters 'of common concern to the whole Province and with those that affect the Communion of the Dioceses with one another and of the Province with other Provinces of the Anglican Communion' – it must leave the dioceses 'to deal with matters which concern only the members of the Church in each Diocese'. The decision as to whether a subject is a diocesan matter or a provincial matter rests with the Provincial Synod. In so deciding, the Provincial Synod must give to all dioceses 'the greatest possible liberty compatible with the unity and good order of the Church . . . and to ensure the fullest consultation with them in matters of legislation'.[99] For some churches the law simply contains a general prohibition against interference,[100] or it assigns to the provincial assembly the function simply of advising dioceses,[101] or else it bases relations on a principle of partnership and co-operation.[102]

[96] LC 1867, Report 1.

[97] Southern Africa, Const. Art. IX; Central Africa, Const. Art. 11.

[98] Philippines, Const. Art. VIII.1–2: the Provincial Synod is competent to deal with 'intra-provincial matters' such as the business of the whole province, the inter-relations of dioceses, any referral made to it by any diocese, relations between itself and another province, and relations between a provincial diocese and the diocese of another province; Papua New Guinea, Const. Art. 16: the Provincial Council 'shall not have authority over the management of the internal affairs of any Diocese, except as [is] otherwise specifically provided' in the constitution; Burundi, Const. Art. 8; Jerusalem, Const. Art. 11; Indian Ocean, Const. Art. 16.1.

[99] West Africa, Const. Art. XXIII.1 and South East Asia, Const. Art. XVI(a),(c).

[100] ECUSA, Cans. I.9: the Provincial Synod has no power 'to regulate or control the internal policy or affairs of any constituent Diocese'; see also Brazil, Const. Art. VIII.

[101] Papua New Guinea, Const. Art. 8: one responsibility of the Provincial Council is to act as 'adviser, consultant and coordinator' for the dioceses.

[102] New Zealand, Cans. B.XX.4: the common life of the church is based on 'a partnership and covenant relationship between the constituent parts of the Church as expressed in the Constitution . . . and regulations of general application'; 'Each partner and its constituent parts shall seek to ensure that adequate provision and support is available to the other partners to assist in the effective proclamation and communication of the Gospel of Jesus Christ and the provision of ministry amongst the people

Executive and Advisory Bodies

Provincial assemblies are assisted by a host of subsidiary institutions, operating both to implement decisions of the assembly and to advise it in the discharge of its functions. Chief amongst these is the provincial Standing Committee (or Executive Council). The existence of the institution is mandatory,[103] and invariably, with the metropolitan as president,[104] its membership is made up of bishops, provincial officers,[105] and other members of the provincial assembly representative of the dioceses.[106] It is obliged to meet at prescribed times,[107] and its functions vary as between churches, but generally it has a leading role to play in the overall policy and strategic planning of the church.[108] It must transact the business of the assembly between its sessions,[109] and is under the direction,[110] and control of the provincial assembly.[111] Commonplace functions

whom each seeks to serve, recognising that in partnership there is common responsibility and mutual interdependence'.

[103] Indian Ocean, Const. Art. 15 and Can. 7; West Indies, Const. Art. 4.1; Uganda, Const. Art. 7(a).

[104] West Indies, Can. 2.1; Southern Cone, Can. 6.2; Melanesia, Const. Art. 7A and Can. D.3; New Zealand, Cans. B.I.3.3; Philippines, Const. VI.2; Uganda, Const. Art. 7(a)(i): the Archbishop is chairman.

[105] Uganda, Const. Art. 7(a) and South East Asia, Const. VIII(c): 'The Standing Committee shall consist of the Archbishop, all the Diocesan Bishops, the Provincial Secretary, the Provincial Treasurer, together with one clergy and two laity from each Diocese elected from amongst themselves by their respective Houses at the Provincial Synod'.

[106] Melanesia, Const. Art. 7A and Can. D.3; Southern Cone, Can. 6.2; Philippines, Const. VI.2: it also includes one representative directly elected by each diocesan convention; see also Rwanda, Draft Const. 1996, Art. 20.

[107] For three meetings each year see Wales, Const. II.64 and Philippines, Cans. I.4.2(a); for annual meetings, at least, see Southern Cone, Can. 6.4; Southern Africa, Can. 43.2; and West Indies, Can. 2.4.

[108] Wales, Const. II.65: it advises the Governing Body on policy (planning, priorities and budgets) and may appoint sub-committees; Uganda, Const. Art. 7: it is 'to examine policy proposals for submission to the Provincial Assembly and implement the decisions' of the assembly; Southern Africa, Can. 43: it acts 'for the furtherance of the Church's mission, well-being and unity'; Rwanda, Draft Const. 1996, Art. 21: the Provincial Standing Committee 'defines the priorities and the direction of the Province, and submits them to the provincial Synod for adoption'; ibid., Art. 24: the Provincial Executive Committee 'assures follow-up and execution of the decisions and projects of the Provincial Standing Committee'.

[109] Southern Africa, Can. 43.1(b); Tanzania, Const. Art. V; Can. 8(a); West Indies, Can. 2.10(b); South East Asia, Const. Art. VIII(a).

[110] Southern Cone, Can. 6.1; Melanesia, Const. Art. 7A; Cans. D.3: the Executive Council must act as the General Synod or Council of Bishops directs (unless a direction of the latter conflicts with one of the former).

[111] Zaire, Const. Art. 6; Philippines, Const. VI.1.

include: presentation of a report on its activities to the assembly;[112] preparation of the agenda of the assembly;[113] deliberation upon and determination of all matters referred to it by the assembly;[114] making rules on prescribed subjects;[115] co-ordinating activities of ecclesiastical institutions;[116] and it is closely involved with the administration of property and finance.[117] In some churches the Standing Committee may institute such enquiries as it may consider necessary into the activities of ecclesiastical bodies or receive reports from other subordinate bodies of the assembly.[118] Sometimes the Standing Committee is responsible for the selection of representatives of the church to the Anglican Consultative Council and other bodies,[119] and commonly it is charged with giving advice to the metropolitan.[120]

In addition to the Standing Committee, the laws of a bare majority of churches assign to a range of assembly commissions, committees, councils and boards various specialist functions related to aspects of provincial church life. Their responsibilities cover both advice to the provincial assembly and the administrative tasks of implementing provincial law and policy in their designated spheres of activity. The membership of such bodies, usually under the leadership of a bishop, consists of appointees of the assembly, normally from its own members: sometimes churches operate general rules applicable to all bodies, and sometimes membership is specifically designed to further the particular objects of the body in question. Laws prescribe for regular meetings and for reports to the ordinary sessions of the provincial assembly. Whereas the law of several churches simply confers a permissive right on the provincial assembly to set up such bodies,[121] a larger number of provincial churches have standing

---

[112] Southern Cone, Can. 6.6; West Indies, Can. 2.10(e); Philippines, Cans. I.4.3; Southern Africa, Can. 43.1(g).

[113] Southern Cone, Can. 6.9; Korea, Const. Art. 37.2; West Indies, Can. 2.10(c).

[114] West Indies, Can. 2.10(a); Korea, Const. Art. 37.1.

[115] Philippines, Const. Art. VI.1: the Executive Council may make by-laws for its own government and for that of its departments; Southern Africa, Can. 43.6; West Indies, Const. Art. 4.5: the body may make rules to give effect to assembly canons.

[116] Uganda, Const. Art. 7(b); Philippines, Const. VI.1; Southern Africa, Can. 43(e).

[117] South East Asia, Const. VIII(e)(i)–(ii): it must 'administer, manage and control all trusts, properties, finances and funds of the Provincial Synod in accordance with the powers delegated to it by the Provincial Synod from time to time' and 'lay before each ordinary meeting of the Provincial Synod the audited accounts of the Province'; see generally Ch. 11.

[118] New Zealand, Cans. B.I.3.3.

[119] Philippines, Cans. I.4.6; Korea, Const. Art. 37.6.

[120] Southern Africa, Can. 43(c).

[121] Tanzania, Const. V and Can. 8(b); New Zealand, Cans. B.I.3; for 'provincial institutions', see Papua New Guinea, Can. No. 8 of 1977; Melanesia, Cans. D.1.M-N: provincial departments must present a written report on their activities to General Synod and their heads must lead discussion and answer questions.

commissions on the constitution and canons, ministry, mission, doctrine, liturgy, and ecumenism;[122] these are discussed, where appropriate, elsewhere in this volume. Other common standing commissions include: social justice and human rights,[123] youth,[124] evangelism,[125] christian stewardship and finance,[126] and publications.[127]

DIOCESAN ASSEMBLIES

The province, constituting either the whole of an individual church or a unit within a national or regional church, is subdivided into dioceses. This section examines the formation and reorganization of dioceses and their institutional organization.

The Diocese

A diocese is, broadly, a territory under the spiritual leadership and oversight of a bishop and governed by a representative assembly,[128] styled, variously, the Diocesan Synod (the most usual title),[129] the Diocesan Convention,[130] or (rarely) the Diocesan Council,[131] or Diocesan Conference.[132] In some churches the law recognizes the diocese to be the

[122] West Indies, Can. 33; Philippines, Cans. I.2.

[123] West Indies, Can. 33.1.C: the Commission on Social Justice and Human Rights is 'to keep under constant review all matters relating to Social Justice and Human Rights in the constituent territories of the Province and to make recommendations to the [Provincial] Synod on the development of strategies'; Philippines, Cans. 1.2: the Provincial Synod has a Commission on Social Concerns.

[124] West Indies, Const. Art. 3.4(ii)(h).

[125] Philippines, Cans. I.2.   [126] Philippines, Cans. I.2.

[127] Korea, Const. Art. 41: the constitutions of the Publications Board, Canons Committee, Liturgical Commission, Evangelism Committee, and Church and Society Committee, are decided on by the National Executive Committee.

[128] LC 1867, Committee Report 'A', 58–60: 'In the organisation of Synodal order for the government of the Church, the Diocesan Synod appears to be the primary and simplest form of such organisation'; Korea, Const. Art. 57: a diocese is 'an independent evangelistic organization administered by a bishop'; North India, Const. II.III.I.1–2: 'Each Diocese is under the charge of a bishop and functions through a Diocesan Council'; 'The objects and purposes of the Diocese shall be to proclaim by word and deed the gospel of Jesus Christ'; Ireland, Const. I.30: dioceses are 'under the government of their respective bishops'; South East Asia, Const. Art. XIV(b): 'A Diocese shall be governed by the Bishop and a Synod'.

[129] Diocesan Synod: England, Synodical Government Measure 1969, s. 5.

[130] ECUSA, Cans. I.9.

[131] North India, Const. II.III.I.1; however, in some churches 'Diocesan Council' is the name given to the diocesan assembly's Standing Committee: see e.g. ECUSA, Diocese of Western New York, Can. 9.

[132] Wales, Const. IV.1; however, in some churches 'Diocesan Conference' is the name given to an assembly other than the Diocesan Synod: see e.g. England, Synodical

primary unit of the church.[133] The laws of all churches deal in some detail with the creation, amalgamation, division, transfer, release and dissolution of dioceses, but formal laws do not normally require the existence of an institution devoted exclusively to diocesan reorganization.[134] Laws differ radically as to the location of the right to carry out diocesan reorganization. Two models emerge. The formation of a new diocese is for the vast majority of churches in the keeping of the national, regional or provincial assembly which may act only with the consent of any diocese and diocesan bishop affected as a result.[135] In line with the terms of Lambeth Conference resolutions, in several churches the law lays down various criteria which must be met before the national or provincial assembly may form a new diocese: typically, that it contains a prescribed number of parishes and priests and that the project is financially viable.[136] By way of contrast, in some churches a central episcopal assembly, rather than the national or provincial assembly, has the determinative voice; again, prescribed criteria must be satisfied about the proposed diocese's capacity for self-government and self-support.[137] Some churches, which reserve the

Government Measure 1969, s. 5(7): in addition to the Diocesan Synod, the bishop may summon 'a conference of persons appearing to him to be representative of the clergy and laity, on such occasions and for such purposes as he thinks fit'.

[133] Australia, Const. III.1: 'A diocese shall in accordance with the historic custom of the One Holy Catholic and Apostolic Church continue to be the unit of organisation of this Church and shall be the see of a bishop'; North India, Const. II.III.I.1: 'The organization of the Church is on a territorial basis. The unit of such territorial organization is the Diocese'; see also LC 1897, Res. 21: 'care should be taken to make the diocese the centre of unity'; LC 1988, Res. 59: 'This Conference requests the Primates Meeting and ACC to give urgent consideration to the situation of the extra-provincial dioceses, that they may be fully part of the structures of the Anglican Communion'; see Ch. 12.

[134] See, however, England, Dioceses Measure 1978, s. 1: the Dioceses Commission advises on diocesan structures and on action 'to improve the episcopal oversight of any diocese . . . or the administration of its affairs'.

[135] West Indies, Can. 12.1: 'The Provincial Synod may, at the request of the Synod of a Diocese, or of its own initiative and with the concurrence of the Bishop or Bishops and the Synod or Synods of the Diocese or Dioceses concerned, form a new Diocese within the province, or re-arrange the boundaries of a Diocese or merge two or more Dioceses'; see also New Zealand, Cans. B.IV.1 and Australia, Const. VIII; South East Asia, Const. Art. XV; Korea, Const. Ch. 8, Art. 102: 'the creation of a new [diocese] shall be resolved by the diocese's synod and decided by National Synod'; see also Brazil, Const. Art. VIII; Japan, Can. XI; Mexico, Const. Art. V.

[136] LC 1978, Res. 17: when a new diocese is created, 'adequate financial support should be underwritten by the member Churches concerned' and for the stipend of the bishop; cases should be referred to ACC; see e.g. ECUSA, Const. Art. V and Cans. I.9.2 and I.10: a new diocese may be formed with the consent of the General Convention provided it contains at least six parishes and six presbyters previously resident in the area for at least one year; compare Philippines, Const. Art. VII: 12 presbyters are required to constitute a diocese; for financial viability, see New Zealand, Cans. B.IV.2–7.

[137] Southern Africa, Can. 21: the formation of dioceses is in the keeping of '[t]he Metropolitan and the Bishops of the Province in Synod'; they must be satisfied that there is 'a need for its formation, that it is capable of being governed by synodical

right to form a new diocese to the provincial assembly, require consultation only with the assembly of affected dioceses when the creation of a new diocese is proposed.[138]

Similarly divergent approaches are to be found with respect to dividing, transferring and uniting dioceses. In many churches the power resides with the central church assembly which may act only with the consent of the assembly and bishop of the affected diocese. The approval of both the provincial assembly and the diocese itself is justified in many laws on the basis that it is a subject of 'common concern' for the whole province.[139] In other churches, the approval of the central church assembly is required but the diocesan assembly simply has a right to be consulted; the central assembly must be satisfied about the spiritual, administrative and financial viability of the proposal.[140] In some churches, in the event of objections, the archbishop and a majority of diocesan bishops may veto the proposal before any submission to the provincial assembly.[141] Sometimes, the matter is decided by an episcopal assembly which is under a duty only to consult with the diocese(s) concerned,[142] or, if a diocesan assembly cannot agree there is a duty to refer the matter to an episcopal assembly for determination.[143] Some churches expressly forbid any division, union or

government and that its staff and finances are sufficient for it to function as a unit of the Church'; Can. 21.4: the consent of any affected diocesan bishop must be obtained; compare Const. Art. XIV: 'The Provincial Synod shall have full power and authority to take all measures and establish all rules that may be necessary for the erection of a new Diocese'; by Can. 21.3, no two dioceses may be united except by act of the Provincial Synod; see also Scotland, Can. 8.1: the Episcopal Synod has the determinative voice.

[138] Tanzania, Const. V, Can. 9.

[139] Melanesia, Const. Art. 17: dioceses cannot be divided without the agreement of the diocese concerned; Wales, Const. II.61–62: the Governing Body may divide a diocese, transfer any part of it to and unite it with any other diocese provided the assent of the Diocesan Conference or Conferences affected and that of the diocesan bishop(s) are obtained; see also Ireland, Const. I.31; West Indies, Const. Art. 3.7; West Africa, Const. Art. XXIII.2; Burundi, Const. Art. 8; Zaire, Const. Art. 8; and nn. 135, 136.

[140] Southern Africa, Can. 21.3: 'No two Dioceses shall be permanently united except by the act of the Provincial Synod'; Can. 21.5: 'No alterations in the limits of a Diocese shall be carried into effect without an opportunity being given to the Synods of the respective Dioceses affected . . . to consider the proposal, and to communicate their opinions thereon to the Synod of Bishops'; Indian Ocean, Can. 8; for a less complex procedure, see Southern Cone, Can. 3: the provincial Executive Council must consent with subsequent approval by the Provincial Synod.

[141] Kenya, Can. I(e).

[142] Scotland, Can. 8.1–2: the Episcopal Synod may divide, unite or transfer a diocese, but the assembly of the diocese(s) concerned has only a right to be consulted; the Episcopal Synod must consider the opinion submitted.

[143] Uganda, Const. Art. 6(c): the Provincial Synod may divide and rearrange dioceses; if the diocesan synod cannot agree, 'the matter shall be referred to the House of Bishops, whose decision . . . shall be accepted by all parties concerned'.

transfer during a vacancy in the diocese.[144] Similar principles apply both to the incorporation of a diocese and to its release from the province.[145] When a diocese is vacant, by the termination of the bishop's ministry there,[146] the guardianship of the diocese invariably devolves upon the metropolitan or his commissary.[147]

The Diocesan Assembly

The institutional organization of dioceses follows the same general pattern as that of the province, with government being vested in a diocesan assembly (synod, convention, council or conference) composed of the diocesan bishop, and representatives of the clergy and laity.[148] The president of the diocesan assembly is the diocesan bishop.[149] The house or order of clergy consists of priests and deacons elected in accordance either with rules found in national, regional or provincial law,[150] or in diocesan legislation.[151] Coadjutor, suffragan and assistant bishops resident in the diocese are also members, usually of the house or order of clergy.[152] The house or order of laity is, similarly, composed of representatives of the laity of the

[144] Scotland, Can. 8.1: no union, division, or transfer may take place during a vacancy in see; compare Wales, Const. II.61–62.

[145] West Indies, Const. Art. 3.7: 'It belongs to the jurisdiction and authority of the Provincial Synod to take all measures necessary . . . for incorporating into the Province an adjacent Diocese . . . [or] for releasing any Diocese . . . from the jurisdiction of the Province'.

[146] See Ch. 4.

[147] See e.g. Southern Africa, Can. 22: 'Whenever any See of this Province shall be vacant by the death of a Bishop or other sufficient cause, the spiritual care and government thereof shall devolve upon the metropolitan, who shall appoint a Vicar General to act until the See be again canonically filled'.

[148] See nn. 129 to 132 for the different titles of the assembly; the assembly is frequently defined legally: see e.g. Southern Africa, Const. Art. VIII: the diocesan synod 'shall resemble, as far as possible, the Provincial Synod in its constitution and mode of procedure'; ibid., Const. XXIV.8: 'By "Diocesan Synod" is and shall be meant an assembly consisting of the Bishop, Clergy, and other members of the . . . Church in the Diocese (being Communicants) and constituted according to such rules as have been or shall be agreed upon in the Diocese and allowed by the Provincial Synod'; see also West Indies, Const. Art. 6.1; Nigeria, Const. Ch. XIII; Tanzania, Const. IV.18: the Diocesan Synod consists of a house of bishops, of clergy and of laity.

[149] Scotland, Can. 50.7; Wales, Const. IV.3; Japan, Can. X, Art. 103.

[150] Melanesia, Const. Art. 16; see also Diocese of Temotu, Can. 1.

[151] New Zealand, Cans. B.II.1; Wales, Const. IV.7.

[152] England, Church Representation Rules, r. 30(4): the house of clergy consists of any bishop not nominated to the Diocesan Synod's house of bishops; compare Diocese of Europe, Const. 34: the house of bishops of the Diocesan Synod consists of 'the diocesan bishop, every suffragan bishop and such other persons, being persons in episcopal orders working in the diocese, as the bishop of the diocese, with the concurrence of the Archbishop of the province, may nominate'.

diocese who are adult communicants.[153] The assembly also has various *ex officio* members and may have co-opted members.[154] Meetings of the assembly are held at prescribed times, usually annually,[155] and these are convened ordinarily by the bishop, or on the requisition of named persons,[156] or bodies.[157] Notice of meetings is required, periods differing as between churches, and the agenda is circulated amongst members.[158] As with regional, national or provincial assemblies, rules are used to fix the quorum necessary to transact business,[159] and decisions are made by majority vote, usually with the members sitting together, but with deliberation and voting by orders at the request of prescribed numbers of assembly members.[160] The laws of a small number of churches allow for the grouping of diocesan assemblies as 'territorial synods'.[161]

There is less consistency as between churches with respect to the func-

---

[153] Ireland, Const. II.2–12; Wales, Const. IV.2: 'All members of the [Diocesan] Conference shall be communicants of the Church . . . over the age of eighteen years'; Scotland, Can. 50.3: lay members include lay representatives for each congregation and lay members of General Synod; ECUSA, Diocese of Mississippi, Const. Art. IV: each parish is represented by delegates chosen by the Vestry or Congregation; see also Brazil, Const. IX.

[154] See e.g. Wales, Const. IV.5; New Zealand, Cans. B.II.1: the diocesan chancellor is *ex officio* a member.

[155] Philippines, Const. VII.2; Scotland, Can. 50.1; ECUSA, Diocese of Western New York, Const. Art. VI and Can. 9; New Zealand, Cans. B.II.2.

[156] Ireland, Const. II.21: a special meeting may be requisitioned by a third of each order; compare Scotland, Can. 50.2: special meetings may be held whenever the bishop sees fit.

[157] Ireland, Const. II.21: one-half of the members of the diocesan council may requisition.

[158] Ireland, Const. II.22: 'Notice of all meetings of the diocesan synod shall be given to every member thereof, at such time and in such manner as the diocesan synod shall determine'; compare Korea, Const. Art. 64: 'The diocesan Bishop shall present all matters received by him for submission to diocesan synod to the Diocesan Executive Committee for discussion and decision, and communicate synod's agenda to all delegates twenty days before the opening of synod'.

[159] Ireland, Const. II.25: the president, one-fourth of clergy and one-fourth of lay members must be present; Korea, Ch. 7, Art. 69: 'The attendance of a majority of delegates constitutes a quorum for synod'; Papua New Guinea, Const. Sched. 2, 9: quorum consists of not less than one-third in each house.

[160] See e.g. New Zealand, Cans. B.II.2: every act of the Diocesan Synod must be supported by a majority in each house; Papua New Guinea, Const. Sched. 2, 11: the houses must sit, deliberate and vote together unless the bishop or any 3 clerical or 3 lay members request voting by houses; Japan, Can. X, Art. 106: membership is simply for one session; see also Wales, Const. IV.32.

[161] Central Africa, Can. 35: 'If the Diocesan Synods of a group of Dioceses so wish they may agree to constitute a Territorial Synod' which 'may exercise such power to legislate for its constituent Dioceses as may be given by its Constitution'; see also New Zealand, Cans. B.XXII: the Inter-Diocesan Conference; Ireland, Const. II.1; see e.g. the Rules and Regulations (1989) of the United Dioceses of Cork, Cloyne and Ross (united in 1870), Standing Orders, I.2.

tions of diocesan assemblies. And very often the subject is left to be dealt with by diocesan law. One basic difference between churches is that in most the diocesan assembly enjoys legislative powers, whilst in other churches this is not the case.[162] Whereas in some churches the law does not place the role of the assembly in a theological context,[163] in several the diocesan assembly has a fundamental task to advance the mission of the church.[164] Occasionally the law expressly requires the bishop to consult the diocesan assembly on matters of general concern and importance to the diocese,[165] but the assembly is expressly forbidden to make any declaration of the doctrine of the church.[166] The diocesan assembly has a general oversight of the lower ecclesiastical units within the diocese,[167] and occasionally a duty is placed on it to keep the lower ecclesiastical units of the diocese informed of the policies and problems of the diocese.[168] Generally, they must consider any matter referred to them by the national, regional or provincial assembly,[169] and are required to obey the lawful

[162] See Ch. 1.

[163] England, Synodical Government Measure 1969, s. 4(2): Diocesan Synods are 'to consider matters concerning the Church . . . and to make provision for such matters in relation to their diocese, and to consider and express their opinion on any other matters of religious or public interest'; New Zealand, Const. C.8: diocesan assemblies must co-operate with each other.

[164] North India, Const. II.III.I.2: 'It is the duty of every Diocese acting as a whole to spread the knowledge of the gospel throughout its territory and to provide for the spiritual needs of the members of the Church who reside within it'; New Zealand, Cans. B.VIII: the diocese of Polynesia must commit itself 'to exploring and developing ways in which the Gospel may most effectively be expressed in the context of the diverse racial, cultural and language traditions of the region'; see also Cans. B.XXII.1: the Inter-Diocesan Conference must consider matters affecting the proclamation of the Gospel, evangelism, and the promotion of the mission of the church; Papua New Guinea, Diocese of Port Moresby, Can. 3: 'the first duty of the Synod is to bring all people in the Diocese to a living faith in their Lord and Saviour, Jesus Christ'.

[165] England, Synodical Government Measure 1969, s. 4(3); Jerusalem and the Middle East, Diocese of Egypt, Const. 1982, 5; South India, Const. VIII.4: the Diocesan Council must 'take executive action for the general management and good government of the Church in the diocese'; see also Korea, Const. Ch. 7, Art. 61: the 'determination of important measures concerning evangelism and the growth of the diocese' belong to the diocesan assembly.

[166] England, Synodical Government Measure 1969, s. 4(2); see Ch. 7.

[167] North India, Const. II.III.III: 'The Diocesan Council shall have supervisory, legislative and executive powers over Pastorates within its jurisdiction'; Papua New Guinea, Const. Sched. 2, 3(h): the assembly effects 'the regulation of parishes, mission districts and those institutions within the Diocese which are not declared to be . . . a Provincial responsibility'; Wales, Const. IV.43: the diocesan conference may control, alter, repeal, or supersede any 'regulation' made by a ruridecanal conference, vestry meeting or parochial church council.

[168] England, Synodical Government Measure 1969, s. 4(5).

[169] Papua New Guinea, Const. Art. 8; England, Synodical Government Measure 1969, s. 4(2)(c); Wales, Const. II.58.

directions of the central assembly.[170] In several churches, the diocesan assembly must make an annual report on the state of the church in the diocese to the regional, national or provincial assembly (or its standing committee).[171] The diocesan assembly is directly involved in the appointment of candidates to episcopal office and in clerical discipline.[172] Finally, the assembly is responsible for a multiplicity of decisions concerning church property and is obliged to arrange for the levying of the quota, the diocesan contribution towards provincial or national church funds.[173] The importance of the institution in the life of the church is reflected, in some laws, by the mandatory nature of the obligation of assembly members to attend its meetings.[174]

It is a general ecclesiastical practice that each diocesan assembly has an executive organ, variously styled the Standing Committee,[175] or Executive Committee,[176] and occasionally the Diocesan Council,[177] or Bishop's Council.[178] The subject is usually left to diocesan laws but those rules appearing in national, regional or provincial law provide that presidency rests with the diocesan bishop and its membership includes others holding episcopal office in the diocese,[179] diocesan officers and representatives of clergy and laity.[180] The body acts with the authority of the diocesan assembly between the sessions of that assembly,[181] and gives advice to the bishop when called upon to do so and discharges any other function assigned to it by the diocesan assembly.[182] Formal laws either oblige or

---

[170] Wales, Const. IV.22 and 29; for the concept of adoption in Australia, see Ch. 1.

[171] ECUSA, Cans, I.6.2.   [172] See Chs. 3 and 4.   [173] See Ch. 11.

[174] ECUSA, Diocese of Western New York, Can. 2.

[175] Wales, Const. IV.16; ECUSA, Const. Art. IV: the standing committee acts also as the bishop's council of advice; if there is no diocesan bishop, or coadjutor or suffragan bishop, it acts as the ecclesiastical authority of the diocese.

[176] South India, Const. VIII.9; Korea, Const. Art. 64; see also Art. 56 for the bishop's conference; Mexico, Const. Art. V.

[177] Southern Cone, Can. 3: 'a Diocesan Council [acts] as the executive instrument of the Synod and advisory body of the Bishop'.

[178] England, Synodical Government Measure 1969, s. 4(4)–(5): the Diocesan Synod may delegate its advisory and consultative functions to the bishop's council and standing committee and its executive functions to deanery synods.

[179] New Zealand, Cans. B.II.3: it consists of the diocesan bishop, assistant bishops and 3 clerical and 3 lay members of the Diocesan Synod; Papua New Guinea, Const. Sched. 3 and Can. No. 1 of 1977: the diocesan council consists of the bishop, elected synod members, assistant bishops, archdeacons, and the diocesan secretary; see also Ireland, Const. II.34.

[180] ECUSA, Diocese of Western New York, Const. Art. VII: the standing committee consists *inter alia* of 4 priests and 4 confirmed and regular communicants.

[181] Melanesia, Const. Art. 16; see e.g. Diocese of Temotu, Can. 1; Papua New Guinea, Diocese of Port Moresby, Can. 4; Can. Jerusalem, Const. 1982, 6; ECUSA, Cans. I.12; Ireland, Const. II.34 and New Zealand, Cans. B.II.3.1: it shall carry out such functions as are assigned to it by the Diocesan Synod; see also North India, Const. II.III.XI.

[182] Philippines, Const. VII.3 and Cans. I.1.9; Papua New Guinea, Const. Sched. 3 and Can. No. 1 of 1977, 12; Japan, Can. XII; see also nn. 175, 177, 181.

empower diocesan assemblies to establish a wide variety of committees, boards, councils and commissions, of which bodies dealing with ministry,[183] liturgy,[184] finance,[185] clergy residences,[186] are typical: generally, these are under the direct control of the diocesan assembly whose lawful decisions they must obey.[187]

LOW LEVEL UNITS AND ASSEMBLIES: PARISHES

Each diocese is, in turn, subdivided into smaller, local ecclesiastical units. Two approaches are used. First, in a small number of churches, the diocese is composed of territorial units constituted as archdeaconries, which are themselves made up of deaneries. An archdeaconry is under the supervision of an archdeacon,[188] and a deanery under that of a (rural) dean and a deanery assembly.[189] However, in the vast majority of churches, the diocese is divided directly into parishes,[190] pastorates,[191] incumbencies,[192]

---

[183] See Chs. 5 and 6.   [184] See Ch. 7.

[185] ECUSA, Cans. I.7.1(1): the diocesan finance committee.

[186] Wales, Const. IV.20: the diocesan parsonage board; see Ch. 11.

[187] England, Diocesan Boards of Finance Measure 1925, ss. 1, 3: it 'shall in the exercise of its powers and duties comply with such directions as may from time to time be given to the board by the Diocesan Synod'.

[188] See e.g. Korea, Const. Ch. 4, Art. 82; for archdeacons see Ch. 5.

[189] See e.g. Ireland, Const. II.42: every archdeaconry must be divided into rural deaneries; England, Can. C23 (for rural deans see Ch. 5) and Synodical Government Measure 1969, s. 5: the deanery synod consists of a house of clergy and a house of laity, the latter elected to it by the annual meeting of parishes in the deanery; its functions include the promotion of the whole mission of the church in the deanery: 'pastoral, evangelistic, social, and ecumenical'; it must obey instructions issued by the diocesan synod from which it may also receive delegated executive functions and from which it must receive information on the policies and problems of the diocese; for similar arrangements, see Wales, Const. V: the ruridecanal conference; see also ECUSA, Diocese of Western New York, Can. 9: the diocesan council fixes the boundaries of deaneries which are governed by the deanery synod; and Philippines, Cans. I.6.

[190] ECUSA, Cans. I.13: parishes are under the 'parochial Cure of the Member of the Clergy having charge thereof'; see also Spain, Const. V; Brazil, Cans. I.1; Ireland, Const. I.30: parishes are 'under the spiritual care of their respective incumbents'; Wales, Const. VI.1: for the purposes of this chapter, on parochial administration, 'parish' means 'every ecclesiastical parish, whether ancient or new', 'every rectorial benefice', 'a united parish' or 'a parish into which another former parish . . . has been merged'; Papua New Guinea, Can. No. 5 of 1977: a 'parish' is 'any district not receiving any subsidy from the Diocese' and a 'parochial district' is one receiving a diocesan subsidy solely with respect to staff; see also Southern Africa, Can. 24.

[191] South India, Const. VII.1: 'A pastorate is an organised congregation or group recognised as such by the Diocesan Council, under the superintendence of a presbyter, who may be in charge of more than one pastorate'; see also North India, Const. II.II.1.

[192] Scotland, Can. 36.1: an incumbency is a congregation, under the charge of an incumbent, with a church or suitable building provided for divine worship and a constitution approved by the bishop.

congregations,[193] regions,[194] or other districts,[195] committed to the spiritual responsibility or cure of an ordained minister and governed by a representative assembly. The law often provides that the precise territorial arrangements of these diocesan units is in the keeping of the diocesan assembly: this may include the union of such districts.[196] This section concentrates on the lowest and most common ecclesiastical units known to regional, national or provincial law. In some churches, however, notably those in Africa, there is little or no regional, national or provincial law on this subject; instead the matter is dealt with by diocesan legislation, an arrangement which itself may reflect a concept of separation of functions.[197]

Each local ecclesiastical unit is governed by an assembly consisting of clergy and representatives of the laity. Many churches share the common practice that the election of lay representatives takes place at an annual meeting of the ecclesiastical unit.[198] Prescribed classes are permitted to attend and to vote: those communicant members of the church, usually over the age of eighteen, whose names appear on the electoral roll or register of the unit.[199] The annual meeting is convened by the minister having

---

[193] Scotland, Can. 37: an independent congregation is a number of people, under a priest-in-charge, living in a locality at an inconvenient distance from an existing church which undertakes to build a church and to provide a stipend for the minister; it is under the control of the bishop who must approve the constitution of the independent congregation; see also Can. 39 for 'dependent congregations'.

[194] Melanesia, Diocese of Temotu, Can. 10: the diocese is divided into 'regions' to which a 'regional priest' is appointed by the bishop; each region is further subdivided into parishes with a priest-in-charge; see also Chile, Cans. C.6.

[195] Papua New Guinea, Const. Can. No. 5 of 1977: the diocese is divided into 'Ecclesiastical districts called respectively Parishes, Parochial Districts and Missionary Districts as the Bishop-in-Council may from time to time determine' (see also n. 190); see Scotland, Can. 38 for districts assigned to congregations; Diocese of Europe, Const. 30: the local units are 'chaplaincies'.

[196] For parishes, see e.g. ECUSA, Cans. I.13; Philippines, Cans. I.6.2; New Zealand, Can. B.V.2; see also Wales, Const. II.60: 'Any Diocesan Bishop, with the consent of the Diocesan Conference, may make any change in the existing territorial arrangement of his diocese, as he may think fit'; for the highly complex legal rules on parochial reorganization in England, see L. Leeder, *Ecclesiastical Law Handbook* (London, 1997), 145ff; for unions and group parishes see also Ireland, Const. III.27 and Japan, Can. XIII.

[197] See e.g. Central Africa, Can. 19: with respect to vestries and church councils, 'Dioceses shall legislate for their own needs'; West Africa, Diocese of Gambia and Guinea, Const. 1982, Art. 15(1): 'A parish is an area of [an] organised congregation or group of congregations' and 'shall be in the charge of a clergyman in priest's orders who shall be called the priest-in-charge'.

[198] Papua New Guinea, Can. No. 5 of 1977, 19; Melanesia, Diocese of Temotu, Can. 10; ECUSA, Dioc. of Mississippi, Cans. II.B.21; West Africa, Diocese of Gambia and Guinea, Const. 1982, Art. 16(4); Wales, Const. VI.10; Australia, Diocese of Sydney, *The 7th Handbook*, 7.21; Japan, Can. XIII, Art. 123.

[199] Japan, Can. XIII, Art. 123 and Southern Africa, Can. 27: the annual vestry is composed of parishioners of 18 or over; Ireland, Const. III.8f: the general vestry; England, Synodical Government Measure 1969, Sched. 3, Church Representation Rules, 6–12.

charge over the unit and at it a report on the state of the unit, its spiritual work, its property and finances is examined and discussed.[200] The assembly itself (variously styled as the Council, Vestry or Committee) is, in turn, composed of various *ex officio* members: the minister in charge, other clergy ministering or resident in the unit, and church officers (such as wardens and treasurers).[201] The bulk of its membership is composed of elected lay representatives: the core qualification is adult communicant membership of the church; sometimes an added qualification is evidence of regular contributions to the funds of the church.[202] Its meetings are under the presidency of the minister in charge,[203] and elaborate rules govern notice of the meeting, quorum and decision-making, normally by a simple majority of members present.[204] Sometimes the law confers upon the minister in charge a casting vote.[205]

There is a remarkable degree of consistency as to the functions of these assemblies. These are described where appropriate in the other studies of this volume, but generally they may be classified as spiritual, governmental, liturgical and proprietorial. A fundamental principle which is shared

[200] Wales, Const. VI.15: it receives and discusses a report for the previous year from the parochial church council concerning: the mission of the church in the parish (pastoral, evangelistic, social and ecumenical); the state of the electoral roll; the state of property; and parochial accounts; for similar arrangements see Ireland, Const. III.8; Southern Africa, Can. 27.5; Papua New Guinea, Can. No. 5 of 1977, 19; Melanesia, Diocese of Temotu, Can. 10.

[201] Wales, Const. VI.24(1): the incumbent, curates, and churchwardens, with the treasurer as a co-opted member; Southern Africa, Can. 28.2; Australia, Diocese of Sydney, *The 7th Handbook*, 7.21, and Papua New Guinea, Can. No. 5 of 1977, 24(a): the incumbent and churchwardens; West Africa, Diocese of Gambia and Guinea, Const. 1982, Art. 15(4); Brazil, Cans. I.11; Chile, Cans. C.5.

[202] Wales, Const. VI.24(1)(b): lay persons elected by the annual vestry meeting over 18; ECUSA, Cans. I.14: the number, mode of selection and term of office of members of the vestry is determined by state law or diocesan law; Diocese of Western New York, Cans. 13: members must be at least 21, baptized, regular attendants at worship and contributors to the parish's expenses; Papua New Guinea, Can. No. 5 of 1977, 23: it consists of not less than 8 communicants chosen annually; New Zealand, Cans. B.V.3.1.1: the vestry consists of up to 10 parishioners being communicants of 18 years or more; see for the same, Australia, Diocese of Sydney, *The 7th Handbook*, 7.24.

[203] ECUSA, Diocese of Mississippi, Cans. II.B.21; Philippines, Cans. I.6.3; West Africa, Diocese of Gambia and Guinea, Const. 1982, Art. 16: the priest-in-charge convenes meetings of the parochial church committee and acts as chairman; Melanesia, Diocese of Temotu, Can. 10; compare Papua New Guinea, Can. No. 5 of 1977, 30: the council elects its chairman.

[204] Wales, Const. VI.22(1): the parochial church council must meet at least four times a year; Australia, Diocese of Sydney, *The 7th Handbook*, 7.25 and ECUSA, Diocese of Mississippi, Cans. II.B.22: monthly meetings are required; Melanesia, Diocese of Temotu, Can. 10: every 3 months; Papua New Guinea, Can. No. 5 of 1977, 25–29: at least every 2 months; 7 days' notice is required and quorum is 20.

[205] Ireland, Const. III.20: at the select vestry; England, Church Representation Rules, App. 2, paras. 10–11.

by the vast majority of churches is that the minister in charge of the ecclesiastical unit and its assembly must both co-operate in the life of that
unit.[206] First, spiritual functions: laws assign to the assembly responsibility for promotion of the whole mission of the church, pastoral, evangelistic, social and ecumenical,[207] with, sometimes, a special responsibility
towards the christian education of children.[208] The assembly may be free
to consider matters of religious and public interest, but prohibitions
against it making any declaration of the church's doctrine are rare.[209] A
common duty is to provide those items necessary for church services, and
the assembly is often involved directly in the choice of services for public
worship.[210] Secondly, its governmental functions include: submission of
reports to the standing committee of the diocesan assembly and of data on
baptisms, confirmations, marriages, burials and numbers of church members;[211] the election of individuals to superior ecclesiastical assemblies;[212]
and the appointment of various officers in the unit, such as the treasurer.[213] A common obligation is to consider and put into effect any matter referred to it by the diocesan bishop,[214] and sometimes the law assigns
to it the function of being the normal channel of communication between
the unit, its members, and the bishop.[215] Thirdly, the assembly is responsible for the administration and maintenance of church property,[216] and
the provision and preservation of ecclesiastical registers and records;[217]
the obligation to co-operate at the time of visitation, or when there is an
inspection of church property in the unit, is commonplace.[218] These
assemblies have special responsibilities for church finances which include

---

[206] Scotland, Can. 60.1: 'The Vestry shall co-operate with and generally assist the
Rector or Priest-in-Charge in all matters relating to the spiritual welfare of the congregation and the mission of the whole Church, subject always to the canonical rights and
duties of the clergy'; Wales, Const. VI.22.2: 'It shall be the duty of the Incumbent and
the Council to consult together and co-operate in all matters of concern and importance
to the parish'; England, Parochial Church Councils (Powers) Measure 1956, s. 2(2);
Australia, Diocese of Sydney, *The 7th Handbook*, 7.23.

[207] Wales, Const. VI.22(3); North India, Const. II.V; Korea, Const. Art. 92.1; in Brazil,
Cans. I.11, functions are fixed by diocesan law.

[208] Korea, Const. Art. 92.6

[209] Wales, Const. VI.22.3; England, Parochial Church Councils (Powers) Measure
1956, s. 2.

[210] Papua New Guinea, Can. No. 5 of 1977, 18(d); Ireland, Const. III.24.

[211] ECUSA, Cans. I.6.1.   [212] Korea, Const. Art. 92.5.

[213] Ireland, Const. III.21; Wales, Const. VI.23; Papua New Guinea, Can. No. 5 of 1977.

[214] Korea, Const. Art. 92.9; Southern Africa, Can. 28.4(f).

[215] Wales, Const. VI.22.3.

[216] Korea, Const. Art. 92.2; Scotland, Can. 60.2; Ireland, Const. III.24; Japan, Can. XIII,
Art. 128.

[217] Papua New Guinea, Can. No. 5 of 1977, 18(f); Scotland, Can. 60.3; Japan, Can. XIII,
Art. 128.

[218] Papua New Guinea, Can. No. 5 of 1977, 18(g); see generally Ch. 4.

preparation of the annual budget,[219] provision for the expenses of clergy,[220] and arranging contributions towards the diocesan quota or assessment.[221] It is common for the law to prescribe that any disputes and disagreements over the discharge of legal functions by the assembly are to be referred to the diocesan bishop.[222]

CONCLUSIONS

Historically, there has been a distinct continuity in the institutional organization of Anglican churches, still arranged on a territorial basis of provinces, dioceses, and local ecclesiastical units such as parishes. Constitutional and canonical arrangements of individual churches clearly indicate a legal unity in the Anglican Communion in terms of institutional church organization. Each unit has its own assembly, and the process of democratization in the church has resulted in a general principle that, whilst individual churches may be episcopally led, government by its assemblies is rooted in the concept of representation of both clerical and lay members of the church acting in concert with the bishops. Laws prescribe carefully both the functions of these assemblies and their relations one with another. One unifying idea is that of the separation of powers or functions. In national or regional churches, the subject-matter jurisdiction of the central church assembly is all embracing, but that of assemblies in the constituent provinces limited; in churches of a single province, the provincial assembly enjoys final authority. Irrespective of the territorial organization of the particular church, whilst the general direction of ecclesiastical life is shaped by the laws and policies of the central church assembly, its administrative work is carried on by a host of committees, commissions and boards: these provide advice in their prescribed fields and implement the decisions of the assembly. A characteristic which emerges in many churches is the precision with which the law defines the subject-matter jurisdiction of these assemblies with respect to the dioceses, for many the primary reality of the church: for these churches this leads to

---

[219] Wales, Const. VI.22.3; Korea, Const. Art. 92.3; Australia, Diocese of Sydney, *The 7th Handbook*, 7.23.

[220] Wales, Const. VI.22.3; Papua New Guinea, Can. No. 5 of 1977, 18(l); Australia, Diocese of Sydney, *The 7th Handbook*, 7.23.

[221] Korea, Const. Art. 92.4.

[222] Southern Africa, Can. 28.5: 'Where differences of opinion may hinder the work of the [Parish] Council the matter may be referred by the Incumbent, the Churchwardens, or by any three members to the Bishop'; see also England, Parochial Church Councils (Powers) Measure 1956, s. 9(3): if the council and minister are unable to fulfil their duty to agree on any matter for which their joint agreement is required, 'such matter shall be dealt with or determined in such manner as the bishop may direct'.

a general principle of the autonomy of the diocese, its protection from interference from superior assemblies in its internal affairs. Whilst churches differ radically in their rules dealing with the formation, union and division of dioceses – some requiring the consent of the diocese for such developments, others not doing so – all churches share the practice of having a diocesan assembly. In some churches, the composition and functions of the diocesan assembly are governed by national, regional or provincial law, and in others by diocesan legislation. In all churches the work of each assembly is carried out by a representative standing committee and other bodies answerable to the assembly itself. Within dioceses, the formal laws of very few churches employ a system of archdeaconries and deaneries. At the lowest ecclesiastical level, the parish, pastorate or other local unit, in addition to the annual meeting of church members, a wide range of spiritual, governmental and administrative responsibilities is assigned to the representative local assembly. All in all, the churches of the Anglican Communion share a high degree of legal unity in their institutional organization.

3

The Resolution of Ecclesiastical Conflict

Modern Anglican canon law provides a very wide range of mechanisms for the internal resolution of disputes between members of the church. Whilst the governance of ecclesiastical discipline is ultimately within the jurisdictional competence of national and provincial legislatures, generally the law reserves to the diocesan bishop oversight concerning disputes involving both ordained clergy and lay persons. When parties to disagreements are unable to settle by negotiation, commonly the law requires referral of the matter to the bishop. The use of visitation, an ancient institution preserved in the laws of the vast majority of churches, is another important means by which quasi-judicial power may be applied to ecclesiastical conflict. A recent innovation in the resolution of conflict is the use of law dealing with the breakdown of pastoral relations. In addition to these legal devices, all Anglican churches operate a hierarchical court or tribunal system to deal with instances of ecclesiastical indiscipline of the clergy and, in many churches, of the laity.[1] The concept of an ecclesiastical offence is a common and fundamental feature of all canonical disciplinary systems. The secular courts of very many states have settled with reasonable clarity the bounds of their competence to intervene in the jurisdiction of ecclesiastical tribunals. This chapter deals with these subjects and ends with some observations on the interpretation of church law and the doctrines of judicial precedent in Anglican canon law.

QUASI-JUDICIAL SETTLEMENTS

Disagreements arising from the application of church law are normally settled by administrative process which often necessitates the making of quasi-judicial decisions. Given the centrality of episcopal jurisdiction in Anglican jurisprudence, it is not surprising that laws channel instances of conflict to the bishop. This section examines three areas of law in which episcopal adjudication, either directly by the bishop or indirectly by ecclesiastical persons exercising ordinary jurisdiction, comes to the fore: refer-

---

[1] For recent historical material on church courts, see J. W. C. Wand (ed.), *The Anglican Communion: A Survey* (Oxford, 1948), 24–27, 31, 170, 257, 264, 275 and for pre-Reformation antecedents and courts in post-Reformation England, see R. H. Helmholz, *Roman Canon in Reformation England* (Cambridge, 1990).

rals to the bishop and analogous devices of administrative recourse; visitatorial powers; and laws treating the breakdown of pastoral relations.

The Principle of Hierarchical Recourse

It is a general practice in Anglican churches that conflicts between church members or complaints about misconduct on the part of the clergy must be referred, at least in the first instance, to the diocesan bishop of the cleric against whom complaint is made. The principal distinction between actual canonical systems is the formal matter of the location of rules regulating referrals. In most churches rules are dispersed amongst laws dealing with discrete topics; only a small number of churches operates a system of rules of general application to all instances of conflict and complaint. Concerning the former, as is seen in the other studies of this volume, there is ample evidence of laws requiring referral of disagreement to the bishop or an episcopal assembly for a quasi-judicial resolution of the problem. The following are typical subjects treated by means of a quasi-judicial decision: removal of a name from a roll of church members;[2] whether a churchwarden's complaint of a minister's conduct is justified;[3] whether a person is eligible to enjoy a financial benefit;[4] the refusal by a cleric to provide liturgical facilities;[5] whether a church building may be used for non-religious purposes;[6] whether a minister may refuse to baptize a person;[7] and whether admission to Holy Communion may be denied.[8] In each of these a decision is made about the application of the law to a given set of facts and often law confers a right of appeal against the bishop's determination to the metropolitan or an episcopal assembly.[9] It must be stressed, however, that episcopal resolution is merely one method amongst many now appearing in Anglican canon law. Frequently rules prescribe referral to a purely administrative body,[10] and it is the case in many churches that

---

[2] E.g. Wales, Const. VI.7: appeal lies to the archdeacon acting under the authority of the bishop.

[3] E.g. Southern Africa, Can. 28.6: this is determined by the bishop.

[4] E.g. Australia, Can. 8 of 1992 and Can. 6 of 1995: the Long Service Leave Board controls pension funds and determines in its 'absolute discretion' entitlement to claims.

[5] E.g. England, Can. B3(4).

[6] E.g. Papua New Guinea, Diocese of Port Moresby, Can. 11: a right of appeal lies to the diocesan council.

[7] E.g. ECUSA, Can. I.17.6: appeal lies to the bishop.

[8] Japan, Cans. XVII, Arts. 174–5; Canada, Can. XXI.26: in cases of remarried persons seeking admission to holy communion, the matter must be referred to the bishop who in his 'judgment' must have due regard for 'the spiritual welfare' of the parties; see generally Ch. 10.

[9] This is particularly the case with revocation of ministerial licences of clergy (see Ch. 5) and lay ministers (see Ch. 6).

[10] See e.g. New Zealand, Cans. B.V.5.2.2: if a vestry refuses to allow a parishioner use of the parish hall, the matter must be referred to the diocesan standing committee.

disputes in the fields of doctrine and liturgy are referred outside the church for informal resolution by institutions of the Anglican Communion.[11]

The second approach, the use of rules of general applicability, has been adopted in a small number of churches,[12] most notably in Scotland and India. In the Scottish church, a single canon (entitled 'Of Differences and Disputes and Appeals') applies 'to any disputes between clergy or other members of this Church as to questions affecting Congregations, Dioceses or the Province'. Disputes not involving the bishop must be referred to the bishop of the diocese in which the dispute has arisen; but where a bishop is 'so personally concerned that it is expedient that another should act', the bishop or the parties may apply to the College of Bishops for it to appoint one of its members to act; he then enjoys the same powers as the diocesan bishop. Disputes directly involving the bishop, and those involving more than one diocese, must be referred to the Episcopal Synod. The canon also deals with those appeals which are expressly allowed (under any canon, congregation constitution or trust deed) to a diocesan bishop or to the Episcopal Synod. In all appeals or references the decision of the bishop or of the Episcopal Synod is final. This is so unless the canons, congregation constitution or trust provide for further recourse to the Episcopal Synod or an appeal in cases where leave is given by the bishop or by the College of Bishops. If a bishop refuses leave to appeal, the College of Bishops may grant it in its discretion. Unless the canons, congregation constitutions or trusts provide otherwise, 'the Bishop in dealing with disputes shall have full power and absolute discretion': to regulate procedure; to hear parties or to dispense with a hearing; to require oral or written contentions; to take evidence formally or informally; and generally to control the process. All parties are entitled to be legally represented.[13]

In India, the bishops are assisted by presbyters and lay persons in their quasi-judicial resolution of administrative disputes. According to the constitution of the church in North India, any 'memoranda, representations, complaints, references, petitions, and appeals related to administrative matters in the Pastorates or the Diocese' must be referred to the assembly

---

[11] See Chs. 7 and 8.

[12] Papua New Guinea, Diocese of Port Moresby, Can. 10(4): complaints against a cleric may be made to the 'immediate ecclesiastical superior', such as the archdeacon or vicar general, who must lay the matter before the bishop; see also Kenya, Can. XV.II(a): if members of a parish council have a complaint of neglect of duty or unbecoming conduct by a minister, 'they shall in the first instance seek an interview with him to discuss the matter and, if possible, resolve it'; if this is not successful referral may be made to the diocesan bishop which may result in judicial proceedings; Southern Africa, Can. 28: 'Where differences of opinion may hinder the work of the [Parish] Council the matter may be referred by the Incumbent, the Churchwardens, or by any three members to the Bishop'.

[13] Scotland, Can. 55.

of the diocese, the Diocesan Council. The Diocesan Council is under a duty to submit complaints or appeals by any aggrieved party against its own decisions to the central Synod.[14] In the constitution of the church in South India, '[a]ll disputes of any nature whatsoever, concerning the affairs of the Synod and/or any matter in relation to the Synod and/or any of its institutions shall be resolved only by Arbitration'. The Synod is obliged to appoint a panel of arbitrators consisting of five bishops, ten presbyters and fifteen lay people. Any member of the church may submit in writing a complaint which must, in the first instance, be resolved 'in a pastoral way'. If this fails, the General Secretary must 'call upon both the parties to the dispute to select from out of the panel of Arbitrators, any one person for each side who he/she/they desire to have as his/her/their Arbitrator'. Two arbitrators, 'one on the side of the person raising the dispute, and the other on the side of the person against whom the dispute is raised shall be Arbitrators for resolving the dispute'; the award of the arbitrators 'shall be binding on all parties to the dispute'. If the award is not acceptable to any party, such party is deemed to be 'ineligible to participate in the Government of the Church at all levels'. Every diocese must incorporate similar provisions in their respective constitutions.[15]

Visitations

The ancient institution of visitation, inherited by English canon law from pre-Reformation law, is a device used extensively in Anglican churches to enable oversight of ecclesiastical discipline, though its judicial character has given way in recent years to a more pastoral understanding of its purpose.[16] Its main object is to provide a first-hand assessment of the condition of ecclesiastical property and the fulfilment of duties placed on clergy and lay officers. It is a general principle of Anglican canon law that visitatorial powers may be exercised by primates, by archbishops, and by bishops; in a handful of churches which have the office, visitation by the archdeacon is also available. First, with respect to primatial visitation, laws of several churches place upon the primate a duty to visit the dioce-

[14] North India, Const. II.III.IX.34; see also New Zealand, Const. D.7: any person aggrieved by any 'act or decision of any Diocesan synod' may appeal to the General Synod.

[15] South India, Const. XI(a): the procedure contained in the secular Indian Arbitration Act 1940 'shall apply'; see also Papua New Guinea, Const. Art. 8.E: when there is a dispute between the province and a diocese a person(s) nominated jointly by the President and the Secretary-General of the Anglican Consultative Council must arbitrate and that decision 'shall be final'.

[16] R. H. Helmholz, *Roman Canon Law in Reformation England* (Cambridge, 1990) 105–109, 165; P. Smith, 'Points of law and practice concerning ecclesiastical visitation', *Ecclesiastical Law Journal*, 2(9) (1990–92), 189.

ses of the province regularly. The pastoral dimension of primatial visitation comes to the fore in the canon law of ECUSA: the presiding bishop must visit every diocese for the purpose of '[h]olding pastoral consultations with the Bishop or Bishops . . . and, with their advice, with the Lay and Clerical leaders of the jurisdiction', preaching the Word and celebrating Holy Communion.[17] This same provision is to be found in the laws of a number of churches,[18] some of which provide for extraordinary primatial visitation when the circumstances of a diocese require this.[19] In other churches the law seems to allow visitation by the primate only at the request of the diocesan bishop.[20]

Secondly, with respect to archiepiscopal visitation, the laws of most churches impose on the archbishop a duty to make an 'official visit' to each diocese: sometimes the duty is expressed in very general terms,[21] but occasionally the law requires metropolitical visitation expressly to ensure compliance by diocesan bishops with the law of the church.[22] The law of most churches is rather more detailed. The constitution of the church in Uganda provides that the archbishop is '[t]o visit officially any Diocese of the Province, whether at the invitation of the Bishop or on his own initiative, provided that reasonable notice is given'.[23] In some churches the pastoral aspect of metropolitical visitation is stressed. In West Africa, for instance, the archbishop is obliged to hold visitations, at the request of the diocesan bishop or on his own initiative, 'for the purpose of holding pastoral consultations with the Bishop or Bishops thereof as well as with the Clerical and Lay Leaders of the Diocese preaching the Word, and celebrating the Sacrament of the Lord's Supper'.[24] In other churches the basic rule is that the archbishop has a right, rather than a duty, to visit the dioceses: in English canon law the archbishop has 'the right to visit, at times and places limited by law or custom, the province' in order 'to correct and supply the defects of other bishops'.[25] In several churches, the law makes express pro-

---

[17] ECUSA, Cans. I.2.4.

[18] Canada, Can. III.8: the primate must maintain a pastoral relationship with the whole of the church.

[19] Philippines, Cans. I.3.1(c): the visitation must take place every three years; if the Council of Bishops consider that 'the affairs of any constituent Diocese gravely require his [i.e. the primate's] attention he shall make an official visitation . . . either in person or through a deputation'.

[20] Korea, Const. Ch. 2, Art. 6.3: '[a]t the request of a diocesan Bishop'.

[21] South East Asia, Const. Art. II(f): one of the archbishop's functions is '[t]o visit the Dioceses of the Province'; Indian Ocean, Const. Art. 11; Melanesia, Const. Art. 9; Kenya, Const. Art. VII(a)(5): the archbishop must 'visit officially any Diocese of the Province as Metropolitan in accordance with any Canon in that behalf'; Burundi, Const. Art. 12; Sudan, Const. Art. 18.24; Rwanda, Draft Const. 1996, Art. 30.

[22] Tanzania, Const. IV.9.   [23] Uganda, Const. Art. 9(d).

[24] West Africa, Const. Art. V(v).

vision for an extraordinary archiepiscopal visitation whenever the metropolitan considers that the circumstances of the diocese require this.[26] In Southern Africa, the metropolitan is 'to visit officially any Diocese of the Province, when invited to do so by the Bishop or Clergy of that Diocese, or whenever it shall seem desirable to himself, after consultation with the other Diocesan Bishops'. The exercise of jurisdiction by the diocesan bishop is not inhibited during the metropolitical visitation 'except there appear to the Metropolitan to be some strong reason for such inhibition'; the Synod of Bishops at their next session is competent to declare whether such reason was sufficient.[27]

Thirdly, with respect to episcopal visitations of the parishes and congregations of the diocese by the diocesan bishop, in some churches the law confers a *discretion* upon the bishop to hold such visitations: this is the case in England and Southern Africa.[28] In Wales this discretion applies both to the time of visitation and its form.[29] By way of contrast, in most churches the bishop is under a *duty* to visit parishes and congregations, either personally or through a deputy, usually at least once in every three years.[30] In the laws of several churches the pastoral and liturgical sides of visitation are stressed as well as examination of 'the life and ministry' of clergy and the laity.[31] Some laws prescribe consequences on the failure of the bishop to visit regularly. According to the canon law of ECUSA, if the bishop fails

[25] England, Can. G5, C17(2); Wales, Const. XI.17: 'Archiepiscopal Visitations shall be held as heretofore, and the law and practice thereto shall be that prevailing' on the date of disestablishment of the church (i.e. 30 March 1920).

[26] Papua New Guinea, Const. Art. 10: the archbishop may make 'pastoral visits to any Diocese . . . at the invitation of the Diocesan Bishop', but if the House of Bishops, a Diocesan Synod or the Provincial Council considers that 'the affairs of any particular Diocese gravely require his attention', the archbishop is 'entitled to make an official visitation either in person or through a deputy appointed by the House of Bishops'; the archbishop may, in consultation with the House of Bishops, 'give orders to put matters right'.

[27] Southern Africa, Can. 2.1(g).

[28] Southern Africa, Can. 39.20: 'Nothing contained in this or other Canons shall be so construed as to affect any right in visitation, or other spiritual authority, which the Bishop of a Diocese may exercise, by virtue of his office, without judicial proceedings'; England, Can. C18(4): the bishop has the right to hold 'visitations at times limited by law or custom to the end that he may get some good knowledge of the state, sufficiency, and ability of the clergy and other persons whom he is to visit'; special provisions apply to episcopal visitation of the cathedral: see Cathedrals Measure 1963, s. 6; Care of Cathedrals Measure 1990, s. 2.

[29] Wales, Const. XI.17: 'Episcopal Visitations shall be held at such intervals as the Bishop may decide, and the form of such a Visitation shall be determined by the Bishop'.

[30] Scotland, Can. 6.1: the bishop must visit each congregation personally at least once every three years and 'formal visitations by the Bishop may from time to time be held'.

[31] ECUSA, Cans. III.24.4(a)–(b): 'Each Diocesan Bishop shall visit the Congregations within the Diocese at least once in three years. Interim visits may be delegated to another Bishop of this Church'. The bishop must preside at Holy Communion and at

or otherwise declines to visit, the minister or vestry, or the bishop himself, may apply to the Presiding Bishop to appoint five neighbouring bishops as a Council of Conciliation to 'determine all matters of difference between the parties, and each party shall conform to the decision of the Council'; it is obliged to resolve amicably any differences between the parties. At the ordinary visitation, the minister and churchwardens must exhibit to the bishop the parish register and give information on the 'spiritual and temporal' state of the congregation.[32] In relation to other churches, occasionally laws require the bishop to report on the results of visitation to the diocesan assembly.[33] Laws do not generally prescribe procedures to be followed at episcopal visitations, but sometimes they expressly insist on full co-operation of the ministers and local church officers in the conducting of the visitation.[34] Lastly, some churches operate a system of annual visitation by the archdeacon: either the procedure to be followed is laid down in canon law,[35] and the archdeacon is required to examine specific items relating to church property,[36] or else the form is left to the discretion of the archdeacon.[37]

the initiatory rites, as required, preach the Word, examine the records of the congregation (as required by Can. III.14.3) and 'examine the life and ministry of the Clergy and Congregation' (according to Cans. III.14.2(e)); see also Mexico, Can. 35; Philippines, Cans. III.15: two years; West Indies, Can. 9.2: 'Every Diocesan Bishop shall visit the parishes within his jurisdiction at least once in every three years for the purpose of examining their condition, administering the Sacrament of Confirmation, preaching the Word, celebrating the Eucharist and giving Communion to the people'.

[32] ECUSA, Cans. III.24.4; Philippines, Cans. III.16.3(f); see Ch. 4 for the appointment of coadjutor and suffragan bishops and Ch. 6 for visitation of religious communities.

[33] See e.g. Philippines, Cans. III.15.5.

[34] ECUSA, Cans. III.14.2(e): 'On notice being received of the Bishop's intention to visit any Congregation, the Clergy shall announce the fact to the Congregation. At every visitation it shall be their duty and that of the Wardens, Vestry or other officers, to exhibit to the Bishop the Parish Register and to give information on the state of the Congregation, spiritual and temporal, in such categories as the Bishop shall have previously requested in writing'; see also England, Can. G6.

[35] England, Can. C22(5), G6: the archdeacon must hold an annual visitation; articles of enquiry must be delivered to the minister and churchwardens, containing specific questions relating to the administration of the parish; the minister and churchwardens must render their account (the presentment) upon these articles.

[36] Southern Africa, Can. 15.4: unless the bishop decides otherwise, 'the Archdeacon shall at least annually examine the financial records, the Inventory of Parochial Property, the Burial Grounds, and the fabric of the Church and other Parochial Property in the Pastoral Charges of his Archdeaconry, and report thereon to the Bishop' (this is listed as a 'visitation').

[37] Wales, Const. XI.17: 'Archdeacons shall conduct regular Visitations of all parishes in their archdeaconries, and subject to any direction by the Governing Body the form of such a Visitation shall be determined by the Archdeacon'; see also Jerusalem and the Middle East, Diocese of Egypt, Const. 1982, 9: this requires 'an annual visitation of inspection' to congregations and chaplaincies.

The Breakdown of Pastoral Relations

Whilst most churches assign to the bishop a general jurisdiction over the discipline of both clergy and laity in the diocese,[38] very few churches possess formal structures for the particular problem of pastoral conflict. Notable exceptions to this general rule are ECUSA and the Church of England. National church law in ECUSA provides two sets of structures to deal with serious pastoral conflict.[39] First, special provisions apply to 'reconciliation of disagreements affecting the pastoral relationship'. When in a parish the pastoral relationship between the rector and vestry is 'imperilled by disagreement or dissension', and the issues are deemed serious by a majority vote of the vestry or by the rector, either party may petition the bishop in writing 'to intervene and assist the parties in their efforts to resolve the disagreement'. The bishop may enlist the assistance of a consultant. The parties are under a duty to labour 'in good faith that [they] may be reconciled'.[40] Secondly, if this fails and for any reason the rector or vestry desires 'a dissolution of the pastoral relation, and the parties cannot agree', either may give written notice to the bishop. Within sixty days of receiving the notice the bishop, as chief pastor of the diocese, must mediate the differences between the rector and vestry 'in every informal way' which the bishop considers proper. The bishop may appoint a committee (composed of at least one priest and one lay person, neither of whom may be members of the parish), to report to the bishop. If the differences have not been resolved, the bishop must give notice to the rector and vestry that 'a godly judgment will be rendered' after consultation with the diocesan standing committee. The parties may confer with the committee within ten days of notice before consultation with the bishop at which conference the parties may be represented. Within thirty days of the conference, if any, or of the bishop's notice, the bishop must confer with the standing committee and receive its recommendation. As 'final arbiter and judge' the bishop decides whether to consent to dissolution and the reasons for the decision must be communicated in writing to the parties. The judgment must include 'such terms and conditions including financial settlements as shall seem to the Bishop to be just and compassionate'. If the pastoral relation is to continue, the bishop must require the parties 'to agree on definitions of responsibility and accountability for the Rector and

---

[38] See e.g. Canada, Can. XVIII.I.1: 'the bishop of a diocese . . . has by virtue of the office of bishop, ecclesiastical jurisdiction, authority and power of discipline over bishops, priests, deacons and lay members of the [church] within the diocese or otherwise under the jurisdiction of the bishop'; see generally Ch. 4.

[39] ECUSA, Cans. III.24.4(c): the bishop may at any time apply to the Presiding Bishop for the establishment of a Council of Conciliation; see n. 32.

[40] Ibid., Cans, III.20.

the Vestry'. In cases where the pastoral relation is to be dissolved, the bishop must direct the Secretary of the Diocesan Convention to record the dissolution. The bishop is obliged to offer 'appropriate supportive services' to the cleric and the parish. In the event that any party fails to comply with the episcopal judgment, the bishop may suspend the rector until compliance and, with respect to the vestry, he may recommend to the diocesan standing committee that the parish be placed under the direct supervision of the bishop until compliance. These arrangements do not apply in any diocese which has made provision by canon on this subject, provided diocesan legislation is consistent with the national canon.[41]

Similar, but far more detailed, arrangements exist in the law of the Church of England. The relevant law and quasi-legislation made under it apply when there has been 'a serious breakdown of the pastoral relationship between the incumbent and the parishioners to which the conduct of the incumbent or of the parishioners or of both has contributed over a substantial period'. Unlike in the ECUSA model, breakdown is legally defined as 'a situation where the relationship between an incumbent and the parishioners . . . is such as to impede the promotion in the parish of the whole mission of the [church], pastoral, evangelistic, social and ecumenical'. In outline, the procedure is as follows. Notice of intent to request an enquiry may be made by the incumbent, the archdeacon or a two-thirds majority of the parochial church council. The bishop must allow a cooling-off period of six months to one year, after notice of intent, before instituting an enquiry. According to the Code of Practice made under the governing legislation, during this period the bishop must appoint a conciliator who must seek to effect a reconciliation. If the conciliator is unsuccessful, the bishop must decide whether to institute the enquiry, after the archdeacon has made a report and has made further efforts to remove the 'cause of their estangement'. Unlike in ECUSA, at this point the matter is taken out of the hands of the diocese: the enquiry is conducted by a provincial tribunal; the incumbent has rights to object to its membership, of appearance, to apply for legal aid, and to be represented legally. The tribunal determines whether there has been a serious breakdown of pastoral relations and, if so, whether the incumbent and/or parishioners have contributed to it and whether the breakdown was due to the age or infirmity of the incumbent. The tribunal reports to the bishop and, if the tribunal so recommends, the bishop may declare the benefice vacant, rebuke the incumbent, rebuke the parishioners or disqualify them (for a period not exceeding five years) from holding office in the parish. The incumbent has a right to be considered for financial compensation in the event of a declaration of avoidance. In disability cases, the bishop may request resignation

---

[41] Ibid., Cans. III.21.

of the incumbent, but only if this is recommended by the enquiry; the bishop may declare the benefice vacant if the incumbent refuses to resign.[42]

ECCLESIASTICAL COURTS AND TRIBUNALS

In addition to provisions enabling quasi-judicial resolution of ecclesiastical conflict by means of hierarchical recourse, visitations and laws on the breakdown of pastoral relations, all churches in the Anglican Communion employ a hierarchical system of courts or tribunals.[43] In most churches, these enjoy only 'criminal' jurisdiction over ecclesiastical offences involving clergy and, in some churches, lay officers and ordinary members of the laity. In a small number of churches, however, courts and tribunals also exercise jurisdiction over 'civil' matters relating to church property.[44] It is a general principle of Anglican canon law that the right to create ecclesiastical offences and to prescribe censures belongs primarily to the national or provincial assembly.[45] The following sections deal with: jurisdiction, particularly ecclesiastical offences; procedures; sanctions; rights of appeal and the superior church courts and tribunals; civil matters including internal review of ecclesiastical legislation; and the supervisory role of the secular courts.

Inferior Courts: Ecclesiastical Discipline

It is rather difficult to generalize about tribunal systems, but, broadly, Anglican churches fall into two basic groups: those with a three-tier hierarchy of courts, the court of the diocese as the tribunal of first instance, the provincial court as an appellate tribunal, and a further final court of appeal;[46] and those with a two-tier system, a court of the diocese and an

---

[42] England, Incumbents (Vacation of Benefices) Measure 1977 (as amended 1993); Incumbents (Vacation of Benefices) Rules 1994; Code of Practice 1994; *Re Flenley* (1981) Fam 64: compensation is payable regardless of the incumbent's fault 'for it is the clear intention of this Measure that the vacation of the benefice is for pastoral reasons and is not punitive in its purpose'.

[43] For Lambeth Conference resolutions on the subject, see n. 126.

[44] The use of tribunals to deal with a range of very diverse ecclesiastical subjects is beginning to make its mark in many churches: for England, see LFCE, Ch. 5.

[45] See e.g. Uganda, Const. Art. 16: 'The Provincial Assembly shall make Canons setting out: (i) What matters are to be deemed to be ecclesiastical offences for which a person may be tried by a Tribunal . . . and (ii) What sentences may be imposed'; Canada, Declaration of Principles, 7A(i)–(ii); for subject-matter jurisdiction see generally Ch. 2.

[46] See e.g. West Indies, Can. 22: the Diocesan Court (for the trial of priests and deacons), the Provincial Court of Appeal (for appeals from the diocese), and the Provincial Court (for the trial of bishops); Central Africa, Can. 26: Diocesan Court, Provincial

appellate provincial court.[47] Few churches have courts at the level of the lower ecclesiastical units; the *panchayats* of the pastorates in the church in India and the archdeacon's court in Wales are unusual.[48] The diocesan tribunal, the composition of which differs from church to church,[49] is in some churches styled the Court of the Bishop: the bishop presides, acting with the assistance of appointees of the Diocesan Synod.[50] In others it is the Consistory Court, presided over by the diocesan chancellor, an episcopal appointee (and usually a person holding secular judicial office or a legally qualified practitioner).[51] In some it is the Court of the Diocesan Synod or Council, composed of the bishop, presbyters and lay persons appointed by the diocesan assembly.[52] Occasionally it is known as the Diocesan Court, sometimes presided over by the bishop acting as judge or by a judge elected by the diocesan assembly,[53] or, simply the Diocesan

Court, and the Final Court; Australia, Const. IX.53–57: the Court of the Bishop (for the trial of priests and deacons) and the Special Court (with original jurisdiction over bishops), the Provincial Tribunal (an appeal court which also has original jurisdiction over matters of faith, ritual and ceremonial), and the Appellate Tribunal; Jerusalem, Const. Art. 14: Diocesan Court, Provincial Tribunal and Supreme Court of Appeal; Canada, Can. XVIII: Diocesan Court, Provincial Court of Appeal and Supreme Court of Appeal.

[47] ECUSA, Cans. IV.4: Diocesan Court (for the trial of priests and deacons and with appeal to the provincial Commission of Review), and the Court for the Trial of a Bishop (with appeal to the Commission of Review for the Trial of a Bishop); Brazil, Cans. IV.2; Papua New Guinea, Const. Art. 17: the Diocesan Court with appeal to the Provincial Court; see also Melanesia, Const. Art. 19; New Zealand, Cans. D.I, 4: Bishop's Court and the Court of Appeal; Ireland, Const. VIII.1: the Diocesan Court with appeal to the Court of the General Synod; the latter also has original jurisdiction in matters of doctrine and ritual.

[48] South India, Const. XI.3–5: rules for the operation of 'local courts or panchayats' continue unless varied by the Diocesan Council; 'The Bishop of the diocese may where necessary appoint a local Court of Panchayat for the administration of discipline of members of the Church' with an appeal lying to the Court of the Diocesan Council; see also North India, Const. II.V.II.1: the Pastorate Committee is the 'primary court of discipline' for 'Church members'; Wales, Const. XI.1(1).

[49] See Ch. 6 for ecclesiastical judges.

[50] Australia, Const. IX.54; New Zealand, Cans. D.I.1.1: the bishop appoints a chancellor as president; see also Scotland, Can. 54.12: the bishop is assisted by the diocesan chancellor.

[51] England, Ecclesiastical Jurisdiction Measure 1963, ss. 1, 2; compare Jerusalem and the Middle East, Diocese of Egypt 1982, 15: the 'Bishop's Court' is composed *inter alia* of the chancellor.

[52] South India, Const. XI.6: 'The Court of a Diocesan Council shall consist of the bishop . . . or a presbyter commissioned by him, together with presbyters and laymen chosen by the bishop out of panels appointed by the Diocesan Council'; North India, II.V.II.2: 'For ministers, the Court of the Diocesan Council' (also called the Judicial Committee) is the 'primary court of discipline'; West Africa, Const. Art. XXII.2.

[53] Central Africa, Can. 26, 27.3: 'The Bishop of every Diocese shall sit as judge in his Diocesan Court in all cases when he thinks fit', with the Diocesan Chancellor acting as assessor; Ireland, Const. VIII.5–6: the bishop is 'the judge in the Diocesan Court' with the chancellor sitting as assessor; compare ECUSA, Const. Art. X, Cans. IV.4: the Diocesan Court for the trial of priests and deacons has a Presiding Judge elected by the Diocesan Convention.

Tribunal.[54] As a general principle the diocesan courts or tribunals enjoy original jurisdiction over the criminal side of ecclesiastical discipline concerning priests and deacons, and in several churches over the laity.[55] The diocesan court has original jurisdiction over the whole spectrum of ecclesiastical offences, and this often includes those offences involving doctrine and liturgy.[56] By way of contrast special courts organized at national or provincial level, and (usually) composed of bishops, have jurisdiction for the trial of bishops.[57] Several churches defy these general categories.[58]

By way of contrast there is considerably greater consistency between churches as to the ecclesiastical offences for which bishops, priests (and in some churches lay persons) may be tried. In the Church of England there are two basic offences in the formal law for which ordained ministers only may be tried: the so-called 'reserved' case, i.e. 'an offence against the laws

[54] Uganda, Const. Art. 17; for exactly the same provision see Burundi, Const. Art. 18; West Africa, Can. XVIII.2: 'Each Diocese shall by canon establish a Tribunal for the trial of any Priest or Deacon in the Diocese'; Southern Cone, Can. 8.

[55] New Zealand, Cans. D.I.1.1: the Bishop's Court has jurisdiction over 'the breach of the laws, rules, regulations, canons and statutes . . . of the Church . . . and the behaviour of and by any minister or office-bearer', that is 'all persons who are members of the Church who shall have assented to the authority of the General Synod'; South India, Const. XI.6ff; Korea, Const. Art. 125: 'In principle, the diocesan bishop shall discipline clergy and laity within his diocese . . . if a bishop does not do so it may be done by the Judicial Committee'; see also Japan, Can. XVII, Art. 172; Southern Cone, Can. 8; and Wales, Const. XI.18.

[56] New Zealand, Cans. D.I.1.1: the Bishop's Court has jurisdiction 'in all matters relating to doctrine'; see also Southern Africa, Can. 40; ECUSA, Cans. IV.4(a); compare Australia, Const. IX.55: the Provincial Tribunal has original jurisdiction over cases of faith, ritual and ceremonial; Central Africa, Can. 26.4: 'The Diocesan Court shall have sole original jurisdiction in the trial of all offences except heresy and false doctrine' and the trial of bishops.

[57] Australia, Const. IX.56: the Special Court is presided over by the primate and two or more diocesan bishops; West Africa, Const. Art. XXII.1; ECUSA, Const. Art. X and Cans. IV.4(b); Central Africa, Can. 28 and Uganda, Const. Art. 17: bishops are tried by the Provincial Court; Scotland, Can. 54.1: the Episcopal Synod; West Africa, Can. XVII: the Episcopal Synod must establish 'a Court for the trial of Bishops consisting of at least three Bishops of the Province'; Southern Cone, Can. 8: 'The House of Bishops has jurisdiction in the trial of Bishops'; Indian Ocean, Const. Art. 17; compare North India, II.V.II.2: 'The primary [court] of discipline . . . [is] . . . for bishops, the Court of the Synod', composed of 4 bishops, 4 presbyters and 6 lay persons.

[58] Wales, Const. XI.18: its courts are the Archdeacon's Court, the Diocesan Court (the business of which is mainly concerning property and complaints against churchwardens and lay parochial church councillors), the Provincial Court (which has original jurisdiction over ecclesiastical offences), the Special Provincial Court (for the trial of bishops) and the Supreme Court (for the trial of the archbishop); Southern Africa, Can. 36: this requires a Bishop's Court (hearing cases concerning archdeacons, churchwardens, and clergy mental incapacity, and presided over by the bishop assisted by a chancellor acting in an advisory capacity), a Diocesan Tribunal (presided over by the bishop hearing disciplinary cases against priests and deacons), a Court for the Trial of Bishops, and a Provincial Court of Appeal.

ecclesiastical involving matters of doctrine, ritual or ceremonial'; and 'conduct' cases, i.e. being 'any other offence against the laws ecclesiastical, including (i) conduct unbecoming the office and work of a clerk in Holy Orders; or (ii) serious, persistent or continuous neglect of duty'.[59] Certain decisions of the secular courts are also considered incompatible with ordained ministry: conviction for a criminal offence resulting in imprisonment; divorce, where the spouse of the cleric relies on adultery, desertion, or unreasonable behaviour; a finding in a matrimonial cause of having committed adultery; an affiliation order having been made against a cleric; and wilful neglect to maintain a spouse or children.[60] In the vast majority of other churches in the Communion there are seven core offences common to each. One obvious feature of these is the striking degree of generality with which the elements of offences are expressed – rarely are they defined in the formal law with any degree of precision.

First: conviction for a criminal offence under the secular law of the state in which the church exists. Mostly, churches treat any 'crime' as sufficient to constitute an offence, but some laws specify crimes involving dishonesty or some other general element of 'immorality'.[61] Second: immorality. Many churches simply use the word 'immorality' or 'immoral conduct',[62] others focus on 'sexual immorality',[63] and others list species of immorality, such as 'drunkenness', 'unchastity', 'adultery', 'dishonesty' and 'corruption'.[64] In this category the canon law of New Zealand includes '[a]ny

[59] England, Ecclesiastical Jurisdiction Measure 1963, s. 14(2): further, no proceedings may be taken 'in respect of the political opinions or activities' of clergy; it is left to the church courts to define the precise terms of these offences; for 'reserved' and 'ordinary' offences, see Chile, Cans. E.2; and for 'canonical offences', see Venezuela, Cans. IV.21.

[60] England, Ecclesiastical Jurisdiction Measure 1963, s. 55; see also *Under Authority*, The Report of the General Synod Working Party reviewing Clergy Discipline and the working of the Ecclesiastical Courts (London, 1996), 6.15ff: this proposes replacing existing offences with: wilful disobedience to or breach of the laws ecclesiastical; neglect, culpable carelessness or gross inefficiency in the performance of the duties of their office; conduct inappropriate or unbecoming the office and work of a clerk in Holy Orders; teaching, preaching, publishing or professing doctrine or belief incompatible with that of the Church of England as expressed within its creeds and formularies; and conviction in a secular court of an offence for which a sentence of imprisonment may be given.

[61] West Africa, Const. Art. XXII.6(a): 'an offence involving dishonesty, fraud, moral turpitude or public immorality which has led to conclusive conviction in the criminal courts'; the same formula appears in Southern Africa, Can. 37.1(a); for crimes of dishonesty, see Brazil, Cans. IV.1; see also Ireland, Const. VIII.53: 'crimes'; New Zealand, Can. D.5.4: 'a crime'; ECUSA, Cans. IV.1.1; and Canada, Can. XVIII.8(a).

[62] ECUSA, Cans. IV.1.1; Scotland, Can. 54.2 and Nigeria, Can. XXXXIX(d): 'immoral conduct'; Canada, Can. XVIII.8(b).

[63] Southern Africa, Can. 37.1(b) and West Africa, Const. Art. XXII.6(b): 'sexual immorality'.

[64] Ireland, Const. VIII.53: 'immorality' and 'drunkenness'; Australia, Cans. 4 of 1962, 7 of 1981 and 12 of 1992: 'unchastity' and 'drunkenness'; North India, Const. II.V.VI.1:

act or habit of dishonesty or immorality, or any gross indecency of life or conversation . . . [a]ny act or habit of sexual harassment or disregard for responsible personal relations' and '[a]ny culpable disregard of the obligations recognised by law in reference to family relationships'.[65] Third: holding and teaching publicly doctrines and opinions contrary to the doctrine of the church. In some churches this is defined as 'publicly and advisedly maintaining doctrines or opinions contrary to the teaching of the church' without formal retraction.[66] Within this category several churches include heresy, schism and apostasy.[67] Fourth: violation of the law of the church, as found in national, provincial or diocesan legislation,[68] or of ordination vows.[69] Fifth: neglect of duty: in some churches this is 'general neglect' and others require 'habitual' or 'wilful' neglect;[70] Scottish canon

adultery, murder, fornication, drunkenness, perjury, theft, dishonesty, and corruption; Papua New Guinea; Can. No. 1 of 1977: unchastity, drunkenness, insolvency, or failure or inability to pay debts; Korea, Const. Art. 125: immorality that brings 'discredit' on the church.

[65] New Zealand, Can. D.II.5.4.

[66] Nigeria, Can. XXXXIX(a); West Indies, Can. 25; ECUSA, Cans. IV.1.1; Wales, Const. XI.18: 'teaching, preaching, publishing or professing doctrine or belief incompatible with that of the Church in Wales'; Scotland, Can. 54.2: 'having taught, published, or otherwise publicly promulgated doctrines or opinions subversive of or opposed to the teaching of the Church, or expressed in its formularies'; Ireland, Const. VIII.53; Canada, Can. XVIII.8(g): 'teaching or advocating doctrines' contrary to those accepted by the church; North India, Const. II.V.VI.1: 'anything in his conduct, worship, belief or teaching which is contrary to the Christian scriptures'.

[67] Southern Africa, Can. 37.1(d)–(f) and West Africa, Const. Art. XXII.6(d)–(f): heresy ('holding and teaching publicly or privately, and advisedly, any doctrine contrary to that held by this Church'); schism ('acceptance or promotion of membership in a religious body not in communion' with the church); 'apostasy from the Christian faith'; Papua New Guinea, Can. No. 1 of 1977: schism, heresy and false doctrine.

[68] Nigeria, Can. XXXXIX(g) and West Indies, Can. 25: 'wilful contravention of any enactment' of the church; Southern Africa, Can. 37.1(g)–(h); West Africa, Can. XXII.6(g): breach of provincial or diocesan law; Papua New Guinea, Can. No. 1 of 1977; ECUSA, Cans. IV.1.1; Wales, Const. XI.18: 'wilful disobedience to or breach of' the constitution or any regulation of the Diocesan Conference; Canada, Can. XVIII.8(d); see also Ireland, Const. VIII.53: for alleged violations of the canons, see *Hick and Others v Wilson* (1941) Journal of the Court of General Synod, 1947, 330: *Chamney and Others v Colquhoun* (1937) Journal of the Court of General Synod, 1947, 368 ; Scotland, Can. 54.2: 'breach of obligations incumbent upon them by the Canons'; New Zealand, Can. D.II.5.4: wilful and knowing contravention of 'any law or regulation' of the General Synod; trustees may also be proceeded against for contravening terms of a trust deed: this is unique.

[69] New Zealand, Can. D.II.2; West Africa, Can. XXII.6(j); ECUSA, Cans. IV.1.1: this includes disregard of episcopal pastoral directions or engaging in secular employment without consent; see also Puerto Rico, Cans. IV.1.

[70] West Indies, Can. 25 and Nigeria, Can. XXXXIX(d): 'general neglect of duty'; West Africa, Can. XXII.6(i) 'habitual neglect' of ministerial duties; Wales, Const. XI.18 and Southern Africa, Can. 37.1(j): 'neglect of duties of office'; Mexico, Cans. IV.37; Canada, Can. XVIII.8(f): 'wilful or habitual neglect of the duties of any office'; see also Australia, Cans. 1962–1992; New Zealand, Can. D.II.2; and Papua New Guinea, Can. No.1 of 1977: 'neglect of duty'.

law forbids 'grave neglect or habitual carelessness or gross inefficiency in the performance of . . . official duties'.[71] Sixth: conduct unbecoming a minister in Holy Orders, sometimes adding that the conduct must be such as to give cause for scandal or offence to the church,[72] or 'discredit' upon it.[73] Seventh: disobedience of any lawful command of the ordinary.[74] To these some laws add: homosexual acts, paedophilia,[75] neglect of public worship or violation of liturgical rubrics,[76] disobedience to the 'pastoral directions' of the bishop,[77] conduct 'disrespectful' to the bishop,[78] and refusing without 'sufficient cause',[79] or 'good cause', 'to perform for any member of the Church, belonging to his cure . . . any act appertaining to his ministerial office'.[80] Occasionally, laws exclude matters which are purely private and more susceptible to resolution by pastoral advice.[81]

[71] Scotland, Can. 54.2.

[72] Scotland, Can. 54.2: 'conduct or behaviour unbecoming the character and office, or calculated to bring scandal on the Church'; Nigeria, Can. XXXXIX(f): 'scandalous conduct or offence unbecoming of a clergyman'; see also Ireland, Const. VIII.53; Wales, Const. XI.18, Southern Africa, Can. 37.1(c) and West Africa, Const. Art. XXII.6(c): 'conduct giving just cause for scandal or offence'; West Indies, Can. 25: 'Conduct giving cause of scandal or offence or otherwise unbecoming a Clergyman'; Papua New Guinea, Can. No. 1 of 1977: '[c]onduct in itself disgraceful or productive of scandal and evil report'.

[73] ECUSA, Cans. IV.1.1: conduct unbecoming is 'any disorder or neglect that prejudices the reputation, good order and discipline of the Church, or any conduct of a nature to bring material discredit upon the Church or the Holy Orders conferred by the Church'.

[74] Canada, Can. XVIII.8(c); New Zealand, Can. D.II.4: it is an offence to 'refuse or neglect to obey the lawful directions of the bishop' or 'to submit to godly admonitions'; for Ireland, see *Bishop of Tuam v Judge* (1947) Journal of the Court of General Synod, 1948, 283: refusal to meet the ordinary.

[75] Papua New Guinea, Diocese of Port Moresby, Can. 10(5): 'bestiality, bigamy . . . homosexual acts, paedophilia or polygamy'.

[76] West Africa, Can. XXII.6(i); ECUSA, Cans. IV.1.1; Spain, Cans. IV.34.

[77] ECUSA, Cans. IV.1.1: for disobedience to or disregard of a pastoral direction of the bishop to constitute breach of ordination vows there must be a warning with reasons for the direction; this must be given in the bishop's capacity as pastor, teacher and overseer and must not be arbitrary or contrary to the constitution and canons, national or diocesan; the direction must have concerned doctrine, discipline or worship or the manner of life of the cleric.

[78] Canada, Can. XVIII.8(h): 'contemptuous or disrespectful conduct' towards the bishop 'in matters pertaining to the administration of the affairs of the diocese or a parish'.

[79] West Indies, Can. 25: 'Refusing without good and sufficient reason to perform for any member of the Church belonging to his cure and not under censure of the Church'.

[80] Nigeria, Can. XXXXIX(c); see also Canada, Can. XVIII.8(e); ECUSA, Cans. IV.1.1.

[81] North India, Const. II.V.IX.1–2: 'The Court shall not entertain matters which are purely civil, or interfere in quarrels, or pry into private conduct or family matters, or scandals more than one year old, unless of a heinous nature or it has become flagrant again. Such matters shall be treated as matters for pastoral advice'.

Procedure

There is a high degree of consistency as between churches with respect to
the processing of disciplinary cases. Laws of only a handful of churches,
however, spell out general principles applicable to procedure: in Canada,
notably, the 'fundamental principles of natural justice' entitle the accused
to be: given full and complete written notice of the particulars of the
charge; presumed innocent until proven guilty 'on a balance of probabil-
ity'; heard in their own defence; represented by counsel of their own
choice; present and accompanied by counsel when evidence or argument
concerning the allegations is received by a bishop, metropolitan or court;
given the opportunity to cross-examine witnesses; tried by persons who
are not biased against them; tried within a reasonable time – they also have
a right to silence and are entitled not to be tried twice for the same
offence.[82] The laws of most churches incorporate provisions approximate
to these, and provisions exist in all churches dealing with the right to bring
a complaint, a preliminary hearing to determine whether to proceed, the
charge and presentment, appointment of the court of trial, and trial.

In order to bring a complaint which may result in judicial proceedings
for an ecclesiastical offence, a person must have *locus standi*. The fundamental requirement is that the person must be a communicant member of
the church; commonly laws require more than one complainant, and provisions vary depending on whether the proceedings are against priests
and deacons,[83] or bishops.[84] Commonly limitation periods apply, ranging
from one year to five after the commission of the offence.[85] Proceedings
continue with a charge, and notice of all charges, with particulars of the

[82] Canada, Principles and General Procedures to be Observed, 16–24; Papua New
Guinea, Diocese of Port Moresby, Can. 10.9: the court must adhere 'to [the] general
principles of . . . Canon Law and Civil Law'; ECUSA, Cans. IV.4(a): the Diocesan Court
is governed by the secular Federal Rules of Civil Procedure; in Japan, Can. XVII, art.
161, procedure is governed by the Diocesan Synod.

[83] See e.g. Scotland, Can. 54.4: at least 3 communicants; Kenya, Can. XV: 5 members
of the parish council; ECUSA, Cans IV.4: rules vary from offence to offence: for disobedience of episcopal pastoral directions only the bishop may proceed; in most other cases
a majority of lay members of a vestry or 3 priests may complain; presentment may occur
only by two-thirds vote of the diocesan standing committee; Southern Africa, Can. 39.1:
a priest, the churchwardens or 3 or more communicants aged 21 or more may complain;
West Africa, Can. XVII.15: 3 priests and 3 lay persons; West Indies, Can. 23.3(ii): the subject is left to diocesan legislation; Wales, Rules of the Provincial Court, III.1: process
begins by the bishop on his own motion or on complaint by 20 members.

[84] New Zealand, Cans. D.III.6: at least 2 priests; West Africa, Can. XVII.15: for doctrine cases, at least 5 priests or a bishop; West Indies, Can. 23.3(i): 2 bishops or 5 priests;
Scotland, Can. 54.4: at least one complainant must be a priest.

[85] Southern Africa, Can. 37.3: 5 years; New Zealand, Can. D.III.3 and West Africa,
Can. XVII.1: 3 years; West Indies, Can. 24.2: 2 years; Scotland, Can. 54.3: 1 year is the
norm.

allegation, the offence, and the time, place and circumstances of its alleged commission, must be given to the accused.[86] It is a general practice for there to be a preliminary enquiry at which it is determined whether there is a *prima facie* case and whether, therefore, proceedings ought to continue;[87] it is at this early stage that a decision may be taken, usually by the bishop, to veto further proceedings.[88] It is normal for laws to confer upon the bishop or metropolitan a power to suspend or inhibit the cleric or bishop, as the case may be, pending a trial,[89] or, with the consent of the accused, action may be taken, including the imposition of a sentence, without further proceedings and the need for a trial,[90] for example when there is an admission of guilt.[91] A wide range of powers enables dismissal of the case if it is frivolous or an early view is taken that the facts do not clearly constitute an offence.[92] Once a date is fixed for trial,[93] individuals are appointed, sometimes known as assessors, to assist the court in reaching a decision,[94] to whom, in some churches, the accused has a right of

[86] Wales, Rules of the Provincial Court, III.1(2), 2, 4: a charge 'shall be laid only by the Bishop' (see also n. 83); Southern Africa, Can. 37.6 and West Africa, Can. XVII.2; South India, Const. XI.9; West Indies, Can. 23.1: particulars including time place and other circumstances; 24.3: in doctrine cases, the doctrine concerned must be specified; New Zealand, Can. D.I.2.1.

[87] For commissions or boards of enquiry, see e.g. Ireland, Const. VIII.15; Southern Africa, Can. 39.3; Australia, Const. IX.54.3.

[88] Papua New Guinea, Diocese of Port Moresby, Can. 10.7; West Indies, Can. 23.4; Philippines, Cans. IV.1; Ireland, Const. VIII.15; North India, Const. II.V.IX.3: the bishop must 'if possible, settle the matter by personal inquiry and advice . . . But if the bishop shall direct or the accused minister demands' the case must be referred to the Court of the Diocesan Council; South India, Const. XI.7; New Zealand, Can. D.I2.1: D.III.4: for bishops, the primate enquires and has a discretion to dismiss the case.

[89] ECUSA, Cans. IV1.2: inhibition; Melanesia, Cans. C.3.A; Scotland, Can. 54.11: in unbecoming conduct cases the accused may be suspended; New Zealand, Can. D.III.9: if 'sufficiently grave', the primate may suspend the bishop; Australia, Const. IX.61; South India, Const. XI.11: the cleric may be suspended if scandal is likely; see also Wales, Const. XI.35; Southern Africa, Can. 39.7.

[90] Scotland, Can. 54.7; ECUSA, Cans. IV.1.3: this allows voluntary submission by which the accused waives all rights to formal charges, presentment and trial and accepts a sentence; New Zealand, Can. D.I.2.9; Ireland, Const. VIII.20.

[91] See e.g. West Indies, Can. 24.13; Southern Africa, Can. 37.14.

[92] Scotland, Can. 54.5, 9; Ireland, Const. VIII.15; Wales, Rules of the Provincial Court, III.6ff; New Zealand, Can. D.I.2.18: North India, Const. II.V.IX,4: judicial process is not to be entered upon unless some competent person undertakes to prove the charges; or the court is satisfied that 'a fama or rumour exists, so specific, so widespread, and with such presumption of truth that the honour of the Church requires it to be investigated'; Melanesia, Cans. C.3.A: the diocesan court sits only when 'all other efforts to settle the matter have failed'.

[93] For an exceptionally speedy process, see Philippines, Cans. IV.2: trial must take place within 21 days of presentment.

[94] Kenya, Can. V; Papua New Guinea, Can. No. 1 of 1977 and Diocese of Port Moresby, Can.10.7: the bishop and the accused each select one assessor from a clergy panel and one from a lay panel; Scotland, Can. 54.12; West Indies, Can. 24.5: trial of

objection.[95] Laws vary as to whether court proceedings are to be held in public or in private.[96] At trial, laws confer on the accused rights to silence,[97] to be legally represented,[98] and usually provisions exist to require attendance of witnesses who are members of the church.[99] In some churches, the verdict must be arrived at by means of a unanimous decision and sometimes by a majority decision of the members of the court.[100]

Ecclesiastical Sanctions

Whilst it is reasonably easy both to enumerate and to define the range of ecclesiastical censures or sanctions available in disciplinary cases, it is rather more difficult to generalize about practices concerning: the location of the right to impose sanctions; the applicability of specific sanctions to specific offences; and the reversibility of censures. Most Anglican churches employ six basic censures which, in order of severity, are as follows. *Deposition* is 'the permanent taking away of the right to perform the duties of every office for which Holy Orders is required'.[101] *Deprivation*

priest for doctrine, 3 priests; ECUSA, Cans. IV.4; Melanesia, Cans. C.3A; for the trial of bishops see e.g. New Zealand, Can. D.III.10: all bishops with at least 3 present and the primate; West Africa, Can. XVII.16: 3 bishops and 3 clerical assessors.

[95] See e.g. West Indies, Can. 24.11; Southern Africa, Can. 39.6.

[96] West Indies, Can. 24.1: 'The proceedings of all Courts Ecclesiastical shall be in private'; ECUSA, Cans. IV.3: the trial of bishops must be private; Ireland, Const. VIII.43: the court has a discretion; Southern Africa, Can. 37.12: trials must be public but the president may exclude 'on the ground of public morals'; New Zealand, Can. D.3.6: proceedings must be public.

[97] See e.g. New Zealand, Can. D.I.3.5: 'The person accused shall not be compelled to give evidence but shall be permitted to do so'; for proceedings in the accused's absence, see West Indies, Can. 24.12; Southern Africa, Can. 37.11.

[98] Nigeria, Can. V; New Zealand, Can. D.III.12; Wales, Rules of the Provincial Court, III.32; West Indies, Can. 24.6: ECUSA, Cans. IV.4; Papua New Guinea, Can. No. 1 of 1977, Arts. 9–15: the court may withdraw permission; Melanesia, Cans. C.3.A; Southern Africa, Can. 37.8: the accused must pay for his own representation.

[99] West Indies, Can. 24.8; Ireland, Const. VIII.46; Australia, Const. IX.62; Wales, Const. XI.28: if any members holding office 'wilfully and without sufficient cause neglect or refuse to attend and give evidence', that office may be declared vacant.

[100] New Zealand, Can. D.I.3.8: unanimous; Philippines, Cans. IV.2: majority verdict and there may be no subsequent trial; for the payment of costs and expenses, for which orders may be made at the discretion of the court, see Wales, Rules of the Provincial Court, I.25f; Ireland, Const. VIII.65; Southern Africa, Can. 37.17; North India, Const. II.V.VIII.4: 'A Court can order the complainant to pay compensation to the respondent, if the complaint is found to be false, frivolous and vexatious, and the Court is convinced that the complainant has acted *mala fide*'.

[101] New Zealand, Can. D.II.1; Nigeria, Can. XL(e): deposition or 'permanent inhibition means the withdrawal from a clergyman of all power to exercise his sacred calling either publicly or privately'; ECUSA, Cans. IV.12: the person is 'deposed entirely from the Sacred Ministry'; North India, Const. II.V.VIII.1; Canada, Can. XVIII.14: deposition has the effect 'as if the person had relinquished the exercise of the ordained ministry'; for degradation see Scotland, Can. 54.18.4 and Southern Africa, Can. 40(f): the consent

is 'the permanent taking away of the right to perform the acts and functions of a particular office or appointment' held by an ordained or lay minister.[102] *Suspension* is 'the temporary taking away of the right to perform acts and functions of the Ministry, or of a particular clerical or lay office or appointment'.[103] *Inhibition* disqualifies a person from exercising certain ministerial functions.[104] *Admonition*, or *monition*, is 'a formal written warning, order, or injunction'.[105] The least severe censure is *rebuke*.[106] In addition, several churches list excommunication as a censure which may be imposed following judicial proceedings.[107] In most churches the court simply determines the question of guilt, and it is empowered only to recommend a sentence, with the right both to choose and to impose sentence vesting in the bishop or the metropolitan,[108] as the case may be. In a small number of churches the court itself imposes the sanction.[109] Rarely is the concept of forgiveness expressly incorporated in law to enable the

of the Synod of Bishops must be obtained; Ireland, Const. VIII.58: only the Court of General Synod may pronounce sentence of deposition.

[102] New Zealand, Can. D.II.1; Nigeria, Can. XL(c): deprivation is 'the final removal of a clergyman from a named charge or office'; for deprivation applicable to lay persons in their 'membership of any body' in the church, see Wales, Const. XI.25(1); ECUSA does not seem to have deprivation: Cans. IV.12 lists only admonition, suspension and deposition; for other systems using only these three sentences see Japan, Can. XVII, Art. 159; Puerto Rico, Cans. IV.9; Mexico, Cans. IV. 46.

[103] New Zealand, Can. D.II.1; ECUSA, Cans. IV.12: the minister must 'refrain temporarily from the exercise of the gifts of ministry conferred at ordination'; West Africa, Can. XVII.5: suspension is 'the removal of a clergyman from a named charge or office for such period as may be determined' in the sentence; Scotland, Can. 54.18.2; Canada, Can. XVIII.12: breach of suspension may lead to deprivation.

[104] England, Ecclesiastical Jurisdiction Measure 1963, s. 49(1)(b); ECUSA, Cans. IV.1.2: inhibition is 'a written command from the Bishop that a Priest or Deacon shall cease from exercising the gifts of ordination in the sacred ministry as specified in the inhibition'; see also West Indies, Can. 25.1(b): inhibition from preaching; and Papua New Guinea, Diocese of Port Moresby, Can. 10.16; inhibition is not listed amongst the censures in *inter alia* New Zealand, Canada, or Scotland.

[105] New Zealand, Can. D.II.1; Nigeria, Can. XL(a): 'a formal admonition is . . . a written warning delivered either in public or private'; for the same idea see Canada, Can. XVIII.11; Southern Africa, Can. 40; West Indies, Can. 25.1(a); ECUSA, Cans. IV.12: admonition is 'a public Reprimand of the Member of the Clergy'.

[106] England, Ecclesiastical Jurisdiction Measure 1963, s. 49(1)(e); for 'notices', see Canada, Can. XVIII.15.

[107] West Indies, Can. 25.1(e); Nigeria, Can. XXXXIX.(h); Papua New Guinea, Can. No. 1 of 1977; Papua New Guinea, Diocese of Port Moresby, Can. 10.16; see generally Ch. 9.

[108] West Africa, Const. Art. XXII.4: 'None but a Bishop shall pronounce sentence of suspension, or removal, or deposition from the Ministry, on any Bishop, Priest or Deacon'; Nigeria, Can. XXXXIX(h); for the idea that the court recommends, see e.g. North India, Const. II.V.VIII.2; Australia, Const. IX.60.1; Papua New Guinea, Diocese of Port Moresby, Can. 10.16.

[109] Ireland, Const. VIII.57.

mitigation or suspension of a sentence,[110] though occasionally the law imposes an explicit duty in sentencing to consider the interests of both the whole and the local church.[111]

In some churches the law does not fix specific penalties to individual offences: a discretion exists as to the severity of the censure depending on the gravity of the offence.[112] In some churches, however, this is not the case. The African churches illustrate well the tariff system, though periods for which the sanction operates usually vary from church to church: for publicly maintaining doctrines contrary to those of the church, inhibition from preaching or suspension for a fixed period; for refusing to perform ministrations for members of the church, admonition or suspension for no more than a fixed period; for neglect of duty, admonition or suspension for not more than (usually) twelve months; for immoral conduct, suspension, deposition or deprivation; for scandalous conduct, admonition, suspension, or deprivation; for wilful contravention of law and disobedience to the bishop, admonition or suspension. In addition, the bishop may suspend the person from receiving Holy Communion for such period as he may determine. Finally, for heresy, schism or apostasy, a sentence of excommunication or deposition may be passed. Sentences may be increased for contumacy, that is, refusal to submit to the sentence.[113] Tariff systems in one form or another are also used in New Zealand,[114] Wales,[115] and the West Indies.[116]

[110] Australia, Const. IX.602: 'The [bishop or metropolitan] to whom the recommendation is made shall give effect thereto, provided that if any sentence is recommended, he may consult with the tribunal and in the exercise of his prerogative of mercy (a) mitigate the sentence or (b) suspend its operation or (c) mitigate the sentence and suspend its operation'; see also e.g. West Indies, Can. 24.16: 'No sentence shall be pronounced until an opportunity shall have been given to the accused to show cause why sentence should not be pronounced and to offer any matter in excuse or palliation for the consideration of the Court'.

[111] New Zealand, Can. D.II.5.3: 'the welfare and interests of the Church, and of the particular parish or ecclesiastical body or organization concerned' must be considered in sentencing; North India, Const. II.V.I.2: 'the ends of the Church Discipline are the good of the offender and the purity of the Church'; for the same notion see South India, Const. XI.1.

[112] England: *Read v Bishop of Lincoln* [1892] AC 644 (PC); *Bland v Archdeacon of Cheltenham* [1972] 1 All ER 1012 at 1016 (Arches Court); North India, Const. II.V.VIII.3

[113] Southern Africa, Can. 40; Nigeria, Can. XXXXIX(a)–(i); West Africa, Can. XVII.5; see also Ireland, Const. VIII.60: 'Disobedience to any sentence or order of any ecclesiastical tribunal shall constitute a separate offence'.

[114] New Zealand, Can. D.II.2: for unauthorized doctrine, unless there is a retraction, suspension or deposition; for refusal to use authorized services, admonition or suspension; for neglect of duty, admonition or suspension; for improper conduct, admonition, suspension, deprivation or deposition.

[115] Wales, Const. XI.25(2): for conduct giving just cause for scandal or offence, 'a judgment, sentence or order of the Provincial Court may include a recommendation to the . . . Bishop that the cleric be deposed from Holy Orders and expelled from the office of cleric'.

[116] See e.g. West Indies, Can. 25.2.

The laws of many churches make express provision for the lifting of sentences. Obviously, with respect to admonition, the censure ceases when there is compliance with the order or injunction. Similarly, suspension loses its effect upon the expiration of the period which, as is mandatory in the majority of churches, must be specified in the sentence.[117] In some churches, the law provides for the lifting of suspension if the individual makes an undertaking within a specified period after sentence is given – once more the African churches have very developed provisions: for maintaining doctrines contrary to those of the church, suspension ceases when the cleric abjures by making a formal retraction; for neglect of duty, the sentence terminates when the cleric 'engages to conform'; for scandalous conduct, the sentence ceases if the cleric undertakes formally not to repeat the conduct in the future.[118] The problem lies with deprivation and deposition, which many laws treat formally as having a permanent character (see above). In some churches, the law allows the reversal of deprivation: in English law, for example, after deprivation as removal from an office and disqualification from preferment in the future, further preferment may be held with the consent of the diocesan bishop, the appropriate archbishop, and the bishop of the diocese where the censure was imposed.[119] In contrast, with deposition from holy orders, 'final removal', the position is a little more problematic: short of possible reversal of the sentence on appeal (see below), in the laws of the vast majority of churches deposition appears to be irreversible; they have no mechanism for reversal. Only the laws of Australia (by means of suspension),[120] New Zealand (by means of dispensation),[121] England (by means of pardon),[122]

---

[117] Scotland, Can. 54.19: nor must it exceed 3 years; Canada, Can. XVIII.12(a); West Africa, Const. Art. XXII.5; ECUSA, Cans. IV.12.

[118] See e.g. Southern Africa, Can. 40; West Africa, Can. XVII.5; Nigeria, Can. XXXXIX; see also New Zealand, Can. D.II.2; West Indies, Can. 25.2.

[119] England, Ecclesiastical Jurisdiction Measure 1963, s. 49(3); Canada, Can. XVIII.13.

[120] For Australia, see n. 110; see also Scotland, Can. 54.21: the sentence of degradation or deposition must state whether 'it implies degradation from an higher to a lower order in the Ministry, or an entire deposition from the Ministry'.

[121] New Zealand, Can. D.II.11: a person under sentence may during its enforcement apply to the Court of Appeal for a declaration that the person 'has given evidence to satisfy the Court of Appeal of such complete reformation . . . and fitness for restoration to that person's former status, as to make it just, having regard to the welfare and interests of the Church, that the further operation of the sentence should be dispensed with'; the declaration has the effect that the offence is 'completely expiated'.

[122] England, Ecclesiastical Jurisdiction Measure 1963, s. 53: a royal pardon will effect termination. Furthermore, under this statute the effects of deposition are to be treated as the same as those for relinquishment of orders (see Ch. 5); one of the effects of relinquishment is the right to petition the archbishop for its reversal: it is arguable, therefore, that one of the effects of deposition is a right to petition for its reversal.

the West Indies (by unanimous vote of the House of Bishops),[123] and ECUSA,[124] would seem to suggest the reversibility of deposition. Reversibility would, needless to say, be neatly accommodated within the doctrine of the indelibility of orders.[125]

Appeals and the Jurisdiction of the Superior Courts

As with diocesan tribunals, it is difficult to generalize about both the appellate and the original jurisdiction of the superior courts of Anglican churches. That appellate tribunals should exist has been recommended by the Lambeth Conference but it has rejected proposals for 'a central appellate tribunal' as 'inconsistent with the spirit of the Anglican Communion'.[126] With respect to appeals, laws share rules concerning: limitation periods; grounds of appeal; leave to appeal; and powers of the appellate tribunal. Rules differ depending on whether the appeal concerns the trial of a bishop or trials of priests and deacons, and, in some churches, lay persons. As to original jurisdiction, in this section examples will be given to illustrate the great diversity of approaches. In churches having a two-tier system of courts, the provincial tribunal acts as the appellate court from decisions of the diocesan tribunal. Typically, churches having only an appellate provincial tribunal vest presidency of the court in the metropolitan,[127] and sometimes membership of the court, assisted by assessors, is confined to bishops,[128] and sometimes bishops, clergy and lay per-

---

[123] West Indies, Can. 25.4: 'The House of Bishops may on petition presented to them, by a unanimous vote, remit or terminate *any* judicial sentence of an Ecclesiastical Court within the Province, or modify the same so far as to designate a precise period of time or specific contingency on the occurrence of which such sentence shall cease and be of no further force or effect'.

[124] ECUSA, Cans. IV.13: the House of Bishops may remit or terminate any sentence imposed on a bishop; a bishop may remit or terminate deposition imposed on a priest or deacon with the advice and consent of two-thirds of the diocesan standing committee, with the consent of four bishops from neighbouring dioceses, and provided the deposed cleric subscribes to the declaration to conform to the doctrine, worship, and discipline of the church; see also Mexico, Can. IV.47 and Chile, Cans. E.9.

[125] See Ch. 5.

[126] LC 1878, Recommendation 8(a): 'Every ecclesiastical province, which has constituted for the exercise of discipline over its clergy a tribunal for receiving appeals from its diocesan courts, should be responsible for its own decisions in the exercise of such discipline'; LC 1930, Res. 51: see also n. 134.

[127] See e.g. South East Asia, Const. Art. II(e): the archbishop must 'preside over such appeals as may be allowed by the regulations of the Province, from decisions of a diocesan authority to a provincial authority'; West Africa, Const. Art. V(a)(vi); Sudan, Const. Art. 24; Burundi, Const. Art. 12; Indian Ocean, Const. Art. 11(v); Kenya, Const. Art. VII(a)(4); Papua New Guinea, Const. Art. 10.

[128] Scotland, Can. 54.22, 26; Southern Africa, Can. 36: the provincial tribunal of appeal consists of the metropolitan and 2 bishops assisted by 2 lay communicants learned in law; Burundi, Const. Art. 21; in some churches the provincial appeals

sons,[129] usually appointed by the national or provincial assembly.[130] In churches with a three-tier system, such as in England,[131] Australia,[132] and Canada,[133] a provincial tribunal has jurisdiction to entertain appeals from the diocesan tribunal with a further right of recourse to a final court of appeal; mostly these are composed of persons from within the church, but occasionally this is not the case.[134]

tribunal is distinguished from the provincial tribunal which hears only cases for the trial of bishops: see below.

[129] Indian Ocean, Const. Art. 17: the House of Bishops acts as a provincial tribunal (it consists of the archbishop, 2 bishops, 2 priests and 2 deacons); Tanzania, Const. IV.20: the court consists of 2 bishops, 2 'clergy' and 2 lay persons; West Africa, Const. Art. XXII.3 and Can. XVII.4(b); Uganda, Const. Art. 17(b): the provincial appeals tribunal hears appeals from diocesan tribunals; ECUSA, Cans. IV.3: the provincial Court of Review of the trial of a presbyter or deacon consists of a bishop, 3 priests and 3 lay persons; the Court of Review of the trial of a bishop consists of 9 bishops; Papua New Guinea, Const. Arts. 10, 17 and Can. No. 1 of 1977.

[130] Southern Cone, Can. 8: 'A Court of Appeal shall be set up to provide for appeals against the ecclesiastical judgment of Priests and Deacons and the discipline of Congregations'; its members are elected by the Provincial Synod; for a regional system see North India, Const. II.V.1: the Court of the Synod is composed of 1 bishop, 2 presbyters and 3 lay members (chosen from a panel set up by the Synod) to hear appeals against the decision of the Court of the Diocesan Council; see also South India, Const. XI.15–20: the bishop of the diocese from which the appeal comes is forbidden to sit; 'No decision or judgment of the Court of the Synod shall be subject to appeal or revision by any person or court outside the Church of South India'; see also Ireland, Const. VIII.2, 26: the Court of General Synod, which has jurisdiction in appeals from diocesan courts of the church's two provinces.

[131] England, Ecclesiastical Jurisdiction Measure 1963: in disciplinary cases involving priests and deacons, appeal lies from the Consistory Court to the provincial court (the Court of Arches in Canterbury and the Chancery Court in York) and then to the Privy Council; in cases involving bishops, appeal lies from the Commission of Enquiry to a Commission of Review; in cases involving doctrine, ritual or ceremonial, appeal lies from the Court of Ecclesiastical Causes Reserved to a Commission of Review; see M. Hill, *Ecclesiastical Law* (London, 1995), Ch. VI.

[132] Australia, Const. IX.53–57: appeal lies from the diocesan tribunal to the provincial tribunal (or, for the trial of bishops, the special tribunal) with a further appeal to the appellate tribunal consisting of 3 bishops and 4 lay persons appointed by the General Synod.

[133] Canada, Cans. XVIII and XX: from the diocesan court appeal lies to the provincial court of appeal and, further, to the Supreme Court of Appeal, if the case relates *inter alia* to doctrine, worship or the trial of a bishop; see also Jerusalem, Const. Art. 14(b) for the Supreme Court of Appeal; West Indies, Can. 22.3, 26: appeal lies from the provincial court of appeal (consisting of the archbishop as president and two other bishops in order of seniority assisted by the provincial chancellor 'as legal assessor') to the Committee of Reference.

[134] Central Africa, Can. 26: 'there shall be a right of appeal from the Provincial Court to a Final Court consisting of the Archbishop of Canterbury, and two Bishops of the Province of Canterbury or the Province of York who shall be elected by the House of Clergy of the Provincial Synod, and who shall summon to their assistance a communicant learned in the Law'; LC 1878, Recommendation 8: there should be no 'central tribunal of appeal', but 'any province desirous that its tribunal of appeal should have power to obtain, in matters of doctrine, or of discipline involving a question of doctrine,

In many churches the law expressly provides that, as a general rule, if an appeal has been lodged, a sentence shall not operate until determination of the appeal.[135] Laws prescribe in detail the limitation periods within which rights of appeal may be exercised,[136] and the grounds of appeal. In most churches an appeal lies on a matter of law (though only for the prosecutor),[137] or a matter of fact,[138] or a mixture of these,[139] or against the severity of the sentence.[140] In many churches leave to appeal must be obtained from the court of trial, or, if it refuses, by leave of the appellate court.[141] As a general principle, every appeal is considered as a review and not as a retrial.[142] The appellate court may make such order, 'as may appear to it to be just', to remit the matter to the inferior court for further hearing.[143] Provisions usually prescribe that the decision must be by majority vote.[144]

There is great diversity as between churches concerning the original jurisdiction of superior church courts and tribunals. Generally, however, to these are assigned the function of determining the trial of bishops, and, in some churches, cases involving matters of doctrine and liturgy and

the opinion of some council of reference . . . the conditions of such reference should be determined by the province itself'; see also Chs. 7, 8 and 12.

[135] Central Africa, Can. 25.7; West Africa, Can. XVII.4(d) and Nigeria, Can. XXXVI: except in cases of immoral conduct or heresy; ECUSA, Cans. IV.32; see also New Zealand, Can. D.I.5.3 and Southern Africa, Can. 41.3: the bishop may inhibit the appellant until determination of the appeal.

[136] See e.g. Nigeria, Can. XXXVII: 30 days; New Zealand, Cans. D.I.4.7: 14 days; West Africa, Can. XVII.4(b): 7 days.

[137] Central Africa, Can. 26.9; West Africa, Can. XVIII.6; England, Ecclesiastical Jurisdiction Measure 1963, ss. 7, 11; Ireland, Const. VIII.26.1

[138] Central Africa, Can. 26.9; compare Southern Africa, Can. 41.2 and Nigeria, Can. XXXIV: there is no appeal 'as regards the facts of any case, but only as to the conclusion to be drawn from those facts'; see also Scotland, Can. 54.22; New Zealand, Can. D.I.4.11: fresh evidence may be adduced with the permission of the Court of Appeal; compare Canada, Can. XX: there is no appeal to the Supreme Court of Appeal on questions of fact.

[139] See e.g. Central Africa, Can. 26.9.

[140] Scotland, Can. 54.22; Central Africa, Can. 26.5; Melanesia, Cans. C.3.B; New Zealand, Can. D.I.4.11: there may be no appeal against a verdict of not guilty.

[141] Central Africa, Can. 26.5; England, Ecclesiastical Jurisdiction Measure 1963, ss. 7, 11; see also Southern Africa, Can. 41.1.

[142] Central Africa, Can. 26.5; compare Australia, Const. IX.55: an appeal to the provincial tribunal is a 're-hearing'.

[143] ECUSA, Cans. IV.3.11; Central Africa, Can. 26.5; Southern Africa, Can. 41.4; Nigeria, Can. XXXVII: 'The Provincial Tribunal may affirm, modify, or amend the judgment or sentence appealed against, or pass any other judgment or sentence in the case, if it thinks just'; West Indies, Can. 22.8: the appellate court may reverse or affirm the diocesan court's decision and it may grant a 'new trial'.

[144] West Indies, Can. 22.9: 'The decision of the [Provincial] Court [of Appeal] shall be that of the majority of the members, whose decision shall be final'; Central Africa, Can. 26.9; compare ECUSA, Cans. IV.3.12: a two-thirds majority is needed in the Court of Review of the trial of a presbyter or deacon.

questions of constitutional difficulty. In general agreement with Lambeth Conference resolutions, in several churches it is the provincial court which tries bishops,[145] though in some churches this function is carried out by a special tribunal.[146] Similarly, in several churches doctrinal and liturgical cases are reserved at first instance to the superior church courts.[147] Some churches assign to superior church courts an original jurisdiction over resolution of constitutional disputes between members of the church and its institutions.[148] In a small number of churches the superior courts are competent to determine the legality of internal church law.[149] Under Australian law, which is exceptionally well-developed on this subject, judicial challenges may be made to both enacted or proposed 'acts' (canons, provisional canons, rules, and resolutions) of the General Synod. A reference must be made to the appellate tribunal by the primate, by twenty-five members of the synod, or a third of each of its three houses. The tribunal may entertain two questions: 'Is any part of the Act or Proposal identified in the reference inconsistent with the Fundamental Declarations or the Ruling Principles' of the church? and 'Does any part of the Act or Proposal identified in the reference deal with or concern or affect the ritual ceremonial or discipline of the Church?'. The tribunal may give its opinion or determination, with reasons, and its decision is final: 'An Act which is inconsistent with the Fundamental Declarations, and an

[145] Southern Africa, Can. 36; Uganda, Const. Art. 17(a): the provincial tribunal consists entirely of bishops; West Indies, Can. 22.14; Papua New Guinea, Const. Art. 17; Melanesia, Cans. C.3; these, and those in n. 146, implement broadly the principles governing the trial of bishops suggested in LC 1878, Recommendation 9.

[146] See e.g. Wales, Const. XI: the special provincial court deals with charges against bishops and the Supreme Court (consisting *inter alia* of the Archbishop of Canterbury) with those against the archbishop; ECUSA, Cans. IV.3; Australia, Const. IX.56: the Special Court; Ireland, Const. VIII.26.2: the Court of General Synod; North India, Const. II.V.4: the Court of the Synod acts as 'a court of original jurisdiction in cases of discipline concerning bishops'.

[147] England, Ecclesiastical Jurisdiction Measure 1963, ss. 38, 42, 45: 'reserved' cases involving doctrine, ritual and ceremonial are dealt with at first instance by the Court of Ecclesiastical Causes Reserved with a right of appeal to a Commission of Review; Australia, Const. IX.55: cases involving charges relating to matters of faith are entertained by the provincial tribunal; Ireland, Const. VIII.26.2: the Court of General Synod has original jurisdiction over matters of doctrine and ritual.

[148] Southern Cone, Can. 8: the Court of Appeal determines cases of 'disagreement between Diocesan Councils and their Bishop'; Wales, Const. XI.18: the Provincial Court may determine any dispute between a member of the church and the Representative Body (the provincial trustees) or a Diocesan Conference.

[149] Canada, Province of Rupert's Land, Const. 1994, 1.10–11: any dispute concerning diocesan regulations 'contrary to or in conflict with an enactment of the Province' must be referred to the national Supreme Court of Appeal; Ireland, Const. III.32: any party aggrieved by 'an act of the diocesan synod', concerning property held or administered by the Diocesan Synod, may appeal to the Court of General Synod; see *MacLaughlin and Macmahon v Diocesan Synod of Cashel* (1893) Journal of the Court of General Synod, 1895, 215.

Act, other than a canon to alter the Ruling Principles, which is inconsistent with the Ruling Principles shall to the extent of the inconsistency, be void'; moreover, 'An Act which deals with concerns or affects the ritual ceremonial or discipline of this Church and which has not been made in accordance with the requirements of this Constitution shall, to the extent to which it so deals concerns or affects, be void'.[150]

PRINCIPLES GOVERNING ADJUDICATION

The making of both quasi-judicial and judicial decisions by ecclesiastical authorities and tribunals is, as has been seen, subject to elaborate rules which are mainly procedural in nature: rights of appearance and appeal are designed primarily to ensure that the use of adjudicative powers is not arbitrary. Indeed, occasionally, laws expressly require disciplinary decisions to be made with reference to large moral ideas of justice, equity and good conscience;[151] sometimes they also prohibit adjudication which results in retrospective censures.[152] In addition, as a matter of practice, the laws of Anglican churches commonly contain general principles applicable to bodies charged with the resolution of ecclesiastical conflict. This section explores three associated subjects: the interpretation of ecclesiastical legislation; the use of judicial precedent; and the need to comply with standards set by the secular courts in their supervisory jurisdiction over church tribunals.

Interpretation

Whilst the process of adjudicating necessarily involves interpretation of church law, many churches have persons or institutions the function of which is to assist in the process of interpretation otherwise than in the context of a trial. A direct consequence of this is the proposition that in Anglican jurisprudence the courts do not have the primary function of interpreting church law. Whilst questions of interpretation may be referred to the legal officers of the church,[153] in many churches they may

---

[150] Australia, Const. V.29; see also Melanesia, Cans. D.1.L.1–2: the Constitutional Review Committee may recommend changes 'to ensure that [laws] are not in conflict with laws which have been previously passed'.

[151] See e.g. North India, Const. II.V.6: the Court of the Synod '[i]n all its work . . . shall be guided by this Constitution and by the general principles of justice, equity and good conscience'.

[152] Burundi, Const. Art. 16(b): 'No tribunal . . . may try any person for any offence or pass any sentence which is not at the time of the commission of the offence so set out in the Canons'; see also Uganda, Const. Art. 16(b).

[153] See Ch. 6.

also be referred to a specially constituted commission or committee. Sometimes the law is silent as to their precise functions,[154] but in several churches such bodies are under obligations to publish their decisions which often enjoy a binding effect.[155] In several churches the interpreting body, which may produce final and binding decisions, is the diocesan assembly or the national or regional assembly,[156] or a central episcopal assembly.[157] In other churches disputes about the interpretation of church law may be referred to a superior court,[158] or an especially constituted tribunal: their decisions are binding and often duties to publish are imposed.[159] Less common are laws which require the referral of disputes about the interpretation of church law to an Anglican body outside the church.[160] Arrangements also exist extensively to govern this process of

[154] England: the Legal Advisory Commission, a subordinate body of General Synod, gives legal advice to a wide range of church bodies and persons; it can advise on contentious cases: if the facts are agreed by all parties concerned; if the matter is referred to it for an opinion by all parties to a dispute; and if the matter is not, and is not expected to become, the subject-matter of proceedings in the courts: *Annual Report* (1996) 1; compare Wales, Const. II.65(4): Governing Body's Standing Committee must appoint a 'Chairman of a Legal Sub-Committee who shall appoint the other members . . . in consultation with the Chairman of the Standing Committee when occasion so requires'; the law defines neither its functions nor the standing of its decisions; nor is there a duty to publish.

[155] Burundi, Const. Art. 18: disputes concerning interpretation of the constitution must be referred by the House of Bishops, the Provincial Assembly Standing Committee, or a Diocesan Synod to 'a Constitutional Interpretation Committee' which decides by majority vote and which must publish its decision; the committee's decision on 'the interpretation or application of this Constitution shall be final'; see also Australia, General Synod Commissions Canons, 1969–92: a commission examines questions of canon law referred to it by the primate, General Synod or its standing committee; see also Sudan, Const. Art. 65; Uganda, Const. Art. 20; Philippines, Cans. I.2.2.

[156] North India, Const. II.VIII: in matters concerning the pastorate, 'the interpreting authority shall be the Diocesan Council or its Executive Committee', and for matters arising in that council, the authority of the Synod; matters of interpretation arising in the Synod are 'finally decided' by the Synod by majority vote; South India, Const. II.20: 'If any questions shall be raised with regard to the interpretation of any part of this Constitution, they shall be finally determined by the Synod of the Church'.

[157] West Indies, Const. Art. 6.2: any question or dispute is determined by the House of Bishops 'whose decision shall be final'; the decision is prospective in effect and 'shall not affect any right, privilege or power acquired or vested, or the validity of any act done under the said provisions' interpreted; see also South East Asia, Const. Art. XVII: the House of Bishops' 'decision or ruling after consultation with the Provincial Chancellor shall be final and binding'.

[158] New Zealand, Cans. C.IV.4: the Judicial Committee; Wales, Const. XI.18(g): 'any matter [may be] referred or reported to the Provincial Court'; Ireland, Const. VIII.26.2: any question of 'a legal nature' may be referred to the Court of General Synod.

[159] Indian Ocean, Const. Art. 17: the House of Bishops acts as provincial tribunal for all questions concerning the interpretation of the constitution.

[160] Central Africa, Can. 32.1: 'If any question should arise as to the interpretation of the canons of this province, or any part thereof . . . [t]he Archbishop shall, at the request of the Episcopal Synod, refer any matter in dispute to the Archbishop of Canterbury,

adjudication: several churches, notably those in Africa, require interpretation to be effected in the light of 'the general principles of Canon Law'.[161] It is, finally, a common practice for church laws to include extensive interpretation sections,[162] and for some churches the same rules of interpretation and construction as apply to secular law apply also to church law.[163]

Doctrines of Judicial Precedent

In the Church of England judicial decisions are themselves creative of law, and elaborate arrangements exist defining their precise authority: broadly, decisions of each provincial court are binding on diocesan courts in that province, and the decision of a diocesan court binds only in that diocese; since the vast majority of the latter are derived from property cases decided under the faculty jurisdiction, in England most judicial decisions are merely of persuasive authority.[164] Rather different conditions prevail in other churches: on the level of general ecclesiastical practice, doctrines of precedent simply do not appear in the formal laws of most Anglican churches. This accords directly with the evidence described in the last section that the function of interpreting law is assigned first and foremost to bodies other than the church courts. Occasionally, however, precedent is mentioned, sometimes in a negative way and sometimes positively. The laws of several churches expressly deny any authority to the decisions of English church courts with respect to prescribed subjects. In Wales, 'the Courts of the Church . . . shall not be bound by any decision of the English Courts in relation to matters of faith, discipline or ceremonial'.[165] A simi-

together with the Archbishop of York and the Bishops of London, Durham and Winchester, who shall decide it in consultation with Canonists of the Anglican Communion'.

[161] Southern Africa, Can. 50: 'It is hereby declared that if any question should arise as to the interpretation of the Canon Law of this Church, or of any part thereof, the interpretation shall be governed by the general principles of Canon Law thereto applicable'; Central Africa, Can. 32; West Africa, Const. Art. XXVII; West Indies, Const. Art. 6.2; Papua New Guinea, Diocese of Port Moresby, Can. 109: court processes are to be governed by 'the principles of Canon Law'.

[162] See e.g. Southern Africa, Const. Art. XXIV; Australia, Interpretation Canon, Can. 10, 1995.

[163] England, Interpretation Act 1978, s. 22: this applies to the interpretation of synodical Measures; Australia, Const. XII.74.7: the constitution must be construed 'as if the Acts Interpretation Act 1901–1948 of the Parliament of the Commonwealth of Australia applied to this Constitution'.

[164] See generally N. Doe, 'Canonical doctrines of judicial precedent: a comparative study', *The Jurist*, 54 (1994), 205.

[165] Wales, Const. XI.36; see also New Zealand, Cans. D.D.II.5.3: the courts 'shall not have regard to precedent of sentences inflicted under any Canon or Statute in operation before . . . 1925 . . . but they may have regard to precedents of sentences inflicted under this Canon'.

lar provision is found in the constitution of the church in Southern Africa: 'in the interpretation of the . . . Standards and Formularies, the Church . . . [is] not held to be bound by decisions . . . in questions of Faith and Doctrine or in questions of Discipline relating to Faith or Doctrine, other than those of its own Ecclesiastical Tribunals, or of such other Tribunal as may be accepted by the Provincial Synod as a Tribunal of Appeal'.[166] ECUSA operates a more positive doctrine of binding judicial precedent,[167] as does the Australian church.

In Australia, where any question arises as to faith, ritual, ceremonial or discipline, or as to the rights and duties of bishops, clergy, lay officers or members generally, recourse may be had to 'the history' of the church and, in determining such questions, any tribunal 'may take into consideration but shall not be bound to follow its previous decisions on any such questions or any decision of any judicial authority in England'. Furthermore, '[a] determination of any tribunal which is inconsistent or at variance with any decision of such a judicial authority in England shall have permissive effect only and shall not be obligatory or coercive'. However, a decision of a provincial tribunal 'shall be binding upon a diocesan tribunal in the province' and a determination of the appellate tribunal 'shall be binding' on the special tribunal, the provincial tribunal and the diocesan tribunal. This is subject to the proviso that 'the synod of any diocese may by ordinance direct that a diocesan tribunal shall not follow or observe a particular determination of the Appellate or provincial tribunal which has permissive effect only'.[168]

Ecclesiastical Adjudication and the Secular Courts

Anglican jurisprudence possesses no coherent set of principles concerning the relationship between church tribunals or other quasi-judicial bodies and the secular courts. Only occasionally does formal church law treat the subject. On the one hand, alongside obligations on clergy and lay officers to undertake to be bound by church court decisions and sentences,[169] some churches have the fundamental principle that recourse to the secular courts ought not generally to be made: disputes should be settled within the church. Two extreme poles of the principle are to be found in North India and in ECUSA. The constitution of the church in North India

[166] Southern Africa, Const. Art. I; see also Chs. 7 and 8.
[167] ECUSA, see e.g. *Stanton (Bishop of Dallas) and Others v Righter* (1996): the Court for the Trial of a Bishop considered that the case of *Bishop Brown* (1924) 'sets precedent for this Court'.
[168] Australia, Const. XII.72, 73.
[169] See Chs. 1, 5 and 6; LC 1878, Recommendation 8(c): 'each diocese must determine how much consensual jurisdiction could be enforced'.

presents the principle as an aspirational norm: 'No bishop, presbyter or any other member of the Church . . . should go to a civil court, for enforcing any of his spiritual and religious rights under the Constitution . . . or the rules framed thereunder . . . but should seek his remedy under this Constitution'.[170] The constitution of ECUSA, which describes its own disciplinary proceedings as 'ecclesiastical in nature' representing 'the polity and order of this hierarchical church', presents the principle as a mandatory obligation: 'No Member of the Clergy of this Church may resort to the secular courts for the purpose of delaying, hindering or reviewing any proceeding' of the church's tribunals. Moreover, '[n]o secular court shall have authority to review, annul, reverse, restrain or otherwise delay any proceeding' of those tribunals.[171] On the other hand, the laws of some churches recognize the authority of secular courts over ecclesiastical tribunals. According to the constitution of the disestablished church in Ireland, the Court of General Synod must not determine 'any matter or question which, in the opinion of the lay judges, is within the jurisdiction and more proper to be submitted to the consideration and decision of a civil tribunal'.[172] A somewhat different arrangement prevails in the established church in England: the church's courts are public statutory bodies, and the secular courts exercise a supervisory function to ensure that they act within their ecclesiastical jurisdiction: a variety of remedies is available to control church courts which exceed their competence, and which violate the common law principles of natural justice.[173]

The status of church courts, and their relationship with the secular courts, may also be defined by the state. This is particularly the case, needless to say, with churches to which the secular doctrine of consensual compact applies.[174] Indeed, laws of some churches use this notion as the

---

[170] North India, Const. II.V.VII; Chile, Cans. E.11: when there is a conflict 'between Christians', and these propose to proceed to the civil courts, the pastor must make every effort to resolve the case; Papua New Guinea, Diocese of Port Moresby, Can. 10: the church courts are not bound by 'any Civil Act' concerning evidence.

[171] ECUSA, Cans. IV.14.2: clergy may not claim 'constitutional guarantees afforded to citizens in other contexts'.

[172] Ireland, Const. VIII.26.4.

[173] England, Ecclesiastical Jurisdiction Measure 1963, s. 83(2)(b): nothing in this legislation affects 'any power of the High Court to control the proper exercise by ecclesiastical courts of their functions'; prohibition may lie if the court exceeds its jurisdiction: *R v Tristram* [1902] 1 KB 816 (CA); *mandamus* may lie for a refusal to exercise jurisdiction: *R v Bishop of London* (1889) 24 QBD 213 (CA); given recent developments in public law, that *certiorari* would not now lie to quash a church court decision is very unlikely: for the view that it does not lie see *R v Chancellor of St Edmundsbury and Ipswich Diocese, ex p White* [1948] 1 KB 195 (CA) and for the opposite view see J. Burrows, 'Judicial review and the Church of England', LL M Dissertation, University of Wales, Cardiff, 1997.

[174] See Ch. 1.

foundation of the competence of their courts.[175] Sometimes it is secular legislation which provides that Anglican tribunals possess no 'coercive power',[176] but more normally the matter is governed by rules made by the secular courts themselves. As was stated in a New Zealand decision concerning the Anglican church, as a voluntary association it is competent 'to constitute a tribunal . . . to decide questions arising out of this association'; moreover, '[s]uch tribunals are not Courts, but their decisions will be binding if they have acted within the scope of their authority, have either observed the prescribed procedure', or, if there is none, 'have proceeded in a manner consonant with the principles of justice, and the Civil Courts will enforce the decision if necessary'.[177] This principle has been applied to the Anglican church in a number of states, including Ireland,[178] and Australia,[179] and it is particularly well-developed in Canada where a recent study adduces considerable evidence that the secular courts require ecclesiastical tribunals: to comply with the church's internal rules; to refer litigants back to the church tribunal, especially where the ecclesiastical appeal system has not been exhausted; and to observe the principles of natural justice.[180] In contrast, the secular courts in the USA have developed the following basic principles applicable to the tribunals of religious societies: a church may establish tribunals to decide on matters dealing with its internal affairs; a person who becomes a member of a church

[175] Uganda, Const. Art. 17: 'The Tribunals shall have such jurisdiction . . . subject to this Constitution and within the limits of such jurisdiction as can be claimed by and may be exercised in a voluntary association upon the footing of mutual contract or agreement'; see also Burundi, Const. Art. 21; for an unlawful trial by the Archdeaconry Board, a 'quasi-ecclesiastical court', see A. Omoyajowo, *The Anglican Church in Nigeria*: *1842–1992* (Lagos, 1994), 51.

[176] For two disestablished churches, see e.g. Wales, Welsh Church Act 1914, s. 3 and Barbados, Anglican Church Act 1969, s. 4(1)(a): the church courts 'shall cease to exercise any jurisdiction as such'; for prohibition against a bishop concerning the exercise of visitatorial power, see Australia, *Ex p King* (1861) 2 Legge 1307 (NSW Sup Ct).

[177] *Baldwin v Pascoe* (1889) 7 NZLR 759 (citing *Long v Bishop of Cape Town* (1863) 1 Moo NS 411); see also *Trustees of the Church of God in the Bahamas v Davis* (1965) [1965–70] 2 Law Reports of the Bahamas, 31.

[178] *Colquhoun v Fitzgibbon* [1937] IR 555 (H Ct): it was held that the Court of General Synod had acted within its competence in entertaining proceedings against the plaintiff.

[179] *Ex p Hay* (1897) 18 LR (NSW) 206: if a member of the church is wrongly deprived of a temporal benefit by a church court, the proper course is to apply 'to the Courts of Equity' for a declaration of his rights; see also West Indies, *Blades and Another v Jaggard and Others* (1961) 4 WIR 207; for its application to non-Anglican churches in Southern Africa, see e.g. *Theron en Andere v Ring van Wellington van die N.G. Sendingkerk in S.A. en Andere* [1974(2)] SALR 505; *Van Vuuren v Kerkraad van die Morelig Gemeente van die Ng Kerk in die OVS* [1979(4)] SALR 548 and *Motaung v Mukubela and Another* [1975(1)] SALR 618.

[180] M. H. Ogilvie, 'Canadian civil court intervention in the exercise of ecclesiastical jurisdiction', *Studia Canonica*, 31 (1997), 49; see e.g. *Bishop of Columbia v Cridge* (1874) 1 BCR (Pt. 1) 5 (BCSC); *Halliwell v Synod of Ontario* (1884) 7 OR 67 (Ch D).

submits to its ecclesiastical jurisdiction and has no legal right to invoke the supervisory power of a secular court so long as no civil right is involved;[181] ecclesiastical questions must be determined by the church's tribunals the decisions of which are binding and not reviewable by the civil courts;[182] and when a church is hierarchical in nature, a civil court may not inquire whether the decisions of the highest internal tribunal complied with the church's own laws or whether that tribunal has conformed to all the rules applicable to civil courts.[183]

CONCLUSIONS

Whilst the laws of many churches distribute a wide range of quasi-judicial powers to bishops, normally with rights of appeal to the metropolitan, few churches have general rules of hierarchical recourse applicable to all administrative or adjudicative decisions. The ancient institution of visitation is to be found in the laws of the vast majority of churches, but without any real degree of precision as to specific rights and duties; in most churches episcopal visitation is cast as a duty, but in some as a right, and in only a few churches is archidiaconal visitation a creature known to law. Only a handful of churches possess laws dealing expressly with the problem of the breakdown of pastoral relations at the most local ecclesiastical unit. However, all churches operate a hierarchical system of church courts or tribunals, either in two tiers or three, and a handful of these enjoy jurisdiction over the laity as well as the clergy. A substantive law of ecclesiastical offences is employed in all churches, but generally offences are expressed with an extraordinarily high degree of generality. Procedures for disciplinary trials make every effort to allow the participation of the peers of the accused, to rights of appearance, representation, unbiased trials, silence and appeals. Whilst church courts in the Anglican Communion decide questions of guilt in disciplinary trials, with sentencing usually reserved to the bishop, the decisions of these courts do not create binding judicial precedents: only a small minority of churches operates a formal doctrine of precedent. Rather, the function of the interpretation of law is carried out by a wide range of commissions, committees and assemblies, not usually by the courts. Anglican jurisprudence is ambivalent to the question of recourse from ecclesiastical tribunals to the secular courts, though in many states, the latter provide a supervisory jurisdiction over the former.

---

[181] *Serbian Eastern Orthodox Diocese for the USA and Canada v Milivojevich*, 99 S Ct 3096 (*certiorari* denied).
[182] *Maxwell v Brougher*, 222 P 2d 910 (Cal).
[183] *Arthur v Norfield Parish Congregational Church Society*, 49 A 73 Conn 718; see also n. 181.

4
Archbishops and Bishops

The office of bishop is central to the government and law of all Anglican churches which, as a matter of ecclesiastical practice, commonly incorporate expressly in their laws a commitment to continue the historic and apostolic ministry of bishops, priests and deacons.[1] Anglican churches have developed complex legal arrangements both to order and to facilitate episcopal ministry which consists of the ministries of primates, archbishops (or metropolitans), diocesan bishops and assistant bishops. Diocesan bishops particularly are involved directly or indirectly with all aspects of ecclesiastical life: pastoral, ministerial, doctrinal, liturgical, governmental and proprietorial. The ministry of assistant bishops is very much in the keeping of diocesan bishops. To the office of archbishop attaches metropolitical jurisdiction in an ecclesiastical province, and national or regional churches have primates or an equivalent presiding bishop exercising a general episcopal ministry of oversight in the church in relation both to archbishops and bishops and to the church in general.[2] This chapter explores the laws of churches regulating appointment, functions and termination of the various episcopal ministries.

PRIMATES AND METROPOLITANS

In national or regional churches, composed of several provinces, a bishop may be assigned to the office of primate, a bishop presiding over the

---

[1] Korea, Fundamental Declaration: 'The Anglican Church of Korea, as a historical church, continues the apostolic ministry and holds as the standard the traditionally received threefold ministry (Bishop, Priest, Deacon)'; see also West Africa, Const. Art. 4; Kenya, Const. Art. V; Indian Ocean, Const. Art. 5; Papua New Guinea, Const. Art. 4: 'the Orders of Bishop, Priest and Deacon are acceptable to Holy Scripture and to the teaching and practice of the Catholic Church'; Uganda, Const. Art. 4(a); compare Philippines, Const. Art. II.1: 'The ministry of this Church includes lay persons, bishops, priests and deacons; LC 1888, Res. 11: this accepts as an 'article' 'The historic episcopate, locally adapted in the methods of its administration to the varying needs of the nations and peoples called of God into the unity of his Church'; see generally, J. Draper (ed.), *Communion and Episcopacy: Essays to Mark the Centenary of the Chicago-Lambeth Quadrilateral* (Oxford, 1988).

[2] See Ch. 12 for the position of the Archbishop of Canterbury in the Anglican Communion as a whole.

provinces comprising the particular church.[3] The principal bishop of a province, whether it is part of a wider national or regional church or whether it comprises the whole church, is styled the archbishop or metropolitan.

Primates

The law of ECUSA contains a comprehensive body of rules on the office of primate. The General Convention must elect a bishop as Presiding Bishop who holds office for nine years and, to do so, must resign any previous episcopal jurisdiction. The Presiding Bishop, 'the Chief Pastor and Primate of the Church', is responsible for leadership in initiating, developing and (as chair of General Convention's Executive Council) implementing the policy and strategy of the church. The primate is 'to [s]peak God's Word to the Church and to the world', as the representative of the church 'and its episcopate in its corporate capacity'. During episcopal vacancies in dioceses he must ensure that adequate episcopal services are provided, and take order for the consecration of bishops. With respect to government, the primate must assemble the House (or Council) of Bishops, preside over these and meetings of the General Convention when it meets in joint session, recommend legislation and visit every diocese. The Presiding Bishop has a special right to issue pastoral letters. If the Presiding Bishop dies or resigns, or by infirmity is incapable of acting, the House of Bishops must elect a successor and the election must be approved by a majority of the standing committees of the dioceses.[4] The main elements of the system in ECUSA are echoed in a number of other churches. Whilst in England appointment to the office of primate is in the keeping of the crown,[5] most churches regulate admission by means of election by a central church assembly.[6] The function of general leadership is commonly stressed as is

[3] For historical material, see H. Lowther Clarke, *Constitutional Church Government* (London, 1924), Ch. 3.

[4] ECUSA, Const. Art. 1; Cans. I.2; for visitation see Ch. 3.

[5] England, Can. C17(1): 'By virtue of their respective offices, the Archbishop of Canterbury is styled Primate of All England and Metropolitan, and the Archbishop of York, Primate of England and Metropolitan'; qualifications for candidature are discussed below.

[6] The following mirror the ECUSA approach: Brazil, Cans. I.3; Chile, Cans. B.15, 17; Brazil, Cans. I.3; Japan, Can. VII; Mexico, Const. Art. II.1; Korea, Const. Ch. 2, Art. 4; Philippines, Const. Art. IV.1–2; see also New Zealand, Const. A.1.7.8: the title 'Archbishop' shall be the 'courtesy title' of the primate; A.1.7.7: the primate 'shall have and may exercise all the powers functions and authorities given . . . under the Constitution and Canons'; compare Scotland, Can. 3.1: election by the Episcopal Synod; Can. 3.2: 'The Primus shall have no powers or prerogatives other than those expressly conferred by these Canons' (the list in Can. 3.3 is standard); for electoral colleges, see Ireland, Const. VI.1 and Australia, Primate Cans. 1985–92, 4; Canada, Can. III.25–49.

that of the primate's responsibility to act as representative of the church in its dealings with other churches and national or international organizations.[7] Some assign to the primate control over the movement of clergy from one diocese to another and various proprietorial functions.[8] Churches differ in terms of the period for which the primate is to hold office,[9] and many assign primatial functions, during the primate's incapacity or vacancy, to a senior bishop, seniority determined either by order of consecration or age.[10] Removal is usually by a special majority vote of the church's central episcopal assembly.[11]

Archbishops or Metropolitans

The principal episcopal office in a province is that of archbishop, an office from which metropolitical jurisdiction is exercised.[12] It is a general principle of Anglican canon law that candidates for archiepiscopal office must already hold episcopal office, and that archiepiscopal office is held concurrently with diocesan episcopal office: in some churches a diocese is designated as a permanent metropolitical see.[13] With the exception of England,[14] invariably admission is by election, a process in which both

[7] Korea, Const. Art. 6; Philippines, Const. Art. IV.1–2: the candidate must be at least 48.

[8] Korea, Const. Art. 6: the primate has pastoral superintendence when there is a vacancy in a diocese, and control over the movement of clergy as between dioceses; Scotland, Can. 3.3: the primus must undertake by declaration to carry out the resolutions of the General Synod, the Episcopal Synod and the College of Bishops; see also Canada, Can. III.8.

[9] Korea, Const. Art. 7 (2 years); Brazil, Cans. I.3: tenure lasts until the primate reaches the age of 68; Australia, Primate Cans. 1985–92, 9 (70); Canada, Can. III.7 (70).

[10] New Zealand, Const. C.13; Scotland, Can. 3.4: written notice to the senior bishop is required; for seniority fixed by order of episcopal consecration, see e.g. Korea, Const. Art. 8; Brazil, Cans. I.3; Canada, Can. III.16–20.

[11] Scotland, Can. 3.6: the Episcopal Synod may by a three-quarters majority declare the office vacant when satisfied that the primus is physically or mentally incapable of discharging the duties of the office; New Zealand, Const. A.1.7.5; Canada, Can. III.21–24: declaration of vacancy by special resolution.

[12] This has been defined recently by the Anglican Consultative Council: see Ch. 12, n. 22.

[13] Australia, Const. III.9; Papua New Guinea, Const. Art. 9: if the archbishop ceases to be a diocesan, tenure as archbishop ceases; Uganda, Const. Art. 10: candidates must be at least 50; compare ECUSA, Cans. I.9.6: the President of each province may be a bishop, presbyter or deacon or lay person of the province: method of election and term of office is to be prescribed by the provincial synod; permanent metropolitical sees are to be found in e.g. England, Ireland, Southern Africa and Australia.

[14] England: the same basic procedure applies as to the appointment of diocesan bishop; see n. 31; Can. C17: the archbishop has throughout the province 'metropolitical jurisdiction', as 'superintendent of all ecclesiastical matters', 'to correct and supply the defects of other bishops'; within the province the archbishop is 'principal minister', presides over the provincial convocation, is the chief consecrator at episcopal consecrations, and on a vacancy in a diocese becomes the 'guardian of the spiritualities' of the diocese.

clergy and lay people are involved. In some churches the central assembly elects.[15] In most, however, election is by a special electoral college; voting, which must take place without fear and bias for the benefit and well-being of the church, is by secret ballot: the election process is usually set within a liturgical context.[16] In most churches the law fixes a period for tenure but reserving a right to be considered for re-election: vacancy occurs usually on death, resignation, completion of the term, the attainment of a fixed age, ceasing to be a diocesan bishop or removal.[17] If the archbishop resigns, or is incapacitated by reason of illness, archiepiscopal functions are carried out by the senior bishop, seniority being determined either by age or order of episcopal consecration.[18]

Under the laws of most churches, candidates for archiepiscopal office must make a declaration, in one form or another, promising to comply with the law of the church and to submit to the authority and decisions of ecclesiastical tribunals or other authorities.[19] Whilst usually laws applicable to bishops also apply *mutatis mutandis* to metropolitans, the laws of several churches contain elaborate provisions for the disciplining and removal of archbishops, particularly in cases of physical or mental incapacity: normally the right to remove belongs to an assembly of bish-

[15] Sudan, Const. Art. 18; Papua New Guinea, Const. Art. 9; South East Asia, Const. Art. 1; Uganda, Const. Art. 8.

[16] Tanzania, Const. IV.8; Melanesia, Const. Art. 8; Southern Africa, Can. 5: other than election of the Archbishop of Cape Town (when the rules governing election of bishops apply: see Can. 4), election is by an Electoral Assembly; Wales, Const. IX; Indian Ocean, Const. Art. 10; Uganda, Const. Art. 10: election by the House of Bishops; Central Africa, Can. 5; Kenya, Const. VI; LC 1930, Res. 55: 'Where the office of metropolitan is attached to a particular see, the other dioceses of the province should have some effective voice in the election of a bishop to that see'; for secret ballot and liturgy see e.g. Tanzania, Const. V.1; Uganda, Const. Art. 10(b); Nigeria, Const. Ch. I, Art. II; Burundi, Const. Art. 11; Zaire, Const. Art. 10.

[17] Tanzania, Const. IV.8: resignation must occur at 65 but the person may continue in office with the consent of the House of Bishops; Sudan, Const. Art. 18.25: the archbishop is elected for 10 years but must retire at 70; Melanesia, Const. Art. 8, Cans. C.1.A: the archbishop may retire at 55 and must retire at 60; Australia, Const. III.9; Sudan, Const. Art. 18.28; South East Asia, Const. Art. 1(b): tenure is for 4 years and vacancy at 55; Uganda, Const. Art. 10(n): tenure is for 10 years with retirement at 65; Indian Ocean, Const. Art. 10: 5 year tenure and retirement at 70.

[18] Papua New Guinea, Const. Art. 11; Melanesia, Const. Art. 11; Southern Africa, Can. 2.2: functions are undertaken by the Dean of the Province. For the right to resign in which case reasons must usually be given to the senior bishop, see e.g. Papua New Guinea, Const. Art. 9.

[19] See e.g. Melanesia, Const. Art. 15.A: the promise is to 'uphold, defend and obey the Constitution' and 'lawfully and honestly keep the Church Laws of the Province' and of the diocese of which he is bishop; compare England, Can. C15(2): the Declaration of Assent concerns only doctrine and liturgy; see also Southern Africa, Acts of the Provincial Synod, IV: 'it is inconsistent with the spirit and intention of the Book of Common Prayer that Metropolitans take an oath of obedience to any other Metropolitan or Archbishop'.

ops.[20] It seems that the formal law of no church contains an explicit definition of 'metropolitical jurisdiction' or 'metropolitical authority'.[21] Rather, definitions of these are implicit in the lists of functions, duties and rights, of metropolitans. The functions of the archbishop, who typically has 'authority, leadership and visitatorial power over the whole province', commonly include: convening and chairing the provincial assembly, its executive council or committee and the house of bishops; the administration and entertainment (with others) of appeals from the decisions of diocesan tribunals; representing the province in its dealings with other churches; and other duties assigned from time to time by the provincial assembly.[22] As is described in the following section, it is a general principle of Anglican canon law that metropolitans are in a legal position of superiority over the bishops of the province and are, as such, owed a duty of obedience by these. In extra-provincial dioceses metropolitical jurisdiction is exercised by episcopal authorities external to the particular church.[23]

DIOCESAN BISHOPS

As with primates and metropolitans, there is a high degree of legal unity between churches of the Anglican Communion concerning eligibility for

[20] Sudan, Const. Art. 18.26–27: removal is possible only for 'inability to perform the functions of his office' or for 'misbehaviour' after a two-thirds majority vote in the Episcopal Council; Tanzania, Const. IV.8: removal may be for neglect of duties or behaviour 'not worthy' of an archbishop; Uganda, Const. Art. 10(o)–(p); Melanesia, Cans. C.2.C.1: after examination by three medical practitioners, the Diocesan Council instructs the senior bishop to declare a vacancy; see also South East Asia, Const. Art. 1(d)–(e) and Regulation B.

[21] See Ch. 12, n. 22.

[22] West Indies, Const. Art. 2.2–3: the archbishop is 'the focus of Provincial unity' and 'shall exercise Metropolitical authority as determined by this Constitution and Canons'; Southern Africa, Can. 2.1; Uganda, Const. Art. 9: this includes 'discipline over the whole Province'; Tanzania, Const. IV.9; Sudan, Const. Art. 18.24; Indian Ocean, Const. Art. 11; South East Asia, Const. Art. II; Southern Cone, Can. 1; Melanesia, Const. Art. 9; for these and particular reponsibility for bishops, see Papua New Guinea, Const. Art. 10; West Africa, Const. Arts. 6, 7; see Jerusalem and the Middle East, Const. Art. 16 for reassumption by Canterbury of metropolitical jurisdiction in the event of its unconstitutional exercise in the province; Wales, Const. II.3: the archbishop takes 'precedence' over all diocesan bishops; II.32: 'Subject to the Constitution, no proceeding of the Governing Body shall interfere with the exercise by the Archbishop of the powers and functions inherent in the Office of Metropolitan'.

[23] Colombo and Kurunagala (Church of Ceylon) and Bermuda are under the jurisdiction of the Archbishop of Canterbury; Costa Rica under that of the House of Bishops of Province IX of ECUSA, Puerto Rico under the President Bishop and the Synod of Province IX, and Cuba under a Metropolitan Council for Cuba (3 Primates); the Lusitanian Church of Portugal and the Spanish Reformed Episcopal Church are under the Metropolitical Authority of the Archbishop of Canterbury; see generally Ch. 12.

the office of diocesan bishop,[24] appointment and ordination,[25] functions, and termination of that episcopal ministry. Perhaps somewhat surprisingly, a significant number of national and provincial churches possess no formal legal statement on eligibility for admission to the office of diocesan bishop, though sometimes this subject is treated by diocesan law. However, in those instances where the formal law of the whole does treat the matter, it reserves candidature to priests who have been in holy orders for a fixed number of years. Minimum ages are commonly prescribed, ranging from thirty to forty, maximum limits are sometimes prescribed,[26] and occasionally express provision is made for the dispensation of an age requirement by means of archiepiscopal faculty.[27] It is usual for laws to require candidates to be 'of comptetent learning', of 'sound mind', and of 'good morals'.[28] In several churches medical examination is mandatory to determine not only the physical but also the mental fitness of the candidate for appointment.[29]

[24] For female bishops, see Ch. 12; in some churches women are not eligible for episcopal office, in others they are; see e.g. Ireland Const. IX.22: 'Men and women alike may be ordained to the holy orders of deacons, of priests and of bishops, without any distinction or discrimination on grounds of sex, and men and women so ordained shall alike be referred to and known as deacons, priests or bishops'.

[25] For acceptance of the principle of election see LC 1867, Res. 10; LC 1930, Ress. 55, 56; LC 1958, Res. 59; for the supervisory role of bishops, see LC 1897, Ress. 26, 50; LC 1908, Res. 10; LC 1958, Res. 90; for jurisdiction as territorial, see LC 1867, Res. 12; LC 1878, Ress. 1, 11; LC 1897, Ress. 9, 24.

[26] For 30 as the minimum age see: England, Can C2(3); New Zealand, Cans. A.1.1: the candidate must also be a priest of this church or of a church in full communion with it (see also Southern Africa, Can. 4); Japan, Const. Art. 2; Australia, Const. XII.74.1; ECUSA, Const. Art. II.2; Melanesia, Cans. A.7.C: the candidate must be over 29; for 35 as the minimum age see: Philippines, Const. Art. V.3; Brazil, Cans. III.16; Jerusalem, Const. Art. 13(i); Rwanda, Draft Const. 1996, Art. 39: this also requires the candidate to have been at least 5 years in priestly ministry; compare North India, Const. II.IV.VIII: experience of 10 years as a presbyter is required and the candidate must be at least 40 and less than 60 years of age; Mexico, Const. IV.3: 40 years or more; Indian Ocean, Can. 2: 30 and less than 60.

[27] See e.g. Papua New Guinea, Const. Art. 14: the candidate, who must be at least 30, must have been in priest's orders for 6 years, but an archiepiscopal faculty may dispense with these requirements; Korea, Const. Art. 11.2: this treats the fixed ages as the 'normal' requirements.

[28] Papua New Guinea, Const. Art. 14; Southern Africa, Can. 7.2; Nigeria, Can. XII; Central Africa, Can. 7.4; Canada, Province of Rupert's Land, Const. 6.02; see also below for challenges to elections for want of canonical fitness and capacity.

[29] Uganda, Const. Art. 4; Burundi, Const. Art. 5; Zaire, Const. Art. 5; ECUSA, Cans. III.22.3: the bishop-elect's medical, psychological and psychiatric condition must be examined.

Appointment: *Election, Confirmation and Consecration*

It is a general principle of Anglican canon law that candidates for admission to the office of diocesan bishop must be elected to that office.[30] Various models are employed but in all there are, basically, four stages to election: nomination, voting, confirmation and pronouncement of the result.[31] The right to nominate is vested in a wide range of ecclesiastical bodies and persons; in most churches it is enjoyed by a special nominating body, usually a diocesan institution consisting of representatives of the episcopate (other bishops ministering in the diocese), clergy and laity.[32] Several churches provide for consultation throughout the diocese in question, sometimes even with the most local of ecclesiastical units within it.[33] Nominations are submitted to the archbishop of the province in which the diocese is situated and commonly at this stage the church's central episcopal assembly may add to the nominations.[34] The second stage of the process is consideration by an electoral body (or college), usually a provincial or national institution.[35] The law normally requires proceedings at this

[30] The underlying assumption is that elections must be lawfully conducted: see e.g. ECUSA, Cans. III.22.1(a): the election must be carried out in accordance with 'rules prescribed by the Convention of the Diocese'; see also Australia, Const. III.8; and Jerusalem, Const. Art. 11(iv).

[31] England: the admission procedure is by nomination, election, confirmation, and ordination or consecration; a diocesan Vacancy in See Committee may discuss names and submit these to the Crown Appointments Commission; two names are agreed and submitted to the appropriate archbishop and the (secular) Prime Minister nominates to the monarch who enjoys a power to appoint under secular parliamentary statute: Appointment of Bishops Act 1534; objection to confirmation is possible for defect of form or if the candidate presented was not the royal appointee: *R v Archbishop of Canterbury* [1902] 2 KB 503; for criticisms of the present appointments procedure see *Episcopal Ministry*, Report of the Archbishops' Commission on the Episcopate (London, 1990).

[32] ECUSA, Cans. III.22; see P. M. Dawley, *The Episcopal Church and Its Work* (New York, 1961), 130ff; Melanesia, Const. Art. 13: the Diocesan Electoral Board nominates to the archbishop; South East Asia, Const. Art. IV and Regulation C: nominations are made by the Diocesan Synod; Uganda, Const. Art. 13: nominations of the Diocesan Synod go to the House of Bishops; Scotland, Can. 4: the Vacancy in See Committee nominates to the Electors of the Diocese; see also Southern Africa, Can. 4.10: the diocesan advisory committee may submit names to the Dean of the Province.

[33] Papua New Guinea, Const. Art. 14.2–3: the Diocesan Selection Committee must visit individually or in groups the parish councils of the diocese; names may be submitted in writing to the Selection Committee by any communicant member of the parish; New Zealand, Cans. A.1.2: the diocesan Electoral College may delegate its right to nominate 'to any person or persons whom it may appoint either absolutely or subject to such conditions as it may think fit to impose'; compare Wales, Const. VIII.27: 'The [Electoral] College shall not be entitled to delegate its power of electing a Bishop'.

[34] Tanzania, Const. IV.12; West Africa, Can II; in ECUSA, Cand. III.22: nominations from the floor of the electoral body are permitted.

[35] Compare ECUSA, Cans. III.22: the Diocesan Convention is the ordinary electing body but it may request an election to be made on its behalf by the provincial House of

point to be conducted in a liturgical setting.[36] Electoral colleges, similarly composed of representatives of the episcopate, clergy and laity,[37] are invariably required to vote by orders and in secret.[38] Most churches operate a system of elimination, based on three or more ballots.[39] The law of several churches provides that, in the event of the electoral college being unable to agree on a name or to agree upon a name within a prescribed period, election passes to an archbishop acting unilaterally.[40]

The decision of the electoral body is subject to confirmation or approval by the archbishop,[41] or else by an episcopal assembly or in some cases by the national or provincial assembly.[42] In many churches, it is only at this stage,

Bishops subject to confirmation by the Provincial Synod; Korea, Const. Art. 11: 'A diocesan bishop is elected by the diocesan synod'; Tanzania, Const. IV.12: the Election Forum merely nominates candidates to the archbishop for forwarding to the House of Bishops; Papua New Guinea, Const. Art. 14: the Bishopric Selection Committee; Scotland, Can. 4 and 5: the Electors of the Diocese.

[36] ECUSA, Diocese of Western New York, Cans. 19.8: the election must be conducted 'in the context of worship and prayer' in which individuals must vote 'religiously and in fear of God, the whole solemnity being an act of religion and part of public worship'; see also Diocese of Mississippi, Const. Art. XIII; Papua New Guinea, Const. Art. 14: this requires celebration of the eucharist 'with the special intention for the guidance of the Holy Spirit'; see also Scotland, Can. 4.22; Ireland, Const. VI.9; Southern Africa, Can. 4.11.

[37] Ireland, Const. VI.4–5; Wales, Const. VIII.9; Southern Africa, Can. 4.5: the Electoral Assembly; Papua New Guinea, Const. Art. 14: the Bishopric Selection Committee is composed of members of the Diocesan Selection Committee, one member from each other Diocesan Selection Committee chosen by the Provincial Council; Canada, Const. Art. 37; North India, Const. II.IV.XIII. Compare, for diocesan electoral colleges: New Zealand, Cans. A.1.2: presided over by the primate; Kenya, Const. Art. X; Scotland, Can. 4.

[38] See e.g. Papua New Guinea, Const. Art. 14: a two-thirds majority is needed; Ireland, Const. VI.13: Wales, Const. VIII.17–23; Southern Africa, Can. 4.16; West Indies, Can. 7; New Zealand, Cans. A.1.2: the diocesan Electoral College determines its own procedure as to consultation, nominations and decision-making; Scotland, Can. 4.2: all meetings must be in private; West Africa, Can. 1: 'The election shall be by secret ballot and shall be determined by a simple majority of those present and voting'.

[39] For elimination, see e.g. Papua New Guinea, Const. Art. 14; and Korea, Const. Art. 11.

[40] West Indies, Can. 7: on failure to elect within six months, the decision passes to the bishops of the province; Papua New Guinea, Const. Art. 14: if the Bishopric Selection Committee fails within 6 months of the vacancy, the House of Bishops selects; Melanesia, Const. Art. 13: if the Diocesan Electoral Board fails to elect within 6 months or has made a nomination which the archbishop rejects, the Council of Bishops must choose; Wales, Const. VIII.26: in the event of disagreement or failure to elect within 3 months of vacancy, 'the vacancy shall be filled up by the Archbishop of Canterbury, unless and until the Governing Body shall have otherwise determined'.

[41] Tanzania, Const. IV.12(a); Cans. 2(a)–(b).

[42] ECUSA, Cans. III.22: a majority of both the bishops and the standing committees of the other dioceses in the province must consent to the election; see also Philippines, Const. Art. V; compare Papua New Guinea, Const. Art. 14: the House of Bishops must consent (see also South East Asia, Const. Art. IV and Regulation C); Korea, Const. Art. 11; New Zealand, Cans. A.1.2: the archbishop decides in consultation with all diocesan

immediately prior to confirmation, that laws allow challenges to the election process, either on substantive grounds, concerning the quality of the candidate, or on procedural grounds, for want of proper form. Challenges are entertained either by a special tribunal or in a quasi-judicial fashion. The canon law of Southern Africa is particularly well-developed on this subject. A valid objection to the election may be made to the Court of Confirmation on the grounds that: the see was not canonically vacant; the election was 'informal'; the candidate was not of canonical age; the candidate was not of 'competent learning, or of sound faith, or of good morals, or is otherwise canonically disqualified, or that he is under such liabilities or contracts as not to be a free agent'. *Locus standi* to object is confined to bishops or a communicant member of the church 'of honest life and good repute'; they must make a declaration that they will accept the decision of the court as final. The metropolitan must summon the bishops (or their commissaries) to a Court of Confirmation consisting of the metropolitan and all diocesan bishops; the metropolitan is president and the court is assisted *inter alia* by the chancellor of the vacant diocese and some other person learned in law. A majority decision is required.[43] A similar judicial model is employed in several other churches,[44] though it is more common for objections to election to be determined by an episcopal assembly which is not styled a court: grounds additional to those appearing in the Southern African canon include doctrinal unsuitability and poor health.[45] In several states, the secular courts have entertained challenges to episcopal elections.[46] Following confirmation the result is pronounced, usually by the archbishop.[47]

bishops and must submit the nomination to General Synod for sanctioning; Jerusalem, Const. Art. 11(v): the Central Synod must approve; Scotland, Can. 4.37: all diocesan bishops must intimate assent or rejection to the primus; see also Chile, Can. B.2.

[43] Southern Africa, Can. 7.

[44] Central Africa, Can. 7; Ireland, *Re Meath Episcopal Election* (1886), Journal of the Court of the General Synod, 1886, 169; see also Canada, *Re Bishop Eric Brays* (1989), Supreme Ct of Appeal (see Const. App. T, 175): the court rejected a challenge to the consecration of a bishop based on the claim that it was conducted under impermissible forms of service.

[45] Papua New Guinea, Const. Art. 14: whether the candidate was of the correct age, a priest of six years, of competent learning, sound mind, or good morals, is determined by the House of Bishops; New Zealand, Can. A.1.5.2: the diocesan bishops may disapprove confirmation on the grounds of doctrine, of character and manner of life, of health, or physical inability to undertake office; Scotland, Can. 4.42: appeal lies to the Episcopal Synod which may upset the election if satisfied that defects in form would have affected the election result.

[46] *Chief Dr Irene Thomas et al v The Most Revd Timothy Omotayo Olufosoye* [1986] 1 All Nigeria Law Reports 215 (Sup Ct of Nigeria): the court would not accept a challenge to the appointment of the Bishop of Lagos, nor would it grant an injunction to prevent translation, on the basis that communicant status was not sufficient to provide *locus standi*; for England, see n. 31.

[47] See e.g. Southern Africa, Can. 7; Papua New Guinea, Const. Art. 14; West Africa, Can. II(d).

Once the election process is completed, it is invariably a metropolitan who must take order for the consecration or ordination of the bishop-elect (if the candidate is not already in episcopal orders) after having obtained that person's consent.[48] A rule commonly appearing either in the formal law or in liturgical rubrics is that consecration may take place by no less than three bishops, of whom the archbishop must be one. If unable to act, the archbishop must appoint a commissary.[49] All consecrations must ordinarily take place (preferably on a Sunday) within the province in which the diocese is situated, unless the archbishop permits otherwise.[50] Consecrations must be carried out in accordance with the prescribed liturgical form and they are effected by the laying on of hands, the recital of the words of consecration and the invocation of the Holy Spirit.[51] Consecration is followed by enthronement or installation in the diocese.[52] The bishop-elect is obliged to make various undertakings in the form of declarations, promises or oaths. These include: assent to the doctrine, liturgy and discipline of the church;[53] compliance with the law of the church, national, provincial or diocesan;[54] submission to the decisions of ecclesiastical tribunals and other authorities;[55] and allegiance to the met-

[48] ECUSA, Cans. III.22.4; Philippines, Cans. III.14.3; Papua New Guinea, Const. Art. 14; Ireland, Const. VI.14; West Africa, Can. II(d); Kenya, Const. X(l); Uganda, Const. Art. 13; West Indies, Can. 8.7; New Zealand, Cans. A.1.5.10. Compare Scotland, Can. 4.40: arrangements must be made by the College of Bishops.

[49] West Indies, Can. 8.8; Papua New Guinea, Const. Art. 14; Australia, Can. 3 1966, Can. 6 1969; ECUSA, Const. Art. II.2 and BCP 1979, Marshall, 621: the Presiding Bishop is 'chief consecrator' with at least two other bishops; Philippines, Const. Art. V.5; Sudan, Const. Arts. 24, 43; Canada, Province of Rupert's Land, Const 1994, 6.26; Southern Africa, Can. 8.1 and *Prayer Book* 1989, 595.

[50] West Indies, Can. 8.9; Australia, Can. 3 1966, Can. 6 1969: consecration may take place in a place of worship of a church in communion with it; for Sundays as the preferred day see e.g. ECUSA, BCP 1979, Marshall, 621.

[51] ECUSA, BCP 1979, Marshall, 637; Southern Africa, *Prayer Book* 1989, 602; Wales, BCP 1984, 716.

[52] West Indies, Can. 8.13: 'Diocesan Bishops shall be enthroned in the customary manner'; see also Korea, Const. Art. 11.8; for installation see e.g. Scotland, Can. 4.41.

[53] ECUSA, Const. Art. VIII; Cans. III.22.8; Philippines, Cans. III.14.1; New Zealand, Cans. A.1 Sched; Central Africa, Can. 9; Indian Ocean, Can. 2. See Ch. 7 for a comparison of the precise terms of declarations.

[54] Southern Africa, Can. 6.3: the bishop-elect 'pledges' 'to acknowledge the Constitution of this Church' and 'to govern his Diocese in conformity with the Constitution, Laws and Canons' of the church; West Indies, Can. 8.10: 'I . . . agree to be bound by all lawful Canons and Regulations which are now in force . . . and by all other Canons and Regulations as may from time to time be made and issued by the authority' of the Provincial Synod; Papua New Guinea, Const. Art. 4: they agree to obey both provincial and diocesan constitutions and canons; Melanesia, Const. Art. 6.D; New Zealand, Cans. A.1 Sched; Sudan, Const. Art. 44; Tanzania, Const. IV.12(b)(v), 13.

[55] See e.g. West Indies, Can. 8.10: 'I . . . do solemnly declare my submission to the authority of the Provincial Synod'; Southern Africa, Can. 8.3: the bishop-elect 'pledges' 'to give due obedience to the decisions of its Synods'.

ropolitan.[56] In some churches the bishop-elect is required to give 'due honour and deference' to the Archbishop of Canterbury.[57]

Functions: Rights and Duties

It is a general principle of Anglican canon law that the functions of diocesan bishops are to teach, to sanctify and to govern, all three functions coming within the general oversight and ordinary jurisdiction which a bishop has as chief minister of the diocese.[58] There are, however, subtle differences between churches in the jurisprudence they employ about episcopal office: episcopal ministry is cast variously in law in terms of service, responsibilities, functions, privileges, duties and rights.[59] Church laws on the subject may be put into two broad categories: those in which functions are scattered amongst rules dealing with discrete subjects; and those which have a separate title presenting a compendium of general functions. With respect to the first class, as may be seen from studies elsewhere in this volume, the diocesan bishop is involved in all aspects of ecclesiastical life in the diocese. In diocesan government the bishop acts as president of the diocesan assembly, and as chairman of diocesan executive bodies. In the process of making diocesan law very often the bishop enjoys a power of veto. The bishop's quasi-judicial functions include the exercise of visitatorial powers and the resolution of disputes concerning liturgy and matters relating to admission to and exclusion from the rites of the church. The bishop is closely involved with the administration of justice in the diocese, particularly in the appointment of legal and judicial officers and in the disciplining of clergy. The function of appointing and licensing ordained and lay persons for ministry in the diocese is vested in the bishop

[56] West Indies, Can. 8.10: 'I . . . do profess all due reverence and obedience to the Archbishop'; Melanesia, Const. Arts. 6, 15: they 'must promise obedience under the laws of the Church to the Archbishop'; Southern Africa, *Prayer Book* 1989, 595: the oath of allegiance; Sudan, Const. Art. 44: the oath of obedience; Korea, Const. Art. 11.9: 'every bishop shall swear an oath of Canonical Obedience to the Primate as Metropolitan, and to his lawful successors'; see also Nigeria, Const. Ch. IV; West Africa, Const. Art. VII.3; Tanzania, Const. IV.12, 13.

[57] West Indies, Can. 8.10: 'I . . . declare that I will pay all due honour and deference to the Archbishop of Canterbury, and will respect and maintain the spiritual rights and privileges of all Churches in the Anglican Communion'; see also Ch. 12.

[58] See generally J. Draper (ed.), *Communion and Episcopacy* (Oxford, 1988); for historical material, H. L. Clarke, *Constitutional Church Government* (London, 1924), Ch. 3.

[59] Papua New Guinea, Const. Art. 14.1: a bishop is 'the servant of Christ and the servant of all', the 'chief shepherd of souls in his diocese and . . . the friend and guide of his clergy and people' (compare Papua New Guinea, Diocese of Port Moresby, Can. 7: this refers to the 'prerogatives' and 'powers' of the bishop); for 'responsibility' see West Africa, Const. Art. 4; Korea, Const. Ch. 3, Art. 12.1: '[t]he duties of the diocesan bishop' include 'the representation and pastoral oversight of the diocese'; West Indies, Can. 9: 'rights and obligations'; Burundi, Const. Art. 17.

and he enjoys rights of consent in matters relating to diocesan finance and property. The diocesan bishop is also involved in the life of the church at provincial, national or regional level, especially through membership of central church assemblies and, which is discussed later in this chapter, through episcopal synods or colleges.

With respect to the second class, laws would seem to fall, in turn, into two further categories: those which present episcopal functions in a strong theological setting and those which emphasize the technical jurisdictional nature of episcopal office. Laws of the Indian churches come within the former. The constitution of the church in South India provides that '[t]he bishop of the diocese has the general pastoral oversight of all the Christian people of the diocese, and more particularly, the ministers of the Church in the diocese'. As 'the Chief Shepherd under Christ of his flock', the bishop is responsible for doing all he can 'to foster the true spiritual unity of the diocese by entering as far as possible into personal relation with every member of the flock', especially by ministering the rite of Confirmation or by presiding at other services in which admission is given into full membership of the church. It is 'the duty of the bishop to take the lead in the evangelistic work of the diocese', and '[t]he office of a bishop is also essentially a teaching office': the bishop should do all that is in his power for 'the edification of the ministers and congregations . . . by instructing them concerning the truths of the Christian faith'. The diocesan bishop has general oversight of worship throughout the diocese and 'authority in the case of grave irregularities in public worship to forbid their continuance'. Responsibility for both ordination and for 'authorization to ministers to officiate and preach in the diocese' is given to the bishop as well as 'authority in disciplinary cases' over both clergy and laity. The bishop is president of the Diocesan Council but 'shall not have any separate controlling authority over the finance of the diocese'.[60]

The Scottish canons may be used as an example of the more technical and overtly jurisdictional approach. In Scottish canon law the diocesan bishop is appointed 'to the charge of a diocese' in which he must be resident; to be absent for more than four months *per annum* the consent of the College of Bishops must be obtained. The Scottish requirement of residence is global, though the right to permit absence, normally for two to four months, may be vested in the diocesan assembly or the metropolitan.[61] In Scotland the

---

[60] South India, Const. IV.1–10; see also North India, Const. I.I.VIII.6.

[61] Scotland, Can. 6.1; for diocesan assemblies: ECUSA, Cans. III.24: absence must be permitted by the Diocesan Convention or its standing committee; Philippines, Can. III.15.2: absence for 6 weeks or more must be approved similarly; Korea, Const. Arts. 13–14: absence for 2 months or more must be sanctioned by the diocesan executive committee; for metropolitans: Southern Africa, Can. 11; West Indies, Can. 9: 6 months; West Africa, Const. Art. X; Central Africa, Can. 12; generally, for the duty to reside, see: Rwanda, Draft Const. 1996, Art. 39; Chile, Cans. B.20; and Spain, Can. 30.9.

bishop is 'the Chief Pastor of all within the Diocese and their Father in God' and to the office attaches the responsibility 'to teach and uphold sound and wholesome doctrine and to banish and drive away all erroneous and strange doctrines contrary to God's Word'.[62] Several churches have an equivalent provision and that in England is almost identical.[63] As to the liturgical life, in Scottish canon law the diocesan bishop is 'the principal minister of the Word and Sacraments in the Diocese, to whom belongs the right of celebrating the rites of Ordination and Confirmation'. In his ministerial capacity 'it is competent for the Bishop to administer the Holy Sacraments, preach the Word of God, preside at all liturgical functions, and perform all other duties pertaining to his office, in every church within the Diocese'.[64] The general thrust of this provision appears expressly in the national or provincial laws of only a few other churches.[65] As to governance, under Scottish canon law, 'No Bishop of one diocese, except as provided in these Canons, shall interfere with the concerns of another diocese'. Consequently, no bishop may perform 'any episcopal function in any other diocese without the sanction, nor exercise any other ecclesiastical function against the will, expressed in writing, of the Bishop' of that diocese.[66] The Scottish prohibition against the exercise of episcopal ministry in the diocese by bishops other than the diocesan is common.[67] In several churches the bishop has an explicit duty to keep a record of all official acts,[68] and in a small number the bishop is formally empowered to deliver a pastoral charge to the clergy and a pastoral letter to the people on points of doctrine, worship and discipline.[69]

[62] Scotland, Can. 6.
[63] See e.g. Korea, Const. Art. 2: responsibilities include '[t]he preservation of the faith, apostolic teaching and catholic truth of the Church' and evangelism; England, Can. C18: the bishop must be 'an example of righteous and godly living' and 'it is his duty to set forward and maintain quietness, love, and peace among all men'.
[64] Scotland, Can. 6.3.
[65] England, Can. C18(4); ECUSA, Cans. III.24; Korea, Const. Art. 12.4: '[t]he administration of Holy Orders and the sacrament of Confirmation' belong to the bishop; for the concept of leadership, see Burundi, Const. Art. 12; and Nigeria, Const. Ch. II, Art. I; see also n. 67.
[66] Scotland, Can. 6.4 and 6.
[67] ECUSA, Cans. III.24; Korea, Const. Art. 15: 'No bishop may confirm or ordain or undertake other episcopal functions in a diocese other than his own without the permission of the diocesan bishop concerned'; North India, Const. I.II.3: a bishop has jurisdiction only over the territory of the diocese; England, Can. C18: 'Every bishop has within his diocese jurisdiction as Ordinary except in places and over persons exempt by law or custom'; see also Diocese of Europe, Const. 5; Wales, Const. II.32: 'Subject to the Constitution, no proceeding of the Governing Body shall interfere with the exercise . . . by the Diocesan Bishops of the powers and functions inherent in the Episcopal Office'.
[68] See e.g. ECUSA, Cans. III.24; and West Indies, Can. 9.9.
[69] ECUSA, Cans. III.24.5; Philippines, Cans. III.15.4; West Indies, Can. 9.3: 'Every Diocesan Bishop may deliver from time to time at his discretion a Charge to the Clergy of his Diocese, and may from time to time address to the people of his Diocese Pastoral

Termination of Ministry

It is a general principle of Anglican canon law that a diocese is vacated on the death, retirement, resignation or removal of the diocesan bishop. During a vacancy it is the primate or (more usually) the metropolitan who is obliged to provide for oversight of the diocese, normally through a commissary though sometimes laws assign oversight to a prescribed diocesan officer such as a vicar general or diocesan administrator.[70] The laws of the vast majority of churches require retirement at a fixed age, the most common being sixty-five or seventy; often, however, laws confer a right to retire at an earlier fixed age (normally sixty and with notice to the metropolitan) and they provide for continuance in office beyond the retirement age usually for five years and with the consent of the metropolitan.[71] The right to offer voluntary resignation at any time is enjoyed by most diocesan bishops: the most widespread practice is for the offer to be made in writing to the metropolitan, who may accept or refuse;[72] sometimes, however, acceptance must be given by an episcopal assembly.[73] Few churches have express provision on compulsory resignation; those that do provide: that resignation may be requested or required, on representations of a fixed number of bishops to the metropolitan; that the bishop must be given a full opportunity to put his case; and that a special majority of all dioce-

Letters on points of Christian doctrine, worship or manners which he may require the Clergy to read to their congregations'; see also Korea, Const. Art. 12.5: the bishop is responsible for the 'disciplining of clergy and laity [for] the maintaining of the good order of the church'.

[70] See e.g. New Zealand, Cans. A.1.6.4: episcopal supervision 'devolves' to the primate who must appoint a commissary; Southern Africa, Can. 22; England, Can. C19(2); see below and, for vicars general, see Ch. 5.

[71] For retirement at 72 see ECUSA, Const. Art. II.9 and Cans. III.28.2; at 70 years see Southern Africa, Can. 14.3; Sudan, Const. Art. 46; and Jerusalem, Const. Art. 13(ii); for the duty to retire at 65 and the right to do so at 60 see e.g. South East Asia, Const. Art. IV(b); and Philippines, Const. V.8; compare Papua New Guinea, Can. No. 1 of 1994: duty to retire at 65, right from 55; Melanesia, Cans. C.1.B: 60 and 55 respectively; Philippines, for continuance in office see e.g. Tanzania, Const. V; Can. 2(e); Korea, Const. Art. 16; some churches use 'resignation' as an equivalent to retirement: Ireland, Const. VI.25, 26: duty to resign at 65 and right to do so at 60; England, Ecclesiastical Offices (Age Limit) Measure 1975, s. 1: retirement at 70 (the archbishop may authorize continuance in office).

[72] For resignation: to the primate, see Scotland, Can. 7.1; to the archbishop, see South East Asia, Const. Art. IV(c), Korea, Const. Art. 17 and England, Bishops (Retirement) Measure 1986, s. 1.

[73] Resignation must be approved by the House of Bishops in ECUSA, Const. Art. II.6; and Cans. III.28.3; see also Philippines, Const. V.6: this requires the consent of the majority of diocesan standing committees and provincial bishops; compare, for unilateral action by the primate, New Zealand, Cans. A.1.6: the primate simply 'advises' the other bishops of the resignation; see also Melanesia, Cans. C.1.B.

san bishops must agree to the resignation.[74] On retirement, the bishop will have rights to a pension.[75]

Episcopal discipline is effected by a wide range of legal devices. In the event that the diocesan bishop might have committed an ecclesiastical offence, judicial proceedings may result in the termination of his ministry: this is treated in Chapter 3. Executive action is the more usual method of correction. This may be achieved by a direction of the metropolitan, with which (provided it is lawful) the diocesan bishop must comply by virtue of the promises of obedience made to the archbishop at consecration and admission to office: this form of correction may result from any complaint to the metropolitan, perhaps through a metropolitical visitation.[76] Special rules enabling removal of the diocesan bishop by executive action apply in cases of mental or physical inability to discharge the functions of office. Typically, if it is certified to the primate, or in some churches to the metropolitan, by (usually two) qualified medical practitioners, psychologists or psychiatrists that a diocesan bishop is incapable of acting, or of authorizing an assistant bishop or other authority to act, then, the primate or metropolitan provides for oversight until the diocesan is competent to resume his functions.[77] A small number of churches expressly employ the terms of secular mental health law to determine incapacity.[78] In some churches process approximating to full judicial proceedings is required to determine incapacity prior to a declaration of vacancy by the metropolitan.[79] In several churches, notably those in Africa, executive removal along these same lines is also permitted in cases of 'misbehaviour',

[74] Southern Africa, Can. 14; Central Africa, Can. 13.3; West Africa, Const. Art. XI; see for a different process South India, Const. IV.13 and Kenya, Can. V.

[75] See Ch. 11.

[76] See Ch. 3 for visitations and see above for the promise.

[77] ECUSA, Cans. III.28.1; Papua New Guinea, Can. No. 1 of 1994; Melanesia, Cans. C.2: 3 doctors are required; Southern Africa, Cans. 13: the metropolitan with the consent of a majority of diocesan bishops may declare the diocese vacant; Korea, Const. Art. 18.1: vacancy occurs when the diocesan executive committee certifies to the episcopal assembly that the bishop 'is permanently unable to discharge his duties'; Scotland, Can. 7.2: the Diocesan Synod must affirm incapacity by a two-thirds majority vote; Ireland, Const. VI.30: incapacity must be 'permanent': after inquiry by the Court of General Synod, vacancy is pronounced by the archbishop; for the equivalent provisions in England, see Bishops (Retirement) Measure 1986, s. 10.

[78] E.g. New Zealand, Cans. A.6.5–9: if the diocesan standing committee has 'cause to believe' that there is incapacity, the primate must put the written opinion of 3 medical practitioners to all the bishops and if they are of the same opinion the diocese is declared vacant.

[79] Australia, Bishop (Incapacity) Canon 1995, Can. 18 1995: a member of the Diocesan Synod may report suspected incapacity to the metropolitan; if the report is contested, the metropolitan must appoint a tribunal from which appeal lies to a special appeal tribunal; before vacancy is declared, the metropolitan must consult the diocese; this canon may be adopted by Diocesan Synods.

'heresy' or persistent absence on the part of the diocesan bishop, as well as for cases of physical or mental incapacity.[80]

Finally, a rule that is employed in some churches, notably in the USA and in south America, seeks to effect termination of episcopal ministry when the bishop abandons the communion of the church. In ECUSA, a bishop does so: by an open renunciation of its doctrine, discipline or worship; by formal admission to any religious body not in communion with the church; or by exercising episcopal acts for a religious body other than the church or for another religious body not in communion with the church. In these circumstances the Presiding Bishop, with the consent of the three senior bishops of the church, must inhibit the bishop until the House of Bishops has investigated the case. If the inhibited bishop makes a 'good faith retraction' or a 'good faith denial', the inhibition may be terminated. Otherwise, the Presiding Bishop, with the consent of the House of Bishops, must terminate the bishop's ministry.[81]

OTHER EPISCOPAL OFFICES

Legal developments allowing the creation of a range of other episcopal offices have been the result of practical considerations rather than of theological principle.[82] The principal episcopal offices designed to provide assistance to the diocesan bishop are coadjutor, suffragan and auxiliary; whilst all churches operate some system of assistant bishop, not all employ these precise titles.[83] A further more recent development has been an increase in posts enabling episcopal ministry to classes of individual. Many of the principles applicable to the office of diocesan are also applicable, *mutatis mutandis*, to other episcopal offices, particularly with respect to: consecration (if they are not already in episcopal orders); declarations

[80] Sudan, Const. Art. 49; Rwanda, Draft Const. 1996, Art. 39; Burundi, Const. Art. 15; Zaire, Art. 13; Nigeria, Const. Ch. VIII.

[81] ECUSA, Cans. IV.9: termination is by deposition: see Ch. 3; see also Chile, Can. B.2(e); Spain, Can. 30.9.

[82] LC 1968, Res. 40: 'This Conference affirms its opinion that all coadjutor, suffragan and full-time assistant bishops should exercise every kind of episcopal function and have their place as bishops in the councils of the Church'; and LC 1988, Res. 46: 'This Conference resolves that each province re-examine the principle that all bishops active in full-time diocesan work be made full members, with seat, voice and vote, of all provincial, national and international gatherings of Anglican bishops'.

[83] Many churches require a diocesan bishop to appoint a commissary to discharge episcopal functions in times of illness or absence: see e.g. South East Asia, Const. Art. V: the commissary must perform 'such of the spiritual and temporal functions of the Diocesan Bishop except such as he may not be qualified to perform'; the appointment may be terminated by the bishop at any time or by the archbishop when the see becomes vacant; see also Scotland, Can. 6.7; Sudan, Const. Arts. 53–55.

accepting the doctrine, worship and discipline of the church; and termination of ministry.

Coadjutor Bishops

Most churches do not have the office of coadjutor bishop. However, the law of ECUSA may be used as the starting point to illustrate the degree of consistency between churches which do. When the diocesan bishop is unable, 'by reason of permanent mental, psychological or psychiatric condition, or by reason of the extent of diocesan work', to discharge the duties of the office, or to provide an orderly transition in the office, a bishop coadjutor may be elected for the diocese in accordance with the provisions regulating election of bishops. The coadjutor has 'the right of succession'. If the reason for appointing a coadjutor is the extent of diocesan work or transition, the consent of the General Convention (or, when not in session, of a majority of diocesan bishops and standing committees) must be obtained. Before election, the diocesan bishop must consent in writing to the appointment and the consent must state the duties to be assigned to the coadjutor. In the case of the inability of the diocesan bishop to issue the required consent, the diocesan standing committee may request the General Convention to act without the diocesan's consent; the request must be accompanied by medical certificates confirming inability. The grounds for the election must be communicated to the General Convention (or its standing committee) and to the Presiding Bishop. There may be one coadjutor only in each diocese (unless the coadjutor himself is unable to act).[84] Laws of the few other churches which possess the office are generally less detailed. All recognize, however, the coadjutor's right of succession to the diocese on vacancy.[85] Moreover, in these churches, all laws require approval of the appointment by a provincial or national assembly.[86] By way of contrast, whereas the ECUSA system focuses on appointment, laws of other churches provide expressly that the coadjutor is subject to the jurisdiction of the diocesan bishop and may perform only those functions assigned by the diocesan.[87] Laws do not generally deal with termination of the coadjutor's ministry.[88]

[84] ECUSA, Cans. III.25; see also Philippines, Cans. III.14.4.

[85] West Africa, Const. Art. VIII.1; West Indies, Can. 11.9; Burundi, Const. Art. 9; Kenya, Const. Art. XI(d); Rwanda, Draft Const. 1996, Art. 40; Brazil, Cans. III.18; Mexico, Const. IV.1.

[86] West Indies, Can. 11.4; West Africa, Const. Art. VIII.3; Burundi, Const. Art. 9: election by Diocesan Synod must be approved by the House of Bishops.

[87] Canada, Can. XVII.2: the coadjutor is 'subject to the jurisdiction of the bishop of the diocese'; Rwanda, Draft Const. 1996, Art. 40; West Indies, Can. 11.8; West Africa, Const. VIII.3(d): the coadjutor's duties may be enlarged by mutual consent.

[88] West Indies, Can. 11.14.

Suffragan Bishops

Canon law on the office of suffragan bishop in Southern Africa is particularly concise and clear.[89] First, the office itself must not be created in any diocese except with the approval of the provincial Synod of Bishops. The procedure is as follows: the diocesan bishop with the concurrence of the Diocesan Synod may apply to the Synod of Bishops and the application must specify 'the powers, authorities and duties' of the proposed office, as well as the territorial or other sphere of responsibility. On receipt of the application the Synod of Bishops must consider the pastoral needs of the diocese and it must be satisfied that adequate provision has been made for the maintenance of the suffragan. The laws of the vast majority of other churches are silent on the mode of creating the office of suffragan bishop.[90]

Secondly, in Southern Africa, the Synod of Bishops 'shall either grant or withhold its approval for the appointment of a bishop suffragan', and no vacancy in the office may be filled without the approval of the Synod of Bishops; this is effected by a fresh application by the diocesan bishop, with the consent of the Diocesan Synod, 'for authority to fill such vacancy'. The method of electing a suffragan is the same as for diocesan bishops – that is, by provincial Electoral Assembly – though the diocesan bishop has a personal right to determine which names are considered. Election is followed by confirmation by the metropolitan. The laws of most other churches require suffragans to be elected by the Diocesan Synod with the consent of the bishop and with subsequent approval by the national or provincial assembly.[91] Some laws explicitly provide that suffragans enjoy no right of succession to the diocese on vacancy.[92]

Thirdly, according to Southern African canon law, the suffragan bishop holds the commission of the diocesan bishop and his successors, and during a vacancy that of the metropolitan, for the powers, authorities and duties specified in the application to the Synod of Bishops. The suffragan bishop must reside in the diocese and minister there in conformity with

[89] Southern Africa, Cans. 8.3 and 10.

[90] England: Dioceses Measure 1978, ss. 15, 18: suffragan sees may be created only upon petition to the sovereign and with the consent of both the Diocesan Synod and General Synod; Suffragan Bishops Act 1534: the diocesan bishop may nominate two candidates by petition to the monarch who is empowered to appoint one of those named; the diocesan is under no legal duty to consult the laity of the diocese; in practice, however, the archbishop, the diocesan bishop's council, and the Diocesan Synod are consulted: *Senior Church Appointments* (1992) para. 5.1; for the functions of suffragans, who are subordinate to the diocesan bishop, see Dioceses Measure 1978, ss. 10, 11.

[91] ECUSA, Cans. III.26.1: a suffragan is elected by a Diocesan Convention with the consent of the diocesan bishop and that of the General Convention; see also Philippines, Cans. III.14.5; Mexico, Const. IV.4; Spain, Can. 31.

[92] ECUSA, Const.Art. II.4: they have a right to sit and vote in the House of Bishops of General Convention.

the constitution and canons of the church and with the terms of his commission. He is 'subject to the authority of the Diocesan Bishop in all matters of policy, doctrine and discipline'; a suffragan having any grievance concerning these against a decision of the diocesan bishop enjoys a right of appeal to the Synod of Bishops. These arrangements are really a sophisticated statement of principles operating in many churches under which the suffragan is subordinate to the diocesan, acting under his direction and control; few churches, however, employ the Southern African system of appeals in cases of disagreement between the diocesan and the suffragan.[93]

Lastly, in Southern Africa, the commission of the suffragan may be withdrawn by a new, incoming diocesan bishop (after a hearing by the Synod of Bishops); it may also be altered 'for any good cause shown to the Synod of Bishops'. The commission may be revoked by the diocesan bishop either: on the representation to the metropolitan of at least three diocesan bishops after consideration by the Synod of Bishops; or: if two-thirds of the Synod of Bishops decide that the suffragan is 'no longer able to discharge adequately [the] duties of his office'. The suffragan has a right to resign by written notice to the diocesan and with the approval of the Synod of Bishops and, in any event, must retire at the age of seventy. These arrangements find a direct parallel in outline in the laws of most churches.[94]

Assistant and Auxiliary Bishops

In Wales any diocesan bishop may, if he so desires, have an assistant bishop or bishops to assist him in the diocese. An assistant bishop has 'no right of succession to any see' and may exercise 'only such powers and functions in the diocese as shall from time to time be committed to him . . . by the Bishop . . . of the diocese by his commission'. The diocesan bishop must nominate a candidate to the archbishop for submission to the Bench of Bishops of which a majority must assent to the appointment; if the Bench is not satisfied as to the candidate's 'fitness', or the candidate does not consent, the diocesan bishop may submit another name. The

---

[93] Canada, Can. XVIII.2: the suffragan is 'subject to the jurisdiction of the bishop of the diocese'; West Africa, Const. Art. VIII.4(a); ECUSA, Cans. III.27.2: 'A Suffragan Bishop shall act as an assistant to and under the direction of the Diocesan Bishop'; for grievances, see e.g. Scotland, Can. 6.8: 'In any case where a Bishop's power to delegate is disputed by any person whose interests are injuriously affected, an appeal . . . shall lie to the Episcopal Synod'.

[94] ECUSA, Cans. III.27.3: 'The tenure of office of a Suffragan Bishop shall not be determined by the tenure of office of the Diocesan Bishop'; Const. Art. II.6: a suffragan may resign only with the consent of the House of Bishops of General Convention; see also West Indies, Can. 11.10 and 13; West Africa, Const. Art. VIII.4.

appointment of an assistant bishop does not prejudice or affect the powers inherent in the office of metropolitan or the exercise by the diocesan
bishop of powers and functions inherent in episcopal office.[95] There are
only partial parallels between the Welsh system and those operative in
other churches. It is rarely the case that the law contains a special procedure for the creation of the office of assistant bishop.[96] In several churches,
the appointment is made by the diocesan bishop with the concurrence of
the Diocesan Synod or other diocesan body with confirmation by the
national or provincial episcopal assembly.[97] As in the Welsh scheme, it is
commonly the case that the assistant bishop is commissioned or otherwise
licensed by the diocesan bishop to undertake such work and perform such
episcopal acts as may be required or permitted by the diocesan bishop.
The assistant continues in office notwithstanding a vacancy in the diocese
but has no right of succession to it.[98] In some churches, the office of auxiliary is equivalent to that of assistant.[99] In the vast majority of churches,
however, the title 'assistant bishop' is reserved to retired bishops holding
special licence of a diocesan bishop to officiate in the diocese: they have no
right of succession to the diocese on vacancy.[100]

[95] Wales, Const. VII.70–75: see D. G. James, 'The office of assistant bishop and the
canon law of the Church in Wales', LL M dissertation, University of Wales, Cardiff,
1994.

[96] Australia, Can. 4 1966: the diocesan synod may create the office; ECUSA, Cans.
III.27: when a diocese, in the opinion of the diocesan bishop, requires additional episcopal services, the bishop may with the consent of the diocesan standing committee
request the Diocesan Convention to approve the creation of the 'position' of assistant
bishop.

[97] Papua New Guinea, Const. Art. 15: the same procedure as for election of diocesans applies but the diocesan bishop has a right of veto; Tanzania, Const, IV.12(b): the
diocesan bishop nominates a candidate (already in episcopal orders) to the standing
council of the diocese which then votes; if the candidate is not in episcopal orders, the
diocesan nominates to the standing council and its decision along with the opinion of
the bishop must be submitted to the archbishop for approval by the House of Bishops;
Rwanda, Draft Const. 1996, Art. 40: the approval of the Diocesan Synod is subject to
confirmation by the House of Bishops; Australia, Can. 4 1966: the bishop must notify
the primate of the intention to appoint and inform him of the stipend provided; no
appointment may be made until the metropolitans of the church are satisfied that a sufficient stipend has been arranged; see also ECUSA, Cans. III.27.

[98] Papua New Guinea, Const. Art. 15: the licence of the assistant does not automatically lapse on vacancy; Tanzania, Const. IV.12(b): assistant bishops have no right of
succession; Melanesia, Const. Arts. 14, 15, Cans. C.4.B; Canada, Can. XVIII.2: the assistant bishop is 'subject to the jurisdiction of the bishop of the diocese'; see also Sudan,
Const. Art. 50; South East Asia, Const. Art. V(d); Korea, Const. Art. 19: North India,
Const. I.I.VIII.8; Zaire, Const. Art. 15.

[99] Indian Ocean, Const. Art. 14.

[100] Southern Africa, Can. 10.18; Central Africa, Can. 11.12.

Non-Territorial Episcopal Ministry

Whilst traditionally episcopal office is fundamentally a territorial jurisdiction,[101] a relatively recent development in Anglican jurisprudence is the concept of episcopal ministry to classes of individuals. In England, the so-called 'flying bishops' provide episcopal ministry to those opposed to the ordination of women as priests; it is a subject governed by ecclesiastical quasi-legislation and not by canon law. Having passed the necessary statutory resolution, a parish opposed to the ministry of women priests may petition the diocesan bishop for the execution of episcopal functions in the parish to be carried out in accordance with arrangements for 'alternative episcopal oversight'. This operates at three levels: diocesan, regional and provincial. Regions comprising two or more dioceses are designated by the appropriate archbishop as areas in which the diocesan bishops, acting together, may nominate one or more opposing bishops to carry out for the parish such episcopal oversight as the diocesan bishop requests. Provincially, the archbishop may appoint additional suffragans to act as 'provincial episcopal visitors'; these carry out in any parish such episcopal duties as the diocesan bishop may request. Due to the general principle that no bishop may exercise ministry in another bishop's diocese without the latter's consent, the entitlements of bishops exercising alternative episcopal oversight derive solely from the authority of the diocesan bishop. When there is a vacancy in these various offices, prior to appointment the archbishop should consult the other episcopal visitor (or visitors) and all other bishops directly concerned.[102] Given the rarity of such arrangements, it is not possible to construct a series of principles of Anglican canon law on this subject.

A well-established episcopal ministry in many churches is that to the armed forces and a recent Australian canon provides perhaps the fullest statement of formal law on this subject in the Anglican Communion. The bishop to the defence force is appointed by the primate, after consultation with the metropolitans of the church and the principal chaplain of each branch of the forces. The bishop acts as an assistant to the primate to whom he is responsible for 'the episcopal oversight of the chaplains' to the armed forces and for 'the ministrations of the church among men and women of the [armed forces] and their families'. Office is held at the discretion of the primate and expires on resignation or the attainment of the

---

[101] For missionary bishops, see e.g. ECUSA, Cans. III.23; Southern Africa, Can. 6: missionary bishops are chosen by the bishops of the province subject to satisfaction that adequate provision can be made for their maintenance; their confirmation and consecration is the same as that for diocesans; as long as they retain the appointment, missionary bishops are usually entitled to all the rights of a diocesan bishop.

[102] England, Act of Synod 1992; a similar system operates in Wales.

age of sixty years. Specific functions include: advice to the primate as to candidates under consideration for appointment as chaplains in the armed forces; the licensing of chaplains; and the duty to inform the appropriate diocesan bishop of the appointment so that the chaplain may present himself to the diocesan 'in order that the bishop may endorse that licence'. Chaplains are 'under the jurisdiction of the Primate and the Bishop to the Defence Force'. The bishop is assisted by the defence force board which must provide resources to enable effective episcopal ministry: in particular the board must consult with the bishop concerning ordinations, promotion of the pastoral and evangelistic work of chaplains, and on the needs and conditions of service.[103]

EPISCOPAL COLLEGIALITY

The theological principle that a collegiality attaches to bishops collectively,[104] that by virtue of their historic and apostolic ministry they share a collective responsibility for leadership in the particular church,[105] is often deployed juridically in institutional terms. The underlying concept, presented in the context of the ministry of the whole church, is nowhere better expressed than in the constitution of the church in North India: 'The pastoral oversight of a diocesan bishop must go hand in hand with this corporate responsibility, shared by bishops, presbyters, deacons and lay people acting together, as well as the corporate responsibility of the episcopate of the Church as a whole'.[106] The laws of all churches assign this responsibility for collective action to national or provincial episcopal assemblies, each institution variously styled as the College of Bishops, the Synod of Bishops, the Council of Bishops or, when it also constitutes a chamber of the central church legislature, the House of Bishops. As a matter of ecclesiastical practice, the membership of these bodies consists either of primates, metropolitans and diocesan bishops,[107] or of these together with suffragan and coadjutor bishops, and assistant bishops equivalent to suffragans.[108] Outside these classes of bishops in active ministry to which

---

[103] Australia, Defence Force Ministry Canon 1985, Can. 19 of 1985.

[104] S. W. Sykes, 'Episcopacy, communion and collegiality', in J. Draper (ed.), *Communion and Episcopacy: Essays to Mark the Centenery of the Chicago-Lambeth Quadrilateral* (Oxford, 1988), 35.

[105] LC 1968, Res. 55; LC 1978, Res. 13; and LC 1988, Res. 8.

[106] North India, Const. I.II.2.

[107] Wales, Const. VIII.1: 'the phrase Bench of Bishops means the Archbishop and the Diocesan Bishops'; Scotland, Can. 51.1; South East Asia, Const. Art. VII(b); Melanesia, Const. Art. 10; Indian Ocean, Const. Art. 7; Zaire, Const. Art. 6; Tanzania, Const. IV.15; see generally, on the House of Bishops, Ch. 2.

[108] See e.g. Burundi, Const. Art. 6: coadjutant bishops are members but have no vote; Japan, Can. VI: suffragans are members of the House of Bishops but have no vote; New

jurisdiction attaches, assistant bishops bearing that title after retirement usually enjoy membershp but not voting rights.[109]

Normally the episcopal assembly meets once a year, but the president, the primate or the metropolitan, as the case may be, may call a special meeting at a fixed time and place with the concurrence of a majority of the diocesan bishops.[110] In some churches the law expressly provides that a meeting of the assembly may also be called on receipt by its president of a written requisition from a majority of the other diocesan bishops; if the president fails to do so within a fixed period after receiving the requisition, a majority of the diocesan bishops may convene the assembly.[111] Prior to its meeting, several churches require the publication (for the information of the church generally) of a statement of the date and venue, and the reason(s) for the meeting.[112] The norm is that no business is to be transacted unless a majority of diocesan bishops are present. For the purposes of decision-making, laws may require unanimity, special majorities or simple majorities depending on the subject for decision.[113] Some laws require meetings to be open to the public, under such regulation as the assembly may adopt, but it is usually empowered to exclude the public during the whole or any part of its proceedings: occasionally the law prescribes that decisions must be announced subsequently in public.[114]

As is seen in this and other chapters in this volume, central episcopal assemblies have a determinative, decision-making power over a very wide range of subjects. Their functions may be summed up as legislative, executive and judicial or quasi-judicial. Commonly laws assign to the episcopal assembly an independent rule-making function, occasionally in the

Zealand, Cans. B.I.1.5: resigned bishops may attend the Order of Bishops but have no vote.

[109] ECUSA, Const. Art. I.2–4 and Philippines, Const. Art. V.1; Melanesia, Const. Art. 7 and Cans. D.2; Uganda, Const. Art. 5: one or two retired bishops must be members.

[110] Papua New Guinea, Can. No. 1 of 1978; Korea, Const. Art. 55: it must meet twice a year; see also Southern Africa, Can. 28; Scotland, Can. 51.2: this requires an annual meeting.

[111] See e.g. Scotland, Can. 51.4: 'The Primus shall call a meeting of the Episcopal Synod on receiving a written requisition to do so from a majority of the other Diocesan Bishops . . . If the Primus fails to call such Synod within two months after receiving such requisition, a majority of the other Bishops may call such Synod and meet and act without the Primus, due notice being given by them to the Primus and to the other Bishops of the time and place of said Synod'.

[112] Scotland, Can. 51.5: 'Before the holding of any Episcopal Synod the Primus shall publish for the information of the Church generally a statement of the time, place and purpose of such Synod'; compare Southern Africa, Can. 28.1: notice only to the bishops.

[113] Melanesia, Const. Art. 10: in the Council of Bishops, they must 'act unanimously in all things and only when they are in agreement shall their acts, deliberations or directions be valid'; Southern Africa, Can. 28.2: 'The business of the Synod shall be determined by the Metropolitan'.

[114] See e.g. Scotland, Can. 51.8.

form of law properly so-called, but more often in the shape of directions or other species of ecclesiastical quasi-legislation.[115] Their administrative functions include: confirmation of the election of bishops and consent to the establishment of ecclesiastical units, notably the formation of dioceses.[116] In a small number of churches the assembly is the designated body to receive and finally determine all appeals allowed under canon law,[117] and in most it is involved in the election of members to courts for the disciplining of bishops.[118] The assembly is particularly involved in the doctrinal and liturgical life of the church: often to it is reserved the right of initiating doctrinal or liturgical development in the church,[119] and commonly, especially in the African churches, it is empowered to determine disputed doctrinal and theological questions.[120] In some churches the assembly has a special power to issue pastoral letters which must then be read by clergy in their congregations.[121]

CONCLUSIONS

Historically the episcopate discharges a fundamental ministry in all Anglican churches which commonly confirm in their laws a full commitment to its continuance and centrality in the life and government of the church. Primatial office is principally a focus for unity and leadership – it is not, as a general principle, superior to that of the metropolitan, the chief episcopal office in an ecclesiastical province. Metropolitical jurisdiction or

[115] See Ch. 1; for rule-making by the Scottish Episcopal Synod, see A. C. McGavin, 'The distribution of legislative power within the Scottish Episcopal Church', LL M dissertation, University of Wales, Cardiff, 1997.

[116] For the re-ordering of dioceses, see e.g. Indian Ocean, Const. Art. 8; Southern Africa, Can. 21; ECUSA, Const. Art. VI.1: the House of Bishops may establish mission areas; see generally Ch. 2.

[117] See e.g. Scotland, Can. 51.11: 'The Episcopal Synod shall receive and finally determine all appeals allowed in these Canons, except such as may be brought before and decided by the Primus'.

[118] See above and e.g. Wales, Const. VIII.32: this deals with the Bench of Bishops' involvement in the removal of the archbishop, bishops and ecclesiastical judges; ECUSA, Cans. IV.3.15: it must elect the Court for the Trial of a Bishop; Tanzania, Const. IV.15; see generally Ch. 3.

[119] See Chs. 7 and 8.

[120] Tanzania, Const. IV.15; Papua New Guinea, Const. Art. 8.A; Philippines, Const. Art. V.1: the Council of Bishops must deliberate on matters of doctrine, discipline and worship; Korea, Const. Art. 56: one function of the Bishops' Conference is the '[d]iscussion of inter-diocesan cooperation and evangelism'.

[121] ECUSA, Cans. III.14.2(g): the House of Bishops may issue pastoral letters which must be read by clergy in their congregations; ibid. III.14.2(h): it may also 'adopt a Position Paper'; Philippines, Const. Art. V.1: it may issue pastoral letters or Statements, on matters of concern to the whole church; see also Spain, Const. V and Mexico, Const. II.(d) and V.6.

authority is expressed legally in a number of key functions which archbishops discharge in relation to the province; it consists of general oversight particularly of the inferior episcopal offices. As a matter of ecclesiastical practice, the elective principle is applied in all churches with respect to the appointment of diocesan bishops. Legal unity in the Anglican Communion is clearly evidenced in the coincidence between laws of churches which reserve to the diocesan bishop a controlling jurisdictional oversight as to the governing, teaching and liturgical life of the diocese. Termination of ministry is regulated in most churches by elaborate provisions enabling retirement, voluntary resignation and, in extreme cases, removal, which is exercisable only by the other bishops of the province or national church. Most churches do not employ the office of coadjutor bishop, who enjoys rights of succession to a diocese on vacancy. Normally, suffragan bishops exercise ministry to aid the diocesan bishop, and it is a ministry of subordination reliant wholly on a grant of authority by the diocesan bishop. The concept of non-territorial episcopal office is increasingly making its mark in the regulatory instruments of churches. Most churches assign, under the doctrine of collegiality, a corporate function to synods of bishops, but the subject-matter jurisdictions of these assemblies vary from church to church.

5

The Ministry of Priests and Deacons

The ordained ministries of priests (or presbyters) and deacons completes the historic threefold ministry, which these share with the episcopate, inherited by all churches in the Anglican Communion and to which the laws of the vast majority pledge continuing commitment.[1] Whilst theologically ordained ministers are treated as called by God to serve the church and the community at large, churches regulate the manner of fulfilling that service by means of law. Rules governing the rights and duties of priests and deacons are scattered throughout laws dealing with discrete subjects, but as a matter of ecclesiastical practice churches deal with the core ministry of priests and deacons under separate titles in their canons. Four bodies of law are associated with their canonical ministry; these regulate: the process of ordination; appointments to the multiplicity of ecclesiastical offices open to ordained persons; the functions of priests and deacons, classed variously in law as responsibilities, privileges, rights and obligations; clerical discipline, rooted in the doctrine of canonical obedience; and termination of ministry. It is the last subject, particularly, that has generated litigation in the secular courts of states in which Anglican churches exist.

ADMISSION TO HOLY ORDERS: ORDINATION

It is a general principle of Anglican canon law that a person may be recognized as a priest and deacon only upon vocation, trial, examination and admission to holy orders in accordance with a church's rite of ordination.[2]

---

[1] See e.g. England, Can. C1(1): 'The Church of England holds and teaches that from the Apostles' time there have been these orders in Christ's Church: bishops, priests and deacons'; for an almost identical formula see New Zealand, Cans. G.XIII.1.1; Wales, BCP 1984, v: 'From New Testament times and through the first two centuries the Christian Church developed a clear pattern of three orders of Ministers. It is the intention and purpose of the Church in Wales to maintain and continue these three orders'; Melanesia, Cans. A.7; New Zealand, *Prayer Book* 1989, 887; compare North India, Const. I.I.VIII: 'The ministry is committed to the Church as a function of the whole Body of Christ, and, therefore, while it is especially exercised by the ordained ministry it is thus exercised as a function of the Body as a whole, and does not belong to the ordained ministry exclusively or in separation from the Body'.

[2] The 'order' of deaconess is normally treated as an 'order of ministry' but not as a holy order: England, Can. D1(1); Scotland, Can. 21.1; Australia, Can. 7 1969, Can. 18 1985; Canada, Can. XIII; West Indies, Can. 19.

The rule in English canon law that no person shall be accounted to be a lawful priest or deacon 'except he be called, tried, examined and admitted thereunto according to the Ordinal', or any other authorized rite of the church,[3] is found in the laws of a great number of churches.[4] But the English rule that the diocesan bishop has a canonical duty to provide, 'as much as in him lies', sufficient priests to minister the Word and the sacraments, surfaces in the laws of a very small number of churches;[5] equivalent arrangements are sometimes expressed as a duty on bishops to foster vocations to the ordained ministry.[6] Very few churches express as an overriding principle governing the process of ordination the provision appearing in the canon law of ECUSA: 'No one shall be denied access to the selection process for ordination in this Church because of race, color, ethnic origin, sex, national origin, marital status, sexual orientation, disabilities or age, except as otherwise specified . . . No right to ordination is hereby established'.[7]

Eligibility and Suitability

A uniform legal practice throughout the Anglican Communion is to reserve to the bishop the final determination of the suitability of candidates for ordained ministry. Yet the bishop does not have an absolute discretion as to whom he may ordain. Laws permit the ordination of defined classes of persons and forbid ordination if the individual does not satisfy the legally prescribed conditions of eligibility. Bars to ordination are framed as disqualifications: these are based on ecclesiastical status, spiritual and moral suitability, age, and mental or physical fitness. The ancient distinction between irregularities and impediments has largely

---

[3] England, Can. C1(1); see also Canons Ecclesiastical 1603, Cans. 31, 32, 34, 35.

[4] For an almost identical provision, see New Zealand, Cans. G.XIII.1.1; Tanzania, Const. III.7: no person is to be regarded a 'true' priest or deacon unless 'called, tried, tested, and ordained'; Wales, BCP 1984, v-vi: 'No person shall be authorized to execute the office of . . . priest or deacon in this Church unless evidence can be produced of ordination with the laying-on of hands by bishops who are themselves duly qualified and authorized to confer Holy Orders'; ECUSA, Const. Art. VII and Cans. III.9: no person is to be ordained unless 'examined' by the bishop and two priests.

[5] England, Can. C18(6); New Zealand, *Prayer Book* 1989, 887: 'The provision of an ordained ministry, to serve the local congregation in the name of Christ and the universal Church is one of the responsibilities of the apostolic Church'.

[6] E.g. ECUSA, Cans. III.4.1.

[7] ECUSA, Cans. III.4.1; Papua New Guinea, Diocese of Port Moresby, Can. 24: 'Ordination is at the sole discretion of the Diocesan Bishop'; England: *R v Archbishop of Dublin* (1833) Alc & N 244: this is commonly understood to confer an 'absolute' discretion on the bishop; in view of the numerous prohibitions imposed upon bishops against ordination in prescribed circumstances, the concept of 'absolute discretion' cannot, it would seem, be sustained in Anglican jurisprudence.

disappeared.[8] At the same time, however, surprisingly few formal laws spell out the criteria necessary for valid ordination, nor do they usually describe the legal consequences which may flow from the ordination of disqualified persons,[9] though occasionally laws allow dispensation from some disqualifications in order to enable ordination.

First, it is generally accepted that baptism and confirmation are necessary qualifications for candidature. Legal differences between churches are simply of form rather than substance. In some churches lack of baptism and confirmation operates as a bar, forbidding the bishop to proceed; in others rules simply require the bishop to be satisfied that the candidate has been baptized and confirmed. For instance, according to English canon law, every bishop must take care that he admit no person into holy orders 'but such as he knows either by himself, or by sufficient testimony, to have been baptised and confirmed'; similarly, in Irish canon law: '[a] bishop shall not admit any person into holy orders unless . . . he has been baptized and confirmed'.[10] Secondly, the bishop must be satisfied about the candidate's spiritual and moral qualities, but laws diverge as to requirements concerning the candidate's basic understanding of the faith and practices of the church. In England, the bishop may not ordain unless satisfied that the candidate is 'sufficiently instructed in holy Scripture and in the doctrine, discipline, and worship' of the church and is 'of virtuous conversation and good repute and . . . a wholesome example and pattern to the flock of Christ'.[11] Formulae equivalent to these are repeated in the laws of a number of churches,[12] though occasionally laws require the candidate to be able to render an account of the church's doctrine.[13] Thirdly, it is a uniform practice for laws to prescribe a particular age for ordination: the vast majority of churches require that candidates for the diaconate must be at least twenty-three years of age and for the priesthood at least

[8] For the use of 'irregularities' and 'impediments' see e.g. R. Phillimore, *Ecclesiastical Law* (London, 1895) I, 93f; as is seen in the following discussion, in some churches today the term 'impediment' is occasionally used: see e.g. England, Can. C4(3A) and Wales, Can. of 1961: 'irregularity of birth' is not a 'canonical impediment'.

[9] See, however, Ireland, Const. IX.24: if 'any bishop shall admit any person to holy orders who is not qualified', the archbishop may suspend the bishop (with the concurrence of one other bishop) from ordaining for up to two years; the decision is subject to a right of appeal to the Court of General Synod.

[10] England, Can. C4(1); Ireland, Const. IX.21; see also Scotland, Can. 11.2; West Indies, Can. 17.6; Australia, Diocese of Sydney, *The 7th Handbook*, 8.17.

[11] England, Can. C4(1).

[12] Scotland, Can. 11.3 and West Indies, Can. 17.6: the candidate must be of 'good life and conversation'; ECUSA, Cans. III.4.2(a): the candidate must be 'a confirmed adult communicant in good standing'; ibid. Cans. III.7: if there is no objection on moral, doctrinal, or spiritual grounds, the bishop may take order for ordination.

[13] Ireland, Const. IX.21: this prescribes that no person may be admitted unless 'he is able to yield an account of his faith according to the Articles of Religion received by the Church, and to confirm the same by sufficient testimonies out of the holy scriptures'.

twenty-four.[14] In a very small number of churches the law expressly confers a power on the archbishop to dispense with these requirements.[15] Recent developments enabling the ordination of women as priests find juridic expression in a number of ways: in some churches there is a large body of law regulating the subject,[16] in others the development has been effected by minimal alteration to the law.[17]

Fourthly, a standard requirement is that the bishop must be satisfied about the physical and mental condition and fitness of the candidate. In some laws the requirement is presented explicitly as a bar. In English canon law the diocesan bishop must not ordain a person who is suffering or has suffered from any physical or mental infirmity which will prevent the ministering of the Word and sacraments or the performance of other ministerial duties. It is the 'opinion of the bishop' which is the determining factor.[18] This approach appears in the laws of several churches.[19] A fifth, rare requirement concerns the marital status of the candidate: this does not appear in the modern formal law of the vast majority of

---

[14] Scotland, Can. 11.5; New Zealand, Cans. G.XIII.3.2; Philippines, Cans. III.11; Korea, Const. Art. 108; North India, Const. I.I.VIII.12; West Africa, Can. XI; compare ECUSA, Cans. III.6 and Japan, Can. II, Art. 15: a person cannot be ordained deacon unless at least 21 years of age and priest until 24; Melanesia, Cans. A.7: deacons must be over 22 and priests over 23; Portugal, Can. VIII, Art. 2: the ages are 24 and 25 respectively.

[15] England, Can. C3(5),(6): in both cases the Archbishop of Canterbury may by faculty dispense with these requirements; see also Southern Africa, Can. 18; West Indies, Can. 17.9; compare Ireland, Const. IX.21: the age requirement may be dispensed with by archiepiscopal faculty only in relation to deacons.

[16] See e.g. England, Priests (Ordination of Women) Measure 1993, Can. C4A: 'A woman may be ordained to the office of priest if she otherwise satisfies the requirements of Canon C4 as to the persons who may be ordained as priests'; the subject is also governed by Act of Synod (1994) and a Code of Practice (1994).

[17] Ireland, Const. IX.22: 'Men and women alike may be ordained to the holy orders' of priest [and] of deacon 'without any distinction or discrimination on grounds of sex, and men and women so ordained shall alike be referred to and known as deacons [or] priests'; ECUSA, Cans. III.8.1; Scotland, Can. 57.6: 'In the Canons and the Ordinals any reference to Deacons or to Presbyters or Priests shall be deemed to include both male and female'; West Indies, Can. 17.1; Southern Africa, Const. Art. XXIV.5: 'Clergy' means 'all persons, male or female, in Holy Orders'; Philippines, Cans. II.8; for other Anglican churches, see N. Doe, 'L'ordination des femmes dans les Eglises anglicanes du Royaume Uni', *Revue de Droit Canonique*, 46 (1996), 59; W. J. Hemmerick, 'The ordination of women – the Canadian experience', *Ecclesiastical Law Journal*, 2(8) (1990–92), 177.

[18] England, Can. C4(2); it has been decided by the secular courts that blindness is not an impediment: *Kensit v Dean and Chapter of St Paul's* [1905] 2 KB 249 at 257.

[19] ECUSA, Cans. III.7: if there is no objection on medical or psychological grounds, the bishop may proceed; Philippines, Cans. III.11; Scotland, Can. 11.3: the bishop must be satisfied of the physical and mental fitness of the candidate; see also West Indies, Can. 17.6; West Africa, Can. XI.5: 'Before the ordination of a Priest, the Bishop shall require the applicant to submit to a thorough examination, covering both mental and physical condition by licensed professionals selected by the Bishop'.

churches.[20] Under English canon law 'no person shall be admitted into holy orders who has re-married and, the other party to that marriage being alive, has a former spouse still living'; nor may a person be admitted who is married to a person who has been previously married and whose former spouse is still living. On an application made by the diocesan bishop, the provincial archbishop may grant a faculty to remove this impediment. According to archiepiscopal directives, the diocesan bishop must interview the applicant, present spouse and two referees (one of whom should be aware of the circumstances surrounding the breakdown of the previous marriage) and make enquiries, if possible, of the former spouse; the case must also be discussed with the incumbent of the parish in which the applicant usually worships. After interview and enquiry the diocesan bishop must decide whether or not to apply to the metropolitan for a faculty: the applicant must be informed but there is no duty to give reasons in the case of a refusal. In deciding whether or not to grant a faculty, the archbishop may make additional enquiries and communicate the decision in writing to the diocesan bishop who must in turn inform the applicant.[21] The canon law of no church expressly lists a person's engagement in sexually active homophile relationships as a bar to ordination.[22] Finally, progression from the diaconate to the priesthood is not automatic: in those churches having legislation on the subject the normal rule is that a deacon may not be ordained priest for at least one year, unless the bishop has good cause to ordain earlier 'so that trial may be made of his behaviour in the office of deacon'; and in some churches, before the bishop proceeds, the consent of the standing committee of the Diocesan Synod is required.[23]

[20] R. Phillimore, *Ecclesiastical Law* (London, 1895), 94: 'by several constitutions of Edmund, archbishop, the following impediments . . . are declared to be causes of suspension from orders received, and consequently . . . if known beforehand, against being ordained at all . . . bigamists'.

[21] England, Can. C4(3 and 3A); Directions (1991): this was considered in 1964 as the introduction of a 'new impediment' created under the Clergy (Ordination and Miscellaneous Provisions) Measure 1964, s. 9 (see e.g. Ecclesiastical Committee of Both Houses of Parliament 114th Report (HL 113, HC 200)); in Wales a policy operates under which both divorce and civil remarriage are treated as impediments. A person born out of lawful wedlock is not impeded: England, Can. C4(4); Wales, Can of 1961.

[22] ECUSA, *Stanton (Bishop of Dallas) v Righter* (1996): the Court for the Trial of a Bishop considered that there was no canonical bar to a bishop ordaining homosexuals; England, *Issues in Human Sexuality*, A Statement by the House of Bishops (1991): with respect to those in a sexually active homophile relationship, a pattern of life which the church does not commend, '[o]rdinarily it should be left to the candidates' own conscience to act responsibly', though in the process of selection it would not be right 'to interrogate on their sexual lives, unless there are strong reasons for doing so'.

[23] England, Can. C3(8); ECUSA, Cans. III.7: a person cannot be ordained priest within one year from admission as a deacon unless the bishop for 'urgent reason' agrees to do so with the consent of the diocesan standing committee; see also Japan, Can. II, Art. 15; New Zealand, Cans. G.XIII.3.4: 'good cause' must be established; Scotland,

Vocation, Examination and Training

In several churches, the process leading to ordination begins with an interview between the candidate and that person's own minister who then submits a report to the diocesan bishop or a diocesan official designated by the bishop. Rules operating in ECUSA are particularly well-developed. Those wishing to be admitted as 'postulants', a stage prior to admission to candidature, must in the first instance consult with the member of clergy in charge of the applicant's congregation; the cleric must make 'a careful inquiry' in consultation with the other leaders of the congregation into 'the physical, intellectual, moral, emotional, and spiritual qualifications' of the persons. The cleric then submits a report to the bishop who, if unable to accept postulancy, may give written consent to the person applying to another diocesan bishop.[24] This initial process is employed in the law,[25] or quasi-legislation,[26] of a number of other churches.

The second part of the process is discernment of vocation by a diocesan or provincial body and examination by the bishop or his appointees. The selection process with which these bodies are concerned results in a recommendation to the bishop, a recommendation which the bishop is free to accept or reject as a matter of discretion.[27] Indeed, in several churches

Can. 11.4: candidates must also furnish evidence of 'their continuing studies, their spiritual development, and growth in the exercise of the ministries entrusted to them'; West Africa, Can. XI.2; Canada, BCP 1962, 644: the bishop must determine whether the deacon has been 'faithful and diligent'.

[24] ECUSA, Cans. III.4; see also Mexico, Cans. II.19; Brazil, Cans. III.3: the candidate must 'justify the reasons for candidature to the local minister'.

[25] Philippines, Cans. III.5; see also Japan, Can. II, Art. 17; Papua New Guinea, Diocese of Port Moresby, Can. 24; North India, Const. IV: 'Any person desirous of offering himself/herself as a candidate for the ordained ministry shall apply to the Bishop of the Diocese in writing through the Presbyter-in-Charge of his/her Pastorate'; the Pastorate Committee must interview the candidate to ascertain 'suitability'; see also Australia, Diocese of Sydney, *The 7th Handbook*, 8.16: 'A prospective candidate for the ministry . . . should first confer with his or her own minister then apply in writing to the Archbishop, who will arrange for an interview with his Ordination Chaplains'; see also Melanesia, Cans. A.7.

[26] England: see e.g. Diocese of Lichfield, *Handbook of Information* (1991) II.1; Diocese of Peterborough, *Diocesan Regulations* (1992–3), I.9: the incumbent must establish whether vocation is 'sufficiently formed'.

[27] ECUSA, Cans. III.4: the postulant has a conference with the bishop who, if he wishes to proceed, reports to the Diocesan Commission on Ministry which, 'with proper regard for confidentiality', then reports back to the bishop with its evaluation of the candidate and reasons for that evaluation. The bishop, if satisfied, then admits the person as a postulant and arranges for training in, *inter alia*, theology, practical experience, emotional development and spiritual formation. The postulant may then apply for candidacy for holy orders (provided six months have elapsed since admission as a postulant and there has been a period of eighteen months of satisfactory study); the bishop may at his discretion remove a candidate from the register of postulants with

these provincial, national or diocesan institutions are employed generally for the purposes of recruitment and the fostering of vocations to the ordained ministry.[28] With respect to episcopal examination, elements of English canon law find a direct parallel in the laws of most churches. The basic English rule is that '[n]o bishop shall admit any person into holy orders, except such person on careful and diligent examination'; the bishop must have 'called to his assistance the archdeacons and other ministers appointed for this purpose'.[29] As to the subject matter of instruction the English canons are rather general: the candidate must possess 'sufficient knowledge of holy Scripture and of the doctrine, discipline, and worship' of the church, as presented in the Thirty-Nine Articles, the Book of Common Prayer and the Ordinal.[30] In contrast, the canon law of several churches specifies that candidates must be instructed in listed subjects: typically, scripture, theology, church history, ministry and worship.[31] In several churches laws assign the responsibility of fixing qualifications to designated bodies,[32] from which occasionally the bishop is able to dis-

written reasons given personally: Cans. III.5 and 6; for the same system see Philippines, Cans. III.5; for almost the same arrangement see West Africa, Can. VIII; Melanesia, Diocese of Temotu, Can. 14: examination is by a Diocesan Selection Board consisting of the bishop, the senior priest of the diocese and two others; and Puerto Rico, Cans. III.4.

[28] ECUSA, Cans. III.2.2: the Diocesan Commission on Ministry has a cluster of responsibilities: to assist the bishop in recruiting and selecting persons for holy orders; to solicit nominations from clergy and laity in the parishes, colleges and universities; to invite individuals to have their vocations discerned and to submit nominations to the bishop; it must submit a report on the person's fitness and readiness for ordained ministry; see Mexico, Cans. III.17; Puerto Rico, Cans. I.14; Philippines, Cans. III.5; Australia, General Synod Commissions Cans. 1969–92: 14.H-J: a commission exists 'to identify and assist in the preservation of the essential character of the Church's ministry as it has been revealed in Holy Scripture and experienced in Christian history'; it must: keep abreast of new understandings and trends in ministry; monitor experiments and dispense information to dioceses and parishes; help establish and maintain the standards required for ministry training; and collaborate with colleges, dioceses and national bodies engaged in training persons for ordained ministry 'so that they may evaluate their work regularly against the established standards'; and study developments in training in Australia and overseas.

[29] England, Can. C7; Ireland, Const. IX.23; New Zealand, Cans. G.XIII.5.

[30] England, Can. C7; New Zealand, Cans. G.XIII.5.

[31] ECUSA, Cans. III.6: the candidate must be examined in holy scripture, church history, Christian theology, liturgics and the theory and practice of ministry; there is a general ordination examination conducted by the General Board of Examining Chaplains; Melanesia, Cans. A.7: the candidate must be examined for admission to theological college; compare Philippines, Cans. III.9: this adds studies in the ecumenical movement, contemporary society (including racial and minority groups) and church music; West Indies, Cans. 16.17: holy scripture, doctrine, church history, liturgy and worship. see also Japan, Can. II, Art. 18 and Korea, Const. Art. 108: the National Priests and Deacons' Examination; North India, Const. IV.

[32] England, Can. C7: candidates for the diaconate must also fulfil 'the requirements as to learning and other qualities which, subject to any directions given by the General Synod, the bishop deems necessary for the office of deacon'.

pense,[33] and sometimes they require prescribed secular educational qualifications.[34]

Thirdly, before proceeding to the service of ordination, the candidate must submit to the diocesan bishop various documents: a birth certificate and testimonials.[35] It is commonly the case that the candidate must also provide a certificate that ecclesiastical office within the diocese is provided, from which ministry may be carried out; often the law presents failure to exhibit such evidence as a bar to ordination.[36] It is generally accepted that if the candidate comes from another diocese, letters dimissory must be exhibited to the ordaining bishop from the bishop of the other diocese.[37] Some churches require before ordination an announcement, in a congregation in which the candidate is known, of the forthcoming ordination in order to receive evidence of support as well as an opportunity for people to make allegations that the candidate is impeded from ordination.[38] Prior to and at ordination, the candidate is obliged to make various undertakings, in the form of declarations, oaths or promises:

[33] Scotland, Can. 11.1: candidates 'must have obtained such qualifications as the College of Bishops may prescribe'; the bishop may dispense with these as 'the sole judge of the propriety of granting such dispensation'; see also Ireland, Const. IX.23: further examination may be required at the discretion of the bishop.

[34] Southern Africa, Act of Provincial Synod, VI: the 'normal qualification for Ordination' is a BA of a recognized university or its equivalent; Ireland, Const. IX.21: the candidate must hold a degree and have attended a course of training approved by the House of Bishops; see also New Zealand, GS Standing Resolutions 1986: the candidate must have competence in the Maori language.

[35] England, Can. C6; ECUSA, Cans. III.9; Scotland, Can. 11.3; New Zealand, Cans. G.XIII.4.1; Australia, Diocese of Sydney, *The 7th Handbook*, 8.17; Philippines, Cans. III.11; West Indies, Can. 17.8; Chile, Cans. B.46.

[36] England, Can. C5(1): there must be an office 'wherein he may attend the cure of souls and execute his ministry'; Ireland, Const. IX.20: the candidate must exhibit 'a certificate that he holds a nomination to some curacy or ecclesiastical preferment then vacant or shortly to become vacant in that diocese, or to some church therein where he may attend the cure of souls and execute his ministry'; Australia, Diocese of Sydney, *The 7th Handbook*, 8.17: 'Nomination to a curacy'; ECUSA, Cans. III.6: no one may be ordained by the bishop without the recommendation of the diocesan standing committee; New Zealand, Cans. G.XIII.3.5: no bishop shall ordain 'unless satisfied such person shall be licensed to an office under the Canons'; Scotland, Can. 11.6: a title must be secured 'setting forth that person's proposed sphere of duty'; West Indies, Can. 17.10: 'a distinct sphere of work in his Diocese' must be available; West Africa, Can. XI.3: the person must have been 'appointed to serve in some Parochial Cure within the Diocese'.

[37] England, Can. C5(4): 'No person shall be admitted into holy orders by any bishop other than the bishop of the diocese in which he is to exercise his ministry, except he shall bring with him Letters Dimissory from the bishop of such diocese'; Ireland, Const. IX.19: 'No bishop shall admit into holy orders any person coming from outside his diocese, unless that person brings letters dimissory from the bishop from whose diocese he comes'; New Zealand, Cans. G.XIII.3.5,6; West Indies, Can. 17.11.

[38] Scotland, Can. 11.3: this requires 'just cause' to be shown; see also resolution 1; New Zealand, Cans. G.XIII.4.3: a certificate must be sent to the bishop; West Indies, Can. 17.7: the form is commonly called '*Si Quis*'.

assent to the doctrine of the church; to use only the lawful services of the church; obedience to the bishop; and compliance with the laws of the church.[39]

The Ordination Service

Ordination must take place in accordance with the Ordinal or with the church's forms of service for ordination.[40] It is usual for either laws or liturgical books to prescribe that the service of ordination must take place on prescribed days or on a day which the diocesan bishop on urgent occasion shall appoint.[41] The venue is also commonly prescribed, either in the cathedral of the diocese or in another church or chapel at the discretion of the bishop; however, the English rule that the candidate must be presented by an archdeacon or his deputy is not common.[42] Whilst the law of many churches echoes the rule of English canon law that no person shall be ordained both priest and deacon on one and the same day, the English provision that this may be permitted by archiepiscopal faculty does not usually appear formally.[43] It is a general principle of Anglican canon law that the minister of ordination is the bishop and that priests present and taking part in the service must together with the bishop lay their hands upon the head of every person who receives the order of priesthood.[44]

[39] England, Cans. C13(1); C15(4) and C14(3); Ireland, Const. IV.67, IX.25; Australia, Oaths and Declarations of Assent Canon 1992, Can. P3 of 1992 and e.g. Diocese of Sydney, *The 7th Handbook*, 6.18; ECUSA, Cans. III.6: at ordination the candidate must declare publicly to 'conform' to the doctrine, liturgy and discipline of the church; see also West Africa, Can. XI.6; Philippines, Cans. III.11; Brazil, Cans. B.8; New Zealand, *Prayer Book* 1989, 922; Korea, Art. 120; Rwanda, Draft Const. 1996, Art. 43; see below for the oath of canonical obedience, for promises to obey the church's law see Ch. 1, and for doctrine and liturgy see Chs. 7 and 8.

[40] See e.g. England, Can. C1(1); Ireland, Const. IX.17.

[41] England, Can. C3(1); Ireland, Const. IX.18: 'in accordance with the ancient custom of the church', ordination must take place on Sundays immediately following Ember days; New Zealand, *Prayer Book* 1989, 922: the bishop appoints the day; Southern Africa, *Prayer Book* 1989, 572: it is 'normally held on a Sunday in Embertide', unless there is 'good reason' not to; Philippines, Cans. III.10.

[42] England, Can. C3(3); Ireland, Const. IX.18: ordination must occur in the presence of the archdeacon or his deputy; Canada, BCP 1962, 645; New Zealand, Cans. G.XIII.3.1: it takes place in the presence of the congregation; Brazil, Cans. III.6; Mexico, Cans. III.22–23.

[43] England, Can. C3(7): only the Archbishop of Canterbury may issue such a faculty; Ireland, Const. IX.18: 'no person shall be made a deacon and a presybter on the same day'; see also e.g. New Zealand, Cans. G.XIII.3.3.

[44] Southern Africa, *Prayer Book* 1989, 571: 'The Bishop is the minister of ordination'; England, Can. C3(4); New Zealand, *Prayer Book* 1989, 923: 'At least some of the priests present shall join with the bishop in the laying on of hands at the ordination of a priest'; Melanesia, Cans. A.7: 'Holy Order' is 'the rite in which the ministers of the Church are ordained'.

According to liturgical norms, valid ordination takes place by the consent of the candidate and by prayer and laying on of hands by the bishop.[45] Very few churches mention the consent of the people generally as a precondition to ordination.[46]

APPOINTMENT AND AUTHORIZATION

A great variety of ecclesiastical ministries is both open and reserved to ordained members of the church. This section examines laws governing appointment to the traditional office of parish priest – or minister to a local pastorate or charge – and to ministerial posts from which assistance is given to the priest, traditionally, the assistant curate. It also contains some material on appointments to sector ministries (such as chaplaincy ministry). Whilst as a uniform practice appointments are in the keeping of the diocesan bishop, one characteristic of Anglican canon law on this subject is the degree to which churches enable the participation of the laity, or their representatives, in the process of appointment. Appointment to a particular ministry is followed by episcopal authorization to minister. Institution is the more traditional method to authorize the ministry of priests in those churches which operate the benefice or incumbency as the local ecclesiastical unit. In these churches authorization of assistant ministers, who may be either priests or deacons, is by episcopal licence.[47] In other churches authorization to all ministries is exclusively by means of licence.

---

[45] England, BCP 1662, 553f; ASB, 338; Southern Africa, *Prayer Book* 1989, 571: 'The central act of ordination consists of the imposition of hands by a bishop, together with prayer for the Holy Spirit to give grace for the particular order being bestowed'; ECUSA, BCP 1979, 577: 'The persons who are chosen and recognized by the Church as being called by God to the ordained ministry are admitted to these sacred orders by solemn prayer and the laying on of episcopal hands' (ibid., 579: at least two presbyters must be present); for English quasi-legislation applicable to the ordination of women as priests, see Episcopal Ministry Act of Synod 1993 and the Priests (Ordination of Women) Measure 1993 Code of Practice; ibid., para. 13–15: 'it would be inappropriate to exclude candidates of one sex from a particular ordination service, or to arrange a separate service for ordinands opposed to the ordination of women to the priesthood'.

[46] New Zealand, *Prayer Book* 1989, 887: 'The assent of the people that the candidate should be ordained is an integral part of the service'; North India, Const. I.I.VIII.2: in ordination 'God . . . bestows on, and assures those, whom He has called and His Church has accepted for any particular form of ministry, a commission for it and the grace appropriate to it'; the authority of the whole church is represented in ordination.

[47] England, Can. C8(5): 'The bishop of a diocese confers such authority on a minister either by instituting him to a benefice, or by admitting him to serve within his diocese by licence under his hand and seal, or by giving him written permission to officiate within the same'; see also Southern Africa, Can. 23.2; and Melanesia, Cans. C.4.B.

The English Model: Presentation and Institution

For those many churches which follow the English model of a benefice, an office covering a prescribed local territorial area in which the ordained minister is entrusted with the cure of souls,[48] admission to office is by presentation or nomination, admission or institution, and induction. First, in English law, where appointment to benefices is the preserve of priests, the right to present vests in the patron; it is exercisable only when the benefice is vacant. The presentation must be approved by the bishop and representatives of the parish chosen by the parochial church council. There is a duty to state the grounds of refusal and the patron has a right of appeal to the archbishop. If there has been no presentation within nine months after vacancy, the right passes to the archbishop who must consult the bishop and the parish representatives.[49] With minor differences, this same basic framework is to be found in the law of many churches. In Scottish canon law, the 'right of presentation' is exercisable by those in whom it is vested; disputes as to possession of the right must be determined by the diocesan bishop with appeal to the Episcopal Synod. Incumbencies are reserved to priests who may not accept until the bishop has approved the presentation. If there is no presentation within six months of the vacancy, or within six months of the bishop's refusal to accept a presentation, the right lapses to the diocesan bishop; if the bishop fails to present and the incumbency remains vacant for a further six months, the appointment lapses to the College of Bishops.[50] In Irish church law, the underlying idea is that arrangements should reflect the interests of the bishop, the diocese at large and the parish. The normal method of appointing incumbents is by a Board of Nomination (comprising the bishop, the diocesan Committee of Patronage and the parochial nominators of the vacant cure). The board cannot be summoned until the diocesan council has certified to the bishop that the approved stipend, expenses and free residence of the incumbent will be available. The diocesan council may not issue the certificate where a parish has failed to meet any of its financial obligations arising under church law. The board must be summoned within two months of the issue of the certificate and each member signs a declaration of secrecy. The board may nominate a cleric in priest's orders, who has signified willing-

---

[48] See below and Ch. 2.

[49] England, Patronage (Benefices) Measure 1986, ss. 3–16; the bishop may suspend the right of presentation with the consent of the diocesan pastoral committee and after consulting the patron, the rural dean and the parochial church council when a pastoral scheme for the reorganization is contemplated: Pastoral Measure 1983, s. 67.

[50] Scotland, Can. 13.

ness to serve.[51] Finally, in Southern Africa, on vacancy of a benefice, the right of presentation is exercisable by those in whom it is vested by law, by 'any Contract that has been sanctioned by the Bishop', or by any Diocesan Synod regulation; if no such contract exists, the right to present vests in the bishop. Every presentation must be either accepted or rejected by the bishop but the presentee or the patron may appeal to the metropolitan whose decision is final. If there has been no presentation within six months the right to present lapses to the bishop.[52] In Wales the concept of a cycle is used, with the right of appointment exercised in turn by the bishop, a diocesan patronage body and a provincial patronage body.[53] The basic process of nomination and episcopal appointment appears in the laws of a number of other churches.[54]

Secondly, as to admission or institution, in English canon law the bishop may refuse on a number of prescribed grounds: if there is no evidence of ordination as priest or of sufficient learning; if not more than three years have elapsed since the presentee's ordination as deacon; if the priest is unfit by reason of mental or physical infirmity or incapacity; if there is evidence of pecuniary embarrassment of a serious character, grave misconduct or neglect of duty in an ecclesiastical office, or evil life (having caused grave scandal since ordination concerning his moral character); and if, in the case of those who have not previously held a benefice, there is an absence of experience (or less than three years' experience) as a full-time assistant curate or curate-in-charge of a parish. The grounds of refusal

---

[51] Ireland, Const. IV; see J. L. B. Deane, *Church of Ireland Handbook* (Dublin, 1982), 62–64; Const. IV.22: nothing in the procedure affects the rights of patrons under the Irish Church Act 1869 (in such cases the bishop must remind the patron of 'his duty to consider the requirements of the benefice and to satisfy himself that the person whom he nominates possesses the doctrine, judgment, honesty, and innocence of life without which he cannot discharge his office adequately'); for finance, see Ch. 11.

[52] Southern Africa, Can. 23.1, 4–5; for Australia, see e.g. Diocese of Sydney, *The 7th Handbook*, 6 (Presentation and Exchange Ordinance 1988): a presentation board for the parish, consisting of the archdeacon, four persons appointed every three years by the Diocesan Synod and five parish representatives, submits a name to the archbishop; the board may surrender to the archbishop its right of presentation; the right to present lapses to the archbishop after one year and one month of its first meeting.

[53] Wales, Const. VII: the right to collate or nominate vests in turns in the bishop, the Diocesan Patronage Board, and the Provincial Patronage Board; ibid, VII.16: the bishop may from time to time summon a meeting of the archdeacons, and the clerical and lay members of the Diocesan Patronage Board elected by the Diocesean Conference 'to confer with him on the general policy of patronage in the diocese'.

[54] Papua New Guinea, Diocese of Port Moresby, Can. 9: the congregation through its parish or district council nominates and the appointment is made at the discretion of the bishop but these are 'normally to be made as a joint decision' between the bishop, the cleric and the parish; Melanesia, Diocese of Temotu, Can. 10: appointment is by the bishop after consultation with the parish council; North India, Const. I.I.VIII.25–26: appointment is by the diocesan bishop after consultation with the Diocesan Council with regard having been made to 'the wishes' of the pastorate.

must be signified in writing to the presentee and the patron; the latter may appeal to a tribunal or, when refusal is based on lack of experience, to the provincial archbishop.[55] The same right of refusal is found in the laws of other churches, but the grounds for refusal are rather narrower. In Irish church law, a candidate must be found to possess 'sufficiency, sobriety, and fitness in every way for the ministrations to which he is to be appointed'; '[i]f he be found worthy by the bishop, he shall be admitted by him by instrument in writing under his hand and seal'. The bishop may, therefore, decline to institute a cleric fully nominated but in so doing reasons must be given for the refusal; an appeal lies to the Court of General Synod at the instance of the nominee or at least half of the Board of Nomination (see above).[56] In Scottish canon law, no institution may take place until the cleric produces Letters of Orders and such testimonials as the bishop requests. Within three months, the bishop must either accept or refuse the presentation in writing; if the bishop refuses, the presentee and the patron have a right of appeal to the Episcopal Synod.[57] In Southern Africa, the bishop must not collate or institute unless the cleric produces Letters of Orders and testimonials to satisfy the bishop of his 'learning, soundness in the faith, and innocency of life and conversation'. When, after the bishop has agreed to institute or collate, evidence comes to light to cause the bishop 'to have grave doubts' as to the candidate's innocency of life and conversation, the bishop must not proceed. The institution or collation is then cancelled but the bishop must give the candidate an opportunity to be heard.[58] Lastly, in English canon law, as in other churches in this group, institution is followed by induction into the temporalities of the benefice.[59]

The American Model: Election and Institution

In the canon law of ECUSA, when a parish is without a rector, the wardens must notify the bishop 'promptly'. During a vacancy it is the duty of the wardens to provide for public services in the parish. If they fail to do so for

---

[55] England, Can. C10; the institution of a person not in holy orders is null: *R v Ellis* (1888) 16 Cox CC 469; see also generally *Willis v Bishop of Oxford* (1877) 2 PD 192; for appeals, see Patronage (Benefices) Measure 1986, s. 18 and Benefices Measure 1972, s. 1.

[56] Ireland, Const. IV.27–30.

[57] Scotland, Can. 13.

[58] Southern Africa, Can. 23; Wales, Const. VII.38: an appeal lies against refusal to the Provincial Court; Australia, Diocese of Sydney, *The 7th Handbook*, 9.2.

[59] England, Can. C11; concerning appointment many churches follow the English requirement (Cans. C14, C15) that the priest makes declarations of assent to the church's doctrine, to use the authorized liturgies, the oath of canonical obedience and the promise to obey the law of the church; see e.g. New Zealand, Cans. A.II.3; Scotland, Can. 13 and App. No. 14.

a period of thirty days, the bishop must take the steps necessary to ensure cover. Rectors are elected: written notice of the election must be sent by the wardens to the bishop who, if satisfied that the candidate is 'duly qualified' as priest, and upon acceptance by the candidate, must arrange for recording the election by the secretary of the Diocesan Convention. The bishop must communicate with the rector and the vestry throughout the election process. The national Board for Church Deployment, which is accountable to the Executive Council of General Convention, is responsible for general oversight of the deployment of clergy: it must study needs and trends, issue reports and information on deployment, co-operate with boards, commissions and agencies concerned with ministry and report on its activities to General Convention.[60] This approach is used in a number of churches, particularly those in Latin America.[61]

Episcopal Licences

Churches either employ a system of episcopal licensing exclusively or in addition to appointment by presentation and institution.[62] In the latter case the system of licensing is applied particularly to assistant curates who may be deacons; in the former it is applied to the appointment of both priests and deacons. The norm is for the law to prescribe that an ordained minister resident in any diocese may exercise ecclesiastical functions only if under a written licence from the diocesan bishop. The authorization may be general or it may be limited as to the functions and duties which may be carried out. Invariably the law provides that the licence may be varied by the bishop as a matter of discretion. If the minister is from another diocese, a licence is not to be issued until the candidate has produced Letters

---

[60] ECUSA, Cans. III.14, 17, 33. Election is followed by institution and induction: BCP 1979, Marshall, I, 649; for the discontinuance of employment see also *Rector, Churchwardens and Vestrymen of Christ Church at Pelham v Collett*, 204 NYS 315, affirmed 240 NYS 563.

[61] Puerto Rico, Cans. III.15; see also Portugal, Cans. VIII.2; Japan, Can. II, Art. 23; Philippines, Cans. III.18; Canada, *Johnson v Glen* (1879) 26 Gr 162 (Ch): Anglican canons requiring consultation by the bishop with churchwardens prior to appointment of a rector were enforced as a matter of contract law.

[62] In some churches appointment is not treated by national or provincial law but rather by diocesan law: see e.g. New Zealand, Cans. A.II.1; ibid. A.II.4: where 'any appointment of an ordained minister to serve in a position of pastoral responsibility or to serve in a worshipping community with a recognized structure' is to be made, representatives of that community must participate in the process prior to appointment by the bishop; Korea, Can. 35: 'Each diocese is to make its own detailed regulations concerning the deployment of clergy but, principles and procedures for movement from one diocese to another are to be decided by the national Executive Committee'; ibid., Can. 36: 'The diocesan bishop makes clerical appointments. However, appointments to churches and other related deployment are made after consultation with the archdeacon, the people's warden and the clergyman concerned'.

of Orders and a testimonial from the bishop of the diocese in which the minister last worked. An ordained minister not normally resident in the diocese may exercise ecclesiastical functions within it only on the bishop's permission to do so. However, laws commonly enable a minister, who is known to be in good standing to the minister of the cure, to carry out ministerial functions for fixed and limited periods: these may be carried out only with the consent of the host minister.[63] Laws vary considerably as to the extent of consultation required in the process of granting licences. In the case of assistant curates, these are appointed on the nomination of the parish priest or other minister in charge with the consent of the bishop.[64] There is judicial authority in England to suggest that reasons need not be given by a bishop in the event of a refusal to grant a licence;[65] certainly, no duty to give reasons appears in the formal laws of any church. For some churches, authority to minister may also be conferred by means of a more informal written permission.[66] It is difficult to generalize about rules governing the appointment of ordained ministers to extra-parochial and sector ministries. Appointment is regulated primarily by the rules of the institution to which the minister is appointed. The laws of some churches, however, expressly provide that such appointments in, for example, schools, colleges, hospitals and prisons, have to be approved by the bishop. When these institutions are located in a territory for which another cleric has cure of souls, the consent of that cleric need not be obtained in

[63] These provisions are taken from Central Africa, Can. 16.1; they are echoed in the following laws: Kenya, Can. VIII; Sudan, Const. Art. 56; North India, Const. III.V; West Indies, Can. 14; Canada, Can XVII, App. L: the licence must also specify the territorial competence of the licensee; ECUSA, Cans. III.16.2: 'No Deacon or Priest shall officiate more than two months by preaching, ministering the Sacraments, or holding any public service, within the limits of any Diocese other than that in which the Deacon or Priest is canonically resident, without a licence from the Ecclesiastical Authority'; for the same principle see also England, C12(1)–(2); Melanesia, Cans. C.4.B; Philippines, Cans. III.16; Southern Africa, Can. 23.6; Papua New Guinea, Diocese of Port Moresby, Can. 10; and Chile, Cans. B.7.

[64] Scotland, Can. 14.1: the rector or priest-in-charge may present to the bishop a person in holy orders (or one ready to be so admitted) to be licensed as an assistant curate; England: the canons are silent, but often diocesan norms require consultation: see e.g. Diocese of Sheffield, *Handbook* (1994), III.E; Ireland, Const. IV.49: assistant curates are nominated by the incumbent to the bishop for licensing; ibid., IV.43: vicars – assistant priests to the incumbent – are nominated by the diocesan Board of Nomination and appointed by the bishop; ibid., V.1–11: a 'curate-in-charge' may be licensed by the bishop to serve in a cure of souls with no parish church (but with a proprietory or other non-parochial church); ECUSA, Cans. III.141(b): assistant clergy are elected by the rector with the approval of the vestry; during the process of election there must be communication between the rector and vestry and the bishop; they serve 'under the direction of the Rector'; see also n. 62.

[65] *R v Bishop of London* (1811) 13 East 419; *Bishop of Down v Miller* (1861) 11 I Ch R App 1; *R v Bishop of Liverpool* (1904) 20 TLR 485.

[66] England, Can. C8(3); New Zealand, Const. C.15.

order for the extra-parochial or sector ministry to be lawfully discharged. Moreover, in order to be authorized to carry out the particular ministry in question, the candidate must in addition be licensed by the bishop; holding and continuing to hold an episcopal licence is a condition of authorization.[67] Appointment to the senior clerical positions of dean, vicar general and archdeacon are discussed in the following section.

THE FUNCTIONS OF DEACONS AND PRIESTS

There is a high degree of consistency as between churches concerning the canonical ministry of priests and deacons. Whilst precise ministerial functions, cast as rights or duties, depend on the subject in question (for which see the other studies in this volume), in the vast majority of churches they are gathered together under a single title in the particular church's body of canons. Ministry is exercised as a result of vocation under the general supervision of the bishop.[68]

Duties Common to Both Orders

In addition to functions peculiar to each of the distinct ministries of priests and deacons, as a matter of ecclesiastical practice Anglican canon law contains a reasonably well-defined set of duties which must be fulfilled by both priests and deacons, in whatever ministry they are placed. First, priests and deacons must be diligent in the liturgical life of the church, particularly in their conformity during public worship to the authorized liturgies, and in the celebration of the eucharist.[69] Secondly, they must apply themselves to personal prayer, self-examination and study, especially of

[67] Central Africa, Can. 16.5; Scotland, Can. 14.5: priests and deacons 'employed' as chaplains and on the staff of a university, college, school, hospital, prison or other institution may be licensed by the bishop; see also ibid., 14.6–7 for 'commissions' and 'warrants'; England, Can. B41; Southern Africa, Can. 23.6: no public ministrations may be conducted by any cleric 'within the limits of a Pastoral Charge without the consent of the Incumbent licensed' except, with the licence of the bishop, in: extra-parochial churches, colleges, schools, hostel chapels, religious houses, naval, military or air force chaplaincies, or chaplaincies to penal institutions, hospitals or universities; the same applies to missions to railway workers, seamen or other special classes of person; for chaplains see also Canada, Can. XVII, App. L.

[68] For vocation generally, see LC 1908, Ress. 3–5, 16; LC 1920, Res. 32; LC 1930, Res. 61; LC 1948, Ress. 82–85; LC 1958, Ress. 72, 81 and 92–94.

[69] England, Can. C26(1): 'every bishop, priest, and deacon is under obligation, not being let by sickness or some other urgent cause, to say daily Morning and Evening Prayer, either privately or openly; and to celebrate the Holy Communion, or be present thereat, on all Sundays and other principal Feast Days'; for almost identical provisions, see Scotland, Can. 17.1 and Southern Africa, Can. 24.1.

holy scripture and other matters pertaining to their ministerial duties.[70] Thirdly, they must not engage in occupations, habits or recreations which are inconsistent with their sacred calling and which will cause scandal to the church and offence to others.[71] Fourthly, priests and deacons must not engage in any secular employment without the permission of the diocesan bishop.[72] In a very few churches, when 'non-ecclesiastical' employment is contemplated without renouncing the exercise of ordained ministry, the priest or deacon must demonstrate to the bishop that 'reasonable opportunities for the exercise of the person's office exist and that good use will be made of such opportunities'; with the consent of the diocesan standing committee, the bishop may then approve the person's continued exercise of ecclesiastical office on condition that the person reports annually to the bishop.[73] Fifthly, both priests and deacons must be resident within the territorial boundaries of the ecclesiastical unit to which they are assigned; absence is permitted only with the consent of the diocesan bishop.[74]

[70] England, Can. C26(1): 'He is also to be diligent in daily prayer and intercession, in examination of his conscience, and in the study of the holy Scriptures and other such studies as pertain to his ministerial duties'; for an identical provision, see Ireland, Const. IX.33; see also Southern Africa, Can. 24.1; Scotland, Can. 17.2: clergy must read holy scripture and apply themselves 'to such studies as help to the knowledge' of holy scripture as well as studies pertaining to their 'clerical duties'; they must also follow courses decided from time to time by the College of Bishops.

[71] England, Can. C26(2): 'A minister shall not give himself to such occupations, habits, or recreations as do not befit his sacred calling, or may be detrimental to the performance of the duties of his office, or tend to be a just cause of offence to others; and at all times he shall be diligent to frame and fashion his life and that of his family according to the doctrine of Christ, and to make himself and them, as much as in him lies, wholesome examples and patterns to the flock of Christ'; see also Ireland, Const. IX.33.

[72] England, Can. C28: 'No minister holding ecclesiastical office shall engage in trade or any other occupation in such manner as to affect the performance of the duties of his office, except as far as he is authorised so to do under the statutory provisions in this behalf for the time being in force or he have a licence so to do granted by the bishop of the diocese'. The bishop may grant or refuse a licence 'after consultation with the parochial church council'; in cases of refusal the minister may appeal to the archbishop of the province; for almost identical provisions, see West Indies, Can. 15.7; Ireland, Const. IX.34; Scotland, Can. 19: 'Any Bishop, Priest or Deacon holding office or a licence to officiate in the Church and desiring to engage at the same time in any secular employment, shall be entitled to do so with the consent . . . of the Diocesan Bishop'; Southern Africa, Can. 26.4; Central Africa, Can. 16.6. 'A stipendiary clergyman may not engage in any other business, trade or profession, whether paid or not, which, in the opinion of the Bishop, will detract from his service to the church, without the consent of the Bishop in writing'.

[73] ECUSA, Cans. III.15; see also Philippines, Cans. III.16.8; Korea, Const. Art. 116: 'A member of the clergy may not undertake other employment whilst exercising his ministry. However, if this cannot be avoided, he must receive the permission from his Diocesan Executive Committee and his diocesan bishop'.

[74] England, Can. 25: the duty to reside applies only to beneficed clergy; absence may be authorized by episcopal licence; Scotland, Can. 17.4: this governs rectors and priests-in-charge who must reside in the house provided unless exempted for 'sufficient

Sixthly, ministers may not officiate or otherwise minister in another diocese without the host bishop's permission,[75] nor in another parish or pastorate in their own diocese without the host minister's permission.[76] Finally, they must obey the directions of their bishops (see below). The rights of clergy to participate in ecclesiastical government, by virtue of membership of provincial, national or other assemblies, and to remuneration, are discussed elsewhere in this volume.

The Ministry of Deacons

As has already been seen, the office of deacon is usually exercised for one year as a transitional ministry prior to ordination as priest; only a small number of churches employs the system of permanent deacons.[77] For several churches diaconal ministry is treated only in liturgical books,[78] though in many (particularly the American, West Indian and Latin American churches) it is defined canonically under a single title. The canon law of the West Indies presents a concise account of the doctrine that the keynote of diaconal ministry is service: the order of deacons 'shall be maintained within the Church of the Province . . . as a distinct order of ministry . . . symbolic of the servant element'.[79] A neat and general

reason' approved by the bishop; and ibid., 17.5: 'The Bishop may require any cleric licensed to a definite sphere of duty to reside in some place conveniently situated for the performance of that duty, to be approved by the Bishop'; see also Ireland, Const. IV.37–39; Southern Africa, Can. 26: the duty of residence applies to incumbents and assistant curates. For an exceptional and explicit treatment of clergy holidays, see Korea, Can. 38: clerics must have 28 days' holiday *per annum*.

[75] England, Can C8(2): 'A minister duly ordained priest or deacon . . . may officiate in any place after he has received authority to do so from the bishop of the diocese'; Brazil, Cans. III.10.5; Melanesia, Cans. C.4.B; Philippines, Cans. III.16.7; West Indies, Can. 15.3; Sudan, Const. Art. 56.

[76] England, Can. C8(4): 'No minister who has such authority to exercise his ministry in any diocese shall do so therein in any place in which he has not the cure of souls without the permission of the minister having such cure'; ECUSA, Cans. III.14; Philippines, Cans. III.16.6; New Zealand, Cans. A.II.2; Southern Africa, Can. 24.6; Korea, Const. Art. 118: 'A member of the clergy wishing to administer the sacraments or preach in another's church requires the invitation or permission of the priest in charge'. The principal exception to this is with regard to sector ministries such as in hospitals, schools and prisons: see above.

[77] Korea, Const. Art. 110; Puerto Rico, Cans. III.7; North India, Const. I.I.VIII.18; South India, Const. V.11; for deaconesses see n. 2.

[78] England BCP Ordinal; ASB, 344; Wales, BCP 1984, 729; Ireland, BCP 1960, 289f; New Zealand, *Prayer Book* 1989, 891; in many churches both the canon law and liturgical books define diaconal ministry: for the latter, see e.g. ECUSA, BCP 1979, Marshall, I, 575; Southern Africa, *Prayer Book* 1989, 434: 'The ministry of a deacon is to represent Christ and his Church, particularly as a servant of those in need; and to assist the bishop and priests in the proclamation of the gospel and the administration of the sacraments'.

[79] West Indies, Const. Art. 5; Australia, Ordination Service for Deacons, Canon No. 16, 1985; for notions of service in the liturgy books see n. 78.

summary of the specific functions of deacons is to be found in Brazilian canon law: to proclaim the Word of God; to serve the presbyter to whom he answers; to care for the poor and the sick; and to baptize when requested. Whilst generally subject to the immediate oversight of the diocesan bishop by whom appointment is made 'to serve as an assistant in a parish', when exercising the functions of an assistant the deacon must act in accordance with the directions of the rector or priest. But at no time may the deacon exercise functions reserved to the order of priests.[80] Laws in other churches particularize diaconal functions more closely; provisions typically include: preparing the table for Holy Communion, assisting with the chalice and reading the gospel at the eucharist; baptizing in the absence of the priest; preaching by the bishop's licence; visiting the sick and disabled and reporting to the incumbent those who are in need; and generally assisting the incumbent in the pastoral work of the parish.[81] The principle that deacons must act under the direction of the priests to whom they are assistants is a general one.[82] Some churches allow deacons to serve in more than one parish but not at the same time in another diocese except with the written permission of its bishop.[83]

The Ministry of Priests with Cure of Souls

Priests who have charge of a local ecclesiastical unit, a parish, incumbency or other pastorate, have the primary authority, spiritual jurisdiction, and responsibility for the cure of souls in that unit.[84] Legally, it is treated as a ministry to which priests are called and commissioned by God and the church,[85] exercisable subject to the law of the church and under the gen-

[80] Brazil, Cans. III.11; Puerto Rico, Cans. III.10; Mexico, Cans. III.27.

[81] West Indies, Const. Art. 5; South India, Const. V.10: 'The functions of deacons shall include . . . assisting the presbyter in the administration of the Lord's Supper and in other services of the Church; administering of baptism; ministering in the temporalities of the Church: giving succour to the poor, the needy and the sick; instructing children and catechumens in the faith; preaching the Word; and generally giving assistance in pastoral and evangelistic work'; North India, Const. I.I.VIII.15.

[82] ECUSA, Cans. III.13: the deacon 'shall act under the direction of the Priest in all ministrations'; Philippines, Cans. III.1(c); West Indies, Can. 17.13; Mexico, Cans. III.27.

[83] ECUSA, Cans. III.6.9(a).

[84] For 'cure of souls', see e.g. England, Can. C24(1); Ireland, Const. V; ECUSA, Cans. III.14.3(a); for 'team ministries' and 'group ministries' in England, see L. Leeder, *Ecclesiastical Law Handbook* (London, 1997), 154–65; see also New Zealand, Cans. B.V.2.8: the diocesan synod may authorize its standing committee to enter agreements to form co-operating parishes; see also B.V.5 for co-vicars and co-pastors.

[85] South India, Const. II.10: 'presbyters are specially called and commissioned by God to be dispensers of His Word and Sacraments, to declare His message of pardon to penitent sinners, to build up the members of the Church in their most holy faith, and, through the councils of the Church and otherwise, to share with the bishops and lay members in its government and in the administration of its discipline'; New Zealand,

eral authority, oversight and pastoral direction of the bishop.[86] The core responsibilities which most commonly appear in Anglican canon law are as follows: to preach the gospel, particularly through sermons; to minister the sacraments and to perform other offices and rites as are authorized by the church; to visit the members of the congregation, especially when they are sick, and to provide opportunities for them to consult him for spiritual counsel and advice; to prepare candidates for baptism, confirmation and reception, and, with respect to confirmation and reception, when satisfied of their fitness to present them to the bishop; to instruct the children of the parish in the Christian faith, and to use such opportunities of teaching and visiting in the schools within the cure as are open to him.[87] Some laws particularize further each of these general duties. For example, in ECUSA, priests in charge of a cure of souls are obliged 'to ensure that children, youth and adults receive instruction . . . in the doctrine, discipline and worship' of the church, 'in the exercise of their ministry as baptized persons' and in 'christian stewardship'; this must include instruction in 'reverence for the creation and the right use of God's gifts' and the 'generous and consistent offering of time, talent, and treasure for the mission and ministry' of the church.[88] Analogous duties which may be found in the laws of a few churches include instruction in the history of the church and in the missionary work of the church, at home and abroad and this is sometimes accompanied by the duty to give suitable opportunity to the people to make offerings towards such missionary work.[89] Rarely is it the

Prayer Book 1989, 901: priests are 'called to build up Christ's congregation', to strengthen the baptized and to lead them as witnesses to Christ in the world; see also ECUSA, BCP 1979, Marshall, I, 575.

[86] See e.g. ECUSA, Cans. III.14.1: 'The authority of and responsibility for the conduct of the worship and the spiritual jurisdiction of the Parish are vested in the Rector, subject to the Rubrics of the Book of Common Prayer, the Constitution and Canons of the Church, and the pastoral direction of the Bishop'; see also Philippines, Cans. II.162(c); West Indies, Can. 15.1: 'The ordering of the worship and the spiritual jurisdiction of a Parish is vested in the Incumbent or Priest-in-Charge subject to Canons and Regulations of the Diocese and the authority of the Bishop'; Southern Africa, Can. 24.2; for the 'cure of souls' see e.g. England, Can. C24(1); for episcopal oversight in matters of clerical discipline, see below.

[87] England, Can. C24; Scotland, Cans. 17.3 and 38.4: clergy having charge of a congregation must 'supply as diligently as possible spiritual ministrations to all persons resident in the district who apply for the same' provided they are members of the church; Southern Africa, Can. 24.2: 'Incumbents are recognized as being leaders, ordained and set apart by God and his Church for the oversight of Pastoral Charges to which they are appointed, particularly in regard to preaching, teaching and liturgical worship'; see ibid. Can. 24.4 for the core list; South India, Const. V.1–2; see also Korea, Const. Arts. 112 and 114: these require 'doctrinal instruction' and the celebration of public worship.

[88] ECUSA, Cans. III.14.2; for much the same provisions see Brazil, Cans. III.12; Mexico, Cans. III.28; Puerto Rico, Cans. III.14; and Portugal, Cans. VIII.3, 4.

[89] West Indies, Can. 15.2

case that Anglican canon law imposes a special duty on clergy towards those who have lapsed from the church; Scottish canon law is exceptional in this regard: clergy must 'endeavour to find out, and establish pastoral relations with, the lapsed and spiritually destitute throughout the district assigned to their charge'.[90] If at any time the priest is unable to discharge these duties, by non-residence or illness, he must provide for the cure to be supplied by a priest licensed or otherwise approved by the bishop.[91] The priest must also keep the church's register books required by law.[92]

Specialist Ministries

The principal senior clerical offices open to ordained clergy of some churches are those of vicar general, archdeacon and rural dean. In a small number of churches, every bishop must appoint a vicar general of the diocese, to hold office for such period and on such terms as the bishop determines. The vicar general must act whenever the diocesan bishop is outside the diocese or is incapacitated or resigns or dies. If for any reason a vicar general is not in office and the bishop is not in a position to make an appointment, the senior priest in the diocese must report the matter to the archbishop who then makes the appointment; the person appointed holds office until the matter has been resolved to the satisfaction of the archbishop. The duties of the vicar general are: to perform all the spiritual and temporal functions of the diocesan bishop, except as otherwise excluded by the law of the church; and to summon and preside at the Diocesan Synod (but synodical legislation has no effect until promulgated by the national or provincial assembly or by the archbishop). The appointment of a vicar general may be terminated at any time by the diocesan bishop or, if the bishop is absent or incapacitated, by the archbishop.[93]

With respect to the office of archdeacon, an office known to the provincial or national law of only a handful of churches, the right to appoint vests

---

[90] Scotland, Can. 38.4.

[91] See e.g. England, Can. C24(8); Scotland, Can. 17.6; ECUSA, Cans. III.15.4(3)(b).

[92] See Ch. 11.

[93] These provisions are taken from Central Africa, Can. 14; see also Portugal, Cans. VI; Melanesia, Can. C.8; South East Asia, Const. Art. V; Papua New Guinea, Diocese of Port Moresby, Can. 14; New Zealand, Cans. A.I.8: the bishop 'may' appoint; England, Ecclesiastical Jurisdiction Measure 1963, s. 83: in practice the chancellor acts as vicar general; functions of the office are largely undefined: see T. Coningsby, 'Chancellor, Vicar-General and Official Principal – a bundle of offices', *Ecclesiastical Law Journal*, 2(10) (1992) 273; Scotland, Can. 43: the equivalent is the diocesan dean: the office is mandatory; appointment is made by the bishop and admission is open to incumbents or priests-in-charge; the dean administers the diocese in a vacancy under the authority of the primus; tenure is for a renewable period of 5 years and the appointment may be terminated by mutual agreement; it may be cancelled with the consent of the Diocesan Synod if the dean is incapable or the subject of judicial proceedings.

in the diocesan bishop. The office may be occupied by either priests or deacons. Termination is at the discretion of the bishop. As to archidiaconal functions, two approaches are used: regulation by law or regulation by the terms of the instrument of appointment. In English and Irish canon law, for example, within the jurisdictional boundaries of the archdeaconry, the archdeacon exercises an ordinary jurisdiction under the bishop, namely: to assist the bishop in his pastoral care and office, particularly to see that those holding ecclesiastical office perform their duties diligently; and to bring to the bishop's attention 'what calls for correction and merits praise'. The archdeacon has a special visitatorial function and duties to inspect church property in the archdeaconry.[94] Somewhat different provisions appear in the canon law of Southern Africa, where the archdeacon is appointed by the bishop for a five-year renewable period which may be terminated only with the agreement of the other diocesan archdeacons. The archdeacon's principal function is 'to share in the pastoral ministry and missionary leadership of the Bishop, in the area to which he has been appointed'. The archdeacon is entitled, '[b]y virtue of his office', to the same obedience as is owed to the bishop in those matters entrusted to him. Specific functions are: to examine annually parish financial records and property; to admit parochial officers; and 'to help, encourage and strengthen the Clergy and Laity of his Archdeaconry'.[95] By way of contrast, as is the case in for example Central Africa, archidiaconal duties, the period of the appointment, the period of notice required for resignation or termination, the geographical area covered and financial provisions or allowances may not be set out in the formal law but instead are dealt with exclusively in the episcopal letter of appointment.[96] The English office of rural dean, an episcopal appointee, is rarely found in the provincial or national laws of other churches: the rural dean must report to the bishop any matter in any parish within the deanery which it may be necessary or useful for the bishop to know, particularly any case of illness or other form of distress amongst the clergy. The rural dean has a special responsibility to ensure the maintenance of the electoral roll in each parish, and to report to the bishop on defects in the fabric, ornaments and furniture of the church.[97]

[94] England, Can. C22: Ireland, Const. II.38–42; Wales, Const. VII.1; Scotland has no archdeacon but see n. 93 for the diocesan dean; for the archdeacon's role in visitations and property see Chs. 3 and 11.

[95] Southern Africa, Can. 15; for very similar provisions see West Indies, Can. 13; see also Portugal, Cans. VII; Australia, Can. 12 of 1995; Papua New Guinea, Diocese of Port Moresby, Can. 14; West Africa, Const. 1992, Art. 14; Jerusalem and the Middle East, Diocese of Egypt, Const. 1982, 9; and Korea, Const. Art. 84.

[96] Central Africa, Can. 15: the bishop may appoint 'lay stewards' to perform such archidiaconal functions as may be set out in their letters of appointment.

[97] England, Can. C23; Ireland, Const. II.43–44; Wales, Const. VII.2; for 'area deans', see Australia, Diocese of Sydney, *The 7th Handbook*, 2.7; ECUSA, Diocese of Western New York, Cans. 9.

Generally, Anglican canon law is undeveloped in relation to those clergy who are engaged in sector ministry where functions are carried out under the terms of a contract of employment.[98] The vast majority of churches have no formal law on the subject. In Central Africa, however, a cleric who is 'employed' by any diocese shall be appointed by the diocesan bishop, in accordance with such diocesan regulations as may exist, and 'the duties of the clergyman shall be sufficiently defined in writing'. It is the responsibility of the bishop and of the diocesan authority concerned 'to provide for reasonable terms of service for clergymen employed by their dioceses'; the terms must provide for the termination of such employment upon reasonable notice. The employment of a cleric is conditional upon his holding and continuing to hold appropriate licence from the bishop.[99]

CLERICAL DISCIPLINE: CANONICAL OBEDIENCE

As has been intimated already, it is a general principle of Anglican canon law that priests and deacons, from whatever ecclesiastical office they exercise ministry, are subordinate to the jurisdiction of the diocesan bishop. The principle is expressed in one way or another in the formal laws of all national, provincial and regional churches.[100] At the same time, though, the laws of many churches assign to the national or provincial assembly (as legislator) the 'final authority' in matters of discipline.[101] A wide range of devices exists in laws to effect clerical discipline, including: systems allowing complaints and quasi-judicial appeals, visitations, arrangements to deal with the breakdown of pastoral relations, judicial proceedings which may result in the imposition of sanctions for the commission of ecclesiastical offences,[102] and (at least in some churches) canonical

[98] In cases other than sector ministry, the classical English doctrine is that, when clergy hold ecclesiastical office, and are subject to ecclesiastical jurisdiction, there is an incompatibility between, on the one hand, the spiritual nature of ministerial functions, their distribution by law rather than by agreement, and, on the other, the existence of a contract: see E. Brodin, 'The employment status of ministers or religion', *Industrial Law Journal*, 25 (1996), 211; the doctrine of incompatibility has not been fully reconciled with the doctrine of consensual compact under which ministers in a fundamental sense 'agree' to carry out spiritual functions: see Ch. 1.

[99] Central Africa, Can. 16.3–5; for model particulars of employment of clergy engaged in sector ministry in England, see *Legal Opinions Concerning the Church of England* (1994), 126–9.

[100] Canada, Can. XVII: 'every priest and deacon of the [Church] shall be subject to the jurisdiction of a diocesan bishop'; Sudan, Const. Art. 1(f): clergy exercise functions 'under the authority and spiritual jurisdiction of [the] Diocesan Bishop'.

[101] Melanesia, Const. Art. 7.A; Uganda, Const. Art. 16: the Provincial Synod defines ecclesiastical offences and sentences; see generally Ch. 2.

[102] See Ch. 3.

schemes for regular clergy appraisals which may themselves result in corrective action.[103] However, at the heart of the whole system of clerical discipline lies the doctrine of canonical obedience. This has two basic aspects: a general duty to comply with the laws of the church; and a particular duty to obey the lawful directions of bishops.

First, in addition to the occasional use of general statements that the law of the church is binding on clergy,[104] the laws of almost all churches contain provisions by which clergy undertake to comply with both provincial or national church law and with diocesan legislation. This is effected by means of undertakings, in the form of declarations, promises or oaths, made or taken at ordination and/or at admission to ecclesiastical office by means of institution or licensing. The form of the undertaking varies from church to church: in some priests and deacons must subscribe and declare that they will 'engage to conform . . . to the Discipline' of the church;[105] in most, more specifically, clergy must 'consent' or 'agree to obey the Constitution and Canons of the Province and of their Diocese'.[106] Scottish canon law contains a unique set of provisions on this subject: clergy promise 'to tender due obedience to the Code of Canons and to what is lawfully ordered thereunder'. However, '[t]he form of subscription promising obedience to the Canons of this Church implies only obedience to their requirements, and not necessarily approval of everything therein contained or that may be supposed to be inferred therefrom'. Moreover, clergy must make 'no promise or lay themselves under any obligation . . . inconsistent with their retaining their lawful liberty of judgment in performing their . . . duties so far as not restrained by their canonical subscriptions'.[107] A related device found in many churches is the duty to undertake to comply with the decisions of ecclesiastical authorities,

---

[103] See e.g. Brazil, Cans. III.10.9: 'An evaluation of the performance of the . . . clergy of the diocese is carried out periodically, every three years. This evaluation must be regulated by the Diocesan Council'.

[104] See e.g. Australia, Const. XII.70; Wales, Const. I.2; for undertakings to comply with the doctrinal and liturgical order of the church, see Chs. 7 and 8.

[105] ECUSA, Const. Art. VIII; ECUSA, BCP 1979, Marshall I, 543; New Zealand, *Prayer Book* 1989, 894, 904: 'Will you accept the order and discipline of this Church?'; Rwanda, Draft Const. 1996, Art. 43: 'I will respect the laws of the Church'; Burundi, Const. Art. 5(d); Zaire, Const. Art. 5.

[106] Papua New Guinea, Const. Art. 4; Southern Africa, Can.16.2(b): 'I consent to be bound by all the Laws and Canons (both present and future)'; Korea, Art. 120: 'I consent to be bound by all the Articles and Canons of the Anglican Church of Korea'; for consent see also West Indies, Can. 14; West Africa, Const. Art. II; Kenya, Can. 9; Central Africa, Can. 9; Melanesia, Const. Art. 6.C: they must promise 'to accept and [to] obey the Constitution of the Church of the Province' and that they 'will keep the laws of the Synod of their Diocese'.

[107] Scotland, Can. 12.1–3, and App. 12.

typically, to submit to the authority of the national or provincial assembly, and to the decisions of the tribunals of the church.[108]

Secondly, the vast majority of churches require clergy to comply with the directions of the diocesan bishop and his successors. This is effected by two devices. One is uncommon, and it seems used only in English canon law, where the church imposes the duty of compliance (with episcopal directions) directly upon clergy by means of a legal rule: 'the inferior clergy who have received authority to minister in any diocese owe canonical obedience in all things lawful and honest to the bishop of the same'.[109] Alternatively, and this is the most common practice, churches require clergy to make an undertaking or oath of canonical obedience. There is widespread consistency as to the basic form. Several churches follow English canon law which requires each cleric to state: 'I swear by Almighty God that I will pay true and canonical obedience to the Lord Bishop of C and his successors in all things lawful and honest'.[110] Other churches require 'due reverence' to lawful and honest episcopal directions,[111] and some simply require a general 'obedience'.[112] The precise meaning of these formulae is a little unclear and the Lambeth Conference has never defined the meaning of the doctrine. Clerical disobedience to an episcopal direction which is a re-presentation of a requirement under the law of the church is itself unlawful: in most churches breach of the oath of canonical obedience is listed as an ecclesiastical offence as is, in some, violation of

---

[108] New Zealand, Const. C.15: they must make 'a declaration of adherence and submission to the authority of the General Synod'; Scotland, Can. 12.1, App. 12: clergy promise submission to 'the decisions and judgments of the tribunals of this Church'; Ireland, Const. IV.67; Korea, Const. Art. 119: they 'undertake to accept . . . any sentence'; West Africa, Const. Art. II; Central Africa, Can. 9.1.

[109] England, Can. C1(3).

[110] England, Can. C14(3); New Zealand, Cans. A.II.3: 'I will pay true and canonical obedience in all things lawful and honest'; see also West Indies, Can. 14; and Chile, Cans. B.8.

[111] Ireland, Const. IV.67: clergy promise to 'render all due reverence and canonical obedience . . . in all lawful and honest commands'; Australia, Can. 7 of 1969: deaconesses must promise to pay 'canonical obedience' to the bishop; Central Africa, Can. 9: 'I will pay due and canonical obedience' (there is no reference to 'all things lawful and honest').

[112] Tanzania, Const. III.7: clergy 'have no choice but to obey the directions of the bishop of the diocese in all things honest and lawful'; Rwanda, Draft Const. 1996, Art. 43: 'I promise to be obedient to the Bishop of this Diocese in all things lawful and honest'; Burundi, Const. Art. 5(c); Zaire, Const. Art. 18; New Zealand, *Prayer Book* 1989, 894, 904: at ordination the candidate is asked whether he will 'accept . . . the guidance and leadership of your bishop'; Southern Africa, Prayer Book 1989, 588: 'Will you reverently obey your Bishop' accepting his 'pastoral direction and leadership?'; Papua New Guinea, Const. Art. 4: clergy 'must promise obedience under the Canons of the Church to their Diocesan Bishop'; for the same formula, see Melanesia, Const. Art. 6.C; Philippines, Const. Art. I.4: they must 'promise obedience under the Laws of the Province to their Diocesan Bishops'.

'pastoral directions' of the bishop.[113] Equally, of course, clerical disobedience to an episcopal direction which is contrary to the law of the church is
itself lawful. One important problem is when the law is silent as to the
bishop's direction: in this case it would seem that clerical obedience is not
required.[114] Generally, the decisons of the secular courts are unhelpful in
clarifying the terms of the doctrine.[115]

TERMINATION OF MINISTRY

It is a general ecclesiastical practice of the Anglican Communion that
churches make provision for the termination of the ministries of ordained
priests and deacons.[116] The laws of churches contain elaborate arrangements for termination of ministry. As a general principle, loss of ecclesiastical office occurs by lapse of time, death, the attainment of a fixed age,
retirement, resignation, transfer, removal or deprivation. It is with regard
to removal that the secular courts have been most involved requiring, as
they do, compliance both with internal church law and with principles of
natural justice appearing in the law of the secular state in which Anglican
churches exist.

Retirement and Resignation

The laws of the vast majority of churches require retirement (or resignation) from the ministry at a fixed age; ages vary but generally range from
sixty-five to seventy-two.[117] Commonly, laws permit continuance in office
beyond the retiring age with the approval of the bishop and for a prescribed period; some churches require the consent of the parochial church

[113] See Ch. 3; the explicit nature of the statement of principle in the following provision is exceptional: Scotland, Can. 6.5: 'The clergy of a diocese shall take no direction for
their official conduct but from their own Bishop, except in the case of a lawful decision
of the Episcopal Synod, or of the College of Bishops'.

[114] *Long v Bishop of Cape Town* (1863) 1 Moo PCCNS 411 at 465; 15 ER 756 at 776 *per*
Lord Kingsdown (PC): 'the oath of canonical obedience does not mean that every clergyman will obey all the commands of the Bishop against which there is no law, but that
he will obey all such commands as the Bishop by law is authorized to impose'.

[115] See e.g. *Ex parte Thakeray* (1874) 13 SCR (NSW) 1: the oath of canonical obedience
means that the cleric must obey only those commands which the bishop is legally
authorized to issue; see also n. 114.

[116] See Ch. 11 for rights to pensions.

[117] For the age fixed at 72: ECUSA, Cans. III.16.5; for retirement at 70 see England,
Ecclesiastical Offices (Age Limit) Measure 1975, s. 1; for 65 but not beyond 70: Scotland,
Can. 62.1; Tanzania, Const. III.7; for mandatory retirement at 65 and the right to retire
at 55, see Papua New Guinea, Can. No. 1 of 1994; for mandatory retirement at 65 see
also Korea, Can. 41; for retirement at 60 see Philippines, Cans. II.16.11; Ireland, Const.
IV.36: retirement is obligatory at 75.

council or its equivalent.[118] The laws of most churches confer on clergy a right to tender a resignation prior to the retiring age on the giving of notice, of a fixed period, to the bishop who may accept or reject the offer.[119] Laws commonly provide for compulsory resignation when the minister is physically or mentally incapable of discharging the duties of office; certificates from registered medical practitioners are invariably required in these circumstances.[120] Formal Anglican canon law is silent on the subject of voluntary and obligatory transfers.[121]

Removal and Revocation of Licences

In those churches where ministers are appointed to benefices or their equivalents (from which they are authorized to minister by means of institution), short of removal resulting from the breakdown of pastoral relations or judicial proceedings for the prosecution of ecclesiastical offences (see Chapter 3), such clergy enjoy a high degree of security of tenure. For example, in England, this is effected by the so-called 'parson's freehold',[122] and in Ireland, removal of incumbents is permitted only in accordance with a resolution of the Diocesan Synod.[123] An unusual arrangement

[118] Ireland, Const. IV.36 and England, Ecclesiastical (Age Limit) Measure 1975, s.1: the consent of the parochial church council is required and continuance may last for no more than 2 years; Southern Africa, Cans. 25.9, 46.3.

[119] England, Church of England (Miscellaneous Provisions) Measure 1992, s. 11: beneficed clergy may offer resignation to the bishop; Pluralities Act 1838, s. 97: assistant curates may resign on giving 3 months' notice to the incumbent and bishop; Ireland, Const. IV.33; Scotland, Can. 13.9: a rector may offer resignation in writing to the bishop (with notice to the patron) who may accept or reject; West Indies, Can. 18.2: 6 months' written notice to the bishop is required; ECUSA, Cans. III.21: the rector may not resign without the consent of the vestry; see also Philippines, Cans. III.17.

[120] See e.g. Scotland, Can. 13.10: an incumbency may be declared vacant when the vestry passes, on a certificate of 2 medical practitioners, a resolution approved by the bishop declaring the rector 'physically or mentally incapable'; appeal lies to the Episcopal Synod in cases of dispute; Ireland, Const. IV.34–36: if mental or physical infirmity is certified by 2 medical practitioners, and the incumbent is incapable of tendering a valid resignation, the bishop must remit the case for enquiry by the Court of the General Synod and subsequently the office may be vacated; Southern Africa, Can. 17: if an incumbent or licensed cleric is reported to be of unsound mind, the bishop must hear and determine the matter (on medical evidence) as 'the laws of the land require for proof'; the cure is then declared vacant or the licence withdrawn as the case may be; see also Papua New Guinea, Can. No. 1 of 1994.

[121] See above for Letters Dimissory when clergy move from one diocese to another; see also Canada Can. XVII.5: letters *bene decessit*; Japan, Can. II, Art. 31f; see also LC 1878, Res. 1; LC 1908, Res. 10.

[122] England: see R. Bursell, 'The parson's freehold', *Ecclesiastical Law Journal*, 2(10) (1992), 259.

[123] Ireland, Const. IV.31: no incumbent may be removed except in accordance with a resolution of the Diocesan Synod and with episcopal approval; a decision of the Court of General Synod or under the procedure contained in IV.36; see also ECUSA, Cans. III.21: a rector may not be removed involuntarily by the vestry.

appears in the canon law of Southern Africa. If the bishop considers that 'the work of God in a Pastoral Charge demands that there should be a change of Incumbent or assistant curate', failing the consent of the minister the bishop must take counsel with the cathedral chapter and, if it agrees after an opportunity is given to the minister to be heard, the bishop must offer the cleric other pastoral work in the diocese. If the minister refuses to accept such work, the bishop 'after satisfying himself by pastoral ministration that no other course is possible', may revoke the minister's letters of institution, collation or licence. If two-thirds of the cathedral chapter agree, the bishop may revoke the minister's authority without offering other work.[124]

Provisions dealing with termination of ministry by means of revocation of licences reveal a considerable diversity of legal arrangements as between churches. All laws on the subject are in agreement that the right to revoke licences belongs to the bishop. However, laws differ as to the procedural safeguards employed and the substantive grounds upon which revocation may take place. With regard to the former, laws are well-developed, but concerning the latter they display a large potential for arbitrary decision-making. Two models emerge: in both, the procedure is clear, but only in the second does the law treat substantive grounds in any detail. In English canon law, the bishop may revoke a licence summarily, and without further process, 'for any cause which appears to him to be good and reasonable after having given the minister sufficient opportunity of showing cause to the contrary'. A right of appeal lies to the appropriate archbishop.[125] The same approach is employed in Scotland.[126] A slightly more rigorous approach to procedure is to be found in the canon law of Central Africa. The bishop may revoke a licence but, if the cleric objects, the bishop must refer the matter to a commission consisting of the bishop himself, two priests of the diocese and one lay person chosen by the bishop, and one priest chosen by the cleric concerned. After having heard

---

[124] Southern Africa, Can. 25; Ireland, Const, IV.32: an incumbent may be removed by a resolution of the Diocesan Synod, with episcopal approval, if there is no longer sufficient work to justify the continued existence of a benefice.

[125] England, Can. C12(5); ibid., C12(6): if the licence is granted for a specified term, the bishop may revoke before the expiration of the term subject to an appeal to the archbishop; see also Pluralities Act 1838, s. 95: an incumbent may terminate the appointment of an assistant curate on six months' notice with the consent of the bishop; if the bishop refuses, the incumbent has a right of appeal to the archbishop who may confirm or overrule the bishop's refusal.

[126] Scotland, Can. 14.10: authorization in the form of a licence, commission, warrant or permission may be withdrawn by the bishop 'at any time': for 'any cause which the Bishop shall judge to be good and reasonable'; and after giving the minister 'sufficient opportunity of showing reason to the contrary'; an appeal lies to the Episcopal Synod and, pending the appeal, unless the cause is immoral conduct or unbecoming behaviour (in which case there is an automatic suspension), the authorization remains valid.

the cleric and such witnesses as the commission may wish to hear, the commission must decide on revocation and its decision is final.[127]

By way of contrast, Canadian canon law provides two procedures for revocation. The bishop may after 'due inquiry' revoke a licence 'for cause' (with suspension pending revocation) – a reasonable opportunity must be given for the minister to show there is no cause for revocation. Alternatively, the bishop may revoke a licence upon 'reasonable notice' in circumstances involving 'dysfunction in the parish or territory or community in which the licensee ministers, financial exigency, or any other matter not amounting to cause'; notice of the date of revocation must be given. A diocese 'may' establish policies and procedures concerning revocation to provide a definition of 'cause', a definition of 'reasonable notice'; and structures by which a bishop may obtain an objective assessment as to whether cause for revocation without notice exists. Notwithstanding these diocesan policies and procedures, cause for revocation exists in three cases: when the licensee is convicted of an ecclesiastical offence under church law, or of a crime under secular law; when the cleric wilfully, persistently or habitually neglects ministerial duties; or when there is evidence that the licensee has been 'incompetent'. A right of appeal lies to a diocesan tribunal.[128] In Kenyan canon law, similarly, an effort is made to spell out permissible grounds for revocation: a bishop may revoke a licence 'if for financial reasons it becomes impossible to continue the services' of the minister; or if the bishop is of 'the opinion that the further services of a Priest or Deacon will not be to the advantage of the Church'; there is both a right to a hearing and a right of appeal to the archbishop.[129] In short, there is little formal legal unity as between churches on the substantive grounds necessary for the revocation of episcopal licences – unity is found simply in the common silence of laws on this subject.

Abandonment of Ministry

For many churches, termination may be effected under the operation of laws governing the abandonment of ministry. In Canada, abandonment is 'presumed' on the occurrence of four events: 'public renunciation of its doctrine or discipline'; 'formal admission into another religious body' not in communion with the church; withdrawal from the practice of the Word and Sacraments; or engagement in secular employment without the consent of the bishop. Abandonment is reversed if the person submits to the bishop a statutory declaration that the facts alleged are untrue, a retraction

[127] Central Africa, Can. 16.2; see also Sudan, Const. Art. 57: 'The Diocesan Bishop may in his discretion revoke a licence . . . but if the clergyman objects, the Bishop shall refer the matter to the Episcopal Council . . . whose decision shall be final'.
[128] Canada, Can. XVII, App. L; see also Chile, Cans. B.7.   [129] Kenya, Can. VIII.3.

or an undertaking to cease the conduct from which abandonment is alleged.[130] A somewhat more theological approach is used in Southern Africa: if an ordained person, without the consent of the bishop, abandons the exercise of ordained ministry, or forsakes the communion of the church, he must not be allowed to resume office 'until he shall have given to the proper authority evidence of the sincerity of his repentance for the fault which he has committed'.[131] In other churches, persistent neglect of duties will constitute for practical purposes an equivalent to abandonment resulting in loss of office.[132] Abandonment of ministry may also be effected by relinquishment of orders, which may be voluntary or compulsory;[133] it results in the person being legally unable to exercise holy orders, though in most churches the law allows episcopal reinstatement.[134] Upon relinquishment and reinstatement, reordination is neither required nor possible.[135] The matter of termination of ministry, more than any other in the area of ordained ministry, has exercised the secular courts considerably in recent years. In several states, notably Australia,[136] Southern

---

[130] Canada, Can. XIX; see also ECUSA, Cans. IV.10, followed generally in: Chile, Cans. B.7b; Brazil, Cans. IV.5, 6; Puerto Rico, Cans. III.5–8; Mexico, Cans. IV.43–45.

[131] Southern Africa, Can. 19; for an almost identical provision, see West Indies, Can. 18.5; see also Scotland, Can. 18: a minister who abandons the ministry of the church, or intimates a decision to do so, is not allowed to resume the exercise of any ministerial office 'until restored thereto' by the bishop.

[132] See e.g. West Indies, Can. 18.4: the bishop may terminate the appointment of a minister, after consulting the Diocesan Council, 'on the ground of absence without leave'; Scotland, Can. 13.12: if a rector is absent for any Sunday without providing adequate cover and this persists without 'satisfactory explanation' to the bishop, the charge may be declared vacant; an appeal lies to the Episcopal Synod; Ireland, Const. IV.35: if the minister performs inadequately or neglects his duties or is physically or mentally incapable, the bishop may appoint an assistant curate.

[133] See Ch. 3.

[134] England, Can. C1(2); Clerical Disabilities Act 1870, s. 3: Ecclesiastical Jurisdiction Measure 1963, ss. 50–53; Clerical Disabilities Act 1970 (Amendment) Measure 1934, ss. 1, 2: a minister may by legal process voluntarily relinquish orders and use himself as a lay person; a deed of relinquishment must be signed and executed; on the recording of the deed the cleric is incapable of officiating, acting, taking or holding any preferment as a minister, and ceases to enjoy all rights, privileges, advantages and exemptions attaching to office, and is discharged from all disabilities, liabilities and disqualifications; see also New Zealand, Cans. G.XIII.8.1; Wales, Can. of 1990; Canada, Can. XIX.1: it 'removes from the priest or deacon the right to exercise that office including spiritual authority as a minister of the Word and Sacraments conferred in ordination'; the bishop may terminate the relinquishment and reinstate (with the same notices); if reinstatement is declined, and mediation is unsuccessful, the case is referred to the Provincial Court.

[135] New Zealand, Cans. G.XIII.8.1: 'No person who has been admitted to the order of Bishop, Priest, or Deacon can ever be divested of the character of that order'; this is a rare appearance of the idea in formal law.

[136] *Gent v Robin* (1958) SASR 328; *Baker v Gough* (1963) NSWR 1340: the bishop was under a duty to give a school chaplain an opportunity to be heard before revocation of a licence for cause; see also *Gladstone v Armstrong* (1908) VLR 454.

Africa,[137] the USA,[138] and England,[139] any action by ecclesiastical authorities resulting in termination of a cleric's ministry must be effected in compliance with the procedural rules of the church concerned and with the principles of natural justice – the secular courts do not, however, enquire into the merits of the substantive grounds for termination.[140]

CONCLUSIONS

Legal arrangements which regulate the ministry of priests and deacons yield a cluster of principles common to all churches in the Anglican Communion. Rules dealing with eligibility impose a direct fetter on the competence of bishops to ordain whomsoever they please, but laws reserve to the bishop the final decision as to the suitability of candidates for ordination. There is no canonical consensus in the Communion as to the precise suitability of individuals in sexually active homophile relationships. Modes of appointment to the many ministries open to ordained ministers vary considerably but with respect to churches operating the traditional process of institution every effort is made to confer a right enabling the participation of the laity in the process of appointment; with regard to authorization to minister by means of episcopal licence, these opportunities are considerably less obvious. Ministerial functions are normally cast, under titles dealing specifically with the subjects, in terms of duties rather than rights. That ministers are obliged to fulfil their duties is effected by a series of legal devices, central to which is the doctrine of canonical obedience to the bishop, a doctrine which is notoriously imprecise. Whilst most churches confer legal rights to retirement and resignation, a particular problem for Anglican canon law concerns the revocation of licences: laws do not generally specify with any degree of detailed precision the substantive grounds for which ministerial licences may be revoked.

[137] *Grundling v Van Rensburg* [1984(3)] SALR 202.
[138] *Stubbs v Vestry of St. John's Church*, 53 A 917; 96 Md 267 (Md): this concerned the legality of summary dismissal with reasonable notice; see also *Rector, Church Wardens and Vestrymen of the Church of Holy Trinity in the City of Brooklyn v Melish*, 88 NYS 2d 764 (NY); and *Diocese of Newark v Burns*, 83 NJ 594 (NJ).
[139] *Re Sinyanki* (1864) 12 WR 825.
[140] For this reason it may by many be thought appropriate for the Lambeth Conference to address by resolution the problem that Anglican canon laws do not spell out substantive grounds for revocation of licences.

6

The Ministry of the Laity

Successive Lambeth Conferences have recommended over the years a more enhanced role for the laity in the life of the church.[1] Their recommendations have been formulated within both the theology that the clergy and the laity together comprise the whole people of God, and the image of the church as a body built up through the interdependent activities of its members, each exercising their individual vocations. A prominent aspect of these understandings are the ideas that the primary function of the laity is in society at large and that most lay people are only secondarily located in the institutional church.[2] It is with the latter that this chapter is primarily concerned – the ministry of the laity within the institutional church and the degree to which the renewed ecclesiological emphasis finds juridic expression. Along with canonical definitions of membership, the following study explores Anglican canon law on the rights and duties associated with the common ministry of all the laity, and the provision and regulation of lay offices in the church.

CLASSES AND ROLLS OF CHURCH MEMBERSHIP

For many churches the need to produce a legal definition of 'member' is stimulated in part by the law of the state in which they exist: in some states only churches with a distinct membership have legal recognition; in others it is essential to determine membership to ascertain the enjoyment of

---

[1] LC 1908, Res. 46: 'The ministry of the laity requires to be more widely recognized, side by side with the ministry of the clergy, in the work, the administration, and the discipline of the Church'; LC 1958, Res. 58: 'The Conference calls on every Church member, clergy and laity alike, to take an active part in the mission of the Church'; LC 1988, Res. 45: the Conference acknowledges 'that God through the Holy Spirit is bringing about a revolution in terms of the total ministry of all the baptized'.

[2] See e.g. LC 1958, Res. 94: 'The Conference, believing that the laity, as baptized members of the Body of Christ, share in the priestly ministry of the Church and in the responsibility for its work, calls upon Anglican men and women throughout the world to realise their Christian vocation both by taking their full part in the Church's life and by Christian witness and dedication in seeking to serve God's purpose in the world'. For the primary location of lay ministry as in secular society, see LC 1908, Res. 45; LC 1958, Res. 125; *All Are Called: Toward a Theology of the Laity* (London, 1985); see also F. H. Thompsett, 'The laity', in Sykes and Booty (eds.), *The Study of Anglicanism* (London 1988), 245.

benefits under a gift to the church; and sometimes only church members have *locus standi* to enforce internal church law in the secular courts.[3] American jurisprudence is very well-developed and is culled from a large number of judicial decisions on the subject. Whether a person is a member of a religious society must, as a basic principle, be determined by reference to the rules of that society as well as by reference, if there is any, to any relevant secular law. Generally membership of a church is dependent on profession of faith, adherence to the doctrines of the church and submission to its government. Membership in a parish, for example, has been treated judicially as rooted in the consent of the parties as evidenced by application for membership and acceptance by the parish. When the signing of church corporation by-laws is a condition precedent to membership, individuals forming a new group who were elected to membership but who failed to sign those by-laws are not members. However, sometimes failure to comply with formality as to reception of candidates for church membership has, by means of 'extending the right hand of fellowship', been held by the secular courts not to preclude such candidates from becoming members. Any provision in a charter of a religious corporation which limits membership to persons with prescribed religious beliefs must be complied with until it is amended: such provisions have been held to be not unconstitutional.[4]

In laws of those very few Anglican churches which operate a formal definition of the word 'laity', a lay person is represented simply as an individual who is not in holy orders.[5] By way of contrast, the laws of the vast

---

[3] Nigeria, *Chief Dr Irene Thomas et al v The Most Revd Timothy Omotayo Olufosoye* [1986] 1 All NLR 215 (Supreme Ct): communicant members had insufficient interest to challenge an episcopal election; Southern Africa, see *Mtshali v Mtambo and Another* [1962(3)] SALR 469: 'a member of a church has *locus standi in judicio* to bring proceedings to protect his rights without joining other members of such church as applicants'. For 'members' in England for the purposes of the law of trusts, see *Re Perry Almshouses* [1898] 1 Ch 391 at 400 and *Schoales v Schoales* [1930] 2 Ch 76 (members are persons who are baptized, confirmed and regular communicants), and *Re Allen, Faith v Allen* [1953] 1 Ch 810 (members are baptized and confirmed persons who attend church regularly and who conform to the church's discipline); see also *Re Barnes, Simpson v Barnes* [1930] 2 Ch 40.

[4] For these principles respectively, see e.g. *Williams v Board of Trustees of Mount Jezreel Baptist Church*, App., 589 A 2d 901 (DC); *Kompier v Thegza*, 13 NE 2d 229, 213 Ind. 542 (Ind); *Korean United Presbyterian Church of Los Angeles v Presbytery of the Pacific*, 2 Dist., 281 Cal Rptr 396, 230 CA 3d 480 (Cal); *Kubilius v Hawes Unitarian Congregational Church*, 79 NE 2d 5, 322 Mass 638 (Mass); *Honey Creek Regular Baptist Church v Wilson*, App., 92 NE 2d 419, 59 Ohio Law Abs. 52, 44 OO 50 (Ohio); *Merman v St Mary's Greek Catholic Church of Nesquehoning*, 176 A 450, 317 Pa 33 (Pa).

[5] Sudan, Const. Art. 1(h): 'the laity' is 'the body of Christians, both men and women, other than those ordained'; Central Africa, Const. Definitions: 'The term "Laity" includes both men and women'; Tanzania, Const. I.2: '"Lay person" is a Christian not in holy orders'; Japan, Const. Art. 6: 'A layman is a person who has become a member of the Holy Catholic Church by Baptism' and 'the Laity includes both baptized members and communicants'; England, see e.g. Church Representation Rules, r.54(2): 'Any

majority of churches contain a definition of 'membership'. Definitions, however, are not uniform. In a minority of churches, baptism is expressly represented as conferring membership of the institutional church as well as providing incorporation into the church universal (for which see Chapter 9). In ECUSA, '[a]ll persons who have received the Sacrament of Holy Baptism . . . whether in this Church or in another Christian Church, and whose Baptisms have been duly recorded in this Church, are members thereof'; this same definition appears in the law of several churches.[6] In other churches baptism and confirmation together seem to give rise to membership within the institutional church,[7] though most commonly to these is added reception of Holy Communion. Under the constitution of the church in Tanzania, 'member' means 'a person baptized and confirmed who has received Holy Communion not less than three times in the past twelve months unless prevented or forbidden from doing so'.[8] A rather different definition appears in the Australian constitution: '"Member of this Church" means a baptized person who attends the public worship of this Church and who declares that he is a member of this Church and of no Church which is not in Communion with this Church'.[9] Perhaps the fullest definition of membership appears in the constitution of the United Church of South India; this 'recognizes as its members those who, being residents in its area, have been baptized . . . are willing to abide by the rules and customs of this Church; and are not members of any Christian body which is not in communion with this Church; and are not excommunicated by lawful excommunication; and are not open apostates to some non-Christian religion'.[10] In short, whilst churches in the Anglican Communion are agreed that baptism effects incorporation in the church universal, there is no legal unity with respect to the concept of membership as applied in individual, particular churches.

reference in these rules to the laity shall be construed as a reference to persons other than Clerks in Holy Orders'; and *Walsh v Lord Advocate* [1956] 3 All ER 129 at 139; see also Melanesia, Const. Art. 6.8. For judicial consideration of 'laity' and 'layman' in Australia, see *AG (ex rel) v Clarke* (1914) VLR 71.

⁶ ECUSA, Can. I.17.1(a); Philippines, Cans. II.2.1; Brazil, Cans. I.12; Chile, Can. A.2; Mexico, Can. 7.1; Japan, Const. Art. 6 (see n.5); for a slight variation see West Indies, Can. 26.1: 'Any person in a Diocese who has been baptised . . . whether in this Church or in another Christian Church, and who has been received into this Church, shall be deemed a Lay Member of the Church'; see also for the general idea North India, Const. I.I.II.1: the church 'acknowledges that the Church is the Body of Christ and that its members are the members of His Body' through baptism; New Zealand, Const. Preamble 1: 'all baptized persons are members' and GS Standing Resolution 1990: 'Baptism confers full membership of the Church'.

⁷ Central Africa, Can. 182: 'The laity, by virtue of their Baptism and Confirmation, share with the clergy in responsibility' for the mission of the church.

⁸ Tanzania, Const. I.2.   ⁹ Australia, Const. XII.74.1.

¹⁰ South India, Const. III.1; see also Japan, Can. 6, Art. 58: 'A Layman who has had no contact with the Church for at least three years shall be regarded as an inactive member'.

Membership is further divided into classes for the purposes of eligibility for admission to individual lay offices in the church.[11] A 'communicant' member is a person who has received Holy Communion in the church (usually) at least three times during the preceding year; only some laws give communicant status to those who have received Holy Communion in another recognized church.[12] Those who have in the preceding year been faithful in corporate worship, in working, praying and giving financially for the work and mission of the church are classified in some laws as 'communicants in good standing'.[13] In many churches 'received members' are those adults who, after appropriate instruction, and having made a mature public affirmation of their faith, have been received by a bishop into the church.[14] In some churches the law further divides classes into, for example, habitual worshippers or regular communicants.[15] Occasionally in churches a member may have the status of a 'parishioner': whilst in some a parishioner is any person resident in a parish,[16] in others a parishioner is equated with an enrolled member, a person whose name is entered in a church register or roll of members.[17]

The purpose of the church roll is to provide eligibility for participation in the government of the church, by membership of ecclesiastical assemblies, as opposed to qualification for holding a specific lay office.[18] The register of members is known variously as the electoral roll (as in England

[11] For 'baptized and confirmed members', see e.g. ECUSA, Can. I.1.17.

[12] For laws giving communicant status to those who may have received Holy Communion in another church, see e.g. Southern Africa, Const. Art. XXIV.6; Indian Ocean, Const. Interpretation section, 2.6; Wales, Const. I.6(a); Central Africa, Const. Definitions, 9; West Indies, Const. Art. 6.1 and Can. 26.2: the person must have received Holy Communion 'at least twelve times in the year'. For laws making no reference to reception of Holy Communion in another church, see e.g. ECUSA, Cans. I.1.17. Compare Sudan, Const. I(g): a communicant is simply 'a baptized and confirmed member' of the church; Japan, Can. 6, Art. 55: 'A Communicant is a layman who has been confirmed and has received Holy Communion' and an 'active communicant' is one who has received at least twice a year.

[13] ECUSA, Cans. I.1.17. Philippines, Cans. II.2.2; West Indies, Const. Art. 6.1: a person must have contributed 'regularly to the support of the Church'.

[14] ECUSA, Cans. I.1.17; Philippines, Cans. II.2.3; England, Can. B28: baptized people may be received by confirmation and confirmed persons with the Form of Reception; South India, Const. III.2, 3.

[15] England, Church Representation Rules, r.1(2) and Can. D2(1).

[16] In England it is a person's status as parishioner which gives rise to rights to the ministrations of the church: see e.g. *R v Dibdin* [1910] P 57; Australia, Const. XII.74.1: 'Parishioner' means 'a member of this Church who is entitled to vote at a meeting of a parish for the election of churchwardens'.

[17] Southern Africa, Can. 27.2: 'parishioner' is a person not being under Church censure who is either a communicant or a habitual worshipper.

[18] This is rarely articulated in law: see, however, Wales, Const. VI.2: '(1) In every parish there shall be an electoral roll. (2) The purpose of the roll shall be the determination of eligibility to exercise voting rights.'

and Wales), the parish roll or register (as in the USA and Japan), and the roll of the congregation (as in Scotland); in addition, some churches (such as in the Philippines) have a communicants' roll and in others (such as New Zealand) there is a roll of regular attendants at public worship.[19] The Church of England possesses by far the most complex body of law on the subject and the fundamentals of it appear in the laws of most other churches. In England, the responsibility for the maintenance of the roll is placed on the parochial church council; normally, in other churches, the roll is to be kept and maintained by an ordained minister (sometimes with the assistance of lay officers such as churchwardens). The English require-ment that it must be revised annually is common. To qualify for entry on the roll in England, the person must be baptized, of sixteen years or more, and must make a declaration of membership of the church or of a church in communion with it; a person may also be enrolled if, not being resident in the parish, he has habitually attended public worship for a six month period or is a member in good standing of another church which sub-scribes to the doctrine of the Holy Trinity. Other churches employ the same age requirement but restrict entry of a name to a person who is a baptized and confirmed communicant member of that church, and that church only; laws also commonly require declarations to this effect and, sometimes, of obedience to the law of the church. In England, as else-where, there is a duty to strike out the names of those who have died, those who are no longer resident in the parish and those who request removal of their names; in other churches, sometimes laws expressly provide that the names of excommunicates must be removed.[20] Seldom do churches

[19] For a register of communicants, see e.g. ECUSA, Diocese of Western New York, Cans. 13.1–7; Diocese of Mississippi, Cans. II.B.21–26; Philippines, Cans. II.2.5: commu-nicant members in good standing must be enrolled as a member of the parish or con-gregation and a certificate must be given to confirm this; New Zealand, Cans. B.V.4.3: this requires a roll of those of 16 years or more who have for at least 4 months 'regularly attended Divine Service'; West Africa, Diocese of Gambia and Guinea, Const. 1982, Art. 17. See also Japan, Can. VI, Art. 60 (and 61–62 for transference of registration); Brazil, Cans. I.12.6; Mexico, Can. 7.1; Portugal, Can. IX, Art. 3. For the 'chaplaincy' electoral roll, see Diocese in Europe, Const. 28.

[20] England, Church Representation Rules, Pt. 1; New Zealand, Cans. B.V.4.2: the vicar and churchwardens must keep the parish roll upon which the names of all per-sons of 16 or over resident in the parish who have declared themselves to be 'baptized and . . . a member' of the church are entered; there is a duty to strike out at least once every year the names of every person who has died, ceased to be resident, or transferred to another parish, or has expressed a desire to have the name removed; Scotland, Can. 41.1: each cleric having charge of a congregation must keep, regularly revise and care-fully preserve, in a manner approved by the bishop, a list of names and addresses of the baptized members and the adherents of their congregation; Ireland, Const. III.1.4, 5. For the responsibility placed on the council, see e.g. Wales, Const. VI.2–9. For the parish register, see ECUSA, Cans. I.1.17; Japan, Can. 6, Art. 55; Central Africa, Diocese of Lake Malani and Southern Malani, Diocesan Acts 1980, 20; Southern Africa, Can. 27; Korea, Const. Art. 95.

give a formal right of appeal against a decision to remove or against a refusal to remove, nor do they have express provisions dealing with termination of membership.[21]

An obvious lacuna in Anglican canon law is a developed treatment of the common ministry of the laity. Whilst many churches operate a system of fundamental anti-discrimination provisions, seldom does the law of churches present a distinct compendium, under a separate title, of the particular rights and duties of non-office holding lay people. Normally, rights and duties are scattered amongst laws treating individual topics – rights and duties are incidental to, or a by-product of, these laws.[22] In this respect the pronouncements of Lambeth Conferences, concerning the share of the laity in the whole ministry of the church, are left without precise juridic expression in most churches. This section explores the little law that exists on the subject.

Fundamental and Other Rights

In accordance with repeated statements of the Lambeth Conference, and in parallel with constitutional developments concerning human rights in the secular sphere,[23] many churches operate a system of fundamental

[21] For appeals see England, Church Representation Rules, rr.43, 45; see also *Stuart v Haughley Parochial Church Council* [1936] Ch 32: the civil courts will not upset a decision of a lay electoral commission unless it was contrary to natural justice; Wales, Const. VI.7: appeal lies to the archdeacon; Scotland, Can. 41.2: questions of removal must be decided by the bishop (subject to an appeal to the Episcopal Synod); Ireland, Const. III.6: appeal is to the Diocesan Council. Termination of membership is usually implicit either in the requirements for membership or in the striking out provisions; see, however, North India, Const. II.II: membership terminates on death, apostasy, resignation or withdrawal, continuous absence for 1 year or joining another denomination.

[22] American jurisprudence contains a clear set of secular legal principles applicable to church members concerning their rights and duties: the rights and obligations of members of churches are governed primarily by the laws of that church (*Canovaro v Brothers of Order of Hermits of St Augustine*, 191 A 140, 326 Pa 76(Pa)); every person entering into a religious society impliedly, if not expressly, agrees to conform to its rules and to submit to its authority and discipline (*First Presbyterian Church of Schenectady v United Presbyterian Church in US*, DCNY, 430 F Supp. 450 (US)); a person has no right to insist upon the exercise of rights as a member if this constitutes an invasion of property rights of the society or of other members: *Blount v Sixteenth St Baptist Church*, 90 So 602, 206 Ala 423 (Ala)). Generally, for the enforcement of lay rights and duties in secular law, see Ch. 1.

[23] LC 1948, Res. 6: 'The Conference declares that all men, irrespective of race or colour, are equally the objects of God's love . . . [e]very individual . . . has certain rights . . . [which] should be declared by the Church'; see Ch. 1 for human rights.

rights within the church. But this is by no means uniform throughout the Communion and often there are subtle substantive differences, included to cater for regional and cultural diversity. Constitutional and canonical declarations of fundamental rights are most common in the American and African churches; in the British Isles churches have no such legal statements.[24] Several principles are to be found. First, commonly laws declare the equality of all individuals before God.[25] This is sometimes presented as a requirement of 'Christian doctrine' and sometimes it is rooted in the rights and dignity of the human person.[26] Secondly, laws prescribe that the church is responsible to provide for the needs, or special needs, of all people committed to its charge.[27] Thirdly, there must be no discrimination 'in the membership and government of the Church'; discrimination is forbidden on grounds of, variously, race alone,[28] ethnicity,[29] nationality,[30] tribe,[31] or (occasionally) region or combinations of these.[32] The canon law of ECUSA contains perhaps the fullest declaration: 'No one shall be denied rights, status, or access to an equal place in the life, worship, and governance of this Church because of race, color, ethnic origin, national origin,

[24] In the United Kingdom, this is doubtless related to the common law approach and the absence of a written secular constitution spelling out fundamental rights formally: for a comparison of the Church of England and the Roman Catholic Church, see LFCE, 225–229.

[25] Papua New Guinea, Const. Art. 3: 'all persons are of equal value in the sight of God'; the same formula appears in Melanesia, Const. Art. 4 and Tanzania, Const. Art. III.5.

[26] Central Africa, Const. Fundamental Declarations, III: 'In conformity with Christian doctrine, the Church of this province proclaims the equal value of all men before the righteous Love of God'; Uganda, Const. Art. 3: in conformity with 'established Christian doctrine' the church proclaims and holds that 'all people have equal value, rights and dignity in the sight of God'; West Africa, Const. Art. I; Burundi, Const. Art. 4.

[27] Melanesia, Const. Art. 4: the church 'will take care to provide for the needs of all people committed to its charge'; the same formula appears in Papua New Guinea, Const. Art. 3; Central Africa, Const. Fundamental Declarations, III: the church must be 'careful to provide for the special needs of different peoples committed to its charge'; Uganda, Const. Art. 3: the church must be 'mindful to provide for the special needs of different people committed to its charge'; Tanzania, Const. Art. III.5: the church must make 'a special effort to fulfil its duties to the faithful'.

[28] Central Africa, Const. Fundamental Declarations, III: the church 'allows no discrimination on grounds of racial difference only, in the membership and government of the Church'; the same formula appears in Sudan, Const. Art. 2(c); a similar formula is to be found in Jerusalem and the Middle East, Const. Art. 5(i).

[29] Indian Ocean, Const. Art. 3: the church 'will not tolerate discrimination on grounds of 'ethnicity' in membership and government of the church; for a prohibition against 'social discrimination', see Zaire, Const. Art. 4.

[30] Tanzania, Const. III.5: the church 'will not allow any discrimination on grounds of nationality'.

[31] Papua New Guinea, Const. Art. 3 (race or tribe).

[32] Uganda, Const. Art. 3: the church 'shall not allow discrimination in the membership and government of the Church solely on grounds of colour, sex, tribe or region'.

marital status, sex, sexual orientation, disabilities or age, except as otherwise specified by Canon'.[33]

Beyond provisions of this sort, as a matter of ecclesiastical practice,
churches do not have a distinct compendium of laws spelling out com-
prehensively the particular rights of the laity. Rights are dispersed
throughout laws dealing with specific subjects, and these are discussed
elsewhere in this book, or else they exist as correlatives to ministerial
duties.[34] In any event, their existence, enjoyment, protection and enforcement are dependent on provision being made by the legislators of the
church concerned.[35] Generally, however, the rights of lay people in
Anglican canon law are distributed according to the individual's status.[36]
In most churches members and their families have formal rights to baptism, confirmation, Holy Communion, marriage, confession, an Anglican
funeral and to the liturgical facilities of the church.[37] Rights to participate
in the government of the church are confined to members whose names
are entered on the church roll and the right to be considered for admission
to church office is usually restricted to communicant members.[38]

A rather different jurisprudence is to be found in the constitutions of the
Indian churches. These do not speak of 'rights' at all but rather of the 'privileges' of lay members; this is placed emphatically within a theological
context. In the United Church of South India, '[t]he full privileges . . . of
membership in the Church . . . belong to those who, having attained years
of discretion and having gained some good measure of experience in the
Christian life', and having received due instruction in Christian truth,
'make public profession of their faith and of their purpose, with God's
help, to serve and to follow Christ as members of His Church'. The 'privilege of participation in the government of this Church is confined to adult

[33] ECUSA, Cans. I.17.5; for a similar approach see Philippines, Cans. II.2.4; for a prohibition against 'sexual discrimination', see Burundi, Const. Art. 4.

[34] See Ch. 5 for the duties of ordained ministers.

[35] Chapter 2 examines principles of which the following is typical: Southern Africa,
Const. Art. XVI: the Provincial Synod has power to determine 'the rights and privileges of
Parishioners in Church matters'; for the same formula see Central Africa, Const. Art. 18.

[36] See e.g. Scotland, Can. 41.2: 'No person whose name is not on the Communicants'
Roll . . . shall have the privileges or rights given by these Canons to communicants'; for
ecumenical law generally see Ch. 12.

[37] See Chs. 8, 9 and 10; New Zealand, Const. Preamble, 12: this recognizes 'the right
of every person to choose any particular cultural expression of the faith'; for an unusual,
but brief, statement, see Southern Africa, Can. 20.3: any lay person may: baptize in an
emergency; conduct divine service and bury the dead, at the request of an ordained
minister, or in an emergency; and at Holy Communion or at other services, read such
scriptures as the ordained minister requests.

[38] See Ch. 2 for government and further in this chapter for admission to lay offices;
in Australia, *AG (ex rel) v Clarke* (1914) VLR 71 it was held that an Act of Synod of
the diocese of Melbourne conferring on women the right to vote for lay members was
lawful.

communicant members of this Church' – the church's central Synod, or a Diocesan Council, 'having power to attach other conditions to the exercise of this privilege'. Moreover, '[i]t is the privilege of every member of the Church to know himself to be a son in the family of God and to rejoice in the experience of his salvation'. Much the same provisions exist in the United Church of North India.[39]

The Duties of Church Members

As a matter of ecclesiastical practice, Anglican canon law is only marginally better developed with respect to the duties of church members. But it is rare for the laws of churches to contain general statements of these. In those which do, the foundation of lay duties is the responsibility which the laity have, by virtue of baptism, for the ministry and mission of the church; in South India, for example, the constitution provides that '[i]t is the duty and privilege of every member of the Church to share in the Church's ministry'.[40] Resolutions of the Lambeth Conference, particularly one resolution from 1948, have treated the subject in some detail: all Church people should 'look upon their membership of Christ in the Church as the central fact in their lives' and '[t]hey should regard themselves as individually sharing responsibility for the corporate life and witness of the Church in the places where they live'; this is to be realized by: 'the regularity of their attendance at public worship and especially at Holy Communion'; the 'practice of private prayer, Bible reading, and self-discipline'; 'bringing the teaching and example of Christ into their every-day lives'; 'the holiness of their spoken witness to their faith in Christ'; 'personal service to Church and community'; and 'the offering of money, according to their means, for the support of the work of the Church, at home and overseas'.[41]

There has been only piecemeal implementation of these recommendations in actual law, in liturgical or catechetical documents, or in quasi-legislation. As with rights, the norm is for duties to be scattered amongst

[39] South India, Const. III.2, 4, 8; North India, Const. I.I.II.3–4, 9: members share 'full privileges' only if they are baptized and confirmed communicants, and if they abide by the constitution and are not apostates or excommunicates; the 'privilege of participating in the government of this Church is confined to those members in full standing' who have attained 21 years of age; this constitution is exceptional in so far as it also demands that '[r]espect for the conscientious convictions of individual members shall be accorded by the Church, as long as they are in harmony with the mind of Christ and are not disruptive of the fellowship of His Body'.

[40] South India, Const. VI.1; for a similar formula, see North India, Const. I.I.VII.1; Melanesia, Const. Art. 6.B: 'The whole people of God, clergy and laity, share in this ministry'; Southern Africa, *Prayer Book* 1989, 434: 'every baptized and confirmed member must share in God's mission to the world'; see also Puerto Rico, Cans. III and Mexico, Can. III.16.

[41] LC 1948, Res. 37; see also LC 1958, Res. 125.

laws on specific topics rather than collected in a separate compendium. In England the terms of the Lambeth Resolution are repeated, almost verbatim, in an Act of Convocation with the additional duty '[t]o uphold the marriage laws of the Church, and to bring up children to love and serve the Lord'. However, the Act concludes that '[t]he rules do not attempt to cover the whole of Christian life and conduct', but '[t]hey assume that every Churchman loyally endeavours to follow the example' of Christ; nor do they 'include all the duties of man as set forth in the Church Catechism; they nevertheless are duties which loyal members of the Church of England should include in their personal rule of life'. Some of these duties appear in the English canons.[42] In Southern Africa, to the Lambeth duties are added working 'for justice and reconciliation' and the upholding of Christian standards in marriage and family life.[43] The South American churches have a neat canonical presentation of duties. The canon law in Chile requires members, both in the personal life of the individual and in the common life of the church: to model their daily lives by the example of Christ; to maintain the practice of daily devotion; to participate in the eucharist and other services of the church; to use and develop their talents for the edification of the church and for the community; and to assist the church financially for the work of God.[44]

Laws of other churches are usually less detailed. The canon law of the church in Korea prescribes under a single title four basic 'duties of the laity': lay people must attend the eucharist every Sunday and Holy Day of Obligation; '[t]he laity must observe the Church's laws of fasting'; the laity 'shall be responsible for the expenses of evangelism and the livelihood of the clergy'; and the laity 'must strive to live according to Christ's teachings, to preach the gospel and to realize God's justice in society'.[45] The constitution of the church in South India has a rare addition, though one which conforms to an idea appearing in a Lambeth Conference resolution: 'members . . . contribute to the total ministry of the Church . . . by responsible participation in secular organizations, legislative bodies, councils and panchayats, and in other areas of public life', so that 'the

---

[42] England, *Acts of Convocation* (1953–4), 173; see also e.g. Can. B6(1): this imposes a duty to observe Sunday and attend worship; Can. B15(1): duty to receive communion regularly; Can. A8: duty to avoid schismatic conduct; Can. B29: duty to examine one's conscience privately and to confess. For a catechetical formulation, see e.g. Wales, BCP 1984, 691: 'The ministry of all its members is to represent Christ and his Church; to bear witness to him wherever they may be; according to the gifts given to them, to carry on Christ's work of reconciliation in the world and to play their part in the worship and life of the Church'.

[43] Southern Africa, *Prayer Book* 1989, 434; for family life, see also Canada, Can. 21.8; New Zealand, Can. G.III.1.4.

[44] Chile, Cans. A.2; for a similar approach see Mexico, Can. 10 and Southern Cone, BCP 1973, 17.

[45] Korea, Cans. 42–45; see also Chs. 7 and 11.

decisions which are made in these areas may be controlled by the mind of Christ and the structures of society transformed according to His will'.[46] The principal methods by which lay discipline is enforced are exclusion from Holy Communion (which is discussed in Chapter 9) and, more rarely, by proceedings in the church courts (which is discussed in Chapter 3).

The Rights of Children

As is outlined in Chapter 9, canon law on the rights of children to baptism and confirmation has been settled for generations, and regulations dealing with admission of unconfirmed children to Holy Communion are developing. By way of contrast, advances in the field of child protection against abuse in the church are very recent, a subject treated usually by means of quasi-legislation rather than by canon law; the specific provision in the canon law of the West Indies, that persons guilty of child abuse shall not receive Holy Communion, is exceptional.[47] It is a problem that has been recognized by the Lambeth Conference which by resolution urges 'Christian leaders to be explicit about the sinfulness of violence and sexual abuse whether of children or adults, and to devise means of providing support for the victims and perpetrators of such exploitation to enable them to break the cycle of abuse'.[48] Churches which seem to be leading in this area are in the British Isles and in North America. In England, for the purposes also of implementing secular law, procedures are intended to be preventative: the House of Bishops has formulated guidelines to regulate the selection and appointment of persons working in the church with children and young people; these require a declaration of convictions for criminal offences which might be considered as impediments to this work and the conducting of the church's own investigations into allegations of child abuse.[49] The Church in Wales has recently proposed similar guidelines and a policy document is currently in the process of being agreed by the church.[50]

---

[46] South India, Const. VI.2; for the Lambeth resolution see n.2; see also Ch. 1 for the church's role in political activity and for the binding effect of laws on the laity; in this regard, see e.g. Scotland, Can. 58: 'The Code of Canons shall be binding on all members, congregations and dioceses of this Church, and, in the case of members, shall so apply whether they are acting individually or corporately as Vestry Members, Trustees or Patrons'.

[47] West Indies, Can. 26.4.

[48] LC 1988, Res. 28: this is intended to reaffirm 'the traditional biblical teaching on the value of the human person who, being made in the image of God, is neither to be exploited nor abused'.

[49] *Policy on Child Abuse* (1995).

[50] *Cure of Souls* (1995) 17–23: the recommendations require full co-operation with secular statutory and voluntary bodies; 'abuse' is understood as including neglect, physical injury, sexual abuse and emotional abuse; and a procedure is set out for dealing with allegations, their investigation and confidentiality.

In Canada, the Diocese of Toronto has very detailed guidance on the subject, formulated in part at least as a response to developments in secular law. The policy that 'sexual abuse or harassment of any kind by any staff person or volunteer will not be tolerated' is placed within a theological context in which abuse is 'to deny Christian identity'. First, the document sets out guiding principles: the protection of children is of fundamental concern; allegations must be taken seriously; an accused person will be presumed innocent until proven otherwise; the protection of the complainant and their family is of paramount concern; and nothing should be done which might impede a secular criminal investigation. Secondly, the mechanisms for response include: a Diocesan Sexual Abuse Resource Person who must work with the bishop to determine the truth of allegations and to recommend action; a Crisis Response Team to visit the parish, consult and recommend action to the bishop; and at this point the bishop may invoke ecclesiastical disciplinary processes. Thirdly, complaints of suspected child abuse must be reported immediately to a secular Children's Aid Society (which is required by the Ontario Child and Family Services Act 1985);[51] if the complaint against a minister is substantiated the bishop may caution, reprimand, censure, inhibit or suspend the minister. Fourthly, the policy makes provision for pastoral care of the victim of the abuse, and disciplinary action is presented as 'a pastoral and caring act, providing for the common good of the church and also offering the possibility for restoration and healing'.[52] By way of contrast, quasi-legislation employed in ECUSA, issued by a committee of the General Convention and designed to operate at a trans-provincial level, treats child protection along with sexual harassment of adults. The guidance prescribes a procedure to be followed by a priest or deacon when approached by a person 'with a story of abuse, exploitation, or harassment' but it is generally less rigorous than the Canadian model and

---

[51] Section 68(2): '[e]very person who believes on reasonable grounds that a child is or may be in need of protection must report promptly the belief and information upon which it is based to a children's aid society'; s. 68(4)(d) lists as a specific category 'priests, rabbis and other members of the clergy'; s. 68(3),(7): '[t]he professional's duty to report overrides the provisions of any other provincial statute, specifically, those provisions that would otherwise prohibit disclosure by the professional or official. The professional must comply with the reporting law even though the report information may be confidential or privileged'.

[52] The policy was accepted by the Diocesan College of Bishops in 1990, endorsed by the diocesan Executive Committee in 1991, and amended in 1992; it may be found in the *Journal of the Church Law Association of Canada*, 1(3) (1994) 325; 'reasonable grounds' are defined as those having 'rational foundation' as e.g. when a complaint is from a child, when there is circumstantial evidence such as physical injury and when there are witnesses (gossip is excluded); 'Confession and absolution should be conducted with care and cannot be considered the sole basis for restoration to ministry'.

recommends only a 'report to appropriate authorities if required by state statutes'.[53]

The Religious Life in Communities

The practice of lay (and ordained) people entering religious communities led the Lambeth Conference in 1930 to advise 'the establishment, by canon or other means, of closer co-operation between the episcopate and the communities'.[54] Several churches, but by no means the majority, have acted on this advice. The most comprehensive canonical treatment is to be found in ECUSA. A religious order is 'a society of Christians (in communion with the See of Canterbury) who voluntarily commit themselves for life, or a term of years: to holding their possessions in common or in trust; to a celibate life in community; and to obedience to their Rule and Constitution'. To be recognized as such, a religious order must have at least six professed members, it must be approved by and registered with the Standing Committee of the House of Bishops on Religious Orders. Each order must have a bishop visitor or a protector who need not be the diocesan bishop. The visitor or protector, if not the bishop of the diocese in which the mother house of the order is located, must not accept election without the consent of the diocesan bishop. The visitor or protector acts as 'the guardian of the Constitution of the Order' and serves as an arbiter in matters which the order or its members cannot resolve through its normal processes. A person wishing to be released from vows who has exhausted the processes of the order may petition the bishop visitor or protector for dispensation; a right of appeal lies to the Presiding Bishop of ECUSA who must institute a board of three bishops to review the petition and to recommend to the Presiding Bishop 'who shall have the highest dispensing power for Religious Orders'. A religious order may establish a house in any diocese only with the permission of the diocesan bishop. The constitution of the order must provide for, *inter alia*, the legal ownership and administration of property and the disposition of its assets in the event of dissolution (which disposition must be effected according to the laws governing non-profit making religious organizations in the State in which the order is incorporated).[55] Similar provisions apply to Christian

[53] ECUSA, *A Clergy Guide to Understanding Title IV*, the Sexual Exploitation Committee of General Convention (1996): behaviour for which disciplinary processes may be instituted includes 'sexual abuse of children, ritual abuse, sexual exploitation of adults, sexual assault of adults, physical abuse of adults, [and] domestic violence'; guidance has also been issued nationally to congregations and vestries: *What a Congregation (and Vestry) should know about the Revised Disciplinary Canons of the Episcopal Church* (1996).

[54] LC 1930, Res. 74.

[55] ECUSA, Cans. III.30.1: a religious order is not, canonically, a parish, mission, congregation or institution of the diocese.

communities, societies of Christians (in communion with the See of
Canterbury) who voluntarily commit themselves for life, or a term of
years, in obedience to their rule and constitution; members of Christian
communities do not hold their possessions in common nor do they commit themselves to celibacy.[56]

These same rules, with differences of form rather than of substance,
appear in the canon law of a handful of other churches; in Papua New
Guinea, a special provincial council has recently been instituted with
canonical powers 'to promote the development and stability' of religious
life and to establish standards to be met and maintained if the province is
to recognize a group as a religious order.[57] In England, the religious life is
regulated by ecclesiastical quasi-legislation which contains similar
arrangements concerning establishment, admission, visitation, ownership
and administration of property and winding up. The English norms differ
from the American canons in so far as they contain in addition very
detailed provisions about the relationship between community members
and ordained clergy of the parish in which they are located, vows, chapter
government, and officers and employees.[58] Scottish canon law provides
expressly for the secularization of ex-members of religious communities:
the College of Bishops may release from the obligations of the religious
state any ex-member of an Anglican religious community having its central house in Scotland.[59]

The Development of Lay Ministry

Whilst Anglican canon law is generally weak on comprehensive statements of the precise rights and duties of the laity, it is rather stronger with
respect to equipping lay people for their share in the whole ministry of the
church. Several resolutions of the Lambeth Conference urge churches to
make arrangements to equip the laity for their ministry.[60] It is a fairly

[56] ECUSA, Cans. 30.2.

[57] Papua New Guinea, Can. No. 1 of 1995; Diocese of Port Moresby, Can. 25; see also
Melanesia, Cans. E.10; Philippines, Cans. III.4.

[58] England, *A Directory of the Religious Life* (1990), issued by the Advisory Council on
the Relations of Bishops and Religious Communities; 5: 'The *Directory* is . . . not a legislative code, but a corpus of norms or authoritative standards'.

[59] Scotland, Can. 56: this is provided that the person has been (with the visitor's consent) released from obligations to the community or has been expelled therefrom by the
authority of the community; Can. 40.5: if a religious community has a private chapel 'it
shall be recognized as a community working in connexion with this Church unless its
chaplain, warden and other clergy ministering therein' are licensed or otherwise sanctioned by the diocesan bishop.

[60] LC 1988, Res. 42: 'The Conference recommends that provinces and dioceses
encourage, train, equip and send out lay people for evangelism and ministry'; see also
LC 1958, Res. 71; LC 1948, Res. 36.

extensive practice for churches to operate at diocesan level institutions for the development of lay ministry, particularly preparation for the holding of lay offices in the church (which is discussed in the next section) and for vocation to the ordained ministry (which is discussed in Chapter 5). Once more, ECUSA seems to lead: each diocese must make provision for 'the development and affirmation of the ministry of all baptized persons in the Church and in the world'. Every diocese is obliged to have a Commission on Ministry, consisting of clergy and lay persons whose number, terms of office and manner of selection is determined by diocesan canons. The Commission must assist the bishop to implement this obligation: in determining present and future needs for ministry in the diocese; in recruiting and selecting lay persons for holy orders; in providing guidance and pastoral care for clergy and lay persons; in promoting continuing education for clergy and lay professionals employed by the church; and in supporting the development, training, utilization and affirmation of the ministry of the laity in the world. The Commission must 'solicit from the clergy and laity' of parishes, colleges, universities, and other communions of faith, nominations of persons for positions of leadership in the church; it may also invite such persons to engage in a process of discernment to ascertain the type of leadership, lay or ordained, to which they may be called for submission to the appropriate church authority. These provisions are adopted in some other churches, but normally, whilst churches have institutions whose function is to encourage vocation and training for the ordained ministry, their terms of reference do not require a general preparation for lay ministry in particular.[61]

LAY OFFICES IN THE CHURCH

One of the achievements of Anglican canon law is the provision of a multiplicity of ecclesiastical offices which are open to the laity at all levels of the church. There is a remarkable degree of consistency as between the laws of churches: all churches regulate eligibility, appointment, functions, and procedures for discipline and removal. As with other areas of the ministry of the laity, the resolutions of Lambeth Conferences have played a reasonably prominent role in the creation of law on lay officers, particularly liturgical offices. With the exception of trustees of church property, state regulation of lay officers is rare. However, the country which has produced an abundance of secular litigation on the subject, possibly the most, is the United States of America. Secular American jurisprudence has a set

[61] ECUSA, Cans. III.2–3; Philippines, Cans. III.1.1 adopts the ECUSA model; see also Puerto Rico, Cans. III.2 and Mexico, Can. 17; see Ch. 5 and, for continuing education in the faith, Ch. 7.

of clearly defined legal principles applicable to church officers. To be eligible for admission to office in a church, individuals must comply with the requirements of the law of that church. The appointment or election of officers is also governed primarily by the law of a church. When the tenure of an office is not limited to a specified period, a person continues in office until duly removed or until another is selected as a successor. The power to dismiss an officer is dependent on, and its exercise must comply with, the terms of internal rules adopted by a church.[62]

Provincial Offices

For churches comprising a single province, and provinces of regional and national churches, the four principal provincial offices are the Provincial Chancellor, the Provincial Secretary, the Provincial Registrar and the Provincial Treasurer. Many churches have the office of Provincial Chancellor. Arrangements in the Province of South East Asia are fairly typical: the chancellor, a communicant who must also be a qualified lawyer, is appointed by the archbishop in consultation with the Provincial Standing Committee; his function, in addition to his judicial activities, is to act as legal adviser to the archbishop and he holds office for such time as the Provincial Synod shall approve.[63] Generally, therefore, in the laws of most churches candidates must be confirmed communicants,[64] and qualified under secular law as judges or lawyers.[65] Some churches require can-

---

[62] For eligibility see *Wall v Mount Calvary Baptist Church*, 64 NYS 2d 200, 188 Misc. 350 (NY); church rules may insist on membership of the church as a pre-condition to appointment: *Mangum v Swearingen*, Civ. App., 565 SW 2d 957 (Tex)); in the absence of provision on the subject, the fact that a person is not a member of a church does not necessarily disqualify that person from holding office in a church: *Bouldin v Alexander*, DC, 82 US 131, 21 LEd 69 (US)); disaffiliation may terminate eligibility: *Diocese of Newark v Burns*, 417 A 2d 31, 83 NJ 594 (NY) and *People ex rel Rector, etc of Church of St Stephens v Blackhurst*, 15 NYS 114, 60 Hun 63 (NY); for election or appointment, see e.g. *Evans v Shiloh Baptist Church*, 77 A 2d 160, 196 Md 543 (Md); for tenure and removal see *Pelley v Hill*, 184 SW 2d 352, 299 Ky 184 (Ky), and for removal see e.g. *Boroyan v Monsesian*, 5 NE 2d 266, 287 Ill App 626.

[63] South East Asia, Const. Art. IX.

[64] ECUSA, Cans. I.2.5: confirmed adult communicants in good standing; West Indies, Const. Pt. IV.12; Philippines, Cans. I.3.3: a communicant; see also Indian Ocean, Const. Art. 13 and Can. 4; for the equivalent office of Dean of Arches and Auditor in England, see M. Hill, *Ecclesiastical Law* (London, 1995), 356–7.

[65] Papua New Guinea, Can. No. 6 of 1977: the candidate must be a judge of the secular Supreme Court or a barrister or solicitor entitled to practise in it; Canada, Const. III.17: a judge of a secular Court of Record or a barrister of 10 years' standing; Melanesia, Cans. C.6.A–K and South East Asia, Const. Art. IX; the person must be 'legally qualified'; Rwanda, Draft Const., Art. 48: a qualified lawyer 'known and respected in his profession'.

didates to be learned both in ecclesisatical law and in secular law.[66] They are normally appointed by the national or provincial assembly, or by the archbishop with the approval of the episcopal assembly.[67] Their function is to act in a judicial capacity in the superior church courts and they are obliged to give legal advice or a legal opinion to the archbishop or presiding bishop on request.[68] There is usually no compulsory age for retirement; they serve 'at the pleasure' of the appointing body and may be removed similarly.[69] Some churches have no provision for removal.[70] Often churches allow for the appointment of a deputy provincial chancellor or legal adviser.[71] Occasionally laws prescribe that the deputy must act 'according to his own conscience and discretion, and without direction from the Chancellor'; if there is a conflict of opinion that of the chancellor prevails.[72]

In the Province of South East Asia, the Provincial Secretary, who must be appointed by the Provincial Synod from amongst its members, is obliged to assist the archbishop with all official correspondence affecting the province; to keep minutes of the proceedings of the synod and its standing committee; to transact such business as is not within the office of the Provincial Chancellor, the Provincial Registrar or the Provincial Treasurer; to undertake such duties as may be assigned by the archbishop

[66] ECUSA, Cans. 1.2.5: the person must be 'learned in both ecclesiastical and secular law'; Philippines, Cans. I.3.3.

[67] For appointment by the provincial assembly see Zaire, Const. Art. 17; Burundi, Const. Art. 23; Papua New Guinea, Can. No. 6 of 1977; for appointment by the Episcopal Council, see Sudan, Const. Art. 32; for appointment by the archbishop with approval by the College of Bishops, see Melanesia, Cans. C.6.A–K; for appointment by the archbishop in consultation with the Provincial Standing Committee, see South East Asia, Const. Art. IX; for appointment by the Council of General Synod on the nomination of the primate, see Canada, Const. III.17; see also Indian Ocean, Can. 4: the 'Official Provincial' is the legal adviser appointed by the archbishop.

[68] Papua New Guinea, Can. No. 6 of 1977: he acts as 'chief legal adviser' to the archbishop and province; see also Melanesia, Cans. C.6.A–K and Uganda, Const. Art. 15(a); ECUSA, Cans. I.2.5: the officer acts as 'counsellor' and as judge; Canada, Const. III.17; Melanesia, Cans. C.6.A–K: the archbishop may permit the chancellor to advise any bishop or other member of the church; see also Sudan, Const. Art. 32; Rwanda, Draft Const., Art. 48: principal legal adviser to the province.

[69] Papua New Guinea, Can. No. 6 of 1977, Can. No. 1 of 1994: he holds office 'at the pleasure' of the Provincial Council and presides over the Provincial Court and all diocesan courts in person or through a deputy appointed by himself; the chancellor is also an *ex officio* member of all Diocesan Synods; ECUSA, Cans. I.2.5: they serve 'as long as the Presiding Bishop may desire'; Melanesia, Cans. C.6.A–K: the archbishop may dismiss the chancellor 'whenever he sees fit'; Philippines, Cans. I.3.3; Canada, Const. III.17: 'at the Primate's pleasure'; Uganda, Const. Art. 15: removal is by the Provincial Assembly Standing Committee or by resignation.

[70] Tanzania, Const. I.2, V and Can. 4.

[71] Canada, Const. III.17; Burundi, Const. Art. 23; Tanzania, Const. I.2, V and Can. 4; Uganda, Const. Art. 1(b).

[72] Melanesia, Cans. C.6.A–K.

or the synod; and to report to each session of the synod the action taken concerning synodical resolutions of the previous session. The Provincial Secretary holds office for such time as the Provincial Synod shall approve.[73] The laws of other churches depart little from these arrangements, though sometimes additional rules may be found: some require candidates for the office to be communicants;[74] occasionally, the officer has wider responsibilities in, for example, administrative and financial planning, co-ordination of the activities of the province and its dioceses, and the development of training programmes for staff;[75] and in some churches mode of appointment is different.[76]

In the Province of South East Asia, the Provincial Registrar, who must be a communicant, is appointed by the archbishop in consultation with the Provincial Standing Committee and holds office for such time as the Provincial Synod determines. The registrar is obliged, in addition to undertaking such duties as may be assigned by the archbishop, to preserve legal documents pertaining to the province and is responsible for the processing of amendments or additions to the provincial constitution and canons.[77] These provisions are echoed almost exactly in the laws of most other churches.[78] The Provincial Treasurer in South East Asia, appointed by the Provincial Synod from amongst its members, is responsible for 'the efficient administration of the Provincial finances and for advice and train-

[73] South East Asia, Const. Art. XI; Tanzania, Const. I.2; Canada, Const. III.16; Sudan, Const. Art. 34; Philippines, Cans. I.2; Southern Africa, Can. 44; Jerusalem and the Middle East, Const. Art. 8; Uganda, Const. Art. 12; Southern Cone, Can. 7.4; Central Africa, Can. 3.3; Japan, Cans. VIII, Art. 76; Indian Ocean, Const. Art. 13; Brazil, Cans. I.6; Mexico, Const. Art. III.3.

[74] Melanesia, Const. Art. 12, Cans. C.5; Papua New Guinea, Can. No. 6 of 1977; Rwanda, Draft Const. 1996 Art. 19: the person 'should' be ordained; Burundi, Const. Art. 10: the candidate 'must be ordained'.

[75] Papua New Guinea, Can. No. 6 of 1977; New Zealand, Cans. B.I.5.1–7; Melanesia, Cans. C.5.

[76] For appointment by the standing or executive committee of the assembly, see e.g. Melanesia, Cans. C.5; Canada, Const. III.16; for appointment by the Episcopal Synod, see Central Africa, Can. 3.2; Rwanda, Draft Const. 1996, Art. 19; the candidate must be of 'irreproachable conduct and integrity' and is bound by confidentiality; for a similar provision see Burundi, Const. Art. 10 and Zaire, Const. Art. 17; for appointment on archiepiscopal nomination see West Indies, Const. Pt II.8; Indian Ocean, Can. 6A: the officer may be nominated by the archbishop; Korea, Const. 6.41: the primate appoints after confirmation by the National Executive Committee.

[77] South East Asia, Const. Art. X: the candidate must be a lawyer.

[78] Sudan, Const. Art. 33; Papua New Guinea, Can. No. 6 of 1977; Kenya, Const. Art. XIV; Southern Africa, Can. 1.15: the registrar is appointed by the metropolitan with the concurrence of the diocesan bishops and in Central Africa, Can. 3.2 by the Episcopal Synod; in England the provincial registrars act as legal adviser to the archbishop and both act as joint registrars to General Synod: Ecclesiastical Judges and Legal Officers Measure 1976, ss. 3, 4. For the publication of laws see Ch. 1 and for the maintenance of records Ch. 11.

ing in financial matters, in co-operation with individual diocesan authorities'; he holds office for such time as the synod shall approve.[79] Once more,
this provision is common.[80]

Diocesan Offices

Generally, diocesan offices mirror those operating at provincial level. With
respect to Diocesan Chancellors, these must be communicant members of
the church, legally qualified under secular law and, sometimes, learned in
ecclesiastical law also. They are appointed by the diocesan bishop, sometimes with the approval of or in consultation with the diocesan assembly.[81] They hold office at the pleasure of the bishop and may be removed
similarly, though in several churches removal requires the approval of the
diocesan or other assembly.[82] Their function is to preside at the diocesan
court but the laws of most churches in addition assign to them a duty to
give legal advice on request to the diocesan bishop and, sometimes, to any
church member.[83] Commonly provision exists for the appointment of
deputy chancellors.[84] A few churches assign to the diocesan registrar (see
below) the function of giving day-to-day legal advice to the bishop.[85] The

[79] South East Asia, Const. Art. XII.

[80] See e.g. ECUSA, Cans. I.1.7; Papua New Guinea, Const. Art. 12; New Zealand,
Cans. B.I.5.1–7; Philippines, Cans. I.2; Canada, Const. III.19; Sudan, Const. Art. 35;
Rwanda, Draft Const. 1996, Art. 19(ii); Jerusalem and the Middle East, Const. Art. 8;
Uganda, Const. Art. 12; Indian Ocean, Can. 6.

[81] England, Can. G2 and Ecclesiastical Jurisdiction Measure 1963, ss. 2, 13; Wales,
Const. XI.8; Scotland, Can. 61, Res. 4: the candidate must be a lay person; Ireland, Const.
VIII.6; Kenya, Can. VII.2: 'A chancellor should normally be a communicant layman'; for
skill in ecclesiastical law, see e.g. ECUSA, Diocese of Western New York, Const. Art.
V.3; Diocese of Mississippi, Cans. I.B.6; see also Puerto Rico, Cans. I.6.

[82] See e.g. England, Care of Churches and Ecclesiastical Jurisdiction Measure 1991, s.
9: retirement is at 72; and Ecclesiastical Jurisdiction Measure 1963, s. 4: removal is by
resolution of the Upper House of Convocation if the person is incapable of acting or
unfit to act; Ireland, Const. VIII.6: removal by the bishop must be founded on a resolution of the Diocesan Synod; Wales, Const. XI.11: retirement is at 75.

[83] Scotland, Can. 61, Res. 4: the officer is 'legal adviser' to the bishop; Uganda, Const.
Art. 15(c); Burundi, Const. Art. 23; Kenya, Can. VII.3: the officer is 'to be available at all
times to the . . . Bishop . . . to advise him on any questions relating to the civil or ecclesiastical law'; ECUSA, Diocese of Mississippi, Cans. B.6.1: 'On the request of the Bishop,
or of any other Cleric, he/she shall give his/her legal opinion in writing'; Diocese of
Western New York Cans. 3.3: the chancellor must on request afford to the bishop and
the diocesan convention 'confidential and public advice on legal and canonical matters'; Ireland, Const. VIII.10: the chancellor must execute the office without fear, favour,
affection or malice; see generally Ch. 3.

[84] For England, see M. Hill, *Ecclesiastical Law* (London, 1995), 346; see also e.g.
Ireland, Const. VIII.9; and Wales, Const. XI.10.

[85] For England, see M. Hill, *Ecclesiastical Law* (London, 1995), 347–8; Wales, Const.
XI.9; no duty to give legal advice appears in Ireland, Const. VIII.8 or Scotland, Can. 61,
Res. 5; Papua New Guinea, Diocese of Port Moresby, Can. 13.3: a diocese may retain a
lawyer, being 'a Christian familiar with Anglican doctrine, discipline and worship'.

office of Diocesan Secretary may be either a creature of diocesan or of national or provincial law. Candidature is confined usually to communicant members of churches and the appointment is made by the diocesan assembly.[86] Functions sometimes vary in their details but normally include recording and attesting proceedings of the diocesan assembly; they hold office at the pleasure of the appointing body and may be dismissed accordingly.[87] Similarly, the Diocesan Treasurer, who normally must be of communicant status, is appointed by the diocesan assembly – the officer's principal function is to receive and disburse moneys collected under the authority of the assembly to which an annual report must be made on the received and audited accounts.[88] The Diocesan Registrar must maintain the diocesan legal records.[89]

Parochial Offices: *The Churchwarden*

The ancient position of churchwarden, existing in post-Reformation English canon law and earlier,[90] still constitutes the principal administrative office open to lay people at the level of the parish (or its equivalent). It is not surprising, therefore, that a number of elements of the law on churchwardens currently operative in the Church of England surface in the law of so many churches in the Anglican Communion. First, as to qualifications and appointment in English law, unless custom prescribes otherwise, there must be two churchwardens in each parish. To qualify a candidate must be a communicant resident in the parish or on its electoral roll. Candidates must consent to serve and they are chosen annually by the joint consent of the minister and a meeting of the parishioners; if this consent is not forthcoming, one warden is appointed by the minister and the other is elected by the parishioners. Instances of dispute may be settled by

---

[86] For appointment by the assembly see e.g. Scotland, Can. 61, Res. 1; England, Church Representation Rules, r. 34; Wales, Const. IV.14: the secretary of the diocesan conference holds office for 4 years at least and in Korea, Const. Art. 47, for 2 years; ECUSA, Diocese of Western New York, Const. Art. V.1. For appointment by the bishop see e.g. Melanesia, SR 14, 1985; Melanesia, Diocese of Temotu, Can. 9: candidates must be communicants; see also generally, Jerusalem and the Middle East, Diocese of Egypt, Const. 1982, 4; South India, Const. IX.6; Puerto Rico, Cans. I.4.

[87] See e.g. ECUSA, Diocese of Mississippi, Cans. I.B.3.

[88] See e.g. Scotland, Can. 61, Res. 2; ECUSA, Diocese of Western New York, Const. Art. V.2: the diocesan council elects on the nomination of the bishop; North India, Const. II.V.

[89] See e.g. Kenya, Const. Art. XV; Scotland, Can. 61, Res. 5–8; Ireland, Const. VIII.8; West Africa, Diocese of Gambia and Guinea, Const. 1982, Art. 12. For the giving of legal advice see n. 85 and for registers and records see Ch. 11.

[90] R. H. Helmholz, *Roman Canon Law in Reformation England* (Cambridge, 1990), 105–7, 192–3.

the bishop.[91] The national or provincial law of many churches requires two wardens to be selected annually, but, unlike in England, the norm is for one to be chosen by the people and the other by the minister; some laws require referral of disputes to the bishop.[92] In several churches the mode of selection is left to diocesan legislation or, sometimes, even to state law.[93]

Secondly, in English church law, the warden is admitted to the office by the ordinary, after making a declaration promising to perform the duties of the office 'faithfully and diligently'. It has been decided judicially that if a warden has been properly selected, the ordinary cannot refuse to admit: tenure lasts until admission of their successors. There is at present no power to dismiss a churchwarden though resignation is permitted, with the consent of the minister and the other churchwarden, upon submission of a written instrument to the bishop.[94] In other churches too the norm is for the office to be held until successors are appointed.[95] Unlike in England, the canon law of Southern Africa allows the archdeacon to object to admission 'for sufficient canonical cause'; there is a right of appeal to the diocesan court.[96] Like England, few churches have express legal provision enabling the dismissal of wardens. The church in Southern Africa, once more, is exceptional: where the incumbent or archdeacon perceives that 'the life and conduct' of a churchwarden is 'inconsistent with that office', the matter may be referred to the bishop who, after further inquiry and giving an opportunity to the warden to be heard, may dismiss or suspend the warden; in cases of removal, the warden has a right of appeal to the diocesan court.[97]

[91] Churchwardens (Appointment and Resignation) Measure 1964, ss. 1–2, 11; Can. E1; see also Diocese of Europe, Const. 31.

[92] For candidates who must be communicants of 18 years or over see New Zealand, Cans. B.V.25 and Wales, Const. VI.10, 17; see also Ireland, Const. III.13(a), 35 (see Diocese of Connor, Regulations 1990, XXVIII for an appeal to the committee of appeal of the diocesan council when there is a dispute concerning appointment); Southern Africa, Can. 29: candidates must be 21 or over and they are elected annually by parishioners with subsequent agreement of the incumbent and a failure to agree is to be referred to the bishop.

[93] ECUSA, Cans. I.14; Philippines, Cans. I.6.3; West Africa, Diocese of Gambia and Guinea, Const. 1982, Art. 16(3); Central Africa, Can. 19: each diocese may legislate on churchwardens 'for their own needs' (see e.g. Diocese of Lake Malani and Southern Malani, Diocesan Acts 1980, 23).

[94] England, Churchwardens (Appointment and Resignation) Measure 1964, ss. 7–9 and Can. E1; *R v Bishop of Sarum* [1916] 1 KB 467. Draft legislation currently before General Synod will allow episcopal suspension of wardens.

[95] Ireland, Const. III.13(a); Philippines, Cans. I.6.3; ECUSA, Cans. I.14.1; Wales, Const. VI.17: wardens have an annual term, they may resign (to the bishop) and there must be no re-election after 6 terms.

[96] Southern Africa, Can. 30.1, 2.

[97] Southern Africa, Cans. 28.6, 30.2; judicial proceedings against wardens in the church courts are possible in those churches in which the courts have jurisdiction over the laity and lay officers: see Ch. 3.

Thirdly, in English canon law functions are governed by the church-warden's legal position as officer of the bishop and the foremost representative of the laity: they include responsibility for the provision of articles necessary for divine worship and management of church property, for which purposes they are treated in secular law as quasi-corporations. Another legal obligation is that they must use their best endeavours 'by example and precept to encourage the parishioners in the practice of true religion and promote unity and peace among them'. They are closely involved in the visitation of the archdeacon and are responsible for the allocation of seats and for keeping order in the church (and churchyard) during the time of divine service.[98] As with England, the law of most churches treats the warden as the officer of the bishop and representative of the laity.[99] In a few churches, unlike in England, the law expressly imposes on wardens a duty to comply with the directions of the bishop.[100] The temporal and pastoral aspects of the warden's ministry are commonly emphasized but usually this is a matter dealt with by diocesan law.[101] In ECUSA, in the Diocese of Mississippi, the wardens must ensure that the parish provides the church with items necessary for divine worship, and that the church and other parish buildings are kept in good repair; moreover, they 'shall co-operate with the Rector in all efforts to develop and set forward the spiritual life of the Parish'.[102] In several secular states, the office of churchwarden has been the subject of both legislation and judicial consideration.[103]

[98] England, Cans. E1, F7(2), F15; see Ch. 3 for visitation and Ch. 11 for property.

[99] Wales, Const. VI.17.2; Southern Africa, Can. 29.7: wardens are the officers of the bishop and 'the principal representatives of the congregation'; they are under a duty to complain to the bishop or the archdeacon 'if there should be anything plainly amiss or reprehensible in the life or doctrine of the Incumbent'.

[100] Southern Africa, Can. 30.3: they must declare 'obedience' to the bishop; in Wales the duty seems to be far narrower: Const. VI.17(2): they must declare, 'I agree to accept and obey the decision of the Bishop or of the Diocesan Chancellor as to any right at any time to hold the office of Churchwarden'.

[101] For direct parallels with the English model, see e.g. Ireland, Const. III.26; Wales, Const. VI.17(2); Southern Africa, Can. 29.7; for law allowing dioceses to formulate functions, see e.g. New Zealand, Cans. B.V.3.5 and Central Africa, Can. 19 (see e.g. Diocese of Lake Malani and Southern Malani, Act 1980, 23.6); for declarations to obey the law of the church, see Ch. 1.

[102] ECUSA, Diocese of Mississippi, Cans. II.B.23; ECUSA, Can. I.14.2: except as provided by diocesan or state law, 'the Vestry shall be agent and legal representative of the parish in all matters concerning its corporate property and the relations of the Parish to its Clergy'.

[103] See e.g. Bermuda, Church of England in Bermuda Act 1975, s. 8: this recognizes the right of the synod to regulate the office of churchwarden; for historical material in America, see E. A. White, *American Church Law* (New York, 1898), 148, 289ff and *Terrett v Taylor* (1815) 13 US (9 Cranch) 43: a warden is not a corporation; compare England, M. Hill, *Ecclesiastical Law* (London, 1995), 95; Australia, *Johnson v Glen* (1879) 26 Gr 162

Liturgical and Pastoral Offices

Resolutions of the Lambeth Conference have consistently encouraged the development in churches of structures enabling qualified lay people to serve in liturgical and pastoral capacities.[104] Law throughout the Anglican Communion is today very well-developed, in terms of regulation of eligibility, appointment, functions and discipline. And from it it is possible to deduce a series of reasonably well-defined principles. In terms of form, three methods of treating the subject seem to be used: a system of general rules applicable to all lay liturgical and pastoral offices; particular law on particular ministries; and a mixture of the two.

First, general rules: a canon of the Australian church may be used as the paradigm. The preamble to the Authorised Lay Ministry Canon 1992, which may be adopted by dioceses, states that 'ministry is of the essence of the life of the whole body of Christ' and 'all baptised persons are called to minister in the Church and in the world'. The canon deals with 'certain persons [who] are called to a public and representative lay ministry within and on behalf of this Church'. A lay minister who is a communicant member of the church may be authorized by the bishop of a diocese 'to exercise within and for this Church' in that diocese one or more of the following ministries: the reading and conduct of authorized services; the preaching of sermons; assistance to the priest in the ministration and distribution of the Holy Communion; and 'any other lay ministry declared by the bishop of the diocese to be an authorised lay ministry for the purposes of this canon'. Authority to minister may, under the canon, be limited by reference to all or any of: the nature of the functions authorized to be performed; the person or persons at whose request or by whose authority the functions may be performed; and the place at which and the period during which the functions may be performed. The bishop may revoke that authority. Except as provided by the Diocesan Synod, the bishop may prescribe: the qualifications of persons who may be authorized to exercise 'a particular lay ministry'; the procedure for authorization; the form of an authority; the duties and functions which may be performed; the manner in which those duties and functions may be performed; and the vesture to be worn performing those functions. The provisions of this canon, however, 'shall not operate to restrict any authority of the bishop or synod of a diocese or to preclude any practice in a diocese relating to a particular lay ministry'.[105] This approach, the use of general rules applicable to all

(Ch): Anglican canons requiring consultation by the bishop with churchwardens prior to the appointment of a rector were enforced as a matter of contract law.

[104] See e.g. LC 1930, Res. 65; LC 1958, Res. 90, 91.

[105] Australia, Can. 17 1992; for diocesan adoption, see e.g. Diocese of Sydney, *The 7th Handbook*, 10 and App. 22: types of authority are for life, periodic and occasional;

lay ministries, is echoed in the law of a number of other churches. In Southern Africa authorization is wholly in the keeping of the bishop,[106] and in Central Africa the law provides that 'when there is no duly licensed person available, any member of the laity, being a communicant, may perform' functions.[107] For the South American churches and the West Indies in particular, lay ministers 'shall conform to the directions of the Incumbent and in all cases to the directions of the Bishop'.[108] Similarly, in New Zealand, general rules apply to lay persons involved in any decision-making process in the church.[109]

Secondly, churches regulate lay liturgical and pastoral ministries by means of particular law on individual offices. This is the approach employed in churches in the British Isles and elsewhere. In English canon law, candidates for the office of reader must be baptized, confirmed and regular communicants. They are nominated to the bishop by the minister and to be admitted must have 'a sufficient knowledge' of Holy Scripture and the doctrine and worship of the church; they must also give obedience to the bishop and comply with the directions of their ordained ministers. Readers must be licensed: to visit the sick, to undertake such pastoral and educational work and to assist any minister as the bishop may direct; to assist in divine service by reading, preaching and receiving and presenting the offerings of the people; to distribute the Holy Communion; and to conduct funerals. The bishop must keep a register of readers in the diocese. Episcopal licences may be revoked summarily, when appeal lies

candidates must be baptized, confirmed, 18 or over, and they must have assented to the doctrine of the church and to obey all lawful and honest commands of the bishop; candidature must be approved by the incumbent and the church committee; lay ministers must use only the authorized services; and posts include: diocesan reader, parish reader, parish worker, youth worker, catechist, counsellor and evangelist.

[106] Southern Africa, Can. 20: 'Lay ministers shall be designated, appointed and admitted in accordance with regulations prescribed by each Diocesan Synod'; they may exercise ministry only by the licence of the bishop 'who may grant, revoke or renew such licence as he deems fit'; the duties of licensed ministers include: instructing and preparing candidates for baptism and confirmation; preaching; assisting in the administration of Holy Communion; and performing such other 'pastoral duties, not reserved to the ordained ministry, as the Bishop may determine'; see also South India, Const. VI.2 for the skeletal approach.

[107] Central Africa, Can. 18 repeats the South African provisions and adds: 'to visit in the name of the Church the homes of the people, especially the sick, the aged and the infirm', to read the order for the burial of the dead, and to baptize in an emergency.

[108] West Indies, Can. 20; for other examples of general rules, see Brazil, Cans. III.1; Chile, Can. 13; Puerto Rico, Cans. III.3.

[109] New Zealand, Can. B.XXI.1–3: this applies to any person who is 'to hold office in or take part in the decision making proceedings of any organisation or body recognising or under the authority of General Synod'; they must be validly baptized, 16 or over, enrolled and have signed the declaration regarding compliance with the constitution.

to the archbishop, or by notice.[110] The law of the Scottish church is similar: it requires communicant status, nomination, testimony of character and fitness, a declaration of compliance with the directions of the bishop and the cleric in charge; the cleric in charge may apply for termination of the licence which 'may be cancelled at any time at the discretion of the Bishop'.[111] The same basic principles apply to the office of lay worker.[112]

Thirdly, churches operate an amalgamation of these two approaches, with both general rules and particular rules applicable to individual ministries. In these churches, a greater variety of offices seems to be open to the laity. According to the canon law of ECUSA, which seems to have been followed in several other churches, a confirmed adult communicant may serve as a lay reader, pastoral leader, lay preacher, lay eucharistic minister, or catechist if licensed by the bishop. Guidelines must be made by the bishop dealing with their training and selection. Licences may be issued only on the recommendation and request of clergy in charge of a congregation. They are issued for a renewable maximum period of three years and may be revoked by the bishop or 'upon request' of the nominating cleric. Renewal is determined on the basis of 'acceptable performance' and endorsement by the cleric. The licensee must 'conform to the directions of the bishop and the Member of the Clergy in charge of the Congregation in which the person is serving'.[113] Pastoral leaders, who are also parish administrators, may be licensed to lead regularly the offices authorized in the service books. They must be trained, examined and found competent in a range of subjects: scripture, the Book of Common Prayer, conduct of public worship, the use of the voice, church history and doctrine, parish administration, the 'appropriate' canon law and pastoral care. A person may not be licensed if the congregation is able to and has a reasonable opportunity to secure a resident member of the clergy in charge.[114] A lay preacher must be trained and examined similarly and they may preach

[110] England, Cans. E4–6; see also Ireland, Const. IX.35 and Japan, Can. VI: unlike England, appeals against revocation may be made to the diocesan court; the Church in Wales seems not to have any modern or comprehensive constitutional or canonical provision for readers.

[111] Scotland, Can. 20 and Resolution 1: functions are prescribed by the diocesan bishop's regulations; see also Korea, Can. 13: the candidate must also have been 'active in the support of his Mission or Parish'; the licence may be granted for a period not exceeding 2 years and may be renewed or revoked 'at any time at the discretion of the Bishop'; and performance is subject to 'periodic assessment'.

[112] See e.g. England, Can. E7; Wales, Const. I.6(b): a lay worker is 'a lay person who officiates in accordance with a licence from the Bishop or with his permission'; see also Japan, Cans. IV and V.

[113] ECUSA, Cans. III.3.1–2; see also Mexico, Cans. 17,18; Melanesia, Cans. C.5.B-D; Philippines, Cans. III.2.3; Papua New Guinea, Diocese of Port Moresby, Can. 22: a licence may be revoked 'with or without cause'.

[114] ECUSA, Cans. III.3.3.

only on the initiative and under the supervision of the clergy in charge.[115] A lay eucharistic minister, licensed 'to this extraordinary ministry', may administer the elements in church, 'in the absence of a sufficient number of Priests or Deacons', and to the sick. The bishop must issue guidelines dealing with selection and training but their ministry 'is not to take the place of the ministry of Priests and Deacons'.[116] Catechists are licensed 'to prepare persons for Baptism, Confirmation, Reception and the Reaffirmation of Baptismal vows'. They must undergo training in scripture, liturgy, church history, doctrine and 'Methods of Catechesis'.[117] A lay reader may regularly lead public worship under the direction of the clergy in charge of the congregation. Training and licensing are under the authority of the bishop as provided by diocesan canons.[118] Finally, a lector is a person licensed by a member of the clergy in charge of a congregation to read the Word of God and to lead prayers.[119] In England, some key posts at parochial level now exist which are not canonical: the position of parish assistant is typical and this is beginning to be regulated by diocesan quasi-legislation.[120]

Employees of the Church

Members of the laity may serve the church in the capacity of an employee rather than as holders of an ecclesiastical office. As a matter of ecclesiastical practice, laws are in the main silent on this subject. If individuals are employed by church bodies, ordinarily the secular law of employment applies and recourse against unlawful dismissal may be had in the secular tribunals.[121] This has led some churches to develop quasi-legislation prescribing good practices for churches towards their employees and the need for contracts to regulate appointment, functions, grievance procedures and dismissal. In the Australian Diocese of Sydney, when a lay minister is employed there should be an exchange of letters between that person and the churchwardens of the principal church which outline the terms and conditions of employment. These should include: a broad description of the hours, days of work and duties to be carried out; the amounts or benefits to be paid; sick leave; provision for housing; an undertaking to apply for any necessary authority from the bishop where relevant; superannuation; annual leave; long service leave and workers

---

[115] ECUSA, Cans. III.3.4. [116] ECUSA, Cans. III.3.5.

[117] ECUSA, Cans. III.3.6.

[118] ECUSA, Cans. III.3.7; see also Diocese of Mississippi, Cans. I.G.17.2 for congregational lay readers.

[119] ECUSA, Cans. III.3.8.

[120] See e.g. Diocese of Worcester, *Diocesan Handbook* (1993), BP.2.1; see generally LFCE, 249–250.

[121] See e.g. England, L. Leeder, *Ecclesiastical Law Handbook* (London, 1997), 87–8.

compensation.[122] It is very rarely the case that the subject is treated canonically, though resolutions of the Lambeth Conference commonly deal with the rights of workers in the secular sphere.[123] Exceptionally, the canon law of ECUSA provides that non-communicants in good standing in other churches not in communion with the church may be employed by ecclesiastical authorities.[124] In Melanesia, all church bodies which employ must structure their personnel contractual arrangements so that they require, as a professional condition of employment, 'compliance with the Christian moral code'.[125]

CONCLUSIONS

Lambeth Conference pronouncements recommending an enhanced role for the laity in its share of responsibility for the ministry of the church are realized throughout the Anglican Communion in complex bodies of law on the subject. The evidence suggests that as a matter of general ecclesiastical practice churches operate reasonably well-defined concepts of membership and systems for the registration of members to enable classes of members to participate in the government of the church. In recent years, many churches have introduced prohibitions against discrimination in the membership and government of the church, but this is by no means the case throughout the Communion. Anglican canon law appears to be weak in terms of presenting a distinct common ministry of the laity in terms of their specific rights and duties; these are, rather, scattered amongst laws dealing with other discrete subjects. And only in a handful of churches is regulation on child protection, religious communities, institutions to develop lay ministry and employees of the church beginning to appear. Laws on lay liturgical and pastoral ministries, however, are very well-developed: provision for these is global and consistent, though laws differ

---

[122] Australia, Diocese of Sydney, *The 7th Handbook*, 10; see for England, *Legal Opinions concerning the Church of England*, Legal Advisory Commission (1994), 120–126.

[123] LC 1908, Res. 49(b); LC 1948, Ress. 22, 43; LC 1958, Res. 127; LC 1978, Res. 1, 3; and LC 1988, Res. 39.

[124] ECUSA, Can. I.4.9; for detailed provisions concerning medical workers in India, see South India, Diocese of Dornakal, Constitutions of Committees under the Diocesan Council 1977, 24.C.

[125] Melanesia, Standing Resolution 27 1989; see also Philippines, Can. III.3: this deals with professional church workers; New Zealand, *Human Rights Commission v Eric Sides Motor Co Ltd and Others* (Equal Opportunities Tribunal No 4/1980, 15 April 1981): a garage proprietor advertised for a 'keen Christian' worker in two newspapers; it was held that the advertisement could be reasonably understood as indicating an intention to commit a breach of s. 15(1) of the Human Rights Commission Act 1977 (i.e. as an employer refusing to employ or giving preference to a person by reason of religious belief): see *Commonwealth Law Bulletin*, 7(4) (1981), 1248.

as to the form of regulation – by general rules applicable to all ministries, by particular laws on individual ministries or by a mixture of these. Liturgical and pastoral lay ministries are in the keeping, usually, of the bishop, but laws on the revocation of licences are, it is submitted, inadequate; the law of no church spells out with any degree of precision the substantive grounds upon which the bishop may revoke and rights of appeal are rare. The law on provincial officers is mirrored at diocesan level and the substantive laws on functions are much the same in all churches; it is in procedural law concerning modes of appointment that churches vary most obviously. The ancient position of churchwarden is still the principal administrative office open to the laity at parochial level. State law, by and large, is silent on church officers: American jurisprudence, however, contains well-defined principles applicable to eligibility, appointment and discipline of these.

7

Faith and Doctrine

The word 'doctrine' has been analysed in the Protestant Episcopal Church in the United States of America in a recent decision of the Court for the Trial of a Bishop: 'doctrine involves more than creedal affirmations'; it embraces 'a spectrum which includes not only faith and belief, but morals and practice'. 'Core Doctrine' is derived from a range of sources and the Anglican Chicago–Lambeth Quadrilateral (1886–88) is 'a reflection of this understanding'. The doctrine of the church is fixed by the whole church 'acting in its corporate capacity, and not by . . . any bishop, priest or deacon speaking individually'. Moreover, doctrine is not 'to be confused with theology which is prayerful reflection on scripture and Core Doctrine in the light of the Christian experience'. In the case it was affirmed that ECUSA is not a confessional church as it had not defined its teaching exhaustively.[1] These ideas provide a useful framework within which to examine doctrine in Anglican canon law, not least because the formal law of churches in the Communion is generally silent as to the meaning of the term – the Australian constitution, in which doctrine means 'the teaching of this Church on any question of faith', seems to be quite exceptional in formal law.[2] Doctrine, then, may be understood in a general sense as that body of faith or teaching which is received and believed by those comprising a religious community.[3] The legal treatment of discrete subjects associated with belief suggests that doctrinal law in Anglican churches has four basic functions: to ensure the public presentation of the faith; to

---

[1] *Stanton (Bishop of Dallas) v Righter* (1996); see also P. M. Dawley, *The Episcopal Church and Its Work* (Revised Edn., New York, 1961), Pt. III.

[2] Australia, Const. XII.74.1: ' "Faith" includes the obligation to hold the faith'; the notion that 'faith is incorporated in the doctrine' of the church is occasionally used: see e.g. Indian Ocean, Const. Art. 2(iii); South East Asia, Const. Fundamental Declaration, 1; sometimes law employs the expression 'the doctrine of Christ' (see e.g. New Zealand, Const. Pt. I, Ch.1, 3).

[3] For Anglican doctrine, see generally J. W. C. Wand (ed.), *The Anglican Communion* (Oxford, 1948), 22–23, 171–2, 188–9, 219–221; G. F. S. Gray, *The Anglican Communion* (London, 1958), 107–120; P. H. E. Thomas, 'The doctrine of the church', in S. Sykes and J. Booty (eds.), *The Study of Anglicanism* (London, 1988), 219; for the Chicago–Lambeth Quadrilateral and LC 1888, Res. 11, see G. R. Evans and J. R. Wright (eds.), *The Anglican Tradition* (London, 1988), 345, 355: Holy Scriptures, the Apostles' Creed (as the baptismal symbol), the Nicene Creed (as the sufficient statement of the Christian faith), the two dominical sacraments (baptism and Holy Communion) and the historic episcopate represent the 'articles' operating as the basis of Anglican doctrine.

define and to protect the faith; to empower the church to develop and reformulate the faith; and to enable a degree of doctrinal discipline.

THE PROCLAMATION OF THE FAITH

The theological principle that the church exists to proclaim the word of God as revealed in Christ finds juridic expression in a variety of forms.[4] The principle is usually repeated in the constitutions of Anglican churches, most of which relate proclamation of the faith directly to the fundamental objectives of the institutional church.[5] Commonly, formal law is purely descriptive, in which proclamation is expressed as a matter of fact: the church 'professes' or 'teaches' faith in Jesus Christ.[6] By way of contrast, in the laws of some churches, proclamation of the faith is cast as a duty placed on the institutional church. The constitution of the United Church of South India prescribes that the church 'purposes to be ever mindful of its missionary calling; and prays that it may not only be greatly used of God for the evangelization of South India, but may also take its share in the preaching of the Gospel and the building up of Christ's Church in other parts of the world'.[7] In others the principle is cast as both a duty and a right: the constitution of the church in the Province of Kenya provides that the church has a 'right and duty to discover the truth as it is in Jesus, and to express that truth in life and in liturgy'.[8] A slightly different idea appears in the constitution of the church in North India which presents the spreading of the gospel as both 'duty and privilege'.[9]

---

[4] LC 1930, Res. 1: 'the Christian Church is the repository and trustee of a revelation of God, given by himself, which all members of the Church are bound to transmit to others'; for the 'teaching office' of the church see LC 1930, Ress. 6, 70, 71; LC 1948, Ress. 20, 30; LC 1958, Res.125; LC 1978, Res. 3; see Ch. 1 for the nature of the church; Korea, Const. Fundamental Declarations: the law is designed 'in order to preserve [the] church's faith'.

[5] Rwanda, Draft Const. 1996, Art. 1: 'The mission of the Province is . . . the proclamation of the Gospel of Jesus Christ'; Chile, Cans. A.1; for a standard statement of the principle in a liturgical document, see e.g. New Zealand, *Prayer Book* 1989, Catechism, 931: the mission of the church is, *inter alia*, '[t]o proclaim the good news of God's Kingdom'.

[6] Southern Cone, Const. Art. 1: the church 'professes the historic faith'; Indian Ocean, Const. Art. 2(iii): the church 'professes' the 'faith of Christ'; Burundi, Const. Art. 3: the church 'accepts and teaches Faith in Jesus Christ'; see also Zaire, Const. Art. 3; and Melanesia, Const. Art. 1.

[7] South India, Const. II.3; see also New Zealand, Const. Pt. I, Ch. 1, 3: 'This Church will ever obey the commands of Christ [and] teach His doctrine'.

[8] Kenya, Const. 1979, Art. II(e).

[9] North India, Const. I.I.VI.1.

Occasionally, constitutions provide that the church is simply 'to hold the faith', without making any reference to 'teaching' it.[10]

Proclamation as a corporate function of the church is not usually accompanied by rules placing individual lay persons under specific canonical duties to proclaim the faith: only occasionally is evangelism listed amongst the duties of the members of the laity; this function is assigned, rather, to ordained clergy and to special classes of lay office-holder.[11] A prime obligation for teaching the faith is placed on the bishop. Arrangements in North India are perhaps the fullest expression of the idea: a constitutional responsibility is placed on the bishop 'of publicly stating, as need may arise, the doctrines of the universal church as understood by the Church of North India, and their application to the problems of the age and of the country'.[12] As to the ordained clergy generally, two duties are employed to enable proclamation of the faith: the preaching of sermons and the instruction of persons within a cure of souls.

First, the duty to preach. Arrangements found in the Church of England may be used to illustrate the diversity of provisions on sermons existing in other churches. The rule in English canon law is that a sermon must be preached in every parish church at least once each Sunday, except for some reasonable cause approved by the diocesan bishop. Ordinarily the sermon is preached by the ordained minister – but it may also be delivered by a lay minister, a reader or lay worker. Moreover, at the invitation of the minister having the cure of souls 'another person may preach with the permission [given occasionally or generally] of the bishop'. In the sermon the preacher 'shall endeavour himself with care and sincerity to minister the word of truth, to the glory of God and to the edification of the people'.[13] There is considerable evidence to suggest that the preaching of a sermon each Sunday is a common legal requirement in Anglican churches as is the relaxation of this rule with episcopal consent; a canon of the Australian church is typical: '[a] sermon must be preached at least once each Sunday

[10] Central Africa, Const. Art. 1: the church simply 'holds' the faith of Christ; see also Uganda, Const. Art. 2(b); Tanzania, Const. III.4; South East Asia, Const. Fundamental Declaration, 1.

[11] For lay duties and lay-office holders see Ch. 6.

[12] North India, Const. I.I.VIII.6; see also England, Can. C18(1): bishops must 'uphold sound and wholesome doctrine'; Brazil, Can.17.2; Venezuela, Cans. III.15: 'The bishop has the authority to direct and supervise the missionary work of the Diocese'; Wales, BCP 1984, 22, General Directions: 'It is the Bishop's right to be the celebrant of the Eucharist and to preach'; see generally, Ch. 4.

[13] England, Can. B18, C24(3); BCP 1662, 241 (a sermon at holy communion is mandatory); *Alternative Service Book* 1980, 116: 'The sermon is an integral part of the Ministry of the Word. A sermon should normally be preached at all celebrations on Sundays and other Holy Days'. For the importance of preaching in Lambeth Conference resolutions, see e.g. LC 1920, Ress. 12, 24, 53; LC 1930, Ress. 6, 64, 70; LC 1958, Ress. 7, 100; LC 1968, Res. 36.

in every cathedral and church in which Divine Service is offered on that Sunday except for some reasonable cause approved by the bishop of the diocese'.[14] In some churches, however, the requirement seems to be expressed in less mandatory terms; under Irish liturgical rubrics '[a] sermon should be preached on Sundays and on the major festivals' and there is a permissive right to preach at any of the church's services.[15] Rarely do laws prescribe in detail the content of sermons. The Southern African and Irish churches are unusual in this respect: in the former, the canons provide that the incumbent must preach, or cause to be preached, 'a sermon expounding and applying Holy Scripture' at least once each Sunday;[16] the constitution of the latter, which echoes but is rather more sophisticated than the English canon, states: '[t]he preacher shall endeavour with care and sincerity to minister the word of truth according to holy scripture', agreeable to the Thirty-Nine Articles and the Book of Common Prayer, and 'to the glory of God and edification of the people'.[17] The English provision concerning invitations to preach does not find an obvious parallel in the laws of other churches.[18]

Secondly, the ministerial duty to instruct. Two sets of contrasting approaches are to be found in the canon law of the Philippines, on the one hand, and in the churches of England and Ireland on the other, where the identical canons of each church are rather narrower in their scope than the Philippine canons. In English and Irish canon law, every minister shall take care that 'the children and young persons within his cure are instructed in the doctrine, sacraments and discipline of Christ, as the Lord has commanded and as they are set forth in the holy scriptures, in the Book of Common Prayer and in the Church Catechism'. To this end, the minister or 'some godly and competent person' appointed by him shall on Sundays or other convenient times, 'instruct and teach them in the same'. Moreover, '[a]ll parents and godparents shall take care that their children receive such instruction'.[19] According to the wider Philippine canon law: the minister must be 'diligent in instructing the children and youth in the Catechisms, and from time to time examine them in the same publicly before the Congregation'; ministers must also inform the youth on the

---

[14] Australia, Can. P6 1992, 5; see also Brazil, Can. 12.2: ministers must preach in order to 'evangelize new members'; Portugal, Can. 8, Arts. 2 and 3.

[15] Ireland, *Alternative Prayer Book*, 1984, 18; compare Const. IX.7 ('must'); BCP 1960, liv: '[a] Sermon may follow any Service'.

[16] Southern Africa, Can. 24.4(a).					[17] Ireland, Const. IX.7.

[18] Churches do, however, provide for invitations of members of other churches: see e.g. Scotland, Can. 16.1 and 2: the bishop may permit 'any lay person in communion with the Scottish Episcopal Church' to address the congregation; generally, of course, in order to exercise the ministry of preaching, persons must be authorized to do so by the bishop: see e.g. Australia, Diocese of Sydney, *The 7th Handbook*, 8.24–29.

[19] England, Can. B26, B28; Ireland, Const. IX.27.

Holy Scriptures and 'the Doctrine, Polity, History and Liturgy of the Church'; finally, they must instruct 'all persons in their Parishes and Cures concerning the missionary work of the Church at home and abroad'.[20] Most churches operate far less detailed rules about instruction; the canon law of Southern Africa is typical: the incumbent is responsible for 'the organization and training of all who instruct children and adults in the Christian faith'.[21] Only Scottish canon law mirrors the Philippine provisions on public examination: clergy must 'set apart a due portion of time on Sundays and other convenient days for publicly examining and instructing the younger members of their congregations in the Catechism contained in the authorized Service Books'. Any other catechism or other manual of instruction may be used in addition if sanctioned by the diocesan bishop.[22] Churches possess far more detailed legal regulation requiring instruction of candidates prior to the celebration of baptism, confirmation and marriage.[23]

INSTITUTIONS OF EVANGELISM AND EDUCATION

There is some evidence that duties to evangelize are distributed to institutions at the lower end of the structures of synodical and conciliar government: the obligation on Deanery Synods and parochial church councils in the Church of England, to promote 'the whole mission of the Church' (which includes the 'evangelical' mission), finds a direct parallel in several churches.[24] The norm today, however, is for churches to assign the work of evangelism and mission to special institutions at national, provincial or diocesan level.[25] Developments are broadly in line with recommendations contained in recent resolutions of the Lambeth Conference.[26] Some

---

[20] Philippines, Cans. III.16.3(a). [21] Southern Africa, Can. 24.4(d).

[22] Scotland, Can. 28; New Zealand, *Prayer Book* 1989, 926: 'This Catechism is a teaching resource expressing the basic Christian beliefs'; it contains material on human nature, God, the Bible, the church and ministry.

[23] See Chs. 9 and 10.

[24] England, Synodical Government Measure 1969, s. 5(3)(b) and Parochial Church Councils (Powers) Measure 1956, s. 2(1)(a); Southern Africa, Can. 24.3: the incumbent and parish council must ensure that 'the educational and evangelistic work' of the pastoral charge is carried out; ibid, Can. 28.4: the parish council is to consider matters effecting evangelism; Wales, Const. VI.22: the parochial church council must promote the 'evangelistic' mission of the church in the parish.

[25] See e.g. North India, Const. I.II.3: 'It is the duty of every Diocese acting as a whole to spread the knowledge of the Gospel throughout its territory'; II.III.IX.41: the diocesan council is to 'further the cause of evangelism'.

[26] For the concept of shared and institutional responsibility for evangelism see e.g. LC 1948, Res. 36, 42, 43; for mission generally, see LC 1978, Ress. 6, 15; LC 1988, Ress. 44, 45, 48.

institutions have a purely advisory role, whilst others also exercise administrative functions.

Boards of Mission and Education

At national level, the General Convention of ECUSA has three permanent advisory commissions on evangelism and mission. The function of Standing Commission on Evangelism (composed of bishops, priests or deacons, and lay persons) is to develop policy on evangelism and to recommend to the General Convention and the dioceses appropriate action. Its Standing Commission of World Mission (composed similarly of bishops, priests or deacons, and lay persons, half from within the USA and half from outside) is obliged 'to review, evaluate, plan and propose policy on overseas mission to the General Convention'. The General Convention also has a Standing Commission to deal with mission in metropolitan areas and a Domestic and Foreign Missionary Society, incorporated under secular law of the state of New York, the constitution of which may be altered by the General Convention. The House of Bishops may establish (and terminate) area missions, and these may be administered ecumenically under the oversight of a bishop appointed by the House of Bishops.[27] Several other churches have similar advisory institutions.[28]

By way of contrast, the Boards of Mission in Australia and New Zealand have more proactive roles. The principal function of the Australian Board is 'to lead, encourage and serve the Church in Christ's mission'. It does so: by educating and stimulating the church in the responsibility of mission; by recruiting, training and supporting persons to serve in the churches of the Anglican Communion; by raising, investing and administering funds and by acting as trustee of funds committed to it; and by reviewing and monitoring missionary policy. The membership of the Board includes the primate, a national director, five bishops, and representatives from the diocesan clergy, laity and youth. The Board may operate within the

---

[27] ECUSA, Cans. I.1.2 and 11: see Ch. 2 for Missionary Dioceses; see also Canada, Can. VII for the Missionary Society (but the canon fails to spell out the body's functions); Australia, General Synod Commissions Cans. 1969–92: the Missionary and Ecumenical Commission is to serve and advise the church in the fulfilment of its missionary task; see also the National Home Mission Fund Canon 1985, Can. 8 1985.

[28] West Indies, Can. 33.1.E: the provincial Standing Commission on Mission and Renewal has 'the duty . . . to keep the Mission of the Church under constant review and to seek out ways and means by which it can renew itself in order to be properly equipped to respond to the challenges of the present time and to undertake its Mission effectively'; for adaptations of the ECUSA model see Philippines, Cans. I.2.2; England, see LFCE, 93 for the national Board of Mission: this is not a canonical institution, but a subordinate body of General Synod which has created the board's constitution; one of its functions is to advise synod 'on issues and proposals concerning mission, evangelism, renewal and inter-faith relations'.

provinces and dioceses, by appointing staff to them, but its powers must not be exercised in such a way as to limit the authority or rights of the diocesan bishop.[29] The New Zealand Board of Mission acts as an agent of the church 'in setting forward the mission of the Church in overseas areas'. The Board is obliged: '[t]o assist and encourage the church at diocesan and local levels to arouse support among parishioners for the objects of the Board'; to give information to assist in the determination of financial grants from within the church, to fix an annual budget and to make and present annual reports and a statement of accounts to the standing committee of General Synod and, biennially, to the General Synod itself. The composition of the Board includes, *inter alia*, diocesan bishops, representatives of Diocesan Synods, youth representatives, and Anglican women; the president is the primate. The Board must have an annual meeting and is empowered to make by-laws, to produce literature, to appropriate funds for expenses, to borrow money and to receive money.[30]

Diocesan institutions charged with the task of evangelism and mission generally mirror those operating at national or provincial levels with lines of accountability directed to the Diocesan Synod or council.[31] Arrangements in India are particularly well-developed: evangelism and mission are the exclusive functions of some institutions and the ancillary functions of others. In North India, the diocesan Christian life, mission and evangelism committee is under an obligation to develop a sense of Christian mission and it is responsible to the diocesan council for policy and programmes of evangelistic work (such as arranging conferences and co-ordinating lay activities); furthermore, one of its objects is to develop 'among the laity . . . a sense of personal evangelism'.[32] In the South Indian diocese of Dornakal, one function of the diocesan medical committee is to

[29] Australia, Can. 8 1995; see also Philippines, Cans. I.4.7: the provincial Executive Council must search for and appoint missionaries of the church 'in accordance with guidelines and criteria' determined beforehand by the Council; New Zealand, Cans. B.XIX.1–10: General Synod's Commission on Communications must facilitate 'the communication of news and information on the mission and ministry of the church, as widely as possible and through all forms of media'; for a similar institution see Melanesia, Cans. E.7: the Christian Resources Development Centre produces literature 'to help the Church in its mission'.

[30] New Zealand, Cans. B.IX; see Cans. B.XXIII for the Mission and Evangelism Conference (inter-diocesan) and B.XXIV for the Nurture and Education Conference (inter-diocesan). The Melanesian Board of Mission is regulated similarly: Cans. E.9–14.

[31] For diocesan boards of mission in England, which are not canonical institutions, see e.g. Diocese of Bradford, *Diocesan Manual* 1987, I.9; Diocese of Salisbury, *Diocesan Handbook* 1991, V.42–53, 46–7; see also West Indies, Can. 33.1.F.(c)(ii): the diocesan Commission on Ministry is obliged to 'formulate and monitor programmes for Christian Education in the Diocese and to liaise with the Provincial Commission on Ministry on matters relating to Christian education'. For ministry commissions, see Chs. 6 and 7.

[32] North India, Const. II.III.XIV.7, II.IV.XVI.4.

'[m]ake known the love of God in Jesus by promoting the treatment and care of the sick without discrimination as to creed or caste'.[33] In North India, the diocesan religious education committee must promote Sunday school programmes, encourage vacation bible school movements and present requests for grants to the diocesan finance committee.[34] Finally, again in the South Indian diocese of Dornakal, the diocesan education committee is 'to promote, order and control all educational activities of the Diocese' – to this end it has the right, 'for sufficient reason', 'to assume the direct management of any or all of the Educational Institutions in the Diocese'.[35]

Many churches have internal organizations involved in an advisory capacity concerning education both in state and in church schools. Some churches have a national or provincial Board of Education and it is common for dioceses to have a local equivalent.[36] In Ireland, the principal duty of the Board of Education of General Synod is 'to define the policy of the Church in education both religious and secular', and, in promotion of this policy, 'to take steps to co-ordinate activities in all fields of education affecting the interests of the Church of Ireland'. The Board must maintain close contact with secular government, diocesan boards of education and schools. The Board has a special duty 'to study any [secular] legislation or proposed legislation likely to affect the educational interests of the Church of Ireland and to act as necessary'. There is an obligation to report annually to General Synod.[37] The Australian canons provide for an institution which performs a mixture of functions related to evangelism, mission and education. The General Board of Religious Education is to encourage and assist in the stimulation, co-ordination and development of the work of: Christian education amongst children, youth and adults; religious education in state and church schools; and education in sunday schools. It also advises on and publishes literature necessary for Christian education work. The Board consists of the primate (who is its president), two bishops, one cleric and one lay representative of each diocese, a director, and one or two diocesan officers engaged in Christian education in each

---

[33] South India, Diocese of Dornakal, Const. 1977, 7.

[34] North India, Const. II.III.XIV.

[35] South India, Diocese of Dornakal, Const. 1977, IV.

[36] Melanesia, Cans. E.16: the Education Board is the education authority for the church as prescribed by the secular Education Act 1978 of the Solomon Islands; the board advises the church on all matters concerning the development of education and proposes education policy for adoption by the General Synod; it advises also on educational funding and liaises with secular government on education; it is accountable to General Synod and must report on its work to each session of the synod or its Executive Committee; for Lambeth Conference resolutions on the subject, see e.g. LC 1948, Ress. 27–31, 46 and LC 1988, Res. 48.

[37] Ireland, Const. approved by General Synod 1965–94: it has two Boards, one for Northern Ireland and the other for the Republic of Ireland.

diocese. The Board has an executive, an annual meeting and it may be incorporated under secular law.[38]

Theological Colleges

As is discussed elsewhere in this volume, knowledge of and examination in church doctrine are prerequisites to ordination and to admission to lay ministries, and often provision is made, by canon (or in some churches by quasi-legislation), for continuing ministerial education.[39] Very few churches, however, have a special body of canon law devoted exclusively to theological colleges – the matter is normally dealt with by trust deeds operative in secular law.[40] The canonical systems of ECUSA and the

[38] Australia, Can. 9 1962, Can. 5 1969, Can. 2 1973, and Can. 1 1989. The subject of church schools is not as a matter of practice treated with any degree of comprehensiveness in national or provincial canon law; regulation is usually under the terms of a secular trust though sometimes diocesan laws effect partial regulation: see e.g. ECUSA, Diocese of Mississippi, Cans. I.F.16: diocesan schools may be established by the diocesan council acting on the recommendation of the bishop and the Executive Committee; they are owned and operated by the diocese or by a separate corporation, and a majority of the school's board of trustees must be adult confirmed lay communicants; each school must set out its aims in a clearly-defined policy statement declaring, *inter alia*, that 'no applicant, otherwise qualified, shall be denied admission because of race, creed or color'; for the subject in England, and the abundance of secular law on it, see R. Charles, 'Church schools and the law', LL M dissertation, University of Wales, Cardiff, 1997.

[39] See Chs. 6 and 7; England: whilst Can. C26(1) requires clergy to study scripture and other matters pertaining to their ministerial duties, arrangements for continuing ministerial education are usually to be found in diocesan quasi-legislation: see e.g. Diocese of Blackburn, *The Blackburn File* 1993, 3.8–9, 12.1–3; Scotland, Can. 17.2: clergy must study and pursue courses determined by the College of Bishops; ECUSA, Diocese of Mississippi, Cans. III.A.39: every minister must be engaged in continuing theological education which is defined as 'a systematic program of conservative and cumulative study focused on concerns where theological import is either centrally or closely related'; every cleric must report annually to the bishop and the vestry or mission committee must give financial assistance; see also Canada, Can. XII: this provides for a Continuing Education Fund for clergy and lay ministers.

[40] Canada, Declaration of Principles, 6.1.(f): it is within the jurisdiction of the General Synod to set 'the basic standards of theological education' for ordination candidates; Australia, Australian College of Theology Cans. 1966–95: these deal *inter alia* with the objects of the college ('to foster and direct systematic study of Theology'), functions, admission and property; Southern Africa, Acts of the Provincial Synod, Act XIV: the Advisory Board on Theological Education and Training for Ministry; New Zealand, Cans. E.II–V: this canonical regulation operates alongside the St John's College Trusts Act 1972. In Australia, the Ministry and Training Commission exists to identify and assist in 'the preservation of the essential character of the Christian ministry as it has been revealed in Holy Scripture and experienced in Christian history and the life' of the church (General Synod Commissions Cans. 1969–92); see also New Zealand, Cans. B.XVIII: the Ministry Education Commission must consider and report to General Synod on 'issues of ministry education', including institutional and distance theological education and training; England, Church Commissioners (Loans to Theological Colleges and Training Houses) Measure 1964.

Melanesian church illustrate two contrasting approaches to the subject. In ECUSA, the General Convention's Board of Theological Education acts as a central advisory authority for seminaries. The Board is composed of bishops, priests, representatives of postulants and lay persons. Its functions are to study needs and trends of theological education, and to recommend action to seminaries, to the General Convention's Executive Council, to the House of Bishops and to the General Convention itself. It must advise and assist seminaries and other training institutions about persons for ordination, promote co-operation between seminaries, and report to the General Convention on statistical and financial data, mission, goals and progress. Not only is the Board obliged to assist in enlistment and selection of ordination candidates, but it must also promote continuing clergy education and lay theological education, aid the General Board of Examining Chaplains, and seek financial support for theological education. Seminaries must submit to the Board statistical reports and statements of their mission, goals and progress.[41]

The canon law of Melanesia is rather more directly regulatory. The visitor of the Bishop Patteson Theological College is the archbishop who, by regular visits, must oversee and encourage the spiritual and material welfare of college members. The Board of Governors consists *inter alia* of the visitor, the diocesan bishops, the provincial General Secretary, the college principal, registrar, the general secretary of the provincial Board of Mission, a student representative, a cleric and a lay person elected by General Synod. The Board of Governors appoints the principal who, as pastor and spiritual leader, is responsible for the quality of teaching, discipline and staffing. The principal must present an annual report on the life, work and finances of the college to the Board and to each session of the General Synod. The Board is, in turn, responsible to General Synod for the fulfilment by the college of its aims and purposes, which are prescribed by canon. As well as powers of appointment, the Board authorizes and pays for all major additions and alterations to college buildings, it subsidises students, sets criteria for selection of students, approves admissions and receives reports on dismissals. The Board is obliged to hear and determine all grievances amongst staff and students and it ratifies the college's internal rules.[42] Given the paucity of legal provisions in the vast majority of churches, it is not possible to construct, from the formal laws of national and provincial churches, general principles of Anglican canon law on this subject.

---

[41] ECUSA, Cans. III.31; see also LC 1930, Res. 63; LC 1948, Ress. 85, 86; LC 1958, Ress. 83, 84.
[42] Melanesia, Cans. E.3 (see Cans. E.2 for the constitution of Selwyn College); for a similar scheme, see Papua New Guinea, Can. No. 9 of 1997.

CANONICAL DOCTRINES

Anglican churches are not confessional denominations possessing formal and definitive legal statements of their beliefs. Instead, laws are employed simply to point to doctrinal documents, extrinsic to the law, which are accepted by the church as normative in matters of faith. It is only in this oblique sense that law is used to define doctrine. What follows, therefore, is a description of the 'official' doctrines of Anglican churches recognized as such by constitutional or canon law.[43] Three broad approaches surface in the formal law.

The first is one in which legal approval is given to doctrine located in the trilogy of documents of the post-Reformation Church of England: the Thirty-Nine Articles 1571, the Book of Common Prayer 1662 and the Ordinal. According to the modern canon law of the Church of England, 'the doctrine of the Church of England . . . [i]n particular is to be found in the Thirty-Nine Articles of Religion, the Book of Common Prayer, and the Ordinal'; this doctrine is, in turn, 'grounded in the Holy Scriptures, and in such teachings of the ancient fathers and Councils of the Church as are agreeable to the said Scriptures'. Moreover, '[t]he Thirty-Nine Articles are agreeable to the Word of God'; '[t]he doctrine contained in the Book of Common Prayer is agreeable to the Word of God'; and the Ordinal 'is not repugnant to the Word of God'.[44] In England a mid-nineteenth-century judicial *dictum* from the provincial court of Canterbury treated the Thirty-Nine Articles as 'the standard of doctrine . . . to be considered, and, in the first instance, appealed to, in order to ascertain the doctrine of the Church'.[45] This English approach corresponds exactly with no other church but broadly with a handful of churches,[46] particularly in the adoption of the Thirty-Nine Articles.[47] In the second approach canonical

[43] For the centrality of Holy Scripture and the Creeds, see LC 1888, Res. 11; 1908, Res. 2; 1920, Res. 9; LC 1930, Res. 3; 1958, Ress. 1–3, 74; LC 1988, Ress. 8, 18, 34.

[44] England, Can. A2–5; Church of England (Worship and Doctrine) Measure 1974, s. 5(1).

[45] *Gorham v Bishop of Exeter* (1849) 2 Rob Ecc 1 at 55 *per* Sir Jenner Fust (Arches Court).

[46] Australia, Const. I.1: the church 'holds the Christian Faith as professed by the Church of Christ from primitive times and in particular as set forth in the creeds known as the Nicene Creed and the Apostles' Creed'; it 'receives all the canonical scriptures . . . as being the ultimate rule and standard of faith given by inspiration of God and containing all things necessary for salvation'; the church also retains and approves 'the doctrine and principles of the Church of England embodied' in the BCP 1662, the Ordinal and the Thirty-Nine Articles; Scotland, Can. 17.2: 'The teaching of the Scottish Episcopal Church is grounded in revelation and reason, on the Holy Scriptures and the Fathers' (no mention is made of the Thirty-Nine Articles).

[47] For adoption of the Thirty-Nine Articles as a source of doctrine, see e.g. Southern Africa, appended to the Constitution and Canons; Zaire, Const. Art. 3(3); Uganda, Const. Art. 2(c); West Africa, Const. Art. 2(a); Chile, Cans. A.1; New Zealand,

approval is given to doctrine located in Holy Scripture, the Creeds and the pronouncements of the early councils. In one sense this is a reversal of the English approach, in which these were the grounds from which doctrine located in the trilogy was derived – here the originals *are* the canonical doctrine. The approach is uncommon and is illustrated by the constitution of the church in South India which 'accepts the Holy Scriptures of the Old and New Testaments as containing all things necessary to salvation and as the supreme standard of faith' as well as the Apostles' and Nicene Creeds.[48]

A final approach, the most common, is based on the principle of reception: here canon law approves doctrinal phenomena received by the institutional church. The provincial churches of the West Indies and of Kenya are fairly typical and their similar but not identical provisions find a direct parallel in the laws of other churches in this group.[49] The West Indian church receives and maintains 'the faith of Our Lord Jesus Christ as taught in the Holy Scriptures, held in the Primitive Church, summed up in the Creeds, and affirmed by the undisputed General Councils'.[50] The equivalent provision in Kenyan constitutional law is a little fuller: the church 'receives all the Canonical Scriptures of the Old and New Testaments, given by inspiration of God, as containing all things necessary for salvation and as being the ulitmate rule and standard of the faith and life of the

Fundamental Provisions, A.1; ECUSA, Marshall, Vol. II, 164ff (for revisions 1801–1979). Compare Melanesia, Standing Resolution 13: the church accepts the Thirty-Nine Articles as 'the historic statement of the Anglican position in faith and practice at the time of the Reformation' but 'without . . . subscribing to every statement contained therein'; see also Kenya, Const. II.(i): 'The absence . . . of any reference to the Thirty-Nine Articles shall not preclude the Synod of any diocese including reference to that document in its own Diocesan Constitution'.

[48] South India, Const. II.5: the constitution restates, in the confessional tradition, the essential elements of the creeds as the 'belief' of the church; see also North India, Const. I.II.III and Korea, Fundamental Declaration of Faith and Rites (there is no mention of the post-Reformation English trilogy): the church 'holds the Old and New Testaments as the word of the everlasting God and declares that they teach all things necessary for salvation and are the standards of faith and morals', and the Creeds; Rwanda, Draft Const. 1996, Art. 5: this lists scripture and the three creeds (Apostles, Nicene and Athanasian); whilst no mention is made in this Article of the BCP 1662 or the Ordinal, these are used as aids to interpretation under Art. 7; Japan, General Principles, 1–4.

[49] West Indies, Declaration of Fundamental Principles, (a)–(c); the following notes, nn. 50 to 55, contain provisions in the laws of other churches equivalent to those of the West Indies and Kenya.

[50] South East Asia, Fundamental Declarations, 1: the church 'holds the Faith of Christ as taught in the Holy Scriptures, preached by the Apostles and summed up in the Catholic Creeds and confirmed by the Councils of the undivided Holy Catholic Church'; Southern Africa, Declaration of Fundamental Principles and Const. Art. I; Sudan, Const. Art. 2(a); Central Africa, Fundamental Declaration, I; for this approach see also Spain, Fundamental Declarations, I; Portugal, Cans. Preamble.

Church'.[51] In addition, the church holds 'the faith of Christ as preached by the Apostles, summed up in the Apostles' Creed, and confirmed by the first Four General Councils of the Holy Catholic Church'.[52] Moreover, the West Indian church receives and maintains 'the Faith, Doctrine, Sacraments and Discipline of the One Holy Catholic and Apostolic Church, according as the Church of England has received the same';[53] it also receives 'the Book of Common Prayer and the Ordering of Bishops, Priests and Deacons, as agreeable to the Word of God'.[54] The Kenyan provisions are a little narrower: the church declares 'its acceptance of the Doctrine, Sacraments and Discipline of the Church' as set forth in the Prayer Book of 1662 and the Ordinal – there is no explicit claim that these are agreeable to the Word of God.[55]

In sum, whilst the canonical evidence suggests three distinct approaches to ecclesiastical understandings about the location and origin of doctrine, each approach shares both the assumption that one function of law is the definition of doctrinal sources and that belief in the primary source, Holy Scripture, is necessary for salvation. These assumptions give rise to a fundamental legal unity for churches in the Anglican Communion, and from them emerge two basic principles of Anglican canon law: each church is competent to define its doctrine and that doctrine operates as the standard of faith governing the church both in the fulfilment of its mission and in its internal governance. And it is this unity, expressed in juridic form, that provides one of the indispensable foundations of the Anglican Communion itself (see Chapter 12). In Anglican

[51] Uganda, Const. Art. 2(a); Burundi, Const. Art. 3; Zaire, Const. Art. 3; Jerusalem and the Middle East, Const. Art. 4(ii); Indian Ocean, Const. Art. 2; Melanesia, Const. Art. 1.

[52] Jerusalem and the Middle East, Const. Art. 4(i); Philippines, Const. Art. I.2; Papua New Guinea, Const. Art. 2; unlike Kenyan law, others using this basic formula do not number the Councils nor, like Kenya, do they identify them: Burundi, Const. Art. 3; Zaire, Const. Art. 2; Uganda, Const. Art. 2(b).

[53] Melanesia, Const. Art. 1: the church accepts 'the faith of our Lord Jesus Christ and the teachings, sacraments and discipline of the One Holy Catholic and Apostolic Church as the Anglican Communion has received them'; the scriptures and creeds function as the 'standards' of faith and 'honour' is given to the teachings of the early church, especially the decisions of the General Councils of the church 'as are accepted by the Eastern and Western Church'.

[54] South East Asia, Fundamental Declarations, 1: unlike the West Indian scheme, this omits the idea that these are agreeable to the Word of God.

[55] Jerusalem and the Middle East, Const. Art. 4(iii); Sudan, Const. Art. 2(a); Southern Africa, Declaration of Fundamental Principles and Const. Art. I; Tanzania, Const. III.4; Indian Ocean, Const. Art. 2(iii); Southern Cone, Const. Art. 1: the church 'professes the historic Faith and Order as contained in the Holy Scriptures, preserved in the Doctrine, Sacraments, Ministry and Discipline of the Anglican Church and observed' in the Prayer Book and Ordinal; Uganda, Const. Art. 2(c) and West Africa, Const. Art. 2(a) (both of these also list the Thirty-Nine Articles); Central Africa, Fundamental Declaration, I; New Zealand, Fundamental Provisions, A.1.

jurisprudence, then, Holy Scripture, the Creeds, the Councils, the Thirty-Nine Articles, the Book of Common Prayer 1662 and the Ordinal are each expressions of canonical doctrine.

THE DEVELOPMENT OF DOCTRINE

Increasingly resolutions of the Lambeth Conference have stressed the need for sensitive doctrinal development so that the faith may be presented intelligibly to each generation and to society at large.[56] As a matter of law, the power to effect doctrinal development is enjoyable only by national or provincial assemblies, not by institutions at lower levels of the church.[57] Its exercise seems to be limited by one fundamental principle of classical Anglicanism: 'it is not lawful for the Church to ordain any thing that is contrary to God's Word written'.[58] Legal provisions dealing with the development of doctrine, from its restatement to its alteration, fall into a wide spectrum of categories: from enabling through limiting to disabling provisions.

The Kenyan constitution is an example of an enabling arrangement: 'The Church of this Province, being a wholly autonomous and self-governing part of the Body of Christ, affirms its right to draw up its own formularies of faith, and to set forth in terms that it considers suitable to the present day and to the needs of the peoples of this Province, the Faith which this church holds'.[59] The law of the majority of churches enables doctrinal development but subject to stringent procedural safeguards. In the Church in Wales proposals to alter, amend or abrogate matters relating to faith, doctrinal statements or the formularies must be effected by bill

---

[56] There has been a shift from a restrictive to a more liberal approach: compare e.g. LC 1867, Res. 8: 'it is necessary that [churches] maintain without alteration the standards of faith and doctrine now in use' in the Church of England; and LC 1930, Res. 2: 'there is an urgent need . . . for a fresh presentation of the Christian doctrine of God'.

[57] Indeed, the laws of several churches expressly forbid inferior church assemblies to declare doctrine: see e.g. England: Diocesan Synods, Deanery Synods and parochial church councils may discuss matters of religious interest but they cannot 'issue . . . any statement purporting to declare the doctrine of the Church of England' (Synodical Government Measure 1969, ss. 4(2), 5(3) and Parochial Church Councils (Powers) Measure 1956, s. 2); slightly different rules operate in Wales, Const. IV.45: 'Nothing in this Chapter shall be construed as giving to a Diocesan Conference any right to pass any resolution or to come to any decision upon any matter concerning . . . faith'; ibid., V.15: the ruridecanal conference may discuss matters of religion 'but the discussion of any doctrinal matters by the Conference shall not extend to any formulation or declaration of doctrine'; a similar rule applies to the parochial church council: ibid., VI.22.

[58] Thirty-Nine Articles, Art. 20.

[59] Kenya, Const. Art. II(c); for a similar approach see West Africa, Const. Art. II(a); see also Chile, Can. E.4; Puerto Rico, Cans. I.13; see ibid. II.2 and Spain, Fundamental Declaration, I.2 for examples of regulation of translations of the Bible.

procedure in the Governing Body; no such bill may be considered unless it has been introduced by a majority of the order of bishops; the bill must receive three readings and, finally, a two-thirds majority in each of the three orders of bishops, clergy and laity voting separately – then the development is operative in the form of a canon which, on promulgation, becomes part of the law of the church.[60] A stricter and more complex refinement of this approach is to be found in North India: in matters of faith and doctrine, proposals are first considered by the diocesan bishops; after submission to Synod and adoption by a two-thirds majority, they are referred to the diocesan councils and if two-thirds of these agree the proposal becomes effective only upon final approval by (a) a simple majority of the bishops, clergy and laity sitting separately *and* (b) a three-quarters majority of the Synod sitting as a unit.[61]

Churches having a connection with the state are subject to additional procedural constraints. According to the celebrated and widely cited English decision of *General Assembly of the Free Church of Scotland v Lord Overtoun* (1904), 'where the state has by legislative acts established a church identified by certain doctrines, that church cannot . . . exercise any power of altering those doctrines without the legislative sanction of the state'.[62] In England this sanction has now been given to the Church of England, at least partially, in the form of parliamentary approval of two synodical measures of 1969 and 1974: '[a] provision touching doctrinal formulae shall, before it is finally approved by the General Synod, be referred to the House of Bishops, and shall be submitted for such approval in terms proposed by the House of Bishops and not otherwise'; a two-thirds majority in each House is required.[63] The quasi-established church in New

[60] Wales, Const. II.34–43; for a similar approach see Ireland, Const. I.25; compare the simple majority voting by orders in Sudan, Const. Art. 4(vi); see also North India, Const. II.IV.XVI.6: a body composed *inter alia* of three bishops, three presbyters and three lay persons shall act as a Committee of Reference on Faith and Order; the decision of the committee 'as to whether a particular proposition is a matter of Faith and Order or not shall be final'; for a similar arrangement in the diocese, see II.III.XXI.2.

[61] North India, Const. I.III.

[62] [1904] AC 515 at 648; for the same principle applicable to non-established churches in the USA, see e.g. *Kuns v Robertson*, 40 NE 343, 154 Ill 394 (Ill); *Commonwealth ex rel. Heil v Stauffer*, 137 A 179, 289 Pa 139 (Pa); with respect to disestablished churches, express recognition of the power to alter doctrine is sometimes given by secular legislation: see e.g. Wales, Welsh Church Act 1914, s. 3(2); Barbados, Anglican Church Act 1969, s. 4; Ireland, Church of Ireland Act 1869, s. 20.

[63] Synodical Government Measure 1969, Sched. 2, Art. 7; Church of England (Worship and Doctrine) Measure 1974, s. 5(1): as this is statutory recognition of the church's legally approved doctrines, so arguably might it be amended only by a new measure which would require parliamentary and royal approval; in this sense the sanction has only 'partially' been given by the state. However, it has been suggested recently by the secular courts that General Synod has *in law* an unfettered competence to change the church's fundamental doctrines: see *R v Ecclesiastical Committee of Both Houses of Parliament, ex p Church Society* (1994) 6 Admin LR 670.

Zealand is in a slightly different position. It is lawful for the General Synod 'in such way and to such extent as may seem expedient', and in accordance with the terms of the secular Church of England Empowering Act 1928, 'to alter, add to, or diminish the Formularies, or any one or more of them, or any part or parts thereof, or to frame or adopt for use in the Church . . . new Formularies in lieu thereof or as alternatives thereto'. But this does not empower General Synod 'to depart from the Doctrine and Sacraments of Christ as defined in the Fundamental Provisions of [the church's] Constitution'. Changes may be made after adoption of a proposal, reference to the Diocesan Synods, and, following a 'fresh election', confirmation of the same in General Synod by a two-thirds majority of the members of each order.[64]

Moving along the spectrum, a few churches employ a reserved right to adopt doctrinal alterations accepted by the Church of England.[65] A variation on this is the right to accept alterations adopted not only by the Church of England but by any Anglican church. According to provisions in Southern Africa, repeated in the Ugandan constitution, 'we disclaim for this Church the right of altering any of the Standards of Faith and Doctrine now in use in the Church of England'; however, nothing shall prevent the church from 'accepting any alterations in the Formularies of the Church (other than the Creeds), which may be adopted by the Church of England or any other Church in the Anglican Communion'.[66] Another small group of churches employs a prohibition against doctrinal change but qualifies this with a reserved right to accept certain doctrinal adjustments provided these are consistent with standards prevailing in the Anglican Communion generally: the Burundi constitution provides that the church 'does not have the right to modify or depart from [its] standards [of faith], but it has the right to accept modifications . . . so long as these conform both to the Holy Scriptures and to the other standards of faith of the Anglican Communion throughout the world'.[67] A variation on this is the right to adopt doctrinal change in the event that this may be permitted, at some time in the future, by a supra-provincial assembly of the Anglican

---

[64] New Zealand, Church of England Empowering Act 1928, Sched. I; Fundamental Provisions, A.2; Const. B.5–6; for historical background see W. P. Morrell, *The Anglican Church in New Zealand* (Dunedin, 1973), 96ff.

[65] Indian Ocean, Const. Art. 2(iv): it may accept all modifications in the BCP 1662 and the Ordinal that are adopted by the Church of England; see also Sudan, Const. Art. 2(c); West Africa, Const. 2(b); Central Africa, Fundamental Declarations, I.

[66] Southern Africa, Declaration of Fundamental Principles 1870; see also Uganda, Const. Art. 2(e): 'The Church of Uganda has power to accept, if it shall so determine through the Provincial Assembly . . . any additional formulations of Doctrine and Discipline which may hereafter be adopted by the Church of England or any other Church within the Anglican Communion'.

[67] See Burundi, Const. Art. 3.3.

Communion. The Declaration of Fundamental Principles of the church in the West Indies states: 'We disclaim for ourselves the right of altering any of the . . . Standards of Faith and Doctrine' referred to in the Declaration. However, it continues: 'We claim for ourselves the right of accepting any alterations in the Formularies of the Church which may be allowed by any General Synod, Council, Congress or other Assembly of the Churches of the Anglican Communion'.[68] Finally, a small number of churches operate an absolute bar to the change of doctrine recognized in their Fundamental Declarations.[69] Others recognize for themselves the authority simply 'to explain the meaning of the norms of faith' or to issue statements 'agreeable to Holy Scripture'.[70]

The formal law of several churches today makes provision for a permanent national or provincial doctrine commission to assist in the process of doctrinal development.[71] These are commissions of the national or provincial assemblies. Composition rules vary from church to church. In Melanesia, the Commission on Doctrine and Theology consists of all the diocesan bishops, members of the theological college faculty, the cathedral dean and co-opted members, and in Australia, members of the Doctrine Commission are selected by the primate in consultation with the standing committee of General Synod.[72] In England, of the fifteen members of the Doctrine Commission three at least must be members of the General Synod.[73] The responsibilities of the New Zealand Doctrine Commission are defined canonically and are probably the most wide-ranging. Composed of twelve persons nominated by the primate in consultation with senior bishops, its functions are: to respond to specific theological questions referred to it by General Synod, its committees or any bishop; to maintain contact with and contribute to international theological exploration in the Anglican Communion; to relate to the theological work of other churches and to participate in ecumenical reflection; to initiate theological study of contemporary issues; and to encourage theological reflection generally within the church. It must present reports on its activities and financial accounts to each ordinary session of General Synod.[74] In comparison, the functions of the West Indian commission are spelt out in the canons

[68] West Indies, Declaration of Fundamental Principles, (d)–(e).

[69] Australia, Const. XI.66; Canada, Declaration of Principles, 6(i): within the jurisdiction of the General Synod is 'the definition of the doctrines of the Church in harmony with the Solemn Declaration', which itself is unalterable.

[70] See respectively Zaire, Const. Art. 3.3; and North India, Const. I.I.III.

[71] See LC 1988, Res. 18 for the Inter-Anglican Theological and Doctrine Commission.

[72] Melanesia, Cans. E.11; Australia, General Synod Commissions Canons 1969–92, 12–14; West Indies, Can. 33.1.A.

[73] General Synod, Boards and Councils Constitutions, 1996–2001, GS Misc. 460, 31–32.

[74] New Zealand, Cans. B.XVII.

with remarkable brevity: 'It shall be the duty of the Commission to study the various doctrinal issues that arise within the Province or that face the Anglican Communion in general'.[75] Like that in New Zealand, the Australian commission acts as a consultative body – to consider and report its findings on matters of Christian doctrine referred to it by the General Synod, the House of Bishops or other agencies, and to serve generally as a consultant body especially for the other General Synod commissions; another of its responsibilities is to examine matters of Christian doctrine that, in the opinion of the Commission, concern the Australian church and require examination.[76] Unlike those of New Zealand and Australia, the English Doctrine Commission is not a canonical institution but a subordinate body of General Synod regulated by a constitution created by the synod – its principal function is to consider and advise the House of Bishops on doctrinal questions referred to it by that House; and it may make suggestions to the House of Bishops as to what issues in its view are of doctrinal concern to the Church of England.[77] The law of none of these churches, however, expressly assigns to these institutions the function of settling doctrinal questions.[78]

SUBSCRIPTION TO DOCTRINE

Doctrinal discipline is effected principally by two devices: rules which require a particular response to the faith of the church, particularly from clergy and lay officers; and rules which enable oversight or enforcement of doctrinal standards by means of executive action or judicial proceedings. This section deals with the first of these. A resolution of the Lambeth Conference 1968 has been influential in the reorganization in recent years of Anglican canon law on subscription: it suggests that 'assent to the Thirty-Nine Articles be no longer required of ordinands' but that 'when subscription is required to the Articles or other elements in the Anglican tradition, it should be required, and given, only in the context of a statement which gives the full range of our inheritance of faith and sets the Articles in their historical context'.[79]

[75] West Indies, Can. 33.1.A; see also Melanesia, Cans. E.11: the Commission on Doctrine and Theology, 'a normative body', deals with matters of faith, order and practice of the church and must report annually to General Synod.

[76] Australia, General Synod Commissions Canons 1969–92: 12–14.

[77] General Synod, Councils and Boards Constitutions 1996–2001, GS Misc. 460, 31–32; for Scotland, Can. 52.18: the Faith and Order Board.

[78] See below.

[79] LC 1968, Res. 43; based on *Subscription and Assent to the 39 Articles*, A Report of the Archbishops of York and Canterbury Commission on Christian Doctrine (London, 1968).

Although an obvious assumption is that ordinary lay members of churches actually hold the faith, very seldom is it the case that formal laws impose upon the ordinary membership a duty to assent intellectually to the legally approved doctrines. Indeed, classical Anglican doctrine itself provides that the church 'ought not to enforce any thing to be believed for necessity of Salvation'.[80] Most often, perhaps as a result, laws are silent on the matter. Three uncommon ideas surface in some formal laws, however. In England, canon law provides only for a right of assent: the Thirty-Nine Articles 'may be assented to with a good conscience by all members of the Church of England' as agreeable to the Word of God; but, as to the canonical statement that '[t[he Church of England . . . belongs to the true and apostolic Church of Christ', 'no member thereof shall be at liberty to maintain or hold the contrary'.[81] In New Zealand, the constitution prescribes that: 'No doctrines which are repugnant to the Doctrines and Sacraments of Christ as held and maintained by this Church shall be advocated or inculcated by any person acknowledging the authority of General Synod'; the same applies to persons involved with the use of funds or property held under the authority of General Synod.[82] Lastly, in Melanesia, all employees of the church must sign 'a doctrinal statement' that they are 'of the Christian faith' at the commencement or renewal of their contracts.[83] Generally, then, with respect to the laity subscription to ecclesiastical doctrine is not the norm. However, whilst forms vary, candidates for judicial office,[84] for some administrative offices,[85] and for teaching, liturgical and pastoral office,[86] must in some churches make a subscription to the church's doctrine.

It is a general principle of Anglican canon law that subscription to doctrine is a precondition to admission to diaconal, priestly or episcopal ordination as well as, in most churches, admission to positions of episcopal and clerical office. The concepts of assent and of belief, and occasionally of respect, are employed as the basis of subscription. Usually candidates subscribe their 'assent' to the doctrines of the church and, occasionally, they subscribe their 'belief' that such doctrines are agreeable to the Word of God. Modes of subscription are variously by affirmation, declaration,

---

[80] Thirty-Nine Articles, Art. 20; see, however, Art. 8: 'The Three Creeds . . . ought thoroughly to be received and believed; for they may be proved by most certain warrants of Holy Scripture'.

[81] England, Cans. A1 and A2.   [82] New Zealand, Const. C.14.

[83] Melanesia, Standing Resolution 28, 1989.

[84] See e.g. England, Can. G2(3): diocesan chancellors must declare their 'belief in the faith' as revealed in Scripture, set forth in the Creeds and attested in the formularies of the church; compare Wales, Const. XI.13.

[85] E.g. England, Can. G4(3): registrars must make the same declaration as in n. 84.

[86] England, Cans. E5 and E6: these govern readers and lay workers; Scotland, Cans. App. No. 11: readers must promise to 'abide by such doctrine in my teaching'.

promise or oath. Elements of the English approach are mirrored in the laws of several churches. In England, at ordination and admission to office, a declaration of assent to the faith and doctrine of the church must be made – archbishops, diocesan and suffragan bishops, archdeacons, priests and deacons are obliged to 'affirm' 'loyalty to this inheritance of faith as [the candidate's] inspiration and guidance under God in bringing the grace and truth of Christ to this generation and making Him known to those in [the minister's] care'. Moreover, they are obliged to 'declare [their] belief in the faith which is revealed in the Holy Scriptures and set forth in the catholic creeds and to which the historic formularies of the Church of England bear witness'.[87] It remains unclear whether 'assent' means a complete adherence to every doctrinal proposition, or acceptability of their main tenor, or preference for them as opposed to any other doctrinal statement, or else their acceptance as portraying the identity of the Church of England.[88] Be that as it may, a statement of the House of Bishops understands such declarations to be made 'without private reservation'.[89]

Whereas the English form requires an 'affirmation of loyalty' to the faith and a 'declaration of belief' of scripture, the creeds and the church's formularies, the Australian declaration of assent, which may be adopted by the dioceses, requires 'belief' in the faith, 'assent' to ecclesiastical doctrine, and 'belief' that the latter is 'agreeable to the word of God'.[90] In New Zealand, canon law requires 'belief' in the faith and an 'affirmation of allegiance' to ecclesiastical doctrine.[91] The undertaking to communicate, woven into the English declaration of assent, is expressed a little differently in the law of Southern Africa where, before ordination, candidates must declare their 'belief in the faith' revealed in Holy Scripture, held by the Primitive Church and summed up in the Creeds, and they declare: 'I will teach and maintain the Faith of our Lord Jesus Christ, and the Doctrine and Discipline by Him delivered to the Church, as acknowledged and set forth by the Church of the Province of Southern Africa in the

---

[87] England, Can. C15.

[88] *Subscription and Assent to the 39 Articles* (1968), 33; see also 12: 'assent' does not mean 'general assent'; '[i]n law, assent must be taken to mean "complete acceptance" '.

[89] *The Nature of Christian Belief* (London, 1986), 4.

[90] Australia, Can. 7 1973: 'I firmly and sincerely believe the Catholic Faith and I give my assent to the doctrine' of the church 'as expressed in the Thirty-Nine Articles and the Book of Common Prayer'; moreover, they must declare: 'I believe that doctrine to be agreeable to the Word of God'; see also Rwanda, Draft Const. 1996, Arts. 42 and 43, for 'belief'.

[91] New Zealand, Can. A.I-II: the form for bishops and clergy is: 'I believe in the faith, which is revealed in the Holy Scriptures and set forth in the Catholic Creeds, as the Church has received and explained it in its Formularies and its authorized worship'; 'I affirm my allegiance to the doctrine' of the church.

Constitution'.[92] Similarly, in Tanzania, bishops must make a promise under oath to 'teach and hold the faith of our Lord Jesus Christ' and the religious teachings and discipline of the church as agreed in its constitution.[93]

Another requirement which is included in a very few forms of subscription is that acceptance of the church's doctrine involves acquiescence that it is agreeable to the Word of God. Under the constitution of the Church of Ireland, candidates at ordination, and clergy at institution or licensing must declare 'assent' to the Thirty-Nine Articles, the Book of Common Prayer and the Ordinal and that they 'believe the doctrine of the Church of Ireland . . . as agreeable to the Word of God'.[94] Scotland is similar but its legal formula makes no reference to the Thirty-Nine Articles: it requires of candidates for episcopal ordination 'assent' to the Scottish Book of Common Prayer, the Ordinal and the liturgical formularies and a 'belief' that 'the doctrine of the Church as therein set forth to be agreeable to the Word of God'.[95] The non-inclusion of the Thirty-Nine Articles in the canonical doctrines of some churches has, needless to say, an effect on forms of subscription: the canon law of Melanesia provides that 'clergy are not required to subscribe to the Thirty-Nine Articles of Religion',[96] and an unusual, but similar, provision from provincial law appears in the Kenyan constitution: the absence of any reference to the Thirty-Nine Articles in the constitutional statement of the official doctrines of the church does not preclude any Diocesan Synod 'from requiring subscription to it in the oaths and declarations made at ordination or licensing of its clergy'.[97]

Finally, the following forms of subscription do not mirror the traditional language of assent and belief. In ECUSA persons to be ordained bishops, priests and deacons must subscribe and declare: 'I do believe the Holy Scriptures of the Old and New Testaments to be the Word of God, and to contain all things necessary to salvation; and I do solemnly engage to conform to the Doctrine, Discipline, and Worship of the Episcopal Church'.[98] On the other hand, in Burundi the constitution requires from priests and deacons a promise 'to faithfully respect the Holy Bible and the Book of

---

[92] Southern Africa, Can. 16.1–2; Central Africa, Can. 9; for the same idea see Spain, Cans. III.25.

[93] Tanzania, Const IV. 14.

[94] Ireland, Const. IV.67; see also Korea, Const. Art. 120: 'I accept and honestly believe all the canonical Scriptures . . . I give assent to the Book of Common Prayer' and the Ordinal and 'I believe the doctrine . . . therein . . . to be agreeable to the Word of God'.

[95] Scotland, Cans. App. No. 1A: 'I assent to the Scottish Book of Common Prayer and of the Ordering of Bishops, Priests and Deacons and to the other authorized liturgical formularies of this Church'; 'I believe the doctrine of the Church as therein set forth to be agreeable to the Word of God'.

[96] Melanesia, Standing Resolution 13.2.   [97] Kenya, Const. Art. III(i).

[98] ECUSA, Con. Art. VIII; Brazil, Const. XI; Mexico, Const. Art. VI.2; Chile, Cans. B.8.

Common Prayer of this Province'.[99] Again, the constitution of the church in Zaire requires the taking of 'an oath of subscription by clergy to the doctrine of the church' (including the Thirty-Nine Articles).[100] Finally in Melanesia, the archbishop, bishops and assistant bishops promise to be 'faithful' to the 'teaching, ordering and faith of the church', each of which, they must declare, 'I believe to be a true part of the Holy Catholic and Apostolic church of Christ'.[101]

THE ENFORCEMENT OF DOCTRINAL STANDARDS

A fundamental principle of traditional Anglican thought is that '[t]he Church hath . . . authority in Controversies of Faith'.[102] This authority, within each church, is vested in a range of ecclesiastical persons and institutions. First and foremost it is placed in the diocesan bishop one of whose functions is to maintain doctrinal standards amongst ministers in the diocese. It is a function recognized time and time again in national and provincial church laws. The English canonical principle, mirrored almost *verbatim* in Scottish canon law, that the bishop is obliged to 'uphold sound and wholesome doctrine, and to banish and drive away all erroneous and strange opinions' finds a direct parallel in many legal systems.[103] In a very small number of churches, the formal law expressly enables the bishop to be assisted in oversight of doctrinal standards by its imposition of duties on officers at the lower levels of the church. In Southern Africa, a canonical duty is placed upon churchwardens to complain to the bishop (or the archdeacon) 'if there should be anything plainly amiss or reprehensible in the life or doctrine of the Incumbent'.[104] In the Church of Ireland, vigilance extends also to the doctrinal standards of the laity: '[e]very minister having within his cure persons holding any erroneous and strange doctrines, contrary to the word of God, shall endeavour to reclaim them from their errors'.[105] This provision is exceptional.

---

[99] Burundi, Const. Art. 25.   [100] Zaire, Const. Art. 18.

[101] Melanesia, Const. Art. 15; Philippines, Cans. III.14.1; see Rwanda, Draft Const. 1996, Art. 43 for a similar formula.

[102] Thirty-Nine Articles, Art. 20.

[103] England, Can. C18(1) and Scotland, Can. 16.2 are almost identical: the word 'doctrine' appears instead of 'opinion' in the Scottish version; see also, for England, the House of Bishops' statement, *The Nature of Christian Belief* (1986) paras. 64–73: this recognizes the episcopal duty to 'guard the faith'; see also e.g. Indian Ocean, Const. Art. 14.4; and Korea, Const. Art. 12: the bishop is responsible for the 'preservation of the Faith'.

[104] Southern Africa, Can. 29.7; for the assistance of the archdeacon generally, see Ch. 6.

[105] Ireland, Const. IX.29.

Doctrinal Offences and Church Courts

As well as executive episcopal correction of doctrinal indiscipline, judicial proceedings are available in serious and appropriate cases. The system of ecclesiastical offences of most churches includes a special offence relating to doctrine, over which church courts possess jurisdiction (see Chapter 3). In a small number of churches, proceedings may be taken against lay people for doctrinal offences. For example, in Wales, 'any member of the Church in Wales', ordained or lay, may be proceeded against in the Provincial Court for 'teaching, preaching, publishing or professing doctrine or belief incompatible with that of the Church in Wales'.[106] Most churches, however, confine judicial proceedings for doctrine offences to the clergy. Definitional elements differ most in terms of their width particularly as to the form of dissent, especially whether either public or private dissent, or both, are actionable. In England proceedings may be instituted against bishops, priests or deacons for an offence against the laws ecclesiastical involving a matter of doctrine: it has recently been held by the church courts that 'a public statement (as in a sermon or a book) denying the doctrine of the Trinity or of the deity of Christ' would 'without hesitation' be referred to the Court of Ecclesiastical Causes Reserved.[107] In the past, maintaining opinions contrary to the Christian religion, depraving the Book of Common Prayer, maintaining doctrines repugnant to the Thirty-Nine Articles, and heresy, have all been treated as doctrinal offences.[108] However, in England today, according to a statement of the House of Bishops, episcopal correction rather than judicial proceedings would be more likely.[109] A similar but somewhat more precise definitional approach is employed in Southern Africa where the doctrinal offences are heresy ('false doctrine'), schism ('acceptance of membership in a religious body not in communion' with the church); and apostasy (abandonment of 'the Christian faith'). For these it must be

---

[106] Wales, Const. XI.1(c)(i); North India, Const. II.V.VI.1: lay or ordained persons may be disciplined for 'belief or teaching which is contrary to the Christian Scriptures'; Canada, Can. XVIII.8(g): proceedings may be brought against clergy and lay officers for 'teaching or advocating doctrines contrary to' those of the church; see also Ireland, Const. VIII.53: the 'teaching or publishing of any doctrine contrary to the doctrines of the [church]' is an offence.

[107] Ecclesiastical Jurisdiction Measure 1963, s. 38; *Bland v Archdeacon of Cheltenham* [1972] 1 All ER 1012 at 1017.

[108] *Gorham v Bishop of Exeter* (1850) Moore's Special Reports 462; *Williams v Bishop of Salisbury* (1864) 2 Moore PCCNS 375. For the celebrated cases of *In re Lord Bishop of Natal* [1864–5] III Moore NS 114 and *Capetown (Bishop of) v Natal (Bishop of)* [1869] VI Moore NS 202, see e.g. A. Ive, *The Church of England in South Africa: A Study of Its History, Principles and Status* (Capetown, 1966), 18ff.

[109] *The Nature of Christian Belief* (1986) 64–73; see generally LFCE, 264ff.

established that the accused has 'taught, published, or otherwise publicly promulgated, some doctrine or opinion repugnant to or at variance with the Faith and Doctrine of the Church', as contained in the Creeds, the Thirty-Nine Articles, the Book of Common Prayer and the Ordinal; a charge must specify 'particular passages of these Standards and Formularies' which are used as the basis of the proceedings.[110] The Scottish canons mirror the Southern African model with only minor differences.[111] Under some laws private withholding of assent is also actionable: in ECUSA, a bishop, deacon or priest may be tried in the church courts for holding and teaching publicly or privately, and advisedly, any doctrine contrary to that held by the church.[112] Express provisions for removal of a bishop for heresy are to be found in a small number of churches.[113]

Arrangements concerning the precise role of the courts in doctrine cases are fairly clear. In England the classical view is that the courts possess no competence to declare, to create or to change ecclesiastical doctrine: one commentator has observed that 'the courts do not claim to declare true

---

[110] Southern Africa, Can. 37.1 and 5; Chile, Cans. E.4: heresy is rejection of the 'divinity of Jesus Christ'; for a comparative study of offences against blasphemy in secular law, see D. W. Elliott, 'Blasphemy and other expressions of offensive opinion', *Ecclesiastical Law Journal*, 3 (13) (1993), 70; Australia, Cans. 4 1962, 7 1981, 12 1992: these seem to contain no explicit reference to a doctrinal offence; for recent developments in the secular law of blasphemy in Australia, see *Commonwealth Law Bulletin*, 18(3) (1992), 964. See also *Osam-Pniako v Lartey* [1967] Ghana Law Reports 380: the Cape Coast High Court declined to grant an injunction to restrain a bishop in the A.M.E. Zion Church on the basis of allegations that he was preaching heresy; *per* Archer J at 383: heresy is 'a belief contrary to the authorised teaching of one's natural religious community. There is no established religion in Ghana recognized as the religion of the State. If a bishop commits heresy by preaching contrary to the precepts of Christ or by propounding religious dogmas opposed to the accepted and established canons of the church, there is nothing that a temporal court can do about it. Only the church authorities can deal with the particular bishop'.

[111] Scotland, Can. 54.2: it is an offence to have 'taught, published or otherwise publicly promulgated doctrines or opinions subversive to the teaching of the Church, as expressed in its formularies'; see also Japan, Can. 17, Art. 158; Brazil, Cans. IV.1.1; New Zealand, Cans. D.II.2: 'If any Minister shall advisedly maintain any Doctrine contrary to Clause 1 of the Constitution', proceedings may be instituted if the minister has not 'retracted such error'.

[112] ECUSA, Cans. IV.1.1; *Stanton (Bishop of Dallas) et al v Righter* (1996): the Court for the Trial of a Bishop held that a bishop who ordained persons living in same gender sexual relationships had not failed to conform to the doctrine of the church; resolutions of the General Convention and the House of Bishops on the subject did not form part of the church's 'core doctrine' but were recommendatory only and did not bind the bishop; see also n. 2. For liability based on public and private dissent, see Mexico, Can. 37.1 and Spain, Cans. IV.34.

[113] Sudan, Const. Art. 49; South East Asia, Const. Art. IV.(h); Papua New Guinea, Can. No. 1 1977, Art. 1; Melanesia, Cans. C.2.A–B: disciplinary action may be taken when a bishop teaches 'wrong teachings against the Foundation of Faith'.

doctrine, but only to state what the law is with regard to doctrine'.[114] According to a judicial *dictum* from the Privy Council '[the] court has no jurisdiction or authority to settle matters of faith or to determine what ought in any case to be the doctrine of the Church of England'.[115] This approach is implicit in the vast majority of churches which reserve these functions only to the national or provincial assembly.[116] Needless to say, however, interpretation of doctrine may be a necessary function of the courts, and sometimes formal laws confine authoritative doctrinal inter-pretations to the courts of the church in question. For Southern Africa, for example, in the interpretation of the standards of faith and the formula-ries, the church is not bound by decisions concerning faith and doctrine other than those of its own ecclesiastical tribunals.[117] The constitution in Wales prescribes that 'the Courts of the Church in Wales shall not be bound by any decision of the English Courts in relation to matters of faith'.[118] It is rarely the case that formal law guides the courts in the status of Anglican teaching generally when reference is made to this in litigation; the formal law of South East Asia is exceptional: '[i]n the interpretation of the . . . standards and formularies and in all questions of faith [and] doc-trine . . . whilst the Province is a fully autonomous part of the Anglican Communion, it shall nevertheless give due weight to the teaching and tra-ditions of the Communion in the deliberations and decisions of its own ecclesiastical tribunals'.[119]

Quasi-Judicial Resolution of Doctrinal Controversy

In cases not involving doctrinal offences under church law, which nevertheless generate disagreement within the church, the law of many

---

[114] T. Briden and B. Hanson (eds.), *Moore's Introduction to English Canon Law* (3rd edn., London, 1992), 50.

[115] *Gorham v Bishop of Exeter* (1850) Moore's Special Reports 462; see also *General Assembly of the Free Church of Scotland v Lord Overtoun* [1904] AC 515 at 648 *per* Lord Halsbury: 'it is to be remembered that a court of law has nothing to do with the sound-ness or unsoundness of a particular doctrine'; however, in *Re St Stephen's, Walbrook* [1987] 2 All ER 578: the Church of England's Court of Ecclesiastical Causes Reserved in determining the question whether there was any legal obstacle to the introduction of an 'altar' clarified eucharistic doctrine and thereby settled a doctrinal dispute.

[116] See above for the development of doctrine and e.g. Indian Ocean, Art. 2(vi): the '[i]nterpretation of norms' concerning questions of faith and doctrine is reached by 'decision' of the ecclesiastical tribunals.

[117] Southern Africa, Const. Art. I; Melanesia, Const. Art. 2; see also West Africa, Const. Art. 2(d): in the interpretation of the standards and formularies 'in all matters of faith and doctrine', the church is not bound by any decision other than those of the church's tribunals; see also Burundi, Const. Art. 3.

[118] Wales, Const. XI.36.   [119] South East Asia, Fundamental Declarations, 5.

churches provides for quasi-judicial process.[120] Three systems seem to be used. In one the church refers a doctrinal problem externally to an institution of the Anglican Communion for consultation and advice. In another it does so for determination. In turn these two systems differ with respect to the body to which the referral is made and whether the referral itself is mandatory. These appear most commonly in the African churches. A third approach is for church law to provide exclusively for resolution within the church.

Under Kenyan constitutional law, if 'any issue of great importance has been raised in the field of Faith and Order', and the Provincial Synod has been unable to reach agreement on the matter and to find an acceptable solution, 'the Archbishop shall, at the request of the Provincial Synod, communicate the problem and the issue raised to the Anglican Consultative Council or such other body as the Provincial Synod may select for advice'. On receipt of the advice the archbishop must commit all the relevant documents to a commission, which may be the provincial tribunal for the hearing of appeals or a commission especially appointed, with instructions to draw up a report. On receiving the report the Bishops of the Province must draw up a statement for presentation to the Provincial Synod at its next meeting. If the Provincial Synod fails to reach agreement, no further action shall be taken. In either case the decision of the Provincial Synod is final. Consequently, '[i]n the interpretation of the . . . standards and formularies and in all questions of Faith [and] Doctrine . . . the Church of this Province is not bound by any decisions other than those of the Provincial Synod'. This scheme is justified on the basis that the Kenyan church claims 'the right and duty to discover for itself' doctrinal truth.[121] In South East Asia 'the Provincial Synod may consult with the Archbishop of Canterbury or the Primates of the Anglican Communion, as appropriate'.[122] For the church in Sudan referral may be made by the General Synod to the Archbishop of Canterbury 'together with the Secretary of the Anglican Consultative Council for advice'.[123] According to the law in West Africa, though referral is to the Archbishop of Canterbury alone, the House of Bishops may seek at any time 'the advice through the Archbishop of Canterbury of the theologians of the Church of England'.[124]

---

[120] Presumably, there would be no legal obstacle, in those churches which have them, for advice to be sought from doctrine commissions (see above) which may then be used by ecclesiastical authorities to resolve the dispute.

[121] Kenya, Const. Art. II(e),(g) and (h).

[122] South East Asia, Fundamental Declarations, 4.

[123] Sudan, Art. 2(d); see also Tanzania, Const. IV.15(d) and (e).

[124] West Africa, Const. Arts. 5 and 14.

For some churches, the law requires external consideration of a doctrinal matter by the Archbishop of Canterbury acting in concert with other bishops. In Central Africa, '[t]he Episcopal Synod has always final authority in matters concerning the preservation of the Truth of the Church's doctrine'; any bishop may require referral of a question to the Archbishop of Canterbury and two other bishops (one nominated by the bishop making the submission and the other by the Episcopal Synod) 'who shall determine the matter in accordance with the formularies and doctrinal teaching of the Church of England, and their decision shall be final'.[125] By way of comparison, the law of some churches seems to fail to define the precise consequence of reference. In Uganda a special procedure becomes active only when the bishops cannot agree: '[i]f questions of interpretation arise concerning Faith [or] Doctrine . . . the jurisdiction to determine any matter of Faith [or] Doctrine . . . is hereby vested in the House of Bishops'. If in the House of Bishops 'doubt or dispute arises concerning a matter of Faith [or] Doctrine . . . which cannot be resolved with general unanimity, the House may, or if two members of that House so require in writing, shall, refer the question to the Anglican Consultative Council'.[126] The treatment of the subject in Ugandan constitutional law ends at this point – it does not describe the status of the Council's response to the referred question.

In line with the principle of the autonomy of each church in the Communion, sometimes the law of a church provides solely for internal resolution of doctrinal controversy without recourse to external bodies. A unique system is employed in New Zealand: rather than determining litigation, a special tribunal on doctrine acts 'for the purposes of deciding all questions of doctrine duly referred to it'. Proceedings are instituted by a notice of application containing a statement of the question or matter of doctrine which the applicants consider 'to involve a departure from the doctrine and sacraments of Christ'. The governing law is mainly procedural and jurisdictional. The applicants must have *locus standi*: applications may be made by at least seven persons, one of whom must be a bishop, one a priest or deacon, and one a baptized lay person. A committee is appointed to present 'perspectives and opinions in answer to the doctrinal propositions being advanced by the applicants'. The tribunal adjudicates on the applicants' and the committee's opposing arguments. The decision, which must be determined with the concurrence of at least two-thirds of the persons hearing the matter, may result in the pronouncement of a judgment, an advice or an opinion. The tribunal is composed of three bishops and priests (or deacons) and baptized lay persons elected by General Synod.[127]

---

[125] Central Africa, Const. Art. V.
[126] Uganda, Const. Art. II(g),(i)–(l); see also Indian Ocean, Const. Art. 7(iii).
[127] New Zealand, Cans. C.V; the tribunal was established under Const. C.10.

CONCLUSIONS

Proclamation of the faith goes to the very nature of the church. Traditionally, in terms of formal law, the function of proclamation has been reserved, by means of canonical duties to preach and to instruct, to the ordained ministers of the church. The imposition of legal duties on members of the laity is not a general practice of Anglican churches. The growing number of canonical institutions involved directly with evangelism and education, at both national or provincial and diocesan levels, may indicate a movement away from the traditional law of individualism in preaching and in instruction; law regulating these institutions provides structures enabling teamwork in the proclamation of the faith. Very few churches have formal law on theological colleges and, therefore, it is not possible to construct general principles of Anglican canon law on this subject. Anglican churches are not confessional: laws do not define in detail the beliefs of churches – they simply point to doctrines located elsewhere. There is widespread legal consensus about the sources of doctrine, derived ultimately from Holy Scripture, and the Thirty-Nine Articles are still recognized as canonical doctrine in a large number of churches. Laws invariably reserve the development of doctrine to national and provincial legislative assemblies which have to comply with special majority procedures to effect doctrinal change or innovation. Only a small number of churches operate explicitly legal arrangements rendering fundamental doctrines unalterable. That subscription to the faith and doctrines of the church is required for admission to ordained ministry is a general principle of Anglican canon law: it is only forms which vary. Executive doctrinal discipline is effected by the oversight of the bishop. The use of doctrinal offences, for which proceedings may be brought in the church courts (in some churches against both lay and ordained persons), is very extensive. Informal resolution of doctrinal controversies, by institutions of a quasi-judicial nature, is beginning to appear in church law.

8

Public Worship and Liturgical Law

Along with proclamation of the faith, worship is one of the central functions of the Christian church. Yet the relationship between public worship and law is often a difficult one. On the one hand, there is the assumption that law intrudes on an occasion of intimacy between the individual and God. On the other hand, there is the desire for order, the organization of worship as formal liturgy, in the enhancement of the corporate identity of the church before God. Today liturgical laws are the direct result of churches seeking to reconcile these values. The Lambeth Conference has played a major role over the years in this development, in its encouragement of liturgical reform throughout the Communion: principles appearing in conference resolutions, about the need for a balance between preservation of the liturgical inheritance and adaptations to local use, about experimentation and about freedom of choice, have all stimulated adjustments in recent years in the liturgical law of churches. This chapter describes the results of these developments along with the centrality of the bishop in the oversight of liturgical worship and liturgical discipline. Secular laws are particularly conspicuous in their protection of places of worship at the time of divine service.

WORSHIP, LITURGY AND LAW

In the secular law of several states essential elements of judicial definitions of worship are that it is a form of ceremony and that it involves veneration, praise, thanksgiving, and prayer.[1] In the formal laws of churches, worship is, needless to say, presented as one of the fundamental purposes and

---

[1] England, *R v Registrar General, ex p Segerdal* [1970] 3 All ER 886 at 892; approved in *Re South Place Ethical Society, Barralet v AG* [1980] 3 All ER 918. For freedom of worship in secular society, see LC 1988, Res. 23 and for the general reluctance of secular courts to get involved with disputes within churches about worship, see e.g. *Lalji Meghji Patel v Karsan Premji* (1976) Kenya LR 112 (CA): the constitutional requirement of religious freedom precluded the courts from interfering with matters of ritual; *R v de Jager* (1931–37) Northern Rhodesia Law Reports 13: 'It is axiomatic . . . that religious matters are subject to the control of the legislature', but it would 'hesitate to indulge in legislation antagonistic to public feelings on any fundamental matter such as Holy Scripture, the Koran or on books of a liturgical nature'.

responsibilities of the church.[2] Resolutions of the Lambeth Conference stress the obligation of the church to engage in corporate worship, in which the whole church, and its individual members, participate in praise, adoration, confession, prayer and thanksgiving.[3] The same concepts surface in the service books and catechetical documents of churches, with emphasis on worship as the individual's or the community's response to God.[4] In Anglican thought 'liturgy', on the other hand, is treated as the public and corporate expression and act of worship in accordance with the service books of the church.[5] As a matter of ecclesiastical practice, however, the term is not usually defined in formal law: the more usual expressions used are 'ritual', 'ceremonial', 'form of service' or 'divine service'.[6] Rather it is defined in service books themselves. In Southern Africa '[l]iturgy is the public worship of the Church of God, a living tradition'.[7] In New Zealand, '[t]he purpose of liturgy is not to protect particular linguistic forms. It is to enable a community to pray . . . the first function of liturgy is to provide conditions in which [God's] presence may be experienced'.[8] In Ireland, 'liturgy becomes worship when the people of God make the prayers their own prayers, and turn in faith, to God'.[9]

---

[2] Chile, Can. D.1: 'The adoration of God is the greatest privilege of a Christian'; Rwanda, Draft Const. 1996, Art. 3: 'The mission of the province is to glorify God through public worship'; Central Africa, Diocese of Mashonaland, *Pastoral Regulations* 1978, p.18: 'All worship is directed to God, the Father, through his Son, our Lord Jesus Christ, and in the power of the Holy Spirit'.

[3] LC 1930, Res. 8: 'we urge upon the Church the absolute obligation of corporate worship' in which individuals 'advance in their knowledge of God's nature, and may hope to penetrate further into his mysteries'; see also LC 1948, Res. 36 and LC 1968, Res. 4; for family prayer see e.g. LC 1958, Ress. 121, 122; but see also, LC 1968, *Message* (Evans and Wright, 470): '[t]he ministry of the laity does not consist solely . . . in the Church's worship'. For the centrality of prayer and the Anglican Cycle of Prayer, see LC 1958, Ress. 69, 101; LC 1908, Res. 33; LC 1920, Res. 61; LC 1958, Res. 69.

[4] Wales, BCP 1984, 695 (Catechism): 'Worship is my response to God's love: first, by joining with others in the Church's corporate offering of prayer, celebration of the Sacraments and reading his holy Word; secondly, by acknowledging him as the Lord of my life, and by doing my work for his honour and glory'; New Zealand, *Prayer Book* 1989, xiv: 'worship is the response of the people of God to the presence of God'.

[5] See generally, R. C. D. Jasper, *The Development of Anglican Liturgy: 1662–1980* (London, 1989); G. J. Cuming, *A History of Anglican Liturgy* (2nd edn., London, 1982).

[6] Australia, Const. XII.74.1: 'ceremonial' includes 'ceremonial according to the use of this Church, and also the obligation to abide by such use'; 'ritual' includes rites according to 'the use of the church, and the obligation to abide by such rites'; for 'forms of service' see Can. P6 1992; England, Church of England (Worship and Doctrine) Measure 1974, s. 5(2): 'form of service', which means 'any order, service, prayer, rite or ceremony', is an equivalent to 'liturgy'; for 'divine service' see Ireland, Const. IX.1.

[7] Southern Africa, *Prayer Book* 1989, 9; for earlier liturgical developments, see P. Hinchliff, *The South African Liturgy* (Oxford, 1959).

[8] New Zealand, *Prayer Book* 1989, xiii–xiv.

[9] Ireland, *Alternative Prayer Book* 1984, 8.

Moving to law, views about the aim of liturgical regulation, particularly by rubrics, have changed radically during recent years. The position, represented in the nineteenth-century English decision of *Martin v Mackonochie*, was that '[i]t is not open to a minister of the Church to draw a distinction in acts which are a departure from or violation of the rubrics [of the 1662 Book of Common Prayer], between those which are important and those which appear to be minor'.[10] Today, liturgical regulation is understood in terms of flexibility and choice with the emphasis, as is expressed neatly in Chilean canon law, on lack of detailed rules and on liturgies as facilities.[11] Rubrics are not to be interpreted in the same way as a statute: some might be classified as mandatory and others as directory or recommendatory;[12] they must be capable of adaptation to meet local circumstances, practices and needs;[13] and, in the processes of revision in some churches, their number in service books has been reduced as a matter of policy.[14] In some churches, canon law is not the principal medium for the regulation of liturgy: regulation is consigned instead to 'directions' or 'notes' contained in the service books themselves; again, recommendatory rather than imperative language is used.[15] This new orientation is not reflected in all churches, however. In some, formal law is deliberately phrased to convey the obligation of compliance with rubrical requirements: 'rubrics' are 'laws'.[16] In others, compliance with rubrics is justified

---

[10] (1868) LR 2 A & E 116.

[11] Chile, Cans. D.2: in view of 'the special characteristics of worship, it is impossible to provide . . . detailed rules; so much depends on the sense of the minister'; New Zealand, *Prayer Book* 1989, ix; see also LC 1878, Res. 7: 'elasticity in the forms of worship is desirable as [it] will give wide scope to all legitimate expressions of devotional feeling'.

[12] See e.g. the English consistory court decision of *Bishopwearmouth* (*Rector and Churchwardens*) *v Adey* [1958] 3 All ER 441; for a Welsh understanding of 'rubrics', see Liturgical Commission, 1949 and 1951: 'rubrics' are 'directions on order, ceremonial, and other matters' (E. Lewis, *Prayer Book Revision in the Church in Wales* (Penarth, 1958), 3).

[13] LC 1908, Res. 27; see also n. 45.

[14] Ireland, *Alternative Prayer Book* 1984, 8: 'Rubrics in this book have been deliberately kept to a minimum'; Wales, Liturgical Commission, 1949 and 1951: 'Rubrics. There is need for the excision of absolute rubrics; for the provision of new ones to regularise a number of practices which have become customary but of whose strict legality there is doubt; and for the expansion of certain rubrics . . . so as to make clear what they allow or do not allow' (see E. Lewis, *Prayer Book Revision in the Church in Wales* (Penarth, 1958), 3).

[15] See e.g. Wales, BCP 1984, v: '[t]he law of worship of the Church in Wales is contained in the Book of Common Prayer'; see ibid., 22 for 'general directions' in which words and expressions such as 'should', 'as far as possible' and 'appropriate' are employed to regulate subjects; for 'notes', see e.g. Australia, *A Prayer Book for Australia* 1995, 654, and England, *Alternative Service Book* 1980, 116; Canada, BCP 1962, 'general rubrics': 'it is desirable that the bell should be rung'; Southern Africa, *Prayer Book* 1989, General Rubrics, 41: 'A bell should be rung, where possible, to invite the people'.

[16] Brazil, Cans. II.1.1: 'The rubrics of the Book of Common Prayer have legal force and should be complied with in the whole church'.

on the basis of order in the fulfilment of clerical and lay roles in liturgical action.[17] Similarly, as we shall see later in this Chapter, on the one hand, modern Anglican laws allow considerable scope for liturgical variation and for rubrical deviation, and yet, at the same time, violation of liturgical laws (and sometimes of rubrics) is still listed amongst the ecclesiastical offences in some churches. In sum, no church has at present any formal canonical expression of the new liturgical outlook. The Anglican church awaits a convincing liturgical jurisprudence in which a convincing synthesis is made of the competing claims of facility and order in worship.[18]

Mandatory canon law, however, plays a more conspicuous role to ensure that the elements of worship described at the opening of this section are realized in liturgical action: worship as a function of the faithful, adoration, praise, and prayer. It is rarely the case that these elements of worship are enumerated in formal law collectively and expressly.[19] Rather, rules about them are dispersed and these elements are implicit within those rules. As a global principle, ultimate responsibility for oversight and control of liturgical practice rests with the bishop.[20] First, laws recognize the responsibility of the members of churches to worship. Attendance at worship, particularly on Sunday, is enjoined (often canonically) for members of the church: the canon law of ECUSA provides that '[a]ll persons within this Church shall celebrate and keep the Lord's Day, commonly called Sunday, by regular participation in the public worship of the Church, by hearing the Word of God read and taught, and by other acts of devotion and works of charity, using all godly and sober conversation'.[21] The equivalent rule in English canon law is marginally narrower: the Lord's Day is to be observed 'particularly by attendance at divine worship, by deeds of charity and by abstention from all unnecessary labour

---

[17] ECUSA, Cans. III.3.2: lay ministers must conform to 'the rubrics and other directions' of the BCP; see also BCP 1979, Marshall I, 75: 'In all services, the entire Christian assembly participates in such a way that the members of each order within the Church, lay persons, bishops, priests and deacons, fulfil the functions proper to their respective orders, as set forth in the rubrical directions for each service'.

[18] See R. D. H. Bursell, *Liturgy, Order and the Law*, (Oxford, 1996) for an English perspective on the 'reasonableness' of the law of worship in the Church of England.

[19] South India, Const. X.2: for example, the communion service consists in the sequence: introductory prayers, the ministry of the Word, the preparation of communicants (by confession and absolution), the offering of gifts, the thanksgiving, intercessions, the Lord's Prayer, administration of communion, and a thanksgiving for the grace received; ibid. 4: '[t]he use of the Creeds in worship is an act of adoration and thanksgiving towards Almighty God for His nature and for His acts of love and mercy, as well as joyful remembrance of the faith which binds together the worshippers'.

[20] For episcopal oversight of liturgy see below and Ch. 4.

[21] ECUSA, Cans. II.1: for the exact same formula, see Philippines, Cans. II.1; see also Southern Africa, Can. 33.5: 'All Public Feasts and Thanksgivings enjoined by authority in this Province shall be religiously observed'.

and business'.[22] There can be no full participation without understanding, and the laws of several churches existing in multilingual societies cater accordingly. In Philippine canon law, for example, in any congregation worshipping in a language other than that of the church's service book, 'it shall be lawful to use a form of service in such language'; prior approval has to be obtained from the bishop who must be satisfied that the text is 'in accordance with the Doctrine and Worship of the Church'.[23] The requirement of episcopal approval, either individual or collective, is standard.[24]

Secondly, a rule which commonly appears in the canon law or rubrics of churches, concerning the acts and words of worship as devotion and adoration, is that the service must be said or sung distinctly, reverently and audibly. In England, the canons deal with the subject in full and mandatory terms. All persons present at divine worship 'shall' audibly with the minister make the answers appointed and in due place join in such parts of the service as are appointed to be said or sung by all present. Moreover, all persons present 'shall give reverent attention in the time of divine service, give due reverence to the name of the Lord Jesus and stand at the Creed and the reading of the Holy Gospel at the Holy Communion'. When the prayers are read and psalms and canticles are said or sung, members of the congregation 'shall have regard to the rubrics of the service and locally established custom in the matter of posture, whether of standing, kneeling or sitting'.[25] Mandatory language is also used in Australia but the scope of the canon is narrower than its English counterpart: '[e]ach service must be said or sung distinctly, reverently and in an audible voice'.[26] For

---

[22] England, Can. B6(1); Ireland, Const. IX.1: the Lord's Day 'shall be observed, according to God's holy will and pleasure and the order of this Church'; see also the secular English parliamentary statute, the Sunday Trading Act 1994, s. 4: if a contract of employment requires Sunday work, a shop worker may give written notice to the employer that he objects to Sunday work: this 'opting-out' notice may be revoked by an 'opting-in' notice and by express agreement to work on Sundays; employees who have opted-out must not be subjected to any detriment by the employer.

[23] Philippines, Cans. II.4.4.

[24] See e.g. Ireland, BCP 1960, General Directions, liv: 'Though all things be here set forth as to be said or sung in the English tongue . . . it is not meant but that, at the discretion of the Minister, and with the consent of the Ordinary, they may be said or sung in Irish or in any other language that is better understood by the people'; for translation to Gaelic and approval by the College of Bishops, see Scotland, Can. 22.6; New Zealand, Cans. G.X.2–4: this governs translation into Maori amongst other languages; ECUSA, BCP 1979, Marshall, Vol. I, 383: at the eucharist, 'When a portion of the congregation is composed of persons whose native tongue is other than English, a reader appointed by the celebrant may read the Gospel in the language of the people'.

[25] England, Can. B9(1)–(2); for a similar provision see Chile, Cans. D.9; see LC 1897, Res. 46 for the 'exclusive right' of the bishop to authorize the use of prayers.

[26] Australia, Can. P6 1992, 6; see also Ireland, Const. IX.8: this imposes a duty 'in public ministrations to speak in a distinct and audible voice'.

other churches, regulation of these subjects is found in liturgical rubrics which are formulated in more recommendatory language.[27]

Thirdly, praise in the form of music is the subject of considerable canonical regulation in a great number of churches. It is a general principle of Anglican canon law that the right to control music belongs to the minister as opposed to the congregation, organist, choirmaster or director of music. Elements of English canon law may be used to illustrate the mainly minor variations as between churches within this principle. In England the minister must ensure that only chants, hymns, anthems, and other settings are chosen as are appropriate, both the words and the music, to the solemn act of worship and prayer as well as to the congregation assembled; ministers must 'banish all irreverence in the practice and in the performance of the same'.[28] Equivalent provisions in other churches require ministers to ensure that words set to music must not be contrary to church doctrine and that the music must glorify God and help the people in worship.[29] Rules in some churches are somewhat more liberal, allowing spontaneity and dancing.[30] The English canon imposes a duty on the minister to heed the advice of the organist or choirmaster in the choice of chants, hymns, anthems, or other settings and in the ordering of the music of the church; however, 'the final responsibility and decision in these matters rests with the minister'. The same basic rules, with variations only in form, are common,[31] but

[27] See e.g. Wales, BCP 1984, The Eucharist, 22, General Directions, 10,12: 'The directions STAND, KNEEL, SIT indicate the postures which are appropriate for the people at various stages of the service . . . The use of silence is commended as a means of recollection'.

[28] England, Can. B20; see also LC 1958, Res. 10: 'The Conference believes that the presentation of the message of the Bible to the world requires great sensitiveness to the outlook of the people of today, and urges that imaginative use be made of all the resources of literature, art, music and drama, and of new techniques appealing to the eye as well as to the ear'.

[29] Ireland, Const. IX.6: hymns must not be contrary to the doctrine of the church as the minister determines; Philippines, Cans. II.4.5: every minister must ensure that 'music is used as an offering for the glory of God and as a help to the people in the worship'; ECUSA, BCP 1979: 'The words of anthems are to be from Holy Scripture, or from [the BCP itself], or from texts congruent with them'; see also Cans. II.6.1 and Diocese of Mississippi, Cans. III.A.37: the minister must 'suppress all light and unseemly music and all irreverence in the rendition thereof'; Australia, *A Prayer Book for Australia* 1995, 654, Notes 7: the 'placing' of hymns belongs to the priest.

[30] Central Africa, Diocese of Mashonaland, *Pastoral Regulations* 1978, p.19: 'Shona people glorify God more by natural and indigenous music, sometimes with drums and dancing, rather than by copying Western forms. Hymns should never be used merely to cover silence which is, in itself, a very vital part of liturgical worship'; delivery should be 'neither too slow and mournful, nor too rapid and clipped'.

[31] Scotland, Can. 22.8: 'overall control' concerning organ, music and choir rests with the rector or priest-in-charge; ECUSA, Cans. II.6.1: the cleric has 'final authority' but must seek assistance from persons skilled in music: '[t]ogether they shall see that music is appropriate to the context in which it is used'; New Zealand, Cans. B.V.4: 'The

Australian canon law is more detailed.[32] By way of contrast, in Southern Africa and the West Indies no hymn may be introduced into the diocese without episcopal consent.[33] In England, according to a judicial authority, if there are disagreements about music, it would seem that the matter should be referred to the bishop.[34] Unlike other churches, the English canon makes provision for the appointment and dismissal of organists.[35] On the other hand, unlike in England, the canon law of some churches places the responsibility for the revision, adaptation and publication of a hymnal on a national or provincial body.[36] Similarly, national or provincial synods of some churches are under a canonical obligation to establish commissions on music to encourage and to produce new compositions, and 'to recommend norms both as to liturgical music and as to the manner of its rendition'.[37] Fourthly, the subject of prayer is not generally addressed in formal law, though occasionally rules may be found recognizing expressly a power in the bishop to control prayer at services of public worship.[38]

formation and management of the choir and the selection of church music shall be subject to the control and direction of the Vicar'.

[32] Australia, Can. P6 1992, 8: 'The minister must determine what parts of Divine Service offered in a church are to be said or sung. No musical instrument may be played in connection with Divine Service in any church without the approval of the minister of that church. The minister must ensure that all music (including any words and accompaniment) is appropriate and reverent'; see also Brazil, Cans. II.1.1: 'It is the duty of the minister to designate hymns . . . together with the appropriate musical instruments to be used in his congregation'.

[33] Southern Africa, Can. 33.4; West Indies, Can. 32.8: 'Hymns and Anthems used during Public Worship shall be subject to the approval of the Bishop of the Diocese'; compare Japan, Can. XIV, Art. 137: the 'Hymns used in Common Prayer and in the Sacraments and other ceremonies must be those appointed and approved by the General Synod' but 'in unavoidable circumstances the Diocesan Bishop may permit other than these to be used'.

[34] *Wyndham v Cole* [1875] 1 PD 130.

[35] England, Can. B20: the person is appointed and may be dismissed by the joint action of the minister and parochial church council; in serious cases the archdeacon may dispense with the requirement of conciliar consent.

[36] See e.g. Canada, Declaration of Principles, 6(g): control is vested in General Synod; Scotland, Can. 22.6: the Episcopal Synod is the controlling authority.

[37] ECUSA, Cans. II.6.2: the Standing Commission on Church Music, composed of bishops, priests, deacons and lay persons of whom a number must be professional musicians, must also organize conferences and courses; see also West Indies, Can. 33.1.D: the church's standing committee on liturgy and church music is obliged 'to encourage the writing of new music for liturgical use and produce such compositions in its own name, collect and collate material bearing upon the production and future revisions of a West Indian Hymn Book and in general serve the Church . . . in matters of music'.

[38] West Indies, Can. 32.2: 'It shall be in the power of each Diocesan Bishop, subject to such restrictions as the House of Bishops may impose, to issue Forms of Prayer and appoint special Psalms and Lessons for such occasions as may seem to him to require them'; Southern Africa, Can. 33.5: at public feasts and thanksgivings 'every Bishop shall

Finally, in this section, mention may be made of rules on the vesture of ministers to be worn at the time of divine service. At times in England a matter of grave controversy (and litigation),[39] today the provincial or national laws of very few churches deal with clerical dress. The Irish canons, which claim for vesture no doctrinal significance, provide that an archbishop or bishop must use at all times of his public ministration of the services of the church 'the customary ecclesiastical apparel of his order'. Every priest and deacon at regular services in a church building 'may' wear a cassock, 'shall' wear a plain white surplice and the customary black scarf or a stole, and 'may' wear bands. A minister is 'at liberty' to wear a plain black gown while preaching, but no other ecclesiastical vestment or ornament. Any questions of the suitableness must be determined by the ordinary with a right of appeal to the Court of General Synod.[40] The English canon is basically the same,[41] but the Scottish canons are rather different. In the performance of public services 'it shall suffice that Priests and Deacons be vested in surplices'. If a 'considerable number' of communicants object in writing to the introduction or proposed introduction of other or additional vesture, or to the disuse of customary vesture, the matter must be referred to the bishop who may forbid or modify such introduction or disuse, subject to appeal to the Episcopal Synod.[42] By way of contrast, in some churches the matter is considered still to be worthy of

give directions to the Clergy of his Diocese as to the form of Prayer which they are to use on such occasions'; Ireland, Const. IX.6: prayers must not be contrary to the doctrine of the church; Wales, BCP 1984, 695: prayer is a person's 'response to God, with or without words', in which God is adored, praised and thanked, and in which sins are confessed and forgiveness requested; prayer is for the individual and for others, and by it the person listens to God and seeks to know his will.

[39] T. J. E. Salter, 'Costume, custom and canon law in the Church of England', LL M dissertation, University of Wales, Cardiff, 1997.

[40] Ireland, Const. IX.12; see *Bishop of Limerick v Cotter*, Ct of GS, Journal of the General Synod, 1897, 258: this dealt with refusal to wear a surplice.

[41] England, Can. B8: 'The Church of England does not attach any particular doctrinal significance to the diversities of vesture permitted by this Canon'; 'no minister shall change the form of vesture in use in the church or chapel in which he officiates unless he has ascertained by consultation with the parochial church council that such changes will be acceptable'; any disagreements must be referred to the bishop 'whose decision shall be obeyed'; unlike the Irish canon (and the Scottish canon: see n. 42), there is no right of appeal in English canon law; at Holy Communion the presiding minister, and at the occasional offices the minister, 'shall' wear either a surplice or alb with scarf or stole; and at Morning and Evening Prayer on Sundays the minister 'shall normally' wear these. For the idea that vestments have no doctrinal significance, see also Chile, Can. D.4.

[42] Scotland, Cans. 34: the cleric may nevertheless wear stole, scarf and hoods; see also Central Africa, Diocese of Mashonaland, *Pastoral Regulations* 1978, 19: 'There is a time and place for splendour of vestments, but a Stole is the only vestment which should always be worn in administering the Sacraments. A clean Alb, with or without a cassock, is always more fitting than Eucharistic vestments which have become creased and thread-bare with travel and constant use'.

explicit and fairly complex regulation. In the Australian church the dioceses enjoy, under national canons, the power to regulate vesture. In the diocese of Sydney an ordinance of the Diocesan Synod 'requires that every minister below the order of Bishop saying the public prayers or ministering the sacraments or other rites . . . shall wear a decent and comely surplice with sleeves to be provided at the charge of the Parish'. No minister when celebrating Holy Communion 'shall wear the alb, the chasuble, the dalmatic, [or] the tunicle'.[43] However, a minister need not wear a surplice while conducting a service in a hospital, private house, or a place which is not licensed for public worship. Nor is a minister obliged to wear a surplice at a service conducted in a place licensed for worship in two prescribed circumstances. Where in that place there is customarily more than one Sunday service, a minister need not wear a surplice while conducting one of those services each Sunday. Furthermore, where in that place there is customarily only one Sunday service, a minister is excused while conducting one of those services in each calendar month. In the course of determining the service(s) at which a surplice need not be worn, the minister must consult with the church committee of the church at which the service(s) is to be held – these provisions do not apply to any service where a bishop is the minister. As an overriding principle, when a decision is made to dispense with a surplice, the minister must have 'due regard to the occasion and the congregation concerned before exercising that relief'.[44]

THE MAKING AND AUTHORIZATION OF LITURGY

Successive resolutions of the Lambeth Conference have stressed that the Book of Common Prayer 1662 is the standard of worship in the public liturgical life of individual churches. However, the resolutions also recognize the right of each church to make revisions in order to adapt to particular needs and circumstances. The Conference has laid down the following 'principles' of liturgical revision: the adaptation of rubrics in a large number of cases to present customs as generally accepted; the omission of parts of services to obviate repetition or redundancy; the framing of additions in the present services in the way of enrichment; the fuller provision of alternatives in the forms of public worship; the provision of greater elasticity in public worship; and the change of words which are

[43] Australia, Diocese of Sydney, Announcement of Divine Service and Clerical Vestures Ordinance 1949; see *The 7th Handbook*, 8.19; the provisional national canon is the Use of Surplice Canon, Can. 5 1977 and Can. 19 1995.

[44] Australia, General Synod – The Use of the Surplice Canon 1977 Adopting Ordinance 1977: see Diocese of Sydney, *The 7th Handbook*, 8.20.

obscure or commonly misunderstood.[45] Churches differ as to the degree to which these principles have been incorporated in formal law but, generally, today the law of most Anglican churches contains implicitly a principle of liturgical subsidiarity, enabling a relatively wide range of bodies within each church to formulate liturgies at the appropriate level of that church: both substantive and procedural limits are used. A key role in liturgical development is played by liturgical commissions, bodies now operating in a great many churches. Functions which these commissions share are: to prepare on request forms of service to submit to the relevant ecclesiastical authority for approval; to advise on liturgical matters generally and in particular on forms of service which are subject to experimentation; to engage in study and make recommendations concerning future liturgical development; and, in some churches, to arrange for the publication and printing of liturgical texts.[46]

In England it is lawful for the General Synod 'to make provision by Canon with respect to worship . . . including provision for empowering the General Synod to approve, amend, continue or discontinue forms of service'. A form of service may not be authorized by canon 'unless it has been approved by the General Synod with a majority in each House thereof of not less than two-thirds of those present and voting'. No regulation may be made by Synod under a canon approving, amending, continuing or discontinuing a form of service without the same majorities. Moreover, a form of service must be such as is in the opinion of the synod 'neither contrary to, nor indicative of, a departure from the doctrine of the Church . . . in any essential matter'.[47] Special provisions exist to ensure the continued availability and use of the Book of Common Prayer 1662.[48]

---

[45] LC 1908, Res. 27: this contains the principles governing liturgical revision; for the idea that the Book of Common Prayer is the normative Anglican liturgical text see LC 1968, Res. 43; 1958, Ress. 73–75; LC 1948, Ress. 78, 105; LC 1930, Res. 49; LC 1920, Ress. 12, 36; LC 1908, Res. 24; for the right of a particular church to make revisions for the purposes of adaptation, see LC 1878, Res. 10; LC 1888, Res. 10; LC 1908, Res. 24.

[46] England: the Liturgical Commission is 'to prepare forms of service at the request of the House of Bishops for submission to that House in the first instance', to advise on the experimental use of forms of service authorized by Synod, and to exchange information and advice on liturgical matters' (it was established by General Synod under the Synodical Government Measure 1969, Sched. 2, Art. 10(2)); for almost identical provisions see West Indies, Can. 33.1.D and ECUSA, Cans. II.4; see also Philippines, Cans. I.2.2(c); Melanesia, Cans. E.8: the Commission on Liturgy and Worship; Australia, General Synod Commissions Cans. 1969–92, 4, 5; Ireland, Const. I.26.3: it is to recommend '[a]ny form of Service and any Lectionary and any Catechism' for experimental use with a view to permanent use; for Wales, see E. Lewis, *Prayer Book Revision in the Church in Wales* (Penarth, 1958), 3; New Zealand, *Prayer Book* 1989, ix and this describes the work of the Prayer Book Commission 1965.

[47] England, Can. B2; Church of England (Worship and Doctrine) Measure 1974, s. 1(1).

[48] England, ibid., s. 4.

The vast majority of Anglican churches have received or adopted the Book of Common Prayer 1662 as a normative standard of faith and worship,[49] but reserve for themselves the right 'of making at any time adaptations and abridgements of, and additions to, the Services of the Church'.[50] As with the Church of England, the national or provincial assembly of the church is the ecclesiastical institution primarily involved with liturgical development. A fundamental substantive limitation which commonly appears in formal laws on the introduction of new services, beyond the requirement that it should be required by the needs of the church, is that liturgical development must be consistent with 'the spirit and teaching' of the 1662 Prayer Book.[51] Several churches employ the requirement that the form of service must be consistent with Anglican faith, its teaching and spirit, or the Word of God as one of the standards of faith.[52] As with doctrinal development, so too with liturgy, commonly compliance with detailed procedures is mandatory, usually with special majorities, voting in the central assembly by houses,[53] and sometimes reference to the dioceses is required.[54]

[49] See e.g. West Indies, Declaration of Fundamental Principles, (c): 'We receive the Book of Common Prayer and the Ordering of Bishops, Priests and Deacons, as agreeable to the Word of God'; Can. 31.1: the church 'acknowledges that the English Book of Common Prayer 1662 together with the Alternative Prayers and Occasional Offices of the English Book of Common Prayer 1928 have been the norm for its worship'; Central Africa, Fundamental Declarations, I: 'We do also accept the principles of Worship set forth in the Book of Common Prayer'; see generally Ch. 7.

[50] See e.g. West Indies, Declaration of Fundamental Principles, (e); Brazil, Const. Art. 38; Uganda, Const. Art. 2(e); Central Africa, Fundamental Declarations, I; Korea, Const. Art. 11; see also Canada, Declaration of Principles, 6(g): within the jurisdiction of General Synod is 'the revision, adaptation and publication of a Book of Common Prayer'.

[51] Southern Africa, Declaration of Fundamental Principles and Const. Art. X; Kenya, Const. Art. II(f): the church 'may make and authorise such deviations from and additions or alternatives to the forms of service provided in the said Book of Common Prayer and such new forms of Service as may, in its judgment, be required to meet the needs of the Church in this Province and shall be consistent with the spirit and teaching of the said Book of Common Prayer'; see also Uganda, Const. Art. 2(f); Jerusalem and the Middle East, Const. Art. 4(iv); Central Africa, Const. Art. 12; Zaire, Const. Art. 3; Indian Ocean, Const. Art. 2(v); South East Asia, Fundamental Declarations, 1; Papua New Guinea, Const. Art. 2(d); Chile, Cans. D.2.

[52] Southern Cone, Can. 9; see also Korea, Const. Art. 11(c): services must be designed 'to meet the needs of this province and are not [to be] contrary to the spirit and teaching of the Anglican Communion'; Rwanda, Draft Const. 1996, Art. 6; see also West Africa, Const. Art. 3; Melanesia, Const. Art. 5: the General Synod has 'the power to authorize forms of worship for the whole province' and these must not conflict with the church's standards of faith.

[53] Scotland, Cans. 22.3–5: the General Synod may by resolution permit the use of services to be listed in the Schedule to the Canon, 'and may in like manner provide for amendment of that Schedule by way of addition, deletion or other alteration'; Can. 52: the Faith and Order Board is responsible for the wording of a liturgical text (and it must decide this by a two-thirds majority) with final confirmation by General Synod; Wales,

With respect to liturgical development outside the church's central assembly, several laws implement the principle recognized in resolutions of the Lambeth Conference that it is 'the exclusive right of each bishop to put forth or sanction additional services for use within his jurisdiction', and also of 'adapting' services; the right is 'subject to such limitations as may be imposed by the provincial or other lawful authority' and the principle that adaptations or additions 'shall not affect the doctrinal teaching or value of the service . . . thus adapted'.[55] English canon law is particularly well-developed: Canon B4 provides that Convocations, the archbishops and individual diocesan bishops may approve forms of service for use on occasions for which no provision is made by means of services contained in the Book of Common Prayer or the authorized liturgies. Such forms of service must be neither contrary to nor indicative of a departure from the doctrine of the church and they must be 'reverent and seemly'. Similar provisions in other churches are few and far between. Under national ecclesiastical law in Canada, the Provincial Synods have jurisdiction over 'the authorization of special forms of prayer, services, and ceremonies for use in the province, for which no provisions have been made under the authority of the General Synod or of the House of Bishops'.[56] In the West Indies, '[a]ny other Service not provided for or approved by Provincial Synod may be arranged and authorised by each Bishop in his own Diocese'.[57] Similar powers are enjoyed by diocesan bishops in Scotland,[58] and in New

---

Const. II.34–43: bill procedure is required for alteration of rites and ceremonies with a two-thirds majority vote in each order; for a similar approach see Ireland, Const. I.25; compare the simple majority voting by orders in Sudan, Const. Art. 4(vi); see also Central Africa, Const. Art. 12.

[54] ECUSA, Const. Art. I.5: no changes are to be made in the BCP 1979 unless proposed at one session of General Convention, referred to all dioceses and adopted by General Convention at the next session with majority support from the House of Bishops and majorities in each order in the House of Deputies; New Zealand, Church of England Empowering Act 1928, Sched. I; Fundamental Provisions, A.2; Const. B.5–6: changes may be made after adoption of a proposal, reference to the Diocesan Synods, and, following a 'fresh election', the Synod confirms the same by a two-thirds majority of the members of each order; see also G.IV.1.

[55] LC 1897, Ress. 45, 46.   [56] Canada, Declaration of Principles, 7(b).

[57] West Indies, Can. 31.2.

[58] Scotland, Can. 22.5: 'A Bishop may in the exercise of the powers traditionally vested in the episcopal office permit the use of services other than those specifically authorized or permitted under this Canon if that Bishop deems such use to be pastorally appropriate'; however, '[t]he Episcopal Synod may . . . restrain such exercise of these powers or impose conditions thereon and may do so either generally or with reference to particular localities, cases or circumstances'; see also Diocese of Europe, Const. 26: 'In addition to the forms of service authorised for use in the Church of England under Canon Law, the bishop may authorise either for use in a chaplaincy where the chaplain and the chaplaincy church council jointly so requests or generally for use throughout his diocese a rite of a Church with which the Church of England is in communion'.

Zealand.[59] By way of contrast, the laws of some churches expressly forbid this sort of liturgical development without the consent of the Diocesan Synod,[60] or without reference to the church's central assembly.[61]

Provisions enabling experimentation are rather more common. In England, when a form of service is in the course of preparation for submission to General Synod for approval, Synod may by canon authorize the two archbishops acting jointly to authorize the use of that draft service after consultation with the House of Bishops.[62] In some churches, only the provincial assembly may authorize experimentation,[63] and in others this competence is assigned to a central episcopal assembly.[64] In the constitutional law of the church in Ireland, a form of service may be used for a period, not exceeding fifteen years, as appointed by the House of Bishops provided it is certified by that House as being 'in its opinion neither contrary to nor indicative of any departure from' the doctrine of the church; '[a]ny such experimental use shall be under the supervision and control of the bishop of the diocese or other the ordinary'; 'the approval of the incumbent and of the churchwardens' is also required.[65] Arrangements in the Philippines are a little more stringent: when the Provincial Synod

[59] New Zealand, Cans. B.VIII.5: 'The Bishop, in consultation with the Diocesan Synod, may from time to time authorize the use of such forms of worship as may be deemed appropriate for the special needs of the Diocese'; but no such form of service shall be 'contrary to the Doctrine and Sacraments of Christ as this Church has received them and declared in the Constitution'; see Brazil, Const. Art. 38 for unilateral action by the bishop when the church's Book of Common Prayer does not make provision.

[60] Jerusalem and the Middle East, Const. Art. 4(v): 'A Diocesan Bishop shall not authorise for general use in his diocese alterations and amendments of Liturgical services unless such alterations and amendments have been approved by the Diocesan Synod or Council of that Diocese, and approved also by the Central Synod'.

[61] Southern Africa, Const. X: 'All adaptations, abridgements, or additions, allowed or made by any Bishop of this Province for his own Diocese, whether in his Diocesan Synod or otherwise, shall be open to revision by the Provincial Synod'; for similar provisions see also Central Africa, Const. Art. 13 and Indian Ocean, Const. Art. 4.

[62] England, Can. B5A. No such right is given to diocesan bishops.

[63] West Indies, Can. 31.4: 'The Provincial Synod may authorise the use of a proposed Form of Service for an experimental period'; see also Burundi, Const. Art. 3: the Provincial Assembly 'shall' provide for 'the possibility' of experimentation with forms of worship 'under the supervision of the Diocesan Bishops'; Rwanda, Draft Const. Art. 8. Some churches impose the requirement that experimental services must be consistent with the teaching and spirit of the 1662 Prayer Book; see e.g. Central Africa, Const. Art. 12; Melanesia, Cans. B.1.A–G; ECUSA, Const. Art. X.

[64] Scotland, Can. 22.4: the College of Bishops may authorize services for use for a definite experimental period; these may then be added by General Synod, at the end of that period, to the services listed in the Schedule to Can. 22.

[65] Ireland, Const. I.26; Wales, Can. of 1956: this permits the experimental use of proposed revisions of the Book of Common Prayer provisionally approved by the Bench of Bishops for a limited period; the bishop may authorize the experimental use for not more than 10 years if the Governing Body has assented to it; see also Melanesia, Cans. B.1.A–G; and Brazil, Const. Art. 38.2.

authorizes for 'trial use' a proposed revision of the Book of Common Prayer the enabling resolution must specify the period, the precise text and special terms and conditions applicable to the trial use. During the trial 'only the material so authorized, and in the exact form in which it has been so authorized, shall be available as an alternative for the . . . Book of Common Prayer'. However, the diocesan bishop may authorize variations, adjustments, or substitutes for or additions to any portion of the text under trial use (on the endorsement of the diocesan Liturgy Commission) 'which seems desirable as a result of such trial use, and which do not change the substance of a rite'; the Provincial Synod too may authorize these.[66]

The right to introduce forms of worship is not generally taken to the lowest level of the church. Only two examples have been found in which this is expressly permitted by formal law. In English canon law the minister, at parochial level, may use forms of service considered suitable for occasions for which no provision is made in existing authorized or approved services; the service must be consistent with church doctrine, reverent and seemly.[67] Similarly, in South India 'a presbyter in charge of any congregation may introduce experimentally the use of an alteration in the accustomed form of worship of that congregation, or a new form of worship, after giving due notice thereof to the congregation, and shall report any such action to the bishop of the diocese'. If after consultation with the congregation, and any three members so desire, the minister must consult a general meeting of communicant members of the congregation 'as to whether the use of the altered or new form shall be continued'; it must not be continued unless two-thirds are in favour. The advice of the bishop 'should be sought in any case of difficulty or serious division of opinion'.[68] These rules are exceptional.

THE ADMINISTRATION OF PUBLIC WORSHIP

At the time of the English Reformation the principle of uniformity, the use of a single liturgy throughout the church, was developed to combat two fears: the anarchy of numerous forms and the anarchy of none. In England, the Act of Uniformity 1549, with its principle of 'one convenient and meet order . . . of common and open prayer and administration of the sacraments . . . and none other or otherwise', was the first of a series of statutes requiring a single liturgy, culminating in the introduction of the Book of Common Prayer 1662.[69] This section deals with the legacy of this

---

[66] Philippines, Const. II.4.2, Cans. 1.2.3(e); ECUSA, Cans. II.5.
[67] England, Can. B5.   [68] South India, Const. X.5.   [69] See n. 5.

legal approach in the Anglican Communion, with law on the variation of forms of service and with the provision of public worship.

The Principles of Uniformity and Conformity

It is a general principle of modern Anglican canon law that ministers must use in public worship only those forms of service authorized or otherwise permitted by the church. However, within this basic principle of liturgical worship, the laws of Anglican churches may be distinguished between those operating a system of conformity, to a multiplicity of authorized forms of service, and those, fewer in number, tending towards the traditional principle of uniformity, the use of a single liturgical form.[70]

The principle of conformity is employed explicitly in the laws of some churches and implicitly in the laws of most. In the Church of England today, the legal requirement of uniformity has been replaced by the principle 'of conformity of worship'. The principle is expressed in the canonical duty that '[e]very minister shall use only the forms of service authorised' by Canon B1. This permits the use of 'authorized' services and 'approved' services; that is: those listed in Canon B1; and those approved by Convocation, the archbishops, or diocesan bishops for which no other provision exists; those authorized for experimental use archiepiscopally (draft forms of service); and those which a minister 'authorizes' (under Canon B5). The canonical duty upon ministers to use only these services is bolstered by the obligation to make a declaration of assent in the form 'I will use only the forms of service which are authorised or allowed by Canon'. The services of Morning and Evening Prayer and of Holy Communion are known as the 'statutory services' and others as the 'occasional offices' (such as rites of marriage and baptism).[71] Much the same approach, the mandatory use of a number of authorized or otherwise allowed forms of service which are listed canonically, is employed: in Australia, where deviations are allowed from the two central liturgical texts if permitted by General Synod canon in force in a diocese;[72] in Ireland, where additional services or special occasion services may be

---

[70] See n. 45 and see n. 84.   [71] England, Can. B1, C15.

[72] Australia, Can. P6 1992, 4: 'The following forms of service are authorised for use in the church in any parish: (a) the forms of service contained in the Book of Common Prayer; (b) the forms of service contained in the Australian Prayer Book; (c) such deviations from those forms as may have been authorised as regards that parish, pursuant to the Constitution or a canon of the General Synod in force in the diocese of which that parish is part'; see *Wylde v AG (NSW)* (1949) ALR 153: the use in church buildings of the Church of England in New South Wales of any order or practice other than the authorized services were breaches of the trusts upon which these churches were held; the Supreme Court also held that making the sign of the cross *coram populo* and ringing the *sanctus* bell were illegal.

used but not 'in substitution' for the prescribed forms of service;[73] in Scotland, where the 'canonical services' are listed;[74] in Southern Africa;[75] in West Africa, where a range of services employed throughout the Anglican Communion is listed;[76] and in New Zealand, where amongst the canonical listings some services are classified expressly as 'alternatives'.[77]

Examples of laws tending towards the principle of uniformity are less numerous. Formal law expresses the idea in a variety of different ways ranging from notions which appear to require rigid adherence to a single liturgical use to those which accommodate flexibility. The draft Rwandan constitution provides: '[t]here shall be a single liturgical model throughout the Province'; and in Wales the law of worship states: '[i]t remains the intention of the Church . . . that there be one Use in this Province'.[78] The constitution of the church in Japan states: '[i]n Common Prayer, in the administration of the Sacraments, and in the conduct of other Rites and Ceremonies of the Church, the Book of Common Prayer According to the

---

[73] Ireland, Const. IX.5: the Book of Common Prayer, the administration of the sacraments, 'or such services as may be otherwise prescribed or authorised, and no other, shall be used in churches'; however, an additional form of service may be used if approved by the ordinary; and a special form of service for use upon a special occasion is permitted if approved by the ordinary – but these must not be used, save with the ordinary's leave, 'in substitution for any of the services prescribed'; see also Ireland, *Alternative Prayer Book* 1984, 18: 'The Holy Communion is the central act of worship, and Morning and Evening Prayer are the regular services of public worship in the Church of Ireland'.

[74] Scotland, Can. 22.1: 'the conduct of divine worship and the administration of the sacraments and other rites and ceremonies of the Church shall at all times be in accordance with the authorised services'; the 'authorised services are those in the Scottish Book of Common Prayer (1929–69), the Liturgy 1970, the Scottish Liturgy 1982; see also Can. 22.9 for the 'canonical services' of, *inter alia*, Morning and Evening Prayer and Holy Communion.

[75] Southern Africa, Can. 33.1: 'In ministering in the congregation no Clergyman may use any other Services but such as are appointed in the Book of Common Prayer' unless 'additions to the Services of the Church are made or allowed in this Church by the Provincial Synod, or allowed exceptionally by the Bishop'.

[76] West Africa, Const. Art. 11(b): 'Until such time as . . . the liturgical worship can be formulated on its own foundations, the Church of this Province allows each of its constituent dioceses to use the Book of Common Prayer of its parent church as well as any other Book of Common Prayer of a church in the Anglican Communion which it wishes to use or such other combinations of services from Books of Common Prayer in the Anglican Communion as may be decided upon by its Diocesan Synod'.

[77] New Zealand, Can. G.IV.1: the Prayer Book 1928 'may be used in a Diocese only with the approval of the Bishop of the Diocese' and is 'to be regarded as alternative or additional' to those services appearing in the BCP 1662; Can. G.V lists the authorised services.

[78] Rwanda, Draft Const. 1996, Art. 8; Wales, BCP 1984, v; ECUSA, Const. Art. I.5 and Art. X: 'The Book of Common Prayer [1979] . . . shall be in use in all the Dioceses'; Philippines, Const. Art. 1: 'The Book of Common Prayer shall be used in all dioceses and episcopal jurisdictions of this Church'; Can. II.4.1: the 'Standard Book of Common Prayer'; see above for the permissible use of experimental forms.

Use of the Nippon Seikokai shall be used'.[79] For Burundi, '[t]he aim and desire of the Church of this Province is to have, as far as possible, one single liturgical model for the whole Province'.[80] In other churches, uniformity is expressed as the norm but the law allows variety in liturgical use. The canon law of the West Indies authorizes 'for use throughout the Province in the public worship of the Church' the liturgy of the Eucharist, the forms of Morning and Evening Prayer (both approved by Provincial Synod, one in 1979, the other in 1986), and the forms approved by Provincial Synod in 1989 for: holy baptism, confirmation, marriage, funerals, reception and conditional baptism. However, '[a]ny other service not provided for or approved by Provincial Synod may be arranged and authorised by each Bishop in his own Diocese'. Importantly, '[n]o forms of Prayer or Non-Liturgical Services not authorised or already allowed by the Bishop shall be used by any clergyman in any Church or Chapel without the permission of the Bishop of his Diocese'.[81] Whichever principle of worship is adopted by a church, it is a general principle of Anglican canon law to require clergy to make a declaration or other type of undertaking in the form: 'in public prayer and administration of the sacraments, I will use only the forms of service which are authorized or allowed by lawful authority';[82] or that 'I engage to conform' to the authorized liturgies of the church.[83]

Liturgical Variation

One of the achievements of Anglican liturgical law in recent years has been the development of permissive rights enabling ministers at the lowest level of the church to effect variations in the conduct of public worship according to the authorized forms of service. Whilst resolutions of Lambeth Conferences are largely silent on the precise issue of liturgical

[79] Japan, Const. Art. 3: also, 'Forms of prayers for special occasions must be authorized or approved by the Diocesan Bishop'.

[80] Burundi, Const. Art. 3; see also Indian Ocean, Const. Art. 24: the aim of the province is to realize 'a common liturgy' for the use of the whole Province; Melanesia, Const. Art. 5; Korea, Const. Art. 132: 'The Anglican Church of Korea shall use the Book of Common Prayer authorised by the National Synod'.

[81] West Indies, Can. 31.

[82] Southern Africa, Can. 16.2; for the same formula, see New Zealand, Can. A.1; Ireland, Const. IV.67 and Sched: 'in public prayer and administration of sacraments I will use the form in the [Book of Common Prayer] prescribed, and none other, except so far as shall be allowed by the lawful authority of the Church'; for much the same formula, see Scotland, Can. 16.4, App. Nos. 1A and 11: 'in public prayer and administration of the Sacraments I will use the form in the said Book and formularies prescribed and none other except so far as shall be allowed by lawful authority in this Church'; see also Korea, Const. Art. 120.

[83] ECUSA, Con. Art. VIII: bishops and clergy must subscribe to and declare that they will 'engage to conform . . . to the Worship of the Episcopal Church'.

variation by ministers within individual services, this general approach is in line with Conference recommendations about greater 'elasticity' in public worship.[84] But these developments surface in the laws of only a small number of churches. Laws fall into two broad categories: those which allow unilateral variation by the minister but with referral to the bishop in difficult cases; and those which require episcopal consent for variation. It would seem that the formal law of no church confers a right on a minister to vary forms of service unilaterally, without any form of recourse to the bishop. Substantive limitations are, however, generally undeveloped.

In those laws which allow unilateral variation sometimes referral of difficult cases to the bishop is mandatory, sometimes there is a right to do so. In Australia, '[t]he minister may make and use variations which are not of substantial importance in any form of service . . . according to particular circumstances'; the variation 'must be reverent and seemly and must not be contrary to or a departure from the doctrine of this Church'; a question concerning the observance of this provision 'may be determined by the bishop of the diocese'.[85] According to Irish canon law, the minister has a discretion to make and use variations not of substantial importance, which are reverent, seemly and consistent with church doctrine and '[i]f any question is raised concerning such variation, or as to whether it is "of substantial importance" ', it 'shall be referred to the bishop in order that he may give such pastoral guidance, advice or directions as he may think fit'.[86] A rather more rigorous arrangement exists in Scottish canon law: before making 'any material change to the conduct of worship or form thereof', the rector or priest-in-charge must consult the vestry and congregation to ensure that the change is 'adequately prepared and explained, and is not unacceptable to the congregation generally'; if 'any serious differences' arise, the minister 'shall endeavour to resolve the same', but 'if requested to do so by the Vestry, shall refer the matter to the Bishop' for determination.[87]

Several churches allow ministerial variation only with direct episcopal approval. Occasionally laws enable the bishop to consent or refuse without any further consultation. The canon law of one Canadian province provides: '[n]o clergyman may alter the services of the Book of Common Prayer or other services authorized by lawful authority, or substitute other liturgical forms for those in the Book of Common Prayer or authorized by

---

[84] See n. 11; see also LC 1988, Res. 47: 'The Conference resolves that each province should be free, subject to essential universal Anglican norms of worship, and to a valuing of traditional liturgical materials, to seek that expression of worship which is appropriate to its Christian people in their cultural context'.

[85] Australia, Can. P6 1992, 5; see England, Can. B5 for an almost identical provision: the matter may be submitted to the bishop who 'may give such pastoral guidance, advice or direction as he may think fit'.

[86] Ireland, Const. IX.6–8.   [87] Scotland, Can. 22.8.

lawful authority without the permission of the Bishop'.[88] The constitution of the church in Kenya, which is typical, requires the bishop to act in consultation with a diocesan body: '[i]t shall be lawful for a Diocesan Bishop in consultation with the Standing Committee of his Diocesan Synod to order or sanction within his Diocese such variation whether by way of deletion, omission, alternative use or otherwise from forms authorised in the Province'. These may be sanctioned when in the bishop's opinion they are 'convenient' and are neither contrary to nor indicative of any departure from the doctrine of the church. Sanction must be reported to the House of Bishops if variation continues beyond a year.[89] In other churches, the consent of the provincial or national assembly, or of its standing committee, is required.[90] Finally, in ECUSA, only variation of experimental liturgical texts seems to be treated by national law: on a written recommendation of the Standing Liturgical Commission, the Presiding Bishop and the President of the House of Deputies of the General Convention may authorize 'variations and adjustments to, or substitutions for, or alterations in, any portion of the texts under trial'. These must seem 'desirable as a result of such trial use', and they must not change 'the substance of the rite'. Variations must be notified to the dioceses by the Custodian of the Book of Common Prayer.[91]

The Provision of Public Worship

A notable omission from the formal laws of most churches is a duty placed on ministers to provide the facility of public services. A rule of the type appearing in the constitution of the church in Japan is exceptional: 'In each Parish there shall be a stated place of worship in which the Priest appointed by the Bishop regularly conducts Common Prayer, administers the Sacraments, and performs other Rites and Ceremonies of the Church with the participation of the Laity'.[92] The canons of a handful of churches oblige clergy to say privately Morning and Evening Prayer, unless hindered by sickness or other 'weighty' or 'urgent' cause, but rarely do they

---

[88] Canada, Province of Rupert's Land, Can. 5; see also Southern Africa, Can. 33.1: the Provincial Synod or 'exceptionally' the bishop may authorize 'alterations, abridgements and additions'.

[89] Kenya, Const. Art. IV.

[90] Indian Ocean, Const. Art. 4; Uganda, Const. Art. 2(f): the Provincial Assembly may authorize 'deviations'.

[91] ECUSA, Cans. II.3.6–8; see also West Indies, Can. 31.4: 'the Provincial Standing Committee may authorise variations, adjustments and alterations' in experimental forms of service 'which may seem desirable as a result of such trial use and which do not change the substance of the rite'.

[92] Japan, Const. Art. 2.

prescribe that these services should be offered publicly.[93] Duties to provide Holy Communion are very much more widespread.[94] Nor is it the case that canons impose duties upon the ordained ministers of the church to give notice of services.[95] Only occasionally do rules deal expressly with the dispensation of services of public worship in times of necessity.[96] The practical reasons for the absence of such provisions in countries with far-flung populations and few ministers are obvious; in countries not of this type they are less obvious. By way of contrast, English canon law has a very well developed scheme dealing with provision, notice and dispensation. Ministers having cure of souls must celebrate or cause to be celebrated Holy Communion on all Sundays, Feast Days and Ash Wednesday, unless prevented for some 'reasonable cause' approved by the bishop, and they must say Morning and Evening Prayer privately and on all Sundays, Feast Days, Ash Wednesday and Good Friday, 'in the absence of reasonable hindrance'. Public notice of these so-called statutory services must be given in the parish. The duty to provide the statutory services may be relaxed in English canon law in two ways: they may be dispensed with on an occasional basis if so authorized by the minister and the parochial church council; and they may be dispensed with on a regular basis if so authorized by the bishop on the request of the minister and parochial

[93] West Indies, Can. 32.1: 'It shall be the duty of every Bishop, Priest and Deacon to say privately or publicly Morning and Evening Prayer daily, unless hindered by sickness or some other urgent cause. So far as circumstances allow, Morning and Evening Prayer shall be said publicly in Parish Churches, and at least on Sundays and the greater Feasts and Ferias'; see also Scotland, Can. 17.1; and Southern Africa, Can. 24: 'in the absence of reasonable hindrance' every cleric must say Morning and Evening Prayer. It is more common for liturgical rubrics to treat this subject: see e.g. Wales, BCP 1984, I, 400: 'It is the duty of the clergy, unless they are prevented by sickness or other weighty cause, to say Morning and Evening Prayer daily, preferably in church after tolling the bell'; Canada, BCP 1962, General Rubrics, lvi: 'All Priests and Deacons, unless prevented by sickness or other urgent cause, are to say daily the Morning and Evening Prayer either privately, or openly in the Church. In the latter case it is desirable that the bell should be rung, in order that the people may come to take part in the Service, or at least may lift up their hearts to God in the midst of their occupations'.

[94] Scotland, Can. 17.1; Korea, Const. Art. 114: 'Except for weighty reasons the clergy shall attend daily public worship and on Sundays and greater Feasts shall celebrate, or be present at, the Eucharist'; Southern Africa, Can. 24.4: every incumbent must, 'in the absence of reasonable hindrance', celebrate or cause to be celebrated Holy Communion on Sundays, Ash Wednesday and other great festivals; see generally Ch. 9.

[95] The following is exceptional: Australia, Can. P6 1992, 2: 'The minister of each church must bring to the knowledge of the people of the suburb, town or locality in which that church is situated, the times and days on which Divine service is to be held in that church'.

[96] See e.g. Ireland, BCP 1960, General Directions, liv: 'Whenever it is found that the use of all the prescribed Services in any Church upon Sundays, Holy-days and Weekdays is attended with serious inconvenience, the Ordinary shall have power to dispense with one or more of them, in whole or in part'.

church council acting jointly. These powers of dispensation, however, may be used only if: the parties are satisfied that there is 'a good reason' for doing so; the parties have regard to the frequency of these services in other parishes in the diocese; finally, no church ceases altogether to be used for public worship.[97]

Much the same applies to the matter of choice of liturgies for public worship. This may be problematic, needless to say, in churches where the law allows public worship to be conducted in accordance with a variety of alternative authorized forms of service. It is rarely the case that the formal laws of churches deal with the subject,[98] unlike in England where there are fairly elaborate provisions: the right to choose a particular liturgy from the church's authorized services vests in the minister and the parochial church council who must act jointly; if they disagree the forms of service to be used are those contained in the Book of Common Prayer 1662, unless other services have been in regular use during at least two of the preceding four years, in which case they must be used either to the exclusion of or in addition to the Book of Common Prayer services. Today there is a large body of diocesan quasi-legislation on the subject of disagreements over choice of liturgy. Choice of forms of services for the occasional offices, such as baptisms, marriages and funerals, lies with the minister who conducts the service but consultation with the parties concerned is required and cases of disagreement must be referred to the bishop for his decision.[99]

It is a general principle of Anglican canon law that the ordained minister of the parish or its equivalent has control over the conduct of public worship in that parish. In English canon law, the incumbent controls directly the performance of public worship throughout the benefice. No cleric can conduct divine services publicly in whole or in part within the benefice without the consent of the resident incumbent.[100] The English position is mirrored in the formal laws of a significant number of churches. For example, in Mexican canon law, '[t]he control of worship and the spiritual jurisdiction of the Parish reside in the Pastor, subject to the rubrics of the Book of Common Prayer, the Constitution and Canons of the Church,

---

[97] England, Cans. B11, B14 and B14A, C24.
[98] Southern Africa, Can. 28.4: one of the functions of the parish council is to consider matters affecting worship; Scotland, Can. 22.8: differences of opinion about changes in form must be referred to the bishop if a request to do so is made by the vestry; South India, Const. X.2: 'every pastor and congregation shall have freedom to determine the form of service which they will use, provided that it includes the essential elements' of worship: see n. 19; North India, Const. I.I.IV: 'No form of worship or ritual to which they conscientiously object shall be imposed on any congregation'.
[99] England, Can. B3; for quasi-legislation see LCFE, 297.
[100] England, Can. C8(4); for secular recognition see *Wood v Headingley-cum-Burley Burial Board* (1892) 1 QB 713 at 729.

and the pastoral direction of the Bishop'.[101] Again, in Southern Africa, 'Incumbents are recognized as leaders . . . for the oversight of the Pastoral Charges . . . in regard to . . . liturgical worship, under the authority of the Bishop'.[102] A direct consequence of provisions assigning liturgical control to the minister is the principle that clergy from another parish or diocese must obtain the consent of the minister to officiate within that parish. This is also associated with the general requirement that ministers must have the permission of the bishop to lead or conduct public worship in the diocese and its parishes.[103] Three slightly contrasting approaches may be found in the laws of the Philippines, Scotland and New Zealand.

In the Philippines, no minister shall officiate, either in preaching or in reading prayers in public worship in any parish or cure of another minister without the consent of the minister of that parish or cure (or one of the churchwardens if in his absence that minister 'fails to provide for services'). Furthermore, no minister may officiate for more than six weeks by ministering the sacraments or holding public services within the limits of any diocese, other than the one in which he is canonically resident, without licence from the bishop. If any minister from disability or other cause neglects to perform the regular services in his congregation and refuses, without good cause, his consent to any other minister to officiate, the churchwardens, vestrypersons or trustees of the congregation may with the consent of the bishop permit any duly qualified minister to officiate.[104] Philippine canon law makes no special provision for breaches of these rules. The position is different in Scotland. According to Scottish canon law, a rector or priest in charge is forbidden to allow any other cleric 'to conduct services . . . for more than two Sundays in any one year' without previously informing the bishop. Moreover, no cleric from another diocese is to officiate for more than five consecutive Sundays in any one year without the written permission of the bishop. In the event that these are done, the bishop may inhibit the offending cleric and, if this is disregarded, the matter must be reported to that cleric's ecclesiastical superior and the grounds for the inhibition to the Episcopal Synod. Clergy who 'knowingly' disregard the inhibition, by allowing an inhibited cleric to

---

[101] Mexico, Can. 28.1(a); ECUSA, Cans. III.14.1: 'the authority of and responsibility for the conduct of worship' in the parish are vested in the rector, subject to the constitution, canons, rubrics of the Book of Common Prayer and 'the directions of the Bishop'; see also Diocese of Mississippi, Cans. III.A.37: basically, this repeats the national canon.

[102] Southern Africa, Can. 24; see Ch. 6 for the role of lay ministers in worship.

[103] See, typically, Melanesia, Cans. C.4.8 and Southern Africa, Can. 33.2: 'No person shall be permitted to officiate in sacred things in any congregation of this Church, except under the authority of the Bishop of the Diocese'.

[104] Philippines, Cans. III.16; see also ECUSA, Cans. III.14; Korea, Const. Art. 118: 'A member of the clergy wishing to administer the sacraments or preach in another's church requires the invitation or permission of the priest in charge'.

officiate, are liable to admonition and if this is disregarded to judicial proceedings.[105] In New Zealand, an additional requirement is grafted onto the basic principle. A minister in charge of a parish may allow only a minister who is in 'good standing' with that minister's own bishop to officiate for up to one week without any other authorization; if for more than one week, the bishop of the inviting minister must authorize.[106]

LITURGICAL DISCIPLINE

Despite the introduction of flexibility as the keynote of modern Anglican liturgical jurisprudence, the existence of mandatory duties in canon law provides ample scope for the imposition of discipline in public worship. The principles of compliance with the authorized forms of service, the promise of clergy to comply, the regulation of music and vesture, the restraints on acceptable variation, and the duties concerning provision of liturgies all conspire to provide a framework within which disciplinary processes may operate. Whilst resolutions of the Lambeth Conference have been largely silent on the issue of liturgical discipline, one 'earnest hope' which it has stressed is that individuals 'will recognize the duty of submitting themselves, for conscience sake, in all matters ritual and ceremonial, to the authoritative judgements of that particular or national Church' in which they are placed.[107] Churches seem to employ two basic devices to effect liturgical discipline: executive and judicial.

Executive Control

Executive control is effected first and foremost by the diocesan bishop in his capacity as principal minister in the diocese: it is a general principle of Anglican canon law that to the bishop belongs the right of ordering public worship. The principle is nowhere more forcefully expressed than in Irish canon law: '[i]t shall be competent for the ordinary to restrain and prohibit in the conduct of public worship any practice not enjoined in the Book of Common Prayer, or in any rubric or canon enacted by lawful authority of the Church of Ireland'.[108] An equally forthright statement of the principle appears in the constitution of the church in South India: the bishop has 'authority in the case of grave irregularities in public worship to forbid their continuance'.[109] As has already been seen in this Chapter,

---

[105] Scotland, Can. 15.
[106] New Zealand, Can. A.II.2.
[107] LC 1878, Res. 7.
[108] Ireland, Const. IX.2.
[109] South India, Const. IV.4; see South India, Diocese of Nandyal, Const. 1977, V.5 and North India, Const. I.I.VIII.6 for an identical provision; see also e.g. England, Can. C18: the bishop has 'the right . . . of conducting, ordering, controlling, and authorising

sometimes the law requires the referral to the bishop of specific problems concerned with liturgy, but occasionally laws of churches recognize a general power of bishops to resolve any instances of dispute and disagreement.[110] The pedigree of such arrangements is ancient: a rule in the Book of Common Prayer 1662 provides that 'to appease all such diversity . . . and for the resolution of all doubts . . . the parties that so doubt . . . shall resort to the Bishop of the Diocese, who by his discretion shall take order for the quieting and appeasing of the same'.[111] Sometimes, particularly in the African churches, the law confers upon the central episcopal assembly the power of resolving collectively questions and disputes about worship; and if the assembly is unable to do so, there is a right (and occasionally a duty) to refer the matter to bishops outside the church.[112] Executive oversight is also possible at lower levels of the church: in several churches, for example, churchwardens are given a special responsibility to ensure decency, order and reverence during the time of divine service,[113] and

all services in churches'; the principle was neatly put in West Africa, Const. (1989 version) Art. 4: bishops have 'a special responsibility and authority . . . for the worthiness of [the church's] worship'.

[110] See e.g. Wales, BCP 1984, vi: 'If any doubt or dispute arises concerning any of the provisions of this book, reference shall in every case be made to the Bishop of the Diocese for his determination of the matter. The Bishop shall not allow any practice which conflicts with the provisions of this Book. In cases of doubt the Bishop may refer any question of interpretation to the Archbishop'.

[111] England, BCP 1662, ix.

[112] Uganda, Const. Art. 3(i): 'The jurisdiction to determine any matter concerning . . . Worship is hereby vested in the House of Bishops'; if there is doubt in that House, and it cannot be settled with 'general unanimity', the matter shall be referred to the Anglican Consultative Council; Central Africa, Const. Art. 5: 'The Episcopal Synod has always final authority in matters concerning . . . the worthiness of [the church's] worship'; if there is no unanimity, any bishop may require that the matter be submitted to the Archbishop of Canterbury and two other bishops (of whom one is nominated by the bishop requiring the submission and the other by a majority vote of the synod) – 'their decision shall be final'; South East Asia, Fundamental Declarations, 4: the Provincial Synod may consult in cases concerning 'adherence to . . . the principles of worship' the Archbishop of Canterbury or the primates of the Anglican Communion.

[113] See e.g. Australia, Can. P6 1992, 9: 'The minister and churchwardens of each church must take all reasonable measures and precautions to ensure that: (a) in the course of and immediately before divine service, there is decency and order and reverence shown by all persons present; and (b) the directions in the forms of service as to the conduct of the persons present are followed'; England, Can. F15(3): churchwardens must maintain order during the time of divine service in the church and in the churchyard; they seem to have a power to apprehend and to eject 'without unnecessary violence': see *Legal Opinions Concerning the Church of England* (1994), 48. For two examples of secular law on the subject, see: England, Ecclesiastical Courts Jurisdiction Act 1860, s. 2 (for judicial consideration see e.g. *Vallancey v Fletcher* [1897] 1 QB 265: the offence may be committed by a clergyman acting in an indecent or violent manner in his own church or churchyard) and Offences Against the Person Act 1861, s. 36 (see also *Williams v Glenister* (1824) 2 B & C 699); and Ghana, Criminal Code, s. 296: this forbids irreverent or indecent acts which disturb a minister celebrating a religious rite in places

occasionally they must report directly to the bishop any instances of clerical wrongdoing.[114]

Judicial Control: Ecclesiastical Offences

The laws of the vast majority of Anglican churches do not list liturgical
indiscipline amongst ecclesiastical offences for which proceedings may be
brought in the church courts. In these churches an allegation of liturgical
indiscipline would come under general offences such as neglect of duty or
breach of the constitutions and canons or of ordination promises.[115] In
some churches, however, liturgical indiscipline is specifically listed. The
terms of the offence differ from church to church, but they may be classified broadly into two groups. First, there are laws in which the offence is
widely or ill-defined: in England proceedings may be instituted in the
church courts charging an offence against the laws ecclesiastical 'involving matters of ritual and ceremonial'; the formal law does not define the
elements of the offence.[116] Secondly, there are offences constituted by failure to provide public worship or by failure to comply with liturgical
rubrics; in ECUSA two ecclesiastical offences are: 'violation of the rubrics
of the Book of Common Prayer' and 'habitual neglect of public worship
and of Holy Communion according to the order and use' of the church.[117]
A slightly less detailed version of the latter offence is found in the canon
law of New Zealand: it is a triable offence to '[r]efuse or neglect to use'
either the Book of Common Prayer or A New Zealand Prayer Book, 'or
other services authorised', or to administer the sacraments as authorised
'except so far as shall be otherwise ordered by lawful authority'.[118] In any
event, in the disposal of such cases generally, some laws prescribe that the

of religious worship: see P. K. Twumasi, *Criminal Law in Ghana* (Tema, Ghana, 1985),
546f.

[114] Southern Africa, Can. 29.7(c): churchwardens must complain to the bishop or
archdeacon if there is anything contrary to 'order or decorum' in the administration of
divine service.

[115] See e.g. Southern Africa, Can. 40(h),(i); Canada, Can. XVIII.8(f); Wales, Const.
XI.18(e); Ireland, Const. VIII.53; Scotland, Can. 54.2; New Zealand, Cans. D.I.1.1.

[116] England, Ecclesiastical Jurisdiction Measure 1963, s. 14(1)(a); judicial decisions
are neither recent nor are they generally helpful in providing precise guidance as to the
definitional elements of the offence appropriate to the modern church: see e.g. *Heywood
v Bishop of Manchester* (1884) 12 QBD 404: non-observance of the BCP 1662 was classified
as an offence 'against ritual'; see also Papua New Guinea, Can. No. 1 of 1977, Art. 1: this
classes as an offence 'breach of ritual discipline'.

[117] ECUSA, Cans. IV.1.1; see also Mexico, Can. 37(c): 'Violation of the rubrics of the
Book of Common Prayer' is an offence.

[118] New Zealand, Cans. D.II.2; see also Central Africa, Can. 24(i): 'Refusing or deliberately neglecting to use in public prayer and in the administration of the Sacraments
and other Holy Offices the forms authorised under these Canons'; Brazil, Cans. IV.1(c):
'the lack of observance of the authorized liturgy'.

church is bound by the decisions of its own tribunals in matters of worship.[119]

CONCLUSIONS

The adoption by so many churches throughout the Anglican Communion of the spirit of the Book of Common Prayer 1662 has resulted in such consistency, as between churches and their laws on public worship, that it is possible to deduce a set of reasonably well-defined principles of Anglican liturgical jurisprudence. And the terms of Lambeth Conference resolutions seem frequently to be echoed in actual laws of individual churches. The right of formulating liturgical texts legitimately belongs to central church assemblies in which the episcopate, clergy and laity are all represented. At the same time, however, a principle of subsidiarity is reflected in the laws of many churches enabling the authorization of forms of services at lower levels of the church: by diocesan bishops, but not by individual congregations. Moreover, formal laws provide ample scope for liturgical experimentation. At whichever level of the church they are authorized, all forms of service must be consistent with the doctrine of the church. It is a general principle of Anglican canon law that public worship must be conducted in accordance with a particular church's authorized forms of service – and in most churches the doctrine of uniformity to a single use has given way to that of conformity to a multiplicity of liturgies. Nevertheless, regulation of liturgical action, of corporate public worship, must be characterized by flexibility: the use of recommendatory norms and of directory rubrics gives substance to this idea as do provisions in the laws of several churches explicitly enabling liturgical variation. These arrangements, together with the ministerial duty to provide the facility of services, are enforced primarily by the bishop who legally has the responsibility in the diocese for upholding the worthiness of worship. The possibility of ministers being subjected to judicial proceedings for liturgical indiscipline exists in many churches, but in very few does liturgical indiscipline appear specifically amongst lists of ecclesiastical offences.

---

[119] See e.g. Burundi, Const. Art. 3: 'the Church of this Province is bound by decisions of its Ecclesiastical Courts' in 'all matters relating to forms of worship'; see also Rwanda, Draft Const. 1996, Art. 7.

9

Baptism, Confirmation and Holy Communion

According to classical Anglican tradition,[1] Christian initiation is effected by participation in the ritual sequence of baptism, confirmation and Holy Communion. Anglican churches regulate the administration of these rites by means of provisions on celebration, preparation, admission and exclusion. This arrangement of provisions is common to all churches and often their terms repeat Lambeth Conference resolutions. Whilst historically church law on initiation has enjoyed a high degree of stability, recent theological debate has resulted in the juridical readjustment of the sequential pattern: admission of the unconfirmed to Holy Communion is the most notable instance where ecclesiastical systems differ. As a matter of form, these subjects are rarely treated in the written constitutions of churches, but appear rather in canonical regulations and liturgical rubrics, though the use of ecclesiastical quasi-legislation, particularly with regard to ritual innovation, is increasingly making its mark in some churches. Generally, state law on these subjects is silent, yet secular judicial decisions on exclusion from Holy Communion represent a significant exception.

BAPTISM

Traditional Anglican doctrine, as contained in the Thirty-Nine Articles, treats baptism as a dominical sacrament, 'a sign of Regeneration or new Birth, whereby . . . they that receive baptism rightly are grafted into the Church'. By baptism 'the promises of forgiveness of sin, and of our adoption to be the sons of God by the Holy Ghost, are visibly signed and sealed; Faith is confirmed, and Grace increased by virtue of prayer unto God'.[2]

---

[1] See generally, K. Stevenson and B. Spinks (eds.), *The Identity of Anglican Worship* (London, 1991), 80; P. J. Jagger, *Christian Initiation: 1552–1969* (London, 1970); T. Simpson, 'The sacraments and personal faith', in J. Wilkinson (ed.), *Catholic Anglicans Today* (London, 1968), 113; D. R. Holeton, 'Initiation', in S. Sykes and J. Booty (eds.), *The Study of Anglicanism* (London, 1988), 261 and D. R. Holeton, 'Christian initiation in some Anglican provinces', *Studia Liturgica*, 12 (1977), 129.

[2] AR, Arts. 25, 27; for judicial adoption of these ideas with respect to the Church of England, see *Kemp v Wickes* (1809) 3 Phillim 264, ER 1320 at 1322, *Escott v Mastin* (1842) 13 ER 241, *Gorham v Bishop of Exeter* (1850) Moore's Special Reports 462, and *Williams v*

That baptism is a sacrament ordained by Christ, a principle affirmed by resolutions of the Lambeth Conference,[3] is one which appears in the law of all churches. However, whilst commonly they express the church's commitment to preserve 'the sacraments',[4] the divine institution of baptism does not usually appear in constitutions.[5] Its dominical character is normally presented in liturgical rubrics,[6] and, exceptionally, in canons.[7] On the one hand, the Anglican doctrine that baptism is 'necessary for salvation' is not itself to be found explicitly in law.[8] On the other hand, it is a general principle of Anglican jurisprudence that baptism is required for Christian initiation. As a matter of ecclesiastical practice, however, churches do not present in their formal law a statement of the spiritual effects of baptism; this descriptive task is performed rather by liturgical and catechetical documents. It cannot be said, therefore, that there is a common *legal* principle of the effects of baptism.[9] Those very few churches which do employ a legal statement present the effects of baptism as: cleansing from sin or regeneration;[10] incorporation into the church uni-

Bishop of Salisbury (1864) 2 Moore PCCNS 375; see also *Re St Barnabas, Kensington* [1990] 1 All ER 169 at 171, for the idea of 'one baptism for the remission of sins'.

[3] LC 1888, Res. 11, LC 1988, Res. 18; for baptism as a prerequisite for ordination, church membership, lay office-holding and marriage, see respectively Chs. 5, 6 and 10.

[4] See for example South East Asia, Const. Fundamental Declaration, 1; South India, Const. II.6; Ireland, Const. I.2; Canada, Declaration of Principles, 1; West Africa, Const. Preamble, (a); Southern Cone, Const. Art. 1; Central Africa, Const. Fundamental Declarations, 1; Kenya, Const. Art. II.(d); Burundi, Const. Art. 3.1; Indian Ocean, Const. Art. 2(iii); Uganda, Const. Art. 2(c); Jersualem, Const. Art. 4(iii); Sudan, Const. Art. 2(a); Philippines, Const. Art. 1.2.

[5] Korea, Const. Fundamental Declaration: 'this Church administers the sacraments of Baptism and the Holy Eucharist which Jesus Christ instituted for the salvation of all and, through his word and ordinance commanded to be continued in his Church'; see also Australia, Const, Pt. I, Ch.1.3; Melanesia, Cans. A (Preamble), and Rwanda, Draft Const. 1996, Art. 5(iii).

[6] See e.g. England, BCP 1662, 236; Wales, BCP 1984, 697; Southern Africa, *Prayer Book* 1989, 361.

[7] Australia, Can. P5, 1992, 1; Chile, Can. F1.

[8] For the doctrine, see G. F. S. Gray, *The Anglican Communion* (London, 1958), 113ff. and for juridical presentations see (e.g.) Korea, Can. 7: 'In order . . . to become a Christian one must . . . be baptized'; Wales, BCP 1984, 654, 660 contains a fundamental qualification: 'Baptism, *where it may be had*, is necessary to salvation'; 'No one can enter the kingdom of God unless he is born again of water and of the Holy Spirit. In Baptism our heavenly Father will make this child a member of Christ, the child of God, and an inheritor of the kingdom of heaven'.

[9] However, those churches which in their constitutions accept the Thirty-Nine Articles (see Ch. 7), the Articles spelling out the effects of baptism (see n. 1), may in a loose and indirect sense be treated as containing a legal statement of the effects of baptism.

[10] North India, Const. I.I.V: baptism is 'a sign of cleansing from sin, of engrafting into Christ, of entrance into the covenant of grace'; Wales, BCP 1984, 697: 'Baptism is the sacrament in which, through the action of the Holy Spirit, we are made Christ's or "christened" ', and in it the candidate receives 'the forgiveness of sins and a new birth into God's family, the Church'.

versal;[11] identification with the death and resurrection of Christ;[12] and, occasionally, the commitment of the candidate to the mission and ministry of the church.[13] These effects apply to adult and infant baptism, both of which are practised.[14] The generally accepted principle that baptism confers an indelible character, and that it cannot be repeated, appears to be an unwritten custom of churches rather than a formal legal rule; it appears expressly only in very few liturgical rubrics.[15]

Celebration

It is a common legal principle that to be valid baptism must be administered with water in the name of the Father, of the Son and of the Holy Spirit.[16] Church laws commonly prescribe precisely the method by which water is to be applied to the candidate and there is general uniformity as between churches: pouring, sprinkling, immersion and submersion are all lawful. In the Church of Papua New Guinea, '[i]n baptism water shall be

[11] Melanesia, Can. A.1.A: it is 'the rite by which we become members of the Church, which is God's family, his people and the Body of Christ'; England, Can. B21: the newly baptized is received 'into Christ's Church' (see generally R. D. H. Bursell, *Liturgy, Order and the Law* (Oxford, 1996), 130f.; in New Zealand, guidelines issued by General Synod provide that baptism is '[t]he sacramental means of entry and incorporation into the Body of Christ', it confers full membership of the Church (New Zealand, GS Standing Res., 1990); see also Brazil, BCP 1987, 162. These provisions are consistent with LC 1920, Res. 9: the baptized person is treated 'as sharing with us membership in the universal Church of Christ which is his Body'; see Ch. 6 for baptism and membership.

[12] North India, Const. I.I.V; England, *Alternative Service Book* 1980, 243; Wales, BCP 1984, 697: 'the outward and visible sign is the water and words' the inward and spiritual gift is 'union with Christ in his death and resurrection'.

[13] Chile, Cans. F1b.6.

[14] AR, Art. 27; the statement in North India, Const. I.I.V, that baptism as an adult or as a child are 'accepted as alternatives', is exceptional. Church laws infrequently define 'adult' for the purposes of baptism; see, however, Southern Africa, *Prayer Book* 1989, 364: 'an adult is a person whom the minister considers able to answer responsibly for himself' or '[w]hen children who are unable to answer responsibly for themselves are baptized at the same time as their parents, the parents answer the questions in the plural both for themselves and for their children'; see also below for adults and preparation.

[15] ECUSA, BCP 1979, Marshall, Vol. II, 233: 'Holy Baptism is full initiation by water and the Holy Spirit into Christ's Body the Church. The bond which God establishes in Baptism is indissoluble'; for the same formula see Canada, *The Book of Alternative Services* 1985, 150; see also Brazil, BCP 1987, 162; England, BCP 1662, 273: a child baptized privately 'ought not to be baptized again'; see also *Kemp v Wickes* (1809) ER 1320 at 1329 and *Re St Barnabas, Kensington* [1991] Fam 1 at 4: 'Baptism can be received only once'; Wales, BCP 1984, 665; the concept of indelibility is implicit in regulations dealing with conditional baptism (see below).

[16] England, *Kemp v Wickes* (1809) 3 Phillim 264 at 269: valid baptism is effected upon 'the use of water with the invocation of the name of the Father, of the Son, and of the Holy Ghost'; Melanesia, Cans. A.1.B–K; Chile, Cans. F1; Australia, Can. P5 1992, 11; Canada, *The Book of Alternative Services* 1985, 150.

poured on the head of the candidate three times, or he may be dipped in the water three times'.[17] In the Melanesian church baptism occurs either by immersion of the person in water or by the pouring of water on the person's head with the words 'I baptize you in the name of the Father and of the Son and of the Holy Spirit'.[18] In one African church diocesan quasi-legislation provides that water used in baptism 'must not be put to common uses afterwards, but must be poured on the ground, if possible on a cultivated piece of ground'.[19] The law of the vast majority of churches is silent on the signing of the cross; in some it is retained, but when (as is rarely the case) this provision is prescribed in law, it is emphasised that signing has no effect upon the validity of the sacrament.[20] Whilst the presence of a baptismal font is required by some churches, baptism at a font in church is not a general legal requirement.[21] It is, however, a legal requirement in most churches that baptisms must be recorded in a register maintained in the parish church especially for this purpose; usually the requirement for registration is canonical, sometimes rubrical and in the Church in Wales it is described as customary.[22] Very few churches require the giving of a certificate of baptism.[23]

There is considerable legal evidence of a general consensus between churches concerning the minister of baptism. In all those churches having legal provisions dealing with the subject, the vast majority are agreed that

[17] Papua New Guinea, *Anglican Prayer Book* 1991, 198; North India, Const. I.I.V: immersion, affusion or sprinkling are all lawful.

[18] Melanesia, Cans. A.1.B–K; Australia, Can. P5 1992, 11 (a canon which may be adopted by dioceses); Southern Africa, *Prayer Book* 1989, 373: pouring thrice; ECUSA, BCP, 1979, Marshall, Vol. II, 345: immersion or pouring; Ireland, *Alternative Prayer Book* 1984, 761; Australia, *A Prayer Book for Australia* 1995, 70, Note 1: 'the symbolism of water should be emphasised' by pouring or immersion.

[19] Central Africa, Diocese of Mashonaland, *Pastoral Regulations* 1978, 6.

[20] Australia, Can. P5 1992, 10: 'the sign of the Cross used in baptism is no part of the substance of the sacrament' but the church 'retains that sign in baptism'; England, Can. B25; signing is retained in Ireland, *Alternative Prayer Book* 1984, 760; and Wales, BCP 1984, 662. For the Canons Ecclesiastical 1603 and 'lawful use of the cross in baptism explained', see Can. 30.

[21] See e.g. England, Can. F1(1); a baptismal pool is lawful (*Re St Barnabas, Kensington* [1991] Fam 1); see also D. Stancliffe, 'Baptism and fonts', *Ecclesiastical Law Journal*, 3(14) (1994), 141; for the requirement of a permanent font see also Central Africa, Diocese of Mashonaland, *Pastoral Regulations* 1978, 6.

[22] Wales, BCP 1984, 665; Chile, Can. F1a.3; Korea, Cans. 12, 13; Philippines, Cans. III.16.3(d); Ireland, Const. 3.5 and BCP 1960, 761; in Australia dioceses may adopt the registration rule found in national law: Can. P5 1992, 12; see also Central Africa, Diocese of Mashonaland, *Pastoral Regulations* 1978, 7. For the duty to maintain baptismal registers, see Ch. 11.

[23] See e.g. Philippines, Can. II.5.4; England, Parochial Registers and Records Measure 1978, s. 2 (as amended by the Church of England (Miscellaneous Provisions) Measure 1992, s. 4). Provisions on registration and certificates are important for the purposes of rules about conditional baptism and 're-baptism': see below.

it may be administered by both ordained and lay people. Baptism by ordained ministers is the norm. If present, the bishop is the minister of baptism: this is a requirement found in liturgical rubrics and not in the canons; indeed, in ECUSA it is 'recommended' that baptism be reserved for when a bishop is present.[24] If the bishop is not present, the 'normal' or 'usual' minister of baptism is a priest and, if a priest is not available, a deacon;[25] occasionally rules allow baptism by a deacon only 'for good reason'.[26] With regard to administration by a lay person, there are no instances in law in which this is not permitted. At the same time, however, not all churches possess formal law on the matter. Those that do limit lay celebration to cases of emergency; no provision exists allowing lay administration outside emergency.[27] Beyond this, the differences that exist within the general principle of permissibility are in the details of rules, some of which are of fundamental importance.

The Melanesian church provides the most comprehensive canonical treatment of emergency baptism. First, baptism may be administered by 'any baptized lay person, male or female'. Laws in other churches are either silent or they do not require the lay minister to be baptized; they provide simply that 'any person' may baptize in emergency.[28] Secondly, Melanesian canon law imposes a duty upon lay persons to baptize in emergencies: they 'should baptize the child'; only the Canadian church has a similar rule.[29] Thirdly, Melanesian canon law prescribes that lay administration is to take place in a case of 'serious sickness', when the candidate is 'very sick and may die'; laws of other churches allow lay

[24] Southern Africa, *Prayer Book* 1989, 364: '[b]y virtue of his office, the Bishop is the minister of baptism in his diocese; Canada, *The Book of Alternative Services* 1985, 150; ECUSA, BCP 1979, Marshall, Vol. II, 233, 265.

[25] Southern Africa, *Prayer Book* 1989, 364; Wales, BCP 1984, 654; Canada, *The Book of Alternative Services* 1985, 163, BCP 1962, 522.

[26] Melanesia, Cans. A.1.B–K; Central Africa, Diocese of Mashonaland, *Pastoral Regulations* 1978, 6: '[t]he normal minister of baptism is a priest. Deacons may not baptize when a priest is readily available, and for priests to absent themselves without serious cause from baptisms and allow deacons to conduct them is to be deprecated'.

[27] See e.g. England, *Kemp v Wickes* (1809) 3 Phillim 264 at 270; Southern Africa, *Prayer Book* 1989, 364; Wales, BCP 1984, 665; Canada, *The Book of Alternative Services* 1985, 165.

[28] Melanesia, Cans. A.1.B–K; in ECUSA, BCP 1979, Marshall Vol. II, 271 and West Indies, *Liturgical Texts* 1989, 49: 'any baptized person' is allowed to baptize in emergency. In the former Province of Uganda, Rwanda and Burundi, the Canon Law and Constitution Commission (meeting at Namirembe 6 June 1968) discussed the rule in the dioceses of Uganda and the Upper Nile that 'in case of urgent necessity any lay confirmed person may administer Baptism in the case of a very small child if he were ill and born in a Christian marriage, and in the case of an older person if he is studying in the Baptism class'.

[29] Melanesia, Cans. A.1.B–K: Canada, BCP 1962, 541 any baptized person present 'should' baptize; Central Africa, Diocese of Mashonaland, *Pastoral Regulations* 1978, 7: readers, catechists and helpers must be told that 'it is their duty to baptize ' in emergencies.

administration similarly in cases of 'critical illness', 'danger of death', and in one church simply '[i]f no ordained minister is available'; but most merely use the blanket word 'emergency'.[30] Fourthly, the Melanesian duty to baptize gives rise to a consequential right to baptism, but this right is enjoyed exclusively by children of church members; only one other instance of a similar rule has been found.[31] The law of most churches contains no such limitation as to parentage. At the same time, however, there is an extensive absence of comprehensive legal treatment in Anglican canonical systems of the problem of the emergency baptism of adults; provisions are confined to children. In this respect the limitation in South African rubrics that in the case of emergency baptism of an adult there must be 'evidence to show that he is desirous of it' would seem to be anomalous.[32] Lastly, the Melanesian canons require the lay person to report the baptism afterwards to the priest. This is a common requirement to enable the priest to be satisfied that a valid baptism has been administered and to register it. The requirement is usually accompanied by insistence that, if the candidate recovers, he is to be received into the church at a public service.[33]

Most churches have detailed legal provisions on the time when baptism is to be celebrated. Provisions reflect a general principle enunciated by Lambeth Conference resolutions that baptism should be administered 'when the most number of people come together . . . in the regular services of the Church'.[34] Public baptism in a full liturgical setting is the norm throughout the Communion. Either church law contains a general requirement that baptism is to take place at 'public worship' or else on Sundays 'in the presence of the congregation'.[35] Several churches prescribe that 'if

[30] Melanesia, Cans. A.1.B–K; Canada, BCP 1962, 541: 'critically ill'; Southern Africa, *Prayer Book* 1989, 396: 'danger of death'; Wales, BCP 1984, 665: if no ordained minister is available.

[31] Melanesia, Cans. A.1.B–K: Central Africa, Diocese of Mashonaland, *Pastoral Regulations* 1978, 7: emergency baptism is restricted to those 'whose homes are Christian'.

[32] Southern Africa, *Prayer Book* 1989, 396.

[33] Melanesia, Cans. A.1.B–K; see also e.g. Wales, BCP 1984, 665; Canada, *The Book of Alternative Services* 1985, 165: there must be recognition at 'a public celebration of the sacrament'; West Indies, *Liturgical Texts* 1989, 49; Central Africa, Diocese of Mashonaland, *Pastoral Regulations* 1978, 7; Australia, *A Prayer Book for Australia* 1995, 71; Diocese of Melbourne, *Guidelines* 1988, p.18; ECUSA, BCP 1979, Marshall Vol. II, 271; Brazil, BCP 1987, 162.

[34] LC 1948, Res. 105; this very same formula appears in England, Can. B21: '[i]t is desirable that every minister having a cure of souls shall normally administer' baptism on Sundays 'at public worship' when 'the most number of people come together'.

[35] See e.g. Australia, Can. P5 1992, 1 (a canon which dioceses may adopt): '[t]he Sacrament of Holy Baptism, wherever possible, shall be administered at public worship'; Melanesia, Cans. A.1.B–K: 'public service'; Spain, Cans. I.10.1; Chile, Can. F1(c); Wales: BCP 1984, 654: as far as possible, baptism must be administered on Sundays or other Holy Days in the presence of the congregation.

possible' it is to be administered in certain seasons, most usually at Easter and at Pentecost,[36] and many express a preference for its celebration at Holy Communion.[37] Occasionally, law incorporates a statement of the justifications for its public celebration: to make it clear that the candidate is being welcomed into the church and to enable witnessing congregations to renew their own baptismal vows.[38] Private baptism, consequently, is permitted as the exception: and sometimes rules prescribe that at such baptisms the congregation must be represented.[39]

Preparation

It is a general principle of Anglican law that candidates for baptism must receive instruction with respect to the sacrament itself and the Christian life they enter through it. The terms of legal provisions on instruction depend on whether the candidate is an infant or an adult. In the case of infants, sponsors must be appointed and instructed as it is they who are responsible for the Christian development of the candidate. If an adult, the candidate must be instructed personally. These principles have been enunciated from time to time by the Lambeth Conference, one resolution of which also recommends an enhanced role for parents and the 'local congregation for bringing a new member, whether infant or adult, into the full fellowship of the Church';[40] only some churches implement in actual law this addition. Church laws uniformly prescribe the number of sponsors (or godparents) for infant candidates: some require one or more, some two and some at least three; similar provisions exist with respect to sponsors

[36] Korea, Can. 11; some add All Saints' Day or the Sunday following the first Sunday after Epiphany: see e.g. America, BCP 1979, Marshall, Vol. II, 233, 265 and Canada, *The Book of Alternative Services* 1985, 163.

[37] Southern Africa, *Prayer Book* 1989, 364; Brazil, BCP 1987, 162; Canada, *The Book of Alternative Services* 1985, 150; New Zealand, GS Standing Resolutions 1990, 1.

[38] West Indies, Can. 28.1; Melanesia, Cans. A.1.B–K; Australia, *A Prayer Book for Australia* 1995, 70: baptism is 'a community event, welcoming new members of Christ's flock, and providing an opportunity for all the baptized to renew their vows'; Diocese of Melbourne, *Pastoral Handbook* 1988, p.16; Canada, BCP 1962, 522; Ireland, *Alternative Service Book* 1984, 755 and BCP 1960, 247.

[39] Scotland, Can. 27.3: baptism 'shall normally be administered in church but clergy may baptize elsewhere when a child cannot be brought to church'; Southern Africa, *Prayer Book* 1989, 364: 'If pastoral needs require, and with the permission of the Bishop', baptisms may 'take place elsewhere than in the church building or in a place commonly used for worship'; representatives of the congregation 'should always be present'; Brazil, BCP 1987, 162; Wales, BCP 1984, 664: 'Children shall not be baptized privately except in an emergency'; Australia, *A Prayer Book for Australia* 1995, 71.

[40] LC 1897, Res. 48 and LC 1948, Res. 104; the requirement of instruction appears in the BCP 1662, 263.

for adult candidates.[41] Many churches prescribe that two sponsors shall be the same sex as the candidate and at least one of the opposite sex.[42] It is very uncommon for rules to require sponsors to have attained a fixed age.[43] Most churches permit parents or guardians to function as sponsors, and occasionally it is recommended that one of the sponsors be a parent.[44] It is with respect to qualifications for eligibility as a sponsor that canonical systems vary most. Indeed, a Lambeth Conference resolution of 1948 provides that no unbaptized person may act as a godparent and that at least one 'should be a practising communicant'.[45] This has been partially implemented in the Communion. In some churches prospective sponsors must be confirmed persons.[46] In others they must be regular communicants or worshipping Christians.[47] In some individuals who are simply baptized are eligible.[48] One church operates the rule that no person may be admitted as a sponsor unless baptized and confirmed but the minister may dispense with the requirement of confirmation if need so requires.[49] Very

[41] Melanesia, Cans. A.1.B–K (two); Southern Africa, *Prayer Book* 1989, 364 (one or more); Canada, *The Book of Alternative Services* 1985, 150; Wales, BCP 1984, 654 (at least two); West Indies, Can. 28.4, 5 (no fewer than three for children, and at least two for adults); Australia, Can. P5 1992, 8 ('usually' at least three; for adults one sponsor suffices); England, Can. B23(1): for infants 'when three cannot conveniently be had, one godfather and godmother shall suffice' and for adults three, 'or at least two' sponsors must be chosen; Scotland, Can. 27.2: in 'cases of necessity', one sponsor 'shall be deemed sufficient'.

[42] See e.g. England, Can. B23(1); Canada, BCP 1962, 552; Australia, Can. P5 1992, 8: this may be adopted by dioceses (see e.g. Diocese of Melbourne, *Pastoral Handbook* 1988, p.16); Wales, BCP 1984, 654.

[43] See e.g. Ireland, Const. IX.26(4): they must be 'persons of discreet age'.

[44] England, BCP 1662, 263: this permits parents to act (compare Can. 29 of the Canons Ecclesiastical 1603); Melanesia, Cans. A.1.B–K; Wales, BCP 1984, 654; West Indies, Can. 28.4, 5; Scotland, Can. 27.1: parents may be sponsors 'in default of others'; ECUSA, BCP 1979, Marshall, Vol. II, 235: '[i]t is fitting that parents be included among the godparents of their own children', a provision which also operates in Canada, *The Book of Alternative Services* 1985, 150; Ireland, *Alternative Prayer Book* 1984, 755, 759: it is 'desirable' that parents be sponsors.

[45] LC 1948, Res. 106.

[46] Chile, Can. F1.c.12; Diocese of Uganda, in the former Province of Uganda, Rwanda and Burundi: in the Diocese of the Upper Nile, people 'living in notorious sin without repentance' were ineligible.

[47] Southern Africa, *Prayer Book* 1989, 364: it is the 'intention' of the church that sponsors be 'communicants'; Wales, BCP 1984, 654: sponsors 'shall be baptized Christians, and it is desirable that they should be regular communicants' and sponsors for adults must be 'regular communicants' of the church or of a church in communion with it (ibid., 670); Scotland, Can. 27.1: they must 'if possible' be communicants; West Indies, Can. 28.4, 5; Papua New Guinea, *Anglican Prayer Book* 1991, 198: they should be 'worshipping Christians'; Spain, Can. I.10.

[48] Australia, Can. P5 1992, 8 (a rule which dioceses may adopt); Ireland, Const. IX.26(4) and *Alternative Prayer Book* 1984, 755: they must be 'members of the Church of Ireland'; Melanesia, Cans. A.1.B–K: a person under public penance is ineligible.

[49] See England, Can. B23(4).

rarely does law present a justification for the appointment of sponsors in the case of infants.[50] Rules about the functions of sponsors are consistent: they are responsible for helping candidates to grow in the knowledge and love of God and in the fellowship of the church, and for support of the candidates by prayer and example of Christian living.[51] Some churches emphasise that at the baptism the parents and sponsors should themselves renew their own commitment to Christ at the baptism of the child.[52]

The common requirement that the sponsors of infant candidates and adult candidates themselves must receive instruction is expressed in a variety of forms. Most usually it is expressed in mandatory terms as a duty imposed upon ordained ministers; in the case of infant candidates, it is the minister's duty 'before baptizing infants or children to prepare the sponsors by instructing both the parents and godparents concerned';[53] in the case of adult candidates, '[t]he minister shall instruct and prepare or cause to be instructed or prepared . . . any person able to answer for himself or herself before baptizing that person'.[54] Very occasionally, rules provide that the reponsibility for preparation and instruction is that of the bishop and that as a matter of practice this function is carried out through delegation by priests, deacons and lay ministers.[55] Provisions vary considerably with regard to the subjects to be included in instruction, some distinguishing between preparation for infant sponsors and preparation for adults.[56] Some laws require adults to be instructed simply in the

---

[50] Melanesia, Cans. A.1.B–K: '[a]s it is impossible for the infant to have faith and repentance this is provided by the congregation and especially by the parents and godparents'; Southern Africa, *Prayer Book* 1989, 364: they are to make 'promises on behalf of the child'; see also Canada, *The Book of Alternative Services* 1985, 150.

[51] Southern Africa, Can. 35.4 and *Prayer Book* 1989, 364; ECUSA, BCP 1979, Marshall, Vol. II, 235; Brazil, BCP 1987, 162: they must be an 'example of the Christian life'; Chile, Can. F1.d; West Indies, Can. 28.6: they are to present the candidate at the font and 'afterwards put him in mind of his Christian profession and duties'; Australia, Can. P5 1992, 8: they must 'faithfully fulfil their reponsibilities both by their care for the children committed to their charge and by the example of their own godly living'; the West Indian and the Australian ideas both appear in England, Can. B23(2); Ireland, *Alternative Prayer Book* 1984, 755, 759: parents and sponsors must 'confess the Christian faith in which [the child] is to be baptized'.

[52] Southern Africa, *Prayer Book* 1989, 364.

[53] West Indies, Can. 28.2; Southern Africa, Can. 35.4; Papua New Guinea, *Anglican Prayer Book* 1991, 198.

[54] Australia, Can. P5 1992, 4; this rule may be adopted in dioceses (see e.g. Diocese of Sydney, *The 7th Handbook*, 8.3).

[55] Southern Africa, *Prayer Book* 1989, 417; Brazil, Cans. III.1.2(c): a lay minister may instruct; for prayer and fasting in the case of adults, see e.g. England, Can. B24(1) and Ireland, BCP 1960, 255.

[56] For two exceptional provisions see Melanesia, Cans. A.1.B–K: arrangements for instruction are made 'at the discretion of the priest'; and Brazil, BCP 1987, 162: the instruction must be determined by the bishop.

'Christian faith' or 'the principles of the Christian religion'.[57] Most churches are rather more specific: some require 'extensive instruction' in the faith of Christ and in biblical doctrine;[58] others require the minister simply to instruct sponsors for children in their responsibilities for the spiritual nurture of the candidate;[59] very few expressly require instruction in the meaning or 'the significance of baptism'.[60] Some churches employ the notion of catechumenate for varying periods.[61] Rarely do church rules present the idea that baptism candidates have a right to instruction nor do they require adult candidates to make confession before baptism.[62]

Admission and Exclusion

The law of the vast majority of Anglican churches concerning admission to and exclusion from baptism is, broadly, a re-presentation of the terms of the Canons Ecclesiastical 1603 and the rubrics of the Book of Common Prayer 1662: these placed the responsibility for bringing infants to church to be baptized upon parents, they required the giving of notice to the minister and they forbade refusal and delay of baptism.[63] The provision in the

---

[57] For 'Christian faith', see Southern Africa, Can. 35.4; Australia, Can. P5 1992, 4 (which may be adopted by dioceses); for 'the principles of the Christian religion' see e.g. Diocese of Sydney, *The 7th Handbook*, 8.3 and England, Can. B24(1); Spain, Cans. I.10: they are to be instructed in 'the principles of the Christian faith'.

[58] Chile, Can. F1c.12; for an 'appointed course of doctrinal education', see Korea, Can. 8; Central Africa, Diocese of Mashonaland, *Pastoral Regulations* 1978, 4: for adults, instruction must cover the Creed, the Lord's Prayer and the Ten Commandments.

[59] Ireland, *Alternative Prayer Book* 1984, 755: they must instruct that 'the same responsibilities rest on [parents and guardians] as are in the service of Holy Baptism required of godparents'; see also England, Can. B22(3); West Indies, Can. 28.2; Papua New Guinea, *Anglican Prayer Book* 1991, 198.

[60] For 'significance' see West Indies, Can. 28.2; Philippines, Cans. III.16.3(b); for 'meaning' see Ireland, *Alternative Prayer Book* 1984, 755: '[t]he Minister of every Parish shall teach the people the meaning of Baptism'; and Southern Africa, *Prayer Book* 1989, 364; New Zealand, GS Standing Resolutions 1990, 1: this provides that 'Education in the Faith, sacraments and mission of the Church precedes and follows Baptism'.

[61] Korea, Can. 9 and Melanesia, Cans. A.1.B–K: at least 1 year for adults; Papua New Guinea, *Anglican Prayer Book* 1991, 193: 2 years for candidates 'old enough to answer for themselves'; Southern Africa, *Prayer Book* 1989, 417: '[t]he Catechumenate is a period of pre-baptismal instruction for adults who desire to become Christians'; Central Africa, Diocese of Mashonaland, *Pastoral Regulations* 1978, 3: 18 months, though in the case of a child of up to 7 years of age, if their parents are Christians of good standing, the child may be baptized without previous instruction'.

[62] However, see Papua New Guinea, *Anglican Prayer Book* 1991, 193: but absolution is not to be given; Central Africa, Diocese of Mashonaland, *Pastoral Regulations* 1978, 4–6: this deals with confession and instruction after emergency baptism, and contains the rule: '[p]riests must warn parents . . . or guardians, who try to prevent anybody's admission to instruction for baptism, of the gravity of resisting God in this matter'.

[63] Can. 68; BCP 1662, 263; see also LC 1897, Res. 48: there must be no deferral for 'training' other than in cases of 'exceptional difficulty'; and LC 1948, Res. 105: 'due

constitution of the Church of North India that 'it is the accepted practice of the [church] that Christian parents are expected to bring their children to Baptism' is unusual as most churches having a rule on the subject cast the parental responsibility not as an expectation but as a duty.[64] Some churches employ a general requirement of notice applicable to both infant and adult baptism; others do not: these are usually in the form either of a week's notice or simply 'due notice'.[65] These provisions exist in order to enable preparation and instruction.

One of the current issues facing Anglican churches is the debate about restrictive or 'indiscriminate' baptism. However, legally, churches operate a general prohibition against refusal but a qualification concerning delay. Generally, it may be said that Anglican churches present a right to baptism.[66] The right is expressed most strongly with regard to infants, though there are subtle differences as between some churches. In the Church of England, no minister 'shall refuse or . . . delay to baptize any infant within his cure that is brought to the church to be baptized'; this is the case whether or not the parent is a Christian.[67] By contrast, in the Australian church '[n]o minister may refuse or, except for the purpose of preparing or instructing the parents or guardians or godparents, delay baptizing a child who has a sponsoring parent, guardian or godparent *who professes to be a Christian*'.[68] Permissible delays of infant baptism to enable the minister to

notice' 'should be required'; for an early example of adoption of these ideas in the Scottish Canons of 1634 (Can. 14), see G. Bray, *The Historic Anglican Canons* (Woodbridge, 1998), 580.

[64] North India, Const. I.I.II.8; Wales, BCP 1984, 654: '[i]t is the duty of Christians to bring their children to Holy Baptism'; England, *Acts of Convocation*, 69; Canada, BCP 1962, 522: the minister of the parish must 'often admonish the people that they bring their children to the Church for Baptism as soon as possible after birth; and that except for urgent cause and necessity they seek not to have their children baptized in their homes'; Ireland, BCP 1960, 247: this fixes the fourth or fifth week after birth as the time for baptism 'unless upon a great and reasonable cause'.

[65] For one week's notice for both children and adults, see Australia, Can. P5 1992, 3: this may be adopted by dioceses; see e.g. Diocese of Sydney, *The 7th Handbook*, 8.3: notice of 1 week is required for adults; for 'due notice' for infants, see Ireland, Const. IX.26.1; *Alternative Service Book* 1984, 755; Canada, BCP 1962, 532; Diocese of Melbourne, *Guidelines* 1988, p.18; Wales, BCP 1984, 654 and for adults 1 week's notice, ibid; Southern Africa, *Prayer Book* 364: this requires 'timely notice' to the bishop if an adult is to be baptized and confirmed.

[66] The provision, in the canons of Puerto Rico (Cans. III.5.3), that there must be no exclusion from the sacraments on grounds of 'race, colour, ethnic origin or nationality', is exceptional; see also: Central Africa, Diocese of Mashonaland, *Pastoral Regulations* 1978, 3, 6: in the case of those who have reached 14 years of age, priests 'should emphasise their right to freedom of choice in regard to baptism'.

[67] England, Can. B22(4): doubtless this is an idea linked to the established position of the church, under which the right is afforded to any parishioner (see LFCE, 315).

[68] Australia, Can. P5 1992, 6: a canon which may be adopted by dioceses; compare Diocese of Sydney, *The 7th Handbook*, 8.3: '[a] minister may not refuse to baptize *any child* living in his parochial unit'.

effect instruction of parents and godparents appear in a number of canon-ical systems.[69] The canon law of the West Indies is perhaps one of the neat-est statements of the basic problem and its solution – it adopts the English model of a right but the right is cast in normative terms: '[no] clergyman *should* refuse absolutely to baptize an infant within his cure whose par-ents/guardians are desirous of having the child baptized'; the cleric 'in the exercise of his pastoral and moral responsibility may, after due notice, postpone baptism until the parents/guardians and godparents have been instructed and in his opinion are in a position to undertake the spiritual, moral and educational obligations required of them'.[70] Other grounds permitting departure from the norm include failure to give notice to the minister, though this is rare,[71] and non-residence in the parish: with regard to the latter, and in line with a resolution of the Lambeth Conference, some churches require ministers to consult with the minister of the parish in which the parents reside before proceeding with the bap-tism.[72] The Lambeth Conference has recommended that both wives and children of polygamous marriages must be admitted to baptism; the implementation of this in actual law is rare.[73] Several churches impose an absolute prohibition on ministers delaying baptism in emergencies but others qualify the duty.[74]

---

[69] West Indies, Can. 28.3; see also North India, Const. I.I.V.9: '[a] Minister who has scruples in regard to the administration of Baptism to infants shall be free to invite some other minister of the Church of North India to perform the rite'.

[70] North India, Const. I.I.II.8. Ireland, Const. IX.26(2); America, Cans. I.17.6; Central Africa, Diocese of Mashonaland, *Pastoral Regulations* 1978, 7: '[n]o child should be refused Baptism because of the sins of the parents provided that there is a real and con-vincing hope that the child will be brought up in the Christian faith and practice'.

[71] See e.g. Australia, Can. P5 1992, 6.

[72] LC 1948, Res. 107: 'The Conference recommends that a minister, baptizing the child of persons not resident in his parish or on his Membership Roll, should consult the minister of the parish in which the parents of the child reside, in order that the child and family concerned may be the more surely linked up with the life of the congrega-tion'; England, Can. B22(5); Australia, Can. P5 1992, 6: '[a] minister shall not normally baptize a child' in these circumstances; compare Southern Africa, Can. 35.5: '[a] priest shall not baptize an infant one or both of whose parents are not his pastoral responsi-bility, or an adult who is not his pastoral responsibility, without the knowledge and consent of the priest whose responsibility they are'.

[73] LC 1988, Res. 26 (compare LC 1888, Res. 5); see e.g. Central Africa, Diocese of Mashonaland, *Pastoral Regulations* 1978, 5: the wife of a polygamist may not be baptized without reference to the bishop; and a polygamous family may only be baptized after 'due preparation', episcopal consent and the approval of the local congregation.

[74] England, Can. B22(6): '[n]o minister being informed of the weakness or danger of death of any infant within his cure and therefore desired to go to baptize the same shall either refuse or delay to do so'; compare Melanesia, Cans. A.1.B–K: sick and dying chil-dren of 'heathen parents' may be baptized if the parents ask for baptism and provided 'they agree that if the child lives it will receive Christian teaching and be brought up a Christian' (the same applies when parents are under public penance).

There is some evidence, but by no means universal throughout the Communion, that rules about refusal and delay are rather different with regard to adult candidates for baptism. Under rubrics in Papua New Guinea '[t]he consent of the diocesan or regional bishop must be obtained before an adult is baptized'.[75] In the canon law of Melanesia, adults must have 'faith and repentance' and the person 'must show that he really wants to put away ways which are not Christian, that he really wants to live the Christian life and that he is truly sorry for what he has done wrong'.[76] According to the canon law of the church in Southern Africa, '[n]o person other than an infant or young child shall be baptized, save in the case of emergency, until he has received such form of instruction in the Christian faith as has been approved by the Bishop of the Diocese'; more- over, '[w]hen adults are to be baptized, the Incumbent shall notify the Bishop of their names before the baptism takes place', and 'they shall be presented to the Bishop for Confirmation at the same time or as soon as possible thereafter'.[77] These provisions are exceptional and the law of most churches is silent on the subject.[78]

Ordinarily, ministerial failure to baptize, other than delay for the pur- pose of instruction, might itself be corrected by executive episcopal action. In serious cases, it may also constitute the ecclesiastical offence of neglect of duty or, in those churches which operate the scheme, the offence of fail- ing to provide ministrations to the members of the church (see Chapter 3). On recent authority from the church courts, the ecclesiastical offence of neglect of duty, is certainly available in the Church of England for refusal to baptize;[79] yet, generally, few churches have formal arrangements

[75] Papua New Guinea, *Anglican Prayer Book* 1991, 193.
[76] Melanesia, Cans. A.1.B–K: this formula also appears in Papua New Guinea, *Anglican Prayer Book* 1991, 193.
[77] Southern Africa, Cans. 35.1–3; Australia, Diocese of Melbourne, *Guidelines* 1988, p.19: baptism should normally be administered 'within a reasonably short time follow- ing a request, unless there is a good reason; requests for preparation over an extended period using the catechumenate pattern should be honoured'.
[78] For treatment of parish baptismal policies in diocesan quasi-legislation, see, for England, LFCE, 315ff. and for Australia, Diocese of Melbourne, *Guidelines* 1988, p.17: parishes' baptismal policies should clearly indicate 'the steps by which a candidate making a request for baptism has that request considered, and may undertake appro- priate preparation'; 'indiscriminate baptism undermines the importance of this sacra- ment, and is a disservice to both candidate and family'; on the other hand, 'strict exclusiveness is alien to the openness which characterizes the gospel of Christ'; '[n]o candidate should be baptized without evidence of faith in Christ', provided by 'active participation, willingness to undertake the vows made, and the desire and intention to become a communicant member'.
[79] *Bland v Archdeacon of Cheltenham* [1972] 1 All ER 1012: the Court of Arches held that evidence of a 'clear and final intention' not to baptize was necessary for a conviction – there is no right of conscientious objection; for the Church in Wales, see *The Cure of Souls*, The Report of a Working Party 1995, p.8: '[t]o refuse to baptize is *prima facie* a

allowing recourse in cases of refusal short of full judicial proceedings. Legal unity in the Communion on this subject is found in the silence of law. However, in a very small number of churches the law does confer an express right of appeal to the bishop of the refusing minister. According to the constitutional law of the Church of Ireland, '[i]f the Minister shall refuse or unduly delay to baptize any such child, the parents or guardians may apply to the bishop who shall, after consultation with the minister, give such directions as he shall think fit'.[80] Similarly, under the canon law of ECUSA, anyone refused admission to baptism may apply for a judgment to the bishop and no one so refused may be admitted without the written direction of the bishop.[81] In neither case does the law provide a right of appeal against the decision of the bishop if this is one which supports the minister's refusal.

Conditional Baptism and Re-Baptism

A rule which occurs very frequently in church laws throughout the Communion, a logical consequence of the principle that baptism is indelible, is that when baptism is requested and it is uncertain whether a prior baptism has already been celebrated, the minister is required to baptize conditionally; re-baptism is neither possible nor permissible. Many churches operate the rule that before a baptism the minister must make certain that candidates have not already been baptized; some laws require determination of this at the time of giving instruction.[82] Laws contain a variety of tests as to the standard of proof required, some of which appear to be mandatory and some directory: they range from 'certainty' to 'doubt' or 'reasonable doubt' that the earlier ceremony was a valid baptism.[83]

breach of duty' under the 1603 Canons Ecclesiastical which are still operative on this subject.

[80] Ireland, Const. IX.26.2; much the same system pertains in England, Can. B22(2): recourse lies for refusal or if the minister 'unduly delay'.

[81] ECUSA, Cans. I.17.6: baptism is not expressly mentioned but the canon deals with 'A person to whom the Sacraments of the church shall have been refused'.

[82] Wales, BCP 1984, 654: the priest must 'make certain that children brought for Baptism have not already been baptized'; Papua New Guinea, *Anglican Prayer Book* 1991, 198: the priest 'should make sure at the time of giving instruction that the child has not been baptized already'; Canada, BCP 1962, 522: the priest 'shall require assurance that the child . . . has not already received this Sacrament'; see also West Indies, Can. 30.5; and Australia, Diocese of Melbourne, *Guidelines* 1988, p.18: 'sensitive investigation should be made to ascertain whether the ceremony performed constituted valid Christian baptism' and where this is believed to be the case, the person is to be treated as having received 'private baptism'.

[83] Ireland, *Alternative Prayer Book* 1984, 755: '[t]he priest shall be assured that the child has not already been baptized'; and BCP 1960, 258: if sponsors of adult candidates 'do make such uncertain answers to the Priest's questions, that it cannot appear whether or not he hath been baptized . . . then let the Priest baptize' conditionally;

Occasionally, churches stress the solemnity of conditional baptism; rubrics in Southern Africa represent one of the most comprehensive treatments of the matter: '[i]t is important that conditional baptism be administered as no mere formality but with the solemnity proper to all the rites of Christian initiation'; '[t]he absence of a baptismal certificate is not in itself a reason for conditional baptism' and '[i]t may be possible to establish by other means that a valid baptism has already taken place'. In such cases, 'it is desirable that a signed statement be obtained from parents, or a member of the family, or a godparent, or a member of the congregation, or a minister. This statement should be attached to the register of baptisms'. The Southern African rubrics also prescribe that '[i]t is desirable that an adult received into the congregation be confirmed either at the same service of reception or as soon as may be convenient afterwards'.[84] Express prohibitions against re-baptism appear in rubrics or quasi-legislation rather than in the canons, and occasionally the prohibition is presented as 'contrary to the teaching of the church'; very rarely do churches prescribe penalties for those who administer re-baptism.[85] In the Australian diocese of Melbourne, for example, guidelines deal with the situation when 'a person who has been baptised under conditions they do not regard as valid or efficacious requests "rebaptism"'. In these circumstances, '[w]here there is a request for "rebaptism", the need for the person concerned to publicly acknowledge their standing in the Church should be recognized and affirmed, and an opportunity for doing so offered' (perhaps with a testimony or renewal of baptismal vows).[86]

Melanesia, Cans. A.1.B–K: if it is not 'certain' that a candidate has already been baptized, or that he has been validly baptized, he should be conditionally baptized ('If you are not already baptized, I baptize you . . .'); if there is doubt whether a person is still living, he should be baptized conditionally ('If you are living, I baptize you . . .'); see also Brazil, BCP 1987, 162; Australia, Diocese of Melbourne, *Guidelines* 1988, p.18: when there is doubt about a prior baptism, the rubrics on 'provisional baptism' must be followed; for 'reasonable doubt, see Southern Africa, *Prayer Book* 1989, 395; Scotland, Can. 27.4; ECUSA, BCP 1979, Marshall, Vol. II, 267, and West Indies, *Liturgical Texts* 1989, 49.

[84] Southern Africa, *Prayer Book* 1989, 395, 397 (see also a Guide produced by the Southern Africa Theological Commission 1983: Evans and Wright, doc. 567); for conditional baptism and reception in England, see Can. B28(1) and R. D. H. Bursell, *Liturgy, Order and the Law* (Oxford 1996), 147; for reception see also Chs. 6, 7 and 12.

[85] See e.g. Melanesia, Standing Res. 18, 1989: persons who re-baptize anyone already baptized 'should be disciplined according to the Constitution and Canons'.

[86] Australia, Diocese of Melbourne, *Guidelines* 1988, p.20; Diocese of Sydney, *The 7th Handbook*, 8.3: '[r]e-baptism is not permitted but conditional baptism can be performed when there is some doubt about a person having been baptized according to the requirements of the Church'; for similar provisions in English diocesan quasi-legislation, see e.g. Diocese of Rochester, *Bishop's Guidelines* (1992), A.4; for an exceptionally comprehensive canonical treatment of re-baptism, see Chile, IACH, Can. F.1c.15.

CONFIRMATION

The relevance of confirmation to Christian initiation and its relation to bap-tism have historically been the subject of considerable debate.[87] According to classical Anglican doctrine, confirmation is 'not to be counted for [a sacrament] of the Gospel' for it has 'not any visible sign or ceremony ordained of God'.[88] Today, laws stress different aspects of the nature of confirmation: a couple treat it as 'a sacrament', several as a rite by which individuals make a profession of the faith and a mature expression of the commitment to Christ made at baptism, some as a reaffirmation of bap-tismal promises, and most state that in it, through the bishop's laying on of hands, the power of the Holy Spirit strengthens the candidate in the Christian life.[89] It is a universal principle of Anglican canon law that the minister of confirmation is the bishop, who celebrates it by the laying on of hands and prayer; in these the bishop is treated as representing the whole church.[90] As to its celebration, many churches require this at a celebration of Holy Communion.[91] In most churches, in the case of adults and children able to answer for themselves, the norm is that confirmation should follow baptism as soon as is convenient; in a minority, however, baptism and con-firmation must normally be administered as 'a single rite'.[92]

[87] For this and its celebration separated chronologically from baptism by the devel-opment of infant baptism, see e.g. D. R. Horeton, 'Initiation', in Sykes and Booty (eds.), *The Study of Anglicanism* (London, 1988), 261, 267ff; J. Martos, *Doors to the Sacred* (London, 1981); G. Dix, *The Theology of Confirmation in Relation to Baptism* (London, 1946); O. C. Quick, *The Christian Sacraments* (London, 1927) 190ff; A. J. Mason, *The Relation of Confirmation to Baptism* (London, 1891).

[88] AR, Art. 25.

[89] For the sacrament idea see West Indies, Can. 30.1; Southern Africa, Can. 35.7; for mature commitment and profession, see e.g. Australia, *A Prayer Book for Australia* 1995, 94; Brazil, BCP 1987, 174; Wales, BCP 1984, 698; for 'embracing' and 'accepting' the faith at confirmation see e.g. Australia, Can. P7 1992, 3. and Southern Africa, *Prayer Book* 1989, 372; for reaffirmation see Chile, Cans. F.2a: this canon contains perhaps the most comprehensive legal statement of the various interpretations of the nature of confirma-tion; New Zealand, GS Standing Res. 1990, 1; Australia, Diocese of Melbourne, *Guidelines* 1988, p.20; Southern Africa, *Prayer Book* 1989, 362, 364; for strengthening by the Holy Spirit, see e.g. Melanesia, Cans. A.3.A–D.

[90] Southern Africa, *Prayer Book* 1989, 362, 364; Australia, Can. P7 1992, 2; New Zealand, GS Standing Res. 1990, 1; England, Can. B27; Scotland, Can. 30.1: it must be administered by the bishop at least once every three years in each ecclesiastical unit in the diocese where there are candidates and more frequently as the circumstances of each ecclesiastical unit may require; it may be administered personally by the bishop or by a bishop commissioned for this purpose; for a similar provision see Ireland, Const. IX.28(2),(3); for antecedents to these rules in the Irish Canons 1634 (Can. 17), see G. Bray, *The Historic Anglican Canons* (Woodbridge, 1998), 581.

[91] Papua New Guinea, *Anglican Prayer Book* 1991, 203.

[92] For the norm, see England, BCP 1662, 288; Ireland, BCP 1960, 259; for the single rite, Korea, Can. 10: 'Baptism and Confirmation shall normally be administered as a

The duty to present candidates for confirmation is placed in most churches upon the baptismal sponsors and sometimes, in addition, upon the parents.[93] A special duty either to seek out or to encourage candidates is only occasionally imposed on ordained ministers.[94] To be eligible for confirmation candidates must, of course, be baptized: this is a universal requirement.[95] Where church laws differ, however, is with respect to additional qualifications. Only a very few churches require adult candidates to be 'regular worshippers'.[96] Some churches fix an appropriate age for confirmation, and this varies as between churches, or else they require the candidate to have attained the age of discretion.[97] Occasionally, in the case of adults, churches require 'evidence of repentance, faith and love towards Jesus Christ'.[98] Witnesses of confirmation are required in some churches as are certificates after confirmation.[99]

Provisions concerning preparation and instruction are similar to those applicable to baptism. As a general principle, all candidates must be instructed.[100] Laws effectively represent the terms of the 1603 Canons

single rite'; Papua New Guinea, *Anglican Prayer Book* 1991, 198: '[i]t is normally expected that baptism and confirmation will take place at the same service'; Brazil, BCP 1987: this treats a single rite as a 'preference'.

[93] Papua New Guinea, *Anglican Prayer Book* 1991, 198; Wales, BCP 1984, 654: it is the 'duty of Christians to see that their children are . . . confirmed'; in ECUSA, confirmation is treated as 'expected': BCP 1979, Marshall, Vol. II, 432.

[94] For the duty to seek, West Indies, Can. 30.2: every minister with cure of souls 'shall diligently seek out persons whom he think meet to be confirmed'; and England, Can. B27(2); for the duty to encourage, Ireland, Const. IX.28(1); and Australia, Can. P7 1992.

[95] See e.g. Scotland, Can. 30.2, 3; Wales, BCP 1984, 704; West Indies, Can. 30.4; England, Can. B27(4).

[96] See e.g. Wales, BCP 1984, 704; Papua New Guinea, *Anglican Prayer Book* 1991, 203.

[97] Melanesia, Can. A.3.A–D: normally the candidate must be at least 12, but the bishop has a discretion to confirm at an earlier age; Puerto Rico, Can. II.5.2: 12 years; Australia, Diocese of Sydney, *The 7th Handbook*, 8.4: 14 years; for those 'who have come to years of discretion', see West Indies, Can. 30.3, Australia, Can. P7 1992, 5 and England, Can. B27(3); Southern Africa, *Prayer Book* 1989, 364: 'an adult is a person whom the minister considers able to answer responsibly for himself'. For an analysis of diocesan practices in England, see J. Behrens, *Confirmation: Sacrament of Grace* (Leominster 1995), 36–49.

[98] North India, Const. I.I.V.5; for anxiety in the United Church of South India over the proposed non-adoption of confirmation in the 1950s, see G. F. S. Gray, *The Anglican Communion* (London, 1958), 157f; for the confirmation of polygamists, see LC 1988, Res. 110.

[99] For notice to the bishop and a list of candidates, see e.g. Philippines, Cans. III.16.3(c) and England, B27(4); Scotland, Can. 30.4: each candidate must have, 'wherever possible', a witness present as godparent at confirmation; for witnesses see also Wales, BCP 1984, 704 and Canada, BCP 1962, 561; for a certificate of confirmation signed by the bishop see Scotland, Can. 30.5.

[100] See e.g. Southern Africa, Can. 35.7: 'No person shall be confirmed unless he has been prepared in accordance with the forms of instruction as have been approved by the Bishop of the Diocese'; see also England, Can. B27(4): the minister shall 'use his best endeavour to instruct'; Chile, Cans. F.4; Scotland, Can. 30.2, 3; Ireland, Const. IX.28(1).

Ecclesiastical,[101] and, sometimes, those of Lambeth Conference resolutions which recommend instruction about repentance and the faith and practice of the church.[102] However, rules about delegation and the subjects and duration of instruction vary as between churches. Most churches allow ordained ministers to delegate the function of instructing to lay ministers.[103] The canon law of Melanesia contains both typical provisions on the subject of instruction and exceptional requirements: candidates 'must normally receive teaching' for two years which includes the Lord's Prayer, the Creed, the Ten Commandments and the provincial catechism; the priest 'must try to be sure of their faith and repentance and their wanting to try to live the Christian life'; and the priest must give candidates 'the chance to make their confession before confirmation'.[104] Whilst some laws simply require instruction in the 'Christian faith',[105] others echo the more specific Melanesian model; the Melanesian requirement about the period of preparation is unusual as is the requirement of confession;[106] the basic test is that candidates should be able to render an account of the subjects in which they receive instruction.[107]

[101] Canons Ecclesiastical 1603, Can. 61: 'none shall be presented to the Bishop for him to lay hands upon, but such as can render an account of their faith, according to the Catechism'; every minister was to 'prepare and make able, and likewise to procure as many as he can to be brought, and by the Bishop to be confirmed'.

[102] LC 1988, Res. 110: 'The Conference recommends that care should be taken to see that before confirmation all candidates are given definite instruction about repentance and about the means provided by God in his Church by which troubled consciences can obtain the assurance of his mercy and forgiveness'; LC 1988, Res. 112: the preparation of candidates should include, from their early years: (a) participation, with their family, in regular worship in church and at home; (b) group instruction in the church's faith and practice; (c) training in fellowship and service through membership of a parochial society or group; candidates 'should be led on to accept a rule of life comprising daily prayer and Bible reading, regular worship, and self-discipline, including almsgiving and personal service'.

[103] Brazil, Cans. III.1.2(c); by implication Wales, BCP 1984, 704; Australia, *A Prayer Book for Australia* 1995, 94: one godparent or sponsor should help candidates prepare; Melanesia, Cans. A.3.A–D: the priest may enlist the assistance of deacons, catechists, and teachers of religious education, 'but the final duty of preparation is his'; see LC 1920, Res. 52 and LC 1930, Res. 70 for delegation to deaconesses.

[104] Melanesia, Cans. A.3.A–D.

[105] Ireland, Const. IX.28(1): the minister must endeavour to instruct 'in the Christian faith and life as set forth in the Holy Scriptures, the Book of Common Prayer and the Church Catechism'; Australia, Can. P7 1992, 4: candidates must be instructed 'in the Christian faith and life, in Holy Scripture and in the Book of Common Prayer and the Catechism; see also Central Africa, Diocese of Mashonaland, *Pastoral Regulations* 1978, 8.

[106] See Papua New Guinea, *Anglican Prayer Book* 1991, 203: '[i]t is desirable that candidates should prepare for their confirmation and first communion by using the Sacrament of Penance'.

[107] See e.g. West Indies, Can. 30.3; Wales, BCP 1984, 704; England, Can. B27(3).

HOLY COMMUNION

According to traditional Anglican doctrine, the Holy Communion (the Eucharist or the Lord's Supper) is a sacrament instituted by Christ;[108] this doctrine appears in resolutions of Lambeth Conferences but only in a very few cases of actual law.[109] Most canons and liturgical rubrics treat the celebration of Holy Communion as 'the central act of worship'; some present it as an act of 'the whole church' or of the 'whole people of God'.[110] Reception of Holy Communion is also treated commonly as the consummation of Christian initiation.[111] Few laws make reference to the early English rejection of transubstantiation, though doctrines of the Eucharist as a memorial, sacrifice and real presence occasionally surface in law; but, as with baptism, there is too little legal evidence to propose that churches in the Communion possess a shared legal statement of the nature of Holy Communion.[112] Indeed, in only one celebrated judicial decision, from Australia, have doctrines of the nature of the Eucharist been considered in recent years by the secular judges.[113]

[108] AR, Arts. 25, 28; BCP 1662, 236; see generally, W. R. Crockett, 'Holy Communion', in Sykes and Booty (eds.), *The Study of Anglicanism* (London, 1988), 272ff; and S. Sykes, *Unashamed Anglicanism* (London, 1995), 30–45.

[109] LC 1888, Res. 11; LC 1988, Res. 18; Southern Africa, *Prayer Book* 1989, 101; Portugal, Can. 8.4.

[110] For the Eucharist as the central or principal act of worship see Chile, Can. D.7; Ireland, *Alternative Service Book* 1984, 18; Brazil, BCP 1987, 11; Wales, BCP 1984, 3; New Zealand, GS Standing Resolutions 1990, 1; for the Eucharist as an act of the 'whole people of God', see e.g. New Zealand, *Prayer Book* 1989, 403; and Canada, *Book of Alternative Services* 1985, 183.

[111] See e.g. Southern Africa, *Prayer Book* 1989, 363: 'Christian initiation is fulfilled in the Holy Communion'.

[112] For the rejection of transubstantiation, see AR, Arts. 31, 36; for the concept of memorial and sacrifice see Portugal, Can. 8.4; Melanesia, Cans. A.2.A–I: 'we believe we receive the true Body and Blood of Christ for our strengthening and for the offering of our souls and bodies to Him as a sacrifice'; New Zealand, GS Standing Resolutions 1990: the Eucharist is '[t]he sacramental means by which members of the Body [of Christ] are sustained and nurtured in that community'; see also *Prayer Book*, 403, 413: '[i]n the celebration of the Eucharist Christ gathers, teaches and nourishes the Church. It is Christ who invites to the meal and presides at it . . . the priest celebrates God's presence with us' (for a similar notion see South India, Const. II.6); Southern Africa, *Prayer Book* 1989: 101: 'his presence is made real among us'; Chile, Can. D.7: Christ is present in the bread and wine. For a discussion of the use of these ideas, and controversies associated with them, see G. F. S. Gray, *The Anglican Communion* (London, 1958), 112, 132, 139, 149.

[113] *Wylde v AG (NSW)* (1949) ALR 153; 22 ALJ 483 at 486 *per* Latham CJ, where he discusses the view that 'the doctrine of the Real Presence . . . [which] was to be distinguished from the doctrine of transubstantiation' could 'properly be held by members of the Church of England'.

Celebration

It is not a general practice of the Anglican Communion for churches to incorporate in national, regional or provincial laws a requirement obliging the regular administration of Holy Communion in churches of the diocese; the existence of such a requirement is exceptional,[114] and laws expressly enabling dispensation from it, in turn, are very rare indeed.[115] In contrast, frequent and regular participation in Holy Communion is often treated as a duty of the faithful; though provisions vary as to the occasions on which it must be received,[116] it may confidently be proposed that the obligation is a general principle of Anglican canon law. Except for the purposes of providing communion for the sick (considered below), Holy Communion must as a general rule be administered in a church building.[117] It is not unusual for church rules to prescribe that a given number of people must be present for the celebration of the Eucharist and generally in its celebration the prescribed orders of service must be used and observed.[118]

Not surprisingly, it is accepted as a matter of law throughout the Communion that the elements for Holy Communion are consecrated

---

[114] Australia, Can. P4 1992, 2: Holy Communion must be celebrated 'sufficiently frequently and at appropriate times so as to provide reasonable opportunity for every parishioner to communicate'; England, Can. B14: it must be celebrated in every parish church at least on all Sundays and principal Feast Days, on Ash Wednesday and Maundy Thursday; Ireland, Const. IX.13(1): it must be celebrated in every church or chapel at least once each month, unless the ordinary orders otherwise.

[115] England, Can. B14A: it may be dispensed with on an occasional basis by the minister and parochial church council acting jointly or on a more permanent basis if the bishop consents.

[116] England, Can. B15(1): '[i]t is the duty of all who have been confirmed to receive the Holy Communion regularly, and especially at the festivals of Christmas, Easter and Whitsun or Pentecost'; compare Australia, Can. P4 1992, 2: 'at least three times a year of which Easter is one'; Wales, BCP 1984, 3: '[e]very confirmed person should communicate regularly and frequently'; for the same formula, see e.g. *The Liturgy of the Church of Nigeria (Anglican Communion): The Order for Holy Communion or the Eucharist* 1983, vii (Direction 3) and Canada, BCP 1962, 66.

[117] See e.g. Korea, Can. 19: '[w]ithout the bishop's permission the Eucharist may not be celebrated outside a church, but, in an emergency or in unavoidable circumstances the place of celebration shall be at the judgment of the celebrant'; Ireland, Const. IX.14: ordinarily it must be celebrated in church but may be administered in any private house or 'other suitable place'; see also Canons Ecclesiastical 1603, Can. 71: ministers were not to administer it in private houses 'except it be in times of necessity'.

[118] See e.g. Ireland, *Alternative Prayer Book* 1984, 19: 'Holy Communion shall not be celebrated unless there is at least one person present to communicate together with the priest'; see also Canada, BCP 1962, 66 and New Zealand, *Prayer Book* 1989, 517. For compliance with liturgical books see Ch. 8; e.g. Ireland, Const. IX.13(2); ibid., (3),(4): the minister must not stand with his back to the people at any time when offering up public prayer; elevation of the paten and chalice beyond what is necessary for taking the same into the hands of the minister, and the ringing of bells during service are not permitted.

bread and wine: a variety of provisions exist. With respect to bread, they range from the idea that it must be 'wholesome' or that it must be made of pure wheat flour to ideas that it must be that which is 'usually eaten' and that wafer bread may be used in some circumstances; with respect to the wine, sometimes it must be fermented grape juice, sometimes pure grape juice – some churches prescribe that the elements must be provided by the churchwardens at the expense of the parish.[119] In accordance with resolutions of the Lambeth Conference, intinction is permissible, but commonly only with episcopal approval.[120] Liturgical rubrics also occasionally implement the principle enunciated by the Lambeth Conference that the giving of Holy Communion in both kinds is the normal practice, something 'according to the example and precept of our Lord'; thus, in rubrics, opportunity 'is always to be given to every communicant to receive the consecrated Bread and Wine separately'.[121]

The current debate about the possibility of lay presidency at the Eucharist has not, as yet, resulted in the alteration of actual law. The norm is that, when present, it is the bishop who presides; the American church

[119] LC 1908, Res. 32: 'the only elements which the Church can sanction for use in . . . Holy Communion are bread and wine, according to the institution of our Lord'; Ireland, Const. IX.13(5): the bread must be 'such as is usually eaten'; England, Can. B17(2): the bread may be leavened or unleavened but must be 'of the best and purest wheat flour', and the wine 'fermented juice of the grape, good and wholesome'; both are to be provided by the churchwardens; Australia, Can. P4, 5: the bread must be 'wholesome' and the wine 'fermented juice of the grape and of good quality'; the wine may be unfermented with episcopal approval; both 'shall be provided by incumbent and churchwardens at the expense of the parish'; see, however, LC 1888, Res. 2: 'the use of unfermented juice of the grape, or any liquid other than wine diluted or undiluted . . . is unwarranted by the example of our Lord, and is an unauthorised departure from the custom of the Catholic Church'; Korea, Can. 17: the bread must be of pure wheat flour and the wine pure grape wine; see Wales, BCP 1984, 22 for 'wheat bread' and 'pure grape wine to which a little water may be added'; for unleavened or leavened bread, see also Canada, BCP 1962, 74; Melanesia, Cans. A.2.A–I: only bread and pure wine mixed with water 'may be used'.

[120] LC 1908, Res. 31, LC 1948, Res. 118: 'any part of the Anglican Communion by provincial regulation according to its own Constitutional procedure has liberty to sanction administration by intinction as an optional alternative'; Ireland, Const. IX.13(5): the use of wafer bread is prohibited except in cases of illness where it is desirable to employ intinction (subject to conditions prescribed by the ordinary); West Indies, Can. 32.5.

[121] LC 1948, Res. 117; America, BCP 1979, Marshall, Vol. I, 385 and Canada, *The Book of Alternative Services* 1985, 184. For distribution from a table, see Wales, BCP 1984, 22; Australia, *A Prayer Book for Australia* 1995, 164; Canada, *Book of Alternative Services* 1985, 183. For the meaning of a 'table' in the Church of England, see *Re St Stephen's, Walbrook* [1987] 2 All ER 578; Ireland, Const. IX.15: the table must be movable, made of wood or other suitable material, with a covering approved by the ordinary (in *Carnduff and Others v Thomas and Another* (1991) GS Journal 1991, 302, the Court of General Synod considered an appeal from the Diocesan Court of Down and Dromore concerning the grant of a faculty to place a cross on the communion table; the appeal was dismissed; see also *Colquhoun and Others v Caithness and Others* (1940) GS Journal 1940, 413).

presents perhaps the strongest version of the principle: '[i]t is the bishop's prerogative, when present, to be the principal celebrant at the Lord's Table'.[122] When a bishop is not present, only episcopally ordained priests may preside.[123] However, today the vast majority of churches permit by law deacons or lay ministers specially licensed by the bishop to assist in the distribution of the elements. A comprehensive arrangement is to be found in regulations of the Church in Wales. The bishop may permit a lay person to assist the incumbent or other priest in the administration of the elements of the Holy Eucharist 'in a particular parish': (a) after consulting with the bishop, the incumbent must apply in writing naming the person and giving the reasons for the application; (b) the application must be accompanied by a certified copy of the resolution of the parochial church council supporting the request; and (c) such permission must be given for one year or a lesser period and 'may be renewed at the bishop's discretion'.[124] The regulation provides for no right of appeal against a refusal by the bishop.

In very many churches, special arrangements are made for administering holy communion to the sick. First, whilst formerly a matter of considerable controversy,[125] reservation of the sacrament in church is now lawful in all those churches which have provisions on the subject. In the canon law of Melanesia the sacrament may be reserved for the sick, dying or those 'in special need', as well as for devotional services, with the permission of the diocesan bishop; it must be kept in a safe place in the church.[126] The same basic scheme, though sometimes with subtle differences, is to be found in other churches but usually with less detail; for example, the canon law of the West Indies provides: '[i]t is the right *and duty* of a Priest with a cure of souls, if he considers it desirable for the spir-

---

[122] ECUSA, BCP 1979, Marshall, Vol. I, 311; Brazil, BCP 1987, 52 follows ECUSA; see also Wales BCP 1984, 22; Korea, Can. 16; Melanesia, Cans. A.2.A–I; compare South India, Const. II.6: '[i]n every communion the true celebrant is Christ alone'.

[123] Korea, Can. 16; Ireland, *Alternative Prayer Book* 1984, 19; North India, Const. I.I.V.17; Melanesia, Can. A.2.A–I; Nigeria, *The Liturgy of the Church of Nigeria (Anglican Communion): The Order for Holy Communion or the Eucharist* 1983, vii (Direction 1); Southern Africa, *Prayer Book* 1989, 103; Australia, Can. P4 1992, 3; Portugal, Can. 8.3; South India, Const. II.6: 'the custom of the church [is] that those only should exercise this function who have received full and solemn commission from the Church to do so; this commission has ordinarily been given by the laying on of hands in ordination'.

[124] Wales, Regulation for the Administration by a Lay Person of the Elements of the Eucharist; provisions in other churches are less detailed: see e.g. Australia, Can. 12 1973: this ceases to have effect in a diocese which adopts Can. 17 1992 concerning lay ministry; Melanesia, Can. A.2.A–I; Ireland, *Alternative Prayer Book* 1984, 19; the idea underlying LC 1958, Res. 91, that lay distribution should occur only in cases of 'pressing need', seems today simply to be implicit in legal arrangements.

[125] For the controversy in England, and the litigation to which it led, see R. D. H. Bursell, *Liturgy, Order and the Law* (Oxford, 1996), 274–277.

[126] Melanesia, Cans. A.2.A–I.

itual well-being of his people, to reserve the Blessed Sacrament permanently in his Church, subject to such Regulations as the Bishop from time to time shall make'.[127] Secondly, sick people enjoy a special right to the administration of Holy Communion in their homes. A typical provision is found in Ireland: ordinarily it is to be celebrated in churches, but it may be administered in any private house or 'other suitable place' (a) where any person due to illness or other sufficient cause is unable to attend church and (b) in any other circumstance, to be approved by the bishop.[128] Some churches place a duty on ministers to exhort the sick to receive Holy Communion, usually after preparation.[129] Other churches limit their right to absence through sickness for 'extended periods' when 'it is desirable that the priest arrange to celebrate the Eucharist . . . on a regular basis'.[130]

Admission

First, in order to qualify for admission to Holy Communion, in all churches the individual must be a baptized person.[131] In most churches,

---

[127] West Indies, Can. 32.4; see also Papua New Guinea, *Anglican Prayer Book* 1991, 214: '[i]t is the custom to reserve the sacrament in one kind'; Central Africa, Diocese of Mashonaland, *Pastoral Regulations* 1978, p. 20; Brazil, BCP 1987, 108; see also, generally, ECUSA, BCP 1979, Marshall, Vol. I, 385ff.; for England, see M. Hill, *Ecclesiastical Law* (London, 1995), 302–3, 408–9 and, especially, *Re Lapford Parish Church* [1954] 3 All ER 484 and *Re St John the Evangelist, Bierley* [1989] 3 All ER 214.

[128] Ireland, Const. IX.14; England, Can. B40; see also Canons Ecclesiastical 1603, Can. 71: ministers were not to administer the communion in private houses, 'except it be in times of necessity'.

[129] England, BCP 1662, 323–5 repeated largely in Canada, BCP 1962, 582: the curate 'shall exhort those who are sick and infirm to the often receiving of the holy Communion'; if they are unable to attend church, due notice must be given (except in cases of urgency) before Communion at home. If the person is too ill to receive the Body and Blood 'he shall be instructed that if he do truly repent him of his sins, and steadfastly believe that Jesus Christ hath suffered death upon the Cross for him, and shed his Blood for his redemption, earnestly remembering the benefits he hath thereby, and giving him hearty thanks therefor; he doth eat and drink the Body and Blood of our Saviour Christ profitably to his soul's health, although he do not receive the Sacrament with his mouth'; for similar provisions, see Ireland, BCP 1960, 278, 279; West Indies, Can. 32.6: it is lawful to give Communion 'to the sick and to those who through no fault of their own are unable to be present at the Celebration of the Holy Eucharist in one kind only, under the species of bread, with the permission of the Bishop and provided that no communicant who desires Communion in both kinds is refused'.

[130] ECUSA, BCP 1979, Marshall, Vol. I, 385ff.; Australia, *A Prayer Book for Australia* 1995, 693: at least two people should join in the celebration with the minister and the sick person.

[131] See e.g. ECUSA, Cans. I.17.7: 'No unbaptized person shall be eligible to receive Holy Communion'; Philippines, Cans. III.16.3(d): the minister must record in the parish register the names of all communicants within his cure; Japan, *The Eucharistic Liturgy* 1971, 3: '[i]f a communicant desires to receive Holy Communion in a Parish other than the one to which he belongs, he must give notice to the celebrant'.

moreover, the individual must be either confirmed or ready and desirous of being confirmed; it would seem that here those who are ready and desirous of confirmation would have a right to admission without, for example, prior episcopal permission.[132] In other churches, however, episcopal approval must be obtained; the canon law of the Scottish Episcopal Church contains perhaps the clearest expression of this approach: '[t]he normal rule of the Church is that none shall be admitted to the Holy Communion until confirmed or be ready and desirous to be confirmed'. However, '[w]ithout prejudice to the normal rule . . . a Bishop may, at the request of a Rector or Priest-in-Charge, and in accordance with the directions of the College of Bishops, admit to the Holy Communion such as are excluded by the normal rule'. In framing directions 'permitting departures from the normal rule, the College of Bishops shall make such reasonable inquiry as they think right, to satisfy themselves that the Causes are good and sufficient and not unacceptable to this Church generally'.[133] The problem of admission of the unconfirmed, particularly children, is dealt with sometimes by canon, sometimes by quasi-legislation and occasionally by a mixture; innovations are, broadly, ahead of Lambeth Conference resolutions.[134] Another interesting formal distinction between churches is that different churches assign competence to regulate the matter to different levels of the church.

For the church in New Zealand the subject is treated at provincial level by both canon law and quasi-legislation. By canon, notwithstanding the rubrics, 'it shall be permitted as alternative practice . . . for Baptized children to be admitted to Holy Communion prior to Confirmation after instruction approved by the Bishop'. The General Synod 'may from time to time approve guidelines which shall be followed in administering the alternative practice'. By quasi-legislation, '[b]aptism provides the ground for admission to the holy communion'; '[a]ll may therefore receive communion from the time of their Baptism irrespective of age'. Moreover, '[v]ariations in pastoral practice in relation to admission to communion may be found, but those once admitted . . . we welcome to receive com-

---

[132] England, Can. B15A: '[t]here shall be admitted to the Holy Communion . . . members of the Church . . . who have been confirmed . . . or are ready and desirous to be so confirmed'; Chile, Can. D.7; Canada, BCP 1962, 561; Melanesia, Cans. A.2.A–I: those who have been confirmed or are 'preparing for confirmation' are to be admitted.

[133] Scotland, Can. 25; Wales, BCP 1984, 704: '[e]xcept with the permission of the bishop no one shall receive Holy Communion until he is confirmed, or is ready and desirous of being confirmed'.

[134] LC 1948, Res. 103: 'it is not desirable to change the present sequence of Baptism, Confirmation, and admission to Holy Communion'; LC 1988: 'This Conference requests all provinces to consider the theological and pastoral issues involved in the admission of those baptized but unconfirmed to communion . . . and report their findings to the Anglican Consultative Council'.

munion in any parish in this Church'. Admission of the unconfirmed may occur 'when judged pastorally appropriate by priest and family, or at a special service after more formal instruction, or after receiving laying on of hands for confirmation'.[135]

For the Australian church, on the other hand, admission is subject to control directly by the representative diocesan assemblies rather than the provincial or national assembly. In Australia dioceses may adopt if they so wish the national canon of the General Synod concerning admission of children to Holy Communion: '[a] child who has been baptized but who has not been confirmed, is eligible to be admitted to the Holy Communion if the minister is satisfied that the child has been adequately instructed, gives evidence of appropriate understanding of the nature and meaning of the Holy Communion and has fulfilled the conditions of repentance and faith'. The child is also eligible if, with the sponsorship of his parents or other confirmed members of the congregation, he seeks admission while awaiting confirmation. The diocesan bishop may make regulations concerning the practice and procedure to be followed and the Diocesan Synod may by ordinance regulate the practice and procedure.[136]

By way of contrast, in the Church of England the subject is governed by quasi-legislation which provides for episcopal rather than synodical control at the level of the diocese – the quasi-legislation itself was created by the national House of Bishops. This prescribes that ' "communion before confirmation" is a departure from our inherited norm, [and] requires special permission'. However, '[a]fter consultation, every diocesan bishop will have the discretion to make a general policy whether or not to entertain new applications for "communion before confirmation" to take place in his diocese'. Individual parishes must seek his agreement before introducing it. The bishop 'should satisfy himself that both the Incumbent and the Parochial Church Council support any application, and that appropriate ecumenical partners have been consulted'. If the parties cannot agree, 'the bishop's direction shall be followed'. Applications should be determined not by the child's age but by 'his or her appreciation of the

---

[135] New Zealand, Cans. G.VIII.1–3: such people, however, are not eligible to take ecclesiastical office until confirmed; GS Standing Resolution, 1990.

[136] Australia, Can. 6 1985; this canon was passed previously as Can. P14 1981; in the Diocese of Melbourne, wishes of parents that children be admitted to Holy Communion before confirmation should be respected, 'but the anomalous standing of an unbaptised person in the congregation and Christian home should be discussed'. Three alternative practices are permitted: confirmation followed by first Communion for adults and young people in their teens; confirmation followed by first Communion from an early age; and admission of children to communion, followed by confirmation as a mature profession of faith. The incumbent and vestry should decide a clear policy and a change of policy should be made at the annual meeting or a special parish meeting convened for this purpose: Guidelines 1988, p. 19 and pp. 28, 29.

significance of the sacrament'; the decision is to be made by the parish priest after consultation with the parents and a serious pattern of preparation should be followed; a register should be kept of every baptized person admitted to Communion before confirmation. Finally, '[n]o baptized person, child or adult, who has once been admitted to Holy Communion and remains in good standing with the Church, should be anywhere deprived of it'.[137]

Exclusion

The pattern for the historic Anglican canon law on exclusion from Holy Communion was to be found, in part at least, in an English parliamentary statute, the Sacrament Act 1547, which conferred a general but conditional right of admission, and in the Canons Ecclesiastical 1603: those 'which be openly known to live in sin notorious, without repentance' and those who had 'maliciously and openly contended with their neighbours, until they shall be reconciled', were 'not to be admitted'.[138] The laws of the vast majority of Anglican churches contain provisions enabling the lifting of the right to Holy Communion, a process variously described as 'exclusion', 'repulsion', 'suspension' or 'excommunication'. There are, however, some important differences in both substantive laws and in procedure.

First, the laws of churches are broadly united as to the grounds for exclusion. Most laws allow exclusion of those who are 'living in grievous sin'; it is invariably required that this must be 'open' and 'without repentance'.[139] Those 'between whom [the minister] perceives malice and

[137] England, House of Bishops' Guidelines on Admission of Baptized Persons to Holy Communion before Confirmation 1997, GS Misc 488; for the debate in 1996 in the General Synod of the Church of Ireland, see M. Davey, 'General Synod of the Church of Ireland 1995', *Ecclesiastical Law Journal*, 3(17) (1995), 434 at 435; for an early example, see Diocese of Mashonaland, *Pastoral Regulations* 1978, 8(iii): this permits experiments with regard 'to the admission to Holy Communion of those not yet ready to commit themselves wholly in Confirmation'; this may be done with the permission of the bishop.

[138] Sacrament Act 1547, s. 8: 'the minister shall not without lawful cause deny the same to any person that will devoutly and humbly desire it'; Canons Ecclesiastical 1603, Can. 26; Can. 27 dealt with exclusion of schismatics; see also AR, Art. 33: 'That person which by open denunciation of the Church is rightly cut off from the unity of the Church, and excommunicated, ought to be taken of the whole multitude of the faithful, as an Heathen and Publican, until he be openly reconciled by penance, and received into the Church by a judge that hath authority thereunto'; for the silence of some churches on the subject today, see T. S. Culver, 'Canon B16: Excommunication in the Church of England', LL M dissertation, University of Wales, Cardiff, 1996, 41ff.

[139] England, Can. B16(1): this requires evidence of 'grave and open sin without repentance'; Scotland, Can. 26: 'living in open and unrepented sin'; see also Ireland, Const. IX.16; Southern Africa, Can. 35.8; ECUSA, BCP 1979, Marshall, Vol. I, 409: 'notoriously evil life'; Japan, *The Eucharistic Liturgy* 1971, 3; Canada, BCP 1962, 66.

hatred', without reconciliation and repentance, is similarly used extensively as a ground.[140] The same may be said of those in 'malicious and
open contention' without forgiveness or reconciliation, though the concept of injury to one's neighbour is rarely used as a ground.[141] Churches
which operate these grounds also permit exclusion of those whose conduct causes 'scandal to the congregation' or 'disrepute to the church'.[142]
Very rarely indeed do laws enable exclusion on the basis of 'contravention
of canonical regulations', though some permit it in the area of divorce and
remarriage.[143]

Secondly, church laws vary concerning the appropriate administrator of
exclusion. Some reserve all decisions of excommunication to the bishop.[144]
However, the normal minister of exclusion is the parish priest: importantly, some laws impose an obligation on the minister to exclude if the
grounds are made out, whilst others confer a discretion.[145] Thirdly, provisions vary as to the procedure to be adopted in cases of exclusion. The
process normally begins with a warning, some laws prescribing that this
must take place when the ground for exclusion comes to the attention of
the minister.[146] If a warning is not heeded, or if there is no evidence of

[140] Canada, BCP 1962, 66; ECUSA, BCP 1979, Marshall, Vol. I, 409; Australia, Can. P4
1992, 6; Japan, *The Eucharistic Liturgy* 1971, 3.
[141] England, Can. B16: this requires proof of 'malicious and open contention with his
neighbours'; Southern Africa, Can. 35.8; ECUSA, BCP 1979, Marshall, Vol. I, 409f.;
Japan, *The Eucharistic Liturgy* 1971, 3: anyone who 'has injured his neighbour' is subject
to exclusion.
[142] England, Can. B16(1): this requires evidence of 'grave and immediate scandal to
the congregation'; Wales, BCP 1984, 3: 'public conduct [which brings] the Church into
disrepute' without amendment of life; see also ECUSA, BCP 1979, Marshall Vol. I, 409;
Japan, *The Eucharistic Liturgy* 1971, 3: word and deed 'so that the congregation is thereby
offended'.
[143] Southern Africa, Can. 35.8: breach of 'canonical regulations of the Church' is a
ground; for excommunication and the divorced, and for those under public penance,
see Ch. 10.
[144] Scotland, Can. 26: 'it is the inherent right of a Bishop of a diocese to repel offend-
ers from Communion'; Wales, BCP 1984, 3: the minister must 'proceed as [the bishop]
directs'; North India, Const. I.I.VIII.6(g); Spain, Cans. I.7: there is to be no 'suspension'
unless the minister obtains prior authorisation from the diocesan bishop.
[145] Ireland, Const. IX.16: if they do not repent or they neglect pastoral advice, the
minister 'shall not admit'; England, Can. B16(1): 'in case of grave and immediate scandal . . . the minister shall not admit'; Canada, BCP 1962, 66: if they do not heed the warning the minister 'shall refuse'. Compare, South Africa, Can. 35.8: if the person fails to
heed admonition, the priest 'may' suspend; Australia, Can. P4 1992, 6: 'in the case of
grave and immediate scandal the minister, in the discretion of that minister, may refuse
to admit pending receipt of a direction from the bishop'; Scotland, Can. 26: in 'an
unforeseen urgent case', the priest, 'if satisfied of urgency, may refuse Communion to
such person until the matter can be brought before the Bishop'.
[146] Southern Africa, Can. 35.8: this requires admonition 'in private' and, if this fails,
'in the presence of other Communicants'; ECUSA, BCP 1979, Marshall, Vol. I, 409;
Brazil, BCP 1987, 108; Scotland, Can. 26; Wales, BCP 1984, 3; Canada, BCP 1962, 66: in

repentance or amendment of life, the minister must report the matter to the bishop; sometimes this duty arises at the same time as the warning.[147] A few churches require the bishop to instigate an investigation of the matter and often a duty is imposed on the bishop to hold an interview with the parties.[148] In the meantime, the individual is under some laws allowed admission and by others this is forbidden; occasionally, laws allow a minister to exclude summarily, particularly when there is an immediate likelihood of scandal.[149] Most churches confer a right of appeal against the bishop's direction, but some do not; in some cases the appeal is either to a court or to an assembly of bishops.[150] Lastly, provisions concerning restoration are equally diverse, though in most churches the law is silent on the matter. Very few laws require restitution in cases of contention,[151] nor do they provide that a minister alone may readmit on evidence of

common with the BCP 1662, this also prescribes that the minister 'shall frequently remind his people of what is required of them who come to receive the Lord's Supper'; Ireland, Const. IX.16: pastoral advice must be given.

[147] Scotland, Can. 26; Canada, BCP 1962, 66: this requires a written account within 14 days and consultation with the bishop or archdeacon; Wales, BCP 1984, 3; Ireland, Const. IX.16: this requires a report 'with details of the case'; Southern Africa, Can. 35.8: within 14 days; England, Can. B16(1): this imposes a duty to give an account and to obey the bishop's direction; ECUSA, BCP 1979, Marshall, Vol. I, 409: process must take place within 14 days and reasons must be given to the bishop; Japan, *The Eucharistic Liturgy* 1971, 3: this imposes a duty to inform the bishop 'with reasons'.

[148] Southern Africa, Can. 35.8: investigation is by the bishop (or the archdeacon or a commissary), 'in order to satisfy himself as to whether or not the priest has acted in accordance with the will of God as disclosed in Christ, the evidence of Holy Scriptures and the Canonical regulations'; for interviews see e.g. England, Can. B16(1); Scotland, Const. IX.16; Australia, Can. P4 1992, 6; ECUSA, Cans. I.17.6: any person repelled 'may lodge a complaint or application with the Bishop'; no cleric is required 'to admit to the Sacraments a person so refused or repelled without the written direction of the Bishop or Ecclesiastical Authority'; if it appears that there is a sufficient cause to justify refusal, 'appropriate steps shall be taken to institute such inquiry as may be directed by the Canons of the Diocese' in question; if no such canons exist, the bishop must proceed 'according to such principles of law and equity as will insure an impartial investigation and judgment'; the same procedure appears in Philippines, Cans. II.2.5.(d); see also E. A. White, *American Church Law* (New York, 1898), 284 for a 19th century case from the Diocese of New York in which Bishop Onderdonk decided that ministers could not exercise the power of repulsion 'in cases of differences or disputes in which [they] themselves or their families were parties'.

[149] See n. 145.

[150] Scotland, Can. 26: a person repelled may require the bishop to consult the College of Bishops as to whether the order of repulsion should be recalled; the bishop must give effect to the College's opinion which must be communicated to the excluded person (the bishop has a similar right of appeal to the College); Ireland, Const. IX.16: right of appeal lies to the diocesan court; compare Southern Africa, Can. 35: the bishop 'may' refer the matter to the diocesan tribunal 'whose decision shall be final'.

[151] This is undefined: see e.g. ECUSA, BCP 1979, Marshall, Vol. I, 409f.; Philippines, Cans. II.2.5(d); Japan, *The Eucharistic Liturgy* 1971, 3.

repentance.[152] More usually the right to restore is reserved to the bishop alone, perhaps acting on the recommendation of the minister.[153] No church requires expressly the giving of reasons for exclusion. Occasionally, laws deal expressly with the legal effects of excommunication.[154]

At this point it may be useful to present in outline the law of a single church in order to draw together the strands of this bewildering array of principles and approaches to exclusion from Holy Communion. The canon law of the Province of the West Indies, whilst untypical in some respects, contains a comprehensive treatment of the subject. It provides that anyone 'guilty' of a prescribed list of acts or other instances of 'uncleanness or wickedness shall not partake of Holy Communion unless they repent'. The canon, uniquely, enumerates the grounds for exclusion as follows: 'adultery, fornication, prostitution, cohabitation outside the bonds of marriage, sodomy, incest, blasphemy, habitual drunkenness or other drug abuse . . . indictable offences including theft, child abuse, crimes of violence and drug trafficking'. Similarly, any communicant member of the church 'who adheres persistently to any of the schismatic sects shall not be admitted . . . until he repents of his error and has been duly restored to the fellowship of the Church'. Moreover, those who have been 'open and notorious evil-livers, being openly known to have offended' may be required to make 'an open declaration of repentance and purpose of amendment, or a private confession to a Priest' before being admitted to the sacrament. Any person refused admission or repelled is entitled to lodge a complaint with the bishop. The bishop may require the person to be readmitted or restored for 'insufficiency of the cause assigned by the Parish Priest'. Rather than ordering restoration, the bishop may institute an enquiry which must be conducted 'according to such principles of law and equity as will serve to secure an impartial decision'. In any event, no priest is required to admit a person so refused or repelled without the written direction of the bishop.[155]

---

[152] See e.g. Canada, BCP 1962, 66.

[153] For episcopal control over restoration, see: Ireland, Const. IX.16: the minister must be satisfied of 'sincere repentance', then notify the bishop who, if also satisfied, 'shall restore the penitent'; Southern Africa, Can. 30.13: restoration is at the discretion of the bishop on the recommendation of the incumbent; if the incumbent declines or refuses to recommend, the parochial church council may do so; the suspended person may also apply directly to the bishop; Puerto Rico, Cans. II.5.8: restoration by the bishop for 'sufficient cause'; ECUSA, Cans. I.17.6; North India, Const. I.I.II.7: '[t]he Church is . . . responsible for persons who have been excommunicated' in order 'to bring them back to full communion'.

[154] See Chs. 6 and 10.

[155] West Indies, Can. 26: elements of this are found in the canon law of ECUSA: see n. 148.

Finally, whereas, by and large, secular states are indifferent to the administration of baptism and confirmation, there is considerable evidence to suggest that with regard to exclusion from holy communion secular courts are prepared to intervene in order to ensure compliance by ecclesiastical authorities with internal church law on the subject. Some of the cases deal specifically with Anglican churches and some with other churches; principles applied to the latter are likely to apply to the former. In England, the courts may intervene because the right to holy communion in the Church of England is one recognized at common law; exclusion must be for 'lawful cause'.[156] On one occasion a Canadian court declined jurisdiction over the refusal by an Anglican priest to admit.[157] In a New Zealand case concerning the Anglican church, the court decided that the matter was most appropriately dealt with by the church tribunals.[158] In the USA, a series of cases concerning exclusion from the rites of religious communities generally establishes that the matter is justiciable: internal procedures must be complied with.[159] The same approach has been adopted in Southern Africa.[160] In India state legislation preventing excommunication on grounds other than religious grounds has been held to be unconstitutional.[161]

CONCLUSIONS

The majority of churches in the Anglican Communion possess law, usually in the form of canons or liturgical rubrics, on all three rites of baptism,

---

[156] *R v Dibdin* [1910] P 57.   [157] *Dunnet v Forneri* (1877) 25 Gr 199.

[158] *Baldwin v Pascoe* (1889) 7 NZLR 759; also, *per* Dennison J: 'If the plaintiff is legally entitled, under certain conditions, to have the sacrament in question administered to her by the defendant, his motive in refusing cannot affect her rights. If she were entitled an honest belief that she was not would not excuse him'; however, '[t]he refusal or neglect to perform them seems to me to be no violation of any duty or breach of duty-contract cognisable by a Court of Law'.

[159] *Kennedy v Gray*, 248 Kan 486, 807 P 2d 670: there must be 'substantial compliance' with internal procedures on expulsion; *Servatlus v Pickee*, 34 Wis 292: the excommunication must be *bona fide* (if it is, the minister is not open to an action for slander); compare, for judicial reluctance, *Merman v St Mary's Greek Catholic Church of Nesquehoning*, 176 A 450, 317 Pa 33 and *Konkel v Metropolitan Baptist Church Inc.*, App., 572 P 2d 99, 117 Ariz 271; *Farmworth v Storrs*, 59 Mass 412: reading a sentence of excommunication from the pulpit is privileged.

[160] *Jamie and Others v African Congregational Church* [1971(3)] SALR 836: the court would not interfere 'at this stage', prior to confirmation of an excommunication by the church's annual conference (the court relied on the idea in the English case of *Kemp v Wickes* (1809) 3 Phillim 264 that excommunication results in exclusion from 'the Christian Church Universal'); see also *Van Vuuren v Kerkraad van die Morelig Gemeente van die NG Kerk in die OVS* [1979(4)] SALR 548.

[161] *Saifuddin Saheb v Bombay* (1962) Supp 2 SCR 496 (concerning the Bombay Prevention of Excommunication Act 1949); see also *Commonwealth Law Bulletin*, 15(3) (1989), 891 and H. M. Seervai, *Constitutional Law of India* (Bombay, 1983), 907ff.

confirmation and Holy Communion. The administration of these rites is, generally, subject to the oversight of the diocesan bishop. Legal unity within the Communion is indicated by the existence of a set of shared or common principles deducible from actual laws. The traditional sequence of the three initiatory rites is maintained as a matter of law in most churches, though in a small minority both canonical provisions and quasi-legislation are beginning to allow for the admission of the unconfirmed to Holy Communion. And there is broad consistency concerning the legal prerequisites for the valid celebration of these rites. Perhaps the most significant achievement of churches is the incorporation in their laws of a system of enforceable rights to baptism, confirmation and Holy Communion. But these rights are conditional and it is the terms of the diverse conditions to be found that produce differences both in substantive law and in procedure. Generally, state intervention operates only with respect to exclusion from Holy Communion: the secular courts interfere only to ensure compliance with internal church laws.

10

Marriage, Divorce, Confession and Funerals

Marriage and confession are two areas of canon law in the Anglican Communion which have undergone radical changes in recent years. In the case of marriage, the stimulus for change has been the shift in secular society and law toward the greater incidence and availability of civil divorce. These developments have resulted in reconsideration by churches of fundamental questions about the nature of marriage and the treatment of 'remarriages' of divorced persons in church. This, in turn, has led to the emergence of sometimes very different legal rules on marriage discipline regulating directly the substantive decision of ministers to solemnize second marriages following civil dissolution. The influence of resolutions of the Lambeth Conference has been prominent in this regard. Developments in the secular sphere, concerning disclosure of information obtained about child abuse and associated subjects, have also led in some instances to a readjustment of the church's traditional stance on the inviolability of the seal of the confessional. This Chapter explores these issues and it describes church law on the use of funeral rites. Needless to say, the following study makes reference to the abundant secular laws on these subjects, in states in which Anglican churches exist, only where appropriate.

MARRIAGE

According to classical Anglican doctrine, marriage is treated not as a sacrament but as sacramental in nature: it is 'an honourable estate, instituted of God in the time of man's innocency, signifying unto us the mystical union that is betwixt Christ and his Church'; it is treated as more than a contract, but it springs from a contract, from the free exchange of consents, a state in which the parties are 'joined together by God'.[1] The concept of the divine institution of marriage, recognized in Lambeth Conference resolutions,[2] commonly surfaces in church law: sometimes it

[1] BCP 1662, 301, 303, 305; AR, Art. 25; see generally G. F. S. Gray, *The Anglican Communion* (London, 1958), 114, 131, 141; and for marriage and divorce see J. W. C. Wand (ed.), *The Anglican Communion* (Oxford, 1948), 25, 45, 131–2, 170, 181, 219, 225 and 284.

[2] LC 1988, Res. 26; LC 1968, Res. 23; LC 1958, Res. 120: these include affirmation of monogamous marriage as a divine institution; see e.g. Nigeria, Cans. Ch.18.3 for the

appears in the canons, when occasionally it is described as a 'sacrament',[3] or that the church affirms its nature 'according to the teaching of Christ',[4] but most usually it appears in liturgical rubrics.[5]

The law of all churches advances the concept of the permanence of marriage. On the one hand, in line with Lambeth Conference resolutions, most laws provide descriptively that marriage 'is' a lifelong union, lasting until the death of one partner.[6] On the other hand, the laws of some churches present marriage as 'intended' to be a permanent union: the church in New Zealand, for example, holds that '[m]arriage is intended by God to be a . . . life-long covenant'; the canon law of the West Indies treats 'the ideal of Christian Marriage as a lifelong union'.[7] This divinely instituted union is exclusive, a 'partnership between one man and one woman'.[8] As to the conduct of married life and its purpose, the classical doctrine is that marriage, which signifies the mystical union between Christ and his church, is for the procreation and nurture of children, to direct the natural instincts and affections, and for the mutual society, help and comfort which the one ought to have for the other, both in prosperity and adversity.[9] The laws of many churches incorporate expressly these traditional elements.[10] Some churches stress the organic nature of marriage. The canon law of New

effect of polygamy; see also *AG v Reid* (1965) LXVII Nigerian Law Reports 25: a person who contracts Christian monogamous marriage has the right to change their religion and contract polygamous marriage.

[3] For the idea of a marriage as a 'divine institution', see e.g. West Africa, Can. 7.1; Nigeria, Cans. Ch.18.5; Southern Africa, Can. 34; Papua New Guinea, Can. No. 2 of 1995, Arts. 1–5: 'marriage is the sacrament endorsed by Christ himself'; Scotland, Can. 31.1: it is 'instituted of God'; Canada, Can. 21.1, 2: the 'union is established by God's grace' and is 'of God's creation'; North India, Const. VI.1. For the idea of marriage as a 'divine vocation', see Australia, Diocese of Melbourne, *Pastoral Handbook* 1988, p. 37.

[4] New Zealand, Cans. G.III.1.1.1: this affirms 'the teaching of our Lord Jesus Christ'; England, Can. B30(1): affirms the nature of marriage 'according to our Lord's teaching'; Ireland, Const. IX.31.1.

[5] Wales, BCP 1984, 699: it is 'instituted by God'; Southern Africa, *Prayer Book* 1989, 457; Brazil, BCP 1987, 182; Canada, BCP 1962, 564; Southern Cone, BCP 1973, 65.

[6] LC 1958, Res. 119; England, Can. B30(1): 'marriage is in its nature a union permanent and lifelong'; Central Africa, Resolution 1969; West Africa, Can. 7; Wales, BCP 1984, 736; Melanesia, Cans. A.4.A–C; Southern Africa, Can. 34; Korea, Can. 25; Brazil, Can. 13; Chile, Can. G.1.

[7] New Zealand, *Prayer Book*, 779; West Indies, Can. 29.1; ECUSA, Cans. I.18.2: it is entered 'with the intent that it be lifelong'; Melanesia, Cans. A.4; North India, Const. VI.8; South India, Const. XII.5.

[8] West Africa, Can. 7.1; England, Can. 30(1); New Zealand, Cans. G.III.1.1.1; Melanesia, Cans. A.4.A–C; ECUSA, Cans. I.18.2(a)–(c); Southern Africa, Can. 34: this affirms that 'marriage is by divine institution a lifelong and exclusive union partnership between one man and one woman'.

[9] BCP 1662, 302; LC 1956, Res. 113.

[10] England, Can. B30(1); Ireland, Const. IX.31.1; Scotland, Can. 31.1: 'The Doctrine of this Church is that Marriage is a physical, spiritual and mystical union'; ECUSA, Cans. I.18.2: marriage is 'a physical and spiritual union'; Philippines, Can. III.16.4.

Zealand has probably the most comprehensive and detailed presentation of the idea. Marriage is 'a relationship which is part of God's fundamental purpose for the human race' – it is 'a creative relationship . . . an invitation to share life together in the spirit of Jesus Christ'. Its purpose is 'the full development of the personalities of husband and wife by the right use of the natural instincts', through mutual help and comfort, 'and the establishment of a home and family life'. The New Zealand canons also state that marriage and the conduct of married life 'both have importance for the wellbeing of society'; '[t]he family is the basic human unit' and the 'social and moral health of the life of any community is bound up with the quality of its family life'. As such, '[a]ll members of this Church share according to their circumstances in the obligation to uphold Christian standards of marriage in human society especially by care for their own families and by neighbourly care for the families of others'.[11]

The Right to Marry in Church

An examination of the canon law of churches in the Anglican Communion discloses two apparently contradictory approaches to marriage in church: in some churches the law recognizes a ministerial duty to solemnize; in most, ministers enjoy a discretion as to whether or not to solemnize. The consequences for those seeking a celebration of holy matrimony are profound. According to the one jurisprudence, they have a right to marry in church; according to the other they do not. In the established Church of England it is commonly assumed that any person resident in a parish has a legal right to be married in the parish church. Ministers are under, therefore, a correlative duty to solemnize the marriages of parishioners on request. Ministerial failure to fulfil this duty may be the subject of judicial proceedings in the church courts for neglect of duty.[12] Much the same sys-

---

[11] New Zealand, Can. G.III.1.1.1; see also Can. G.III.1.1.4: 'In marriage the sexual act is recognized as the means of declaring the deepest and most complete personal exchange of love and its significance is fully experienced and expressed in a life-long commitment . . . [it] symbolise[s] . . . the complete committing of one human being to another'; see also *Prayer Book* 1989, 779; for almost exactly the same approach and formulae, see Canada, Can. 21 which includes the principle: '[t]he purposes of marriage are mutual fellowship, support, and comfort . . . and the creation of a relationship in which sexuality may serve personal fulfilment in a community of faithful love'; Southern Africa, *Prayer Book* 1989, 459.

[12] The right is associated with the established position of the church and the idea that any resident may call upon its ministrations; the right has been recognized both in the church courts and in the secular law courts: see e.g. *Argar v Holdsworth* (1758) 2 Lee 515, 161 ER 424; *Tuckness v Alexander* (1863) 32 Ch 794; see also the secular cases of *Davis v Black* (1841) 1 QB 900; *R v James* (1850) 3 Car & Kir 167; 175 ER 506. For a critical study of this see LFCE, 358ff.

tem is said to apply to the disestablished Church in Wales.[13] By way of contrast, the laws of the vast majority of churches in the Anglican Communion contain no explicit reference to 'a right to marry in church'. On the contrary, when the subject is treated the laws of churches instead emphasise the discretionary nature of admission to church for marriage. The canon law of ECUSA provides that '[i]t shall be within the discretion of any Member of the Clergy of this Church to decline to solemnize any marriage'. This is typical of the laws of a number of churches, some of which, in turn, expressly enable ministerial refusal to solemnize by means of a right of conscientious objection.[14] Whichever model is employed, in relation to both approaches the church is not free to solemnize any marriage it pleases; the church must not solemnize marriages if they are contrary to the law of the state. Indeed, this overriding condition is of itself recognized in the laws of most Anglican churches: no minister of the church may solemnize a marriage unless the proposed union satisfies the secular legal criteria on validity (see below). In other words, what all churches have in common is that ministerial execution of both the duty to marry (the English model) and the discretion to marry (the ECUSA model) is contingent upon the proposed marriage being valid under secular law. In each case the hands of the church are tied – it is this feature of the wider, secular legal environment that produces a legal unity for churches in the Anglican Communion.

Whilst churches are not at liberty to solemnize marriages forbidden by secular law, they may be at liberty to impose additional ecclesiastical conditions for the purposes of marriage in church. Even though parties have capacity under secular law, admission to marriage in church is barred if the ecclesiastical condition is not met. The classical doctrine, needless to say, is that Christian marriage is a union of two Christians. In several churches, therefore, canon law forbids clergy to solemnize proposed

[13] In Wales the right to marry in the parish church has survived disestablishment: *Cure of Souls* (1995), 9 and T. G. Watkin, 'Disestablishment, self-determination and the constitutional development of the Church in Wales', in N. Doe (ed.), *Essays in Canon Law* (Cardiff, 1992), 25 at 33.

[14] ECUSA, Can. I.18.4; Philippines, Cans. III.16.4(d); New Zealand, Can. G.III.2.9.3: 'The discretion of a minister to decline to solemnize any particular marriage shall not be abrogated by this Canon'; for the same formula see Canada, Can. 21.11; Kenya, Can. 14: 'No minister shall be compelled to solemnize any marriage' nor shall he be 'required without his consent to make his Church available for the solemnization of any marriage by another minister provided that if he shall refuse consent the aggrieved parties may appeal to the Bishop whose decision shall be final'; for a ministerial right of conscientious objection, see Brazil, Can. 13, Art. 7; North India, Const. VI.5 and West Indies, Can. 29.6: 'It shall be within the discretion of any Clergyman to decline to solemnize any marriage on grounds of conscience only'; Korea, Can. 24: 'One who is suspended from Holy Communion or excommunicated may not receive the Sacrament of Holy Matrimony' according to the rites of the Church'.

marriages of those who are not baptized. Once more, however, there is little overall legal unity in the Anglican Communion on this subject: whilst some churches treat baptism as an ecclesiastical precondition to solemnization, others do not. On the one hand, in the Church of England, the right to marry in the parish church is enjoyed irrespective of whether the person is a Christian – generally, there is no ecclesiastical requirement that both parties, or indeed either of them, be baptized. Consequently, a minister may not refuse to solemnize the marriage of a Christian to a non-Christian nor that of two non-Christians.[15] This is not the norm in Anglican canon law. On the other hand, therefore, the laws of most churches in the Communion refer in one way or another to baptism as a precondition. Two very separate rules are used. First, some churches require one of the parties at least to be baptized – solemnization is forbidden if both are unbaptized. In these the basic rule is expressed in two forms: there is to be no marriage in church unless one of the parties is baptized;[16] or else, there is to be no marriage in church when neither party has been baptized.[17] These are differences of form only. Secondly, in a small number of churches laws expressly state that marriage is permitted only if both parties are baptized: under the canon law of Korea '[t]he marriage service may only be used by Christians who are baptized'.[18] The laws of a few African provinces employ the concept of 'reservation' of holy matri-

[15] England, House of Bishops' *Guidelines for the Celebration of Mixed-Faith Marriages in Church* (1992), para. 2: this applies to marriage by banns; however, marriage by episcopal common licence or archiepiscopal special licence may be refused for lack of baptism; the Court Arches in *Jenkins v Barrett* (1827) 1 Hag Ecc 12 declined to decide the point. The matter has been the subject of debate: *Acts of Convocation*, 93: 'the clergy should not be bound by the law of England to celebrate the marriage in church of two persons of whom neither has been or is willing to be baptized'; see also *The Canon Law of the Church of England*, Report of the Archbishops' Commission (London, 1947), 126, draft Can. 37. Also, some diocesan norms prescribe that where both are unbaptized 'they should not be married': see e.g. Diocese of Carlisle, *Diocesan Handbook* (1990), 100, 101. The canons of both the Episcopal Scottish Church and the Church of Ireland seem to be silent on the matter.

[16] Australia, Can. 3 1981, 3(b): 'Matrimony shall not be solemnized according to the rites and ceremonies of this Church . . . unless at least one of the parties to be married has been baptized'; ECUSA, Can. I.18.2(d); Papua New Guinea, Can. No. 2 of 1995, Art. 8f; Philippines, Cans. III.16.4; Brazil, BCP 1987, 182.

[17] New Zealand, Can. G.III.2.8: '[n]o minister shall solemnize Matrimony between two persons neither of whom has been baptized'; Southern Africa, Can. 34.2: '[n]o clergyman shall join in matrimony two unbaptized persons'; Canada, Can. 21.10: 'No minister shall solemnize matrimony between two persons neither of whom has been baptized'; for exactly the same formula see Central Africa, Can. 22.1; West Indies, Can. 29.2.

[18] Korea, Can. 22; North India, Const. VI.9: 'No minister of the Church may solemnize the marriage of a Christian with a non-Christian'; Kenya, Can. 14.v.1: 'A Minister shall not solemnize Matrimony or allow Matrimony to be solemnized in this Church except between two persons both of whom have been baptized or who show a serious desire to be baptized'.

mony to the baptized.[19] Those laws which forbid marriage if both parties are unbaptized contain express provision allowing relaxation of the basic rule.[20] It is usual for those churches whose laws allow marriage when one party is unbaptized, to control such cases by referral to the diocesan bishop – though, occasionally, churches permit marriage without involving the bishop if the unbaptized partner is under instruction for baptism.[21] Sometimes, where a referral is required, the law prescribes that the minister must follow the bishop's direction.[22] For several churches, notably those in Africa, the law enables relaxation from a general bar by means of episcopal dispensation. According to the law of the church in West Africa, 'a dispensation [may] be granted by the Bishop' provided listed conditions are satisfied; these are as follows: that 'both parties . . . recognize that the marriage will be a Christian marriage identical in status to a marriage' between two baptized persons; that the unbaptized person intends to live 'according to the Christian law of marriage'; and that both parties 'intend and will give an undertaking that any children resulting from the marriage shall be baptized and brought up as Christians'.[23]

The use of conditions, assurances and undertakings about the future conduct in the marriage of the unbaptized partner, is dealt with in a small number of churches under the canonical title of *mixed marriages* – those between baptized Anglicans and members of other religious faiths. Sometimes conditions are treated by ecclesiastical quasi-legislation, expressed in directory rather than in mandatory terms. In England mixed

[19] Kenya, Can. 14.ii; see Nigeria, Cans. Ch.18.1(a) and Central Africa, Can. 7.3(a) for the idea that matrimony is 'reserved' to those who are baptized.

[20] For an exception, see Kenya, Can. 14.v.2: 'The marriage of a baptized person with an unbaptized person or of two unbaptized persons shall not take place without the prior permission of the Bishop, who shall decide upon what conditions such marriage may take place' and upon the form of service; Korea, Can. 23: 'When a member of the church wishes to marry a non-Christian or a member of another denomination he must seek a dispensation from the bishop'; North India, Const. VI.9: 'The bishop of the Diocese . . . may in special cases permit after due investigation the marriage of a Christian with a catechumen'; see also South India, Const. XII.6: marriage of those unbaptized but under 'regular instruction for baptism' may be authorized by the diocesan council.

[21] Southern Africa, Can. 34.2: 'A baptized person may be joined in matrimony to one who is under instruction for baptism'; Papua New Guinea, Can. No. 2 1995, Arts. 8–15.

[22] Wales, BCP 1984, 736: 'If one of the parties is unbaptized the Minister shall act in accordance with the Bishop's direction'; Canada, Can. 21.10: 'If two persons, one of whom has not been baptized, desire to be married, the minister shall refer the matter to the bishop of the diocese whose order and direction shall be followed'; West Indies, Can. 29.2: the bishop's decision 'shall be final'.

[23] West Africa, Can. 7.3(a)–(b); for a similar arrangement see Nigeria, Cans. Ch. 18.1; Central Africa, Can. 22: prior dispensation is required; Kenya, Can. 14.v.2–3; Southern Africa, Can. 34.2: 'The Bishop may allow the marriage of a baptized person with an unbaptized person (not under instruction for baptism) under such conditions and with such forms of service as he shall direct'.

marriages are dealt with by ecclesiastical quasi-legislation under which ministers should be satisfied that the party of a faith other than Christianity does not, nor is likely to, reject the Christian faith. This English ecclesiastical quasi-legislation does not, of course, generate any enforceable rights or duties: the minister cannot refuse to solemnize even if the non-Christian party is antagonistic to Christianity – as a matter of law, all parishioners, including parishioners of other faiths, have a right to marriage in the parish church.[24] The canon law of Kenya contains perhaps the most sophisticated treatment of conditions applicable to mixed marriages. It provides that '[a] baptized member of the Church ought not to enter into [a] marriage with a person other than a member of the Anglican Church' when this may involve 'the acceptance of conditions imposed without option by any other religion or denomination'. Moreover, the church recognizes 'no legal or moral obligation to accept such conditions'. Similarly, under Kenyan canon law, 'a baptized member of the Church who wishes to marry a baptized member of another Christian denomination may be married according to the rites of either Church provided that no such conditions are imposed'.[25]

Preparation and Preliminaries

It is a general principle of Anglican canon law, deduced from the actual laws of churches, that parties to marriage must undergo preparation. The form and duration of preparation, and requirements as to the effect of instruction upon the parties, vary from church to church. Some churches, such as in the Province of Southern Africa, forbid marriage of persons 'until they have received such instruction on Christian Marriage as has been approved by the Bishop of the Diocese'.[26] Others do not require episcopal approval of the form of instruction.[27] Often laws require that the parties understand the nature, meaning and purpose of marriage: in West Africa, the canons forbid a minister to solemnize a marriage unless '[h]e shall have ascertained that both parties understand that Holy Matrimony

---

[24] England, House of Bishops' *Guidelines for the Celebration of Mixed-Faith Marriages in Church* (1992): with marriage by banns, there is a legal duty to marry; when marriage is by episcopal common licence or by archiepiscopal special licence the granting of permission and the imposition conditions are discretionary.

[25] Kenya, Can. 14.vii; see also Korea, Can. 28: 'A "mixed marriage" for which a bishop's dispensation has been obtained must be celebrated by the priest in charge of the church to which the Christian partner belongs and in accordance with the rites of the Anglican Church of Korea. The bishop's dispensation must be obtained to omit the Nuptial Mass'.

[26] Southern Africa, Can. 35.6.

[27] Japan, Can. 16; Puerto Rico, Cans. II.6; Wales, BCP 1984, 736: 'All who wish to be married . . . are to receive due instruction from the Minister of the parish'.

is a physical and spiritual union . . . entered into within the community of faith, by actual consent of heart, mind and will, and with the intent that it be lifelong'.[28] In marked contrast, other churches simply require 'explanation' of marriage; in England there is a duty on the minister only 'to explain to the two persons who desire to be married the Church's doctrine of marriage . . . and the need of God's grace in order that they may discharge aright their obligations as married persons'; Kenya only, it seems, mixes these two contrasting approaches.[29] The canon law of one church, the Canadian, requires additionally that the minister embarks on a detailed investigation as to how the couple will deal with financial planning, potential religious differences, the reaction of families, lifestyle, home relationships, sexual relations, the rearing and education of children, and even career conflicts – but this approach to preparation is exceptional.[30]

As a fundamental preliminary, laws generally impose the duty on parties to give notice of the proposed marriage; prescribed periods vary and often provisions concerning notice allow for ministerial dispensation.[31] Usually, notice is accompanied by the requirement that banns must be published in church on three occasions during the weeks before the day of solemnization. This is an ancient requirement of English ecclesiastical law and it is to be found in the laws of many Anglican churches.[32] A related duty, placed on the minister, is to make enquiry as to possible legal impediments to the marriage.[33] Seldom, however, do church laws expressly spell out the legal consequences for the minister in the event of a failure to make

[28] West Africa, Can. 7.4(b); ECUSA, Cans. I.18.2(a)–(c); Philippines, Cans. III.16.4; Melanesia, Cans. A.4.D-G; Papua New Guinea, Can. No. 2 of 1995, Arts. 8–15: they must receive 'suitable preparation'; West Indies, Can. 29.3.

[29] England, Can. B30(3); New Zealand, Can. G.III.1.3.1: instruction 'should include serious consideration of all the responsibilities of life in marriage and home'; there is also a duty to provide continuing education (1.3.2). For a mixture of the two approaches, see Kenya, Can. 14.ii.3: '[i]t is the duty of the parish priest to interview those who desire to be married, to explain to them the nature and the obligations of Christian marriage, and, as far as lies in his power, to make sure that when they come to the Church to be married they will understand the promises which they will make in the presence of God and of the congregation'.

[30] Canada, Can. 21.2 and Sched. E; see n. 23 for instruction of an unbaptized party.

[31] For 30 days, see ECUSA, Can. I.18.3; Philippines, Can. III.16.4(c); New Zealand, Can. G.III.2.1; West Africa, Can. 7.5(a); for 60 days, see Canada, Can. 21.1.

[32] England, Can. B34: this also allows marriage by a bishop's common licence or by the Archbishop of Canterbury's special licence; Wales, BCP 1984, 736; Ireland, BCP 1960, 266; Japan, Can. 16; Brazil, Cans. III.13; Canada, Can. 21.6, 7; Korea, Can. 30: episcopal dispensation is permitted; Melanesia, Cans. A.4.D-G; ECUSA, BCP 1979, Marshall, Vol. II, 439: it is optional; Nigeria, Can. 18.

[33] England, Can. B33; West Africa, Can. 7.4(a); New Zealand, Can. G.III.2.2; Canada, Can. 21.2; North India, Const. VI.10, 11; South India, Const. XII.8; Philippines, Cans. III.16.4.

the necessary enquiries – in so far as churches cast this duty, it may be presumed that failure to comply with it might constitute an ecclesiastical offence of neglect of duty, for which in serious cases proceedings may be brought in the church courts (see Chapter 3). In addition to challenges on the basis of impediments under secular law, churches sometimes allow challenges to the proposed marriage grounded on 'the law of God'; this right of challenge ordinarily appears in liturgical rubrics.[34] Occasionally, these require the payment of a surety to cover consequential loss. In Australia, for example, rubrics contain the principle that '[a]ny person alleging an impediment on the occasion of marriage must give an indemnity against any pecuniary loss, in the event of the allegation failing, which the action brings upon the parties'; if the allegation is made 'the marriage must be deferred until the truth has been tried'.[35] Rules of this sort lack precision as to the procedure to be employed: no church has formal law as to whether such cases are to be referred to the bishop, or whether there is a right of appeal if the challenge is allowed or rejected.

Solemnization and Validity

Church laws normally contain explicitly the principle that every minister of the church must conform both to the laws of the state governing the creation of the civil status of marriage and to the laws of the church governing the solemnization of marriage in church.[36] When the matter is expressly treated, and seldom is it not, the canon law of churches simply represents the requirements of validity operative under secular law. In short, on this subject, Anglican churches follow the laws of the states in which they exist. And when the parties concerned do not satisfy these conditions for validity the minister is under a duty to refuse solemnization. Consequently, the majority of church laws include the following

---

[34] England, BCP 1662, 303: the objection may be made under 'God's law, or the laws of this Realm'; Ireland, BCP 1960, 266; Canada, BCP 1962, 565; Southern Africa, *Prayer Book* 1989, 462: the objection may be based on 'God's word'.

[35] Australia, *A Prayer Book for Australia* 1995, 654; for deferral to establish the truth, see also e.g. Southern Africa, *Prayer Book* 1989, 460.

[36] See e.g. England, Can. B35(1); Scotland, Can. 31.2; Chile, Can. G.2; Puerto Rico, Cans. II.6; West Africa, Can. 7.2; Kenya, Can. 14.ii.4; New Zealand, Can. G.III.2.4; ECUSA, Cans. I.181; Philippines, Cans. III.16.4(a); for law applicable to the Spanish Reformed Episcopal Church, see I. C. Iban, 'Church and state in Spain', in G. Robbers (ed.), *State and Church in the European Union* (Baden-Baden, 1996), 93 at 115; see also E. I. Nwogugu, 'The validity of church marriages in Nigeria', *Nigerian Law Journal*, 8 (1974), 142; for the influence of English ecclesiastical matrimonial law in Papua New Guinea, see O. Jessep and J. Luluaki, *Principles of Family Law in Papua New Guinea* (University of PNG Press, 1994), 12, 22, 28ff; see also J. Y. Luluaki, 'When is rape not rape: the marital rape exceptions rule under the Papua New Guinea Criminal Code and related issues', *Melanesian Law Journal*, 22 (1994), 59.

requirements for a valid ecclesiastical marriage, and upon each the minister must be satisfied in advance: (1) that the parties have a right under secular law to contract a marriage; (2) that both parties freely and knowingly
consent to the marriage, without fraud, coercion, or mistake as to the identity of a partner or the mental condition of the other party; (3) that the parties do not fall within the prohibited degrees of relationship; (4) that the
parties have attained the legal age for marriage, and (5) where required in
the case of minors, that their parents or guardians have consented to it.[37]
As has already been seen, additional and purely ecclesiastical requirements include prior baptism (of one or both of the parties), and prior
instruction in or understanding of the nature, meaning and purpose of
marriage.

Turning to the ceremony of solemnization, there is considerable legal
unity as between the churches of the Communion. First, it is a general
principle of Anglican canon law that the ordinary minister of holy matrimony is a priest, though some churches, such as in Papua New Guinea,
state canonically that 'the man and the woman are both the recipients and
the ministers of the marriage' – the priest merely confects the marriage.[38]
However, if a priest is not available to conduct the marriage service, it is
lawful in many churches for deacons to do so – but some churches do not
recommend solemnization by deacons in the first year of their diaconate.[39]
Similarly, marriage must ordinarily be solemnized in a church, though in

---

[37] West Africa, Can. 7.4; ECUSA, Cans. I.18.2; Philippines, Cans. III.16.3; Papua New
Guinea, Can. No. 2 of 1995: they must not marry 'if the family relationship between
them is such that the marriage is forbidden by their culture and the customs of the fam-
ily line or clan'; see also Melanesia, Cans. A.4.A–C; England, Can. B31, B32; Ireland,
Const. IX.31 (see also the ecclesiastical decision in *Re the Deceased Wife's Sister Marriage
Act 1907* (1908), Journal of the General Synod of the Church of Ireland, 1908, 333);
Australia, Can. 3 1991 and Can. 15 1981; Canada, Can. 21.3–5; Korea, Cans. 26, 32; South
Africa, Can. 34.4; Nigeria, Cans. Ch. 18.5; Central Africa, Can. 23; Kenya, Can. 14.ii to
vii; West Indies, Can. 29.3, 7; Chile, Can. G.3; Brazil, BCP 1987, 182ff.; South India,
Const. XII.4: 'The Bishop of the diocese shall have power to suspend or modify in spe-
cial cases, if there seem good cause, the strict letter of the law of the Church with regard
to marriages prohibited on the ground of consanguinity or affinity'.

[38] Papua New Guinea, Can. No. 2 of 1995, Arts. 1–5.

[39] See e.g. England, Archiepiscopal Guidelines 1992, 187; and Brazil, BCP 1987, 182;
for the rule that ministers must be registered under secular law, see e.g. Papua New
Guinea, Can. No. 2 of 1995, Arts. 8–15; Melanesia, Cans. A.4.D-G; New Zealand, Can.
G.III.2.5 and 2.9: the minister must be nominated by the bishop to the Registrar General
of marriages as an 'officiating minister'; ECUSA, BCP 1979, Marshall, Vol. II, 441:
'Where it is permitted by civil law that deacons may perform marriages, and no priest
or bishop is available, a deacon may use the service . . . omitting the nuptial blessing';
compare e.g. Korea, Can. 27.1: this does not mention deacons; one idea in England is
that solemnization by a deacon is 'irregular': *Cope v Barber* (1872) LR 7 CP; and *Beamish
v Beamish* (1861) 9 HL Cas 274; *Re Ogola's Estate* (1978) Kenya LR 18 citing *Jembe v Nyondo*
(1912) 4 Kenya LR 160: Anglican marriage did not affect succession rights; for 'Christian
marriage' see also *State v Kwaku Brenyah* [1961] Ghana Law Reports 250.

some churches provision exists for it to be celebrated elsewhere with episcopal approval.[40] It is not uncommon for solemnization to be confined to
prescribed seasons, though provisions are normally directory on this subject.[41] Some churches recommend solemnization at a celebration of the
Holy Communion, and often liturgical rubrics prescribe that it is desirable
(or 'convenient') for the couple to receive communion.[42] This is permitted,
needless to say, if the parties are otherwise qualified under church law to
receive the sacrament. Choice of liturgy for solemnization, from amongst
the services for holy matrimony provided by churches, invariably belongs
to the minister as does that of the music to be used in the service.[43]
Secondly, the key element in the rite necessary to effect a valid marriage –
and here laws of churches mirror those of the secular state – is the
exchange of consents between the parties. Perhaps the clearest expression
of the principle is to be found in the canon law of the church in New
Zealand: 'A marriage is created by the free, competent and open consent
of the parties who contract it, in the presence of witnesses and of an authorized minister'.[44] In accordance with secular law, canon law frequently
requires that the marriage be witnessed (usually by two persons), as well
as registration of the marriage in books provided and maintained in the
church for this purpose.[45]

[40] Scotland, Can. 31.6: the bishop must sanction it in writing; Southern Africa, Can.
34.12: marriage may take place in a church or chapel or 'other place customarily used
for worship'; Australia, Can. 3 1981, 3(c): the bishop must give 'express permission' for
marriages outside church; Canada, Can. 21.12; Korea, Can. 27; Central Africa, Can. 22.4;
Kenya, Can. 14.ii.2; for Anglican marriage on the high seas, see *Australian Law Journal*,
62 (1988), 716 at 717 for *Culling v Culling* [1896] P 116.

[41] For the express prohibition against solemnization in Lent, see e.g. Central Africa,
Can. 22.5; Papua New Guinea, Can. No. 2 of 1995, Arts. 8–15: it is forbidden unless a
special dispensation is given by the bishop; Melanesia, Cans. A.4.H-J; Wales, BCP 1984,
736: '[i]t is an ancient tradition of the Church that marriages should not take place in
Lent'.

[42] New Zealand, *Prayer Book* 1989, 807; Australia, *A Prayer Book for Australia* 1995, 654;
Southern Africa, *Prayer Book* 1989, 459, 460; ECUSA, BCP 1979, Marshall, Vol. II, 475; see
also Southern Africa, Can. 34.14: marriages 'shall not be solemnized from Palm Sunday
to Easter Eve inclusive without dispensation from the Bishop'; this is repeated in Korea,
Can. 33.

[43] See e.g. England, Cans. B3(4), B35(5); compare New Zealand, Can. G.III.3 and
Prayer Book 1989, 808: '[t]he selection of the service . . . should be made by the couple in
consultation with the priest'; and Kenya, Can. 14.xi.1: the minister's function is to
'advise' concerning the music.

[44] New Zealand, Can. G.III.1.1.2; West Africa, Can. 7.4(c); Korea, Can. 32.2; for
England, see *Harrod v Harrod* (1854) 1 K & J 4; see also generally *Quick v Quick* [1953]
VLR 224.

[45] For 2 witnesses, see e.g. West Africa, Can. 7.5(b); ECUSA, Cans. I.18.3; Philippines,
Cans. III.16.4(c); New Zealand, Can. G.III.3.1; Canada, Can. 21.12; England, Can. B35(4):
2 or more. For registration, see New Zealand, Can. G.III.3.4; Australia, Can. 3 1981, 3(f);
West Africa, Can. 75(c); ECUSA, Cans. I.18.3: the entry must include a declaration as
to lifelong union; Philippines, Cans. III.16.4(d); Melanesia, Cans. A.4.D–G: the

One aspect of matrimonial discipline over which churches in the Communion are united by the silence of their laws, concerns the laity and their maintenance of married life. Canon law in the Anglican Communion neither imposes duties on the laity to support the married life of couples after solemnization in church, nor does it regulate the conduct of married life. There are two notable exceptions to this general rule. The canon law of New Zealand and of Canada gives partial effect to recommendations of Lambeth Conference resolutions in this regard. In almost identical provisions the canons of both churches place on the laity a series of duties to share with the clergy 'the responsibility for upholding family life', both that of the newly wed and their own. This may be effected in various ways: by their presence with friends and neighbours at weddings to bear witness to their support of those who marry; and by promoting and encouraging the use of professional skills that may be employed to serve family life. It is also the responsibility of the laity generally: as spouses 'to be faithful to their own marriage vows'; as parents, guardians, godparents and teachers, 'to guide children and young persons in preparation for family life'; as neighbours, to promote the welfare of families and to seek reconciliation of any whose family life is 'impaired or broken'; as communicants, to uphold the church's discipline on marriage; and as citizens, to work for the maintenance of just laws for the welfare of family life. The Canadian canon obliges the laity, in addition, 'to safeguard the legality of marriages by readiness to allege promptly any cause or just impediment which might make a proposed marriage unlawful'.[46] It is to be emphasised that these canonical provisions are thoroughly exceptional. In short, from actual law, the evidence is too scant to sustain the proposition that there are general principles of Anglican canon law concerning the maintenance of Christian marriage by the laity generally.

DIVORCE AND REMARRIAGE

When there has been a civil decision that a prior marriage was null, Anglican churches generally follow the state and subsequent 'second' marriages in church are permitted. However, this is not always the case and several churches operate a system of ecclesiastical nullity, following civil proceedings, under which church authorities may declare that a previous marriage was void thereby enabling the solemnization of a subsequent marriage in accordance with ecclesiastical rites in church. The

'bride-price' fixed by the local council 'should be followed'; Canada, Can. 21.5 and 15; Korea, Can. 34; North India, Const. VI.15: registration must occur in accordance with the Indian Christian Marriage Act 1872.

[46] New Zealand, Can. G.III.1.4; Canada, Can. 21.8; LC 1988, Res. 34; LC 1978, Res. 10.

position is more problematic with respect to the civil dissolution of marriages. Traditional Anglican doctrine teaches the indissolubility of marriage, that the union is dissolved only by the death of one of the parties.[47] The doctrine is implicit in canonical definitions of the nature of marriage as a permanent and lifelong union, some of which present indissolubility as a descriptive fact and others as a normative ideal.[48] Indissolubility is, of course, most relevant as to whether clergy may solemnize subsequent marriages of persons divorced by dissolution under secular law. In some churches the law allows remarriage when there has been a civil dissolution in addition to cases where there has been a civil annulment; other churches do not. The issue is important, moreover, because in many churches remarriage after a civil divorce short of nullity has a legal effect upon the ecclesiastical status and, therefore, the rights of individuals as members of the church – this is particularly so in relation to admission to Holy Communion.

Ecclesiastical Nullity Proceedings

Given the general practice of Anglican churches to stress the permanence of marriage (as fact or ideal), it may not be thought surprising that the possibility of marital breakdown is rarely acknowledged formally in canon law. A provision appearing in the canons of the church in Kenya, therefore, is exceptional: 'Even when everything has been done, it may still come about that the situation between married persons has become such that a marriage has in point of fact ceased to exist'. In such cases, '[it] may then be the duty of the Church to concur that, though divorce is always bad, it may be less bad than the continuance of an impossible situation, in which the pretence is maintained that what is now a non-existent marriage still exists'.[49] Several churches, therefore, operate a system under which serious marital difficulties, which may lead to the breakdown of the union, must be addressed by both the couple in question and the clergy in order to prevent the destruction of the marriage. Under the canon law of ECUSA, for instance, '[w]hen marital unity is imperilled by dissension, it shall be the duty of either or both parties, before contemplating legal action, to lay the matter before a Member of the Clergy; and it shall be the

---

[47] See e.g. England, *Acts of Convocation*, 90, 91: 'according to God's will, declared by Our Lord, marriage is in its true principle . . . indissoluble save by death'.

[48] See nn. 6–8.

[49] Kenya, Can. 14.iv.3; see also North India, Const. VI.9: 'the Christian Church has always recognized that there are circumstances in which the ideals of Christian marriage cannot be attained . . . and that there are special cases in which the law of the Church should not be applied with rigidity lest greater evils follow'; South India, Const. XII.5.

duty of such Member to labor that the parties may be reconciled'; this preventative scheme is not entirely uncommon.[50]

When reconciliation fails and the parties obtain from the civil authorities either an annulment or a dissolution of the marriage, the canon law of several churches provides a mechanism by which a decision is made within the church about the marital status of the parties for the purposes of the church itself. In ECUSA, once more, canon law permits an ecclesiastical decision about the effect of civil proceedings with regard to both annulled marriages and dissolved marriages. The canons state: 'Any member of this Church whose marriage has been annulled or dissolved by a civil court may apply to the Bishop . . . for a written judgment as to his or her marital status in the eyes of the Church'. Such judgment may be 'a recognition of the nullity, or of the termination of the said marriage'. But the judgment must not be construed as affecting in any way the legitimacy of children or the civil validity of the former relationship. These same provisions appear in the laws of a number of churches.[51] In other churches, ecclesiastical decisions about the effects of a civil annulment are made by a range of church authorities. In Canada, the question of the validity of the former marriage, and of whether it has been annulled under civil law for the purposes of the church, is determined by a special diocesan authority, the Ecclesiastical Matrimonial Commission whose decision, to be effective, must be confirmed by the bishop; in Central Africa, this function is performed by a Diocesan Board, and in Kenya by the Bishop's Court – indeed, provisions such as these have been recommended by Lambeth Conference resolutions.[52]

---

[50] ECUSA, Cans. I.19.1; New Zealand, Can. G.III.1.3.4: clergy must 'minister to those whose marriages experience tensions and difficulties to encourage them to seek such a ministry of reconciliation, and to obtain such training as may assist them in such a ministry'; Kenya, Can. 14.iv.2: 'If it comes to the notice of the parish priest that the marriage of two members of the Church is undergoing strain, it shall be his duty to visit the said persons, with at his discretion godly layfolk of the parish, to remind them of the obligations into which they have entered, to enquire into the causes of dissension and if possible to remove them, and by all means to effect reconciliation between those who have become estranged'; see also n. 46.

[51] ECUSA, Cans. I.19.2; Korea, Can. 25: the bishop may declare the marriage void 'thereby setting both parties free to marry'; West Africa, Can. 7.7; Nigeria, Cans. Ch. 18.1.

[52] Canada, Can. 21.16–33: the bishop or his appointee is president of the Commission and the bishop must appoint 2 or more communicants to act as members, and others to act as consultants; one member must have knowledge of civil law and another of canon law; dioceses may set up joint Commissions; Central Africa, Can. 23; Kenya, Can. 14.iii; Chile, Can. G.5; Puerto Rico, Cans. II.7; see also n. 53. For the Lambeth Conference, see LC 1958, Res. 118: 'The Conference recognizes that divorce is granted by the secular authority in many lands on grounds which the Church cannot acknowledge, and recognizes also that in certain cases, where a decree of divorce has been sought and may even have been granted, there may in fact have been no marital bond in the eyes of the Church. It therefore commends for further consideration by the Churches and provinces of the Anglican Communion a procedure for defining marital status, such as already exists in some of its provinces'.

Canon law in Southern Africa employs a similar system: there may be no solemnization of a subsequent marriage following a civil annulment without an ecclesiastical declaration of invalidity; the procedure, the mode of determination, and the grounds for the declaration of nullity are all carefully prescribed. Every application for a declaration of the invalidity of a former marriage must be made to the bishop. This is to be done either through the incumbent of the pastoral charge in which the applicant resides or habitually worships, or directly to the bishop. If a direct application is made to the bishop, the bishop must always consult with the incumbent and any other priest who may be concerned with the application. The bishop, who may be assisted by other persons whose advice he desires, is under a duty to consider the application and has authority to grant or decline such application. After consultation with 'a person learned in the law who is a Communicant of this Province he shall inform the applicant in writing of his decision and issue a certificate of invalidity if the application is approved'. The bishop has discretion to withhold any declaration of invalidity 'if he is of the opinion that the granting of it, though technically in accordance with ecclesiastical law, would be contrary to the principles of equity'.[53] The grounds upon which the ecclesiastical declaration of invalidity may be made are conditioned, as is the case in other churches employing this system, by those appearing in civil law; they include cases in which: consent had not freely been given and received; either party was not of the legal age to marry; the parties were within the prohibited degrees; the marriage has not been consummated; or the parties had entered the relationship without the intention of it being until death.[54] Laws of churches in the British Isles, in Australia and in New Zealand do not operate a system for formal ecclesiastical recognition of civil annulment.[55]

[53] Southern Africa, Can. 34.4(a),(b),(d); see also Papua New Guinea, Can. No. 2 of 1995, Art. 17: remarriage may not take place unless the prior marriage is found to be null and void or one of the parties has died; Melanesia, Cans. A.4.L: a person who has a partner still living 'should not' remarry; see nn. 61 and 63 for prohibitions against subsequent marriages following civil annulment, except with episcopal approval, in Scotland and Ireland.

[54] Southern Africa, Can. 34.4(c); for the same approach see Central Africa, Can. 23.3; see also Papua New Guinea, Can. No. 2 of 1995, Art. 16; Melanesia, Cans. A.4.K; Nigeria, Cans. Ch.18.1; and Canada, Can. 21.17.

[55] For the transference in England in the 1850s of ecclesiastical matrimonial jurisdiction to the state courts, and for a critical and comparative analysis of the modern position, see J. Owen, 'Nullity of marriage in the Church of England and in the Roman Catholic Church', LL M dissertation, University of Wales, Cardiff, 1995.

Remarriage

When civil proceedings result in a declaration of annulment, and in those churches which have an ecclesiastical nullity system that annulment is formally recognized for ecclesiastical purposes, there is no bar to the celebration of a subsequent marriage. Nor is there a bar in the case of the death of a spouse. In these cases the proposed marriage is treated as a first marriage and the rules, varying from church to church, about the ministerial duty to solemnize or the discretion to do so become active. However, in cases of civil dissolution, where the union is ended on grounds other than invalidity, the picture emerging from actual laws is rather more complex. The more usual method by which churches regulate remarriages, when the former spouses of dissolved marriages are still living, is by provisions dealing directly with the use of the church's rites at the celebration of a proposed marriage.[56] Despite the standard notion of indissolubility, seldom do churches operate a blanket rule forbidding clergy to solemnize such marriages.[57] When remarriage is permitted, the basis of the permission, and the procedures to be followed, vary. Three models seem to be used: all enable the minister who so wishes to proceed with solemnization – it is the conditions which differ.

First, though only occasionally, laws confer upon ministers a right to refuse: the canon law of New Zealand provides that '[a]ny Bishop or Priest shall be entitled to refuse to solemnize the marriage of a divorced person'.[58] Very occasionally, the right to refuse is cast as a right of conscientious objection – here there is an implicit precondition to refusal: that the minister actually holds a genuine conscientious objection.[59] Secondly, and more commonly, laws require those ministers who are prepared to

[56] LC 1948, Res. 92 and Res. 94: 'The Conference affirms that the marriage of one whose former partner is still living may not be celebrated according to the rites of the Church, unless it has been established that there exists no marriage bond recognised by the Church'.

[57] In Wales a 'policy' of the Bench of Bishops seems to be the basis of the prohibition along with the principle in the BCP 1984, 736 that 'marriage is a lifelong union . . . and is dissolved only by the death of either party': it is difficult to reconcile the rule of practice with the secular Matrimonial Causes Act 1965, s. 8 which may be interpreted as conferring a statutory discretion in the matter.

[58] New Zealand, Can. G.III.4.1–2; Ireland, Const. IX.31: 'When any clergyman is approached with a view to solemnizing a marriage between parties either of whom has been party to a ceremony of marriage with another person still living he shall, if he is unwilling to perform the ceremony, so inform the parties immediately'; Australia, Can. 7 1985, 4: 'A minister of this Church may refuse to solemnize the marriage of any divorced person during the life of the person's former spouse'; 1: ' "divorced person" means a person who was party to a marriage which has been dissolved in accordance with law'.

[59] Scotland, College of Bishops Guidelines (1981), 4: no priest can 'be required to officiate at a marriage contrary to his conscience'; see also n. 14.

solemnize a second marriage to obtain the consent of the bishop: prior episcopal consent is a precondition to proceeding. In Southern Africa this is in the form of an episcopal licence, though once it is issued, whilst no cleric 'shall be obliged to solemnize', 'the rite shall be performed by such clergyman and in such place as the Bishop shall decide'.[60] In Scotland a certificate of authorization must be obtained and '[n]o Bishop shall entertain an application which has already been before another Diocesan Bishop . . . without the agreement of the Bishop of the other Diocese and the Episcopal Synod'.[61] In West Africa the general term 'consent' is used and, moreover, the subsequent solemnization must be reported to the bishop.[62] Thirdly, the matter is sometimes left to the discretion of the minister who, in exercising that discretion, is required (or recommended) to consult with the diocesan bishop and to take into account the opinion of the bishop. In Ireland, the minister must not solemnize such a marriage 'unless he has first sought from the bishop his opinion as to the advisability of solemnizing the marriage'; the minister 'shall consider and take into account the opinion of the bishop in exercising the discretion, vested in him by law, as to whether or not he should solemnize the marriage'.[63]

Lawful grounds for allowing the solemnization of such marriages vary as between churches. Probably the fullest canonical treatment as to grounds is to be found in the church in Southern Africa. Following civil

---

[60] Southern Africa, Can. 34.3: 'No clergyman shall solemnize the marriage of any person whose marriage has been annulled or dissolved by secular authority during the lifetime of the partner' unless the marriage has been declared by the bishop as invalid or 'the clergyman has obtained a licence from the Bishop'; Australia, Can. 7 1985, 3: there is to be no solemnization 'unless, upon application made by the proposed celebrant, the bishop of the diocese . . . has consented' (this canon may be adopted by the dioceses: see e.g. Diocese of Sydney, *The 7th Handbook*, 8.13); West Indies, Can. 29.4, 5.

[61] Scotland, Can. 31.4: after civil nullity or dissolution the minister must refer the matter to the bishop who must 'make such enquiries into the circumstances of the case, and take such pastoral and legal advice, as shall seem appropriate'; thereafter the bishop 'may issue, or decline to issue' a Certificate of Authorisation (see Appendix 27) of the cleric's officiating at the solemnization according to the church's rites; see also Nigeria, Cans. Ch.18.1.ix: permission given in one diocese is not operative in another without the consent of the bishop of the other diocese.

[62] West Africa, Can. 7.6; see also Nigeria, Cans. Ch. 18.1.

[63] Ireland, Const. IX.31.3–6: the minister must furnish the bishop with 'all the information' required; in cases 'where a decree of nullity has been granted on grounds acceptable to the Church of Ireland, he shall declare that the applicant is free to marry in church'; in other cases, the minister must conduct a private service of preparation before solemnization. In England, though solemnization is forbidden by Acts of Convocation (see *Acts of Convocation*, 91–4), guidelines of the House of Bishops 1985 recommend that the decision is ultimately one for the cleric (who is to consult the bishop); see LFCE, 377ff.; the secular Matrimonial Causes Act 1965, s. 8 provides that no minister of the church shall be compelled to solemnize the marriages of divorced persons; see also Philippines, Can. III.16.4(d): '[i]t shall be within the discretion of any Minister of this Church to decline to solemnize any marriage'.

dissolution, an episcopal licence may be issued to authorize a second marriage on condition that: (1) there is 'no prospect of re-establishing a true
marriage relationship between the partners of any former marriage';
(2) the person acknowledges a share 'in the sin which led to the breakdown of the former marriage, is repentant for the failure to keep vows . . .
knows the forgiveness of God and therefore considers himself able in good
conscience to make new vows, and is genuinely forgiving'; (3) the persons
'understand the Church's teaching concerning marriage . . . and truly
intend to enter such a marriage'; (4) 'such provision as is in the power of
the applicant has been made for the spiritual welfare, happiness, care,
maintenance, education and advancement of minor, disabled or otherwise
dependent children of a prior marriage'; and (5) the applicant is prepared
'to fulfil his responsibilities, both moral and legal, in respect of any former
marriage'. The canon law of Southern Africa confers a right to petition the
bishop to reconsider the case in the event of a refusal.[64] Several other
churches employ a similar system and sometimes conditions are included
which do not appear in the law of Southern Africa.[65] An interesting overriding principle appears in the national canons of the Australian church,
which dioceses may adopt. Episcopal consent must not be given if at least
one of the parties is not ordinarily resident in the diocese and if the bishop
and the proposed celebrant are not satisfied that the marriage 'would not
contravene the teachings of Holy Scripture or the doctrines and principles
of the Church'.[66]

In addition to the consequences for remarriage, civil divorce has in
many churches a direct effect upon the individual's admission to Holy
Communion. Lambeth Conference resolutions have permitted exclusion
in certain cases in this context and actual laws are generally in line with
these.[67] No laws prescribe suspension from Holy Communion of persons

[64] Southern Africa, Can. 34.5, 7; for reconsideration see also Central Africa, Can.
23.10.

[65] For almost the same arrangement (though here the matter is to be decided by the
diocesan Ecclesiastical Matrimonial Commission with subsequent ratification by the
bishop), see Canada, Can. 21.22–5; see also New Zealand, Can. G.III.4.1: there must be
'good and sufficient grounds after full and adequate inquiry to believe' that (a) any
divorced person intending marriage sincerely regrets that the promises made in any
previous marriage were not kept, and (b) both parties to an intended marriage have an
avowed intention to abide by the lifelong intent of the proposed marriage; West Africa,
Can. 7.6: the minister must have (1) satisfied himself by appropriate evidence that the
prior marriage has been annulled or dissolved by a final judgment or decree of a civil
court of competent jurisdiction; and (2) instructed the parties that 'continuing concern
should be shown for the well-being of the former spouse, and of any children of the
prior marriage'; for much the same, see ECUSA, Cans. I.19.3.

[66] Australia, Can. 7 1985, 4.

[67] LC 1948, Res. 96 which endorses LC 1930, Res. 11: 'That in every case where a person with a former partner still living is remarried and desires to be admitted to Holy
Communion the case should be referred to the bishop, subject to provincial or regional

who have obtained a civil divorce only. However, many laws allow suspension of divorced persons who remarry; suspension is rarely automatic
– it is most usually a matter either to be decided by the minister or by a reference to the bishop for his unilateral decision or to an episcopal assembly
for its collective decision.[68] In Papua New Guinea those who have had a
civil divorce but do not take a new partner are not excluded from Holy
Communion – those who remarry are excluded by the minister; there is a
right of recourse to the House of Bishops.[69] Suspension of remarried persons may occur under Canadian canon law only after reference to the
bishop. Unless the bishop has sanctioned remarriage, in every case where
a person who has been remarried (and the former spouse is still living)
desires a ruling with respect to admission to Holy Communion, the case
must be referred by the incumbent to the bishop for judgment. In arriving
at his decision the bishop must have 'due regard for the spiritual welfare
of the petitioner'; the bishop must give a written judgment to both the
incumbent and the petitioner.[70] In Southern Africa, the basic rule is wider:
both persons who remarry and 'those married to them' may be admitted
to Holy Communion only if: (1) the previous marriage was declared
invalid; or, (2) following dissolution, an episcopal licence to remarry has
been issued; or, (3) they have received a dispensation from exclusion from
Holy Communion; or, (4) they have had their marriage blessed in church;
or, (5) they have received permission from the bishop (who shall determine the conditions under which such admission may be granted); or,
finally, (6) they have been received as communicants within a church in
full communion with the church in Southern Africa.[71] Often Anglican
canon law requires or permits civil marriage to be followed by a blessing
of that marriage in church.[72] Occasionally, laws provide that a Christian

regulations'; see Ch. 5 for the effect of divorce and remarriage on candidature for ordination.

[68] West Africa, Can. 7.10(b): there is no express provision for the matter to be referred
to the bishop; the person 'may be suspended from the reception of holy communion';
West Indies, Can. 29.9: 'When in the case of a divorced person the Bishop considers that
a decree of nullity could have been granted, having taken the advice of Canonists and
the Advisory Committee the Bishop may exercise his discretion and admit the said person to the Sacraments of the Church'; Korea, Can. 29: '[i]n the case of a deliberate violation of the marriage canons the bishop may punish those married and the celebrant
with suspension from communion or excommunication'; in Wales it is said that there is
a policy that where a civil divorce has taken place, the parties should be advised to
abstain from Holy Communion unless the bishop decides otherwise.

[69] Papua New Guinea, Can. No. 2 of 1995, Art. 18.

[70] Canada, Can. 21.26; for a similar provision in England, see *Acts of Convocation*, 90,
91.

[71] Southern Africa, Can. 34.8.

[72] See e.g. England, Can. B36; Wales, BCP 1984, 751; Scotland, Can. 31.5; New
Zealand, Can. G.III.3.5; Southern Africa, Can. 34.9 (and 10 for blessings following customary marriages); Papua New Guinea, Can. No. 2 of 1995, Arts. 8–15: those who have

partner may not divorce a non-Christian partner, but if the non-Christian partner wishes for a divorce the Christian partner is free to remarry.[73]

CONFESSION

The English Reformation led to the abandonment of obligatory private auricular confession, required under the pre-Reformation Roman canon law, as the norm.[74] Today, the canon law of Anglican churches normally provides for both public and private confession as a matter of permissive right – ordinarily private confession is voluntary, not mandatory. Provisions for public penance are rare. This section examines these and the place in modern canon law of the traditional principle that the seal of the confessional is absolute.

Confession, Absolution and Penance

Without doubt the church in Melanesia has the most comprehensive canonical treatment of the subject.[75] In some respects the Melanesian canons are exceptional and, when measured against those of other churches, they prove the rule throughout the Anglican Communion. First, in Melanesia penance is treated as a sacrament, the rite by which sins committed after baptism are forgiven. Whilst churches commonly agree on the nature of the rite as effecting reconciliation with God, that it is a sacrament does not square with traditional Anglican thought and seldom do laws incorporate the same idea.[76] Secondly, the Melanesian church holds that

contracted civil or customary marriages 'should be encouraged to ask the Church to bless their marriage'; Melanesia, Cans. A.4.H–J.

[73] Korea, Can. 21; Papua New Guinea, Can. No. 2 of 1995, Arts. 8–15; Canada, Can. 21.4; West Africa, Can. 7.8; for the so-called 'Matthean exception', see Matt. 5.32, 19.9: 'whoever divorces his wife, except for unchastity, and marries another, commits adultery'; and for the 'Pauline privilege', I Cor. 7.14, 15: 'If the unbelieving partner desires to separate, let it be so'.

[74] R. H. Helmholz, *Roman Canon Law in Reformation England* (Cambridge, 1990), 113–14.

[75] Melanesia, Cans. A.6.A.1–5.

[76] AR, Art. 23; see, however, Scotland, Can. 29.1: this treats the 'Sacrament of penance'. Usually churches speak of the 'ministry of reconciliation': Canada, *Book of Alternative Services* 1985, 166; Australia, *A Prayer Book for Australia* 1995, 774; Southern Africa, *Prayer Book* 1989, 447–8; New Zealand, *Prayer Book* 1989, 750; England, Can. B29(1): '[i]t is the duty of baptised persons at all times to the best of their understanding to examine their lives and conversations by the rule of God's commandments, and wherever they perceive themselves to have offended by will, act, or omission, there to bewail their own sinfulness and to confess themselves to Almighty God with full purpose of amendment of life, that they receive from him the forgiveness of their sins which he has promised to all who turn to him with hearty repentance and true faith'.

'the power to forgive sins is given by God to a priest at his Ordination and the priest uses this power when he forgives sins'. The confinement of the right to pronounce absolution (a declaration of forgiveness by God) exclusively to priests commonly appears in canonical and liturgical provisions in the Communion, though (not surprisingly) sometimes bishops are expressly included.[77] Thirdly, in Melanesia, private confession to God in the presence of a priest may be made when a person comes with sorrow for the past and intends to lead a new life in the future. This is not exceptional: in all churches confession and absolution are lawful and in some, notably Scotland, the law confers a right to confession; in the ministry both repentance and an intention of amendment of life are required.[78] In a few churches, private auricular confession in the presence of a priest is permitted only when the person is unable to quieten his own conscience by public general confession in the context of a church service or by personal confession to God.[79] Fourthly, in the Melanesian canons, when a person makes a private confession 'the priest will give advice' and pronounce absolution 'if he thinks this is right'. In most churches the giving of spiritual and pastoral counsel is at the discretion of the priest; seldom is it obligatory.[80] However, sometimes absolution by the priest is obligatory and sometimes discretionary.[81] Fifthly, in Melanesia, when a person pro-

[77] Wales, BCP 1984, 763; Ireland, *Alternative Prayer Book* 1984, 30, 51; Central Africa, Diocese of Mashonaland, *Pastoral Regulations* 1978, p. 13; England, it is implicit in Can. B29(1); New Zealand, *Prayer Book* 1989, 750: in it 'the priest, on behalf of the Christian community, listens to the penitent and declares God's forgiveness' (the same formula is used in *A Prayer Book for Australia* 1995, 774); Southern Africa, *Prayer Book* 1989, 452: the priest 'declares God's forgiveness'.

[78] Scotland, Can. 29.1: 'All priests who are eligible by reason of holding a pastoral charge . . . or by permission granted by the Diocesan Bishop, shall make themselves available for the ministration of the Sacrament of Penance as may be convenient, and no priest may refuse to hear a confession unless able to direct the penitent to some other competent priest'; Southern Africa, *Prayer Book* 1989, 448: 'The Church does not require anyone to confess in the presence of a priest in order to receive forgiveness. It requires only that all may be honestly assured in their own conscience of their duty in this matter'; see also ECUSA, BCP 1979, Marshall, Vol. II, 389; Canada, *Book of Alternative Services* 1985, 166: 'The Reconciliation of a Penitent is available for all who desire it. It is not restricted to time of sickness'.

[79] England, Can. B29(2): '[i]f there be any who . . . cannot quiet his own conscience, but requires further comfort or counsel, let him come to some discreet and learned minister of God's Word; that by the ministry of God's holy Word he may receive the benefit of absolution'; Australia, Can. 10 1992, 2.

[80] Wales, BCP 1984, 763: here is 'the opportunity to ask for informed counsel'; Southern Africa, *Prayer Book* 1989, 449: 'The Priest . . . may give advice if it is requested or if he judges it appropriate'; in England, it seems to be discretionary: Can. B29(2) (see n. 79); Scotland, Can. 17.3: all clergy having cure of souls 'shall provide opportunity for those who may wish to come to them for spiritual counsel and advice'.

[81] Scotland, Can. 17.3: all clergy with cure of souls 'shall provide opportunity . . . for . . . absolution'; England, B29(2): only the word 'may' is used; for Mashonaland, see n. 82.

poses to make confession in a language not known to the priest, the priest 'may not refuse' to hear it and may absolve on the assumption that the confession was *bona fide*. This rule is rarely used in other canonical systems.[82] In sum, fundamental Anglican canon law, deduced from actual laws, confers a right to private confession and a conditional right to absolution, which itself may be pronounced only by priests.

Melanesian canon law differs most radically from that of other churches in that it permits public penance. This has two objects: to help a person who has sinned to come to true repentance and to be fully restored to the fellowship of the church; and to guard the church against scandal. However, public penance 'must not be thought of as a punishment for sin' and 'the priest may put [the person] under public penance', for not more than three months, only when a serious sin is 'known publicly' and the person has not confessed and received absolution privately. If there has been a private confession, the priest must 'tell the people that [the penitent] has already received absolution and ask them to forgive the sinner, just as God has already forgiven him'. During the period of public penance the person must not receive Holy Communion (but must attend the Eucharist) and the priest has 'a heavy pastoral duty to visit' the penitent and 'try to help him to come to true repentance'. Written details should be kept by the priest. At the end of the period the penitent is restored before the congregation at a public service. In cases where the person is unrepentant at the end of the period, the priest may impose public penance for a further three months. If the person is unrepentant at the end of this second period, the priest must report the matter to the bishop.[83]

It must be stressed that these Melanesian provisions are exceptional: the institution of public penance is not one generally known to Anglican canon law. However, public confession is an institution known to Anglican canon law. Most churches incorporate in their liturgies an opportunity for general confession and absolution in the context of public worship in accordance with the service books of the church.[84] Finally, special rules are used to regulate the place of exercising the ministry of absolution. Whilst in practice the normal place for hearing private confessions may be in church (but laws do not usually expressly prescribe this),

---

[82] Central Africa, Diocese of Mashonaland, *Pastoral Regulations* 1978, p. 12: confession 'may not be made through an interpreter', and if a priest has so little knowledge of the penitent's language 'that he cannot understand fully the confession made, he shall give absolution, unless he has any grave cause for doubt of the sincerity of the penitent'.

[83] Melanesia, Cans. A.6.B.1–11; see for a hint of the idea, West Indies, Can. 26.5: 'notorious evil livers' must make 'an open declaration of repentance' before admission to Holy Communion.

[84] Wales, BCP 1984, 763; England, Can. B29(1): the baptized must acknowledge their sins and seek forgiveness, 'especially in the general Confessions of the congregation and in the Absolution pronounced by the priest in the services of the Church'.

commonly this is not required in the case of sick persons.[85] Occasionally churches forbid the exercise of the ministry of absolution without the permission of the minister having cure of souls of the parish in which it is performed.[86] However, in some churches this rule does not apply when a person is in danger of death, in which case the ministry may be exercised anywhere; frequently canon law confers an absolute right to receive absolution in the event of imminent death; and occasionally rules cast a duty on sick persons to make confession.[87] In the Church of England, the law allows a parochial church council to pass a resolution barring a woman priest from pronouncing the absolution at a church service.[88] Seldom do laws require the performance of acts of penance.[89]

The Seal of the Confessional

Canon 113 of the Canons Ecclesiastical 1603 has played an important part in the provision of rules regulating the disclosure of information given and received in private auricular confession. It provides that 'if any man confess his secret and hidden sins to the Minister, for the unburdening of his conscience, and to receive spiritual consolation and ease of mind from him; we do not any way bind the said minister by this our Constitution, but do straitly charge and admonish him, that he do not at any time reveal and make known to any person whatsoever any crime or offence so committed to his trust and secrecy . . . under pain of irregularity'. The canon is still operative in England.[90] Remarkably, the canon law of the vast majority of Anglican churches makes no explicit reference to the seal of the confessional. The prohibition against disclosure, therefore, may more properly be classified as an unwritten ecclesiastical convention or custom. However, in those few churches having formal law on the subject, various

[85] New Zealand, *Prayer Book* 1989, 728; Australia, *A Prayer Book for Australia* 1995, 778: the ministry may take place 'in a church or elsewhere'; Canada, *Book of Alternative Services* 1985, 166: at any time and 'in any suitable place'; England, Can. B29(3): '[i]n particular a sick person, if he feels his conscience troubled in any weighty matter, should make a special confession of his sins, that the priest may absolve him if he humbly and heartily desire it'; Papua New Guinea, *Anglican Prayer Book* 1991, 214: '[s]ick persons should be given the opportunity to make a sacramental confession if they so desire'.

[86] England, Can. B29(4).

[87] England, Can. B29(4): 'a priest may exercise the ministry of absolution anywhere in respect of any person who is in danger of death or if there is some other urgent or weighty cause'; Central Africa, Diocese of Mashonaland, *Pastoral Regulations* 1978, 10(iii).

[88] Priests (Ordination of Women) Measure 1993, Scheds. 1, 2; contravention is an ecclesiastical offence (s. 5).

[89] Southern Africa, *Prayer Book* 1989, 452: 'The penitent may make an act of contrition' and the priest may suggest 'some prayer or action as a token of repentance'.

[90] R. Bursell, 'The seal of the confessional', *Ecclesiastical Law Journal*, 1(7) (1990), 84: this includes detail of the position in pre-Reformation canon law.

principles surface and there is a fairly high degree of variety as to its nature and scope.

For some churches canon law presents the seal as an absolute moral duty; it is to be presumed that the appearance of this moral prohibition in a canon converts it also into a legal duty. The canons of ECUSA prescribe that 'the secrecy of a confession is morally absolute for the confessor, and must under no circumstances be broken'.[91] Similarly, under liturgical regulations in Canada, '[t]he secrecy of a confession of sin is morally absolute for the confessor, and must under no circumstances be broken'.[92] In Southern Africa, the prohibition is applied to all information received in confession: '[e]very priest in exercising the ministry of reconciliation . . . is solemnly bound to observe secrecy concerning all those matters which are confessed before him'.[93] Occasionally, the rule against disclosure extends to priests outside sacramental confession, to ordinary pastoral circumstances which result in ministers receiving information given in confidence: in Canada, again, it is 'the historic obligation of the members of the clergy . . . to regard as a sacred trust all confidential information imparted to them either under the seal of the confessional or revealed to them in their capacity as pastors'. This rule is exceptional and it is to be found in the canon law of only one other church.[94]

Rarely is it the case that the purposes of the basic rule are spelt out: exceptionally, in New Zealand, '[t]he priest exercises the ministry in complete confidentiality' so that the penitent is 'able to confess in the assurance that the priest will not refer to the matter again'.[95] In Scottish canon law the confessor's duty continues after the penitent has died: '[t]he seal is absolute and is not abrogated on the death of the penitent'; this is an equally unusual requirement.[96] Occasionally, laws apply the principle both to the priest and to the penitent: in Melanesian canon law '[u]nder no circumstances may the priest or the person repeat to any other person what has been said by the priest or the person in the Confessional'.[97] Laws are also generally silent as to the mode by which disclosure might occur: pastoral regulations in the Diocese of Mashonaland, in Central Africa, provide untypically that '[i]n no circumstances whatever may the material of

---

[91] ECUSA, Cans. IV.14.23.

[92] Canada, *Book of Alternative Services* 1985, 166; Wales, BCP 1984, 763: this speaks of 'the seal of secrecy'.

[93] Southern Africa, *Prayer Book* 1989, 448.

[94] Canada, Const. 156, Appendix M; see also ECUSA, Cans. IV.15.1: it applies to 'disclosures in confidence made by a person to a Member of the Clergy with the purposes of seeking religious counsel, advice, solace, absolution or ministration wherein the Member of Clergy is acting in the capacity of spiritual adviser to that person, and where the person making the disclosures has a reasonable expectation that the communication will be kept in confidence'.

[95] New Zealand, *Prayer Book* 1989, 750.   [96] Scotland, Can. 29.2.

[97] Melanesia, Cans. A.6.A.6.

confessions made be made known by the priest to any person either by word or action or attitude in such a way that the penitent could possibly be identified'.[98]

In some churches, whilst the prohibition is expressed as 'absolute', provisions exist to enable disclosure with the permission of the penitent. According to Scottish canon law '[a] priest may not divulge anything that has been revealed in Confession, nor refer subsequently to such matter without leave of the penitent';[99] in Australia dioceses may adopt the canonical provision that disclosure must not occur 'without the consent of that person'.[100] Whereas in Australia and Scotland it would seem that the minister may suggest disclosure, in New Zealand it may occur only 'at the penitent's request'.[101] Similarly, in the Diocese of Mashonaland regulations forbid disclosure 'except in the rare cases where a penitent himself has of his own free will given permission to the priest'; but such permissions 'may never be exacted, or required of the penitent'.[102] A refinement of this approach appears in Melanesian canon law: this provides that 'a person may give the priest permission to seek advice so that more help may be given to him to overcome his difficulties and temptations'; also, '[t]he priest may not at any time reveal the name of the person who has given this permission, and at any time the person may withdraw the permission'.[103]

Whether communications between priest and penitent are privileged under the secular laws of the state in which an Anglican church exists has been a matter of debate in recent years, at least in the English-speaking world – in some states they are privileged, in others they are not.[104] In most states, the courts display a general reluctance to require disclosure, but in an extreme case where the interests of the administration of justice demand, disclosure may be compelled by secular laws under which refusal to give evidence may constitute contempt of court.[105] This has led two Anglican churches in their internal rules to make mention of the diffi-

[98] Central Africa, Diocese of Mashonaland, *Pastoral Regulations* 1978, p. 13.
[99] Scotland, Can. 292.   [100] Australia, Can. 10 1992, 2.
[101] New Zealand, *Prayer Book* 1989, 750.
[102] Central Africa, Diocese of Mashonaland, *Pastoral Regulations* 1978, p. 13.
[103] Melanesia, Cans. A.6.A.6.
[104] For a survey of judicial decisions in England, the USA and Canada see e.g. D. W. Elliott, 'An evidential privilege for priest–penitent communications', *Ecclesiastical Law Journal*, 3(16) (1995), 272; D. Nokes, 'Professional privilege', *Law Quarterly Review*, 66 (1950), 88; J. N. Lyon, 'Privileged communications – penitent and priest', *Criminal Law Quarterly* (Toronto), 7 (1964–5), 327.
[105] See e.g. Southern Africa, *Smit v Van Niekerk* [1976(4)] SALR 1 (Supreme Ct): 'It cannot be accepted that the public policy of our country required in the past and today requires a right of a clergyman to remain silent and in any event such right has not been recognised by the Criminal Procedure Act, 56 of 1955'.

culty for priests.[106] According to the canon law of ECUSA, 'communications under the law of the state and applicable federal law' and 'such other
communications as defined under The Federal Rules of Evidence' may be
privileged, and in disciplinary proceedings against clergy in the church
courts '[n]o communication privileged under the law of the state or . . . federal law shall be required to be disclosed'.[107] In the church in Canada a
recent statement recognizes both that communications are not privileged
under either federal law or the laws of some provinces, and that 'the obligation to give evidence under compulsion of a court of law or other legally
authorized body' is an enforceable one in secular law. However, it
provides that priests 'compelled to testify must always have in mind the
historic obligation of confidentiality'. The statement recommends, therefore, that priests should declare that obligation in court. If 'the judge
requires that the priest so testify, the priest should seek permission to
consult the diocesan [bishop] and chancellor'; the priest ought also to
obtain legal representation in such cases. The same procedure should be
followed in any 'other circumstances where the sacred obligation of confidentiality imposes a serious dilemma for the priest concerned'.[108] These
arrangements are exceptional: generally, Anglican churches provide no
formal guidance concerning the problem in secular legal proceedings of
compulsory disclosure by clergy of information given in confidence.

THE DISPOSAL OF HUMAN REMAINS

Cultural circumstances have led to a great diversity between Anglican
churches with respect to death, funerals and the disposal of human
remains. At the same time, however, there is a distinct paucity of formal
law in the Communion on these matters. Although care for the dying and
the bereaved is enjoined by the general duty of clergy to minister to those

---

[106] See e.g. Australia, *A Prayer Book for Australia* 1995, 778: 'Canon law makes confidentiality absolute, but this is not recognised in the laws of some Australian States'.

[107] ECUSA, Cans. IV.14.23 and 15.1; see also W. Wantland, 'The seal of confession
and the Episcopal Church in the USA', *Ecclesiastical Law Journal*, 4(19) (1996), 580 and a
reply by Francis Helminski, ibid., 4(20) (1997), 691. A spiritual adviser's disclosure does
not 'invest tort liability' even if there is a statute rendering a cleric incompetent to
testify concerning a communication made to him as spiritual adviser: *Hester v Barnett*,
App, 723 SW 2d 544 (Mo); for some old USA cases, see C. Zollmann, *American Civil
Church Law* (Columbia, 1917), 333f.

[108] Canada, Const. 156, Appendix M; see also *Journal of Church Law Association of
Canada*, 1(3) (1994), 260ff. for discussion of *B(DA) v Children's Aid Society of Durham
Region* (1993): the Diocese of Toronto successfully obtained a ruling that files held by it
containing documentation relating to an Anglican priest and Children's Aid Society
proceedings were privileged (see also *Slavutych v Baker*, DLR (3d) 224 (SCC) and *R v
Gruenke* (1991) 3 SCR 263).

in their cure of souls (see Chapter 5), very few churches employ canon law to provide a specific ministry to these. Instead the subject is treated by liturgical norms or quasi-legislation. Sometimes preparation of an individual for death is recommended and many churches offer the rite of anointing or laying on of hands for this purpose. The canon law of Melanesia is untypically detailed on the subject: holy anointing, a sacrament administered by a priest with oil consecrated by a bishop, may be given to any baptized person who is seriously ill, particularly before surgery, or on the point of death; normally it should be employed after confession and Holy Communion, but priests must not anoint dead persons – however, when it is uncertain whether a person is dead, the priest may anoint conditionally.[109] In some churches, to allow for preparation, rules prescribe that the death of a member of the church should be reported as soon as possible to the minister.[110] In New Zealand, prayer ought to be offered in a house after death and '[i]f it is the custom of the people concerned that the house should be sprinkled with water, the water should be sanctified' beforehand.[111]

A key issue is whether members of the church and others have a right to insist upon a funeral according to the rites of the church. For some churches, the principle in Canon 68 of the Canons Ecclesiastical 1603 seems to enjoy continuing influence; this forbade ministers to refuse or delay to bury the corpse of any person that was brought to the church or churchyard. In England today, any person who dies in a parish has a legal right to be buried in the parish churchyard in accordance with the funeral rites of the Church of England.[112] A similar approach is adopted in Wales

---

[109] Melanesia, Cans. A.4.D-G; see also New Zealand, *Prayer Book* 1989, 812: '[w]here possible the minister ensures that the dying person is prepared before hand'; England, *Funerals and Ministry to the Bereaved: A Handbook of Funeral Practices and Procedures* (London, 1989) and *The Role of the Minister in Bereavement: Guidelines and Training Suggestions* (London, 1989). For anointing and laying on of hands, see e.g. Southern Africa, *Prayer Book* 1989, 500, 502; ECUSA, BCP 1979, Marshall, Vol. II, 475, 489, 505; Canada, BCP 1962, 584 and *Book of Alternative Services* 1985, 559; Australia, Ministry to the Sick Canon, Can. 5 1981, 4: 'A minister of this Church is not bound to lay hands on or anoint the sick'; and *A Prayer Book for Australia* 1995, 771.

[110] See e.g. ECUSA, BCP 1979, Marshall, Vol. II, 531; Canada, *Book of Alternative Services* 1985, 570.

[111] New Zealand, *Prayer Book* 1989, 871.

[112] England, Can. B38(2): 'It shall be the duty of every minister to bury, according to the rites of the Church of England, the corpse or ashes of any person deceased within his cure of souls or of any parishioners or persons whose names are entered on the electoral roll'; *Re Kerr* [1894] P 284 at 293 *per* Tristram Ch: 'by the Common Law as well as by Ecclesiastical Law any person (subject to certain exceptions) dying in England is entitled to a Christian burial . . . in a consecrated burial-ground belonging to his own parish'; see also *Re West Pennard Churchyard* [1991] 4 All ER 124 at 126: the right 'crystallises' on death.

and Ireland.[113] However, for most churches the principle is implicit within provisions dealing with denial of funeral rites to those who have died unbaptized, to suicides and to excommunicate persons.[114] In some churches these classes are excluded from enjoyment of funeral rites and a special episcopally approved form of service must be used, usually where there is no evidence of repentance before death.[115] The laws of a few churches confer on the minister a discretion to refuse to use the church's funeral rites in these cases.[116] Formal law occasionally provides for the non-application of the rule to unbaptized infants.[117] More often than not church laws are silent as to excluded classes.

A lack of evidence from formal laws on funerals makes it difficult to deduce general principles running throughout the Communion. The following represent a miscellany of rules on the subject. The normal minister of funeral rites is an ordained cleric, either a priest or if a priest is unavailable a deacon, though commonly churches allow lay ministers to conduct funerals.[118] Choice of funeral rite normally belongs to the minister, but sometimes arrangements exist to consult with the family or friends of the deceased person.[119] A church is the appropriate place for the funeral of a church member.[120] Disposal of the remains of a Christian should be in consecrated ground; if the ground is unconsecrated, the site should be

[113] Wales, Can. 68 of the 1603 Canons (see n. 114) continues to operate: *Cure of Souls* (1995), 9; Ireland, Const. IX.32.1: 'No minister shall, where reasonable notice has been given to him, refuse to read the burial service . . . at . . . the burial within his cure of a person who may have died within it'; see also *Correll v Robinson* (1914) Journal of the Court of General Synod (1915) 459.

[114] The rule is ancient: Canons Ecclesiastical 1603, Can. 68: refusal was allowed of one who died excommunicate; see generally R. Phillimore, *Ecclesiastical Law* (2nd edn., London, 1895), 670.

[115] England, Can. B38(2): suicides of unsound mind are excluded and excommunication must be for 'some grievous and notorious crime'; see also Central Africa, Diocese of Mashonaland, *Pastoral Regulations* 1978, 15: Christians are allowed to attend the funerals of their heathen relatives or friends.

[116] For the reading of such parts of the service as the minister sees fit, see e.g. Ireland, Const. IX.32.2–3: this adds to the classes those who had 'committed some grievous and notorious sin' as does Southern Africa, *Prayer Book* 1989, 530.

[117] Ireland, Const. IX.32.2: the minister should consult the bishop if possible; compare Melanesia, Cans. B.2.A–D: unbaptized children and still-born babies are excluded.

[118] Brazil, BCP 1987, 192; ECUSA, BCP 1979, Marshall, Vol. II, 531; Southern Africa, *Prayer Book* 1989, 528; Scotland, Can. 33: 'At the burial of the dead the rubrical directions of the authorized Service Books of this Church shall be complied with so far as circumstances permit'; for provisions allowing the funeral to be conducted by a person other than the parish clergy, see Australia, Diocese of Sydney, *The 7th Handbook*, 8.6.

[119] England, Can. B3(4); Southern Africa, *Prayer Book* 1989, 528.

[120] ECUSA, BCP 1979, Marshall, Vol. II, 531; New Zealand, *Prayer Book* 1989, 867: at a church or a 'marae' (a Maori tribal meeting place).

blessed.[121] Some churches forbid funerals to take place on Sundays.[122] In most churches disposal of a body either by burial or by cremation is lawful.[123] With respect to burial in some churches it is the incumbent of a parish who has the right to determine the position of the grave.[124] Provision for exclusive rights of burial in reserved plots is exceptional.[125] The mode of disposal of ashes is sometimes regulated closely.[126] Express arrangements seldom exist concerning memorial services.[127] It may be mentioned, finally, that several churches have explicit provisions regulating exorcism, or the ministry of deliverance as it is sometimes known; usually the ministry may be exercised only after instruction and with permission from the bishop.[128]

CONCLUSIONS

There is extensive agreement within the canonical systems of the Anglican Communion about the nature and purposes of marriage. Formal laws are beginning to reflect, however, a subtle change from propositions about the permanence of marriage as a fact, to permanence as an ideal. In the vast majority of churches canon law does not recognize a right to marry in

[121] For England, see LFCE, 384f.; for blessing of a grave, see e.g. ECUSA, BCP 1979, Marshall, Vol. II, 559: it 'may' be blessed; Melanesia, Cans. B.2.A–D: it 'should' be blessed. For property issues related to burial, including the payment of fees and the keeping of registers, see Ch. 11.

[122] See e.g. Wales, Rules made under the Welsh Church (Burial Grounds) Act 1945, s. 4: this is so except in cases of emergency.

[123] England, Can. B38(2) and *Re Atkins* [1989] 1 All ER 14; Australia, *A Prayer Book for Australia* 1995, 771.

[124] England, *Re West Pennard Churchyard* [1991] 4 All ER 124; Wales, Rules made under the Welsh Church (Burial Grounds) Act 1945, s. 4.

[125] A faculty is required in Wales, ibid., r. 8; Ireland, Const. XII.3; and England: see P. Sparkes, 'Exclusive burial rights', *Ecclesiastical Law Journal*, 2(8) (1991), 133.

[126] Wales, BCP 1984, 797: ashes 'should be buried in consecrated ground' and may not be scattered; Southern Africa, *Prayer Book* 1989, 530: '[t]he ashes after cremation are placed either in a grave or in some place set apart for that purpose'; New Zealand, *Prayer Book* 1989, 877: this requires 'reverent disposal of the ashes in a dignified way'; Australia, *A Prayer Book for Australia* 1995, 771: '[t]he act of cremation . . . is symbolically incomplete without interment'.

[127] Australia, *A Prayer Book for Australia* 1995, 772; Southern Africa, *Prayer Book* 1989, 553.

[128] Australia, Can. P6 1992, 10: 'No minister may exorcise except when authorized so to do by the bishop of the diocese' (this may be adopted in the dioceses); Diocese of Sydney, *The 7th Handbook*, 8.31: 'Any licensed member of the clergy proposing to engage in an exorcism, except in special emergency, should act only after consultation with the assistant bishop'; Melanesia, Cans. B.3.A–C; Southern Africa, *Prayer Book* 1989, 489; Wales, BCP 1984, 770: this also requires 'co-operation with the medical profession'; in England, since the repeal of Can. 72 of the 1603 Canons, the matter is regulated by quasi-legislation: see LFCE, 401.

church – admission lies at the discretion of the minister. Lack of baptism, in one or both parties, is generally a good ground in Anglican canon law for refusal to solemnize but commonly churches confer a ministerial right of refusal on grounds of conscientious objection with respect to any proposed marriage. Equally, there is consistency as to the requirement that parties be instructed, as to criteria for validity (where basically churches seem to follow the state), and in the lack of formal provision for the support of a couple after solemnization. Resolutions of the Lambeth Conference have been influential, it would seem, in the response of churches to the greater availability of civil divorce – but the adoption of systems enabling ecclesiastical declarations of nullity is by no means universal. Most churches, however, allow remarriage in church following a civil divorce, either with episcopal consent or by means of ministerial consultation with the bishop. At the same time most churches do not seem to have implemented in law the Lambeth Conference recommendation that divorced and remarried people be excluded from Holy Communion. Quite remarkably, canon laws are generally silent on the seal of the confessional; prohibition against disclosure of information received in confession appears to be, therefore, an unwritten usage of Anglican churches. Whether the absence in most churches of formal rules denying funeral rites to the unbaptized, to suicides and excommunicates points to a general practice allowing an Anglican funeral is purely speculative.

11
Church Property and Finance

The interplay of canon law and secular law is perhaps most evident with regard to the management of church property. Generally, individual churches lack the capacity under the civil laws of the states within which they exist to hold and administer property. As a result property is held by trustees acting as representatives of the church with juridic personality under secular law. The doctrine of Christian stewardship, which increasingly is becoming a key concept in this field, provides a theological framework within which churches have developed legal structures enabling the responsible management of property and financial resources. Ownership of property is vested under secular law in trustees who function under the direct control of National, Provincial or Diocesan Synods and other assemblies. This chapter explores legal arrangements for the acquisition, use, maintenance and disposal of real and personal church property, particularly property used at the most local level, and the control and management of the finances of the church. Resolutions of the Lambeth Conference would seem to have been especially influential in the implementation of the principle of financial independence and in the widespread use of rights to stipends and pensions. Detailed legal provisions in many churches on the quota system represent a major development in recent years and may be of special interest to English canon lawyers unfamiliar with canonical regulation of this subject.[1]

TRUSTEESHIP OF PROPERTY AND ITS CONTROL

It is a general concept in Anglican canon law that all property is entrusted to ecclesiastical bodies for the benefit of the church. Effect is given to this idea in a number of ways, particularly in the widespread notion that the overall responsibility for oversight of the administration of church property resides in the provincial, national or regional assembly of individual

---

[1] The most complex body of law which churches possess is that relating to property. In order to illustrate this complexity, and to enable closer comparative scrutiny of the exact terms of the laws of different churches, the footnotes in this Chapter carry rather more detail than those of earlier Chapters. For discussion of property and finance generally, see J. W. G. Wand (ed.), *The Anglican Communion* (Oxford, 1948), 25, 56–61, 103–105, 132–3, 166–8, 232–4.

churches. Church laws differ most radically in relation to the vesting of property. Sometimes all church property, realty and personalty, is vested in national or provincial trustees both appointed by and acting under the direct control of the central assembly. Several churches do not operate a system of centralized ownership but rather assign the function of holding church property to diocesan trustees acting under the direction of the diocesan assembly. The laws of other churches allow a combination of these schemes. Whichever approach is employed, a dualist system seems to be the norm. On the one hand, the appropriate assembly determines the purposes to which realty or personalty must be put, and the priorities as between purposes, in accordance with any limitations imposed by national or provincial law. On the other hand, whilst they are directed accordingly, in turn trustees must ensure that those purposes and their implementation accord with the requirements of secular law.

First, in many churches the law promotes a centralized system of ownership. According to the constitution of the church in Southern Africa the Provincial Synod is empowered to frame regulations for the management and use of property held in trust for the church (except for the Dioceses of Cape Town and Grahamstown). Its regulations operate in so far as they do not conflict with secular law or the terms of any special trust. All property, movable or immovable, real or personal, which is given, obtained and held for the benefit of the church must wherever practicable be transferred to the Provincial Trustees acting on behalf of the Provincial Synod. Such property must be held as the Provincial Synod directs for the purpose of any ecclesiastical, missionary, religious, scholastic or charitable object; always, the trustees themselves are 'subject to all and singular the rules and directions . . . issued by or under the authority of the Provincial Synod'; they are also 'bound to obey and give effect to all decisions of the Tribunals for the exercise of Ecclesiastical Discipline'. The Provincial Trustees may sell (by public sale or private auction) and exchange property. They are empowered, in the application of proceeds, to purchase other property. However, the Provincial Synod may delegate to any Diocesan Synod, board, committee or other body 'any powers which may be required for the management of property' in the diocese.[2] This approach is employed in the laws of most African churches.[3] In Uganda,

---

[2] Southern Africa, Const. Arts. XVI–XX; see also Can. 42 which contains rules applicable to all trusts.

[3] Burundi, Const. Art. 22; Kenya, Const. Art. XVII and Can. IX; Tanzania, Const. IV.21: trustees must fulfil the terms of secular law as to trusteeship; Rwanda, Draft Const. 1996, Art. 13: land, buildings, funds and endowments are to be held by trustees elected and removable by the Provincial Synod; Nigeria, Const. Art. VII: trustees are subject to the jurisdiction of the church tribunals; Zaire, Const. Art. 20; West Africa, Const. Art. XX; Sudan, Const. Art. 62: General Synod is to appoint a Board of Trustees 'to receive and look after the real and immovable property, funds and endowments'

for example, a Board of Trustees of the Province of Uganda, incorporated under the secular Ugandan Trustees Incorporation Act, holds all land and property entrusted to it lawfully for any purpose of the church; the Board must 'give effect to any trusts whether general or special'; if the trust is for general purposes, the Trustees 'shall be guided by, the Diocesan Synod or Synods concerned. The Provincial Assembly is empowered to establish by canon a body known as 'Church Commissioners' with expert knowledge to assist and advise the Board of Trustees in the development and administration of any land or property held by the trustees.[4] The same duty, to appoint a Board of Trustees, appears in the church in Melanesia,[5] and Korea,[6] though in the Philippines it is the Executive Council of the Provincial Synod that acts as the Board of Trustees,[7] and in the Indian Ocean it is the Provincial Synod itself which holds the property of the church.[8]

For several churches, the secular law makes express provision for the holding of church property in this centralized fashion. Under the terms of secular parliamentary legislation, in the Church in Wales, the Representative Body, a charitable trustee corporation, holds and administers all church property vested in it for the uses and purposes of the arch-

belonging to the church; see also *Sibanda v Church of Christ* [1994)(1)] Zimbabwe Law Reports 74: this required compliance with the charter of incorporation and trusts deeds governing alienation of property.

[4] Uganda, Const. Art. 18.

[5] Melanesia, Const. Arts. 19, 21: the General Synod must appoint a Board of Trustees to receive and look after the property, funds and endowments belonging to the province; the terms of trusts for the benefit of the church prevail over any inconsistent provisions in the constitution; see also Chile, Cans. H.2: the Corporation; Brazil, Cans. I.7: the properties of the diocese are registered; Spain, Can. 18: this employs the concept of usufruct.

[6] Korea, Const. Art. 49: the church must establish the Anglican Church of Korea Church Property Trust which owns all land, church buildings and other property used for the benefit of the church; Art. 50: the Board is constituted by an equal number (determined by the National Synod) of representatives from each diocese chosen by the Diocesan Synod; Art. 51: the Board's statutes must be approved by the National Synod and 'the appropriate government authority'. The Church Property Trust must report on the land, buildings and property it holds, and other trust business, at each regular meeting of the National Synod.

[7] Philippines, Const. VI.1: the Executive Council of the Provincial Synod is the Board of Trustees and is incorporated as such under Philippine secular law; it is empowered to 'enter into contract with any legal entity, acquire, alienate or encumber properties . . . and may sue and be sued'; see the secular decision of *Metropolitan See of the Episcopal Church in the Philippines Inc v Prime Bishop Ticobay and Others* (1996) Securities and Exchange Commission, EB Case 471: the Executive Council has competence under the constitution and canons to alienate property without the consent of the metropolitical see.

[8] Indian Ocean, Const. Art. 18: the Provincial Synod is authorized to acquire movable and immovable property and to receive gifts or legacies the administration of which may be delegated to the diocese where the property is situated.

bishop, bishop, clergy and laity of the church. Subject to its statutory authority, powers and duties, and the terms of secular charitable trusts law, the Representative Body is obliged to perform its functions under the order and control of the Governing Body. Subject to the provisions of the Welsh Church Act 1914 and its royal charter of incorporation, the Governing Body is empowered to 'make alteration . . . in the powers and duties' of the Representative Body. The members of the Representative Body are elected by the dioceses but its *ex officio* members include the diocesan bishops. The Governing Body may remove any of its members 'for sufficient cause', of which the Governing Body is final judge. The Representative Body is empowered to sell, exchange, lease, and manage all real and personal property vested in it. It is also empowered to sell property vested in it but certain types of property, church plate, furniture, buildings and vessels may be sold only with the written consent of the diocesan bishop.[9] Much the same system operates in Ireland,[10] and in Papua New Guinea.[11]

Secondly, by way of contrast, the norm in other churches is for property to be held at diocesan level, with trustees acting under the direct control of the Diocesan Synod or council. In New Zealand, where the Charitable Trusts Act 1957 requires the vesting in trustees of freehold and leasehold property acquired by or on behalf of any religious denomination, the Diocesan Trusts Board, appointed by the Diocesan Synod, is empowered to appoint trustees to administer the property of the diocese. All property held for the use of the diocese must be transferred to the Diocesan Trusts Board and 'the specific application [of land] shall be determined by the Diocesan Synod, subject to the control of the General Synod'. The diocesan

[9] Wales, Welsh Church Act 1914, s. 13; Const. II.56, III.2, 3–5, 17, 20–21, 26.

[10] Ireland, Irish Church Act 1869; Trustee Churches (Ireland) Act 1884; Const. XI.11, 12: the Representative Body holds property for the use and purposes of the church subject to the order and control of the General Synod; it may lease or sell by public auction or by private contract any see lands and sites of churches, which are found unnecessary, with the consent of the Diocesan Council; it may also grant loans for the purchase, repair or improvement of church real property; Const. X.11: all movable property for use in church services vests in it 'subject to any trust affecting the same'; movable property which has ceased to be required by a parish shall be disposed of as the Body thinks fit: proceeds must be applied for the purposes of the parish or in such other manner as the diocesan council determines; see also *RCB v AG* [1988] IR 19: when purposes fail the court may permit application of trust property *cy-près*.

[11] Papua New Guinea, Const. Arts. 8, 18 and the Anglican Church of Papua New Guinea Property Trust Act 1993: the Provincial Council is responsible for property and must appoint Provincial Trustees to hold and administer it for the erection of church houses, schools, hospitals and other buildings 'in connection with or for the benefit or maintenance of the church or of the members thereof'; the Trustees may purchase, lease, acquire by gift, devise, exchange or otherwise, realty and personalty and sell it by public auction or private contract. Every trustee must be indemnified against loss unless by his own wilful act or default; the trustees may sue and be sued.

trustees must 'carry out the objects of each Trust in such manner . . . as the Diocesan Synod shall . . . direct'.[12] Similarly, in Scotland the supervision of all properties within each diocese rests with the Diocesan Synod which, annually and from its membership, appoints a Committee to perform the function of supervision. The diocesan trustees must obtain the consent of the standing committee of the Synod concerning the sale of church property.[13] In some churches, the system of diocesan trustees operates alongside the centralized system of provincial trustees,[14] and in a small number the vesting of property in diocesan trustees is effected by secular law.[15] In other churches, property used in a diocese is held by a national body of trustees but oversight of its administration is effected by the diocesan assembly.[16] In turn, sometimes, the law of the church enables property to be held nationally under the supervision of authorities responsible to the diocesan assembly. In Australia, the national Anglican Church of Australia Trust Corporation is empowered to acquire and to hold realty and personalty. The Corporation may be appointed as trustees of any church property: it may act as trustee of property in a diocese, with the consent of the Diocesan Synod, in which case that property is then held subject to the direction of the Diocesan Synod.[17]

---

[12] New Zealand, Cans. F.I.1, F.III, F.VIII.1; see also the Anglican Church Trusts Act 1981.

[13] Scotland, Digest of Resolutions, 37: the committee's duties include supervision and enquiry as to: congregational capital funds and the propriety of their investment; the condition and repair of buildings; due payment of feuduties and other charges on property; and adequate insurance; Digest of Resolutions, 36.2: the diocesan trustees must obtain the consent of the standing committee concerning the sale of property.

[14] Southern Africa, Const. Arts. XVI–XVII: Diocesan Synods similarly enjoy a legislative power over property but any diocesan regulations are subject to those made by the Provincial Synod; see also Can. 42.11: the Diocesan Trusts' Board, appointed by the Diocesan Synod, is authorized to act on behalf of the Synod; the trustees must 'carry out the objects of the Trust in such manner, not inconsistent with the terms of the Trust, as the several Diocesan Synods shall from time to time direct'.

[15] See e.g. Barbados, Anglican Church Act 1969, s. 6: property vests in the Barbados Diocesan Trustees.

[16] North India, Const. II.III.IX.25: the diocesan council has 'the supervision of properties in the use of the Church within the Diocese' and acts on behalf of the North India Trust Association; the council is under a duty to ensure 'that right use is made of the Church property'; ibid., II.III.XIV.3: the function of the diocesan property committee is to manage and/or supervise properties in use in the diocese and its pastorates; it is responsible to the Church of North India Trust Association for the care, maintenance and protection of church property.

[17] Australia, Const. X.64; and Corporate Trustees Canon, Can. 2 1962: the primate is chair and membership includes four trustees elected by General Synod who hold office until death or resignation or if declared by a court to be incapable of managing their affairs; they must present a report of their activities at each session of the General Synod; see also *Church of England Property Trust Diocese of Goulburn v Rossi* (1893) 14 LR (NSW) Eq 186: trustees who purported to have been appointed under state legislation never had the trust estate conveyed to them; *AG v Church of England Property Trust*

Finally, there are those churches which enable the holding of property by trustees at the lowest levels of the church. In England, the church is not of itself a corporation and as such it does not therefore hold property; it does so through representative owners: archbishops, bishops, archdeacons and incumbents are corporations sole; corporations aggregate include parochial church councils, and, for some purposes, church-wardens; alongside these arrangements, at the national level the Church Commissioners may acquire and hold a wide range of properties.[18] A similar approach operates with respect to ECUSA in which vestries and other trustees may hold property. All real and personal property held by or for the benefit of the parish, mission or congregation is held in trust for the church and the diocese in which it is located: however, the existence of this trust in no way limits the power and authority of a parish, mission or congregation otherwise existing over such property so long as it remains part of and subject to the governing authorities of the church, its constitution and canons.[19]

Diocese of Sydney (1933) 34 SR (NSW) 36: in declaring new trusts to take effect outside a parish, where it had become impossible to operate existing trusts, it was not necessary to specify the new beneficiaries. For guidance of the applicability of secular law to the administration of trusts, see e.g. Diocese of Sydney, *The 7th Handbook*, 12; *AG (Queensland) v Corporation of the Lesser Chapter of Brisbane Cathedral* [1975–8] 136 CLR 353: this contains discussion of the effects of the incorporation of Diocesan Synods under secular law.

[18] See generally L. Leeder, *Ecclesiastical Law Handbook* (London, 1997), Ch. 8; it has been held that the freehold of the church usually vested in the incumbent and is held for the use of the parishioners: *Ritchings v Cordingley* (1868) LR 3 A & E 113.

[19] ECUSA, Cans. I.7.3–4; it has been decided judicially that, when there is a schism in a church, a court cannot quiet title to church property on the basis of doctrine; but, some courts have deferred to the resolution of a property dispute by a higher authority of the church under which parties seceding from a hierarchical church lose all rights to church property: see e.g. *Protestant Episcopal Church in the Diocese of New Jersey v Graves*, 83 NJ 572 (NJ); *Moore's Protestant Episcopal Church in the Diocese of New Jersey*, 449 US 1131 (NJ); see also *Hunter v Rector, Wardens and Vestrymen of St. Anna's Chapel*, 168 So 780, 185 La 217 (La): a deed to the trustees of the church for its benefit vests legal title in those trustees, and whether they are a corporation is immaterial so long as they are a legal body capable of taking estates by grant; *Edwards v Rector, Churchwardens and Vestrymen of Trinity Church in the City of New York*, 296 US 628 (US): it is presumed that a royal grant of land to a church is legal in all respects; *Town of Pawlet v Clark* (1815) 13 US (9 Cranch) 292 (US): the Church of England was not a corporate body; *Terrett v Taylor* (1915) 13 US (9 Cranch) 43 (US): the churchwardens are not a corporation for the holding of church lands which cannot be sold without the consent of the parson and vestry; *Rector, Wardens and Vestrymen of Trinity-St Michael's Parish Inc v Episcopal Church in the Diocese of Connecticut* (1993), 224 Conn 797, 620 A 2d. 1289 (Conn): parishes have held their property in trust for the larger church even though this trust was not expressed in the canons until the 1970s.

FORMS OF CHURCH PROPERTY

The principal forms of real and personal property used at the lowest level of the church include: places of public worship and their contents, associated buildings (such as church halls), churchyards and burial grounds, residence houses for clergy, and ecclesiastical registers and records. Whilst the ownership of church property vests in a wide variety of ecclesiastical trustees – provincial, diocesan or local, depending on the church in question – responsibility for the day-to-day care and maintenance is assigned to parishes or pastorates and their clergy, councils and congregations.

The Church Building and its Contents

In several churches, legally a building does not acquire the status of a church designated for public worship until it is set apart for that purpose by means of consecration or dedication.[20] The act of consecration or dedication, for which a special service may be used,[21] is reserved to the bishop.[22] In some churches the law provides that the effects of consecration or dedication may be removed, usually by an episcopal act.[23] Occasionally, laws forbid the setting aside of a building as a place of public worship unless and until the bishop is satisfied that the building is free from secular legal incumbrances.[24] It is, needless to say, an assumption that once a building has been set aside for a sacred purpose, no acts which are contrary to that purpose may be performed in the building. However, seldom is it the case that express provision is made in law to ensure this.

[20] England, Pastoral Measure 1983, s. 87: a building does not become a church until consecrated for the purpose of public worship; Ireland, Const. IX.36: 'As often as churches are newly built or rebuilt, or churchyards are appointed for burial, they shall be dedicated and consecrated'; Australia, Diocese of Sydney, *The 7th Handbook*, 11: a church is a building which has been duly consecrated or licensed by the bishop for divine service.

[21] See e.g. ECUSA, BCP 1979, Marshall, Vol. II, 687: 'Accept us now, as we dedicate this place to which we come to praise your Name, to ask forgiveness, to know your healing power, to hear your Word, and to be nourished by the Body and Blood of your Son. Be present always to guide and to judge, to illuminate and to bless your people'.

[22] Korea, Const. Art. 12.4: 'the consecration of churches within his diocese' is one of the duties of the bishop; Melanesia, Diocese of Temotu, Can. 5: the bishop may consecrate or dedicate a church.

[23] England, Care of Churches and Ecclesiastical Jurisdiction Measure, 1991, s. 22.

[24] ECUSA, Cans. II.7.1: no church shall be consecrated until the bishop is satisfied that the building is secured for ownership; see also Diocese of Mississippi, Cans. II.C.30: consecration is forbidden until the bishop is satisfied that the property has been fully paid for and is free from any lien or other incumbrance; Australia, Diocese of Sydney, *The 7th Handbook*, 11.4: 'A church may be consecrated when it is free of debt and complete in its structure and furnishings'.

The few laws which deal with the matter provide enforcement in a number of different ways. In English canon law a consecrated church cannot be used for purposes inconsistent with the object of consecration. The primary responsibility for ensuring use consistent with consecration lies with the churchwardens: they must not allow it to be profaned by any meeting for temporal purposes inconsistent with the sanctity of the place. When it is proposed to use it for a play, concert or exhibition of films or pictures, the minister must ensure that the words and music are such as befit the house of God, are consonant with sound doctrine and make for the edifying of the people.[25] Irish canon law contains much the same system of regulation.[26] In Scottish canon law, however, any use which is not 'religious' or 'ecclesiastical' must be sanctioned by the bishop.[27] In some churches the law seeks to control use of the building beyond the time when it has ceased to be used for public worship.[28]

It is a general principle of Anglican canon law that the day-to-day control of the church building is vested in the local parish or pastorate council. The law of Southern Africa is typical: the parish council is 'to have direction and control of the properties . . . of the Parish' subject to the overriding control of the Provincial Trustees when this has been assigned to them and the rules and canons of the diocese.[29] With respect to some

[25] England, Can. F15, F16: the minister is obliged to obey the directions of the ordinary; see also North India, Const. II.II.XXI.1: the pastorate committee is responsible for 'the protection of the property from encroachment and/or from any other kind of misuse'; ibid., II.II.XXI.2: 'Property belonging to the Church shall not be available for use by political parties for propaganda purposes or for public worship contrary to the Christian Faith'.

[26] Ireland, Const. IX.27: this lists purposes to which a church may be put other than public worship: when a church is to be used for a play, concert, exhibition of films or pictures or similar purpose, 'the minister shall take care that the words, music, pictures and performance are such as befit the house of God, are consonant with sound doctrine, and contribute to the edifying of the people'; the minister must obey any directions relating to such use as may be issued from time to time by the ordinary; ibid., IX.40: this prohibits incense or 'any substitution' or 'imitation'; ibid, IX.41: this regulates processions.

[27] Scotland, Can. 35.4: 'No church that is consecrated or set apart for public worship shall be used for any purpose not religious or ecclesiastical without the consent of the Bishop'; see also Australia, Diocese of Sydney, *The 7th Handbook*, 11.6: the church must not be used for 'a purpose not sanctioned by the minister', but: for divine worship or religious instruction, a vestry or prayer meeting, or any similar purposes approved by the bishop.

[28] See e.g. Ireland, Const. IX.36: 'No church which has ceased to be required for worship, nor any churchyard, shall be put to any base or unworthy use'; ECUSA, Cans. II.7.3: this forbids disposal for 'wordly' use without the consent of the diocesan standing committee.

[29] Southern Africa, Can. 28.4; see also North India, Const. II.II.XXI.1: the pastorate committee is responsible to the Diocesan Council for 'the right use of Church property, both movable and immovable such as the church building, chapel, Sunday School rooms, parsonage, parish hall, graveyard and other property allocated for the use of the Pastorate'.

churches, this right has been recognized in the secular courts.[30] In a number of churches, however, primary control is assigned to the minister who acts with the assistance of the parish council.[31] Some laws confer a right upon parishioners to appeal to the bishop in cases of dispute.[32] Occasionally, laws expressly confer upon the minister a right of access.[33] A fundamental aspect of this general right of control is responsibility for the care and maintenance of the church and its contents. It is nowhere better represented than in Scottish canon law: the vestry with the rector or priest-in-charge 'shall cause all proper and reasonable care' to be taken of places of worship within its charge, and of the furniture and ornaments, and they must endeavour to keep them 'decent, clean and in good repair'.[34] The same principle appears in the laws of very many churches,[35]

---

[30] See e.g. ECUSA, *Cushman v Rector etc of the Church of the Good Shepherd of Radnor*, 162 Pa 290 (Pa): the church has the right to regulate the use of the church building in conformity with the church's own rules and, if held under special trusts, in conformity with the requirements of the deed; it may carry out repairs unless this is contrary to the trust.

[31] Brazil, Cans. I.7: it is the duty of each minister to provide control over the use of the property of the church which the minister shares with the bishop and the parochial church board; Chile, Cans. H.3; Philippines, Cans. III.15.2: the rector is 'entitled to use and control the Church and Parish buildings with appurtenances and furniture'; compare Korea, Const. Art. 49.4: the use of any property situated in a diocese is determined by the Diocesan Synod.

[32] Papua New Guinea, Diocese of Port Moresby, Can. 11.28: the incumbent assisted by the parish executive has control of all buildings designated to the care of the parish, but '[p]arishioners shall have the right of appeal to the Diocesan Council about the use of such buildings and decisions of the Diocesan Council shall be final'; see also New Zealand, Cans. B.V.5.3.1: 'The Vestry shall have control and management of the Parish Hall'; if the vestry fails or refuses to allow any use of the parish hall 'desired by any Parishioner, then such Parishioner shall have the right to appeal to the Standing Committee of the Diocese against such failure or refusal'; the committee 'may in its discretion either refuse or allow such proposed use of the Parish Hall and in any such case the decision of the Standing Committee shall be final'.

[33] New Zealand, Cans. B.V.5.3.1: 'The Vicar of the Parish shall have possession of the keys of [the] Vicarage and the Churches'; for the same rule in England, see *Daunt v Crocker* (1867) LR 2 A & E 41; Australia, Diocese of Sydney, *The 7th Handbook*, 11.6: 'the minister is entitled to access to the church at all times'; see also the Australian case of *Long v Rawlins* (1874) 4 QSCR 86: whether a member of the public has a right to enter a church depends on the rules of the church and its trust deed; see also Central Africa, Diocese of Mashonaland, *Pastoral Regulations* 1978, 20: the whereabouts of the key to the aumbry should be known only to the local priests, and to the sacristan or other person who has charge of the Church in the priest's absence, and to no one else.

[34] Scotland, Can. 35.3; see also Central Africa, Diocese of Lake Malani and Southern Malani, *Diocesan Acts* 1980, 8.8: the parochial church council must provide for the safety of communion vessels, valuables and records to the satisfaction of the Archdeacon.

[35] Ireland, Const. III.24: the select vestry of a parish must ensure that churches and other parochial buildings are kept in 'a proper state of repair and maintenance' and that 'churches and their furnishings are kept in a proper state of cleanliness'; England, Can. F13: churches must be decently kept and repaired; all things in them must be maintained in such an orderly and decent fashion as best becomes the house of God; this

and sometimes laws prescribe in detail the objects which must be provided and maintained in a church for the purposes of public worship.[36]

As a matter of ecclesiastical practice, churches throughout the Anglican Communion contain detailed provisions concerning the procedures to be employed when works are proposed to be carried out involving the church building and its contents. It is a general principle that episcopal consent must, in one form or another, be obtained for any alteration, addition or removal. First, in some churches, a judicial system is employed under which the chancellor in the diocesan tribunal, acting under the ordinary jurisdiction of the bishop, permits works to be carried out under the authority of a faculty. This judicial system operates in England,[37] and Wales.[38] Secondly, in other churches, the direct consent of the bishop is required: in the West Indies, a faculty must be obtained from the bishop,[39]

responsibility falls on the parochial church council (F14); Wales, Church Fabric Regulations, 1–4: 'The Parochial Church Council shall keep all churches in the parish in repair and shall be responsible to the Representative Body for the proper care, maintenance and upkeep of such churches and their contents'; Japan, Can. XIII. Art. 128: the vestry has custody over the vessels and the maintenance of buildings; Portugal, Can. IX, Art. 5: care and maintenance is a duty of the parish council.

[36] England, Can. F1–10: there must be a font, holy table, communion plate, communion linen, surplices, reading desks and pulpit, seats, church bells, bible and prayer book and alms box; Ireland, Const. III.24: the select vestry must provide from the funds at its disposal the requisites for divine service including prayer books, hymnals, reading desk, pulpit, font, table, chalice, patten and linen cloth, and bread and wine subject to the direction of the minister; Wales, BCP 1984, 22, General Directions, 2: 'The bread and wine are to be provided by the churchwardens at the expense of the parish'.

[37] England, Can. F13(3): 'It shall be the duty of the minister and churchwardens, if any alterations, additions, removals, or repairs are proposed to be made in the fabric, ornaments, or furniture of the church, to obtain a faculty or licence of the ordinary before proceeding to execute the same'; Care of Churches and Ecclesiastical Jurisdiction Measure 1991, s. 11: the diocesan chancellor must give written guidance to all parochial church councils, ministers and churchwardens 'as to those matters within the jurisdiction of the consistory court which he for the time being considers, after consultation with the diocesan advisory committee, to be matters of such a nature that they may be undertaken without a faculty': the archdeacon may grant unopposed faculties. A very large body of judicial decisions provides guidance on the issuing of faculties which, generally, is at the discretion of the diocesan chancellor: see generally, G. H. Newsom and G. L. Newsom, *Faculty Jurisdiction of the Church of England* (2nd edn., London, 1993).

[38] Wales, Rules of the Diocesan Courts, 2, 5: the following require a faculty: the change of use of a consecrated church or land; any alteration, addition or repair to, decoration, redecoration or demolition of, and removal from, the fabric of a consecrated church or land; the introduction, removal, and alteration or repositioning of, furniture, fittings, murals, monuments (including gravestones), plate and other precious objects, into, from or in, a consecrated church or consecrated land, or the repair of any such furniture, fittings, murals or objects. Unconsecrated churches and churchyards are subject to the faculty procedure if the bishop so decrees in writing; under the Church Fabric Regulations, parochial church councils 'shall observe' the Faculty Rules.

[39] In the West Indies, Can. 27: 'No Church . . . shall be erected, demolished, removed or substantially altered, externally or internally, without the written approval and consent of the Bishop of the Diocese, given upon application therefor in writing'; episcopal

acting in a quasi-judicial manner, a process which may be susceptible to review by the secular courts.[40] Indeed, an episcopal faculty system is employed in New Zealand,[41] in dioceses in Australia,[42] and in Papua New Guinea.[43] But in some churches, such as Ireland,[44] Scotland,[45] where the

consent is also required for '[t]he erection, substantial alteration, or removal of Altars, Fonts, Pulpits, Lecterns, Organ, Seats, Screens, or Bells, or any notable ornament, or the installation of electric lighting, fans and the erection or removal of permanent Memorials in Churches or on the external fabric thereof or in Church-yards or Cemeteries'; every application to the bishop must certify that due notice has been given to the congregation to indicate objections: 'Where there are objections the Bishop assisted by his Chancellor shall hear and determine the issue and the decision shall be final'; where diocesan laws so require, 'a faculty shall be issued in accordance with the provisions of the said Canons and Regulations of the Diocese'.

[40] Barbados, *Blades and Another v Jaggard and Others* (1961) 4 West Indian Reports 207 at 217 *per* Stoby CJ: 'while the Bishop or Chancellor . . . always has a discretion whether a faculty will be granted or not, it is the duty of an applicant for a faculty . . . to obtain the views of the parishioners and in the petition to state whether the application is supported by a majority or minority of parishioners'; this procedure is necessary only when alterations will result in the parishioners being put to expense; the court cited the celebrated English decision of *Nickalls v Briscoe* [1892] P 269.

[41] New Zealand, Cans. F.III.15–17: 'No alteration of an important kind, affecting the stability and general plan of the church, and no new arrangement of seats or erection of monuments shall take place without the written consent of the Trustees, the Minister and Churchwardens'; 'A Faculty for such alteration . . . may be issued by the Bishop' if satisfied *inter alia* that there is adequate insurance: no alteration may occur until the faculty is issued and any questions arising between trustees and the ministers or officers of the parish 'shall be decided by the Bishop and the Standing Committee of the Diocese'.

[42] Australia, Diocese of Sydney, *The 7th Handbook*, 11.7: 'It is unlawful to alter, add to or take away from the fabric, utensils, ornaments or furniture of a church; or to place any monument, memorial or tablet in or on any part of a church, except with approval of the [bishop] given by faculty'; *Re Trusts of the Church of St. Jude, Brighton* (1956) SASR 46: a power given by a trust deed to enlarge, alter, repair and reinstate a church did not extend to authorize the demolition of a church and the erection of a new and larger one.

[43] Papua New Guinea, Diocese of Port Moresby, Can. 11.36: no alteration may be made of 'the principal fabric, furniture, monuments or ornaments of any Church' without an episcopal faculty – this does not apply to 'ordinary maintenance'.

[44] Ireland, Const. IX.38: 'No change shall be made in the structure, ornaments, furnishings or monuments of any church (whether by introduction, alteration or removal), unless with the consent of the incumbent and select vestry, and until an accurate description or design of the proposed change shall have been approved of by the ordinary: provided always that any person aggrieved by any such proposed change, or by the refusal of the ordinary, incumbent or the select vestry to consent or approve thereof, shall have a right of appeal'.

[45] Scotland, Can. 35.1: 'No change (whether by introduction, alteration or removal) shall be made in the structure, ecclesiastical furniture or ornaments, monuments, mural tablets, or painted windows of any church used for public worship, nor shall any scheme of redecoration or any alteration of lighting or heating system be undertaken', without the consent of the rector or priest-in-charge and the vestry and until the bishop (or an advisory committee appointed by the bishop) is consulted and approves in writing. An appeal by the proposers or opponents lies to the bishop. If any of the proposers or opponents feel aggrieved by the bishop's decision, an appeal lies to the Episcopal Synod.

law also confers a right of appeal in the event of refusal, Melanesia,[46] and Southern Africa,[47] episcopal authorization is not in the technical form of a faculty. Thirdly, in several churches, for the erection of or additions to church buildings the consent of the bishop and/or the diocesan standing committee is required.[48] Occasionally, the system of care and maintenance is supported by a duty to keep an inventory of the contents of the church, which is subject to inspection at prescribed times, usually by the archdeacon or some other officer: this is the case in England,[49] Ireland,[50] Wales,[51] and Scotland,[52] but there is little evidence of the practice in the formal laws of other churches.[53] Oversight is also supported in a number of churches

[46] Melanesia, Diocese of Temotu, Can. 5: nothing may be introduced or removed from a church without episcopal consent.

[47] Southern Africa, Can. 31: it is not lawful for any incumbent, churchwarden or other person to make any alteration in the construction or arrangements of any church without 'the written permission of the bishop'.

[48] ECUSA, Cans. II.7.1 and Diocese of Mississippi, Cans. II.C.30; Papua New Guinea, Diocese of Port Moresby, Can. 11.34: the advice of the diocesan council must be obtained before any building is erected on church property; see also West Indies, Can. 27.1; Central Africa, Diocese of Lake Malani and Southern Malani, *Diocesan Acts* 1980, 8.1: no buildings are to be erected on church land nor their use altered without the consent of the diocesan standing committee; New Zealand, Cans. F.III.13: no building is to be erected on a church until plans are submitted to the bishop for approval; and Melanesia, Diocese of Temotu, Can. 5: when a congregation wishes to build a new permanent church, the diocesan bishop must consent; it is for the bishop to determine questions relating to churches which are 'too old for further use'.

[49] England, Can. F17: a record must be kept of all alterations and the archdeacon at least once every 3 years must satisfy himself that a full note and terrier of all lands, goods and other possessions is maintained; see also Southern Africa, Can. 15.7: the archdeacon must examine and report to the bishop on 'all plans for the building or restoration or alteration of churches and other buildings'.

[50] Ireland, Const. III.38: the incumbent and churchwardens must furnish the representative body with 'a complete statement of the church plate and parochial documents' in their custody; the rural dean must examine the church annually and report to the diocesan council; he is responsible for safe custody of plate and documents during a vacancy.

[51] Wales, Const. VI.21: 'It shall be the duty of the Incumbent and Churchwardens of every parish to ensure that particulars of all church plate and other valuable articles belonging to the church or used in the worship of any church or mission room in the parish, are entered in the inventory of such church or mission room'; the inventory is under the control of the incumbent and churchwardens; entries must state the name of the donor if known; and gifts must be reported to the bishop and the representative body; VI.21A: the incumbent and churchwardens must keep a log book and terrier.

[52] Scotland, Can. 35, Resolution 1: unless the constitution of the charge places the duty on the churchwardens, the vestry must see that a detailed inventory of all church goods, ornaments and registers be prepared and kept up to date; a copy must be sent to the registrar and it is to be compiled in accordance with the form issued by the standing committee of General Synod.

[53] See, however, e.g. West Africa, Diocese of Gambia and Guinea, Const. 1982, Art. 22; ECUSA, Cans. I.6.1: each parish must submit an annual report to the diocesan bishop itemizing all holdings of realty and personalty, with an appraisal of their value.

by a system of regular inspection of the church building and its contents, annually,[54] every three years,[55] or every five years.[56]

Similar systems of control exist with respect to the disposal of the church building and its contents by way of sale, leasing or exchange. Some churches require the consent of the bishop,[57] others that of the Diocesan Synod,[58] or of its standing committee,[59] or that of both the bishop and the standing committee (as is the case in ECUSA),[60] or of some other desig-

---

[54] Southern Africa, Can. 15: the archdeacon must examine annually the inventory, burial grounds and fabric and report to the bishop; Scotland, Can. 35, Digest of Resolutions, 37: the administration board must make an annual enquiry of vestries concerning: the ownership of any property; the date of the last comprehensive survey of all buildings; any change in the architect; the date of last full review of insurance and a note of the present levels of cover.

[55] England, Can. F18: the archdeacon must survey at least once in 3 years the churches and churchyards and 'give direction for the amendment of all defects in the fabric, ornaments and furniture' (see also the Inspection of Churches Measure 1955); any person or body carrying out functions of care and maintenance must have 'due regard to the role of the church as a local centre of worship and mission': Care of Churches and Ecclesiastical Jurisdiction Measure, 1991 s. 2.

[56] Wales, Const. IV.17: the Diocesan Board of Finance must provide a quinquennial inspection of every church; Church Fabric Regulations: the parochial church council must co-operate in the inspection and must effect all repairs reasonably advised as a result; also churchwardens must report annually to the council and the archdeacon on 'the state of repair of all churches . . . and their contents and any outstanding and necessary work'; Scotland, Can. 35, Digest of Resolutions, 37: each vestry (or, if it fails, the diocese) must appoint an architect or chartered surveyor to supervise buildings under its charge and must receive a written report every 5 years.

[57] Wales, Const. III.26: for the sale of church plate, furniture, or other movable chattels used for divine worship, consecrated sites and ecclesiastical residences, the consent of the diocesan bishop must be obtained; Redundant Churches Regulations: no church may be declared redundant by the bishop without first seeking and considering the advice of the Diocesan Churches Committee and the archdeacons; the committee must in turn seek and consider the advice *inter alia* of the parochial church council, the incumbent and churchwardens. On a declaration of redundancy, the management and insurance of the church building and contents ceases to be the responsibility of the incumbent, churchwardens and council and becomes the responsibility of the representative body.

[58] Southern Africa, Can. 31: no consecrated building is to be sold, exchanged or otherwise disposed of unless this is authorized by the Diocesan Synod pursuant to a report of a commission appointed by the bishop; there must be a revocation of consecration.

[59] North India, Const. II.II.XXI.2: 'The Pastorate Committee shall have no authority to lease, rent out, mortgage, sell, pledge as security or alienate in any manner whatsoever, church property in the use of the Pastorate'; any scheme regarding development of the immovable property must be approved by the diocesan council or its executive committee through the diocesan property committee; the final decision rests with the Church of North India Trust Asssociation.

[60] ECUSA, Cans. II.7.1–3: consecrated or dedicated churches used solely for divine service may not be alienated by any vestry, trustees or other body, without the prior consent of the bishop acting on the advice and with the consent of the diocesan standing committee; nor may they be removed, taken down, or otherwise disposed of for 'any worldly or common use' without the consent of the diocesan standing committee;

nated ecclesiastical authority.[61] Churches commonly incorporate into their laws rules governing the application of proceeds derived from the sale of church property.[62] In some states, the law regulates alterations to church buildings and this has from time to time resulted in litigation in the secular courts.[63] With the notable exceptions of the church in Wales,[64] Ireland,[65]

see also *Wilkeson v Rector, Wardens and Vestry of St. Luke's Parish of Tacoma*, 176 Wash 377 (Wash): property may be sold subject to the terms of the charter of incorporation; *Rector, Churchwardens and Vestrymen of the Church of the Nativity v Fleming*, 20 NYS 2d 597 (NY): property can be sold to satisfy a judgment against a church. See also Philippines, Cans. II.5; and Mexico, Can. 15.

[61] Scotland, Can. 35.2: 'No holy vessel or ecclesiastical furniture or ornaments are to be sold, exchanged or otherwise disposed of without the written consent of the bishop, the dean and the registrar of the diocese'.

[62] Ireland, Const. X.19ff.: money received by the representative body from any sale or insurance compensation may be used only for the building or repair of an equivalent building reasonably suited to the existing needs of the parish at a cost determined by the diocesan council; *Johnson and Others v Robinson* (1922) Ct. of GS, Journal of the General Synod, 1992, 333: this dealt with alleged sub-letting of glebe without permission; the petition was withdrawn. See also Wales, Redundant Churches Regulations: proceeds from the sale, leasing or licensing of churches and churchyards may be applied to, *inter alia*, the purchase of burial grounds in the parish; the repair of places of worship, churchyards, burial grounds, and church halls in the parish.

[63] ECUSA, *St Bartholomew's Church v City of New York* (1990) 914 F 2d 348: US Ct of Appeals: ECUSA unsuccessfully challenged the constitutionality of legislation after an application under it to demolish a community house adjacent to a church, both designated as 'landmarks', had been refused; the legislation was 'valid, neutral regulation of general applicability' – ECUSA had not objected to the original designation; Australia, Diocese of Sydney, *The 7th Handbook*, 11.17ff.: churches and church buildings, if they fall within the Heritage Act 1977, enjoy special protection to which church authorities are subject: if a Permanent Conservation Order exists there can be no alteration, development or demolition without the consent of the Heritage Council; in England and Wales, places of worship are exempt from the Planning (Listed Buildings and Conservation) Act 1990 and they are not monuments for the purposes of control under the Ancient Monuments and Archeological Areas Act 1979: the faculty system is allowed to operate instead of secular control.

[64] Wales, Regulations for the Administration of Churchyards: the incumbent is responsible for the 'general supervision' of the churchyard, but the parochial church council is responsible for its 'proper care, maintenance and upkeep' and for the repair of any damage; Rules of the Diocesan Courts, 2, 5: a faculty is required for the acquisition of a permanent or exclusive right of burial and for the removal of a corpse or cremated remains; the bishop may place unconsecrated churchyards and burial grounds under the faculty rules by written decree; these are subject to faculty rules in any event if listed under secular legislation as being of special architectural or historic interest or if situated in a conservation area.

[65] Ireland, Const. XII.1: the care of all burial grounds vested in the representative body is entrusted to the minister and churchwardens; they may prevent trespass or other unlawful use and act on behalf of the trustees in legal proceedings; ibid., XII.3, 10: if a family has by faculty or prescription acquired a right to be buried in a particular place, the exercise of that right (in conformity with the Irish Church Act 1869) must be allowed by the ministers and churchwardens; any person aggrieved by a decision of the ordinary, minister or churchwardens has a right of appeal to the Court of General Synod; Australia, *Beard v Baulkham Hills Shire Council* [1986(7)] NSWLR 273: this deals

and England,[66] as a matter of ecclesiastical practice there is little formal canon law in the Anglican Communion on the subject of churchyards and burial grounds.[67]

Clergy Residences

An insufficient number of churches possess formal law on clergy residences, or parsonages,[68] from which to construct a set of general principles applicable throughout the Communion. Provisions are to be found rather within rules applying to church property generally. It is rarely the case that canon law confers upon clergy an explicit right to a residence:[69] normally such rights are assumed. In those churches which have national or provincial laws especially devoted to this subject, rules deal mainly with use, care and maintenance, alteration and disposal. Several of the elements of English church law find direct parallels in the laws of other churches. In England, responsibility for care and maintenance is shared by the incumbent and the diocese which, through its parsonages board, must organize quinquennial inspections and carry out repairs to the property. The incumbent, obliged to take 'proper care of the parsonage house, being a duty equivalent to that of a tenant, to use the premises in a tenant-like manner', is liable for deliberate acts damaging to it. During a vacancy responsibility for care and maintenance rests on the bishop. The incumbent has powers of disposal subject to the consent of the Church Commissioners, the diocesan parsonages board and the bishop – and the parochial church council has rights to be notified and to object but not to veto disposal.[70] These arrangements find a direct parallel: in Australia, where use of the house is under the control of the minister;[71] in New

---

with ecclesiastical custom and usage concerning the sale of rights to burial; it was held that English ecclesiastical law did not apply to the case.

[66] England, Can. F13: churchyards must be decently maintained and kept in sufficient repair; they must be duly fenced and kept in an orderly and decent manner as become consecrated ground; the responsibility for doing so rests on the parochial church council; for the applicability of faculty jurisdiction see Hill, *Ecclesiastical Law*, Ch. 7.

[67] Regulation is to be found implicitly in rules governing church property generally (see above); see also Ch. 10.

[68] Scotland, Digest of Resolutions, 42: 'parsonage' means 'the residence of any of the clergy instituted or licenced by a Bishop'.

[69] Ireland, Const. IV.51.5: the incumbent, vicar or curate's assistant is 'entitled to the enjoyment of a free residence'; see also New Zealand, Cans. F.III.19.

[70] England, Parsonages Measure 1938 and Repair of Benefice Buildings Measure 1972.

[71] Australia, Diocese of Sydney, *The 7th Handbook*, 11.9: 'The rectory is the home of the minister and his family and must not be used for any purpose not sanctioned by the minister'.

Zealand, where no additions may be made without episcopal consent;[72] in Wales, where if a dispute results from the quinquennial inspection the matter is settled by arbitrators with appeal to the diocesan chancellor;[73] in the West Indies, where no parsonage may be disposed of without episcopal consent;[74] and in Papua New Guinea, where, in one diocese, during a vacancy in the parish, the incumbent's house must be used at the joint decision of the parish council and the Bishop.[75]

Ecclesiastical Registers and Records

It is a general principle of Anglican canon law that each local ecclesiastical unit must keep registers and records of services, baptisms, confirmations, marriages, communicants, and, where appropriate, of parishioners, and burials and funerals.[76] Churches differ as to the bearer of the responsibility for safeguarding these documents, but most commonly their safe custody is the duty of the minister and churchwardens acting individually, jointly, or in concert with the local parish or pastorate council or committee.[77] Laws of most churches require regular inspection of registers and records,[78] and often detailed rules prescribe methodically the manner of

---

[72] New Zealand, Cans. F.III.19: also, the trustees must 'allow the free use of the Parsonage House to the Ordained Minister of the Parish' and must not interfere with the right of occupation but they have a right of entry at reasonable times to inspect; they must report annually to the Diocesan Synod and liability to repair is decided by the Diocesan Synod; a surviving spouse has a right to occupy for 3 months.

[73] Wales, Const. IV.19 and X: the incumbent must: pay all rates, charges and taxes (excluding insurance); maintain and decorate the interior; pay for negligent or wilful damage; and he cannot let the property or make structural alterations without the consent of the parsonages board.

[74] West Indies, Can. 27: no 'Rectory, Vicarage, Presbytery or Parsonage' may be erected, demolished, or altered without episcopal consent.

[75] Papua New Guinea, Diocese of Port Moresby, Can. 11.29.

[76] Philippines, Cans. III.16.3: the minister must record in the parish register all baptisms, confirmations, marriages, burials and the names of communicants; Melanesia, Diocese of Temotu, Can. 6: this is identical but adds registers for services and ordinations – they must be examined on each visitation; England, Can. F11, F12: there must be register books of services, baptisms, confirmations, banns and marriages, and if appropriate, of burials; Scotland, Can. 42.1: every cleric in charge of a congregation must 'keep and safely preserve in a manner approved by the Bishop correct registers of Baptisms, Confirmations, Marriages, Funerals and Burials' and a register of the number of persons who have communicated publicly or privately on each separate occasion; in a vacancy these must be held by a person designated by the bishop.

[77] Japan, Can. XIII, Art. 128: the vestry has custody of the archives.

[78] See e.g. Scotland, Can. 42, Resolution 1: the dean of the diocese must inspect registers, inventories and records of each congregation (including the communicants' roll and the members' roll) once in every 4 years and report to the bishop in synod; Ireland, Const. III.25: the select vestry must provide for each church a register, of which the incumbent has custody, of baptisms, marriages and burials; the incumbent must at all reasonable times on demand allow searches in such registers (and give a copy on payment of a fee).

their safe-keeping.[79] In the event that the local church is unable to meet, or fails to comply with, legal standards governing maintenance, occasionally laws allow the depositing of documents with a diocesan archive,[80] and in some cases this may be done compulsorily.[81] In a small number of churches the law imposes a duty to allow reasonable access to these documents on request and, sometimes, it provides for the episcopal resolution of disputes.[82] The canon law of Southern Africa, echoing in key respects English church law, presents a comprehensive treatment of the subject. The incumbent and churchwardens must keep: a register of all parishioners and communicants in the parish; a record of all baptisms and marriages; an inventory of all movable property belonging to the parish; a register of all immovable property; and the financial records of the parish. All registers and records must be kept in a safe or other secure place. Records and registers are retained by the parish for a period prescribed by the Diocesan Synod and then they are transferred to the Diocesan Office; they may then be transmitted, at the discretion of the diocese, to the provincial archives or a state library.[83] In some churches, the collection, maintenance and preservation of ecclesiastical documents is discharged by national or provincial archival bodies.[84] A particularly mature system operates in New Zealand.

According to the canon law of New Zealand, archives are deemed to include 'all non-current records of permanent value' to the General Synod, its commissions and working parties, the primate, General Secretary, insti-

---

[79] England, Parochial Registers and Records Measure 1978, Sched. 2, as amended by the Church of England (Miscellaneous Provisions) Measure 1992, Sched. 1, para. 12: every register must be kept in a wood-lined, rust-proof, vented steel cabinet, the door of which must be fitted with a multi-lever lock, or in a fire-proof muniment room; these rules also deal with temperature and humidity.

[80] England, Parochial Registers and Records Measure 1978, ss. 7, 10.

[81] Ibid., ss. 12, 13: the bishop may apply to the secular county court for an order to deliver the documents to the diocesan archives.

[82] Scotland, Can. 42.2: registers are 'the property of this Church'; they are held on behalf of the congregation to which they refer by the cleric and subject to any direction of the bishop as to custody if they are non-current; they must be exhibited to the bishop or the dean for inspection on request and anyone wishing to inspect may apply to the cleric 'who shall have discretion to grant access, and in what circumstances, to parts of the registers relevant to the application'; disputes over access must be referred to the bishop with an appeal to the Episcopal Synod.

[83] Southern Africa, Can. 32: Can. 15.4: the archdeacon must inspect registers to ensure compliance with Can. 32; see also West Africa, Can. XIV.

[84] ECUSA, Cans. I.1.4 and I.5: the Board of Archives; Canada, Can. V: the Archives Advisory Board must: develop and propose policy for the maintenance of archives and documents of the church; develop increased awareness of the heritage of the church; and promote historical research and writing; Papua New Guinea, Can. No. 6 of 1977, 1.C: the Provincial Registrar is appointed by the Provincial Council to be the guardian of all the records, deeds, and other documents of the province and any diocese; for Provincial Registrars, see Ch. 6.

tutions and bodies, 'which relate primarily to the common life of this Church'. An Archives Committee must: administer the archives; advise General Synod thereon; ensure ready access; and encourage diocesan authorities to have 'a proper care for diocesan and parochial archives either in secure conditions within their own offices, or in recognized regional archival repositories'. The Committee must also draw up guidelines for these purposes and report to each session of the General Synod. Furthermore, there is a duty on church authorities to offer their records which have 'passed out of current use' to the Archives Committee before destruction or disposal. Each Diocesan Synod must arrange for maintenance of its own and parochial archives worthy of preservation. In turn, each parish is obliged to maintain as archives 'such of its records and registers as the Diocesan Synod may deem worthy of permanent preservation for historical research and other purposes, having proper regard for the guidelines as may be laid down from time to time by the Archives Committee'.[85]

FINANCE: THE ADMINISTRATION OF FUNDS

Anglican church law dealing with the control and management of finance is, in many key respects, a mirror image of that dealing with real and personal property. Rules are employed to enable the accountability of ecclesiastical fund-holders and regulation of ecclesiastical income and expenditure. Churches deploy law to secure income in three basic ways: voluntary contributions (including almsgiving), compulsory contributions (used for distribution within the church under the quota system) and investment. The law requires expenditure in relation to a host of matters, notably insurance and the provision of ministers' stipends and pensions. The entire legal structure of a church's financial organization may conveniently be set within the principle of stewardship.

The Principle of Stewardship

Successive Lambeth Conferences have recommended the adoption throughout the Anglican Communion of three basic principles: the 'principle of financial independence' stresses the need for individual churches to be self-supporting;[86] local church units should be entrusted with 'a real

---

[85] New Zealand, Cans. B.V.6 and B.X.1–7.

[86] LC 1897, Res. 18: 'the management and financial support of the Church should be theirs from the first'; Res. 56: 'the whole principle of gradual withdrawal of home aid to the Church in the colonies . . . is a sound policy'; LC 1958, Res. 64: 'The Conference urges that the Church in every field be encouraged to become self-supporting'.

share in the financial control and general direction' of the church;[87] and, one of the duties of church membership is for individuals to contribute according to their means to the work of the church 'at home and overseas'.[88] The doctrine of stewardship has been employed canonically in several churches as the basis of a set of general rules or 'business standards' applicable to all ecclesiastical bodies and persons involved with church finances; this has been the case in New Zealand,[89] ECUSA,[90] the Philippines,[91] and West Africa.[92] In some churches, misconduct by ecclesiastical trustees may be the subject of disciplinary proceedings in the church courts.[93] A particularly advanced set of rules is to be found in Australia.

In Australia, a national canon has recently been promulgated 'to assist in the responsible financial management of the Church and its associated organisations'. Organizations, listed in the schedule to the canon and including the Anglican Church of Australia Trust Corporation, must submit annually to the standing committee of the General Synod a report which contains audited financial statements. Each organization must maintain 'such financial procedures and controls' as are prescribed by the standing committee. The primate may appoint a person, on sufficient cause being demonstrated, to review the management and financial affairs of an organization and report the review to the standing committee. The

---

[87] LC 1920, Res. 34.

[88] LC 1948, Res. 37; LC 1958, Res. 64: 'The Conference recalls Church people to the duty and privilege of stewardship, of which sacrificial, planned, and systematic giving is a part, to the end that the souls of the people may be enriched, and the needs of the Church met, including the adequate support of the ministry and provision for the extension of its work'; LC 1978, Res. 9: 'We commend the biblical principle of tithing as a guide for normal Christian living'.

[89] New Zealand, Cans. F.III.4: any trustees holding land or personalty for the General Synod, for general church purposes, or for a diocese or parish, must report annually to the Diocesan Synod showing investments, assets and liabilities as the Diocesan Synod directs; yearly accounts must be audited.

[90] ECUSA, Cans. I.1.2(n)(10): General Convention's Standing Commission on Stewardship and Development must 'hold up before the Church the responsibility of faithful stewardship of time, talent and treasure in grateful thanksgiving of God's gifts' and co-ordinate church-wide fund-raising activities; Cans. I.7: standards on business methods in church affairs, which 'shall be observed', require the deposit of funds, records of trust funds, the keeping of books and accounts, and adequate insurance of property – the dioceses are obliged to enforce these canonical standards and establish a finance committee, a department of finance or other appropriate diocesan body for this purpose.

[91] Philippines, Cans. I.2.2: this follows ECUSA: the Provincial Synod's Commission on Stewardship and Finance must also evolve a long-term plan to build up the resources and capacities of the church for 'self-reliance'.

[92] West Africa, Can. XV: the provisions are entitled 'Of Business Methods in the Church'; records must be kept, treasurers adequately bonded, accounts audited and buildings adequately insured.

[93] See Ch. 3.

organization under review must co-operate fully with the appointee and disclose 'a true full and fair account of its activities'. If the standing committee 'in its absolute discretion' considers it necessary, it may compel the organization to give information on its activities. Importantly, '[i]t is not a breach of the duty of confidentiality owed by a member of a board or an employee of an Organisation to disclose information . . . concerning [its] financial affairs . . . to the Primate, General Secretary or Treasurer of General Synod'. This is so if that person considers such information to be of sufficient importance as to be in the possession of the General Synod's officers 'for the good of this Church as a whole'.[94]

The Distribution and Control of Funds

It is a general principle of Anglican canon law that control over church finances belongs primarily to the national or provincial assembly. Most churches list the control of finance amongst the subjects within the jurisdiction of that body.[95] Oversight is effected by rules requiring: budgets of central church trustees, commissions, boards and other bodies responsible to the central assembly to be approved by that assembly;[96] and annual reports on the financial activities of ecclesiastical authorities, reports which invariably must be accompanied by an audited statement of accounts.[97] Funds to cover the expenses of the central church assembly,[98]

[94] Australia, Financial Protection Canon 1995, Can. 16 1995.

[95] North India, Const. II.IV.IV.15: the Synod shall be 'the final authority in all matters pertaining to the financial administration' of the church; Papua New Guinea, Const. Arts. 6, 8; see also Canada, Fundamental Principles, 7: the Provincial Synod has jurisdiction over 'the administration of any fund or trust established in respect of the Synod'.

[96] Wales, Const. III.32: the Finance and Resources Committee of the Representative Body, which carries out executive functions of the Body, must review resources and deployment in consultation with the standing committee of the Governing Body; it must formulate an annual provincial budget, submitted to the standing committee of the Governing Body, and present annual accounts of the Representative Body to the Governing Body; for a similar system see Ireland, Const. X.17.

[97] Papua New Guinea, Const, Arts. 6, 8: Provincial Trustees must keep 'true accounts' audited annually with a report to the Provincial Council; see also Melanesia, Const. Art. 21; North India, Const. II.IV.V: Synod funds consist of: assessments, voluntary contributions, offerings, gifts, donations, aids, income from properties, endowments, and investments; accounts must be audited annually and these with the auditor's report must be submitted through the Finance Committee to the Executive Council; Philippines, Cans. I.4.4.5: the Executive Council, as Board of Trustees, must at the end of each fiscal year publish a full report of its work in the church, containing an itemized statement of receipts and expenditure, of trust funds and a schedule of salaries paid to all its officers, employees and agents.

[98] Jerusalem and the Middle East, Const. Art.15(i): the financial responsibility of the Central Synod is confined to its own expenses and the administration of projects initiated by it for which purposes 'the Central Synod may raise money whether by assessments on the dioceses or otherwise'; ECUSA, Cans. I.1.8; New Zealand, Cans. B.I.4: 'All appropriations of money by the General Synod . . . shall be made by statute'.

the primate or metropolitan,[99] are uniformly in the keeping of the central church assembly, or its financial executive.[100] The same applies, needless to say, to central church funds devoted to the payment of clergy stipends, pensions, ministerial education and training.[101] Often constitutions limit the financial liberty of central assemblies by listing objects towards which funds may legitimately be applied,[102] and generally funds must be applied in accordance with the terms of the gift under which they were acquired.[103]

Equally, it is a general principle of Anglican church law that oversight of funds held at the diocesan level are under the control of the diocesan assembly. The law of the church in North India contains arrangements many of which are shared with other churches.[104] The law denies to the bishop any unilateral controlling power over finance within the diocese.[105] The administration of diocesan funds is carried out by the financial executive of the diocesan council, under the direction and control of the

---

[99] Sudan, Const. Art. 60: the Provincial Fund, administered under the authority of the standing committee of the General Synod, is used for the expenses of the archbishop, the Episcopal Council, the General Synod and its standing committee; see also Tanzania, Const. V.

[100] England: for the Central Board of Finance, see LFCE, 463; Canada, Fundamental Principles, 7: a Finance Committee has 'the control, oversight and supervision of the administrative and financial concerns' of the General Synod; it must supervise the accounting systems of all boards and committees of the Synod.

[101] Scotland, Digest of Resolutions, 2–16: the funds of the General Synod, vested in six trustees (under the Trustees (Scotland) Act 1921 (as amended)) may be disposed to: clergy pensions; the maintenance of churches, halls, episcopal residences, parsonages; education and training of candidates for holy orders; and advancement of the church's educational work; South East Asia, Const. Art. XIII: the province must establish the provincial General fund and other funds necessary to meet the expenses and future development of the province.

[102] Southern Africa, Can. 45: the Provincial Synod holds and administers the Common Provincial Fund which is used: to increase the stipend of the metropolitan; to provide for the expenses of the metropolitan; to maintain and develop theological colleges; and to contribute to the expenses of provincial boards and committees; Central Africa, Can. 30: the Common Provincial Fund is administered under 'the authority of the Provincial Standing Committee' for the maintenance and development of any provincial institution or works approved by the Provincial Synod.

[103] Jerusalem and the Middle East, Const. Art. 15(iii): a gift of money to the church must be used exclusively towards the objects for which it was made 'unless the donors have agreed in writing to a variation of that purpose'; if the donor has died and 'the specific and defined purpose has failed', the Central Synod may reallocate its use for another purpose 'provided that such a change is approved by a two-thirds majority of the members present'.

[104] North India, Const. II.III.IX.13: 'The Diocesan Council shall be the ultimate financial authority of the Church in its Diocese in all matters concerning its internal administration'.

[105] South India, Diocese of Nandyal, Const. 1990, V.10: 'The Bishop of the Diocese shall not as the Bishop or as President of the Diocesan Council have any separate controlling authority over the finances of the Diocese'.

council.[106] The function of the executive is to present and scrutinize the annual budget before submission for approval to the diocesan council.[107] Accounts of diocesan bodies must be audited annually and a report with the audited accounts is submitted to the diocesan council.[108] The allocation of all funds under the control of the diocesan assembly is determined ultimately by that body.[109] Investigation of complaints of financial mismanagement in the diocese is carried out by a finance committee and an appeal lies to the central church assembly.[110] At the lowest level of the church, financial administration is the responsibility of the parochial church council, vestry, pastorate committee or equivalent body.[111] As at the diocesan level, the assembly must receive audited accounts annually.[112] It controls the distribution of funds in the unit to the various objects

[106] England, Diocesan Boards of Finance Measure 1925; Diocese of Europe, Const. 44; Wales, Const. IV.16: the Diocesan Board of Finance is appointed by the Diocesan Conference; Melanesia, Const. Art. 19: the General Synod must appoint Diocesan Boards of Trustees; Scotland, Digest of Resolutions, 36: every Diocesan Synod controls all funds and properties committed to it.

[107] North India, Const. II.III.IX.14: the executive committee shall 'scrutinize and approve the annual budget . . . and . . . present to the Diocesan Council for consideration and approval the financial report of the Diocese'.

[108] North India, Const. II.III.IX.15, 20: all diocesan accounts must be audited annually by chartered accountants appointed by the executive committee; the auditor's report with the audited statement of the accounts must be submitted to the executive committee through the finance committee and to the diocesan council; see also Rwanda, Draft Const. 1996, Art. 12 (audit); ECUSA, Diocese of Western New York, Can. 6: an audited statement showing the condition of the funds held by diocesan trustees must be reported to the Annual Convention; Scotland, Can. 61, Res. 3: the diocesan auditor submits to the bishop and Synod before its annual meeting 'a report in writing upon the whole of its accounts relating to the preceding year'.

[109] North India, Const. II.III.XIV.1: the finance committee of the diocesan council must determine the allocation of all funds at the disposal of the council and submit the proposals to the executive committee for approval; the stewardship committee must conduct stewardship campaigns in the pastorate and arrange seminars and conferences to lead pastorates to self-support.

[110] North India, Const. II.III.IX.22: 'In the event of grave financial maladministration or irregularity in any Diocese' having been brought to the attention of the Synod, its finance committee may investigate and submit its report to the executive committee of the central Synod; diocesan council officers must make available all necessary papers, account books, and bank statements; the diocese has a right of appeal to the synod's executive committee whose decision is final.

[111] Ireland, Const. III.24: the select vestry has control and charge of 'all parochial charity and church funds not excluded from the operation of this clause by the trusts on which the same are held'; Wales, Const. VI.23: all parish finance, subject to special trusts and the incumbent's discretionary fund, is under the control of the parochial church council; North India, Const. II.II.X: 'the Pastorate Committee shall act as the Finance Committee of the Pastorate'; see also Portugal, Can. IX, Art. 4.4: the parish council oversees finance.

[112] North India, Const. II.II.IX.6: the pastorate committee must arrange for audit of its accounts every year; a copy of the financial statement and the auditor's report must be sent to the treasurer of the diocesan council; any grave financial maladministration

of the church.[113] The terms of trusts for the benefit of the church must be adhered to by trustees operating at this level of the church.[114]

For a very small number of churches, one source of income is derived from fees payable on the performance of some of the ministrations of the church: in England, for example, the church may charge fees for the solemnization of marriage, the conducting of burials and the issuing of various certificates confirming entries in ecclesiastical registers.[115] For all churches the most important sources of income are gifts, offerings and alms, money derived under the quota system and investments.

Offerings and Alms

Rules governing the making of offerings are directed to individual members of the church. In several churches the law imposes a duty on clergy to educate the faithful about the need to give generously to the church. Philippine canon law is typical: ministers must instruct 'all persons in their Parishes and Cures concerning the missionary work of the Church at home and abroad, and give suitable opportunities for offerings to maintain that work'.[116] Sometimes laws repeat the principle appearing in

or irregularities in the accounts must be investigated by the executive committee of the diocesan council and its decision is 'final and binding'.

[113] Southern Africa, Can. 28.4: the parish council has 'direction and control of the . . . revenues and expenditure of the Parish', and it receives, considers and approves the estimates for the financial year; Can. 15.4: the archdeacon must examine annually the financial records of the parish; Ireland, United Dioceses of Cork, Cloyne and Ross, *Rules and Regulations* 1989, IV.3: the select vestry must appoint auditors and adopt audited accounts; Scotland, Digest of Resolutions, 39, 40: 'Each congregation shall annually submit audited accounts through the Diocesan Synod to the General Synod'; see also Japan, Can. XIII, Art. 128 and ECUSA, Cans. I.6.1: each parish must submit an annual report to the diocesan bishop itemizing receipts, outgoings, debts, and insurance.

[114] New Zealand, *Re Filshie, Raymond v Butcher* [1939] NZLR 91: a private trust for a memorial is not charitable; *Rowe v Public Trustee* [1928] NZLR 51: a fund for the repair of a spire is charitable; Southern Africa, *Ex p Hart* [1947(4)] SA 46 (W): the boundaries of 'religion' are explored to determine the necessary requirement of public benefit; see also *Lindley v Jones (Archbishop of Cape Town) and Others* (1906) 16 CTR 695; *Mills v Registrar of Deeds* (1936) CPD 417.

[115] Ireland, Const. III.25; see also Const. XII.7: ministers and churchwardens are entitled to charge fees for the erection of headstones etc. in burial grounds, and the fees must be spent to keep the churchyard in good order and repair; any surplus may be applied as the select vestry determines and an account of receipts and expenditure must be furnished to the Representative Body on demand.

[116] Philippines, Cans. III.16.3(a).

Lambeth Conference resolutions that the church confirms the biblical notion of the tithe, with the qualification that the faithful should give according to their means.[117] It is an ecclesiastical practice throughout the Communion for opportunities, to make offerings and alms for the needy, to form an essential element of liturgical worship of churches,[118] and forms of service in several churches cast giving as a duty on all parishioners.[119] The responsibility for collecting offerings during the time of divine service is commonly assigned to churchwardens.[120] The disposal of income from offerings rests with the parish or pastorate council,[121] whilst norms confer upon the minister,[122] or the minister and churchwardens, the right to dispose of offertory alms; commonly rules provide that disputes must be referred to the bishop.[123]

The Quota System

It is a general principle of Anglican canon law that each diocese is obliged to contribute a sum of money to the national or provincial assembly,

[117] Central Africa, Diocese of Mashonaland, *Pastoral Regulations* 1978, 19: 'Almsgiving must regularly be taught as a part of worship. This should be in proportion to the giver's wealth. For very poor people, 1% of income may be the most possible. For the wealthy, 10% is not an undue sacrifice. Between the proportions each person should honestly set their regular giving either as a "pledge" or at the offertory'.
[118] See e.g. Southern Africa, *Prayer Book* 1989, 116: 'Alms, and other gifts for the church and the poor', may be presented before the Great Thanksgiving in the Eucharist.
[119] Canada, BCP 1962, 66: 'It is the duty of every parishioner to contribute regularly of his substance, as God shall prosper him, to the maintenance of the worship of God and the spread of the Gospel'; Nigeria, *Liturgy of the Church of Nigeria* (*The Anglican Communion*): *The Order for Holy Communion or the Eucharist* (1983), vii, Directions, 4: 'It is the duty of every parishioner to contribute generously, according to his means, to the maintenance of the worship of God, to the spread of the Gospel, and to works of charity'; Wales, BCP 1984, 3: 'It is the duty of a Christian to contribute gladly and liberally to the maintenance of the worship of God and the proclamation of the Gospel'.
[120] Central Africa, Diocese of Lake Malani and Southern Malani, *Diocesan Acts* 1980, 23.6: the churchwardens are responsible for the offerings; Canada, BCP 1962, 74: the churchwardens, or their appointees, are charged with collecting the offerings of the people.
[121] England, Parochial Church Councils (Powers) Measure 1956, s. 7(i)(b): the council is empowered jointly with the minister 'to determine the objects to which all moneys to be given or collected in church shall be allocated'.
[122] Philippines, Cans. III.16.3: alms and other offerings for the poor must be deposited with the minister 'to be applied by the Minister, or under his superintendence, to such pious and charitable works as shall by him be thought to be fit'; during a vacancy, the vestry must appoint a person responsible 'to serve as Almoner'; see also ECUSA, Cans. III.14.2(f).
[123] Nigeria, *The Liturgy of the Church of Nigeria* (*Anglican Communion*): *The Order for Holy Communion or the Eucharist* 1983, vii, Directions, 5: 'The Minister and Churchwardens decide on the disposal of the offertory alms. If they disagree, the Ordinary shall make the decision'.

through its financial executive, for the purpose of funding schemes organized nationally or provincially (such as stipends or pensions). This is known variously as the provincial or national quota (or sometimes, as it is paid by the diocese, the diocesan quota). In turn, local ecclesiastical units, parishes and pastorates, through their assemblies, are obliged to make payments to the diocesan assembly, through its financial executive, to fund diocesan expenses including the provincial or national quota. This is commonly known as the parish share or parochial charge (though, confusingly, as it is paid to the diocese, it is sometimes called the diocesan quota). The quota is in effect an ecclesiastical charge or levy and laws regulating its administration deal with: the duty to pay; calculation of the assessment; timing of its payment; appeals against the assessment; and sanctions for its non-payment.

With respect to the national or provincial quota, paid by the diocese, laws commonly present this as one of the primary sources of church income.[124] Sometimes a duty is cast on the national or provincial assembly to levy the quota,[125] but more usually law confers a right upon the national or provincial assembly to do so with a direct duty to pay placed on the diocese: the most common formula is that the financial requirements of the assembly 'shall be provided' by the dioceses through the provincial or national quota.[126] The duty sometimes appears in church constitutions,[127] but more usually the quota is regulated canonically.[128] Laws differ as to the timing of the quota: sometimes it must be paid by the diocese in quarterly instalments,[129] or, more usually, annually.[130] Commonly laws require from dioceses a statement of their commitment to pay, or of their

---

[124] Rwanda, Draft Const. 1996, Art. 11: the province's financial resources come from 'Diocesan contributions, loans, subsidies, gifts and legacies and income from its own activities'; 'Diocesan quotas are fixed by the Provincial Synod or by the Provincial Standing Committee'; see also n. 97.

[125] ECUSA, Cans. I.4.6: 'an assessment shall be levied upon the Dioceses of the Church in accordance with a formula which the Convention shall adopt'; the Executive Council of the General Convention must present a full report on its work and a budget to General Convention, and an apportionment to the diocesan bishops; it is authorized to expend sums granted by General Convention; see also Philippines, Cans. I.1.11.

[126] Canada, Const. V.30: the financial requirements of the General Synod must be provided for by an assessment of the dioceses represented in the General Synod by means of an apportionment allocated to each diocese.

[127] Canada, Const. V.30: the assessment 'shall be paid by each diocese' to the General Synod.

[128] ECUSA, Cans. I.4.6: 'It shall be the duty of each Diocesan Convention to forward . . . the amount of the assessment levied upon that Diocese'; New Zealand, Cans. B.I.4.

[129] Canada, Const. V.30.

[130] South East Asia, Const. Art. XIII(b): 'Annual contributions to the Provincial General Fund shall be made by the dioceses as may be determined from time to time by the Provincial Synod'; ECUSA, Cans. I.4.6; Southern Africa, Can. 45.

acceptance of, the assessment.[131] In some churches each quota must be introduced by means of formal legislation,[132] and occasionally the assessment is seen as a necessary exception to the principle that the central assembly must impose no financial liability on the dioceses.[133] It is rarely the case that laws contain precise formulae for the calculation of the provincial or national quota: rather this is left to the discretion of the central assembly.[134] On occasions, however, laws refer to general principles governing the quota, requiring the assessment to be 'fair' or 'equitable'.[135] In some churches the assessment must be determined in consultation with the diocesan bishops.[136] It is rarely the case that provision is made for objections to the assessment, but when laws allow for this, determination of the matter is made by the standing committee of the central assembly.[137]

[131] Canada, Const. V.30: General Synod's Financial Management and Development Committee must 'advise the several dioceses of their suggested share of the General Synod apportionment and shall secure from each diocese the acceptance of its share'.

[132] New Zealand, Cans. B.I.4: 'All appropriations of money by the General Synod . . . shall be made by statute'; finance bills are introduced by the standing committee.

[133] Australia, Const. V.32: General Synod must not make 'any canon or rule imposing any financial liability on any diocese' except to meet the cost of the implementation of the constitution and canons, when the Diocesan Synod by ordinance assents.

[134] Australia, Const. V.32: General Synod may provide for 'the levying of assessments on dioceses . . . the method of calculating such assessments', and their apportionment between the dioceses; West Africa, Const. Art. XXI.2: 'The Provincial Synod shall determine and may, from time to time, increase or diminish the contribution to be paid annually by each diocese of the Province to the Common Provincial Fund'; Southern Africa, Can. 45: the Provincial Synod must determine 'the maximum percentage on income from parochial and diocesan sources, which the several dioceses . . . may be called upon to contribute', 'in such proportion as it may determine'.

[135] New Zealand, Cans. B.I.4: the Distribution Advisory Committee advises the standing committee on allocations with 'regard to the principles of partnership and the covenant relationship' expressed in the Constitution 'and the need for fair and equitable sharing and allocation of financial resources in this Church'; Philippines, Cans. I.1.11; I.4.4, 5: it is based on 'a formula which the [Provincial] Synod shall adopt . . . upon an equitable basis'.

[136] Sudan, Const. Art. 61: 'The annual contribution of each diocese shall be determined by the Provincial Treasurer in consultation with the Diocesan Bishops and subject to confirmation by the Standing Committee of the General Synod'; Central Africa, Can. 30.4: 'The annual contribution of each diocese, or group of dioceses, within the province shall be determined by the Provincial Treasurer in consultation with the Diocesan Bishops'; any contribution so determined is subject to confirmation by the Provincial standing committee.

[137] Southern Africa, Can. 45.4: 'Any objection to a contribution, with the reason therefor, must be lodged by the Provincial Secretary at least thirty days before the meeting . . . and all such objections shall be considered by the Provincial Synod' or its standing committee; compare Central Africa, Can. 30.4: 'Any objection to a contribution, with the reasons therefor, must be lodged with the Provincial Treasurer within six weeks of its being notified to the diocese concerned'; all such objections are determined by the standing committee.

The diocesan quota due to the province is fed, along with diocesan expenses themselves, by the parish charge. Laws are generally more developed and detailed with respect to the assessment levied by the diocese upon local ecclesiastical units, particularly in relation to sanctions for non-payment and appeals. As is the case with provincial or national quotas, the assessment is often listed amongst the permitted sources of diocesan income.[138] An apportionment is made as between the parishes or other ecclesiastical units.[139] Various methods are used to determine the assessment: it may be fixed by law,[140] or calculation is left to the diocesan assembly,[141] to be exercised, sometimes, in accordance with general notions of fairness and equity.[142] The parishes are notified of the assessment,[143] and constitutions and canons uniformly treat its payment as an

---

[138] North India, Const. II.III.IX.17: the money of the diocesan council shall consist of 'voluntary contributions, gifts, grants from the Synod, trust associations, churches and missionary societies' and an 'assessment from Pastorates or institutions, income from properties, endowments and other sources approved by the Diocesan Council or the Synod'; Papua New Guinea, Diocese of Port Moresby, Can. 12: 'The purpose of [the] diocesan assessment is to assist the diocese in providing for the expenses of Diocesan Administration and for augmenting the general income of the Diocese, especially with a view to pastoral needs, evangelism and mission'; ECUSA, Diocese of Western New York, Cans. 7.1–6: it is used to support the episcopate, the expenses and programme of the diocese and of the national church.

[139] Papua New Guinea, Diocese of Port Moresby, Can. 12: the Diocesan Treasurer prepares a budget and 'a list showing the assessment for each Parish and District which shall be brought before Diocesan Council for acceptance or amendment prior to distribution'; Wales, Const. V.15: the Ruridecanal Conference arranges the ruridecanal budget and 'the allocation of the diocesan quota between the parishes'; Scotland, Digest of Resolutions, 36: 'A Diocesan Synod may . . . require congregations to contribute annually to the funds of the Diocese'.

[140] Papua New Guinea, Diocese of Port Moresby, Can. 12: 'The general principle for the assessment of each Parish and District shall be the Biblical tithe; that is, each parish and District shall forward to the diocese, on a monthly basis, ten percent of its general income'; Ireland, Diocese of Connor, *Diocesan Regulations* 1990, 17: the scheme is based on a 'grading of all parishes' with an annual increase and a triennial review by the diocesan council 'to take account of changes in relative parochial incomes and to allow for movement of parishes from grade to grade as appropriate'.

[141] North India, Const. II.III.IX.29: the diocesan council has 'the power to assess and to determine the amount of the assessment to be paid by each Pastorate and any other institution to the Diocesan Central Fund'; Ireland, Diocese of Connor, *Diocesan Regulations* 1990, 17: 'the Diocesan Council may assess the parish for such sum as may be required to pay' the clergy stipends and allowances in the parish; 'Such assessments shall be payable at such times as may be determined by the Diocesan Council'.

[142] ECUSA, Diocese of Western New York, Cans. 7.1–6: the diocesan council submits to the Annual Convention its proposed 'Operating Budget of the Diocese' for the ensuing year and 'a schedule of recommended fair share contribution guidelines for parishes and missions'.

[143] ECUSA, Cans. I.4.6: the diocese must notify parishes of the objective allotted to it and the amount to be raised; the dioceses must report annually to the Council on all receipts and distributions of money; Philippines, Cans. I.4.4.5: the diocese must notify each parish, mission or institution 'of the amount allotted to each diocese, and the

obligation.[144] As with the system of national and provincial assessment, laws require periodic payment, which is usually annual.[145] In a number of churches, the law confers a right of appeal against the assessment to a designated ecclesiastical authority in the diocese.[146] The laws of several churches expressly prescribe the consequences of non-payment: these may be in the form of remedial action or sanctions,[147] and in some churches non-contributing parishes are put on a special defaulters' list.[148]

amount of such objective to be raised by each Parish, Mission or Institution'; Scotland, Digest of Resolutions 39.3: 'It shall be the duty of the Vestry in each congregation to arrange for the collection of contributions to Diocesan and Provincial Quotas'.

[144] Scotland, Digest of Resolutions, 39: it is a secondary 'duty' of every congregation (after providing for the stipend) 'to contribute, either directly or through such general levy or Quota as the Diocesan Synod may require, to the Diocese and to the general funds of the General Synod'; Wales, Const. VI.22: one of the functions of the parochial church council is to prepare an annual parochial budget which must include 'the various church expenses, the parochial contribution to the diocesan quota and home and overseas mission'; ECUSA, Diocese of Western New York, Cans. 7.1–16: by the end of each year (31/12) the vestry or advisory council of each parish and mission must report to the Board of Trustees and diocesan council the amount of its 'pledge' to support the diocese for the ensuing year: this is then paid monthly to the Diocesan Treasurer; no moneys may be expended from diocesan funds without the approval of the diocesan council or the Treasurer; and the council may require reports and statements from parishes.

[145] Central Africa, Diocese of Lake Malani and Southern Malani, *Diocesan Acts* 1980, 24.4: the quota is a sum contributed monthly to the diocese to pay for the salaries of clergy and lay ministers; it is fixed by the diocesan standing committee which directs parish church councils to pay directly to the ministers or to the committee; there is a right of appeal against the assessment; Ireland, Diocese of Connor, *Diocesan Regulations* 1990, 17: the Diocesan General Fund consists of 'An annual contribution as determined by the Diocesan Council from each parish in the Diocese, payable in four moieties'; Ireland, United Dioceses of Cork, Cloyne and Ross, *Rules and Regulations* 1989, III.1(b): 'Every parish shall be assessed annually for such amount as may be decided by the Diocesan Council'.

[146] See e.g. Papua New Guinea, Diocese of Port Moresby, Can. 12: in the event that any parish or district considers the amount 'too great or unfair' an appeal may be made in writing to the diocesan council; 'If the Council of a Parish or District makes default in payment of any assessment due for a period of twelve months the Diocesan Council may take such action as it deems fit'; see also n. 145.

[147] North India, Const. II.II.IX.4: where the pastorate committee along with the presbyter-in-charge act in 'a prejudicial manner and refuse to send the Pastorate's assessment and contribution to the Diocesan Central Fund, the Executive Committee of the Diocesan Council shall take immediate steps to intervene and bring about normalcy in the Pastorate'; Ireland, Const. IV.13: if a parish fails to pay for two successive years the assessment for stipends, expenses of office, allowances, locomotory allowances, and a free residence, or has failed to satisfy state requirements concerning social security, no nomination is to be made on a vacancy until arrears are paid and satisfactory provision has been made for these; see also n. 146.

[148] Wales, Const. IV.12: the diocesan conference may exclude from its membership persons from a district which has failed 'to make payment of any sums for which it has been assessed by the Conference, or which it has been called upon by the Conference to pay'; IV.18: the diocesan board of finance, with the approval of the diocesan bishop,

Investment

One aspect of the principle of stewardship developed in resolutions of the Lambeth Conference is that churches have a responsibility to make investments which are not only financially prudent but also morally sound.[149] The first of these recommendations, prudent investment, is commonly reflected in the formal laws of churches; the second is not.[150] The principal elements of laws on investment by ecclesiastical trustees may be summed up as follows. First, the vast majority of provincial and national laws confer powers of investment upon fund-holding trustees at all levels of the church, and their exercise is normally subject to the direction and control of the appropriate assembly, national or regional,[151] provincial,[152] diocesan,[153] or at the lowest level of the local ecclesiastical unit, the parish or pastorate.[154] Sometimes investment is cast as a duty.[155] Secondly, a gen-

may place on 'a defaulters' list a parish which culpably neglects to meet its financial obligations; the parochial church council must be given a 'full opportunity of stating the case for the parish'; when a vacancy occurs, the incumbency may be suspended (or a new incumbent appointed under Const. VII.6); any person aggrieved by an act of the diocesan conference concerning property may appeal to the Provincial Court: Const IV.28.

[149] LC 1908, Res. 49: 'The Conference urges upon members of the Church practical recognition of the moral responsibility involved in their investments'; this extends to consideration of: 'the character and general social effect of any business or enterprise in which their money is invested'; the treatment of the persons employed in that business or enterprise; the due observance of the requirements of the law relating thereto; and 'the payment of a just wage' to employees.

[150] England, *Harries (Bishop of Oxford) v Church Commissioners* [1992] 1 WLR 1241: the Church Commissioners in the exercise of their powers of investment (under the Church Commissioners Measure 1947, s. 6), may take into account non-financial ethical considerations only in so far as this does not jeopardize the profitability of those investments; their principal duty is 'generating money'.

[151] Ireland, Const. X.10: the Representative Body's powers of investment are subject to the control of the General Synod; see also North India, Const. II.IV.IV.22.

[152] Southern Africa, Const. Art. XIX, Sched. A: the Provincial Trustees may invest 'under the special leave and sanction' of the Provincial Synod; see also New Zealand, Cans. B.XIV.4: the Church Pension Board has a power of investment.

[153] Scotland, Digest of Resolutions, 36.2(d): diocesan funds vest in trustees, acting on behalf of the Diocesan Synod, who enjoy powers arising under 'statute and the common law of Scotland'; these include the power to invest; see also New Zealand, Cans. F.III.11: investment by trustees must accord with the terms of the Anglican Church Trusts Act 1981; for diocesan rules regulating investment, see e.g. Australia, Diocese of Sydney, *The 7th Handbook*, 14.

[154] England, Church Funds Investment Measure 1958, s. 2; whilst ordinarily the parochial church council may act only with the consent of the diocesan authority as custodian trustee (see Parochial Church Councils (Powers) Measure 1956, s. 6(3)), with respect to investments the decision lies wholly with the council: *Legal Opinions Concerning the Church of England* (1994), 203.

[155] Canada, Can. VIII: the Board of Trustees of the Pension Fund is under a duty to invest; see also North India, Const. II.III.IX.18: the bishop and the executive committee

eral principle which is commonly incorporated into church laws in express terms, is that trustees are not liable personally for any loss resulting from an investment unless this is due to their own wilful default or negligence.[156] Thirdly, laws rarely list permitted investments in any meaningful detail.[157] Choice of investment is, rather, left to the discretion of the fund-holding trustees.[158] Very occasionally, canon law forbids trustees to invest in any business owned or managed by the church itself.[159] Some churches have designated advisory bodies specializing in investment matters.[160]

ECCLESIASTICAL EXPENDITURE

As has been seen, the laws of Anglican churches confer upon trustees discretionary powers to dispose of funds as they think fit, subject to the overriding control of church assemblies. Normally, therefore, expenditure is a matter of choice. By way of contrast, in three major instances, the law imposes duties on ecclesiastical authorities to apply funds for: insurance; ministerial stipends (and expenses); and pensions. Such arrangements, containing rules of mandatory expenditure, result in the conferral of rights which entitle bodies and persons to make claims upon the funds of the church.

of the diocesan council are obliged 'to explore ways and means for augmenting the income of the Diocese'.

[156] Southern Africa, Const. Art. XIX, Sched. A: no liability attaches to the trustees unless loss occurs through their 'own wilful neglect or default'; Scotland, Digest of Resolutions, 36.2: no member of a Diocesan Synod, committee, board, or trustees shall be personally liable for any loss in investments and these are indemnified by the Diocesan Synod against such claims; Wales, Const. III.25: no member of the Representative Body is liable for 'any loss occasioned by the depreciation or failure of any investment, or otherwise, save when caused by the wilful default of such member'; Ireland, Const. X.10: this uses an almost identical formula.

[157] England, Church Funds Investment Measure 1958, Sched.

[158] Ireland, Const. X.10: the Representative Body is 'at liberty to invest any property vested in it in trust for the Church . . . in any investment that it may think fit and it may borrow such sums of money'; it must be satisfied as to 'the prudence and advisability in all the circumstances'; Wales, Const. III.23: '[a]ll monies . . . held by the Representative Body in trust for the Church . . . may be invested in the purchase or upon the security' of named properties including freehold land and stock funds.

[159] Papua New Guinea, Can. No. 3 of 1992.

[160] Melanesia, Standing Resolution 26, 1989: each diocese must have a diocesan development investment committee to recommend investments for authorization by the diocesan council and to draw up policies and guidelines on investments.

Insurance

For those churches which operate rules of general applicability to all fund-holding trustees, the obligation to insure personal and real property is listed amongst the business standards of the church.[161] For most churches, however, duties to insure are scattered amongst rules dealing with the responsibilities of ecclesiastical trustees and other bodies, particularly at the lower levels of the local church. In most churches duties to insure, imposed on parochial church councils or pastorate committees,[162] are cast in very general terms, leaving a wide discretion as to forms of insurance. In several churches, the law is more precise: sometimes it prescribes that insurance must be with companies of proven reliability;[163] and sometimes the duty is to insure against listed risks.[164] Occasionally the law requires bodies to provide insurance in accordance with directions of the Diocesan Synod.[165] In many churches the law requires a regular review of insurance policies.[166] However, rarely is it the case that laws demand insurance against third-party liability.[167]

---

[161] See e.g. ECUSA, Cans. I.7.

[162] England, Parochial Church Councils (Powers) Measure 1956, s. 4(1)(ii)(b): the parochial church council must arrange 'insurance of the fabric of the church and the goods and ornaments thereof'; Scotland, Can. 35.3: 'The Vestry shall make provision for the adequate protection and insurance of all church fabric and property'.

[163] Brazil, Cans. I.7: the properties of the church must be insured with insurance companies of 'proven competence', against the risk of fire and other risks; Scotland, Can. 35, Digest of Resolutions, 37: the Diocesan Synod is responsible for ensuring adequate insurance of all property with insurance companies of 'good standing' and the proper custody of policies of insurance.

[164] Ireland, Const III.24.4: the select vestry must 'keep the churches and other parochial buildings insured against fire'; New Zealand, Cans. F.III.14: all buildings and their contents held by trustees under the authority of the General Synod must be insured in the name of the trustees 'for such sums and for such risks as the Trustees shall consider prudently appropriate'; compare West Africa, Can. XV: buildings must be 'adequately insured'.

[165] Ireland, Const. III.24.4: insurance of the church must not be less than that fixed by the diocesan council 'having taken account of all the circumstances of the particular case'; see also Wales, Church Fabric Regulations, 5: the parochial church council must ensure that 'all churches . . . and their contents are insured in accordance with the advice of the insurer, provided that other terms may be agreed with the insurer if the archdeacon also approves, and provided that the Representative Body may require the insurance to be upon such terms and for such amounts as it thinks fit'.

[166] Scotland, Can. 35, Digest of Resolutions, 37: the diocesan administration board must make an annual enquiry of the vestry concerning the date of the last review of insurance and a note of the present levels of cover; Brazil, Cans. I.7: policies should be revised annually; see also Chile, Cans. H.4.

[167] Wales, Church Fabric Regulations, 6: 'The Parochial Church Council shall ensure that insurance is effected against employer's liability and against liability to third parties upon such terms and for such amounts as the Representative Body may from time to time require'; ECUSA, Diocese of Western New York, Cans. 7.7(2): all diocesan

Clergy Stipends and Expenses

That ordained clergy have a right to financial maintenance, in order to liberate them to realize their vocation and ministry, is now understood to be a fundamental of ecclesiastical life. However, the concept of a ministerial right to a stipend, or other form of pecuniary support, is not one which commonly surfaces in express terms in the laws of Anglican churches: more usually, the entitlement is assumed. For this reason, Irish church law is unusual: 'all stipends and salaries . . . paid to [the minister] by right of his office for the performance of his duties', are such as 'he might reasonably be expected to have'.[168] Arrangements for the payment of stipends vary considerably from church to church and thus it is difficult to deduce general principles on this subject. In some churches stipends are organized nationally or provincially and control over them rests with the central church assembly: funds are held by national or provincial trustees for the purposes of providing stipends, and the central assembly determines the rate.[169] In other churches, the diocese itself is the unit responsible for stipends: the diocesan assembly has a controlling hand in the determination of the rate,[170] or else the bishop controls the sum acting on the advice of the diocesan assembly.[171] Occasionally, churches employ a national stipend system with each diocesan bishop empowered to call on funds, held nationally for the diocese, to provide for the maintenance of the clergy in that diocese.[172] In several churches, it is the local church, the

property must be insured against fire and public liability damage claims in amounts to be determined by the diocesan Board of Trustees.

[168] Ireland, Const. IV.51.

[169] Korea, Can. 40: the National Synod shall decide the basic 'salary' of the clergy; Wales, Const. III.33: the Representative Body may reduce any stipend upon 3 months' notice.

[170] North India, Const. II.III.IX.7: 'It shall be the responsibility of the bishop and the Diocesan Council to see that, as far as possible, every presbyter who holds the bishop's authorization and who has not been superannuated is suitably engaged in the work of the Church, provided the funds of the diocese so permit'; ibid., II.III.IX.21: 'The Diocesan Council shall set up a Diocesan Central Fund and frame rules for the same'; the fund 'shall be used to maintain presbyters or other full-time employees, for administration and programmes of the diocese'.

[171] Diocese of Europe, Const. 45: The diocesan bishop, acting on the advice of the Bishop's Council, must establish minimum stipends for full-time clergy licensed to the Diocese 'having regard to the economic circumstances of the country in which they are serving'; there must be an annual review and each chaplaincy council must ensure that its minister receives not less than the minimum stipend or show cause to the bishop why this is not possible.

[172] England, Diocesan Stipend Funds Measure 1953: the Church Commissioners act as the Central Stipends Authority; the fund must be applied 'in accordance with directions from time to time given, with the concurrence of the Diocesan Board of Finance, by the bishop'; episcopal directions must, in turn, be 'consistent with any directions given by the Commissioners, in the exercise of their functions as the Central Stipends Authority, with respect to the forms and levels of the pay of those persons'.

parish or pastorate, which is responsible for the payment of clergy stipends.[173] In any event, at whichever level of the church they are administered, it is a practice throughout the Anglican Communion that stipends are payable to those bishops, priests and deacons who are active in full-time ministry.[174] Much the same arrangements apply, at least in some cases, to lay ministers of the church.[175] Sometimes a designated institution exists to give specialist advice on the subject of financial maintenance of ministry.[176] Rarely is it the case that stipends are regulated directly by secular legislation.[177] It is, equally, a general principle of Anglican canon law that the local church assembly pays the recurring expenses of clergy.[178] In order to provide an outline picture of a canonical stipend and expenses system, this section may be concluded with a short description of the system in the Scottish Episcopal Church.

In Scotland, it is the duty of every congregation to provide, as far as it reasonably can, both a minimum stipend and allowances for its clergy. The minimum stipend is determined from time to time by the General Synod – though the Synod may delegate this function to its Admin-

[173] Ireland, Const. IV.51: the diocesan council determines the 'approved stipend' but this must not exceed 110% of the 'minimum stipend' fixed by General Synod; Diocese of Connor, *Diocesan Regulations* 1990, 16: the select vestry of each parish must pay to its incumbent, vicar or assistant curate 'such stipend and expenses allowances as determined by the Diocesan Council'; if in default the diocesan council must take 'all steps necessary to comply with' the incumbent's request; Melanesia, Cans. A.7.D and Diocese of Temotu, Can. 10: the parish must pay the stipend and expenses of full-time clergy.

[174] See e.g. Philippines, Cans. I.3.5: the prime bishop has a canonical right to receive an honorarium in addition to the basic 'salary' paid to a diocesan bishop, as set by the provincial Executive Council; Ireland, Const. VI.31; see also *Kempthorne v Kempthorne* [1956] Fiji Law Reports 39: this concerned the applicability of imperial laws to the endowment of a see; see also *Twitchell v Floyd* [1909] Fiji Law Reports 19; many churches also operate a system of non-stipendiary ministry.

[175] North India, Const. II.III.IX.7: the diocesan council has 'power to fix salary scales and rate of allowances of . . . all . . . employees of the Diocese on the recommendation of the Finance Committee and the Executive Committee'.

[176] Melanesia, Cans. E.5: the Salaries and Service Commission recommends to the Executive Council on, *inter alia*: the establishment of 'a fair grading system for all lay persons employed' by the church; 'the application to each grade of a fair annual salary and other allowances and conditions of service as may be appropriate'; and salaries, allowances and conditions of service for clergy; the Commission must issue guidelines to dioceses on stipends and allowances for clergy.

[177] Barbados, Anglican Church Act 1969, ss. 14–18: this forbids the payment of stipends from the secular Consolidated Fund.

[178] Ireland, Const. IV.51: the select vestry must pay allowances for locomotor expenses, and the expenses of office allowance (to cover telephone, stationery etc); the diocesan council determines the amount and the vestry has a right of appeal against the council's determination; Philippines, Cans. I.1.11: the travel and accommodation expenses of clergy for their attendance at the Provincial Synod are covered by the expenses of the Synod; Wales, Const. VI.22: the parochial church council must review expenses 'for which the clergy should be reimbursed by the parish'.

istration Board. When the Administration Board determines the matter, it may take into account the 'Government norms for wage increases'. The minimum stipend itself may be abated by a sum equal to any allowance paid to a cleric for the heating, lighting and cleaning of his official residence and for the upkeep of the garden. A Clergy Stipend Fund and a Diocesan Stipend and Allowances Fund may be used to top up stipends and allowances when a congregation is unable to meet the minimum stipend fixed by the General Synod or the Administration Board. In those cases where a congregation receives a grant from the Diocesan Stipend and Allowances Fund, to augment the cleric's stipend, 'it should direct its efforts to increasing the local stipend and this fact should be taken into account by Diocesan Treasurers in reckoning its assessment for Diocesan and Provincial Quotas'. If the cleric is ill or disabled, the minimum stipend must still be paid and National Insurance benefits recoverable must, in turn, be paid to the congregation. Every diocese or congregation must pay clergy, in accordance with the rules of the Administration Board, the following: local rates for the parsonage; expenses for the services of a *locum tenens*; telephone, travelling expenses, and contributions to the Pension Fund. Income for clergy will also include the Easter offerings and pay received from, for example, chaplaincy and secular work.[179]

Pensions

In line with several resolutions of the Lambeth Conference, legal structures are today in place in all churches in the Anglican Communion which seek to make provision for clergy on retirement or during illness.[180] It is a general principle of Anglican canon law that clergy have a right to a pension.[181] In contrast with laws on stipends, normally clergy pensions are organized on the national or provincial level.[182] Special pension funds

---

[179] Scotland, Digest of Resolutions, 20–22, 39.

[180] LC 1908, Res. 6: 'It is of the greatest importance that the conscience of the Church at large should be awakened as to its primary responsibility for providing for the training, maintenance, and superannuation of the clergy'; see also LC 1948, Res. 88 and LC 1978, Res. 27: churches must ensure that 'ultimate retirement and other relevant provisions are fully protected'.

[181] The concept of a clergy right to a holiday has not made any significant impact in formal law; see, however, Korea, Can. 38: 'A clergyman may have twenty-eight days vacation each year but he must make application to the archdeacon four weeks beforehand; vacations may not be taken between 21–26 December or from Ash Wednesday to the Monday after Easter; every ten years a clergyman may, with the bishop's permission, take a three month holiday'.

[182] Korea, Can. 40: clergy pensions and severance pay are determined by the National Synod; see also Melanesia, Standing Resolution, 1 1979; 22 1989; Japan, Can. XV, Art. 150.

must be established as a legal requirement.[183] In some instances, internal church laws expressly provide for regulation of a pension fund by secular law.[184] In the vast majority of churches the fund is administered by trustees appointed by the national or provincial assembly.[185] Very many churches operate as the basis of the administration of the fund the following formula: 'The general principle to be observed shall be the maintenance of a proper actuarial relationship between the contributions made, levied and collected and the several benefits proposed to be paid'.[186] The annual report of trustees operates to enable accountability for compliance with this principle and it must contain a statement of the audited accounts.[187] Most church laws adopt the principle, however, that trustees are not liable for losses to the fund unless these have occurred as a result of wilful default or neglect on the part of those trustees.[188] The object of the fund is to provide pensions on retirement,[189] maintenance for spouses and dependants,[190] and awards during periods of disability or

[183] ECUSA, Cans. I.1.8: the Church Pensions Fund, a corporation under the civil law of the state of New York, is authorized to establish a clergy pension system including life, accident and health benefits for those clergy who are retired or disabled by age or infirmity and for their surviving spouses and children.

[184] Brazil, Cans. I.8: the Retirement and Pensions Fund is regulated by the social welfare rules of secular law; see also n. 190.

[185] Canada, Declaration of Principles, 6(m): within the jurisdiction of the General Synod is 'the establishment, operation and maintenance of a general pension fund'; Can. VIII: the Pension Plan is to provide pensions and ancillary benefits to Members of the Pension Fund, a trust; the Pension Committee (a corporation) must appoint a Board of Trustees to administer a system of contributions and pensions established under the regulations of the committee; see also Southern Africa, Can. 46: the Fund is administered by the Provincial Pensions Board.

[186] See e.g. Canada, Can. VIII; Ireland, Const. XIV.

[187] Southern Africa, Can. 46; Canada, Can. VIII: see n. 185; the trustees must report annually to the Pension Committee.

[188] Canada, Can. VIII: there is no liability for 'honest error' but there is liability for 'bad faith, gross negligence and wilful misconduct'.

[189] Southern Africa, Can. 46: the Provincial Pension Fund is 'to provide for pensions for Members who have attained normal retirement age or who have become disabled by infirmity from the due discharge of their ministerial or official duties'; it is also to provide for their dependants upon their death; the Board at its discretion may grant an early retirement pension, a permanent disability pension and make provision for temporary disablement; see also West Indies, Can. 34.

[190] New Zealand, Cans. B.XIV; New Zealand Anglican Church Pension Fund Act 1972: the Church Pension Board, a body corporate under the Charitable Trusts Act 1957, administers the superannuation scheme, 'for the benefit of ordained ministers, their surviving spouses and dependants', and it acts as trustee of 'The Retire Fund' (under the Superannuation Schemes Act 1989); it may establish a superannuation scheme for 'natural persons employed by or in the service of or associated with the Church', their spouses and dependants; it may also provide schemes for personal sickness and accident insurance and financial provision for retirement housing for clergy, employees or servants; the Board determines the rate of pensions.

illness.[191] Rights to pensions arise by way of membership of the fund,[192] which generates duties to contribute,[193] on the basis of service in the ministry of the church.[194]

CONCLUSIONS

The overriding principle which emerges in the laws of all churches of the Anglican Communion is that ecclesiastical authorities are the stewards of church property. General oversight of church property falls under the jurisdiction of national and provincial assemblies, and sometimes under that of diocesan assemblies, though ownership is vested in trustees enjoying juridic personality under secular law. Management and control over the major forms of church property in use at the local level is vested in parish councils and their equivalents: elaborate schemes are used to ensure episcopal control over the use, care and maintenance, alteration and disposal of real and personal church property. Much the same arrangements operate with respect to church finances. Laws sometimes contain rules of general application to all church fund-holding bodies, but

[191] See e.g. Wales, Can. of 1982: this provides for the maintenance of ministry when an incumbent is incapacitated: for the first 4 weeks the full stipend is paid and a medical certificate must be supplied if incapacity continues beyond 7 days; during the first 4 weeks the incumbent must meet the costs of cover and after 4 weeks these are borne by the Maintenance of Ministry Fund of the Diocese; after 26 weeks, the incumbent receives half the stipend; and the bishop may require the cleric's appearance at a medical board.

[192] Ireland, Const. XIV: the Clergy Pension Fund is for the financial assistance of clergy who are members of the fund and who retire or become unable to continue in their ministry by reason of infirmity, accident or disease, and for that of spouses and orphans of fund members; it consists of capital held by the Representative Body, income, contributions and donations; the Representative Body are the trustees and it is administered by the Pensions Board which decides on every question of membership, contribution and benefit with a right of appeal to the Court of General Synod; membership of the fund is compulsory for all clergy who are in service unless they are exempt by the Board with the consent of the bishop; contributions are linked to the rate of the minimum approved stipend.

[193] Australia, Can. 2 1981: a common minimum level of contributions and benefits must be established; Can. 8 1992, Can. 6 1995: the Long Service Leave Board manages and controls the fund in its 'absolute discretion'; it must keep accounts which are to be audited and reported annually to the standing committee of the General Synod; contributions of members of the fund, which include clergy, are determined by the Board and entitlements of members are based on 'qualifying service'.

[194] Scotland, Digest of Resolutions, App. 1: the Scottish Episcopal Church Retirement Fund is for the benefit *inter alia* of full-time stipendiary clergy and full-time salaried lay workers; Wales, Const. XII.II.4: 'On the retirement of clerics or deaconesses, pensions shall be paid in accordance with the provisions of the Clerics and Deaconesses Pension Scheme'; 5: pensions, which are 'non-contributory', are paid by the Representative Body; and pensionable service includes full-time stipendiary ministry.

more often than not rules are dispersed, imposing duties of accountability to designated ecclesiastical authorities under the broad control of national, provincial and diocesan assemblies. The principal sources of income are offerings, investments and money derived from the quota system, under which duties are imposed to contribute to diocesan funds which, in turn, are employed to fund projects organized at national and provincial level. One of the key achievements of Anglican canon law is the widespread provision of rights to stipends and pensions.

12

Inter-Church Relations and Ecumenical Law

The traditional understanding is that each individual Anglican church is independent, enjoying an authority and freedom to govern itself according to its own constitutional and canonical system. The principle of autonomy has been both enunciated and developed by institutions of the Anglican Communion and it is one which commonly appears in the formal laws of individual churches. However, the opportunity for collective approaches to single subjects and problems has always been possible as a direct result of the institutional organization of the Anglican Communion, particularly since the establishment of the Lambeth Conference in the 1860s. From a legal perspective, these institutions are of importance in so far as their decisions, as a matter of ecclesiastical practice, have themselves shaped the legal systems of individual churches. The relations between Anglican churches are sometimes defined in decisions of Communion institutions, but more commonly they are defined unilaterally by the laws of particular churches. However, this subject of inter-church relations is not one from which very many principles may be deduced. By way of contrast, especially as a consequence of a series of decisions by the Lambeth Conference, and by individual churches, the subject of the relationship between Anglican churches and non-Anglican churches has led to the creation of a large and growing body of law. From a study of this, the ecumenical laws of individual churches, it is possible to deduce several principles applicable throughout the Communion on this subject.

There is no formal Anglican canon law globally applicable to and binding upon member churches of the Communion. No central institution exists with competence to create such a body of law. Instead, for the purposes of government member churches, and the Communion itself, are bound together by a *corpus* of ecclesiastical conventions. These conventions are based upon both explicit and tacit agreement amongst member churches and many of them have been enunciated in the resolutions of the Lambeth Conference, the assembly of world-wide Anglican bishops. Conventions

are expressed in the form of general principles, particular rules, or ecclesiastical practices. Whilst formally by their very nature conventions are non-
legal, still, in view of their strong persuasive authority, some lawyers may
conceive them as quasi-legal in nature – so powerful are many of these
conventions, that they are treated as if they were law. Their function is, in
part, to define the relationship of church to church, and to define the competence of the central institutions of the Communion *vis-à-vis* the member
churches. They also serve, needless to say, to sustain Anglicanism itself
and the unity of its traditions. Two fundamental conventions concern the
nature of the Communion and the independence of individual churches.

The principle that each church in the Communion is autonomous, for
the purposes of its own self-government and law, has emerged as a direct
result of discussion amongst Anglicans about the nature of the Anglican
Communion and the nature and location of authority within it.[1] The
Lambeth Conference has adopted the idea that '[t]he Anglican
Communion is a fellowship, within the One Holy Catholic and Apostolic
Church, of those duly constituted dioceses, provinces and regional
Churches in communion with the See of Canterbury'. These churches have
the following characteristics in common: 'they uphold and propagate the
Catholic and Apostolic faith and order as they are generally set forth in the
Book of Common Prayer as authorized in [these] several Churches'; they
are particular or national churches and, as such, 'promote within each of
their territories a national expression of Christian faith, life and worship';
and 'they are bound together not by a central legislative and executive
authority, but by mutual loyalty maintained through the common counsel
of the bishops in conference'.[2] More particularly, communion is reflected
in the shared allegiance of churches to: Holy Scripture, 'as containing all
things necessary to salvation'; the Apostles' Creed, 'as the baptismal symbol', and the Nicene Creed, 'as the sufficient statement of the Christian
faith'; the two sacraments 'ordained by Christ himself', baptism and the
Eucharist; and the threefold ministry of bishops (comprising 'the historic

---

[1] For theological discussion about the nature of authority see the studies in: S. W.
Sykes (ed.), *Authority in the Anglican Communion: Essays Presented to Bishop John Howe*
(Toronto, 1987); S. W. Sykes, *Unashamed Anglicanism* (London, 1995), 140–162.

[2] LC 1930, Res. 49; for adoption of these ideas by lawyers, see: Halsbury, *Laws of
England*, Vol. 14, *Ecclesiastical Law* (4th edn., London, 1975), para. 313: it is 'a fellowship
of churches historically associated with the British Isles which have certain characteristics in common, including standards of faith and doctrine, and to some extent, forms of
worship'; it embraces 'all those churches and dioceses which are in communion with
the See of Canterbury, recognise the Archbishop of Canterbury as the focus of unity',
and propagate 'the catholic and apostolic faith based upon the scriptures interpreted in
the light of Christian tradition, scholarship and reason as expressed in the Book of
Common Prayer [1662] and the Ordinal and their derivatives'; see also L. Leeder,
Ecclesiastical Law Handbook (London, 1997), 422.

episcopate'), priests and deacons.[3] Admission to membership of the Communion is based on an individual church satisfying these general requirements, and one Lambeth Conference resolution recommends a procedure in the event that a church wishes to withdraw from the Communion.[4] Indeed, that these arrangements are actually applied may be construed as further indication of the quasi-legal nature of Communion practices.

The twin concepts of communion and autonomy have been particularized by a small cluster of additional global ecclesiastical conventions, some of which have been codified in the actual laws of member churches. Sometimes churches assert legally their own membership of the Communion and, therefore, their full communion with member churches and with the See of Canterbury;[5] interestingly, in some laws membership is treated as indissoluble,[6] and often the Lambeth Conference definitions of the Anglican Communion appear in the formal laws or other legally approved documents of individual churches.[7] Full communion has been

---

[3] LC 1888, Res. 11; see also Res. 19.

[4] LC 1958, Res. 14; compare LC 1888, Res. 19: as regards newly constituted churches, 'especially in non-Christian lands, it should be a condition of the recognition of them in complete intercommunion with us, and especially of their receiving from us episcopal succession, that we should first receive from them satisfactory evidence that they hold substantially the same doctrine as our own, and that their clergy subscribe to articles in accordance with the express statements of our own standards of doctrine and worship'; see also LC 1978, Res. 30: 'The Conference requests the Anglican Consultative Council, in consultation with other Churches, to formulate appropriate definitions of terms used in inter-Church relations'; LC 1948, Res. 56(e): 'Because the Anglican Communion is itself a treasured unity with a special vocation, a part of our Communion contemplating a step which would involve its withdrawal from the Anglican family of Churches should consult the Lambeth Conference or the provinces and member Churches of this family before final commitment to such a course'.

[5] Indian Ocean, Const. Historical Introduction: the province is 'in full communion with the Church of England and the Anglican Communion of Churches around the world'; Mexico, Const. Preamble and Declaration: the church is 'in communion with the See of Canterbury'; Ireland, Const. Preamble: 'The Church of Ireland will maintain communion with the sister Church of England, and with all other Christian Churches agreeing in the principles of this Declaration'; Chile, Cans. A.7: 'The Anglican Communion is a federation of autonomous provinces which maintain fraternal contact on a global level'.

[6] Venezuela, Const. Art.I: 'The Anglican Church in Venezuela is an ecclesiastical jurisdiction which forms an indissoluble part of the Anglican Communion . . . subject to the metropolitical canonical authority' of Province IX of ECUSA; the constitution and canons are amended internally by the Diocesan Convention: Const. Art. X and Cans. V.22.

[7] Wales, BCP 1984, Catechism, 692: 'The Anglican Communion is a family of Churches within the Catholic Church of Christ, maintaining apostolic doctrine and order and in full communion with one another and with the See of Canterbury'; New Zealand, *Prayer Book* 1989, 936: the Anglican Communion is 'a world-wide fellowship of self-governing churches holding the doctrine and ministry of the one, holy, catholic and apostolic church, and in communion with the Archbishop of Canterbury'.

understood by the Lambeth Conference as 'unrestricted *communio in sacris*' which includes 'mutual recognition and acceptance of ministries' exercised in each of the member churches. As is seen later in this Chapter, in the section on ecumenical law, this relation may also exist between Anglican churches and non-Anglican churches, those of another 'denominational or confessional family'. Full communion is sometimes distinguished, in turn, from *inter-communion*, 'where varying degrees of relation other than "full communion" are established by agreement between' two churches.[8] Moreover, ecclesiastical independence, a funda-mental of the global conventional order, finds expression in resolutions of the Lambeth Conference in the idea that 'the true constitution of the Catholic Church involves the principle of autonomy of particular Churches based upon a common faith and order'.[9] Not only, however, is global ecclesiastical convention power-conferring – it also has a power-limiting aspect. Unless the formal law of an individual church so pro-vides,[10] convention forbids interference by one church in the internal affairs of another member church.[11] A related principle is the requirement that particular churches must adapt themselves to their own local needs, which itself militates against the blind adoption of the ecclesiastical sys-tems and structures of fellow churches.[12] Perhaps the most far-reaching power-limiting principle of global ecclesiastical convention is that, in the exercise of autonomy, churches must take no unilateral action in matters of concern to the whole of the Anglican Communion; the precise terms of this limitation have not found expression in these developing ecclesiasti-cal conventions.[13]

[8] LC 1958, Res. 14; for the distinction between 'full communion' and 'inter-commu-nion', see also *Intercommunion Today*, the Report of the Archbishops' Commission on Intercommunion (1968).

[9] LC 1930, Res. 48.

[10] See e.g. Southern Africa, Const. Art. VI: 'the Provincial Synod . . . shall be subordi-nate to the higher authority of a General Synod of the Churches of the Anglican Communion to which this Province shall be invited to send representatives, whenever such General Synod shall be convened'; no such synod at present exists (see below for the role of the Lambeth Conference) though the idea has been mooted: LC 1867, Res. 4: 'unity in faith and discipline will be best maintained among the several branches of the Anglican Communion by due and canonical subordination of the synods of the several branches to the higher authority of a synod or synods above them'.

[11] LC 1878, Committee Report: 'the duly-certified action of every national or particu-lar Church, and of each ecclesiastical province (or Diocese not included in a Province), in the exercise of its own discipline, should be respected by all other Churches, and by their individual members'.

[12] LC 1897, Res. 19: 'so far as possible, the Church should be adapted to local cir-cumstances, and the people brought to feel in all ways that no burdens in the way of foreign customs are laid upon them, and nothing is required of them but what is of the essence of the faith, and belongs to the due order of the Catholic Church'.

[13] LC 1978, Res. 11: 'The Conference advises member Churches not to take action regarding issues which are of concern to the whole Anglican Communion without

OFFICES AND INSTITUTIONS OF THE ANGLICAN COMMUNION

The principal institutions of the Anglican Communion are the office of Archbishop of Canterbury, the Lambeth Conference and the Anglican Consultative Council. The functions of the Conference and the Council, particularly, are regulated principally by ecclesiastical convention – though sometimes these institutions enjoy a legal status in the constitutions or canons of individual churches. The following section deals with these and other ancillary organs of the Communion concerned with co-ordinating the activities of member churches.

The Archbishop of Canterbury

The office of Archbishop of Canterbury is governed both by the laws of individual churches and by ecclesiastical convention of the Anglican Communion. Under English ecclesiastical law, for the purposes of the Church of England, the archbishop is 'Primate of All England' and metropolitan of the Province of Canterbury.[14] According to ecclesiastical convention, and for the purposes of the Anglican fellowship of churches, 'the Archbishop of Canterbury . . . serves as the principal focus of unity in the Communion'.[15] Juridic expression is given to both of these ideas in the laws of many churches. The churches fall into two broad groups: those in which the law assigns a limited jurisdiction to the archbishop; and those in which the archbishop is given full metropolitical authority. With respect to the first group, in several national and provincial churches formal laws distribute to the archbishop, who enjoys 'the first place' amongst Anglican metropolitans,[16] a miscellany of functions; to the archbishop they: require newly-elected bishops to pay deference;[17] provide for an

consultation with a Lambeth Conference or with the episcopate through the Primates Committee, and requests the primates to initiate a study of the nature of authority within the Anglican Communion'.

[14] England, Can. C17(1); see below for the archbishop's legal involvement in the consecration of bishops for 'foreign lands' and permission for 'overseas' clergy to minister in England.

[15] See also LC 1988, Res. 18.2(b): this recommends that 'in the appointment of any future Archbishop of Canterbury, the Crown Appointments Commission be asked to bring the primates of the Communion into the process of consultation'.

[16] Sudan, Const. Art. 2 and Central Africa, Fundamental Declarations, II: the church 'accepts the Archbishop of Canterbury as holding the first place among the Metropolitans of the Anglican Communion'.

[17] West Indies, Can. 8: the episcopal declaration is presented as 'pursuant to' LC 1897, Res. 9: 'I. A.B. do solemnly declare that I will pay all due honour and deference to the Archbishop of Canterbury'.

appeal in cases of doctrinal and liturgical controversy;[18] assign the function of deciding upon the appointment of bishops in the event that the electoral college of the particular church fails to elect;[19] and, assign the legislative function of confirming that proposed constitutional amendment will not take a church outside the Anglican Communion.[20] For the second group of churches, those which have the status of extra-provincial dioceses, the Archbishop of Canterbury acts as metropolitan.[21] Metropolitical jurisdiction itself may embrace a multiplicity of archiepiscopal competences,[22] and these are illustrated in the case of the Lusitanian church.

[18] See Chs. 7 and 8; see also Spain, Second Transitional Canon: 'all questions of Faith and Order are subject to the authority of the Archbishop of Canterbury'; LC 1878, Res. 8: this recommended that in dioceses not forming part of a province appeals in matters of doctrine or disciplinary cases involving doctrine should lie from the diocesan court to the Archbishop of Canterbury.

[19] Central Africa, Can. 3: if after 3 successive votes, the Electoral College fails to elect a new archbishop, the college must reassemble; if after a further 5 successive votes no decision is reached finally 'the appointment shall be delegated to the Archbishop of Canterbury, acting in conjunction with two other Bishops of the Anglican Communion nominated by the College'; see generally Ch. 4.

[20] Central Africa, Fundamental Declarations, VII: any alteration of these is effective only if 'endorsed by the Archbishop of Canterbury as not affecting the terms of Communion between the Church of this Province, the Church of England and the rest of the Anglican Communion'.

[21] Compare Puerto Rico, Const. II.5: 'Metropolitical Authority' over the Extra-Provincial Diocese of Puerto Rico belongs to the Provincial Synod of the Province IX of ECUSA; Art. X: the constitution is amended internally, by the Diocesan Assembly, there being no reference to ECUSA.

[22] ACC – 4, 1979, Ontario, 6.B: the following is a rare attempt to define the term: metropolitical authority is 'the focus of ultimate decision-making in a Province, and the process by which it is exercised'; it 'relates to [the] general welfare and growth of the whole Church in which it is exercised' to help the church grow within 'the general Anglican ethos'; it is 'expressed through canonical responsibilities laid upon bishops' and it is exercised within 'synodical structures, but sometimes may still be exercised individually by the Metropolitan'; metropolitans exercise 'their authority synodically with the clergy and laity for the government and good ordering of the Church'; '[t]he degree to which Metropolitical Authority is exercised individually or corporately in association with the House of Bishops or the Provincial Synod, is determined by the Constitution and Canons of the particular Church'; it includes: the exercise of pastoral oversight, 'ensuring that both the Provincial constitution and canonical development are in accordance with general Anglican tradition and practice, and that the provisions of the Provincial Constitution and Canons are adhered to'; authorizing the amalgamation or division of dioceses and the creation of new dioceses; authorizing and confirming the election of bishops; consecrating or issuing a mandate for the consecration of bishops; provision of adequate episcopal oversight in the case of vacancies; provision for effecting changes in the constitution and canons of dioceses in so far as they pertain to faith and order, or relations with other parts of the Anglican Communion; ensuring the calling of meetings of the synods of the jurisdiction; receiving and hearing appeals under the constitution and canons. This definition was formulated by the Commission appointed 'to consider the application by the Lusitanian Church and the Spanish Reformed Episcopal Church for full integration into the Anglican Communion'; see also *The Iberian Churches* (1979), Report to the Archbishop of Canterbury, 6–10.

Under its canon law, metropolitical authority is exercised by the Archbishop of Canterbury and it comprises, *inter alia*, ratification of: the election of bishops; liturgical and canonical alteration; the revision of doctrinal formularies; the establishment of concordats of full communion with other Anglican churches; participation in and authorization of acts of integration of ministries of other churches of the historic episcopate; determination of doctrinal and disciplinary matters; and approval of the formation of new dioceses.[23] Whereas the canon law of the Lusitanian church provides for the actual exercise of metropolitical jurisdiction by the Archbishop of Canterbury, the constitution of the church in Jerusalem and the Middle East provides for its assumption by the archbishop on the occurrence of prescribed events. The constitution places a duty on the archbishop to assume or to make arrangements for the maintenance of metropolitical jurisdiction: if the church decides to dissolve the unity of its dioceses;[24] if the church informs the archbishop that 'a situation has arisen in which metropolitical jurisdiction can no longer be exercised in accordance with the Constitution of that Church';[25] if the constituted authority of the church can 'no longer exercise its functions according to the Constitution';[26] and over any diocese of the church which may withdraw from it with the consent of the Central Synod.[27]

The Lambeth Conference

In 1863 the Provincial Synod of the Church of Canada urged the Archbishop of Canterbury and the Convocation of the Province of Canterbury to establish a General Council, composed of bishops consecrated in England and serving overseas, to discuss issues then facing the Canadian church.[28] Despite some opposition from a number of English bishops, Archbishop Longley invited Anglican bishops to the first Conference held at Lambeth Palace in 1867, which seventy-six bishops attended.[29] With the exception of 1920, as a matter of ecclesiastical convention Anglican bishops have assembled for the Conference, at periodic

[23] Portugal (the Lusitanian Catholic Apostolic and Evangelical Church), Const. Preamble, 7: the church is 'an Extra-Provincial Diocese of the Anglican Communion'; Can. I.

[24] Jerusalem and the Middle East, Const. Art. 16.1.

[25] Ibid., Const. Art. 16.2(a) and Res. 23 ACC–2, Dublin.

[26] Jerusalem and the Middle East, Const. Art. 16.2(b) and Res. 23 ACC–2, Dublin.

[27] Jerusalem and the Middle East, Const. Art. 16.3.

[28] The request was stimulated in large measure by the celebrated dispute between Robert Gray, Archbishop of Cape Town, and Bishop Colenso, Bishop of Natal: see LC 1867, Res. 6.

[29] Evans and Wright, *The Anglican Tradition*, Doc. 327: the Archbishop's Letter of Invitation.

intervals of roughly ten years,[30] at the invitation and under the presidency of the Archbishop of Canterbury.[31] The Conference has no formal constitution as such, but decisions of successive Conferences have defined its sphere of competence: the intent underlying the first Conference, as expressed by Archbishop Longley at the time, was that '[i]t should be distinctly understood that at this meeting . . . no decision [shall be] come to that shall affect generally the interests of the Church, but that we shall meet together for brotherly counsel and encouragement'.[32] The decisions of the Conference are cast usually in the form of resolutions, which 'should be formally communicated to the various national Churches, provinces, and extra-provincial dioceses of the Anglican Communion for their consideration, and for such action as may seem to them desirable'.[33]

Two very different views are commonly held about the nature of resolutions of the Lambeth Conference: the one denies to them the status of binding 'law'; the other treats them as a form of 'legislation'. On the one hand, therefore, is the understanding that the Conference has no formal legislative power,[34] no competence to create binding law for individual

[30] LC 1897, Res. 2: 'That whereas the Lambeth Conference has been called into existence by the invitation of the Archbishop of Canterbury, we desire that similar Conferences should be held, at intervals of about ten years, on the invitation of the Archbishop, if he is willing to give it'.

[31] Pan-Anglican Congresses, attended by ordained and lay representatives from all the dioceses in the Anglican Communion, have also been held: London 1908, Minneapolis 1954, and Toronto 1963; the LC 1978 requested that a Primates' Meeting be established to enable greater consultation between primates of the Communion; its first meeting took place in 1979 and meetings occur every 2 to 3 years; see LC 1988, Res. 18: the Conference urges 'that encouragement be given to a developing collegial role for the Primates' Meeting under the presidency of the Archbishop of Canterbury, so that the Primates' Meeting is able to exercise an enhanced responsibility in offering guidance on doctrinal, moral and pastoral matters'.

[32] Coleman, E. (ed.), *Resolutions of the Twelve Lambeth Conferences 1867–1988* (Toronto, 1992), viii; A. M. G. Stephenson, *Anglicans and the Lambeth Conferences* (London, 1978), 79 (extract from Archbishop Benson's *Diary* (1888)): 'I opened the Conference by pointing out that the Conference was in no sense a Synod, and not adapted, or competent, or within its powers, if it should attempt to make binding decisions on doctrines or discipline': see Evans and Wright, Doc. 345.

[33] LC 1897, Res. 3; decisions have also been cast as 'Recommendations' and 'Encyclicals' (see e.g. LC 1878, Recommendation 12 which is also Encyclical Letter 4.1 concerning Anglican chaplaincies).

[34] LC 1930, Res. 49: Anglican Churches 'are bound together not by a central legislative and executive authority', but by mutual loyalty; LC 1930, Encyclical Letter: the Communion is 'a commonwealth of Churches without a central constitution: it is a federation without a federal government'; the denial of competence is implicit in LC 1897, Res. 24: concerning the prohibition against parallel episcopal jurisdictions, 'the Conference recommends every bishop to use his influence in the diocesan and provincial synods of his particular Church to gain the adhesion of the synods to these principles, with a view to the framing of canons or resolutions in accord therewith'.

churches or for the Communion as a whole.[35] For commentators on English ecclesiastical law, the Conference has 'no legal basis': the implementation of 'any resolution that it passes' depends on 'the voluntary acts of the individuals composing it and their acceptance by churches represented by them'. Resolutions may enjoy 'an authoritative character' on a 'consensual basis', but they do not have the force of law.[36] On the other hand, some treat resolutions of the Conference as species of 'church law'. Whilst it is accepted that the Conference is convened 'not to make law but to take resolutions which should be a guide to the various . . . Churches in their making of law', resolutions are 'of such weight that they [are] more than "not binding" ': it is '[i]n this way the Lambeth Conference started to make a new body of legislation'.[37] These views are not entirely contradictory: their proponents are merely using different definitions of 'law'. Resolutions are clearly not law properly so called: they only bind a church by its adoption of them, when they are incorporated in its own law; moreover, resolutions do not appear amongst the categories of law recognized in the constitutions or canons of individual churches. Any church is competent, however, to legislate to the effect that resolutions are law for the purposes of that church. At the same time, it is not the case that resolutions of the Conference lack any authority. As earlier Chapters indicate, the implementation of Conference resolutions in the laws of individual churches is a reasonably widespread practice. The adoption of resolutions in particular laws may of itself be a direct result of them being treated 'as if' they were law. Like the ecclesiastical conventions of the Anglican Communion, it may be more accurate to classify Conference resolutions as forms of 'quasi-legislation'. Some support for this approach is found in the language used in resolutions. Language, and the underlying intent which may be inferred from it, suggests a spectrum of positions about the authority and nature of Conference resolutions. Some resolutions affirm that they have no material effect on the laws of particular churches,[38] or they

---

[35] See E. Kemp, 'Legal implications of Lambeth', *Ecclesiastical Law Journal*, 1(5) (1989), 15: the author states that at the 1988 Conference of the 70 or so resolutions 'none of them, with one possible exception, has any legal effect of any kind'; this was Resolution 18 concerning the Anglican-Roman Catholic International Commission: the commission's report has been circulated to all churches and it has been accepted that the results of discussions should be collated by the Anglican Consultative Council and presented to the Conference which 'should have the authority to say whether or not the Statements on Eucharistic Doctrine, Ministry and Ordination . . . are or are not consistent with the faith of Anglicans'.

[36] Halsbury, *Ecclesiastical Law*, para. 314; L. Leeder, *Ecclesiastical Law Handbook* (London, 1997), 422.

[37] O. Chadwick, 'Introduction', in Coleman, E. (ed.), *Resolutions of the Twelve Lambeth Conferences 1867–1988* (Toronto, 1992), xv–xviii.

[38] LC 1930, Res. 54: 'Without prejudice to the provisions of any constitution already adopted by any province or regional Church', arrangements should exist dealing with

disclaim the effect of establishing rules,[39] or they simply prescribe a 'recognized practice'.[40] Moving along the spectrum, commonly resolutions assert the existence of rights,[41] or of duties,[42] applicable to churches and their members. Sometimes resolutions take the form of administrative instructions requiring the consistent application of church law on particular subjects.[43] Similarly, often they contain prohibitions of proposed canonical development as contrary to Anglican 'tradition',[44] or precepts that in any change of a rule or usage regard must be had to Anglican tradition.[45] Occasionally they purport to be declaratory of 'universal custom'.[46]

subscription to the constitution of a new province; LC 1920, Res. 12: this resolution, dealing with the problems of reunion, was 'not to be regarded as calling into question any canons or official declarations of any synod or House of Bishops of a national, regional, or provincial Church which had already dealt with these matters'.

[39] LC 1897, Res. 41: 'That this Conference, while disclaiming any purpose of laying down rules for the conduct of international arbitration . . . desires to affirm its profound conviction of the value of the principle of international arbitration, and its essential consistency with the religion of Jesus Christ'.

[40] LC 1908, Res. 62: 'it should be the recognised practice of the Churches of our Communion' to admit members of Eastern Orthodox Churches to Holy Communion; LC 1908, Res. 31: concerning health and the administration of the Holy Communion, '[s]pecial cases involving exceptional risk should be referred to the bishop and dealt with according to his direction'.

[41] LC 1897, Res. 45: 'That this Conference recognises the exclusive right of each bishop to put forth or sanction additional services for use within his jurisdiction, subject to such limitations as may be imposed by the provincial or other lawful authority'.

[42] LC 1958, Res. 125: the duties of the laity; LC 1948, Res. 93: 'The Church has a primary duty in the pastoral care of those who are married or are about to be married'; LC 1897, Res. 24: 'it is the duty of the whole Church to make disciples of all nations'; Res. 60: 'That it is the duty of the Church to give all possible assistance to the bishops and clergy of the colonies in their endeavour to protect native races from the introduction among them of demoralising influences and from every form of injustice or oppression'; LC 1908, Res. 8: 'It is of the greatest importance that the conscience of the Church at large should be awakened as to the primary responsibility for providing for the training, maintenance, and superannuation of the clergy'.

[43] LC 1920, Res. 39: 'It is of real importance that the marriage law of the Church should be understood and administered as far as possible consistently, in all parts of the Anglican Communion'.

[44] LC 1948, Res. 113: concerning the proposed canon of the General Synod of the Church in China that for an experimental period of twenty years a deaconess might be ordained priest, 'the Conference feels bound to reply that in its opinion such an experiment would be against [Anglican] tradition and order'.

[45] LC 1908, Res. 30: concerning the use of the *Quicunque Vult*: 'inasmuch as the use or disuse of this hymn is not a term of communion, the several Churches of the Anglican Communion may rightly decide for themselves what in their varying circumstances is desirable; but . . . if any change of rule or usage is made, full regard be had to the maintenance of the Catholic faith in its integrity'.

[46] LC 1897, Res. 6: 'Recognising the almost universal custom in the Western Church of attaching the title of Archbishop to the rank of Metropolitan, we are of the opinion that the revival and extension of this custom among ourselves is justifiable and desirable'.

The Anglican Consultative Council

The Lambeth Conference of 1968 endorsed proposals for the establishment of the Anglican Consultative Council. The proposals, including a
draft constitution, were submitted to the member churches for approval,
and they were to become operative when adopted by a two-thirds majority of those churches. Unlike the Conference, the Council is regulated by a
formal written constitution. The Council is composed of the Archbishop of
Canterbury as President, the Chair and Secretary General, three persons (a
bishop, a priest or deacon, and a lay person) chosen by each member
church, and six co-opted members two of whom must be women and
two under the age of twenty-eight. It meets every two or three years and
its standing committee administers its affairs between sessions. The
Council's functions are defined in its constitution. It acts as 'an instrument
of common action' and must advise on inter-Anglican relations, including
the division or formation of new provinces and the establishment of
regional councils; it has a special responsibility towards extra-provincial
dioceses. A key obligation is to develop as far as possible agreed Anglican
policies in the world mission of the Church and to encourage national and
regional churches 'to engage together in developing and implementing
such policies by sharing their resources of manpower, money and experience to the best advantage of all'. The constitution emphasizes the
Council's role in ecumenism; it must: promote the fullest possible
Anglican collaboration with other Christian churches; encourage and
guide Anglican participation in the ecumenical movement and organizations – particularly the World Council of Churches; and arrange for Pan-
Anglican conversations with the Roman Catholic Church and the
Orthodox Churches. The Council is also responsible for advising on proposed unions between Anglican and other churches, and on subsequent
relations between the Communion and united churches. Finally, it must
advise on problems of inter-Anglican communication, help in the dissem-
ination of Anglican and ecumenical information, and promote enquiry
and research.[47] The laws of a very few churches occasionally provide for
the submission of matters to the Council.[48] As with the Lambeth
Conference, the Council possesses no formal law-making power,[49] an
understanding occasionally represented in the laws of individual

---

[47] LC 1968, Res. 69.

[48] See e.g. Tanzania, Const. IV.15: in matters of faith and doctrine, the House of
Bishops may refer the case to the Council of the Lambeth Conference; Kenya, Can. II:
proposed schemes for union with other churches must be submitted to ACC; see also
New Zealand, Can. B.XVIII.10: this places a duty on the church's Ecumenical Council
to represent to the ACC ecumenical matters of concern to the church.

[49] W. J. Hankey, 'Canon law', in Sykes and Booty, 200 at 202.

churches.[50] However, whilst no legislative competence is given by its written constitution, in the exercise of its advisory functions the Council often issues quasi-legislation – policy documents and other such instruments sometimes give rise to 'expectations' of their adoption by member churches.[51] For instance, in the legal field, one of the most important documents produced by the Council has been its 'Guidelines for Provincial Constitutions'.[52] This document contains principles with which churches should comply in the process of constitutional reform and revision; these principles govern both the form of the proposed constitution, and the subjects with which it should properly deal.[53]

[50] Chile, Cans. A.7: the Anglican Consultative Council is 'an organization having no legislative character which is obligatory for the provinces' of the Communion.

[51] See e.g. ACC – 1, 1971, 21: Lumuru, Africa: a province is 'the smallest complete unit of the Anglican Communion because it exists under a College of Bishops' which 'requires to be more than a mere trio of bishops'; '[a] province must have some common constitution'; '[i]t is expected that a new province should normally contain at least four dioceses'; '[i]t must be ensured that the remaining area of the former province is not unduly weakened in finance, personnel, or institutions'; the proposed province 'must have financial stability, adequate leadership, proper administration, and accessibility to and from each diocese'; '[b]efore the creation of a new province there should be consultation with the [Council] or its Standing Committee for guidance and advice, especially in regard to the form of constitution most appropriate'.

[52] ACC – 4, 1979, 6: Ontario, Canada: the existing guidelines were criticized in a review by the Council's Standing Committee which indicated that: 'the terminology at present in use not only reflects excessively its origins in English ecclesiastical and civil law, but the same terms are often used with different meanings by different Provinces'; technical terms are sometimes used 'without definition of their meaning'; and 'the structure of the constitutions varies as between one Province and another'.

[53] In the process of constitutional reform, churches should observe the following: (1) only matters should be included which affect each and all of the dioceses of the province, the criteria by which a province 'may be validly accepted or remain part' of the Communion, relationships with other provinces of the Communion, and relationships between the province and other churches or communions; (2) technical terms should be clearly defined; (3) constitutions 'should follow the same broad outline'; (4) '[u]niformity of structure does not imply uniformity of expression and content'; (5) the requirements of a church covering more than one country are different from those where a province is coterminous with a nation; (6) constitutions 'should allow on the one hand for the operation of the Holy Spirit in continuous growth, development and adjustment to changing ecclesiastical and social environments, while on the other hand providing a basis of stability from which to make appropriate alterations from time to time' – thus, 'Constitutions should be as short, clear and simple as is consistent with their being comprehensive'; (7) the 'outline Constitution should be used in the drafting or revising of Provincial Constitutions'. An outline constitution is provided: it should consist of three parts. The first, containing a preamble, setting out the fundamental declarations of the church with respect to doctrine, worship, ministry, the relation of provinces to dioceses and of the province to other provinces and other churches and communions, and the procedure for constitutional amendment. The second part should deal with: metropolitical authority, bishops (appointment, functions, and procedure for absence, incapacity, resignation and retirement), the provincial assembly, liturgical matters, declarations (of ordained and lay ministers) and ecclesiastical discipline, funds

LEGAL RELATIONS BETWEEN ANGLICAN CHURCHES

Quasi-legislation of the Lambeth Conference provides a basic framework to govern relations between churches in the Anglican Communion. The framework is based, in turn, on the ecclesiastical conventions of communion and autonomy. First, each church has an obligation to respect the autonomy of each other church,[54] and this is particularly the case when it is proposed to establish foreign missionary jurisdictions.[55] Secondly, 'two bishops of [the] Communion may not exercise jurisdiction in the same place'.[56] Thirdly, no bishop or cleric should exercise their ministries in another diocese without the consent of the bishop of the host diocese; and no priest or deacon may minister in another diocese without letters testimonial from their own bishop.[57] Fourthly, each church must inform member churches, and the Archbishop of Canterbury, of all new metropolitical and episcopal appointments.[58] Lastly, member churches should co-operate to further the mission of the whole church.[59] Turning to the actual

and property, definitions of listed terms, and procedure for the creation and amendment of articles, canons and other species of church law. Part three should contain rules on order and procedure. See also the Joint Meeting of the Primates of the Anglican Communion and the ACC, Cape Town 1993, Res. 52: constitutions should incorporate the rule that a bishop must undertake canonical obedience in all things lawful and honest to the metropolitan and to uphold the provincial and diocesan constitutions.

[54] LC 1878, Recommendation 1: one of the 'principles of church order' is that 'the duly certified action of every national or particular Church, and of each ecclesiastical province (or diocese not included in a province), in the exercise of its own discipline, should be respected by all the other Churches, and by their individual members'.

[55] LC 1897, Res. 24: 'independent Churches of the Anglican Communion ought to recognise the equal rights of each other when establishing foreign missionary jurisdictions, so that two bishops of that Communion may not exercise jurisdiction in the same place'; bishops should use their influence to ensure 'canons and resolutions' are framed accordingly; '[w]here such rights have, through inadvertence, been infringed in the past, an adjustment of the respective positions of the bishops concerned ought to be made by an amicable arrangement between them, with a view to correcting as far as possible the evils arising from such infringement'.

[56] LC 1897, Res. 24; see also LC 1968, Res. 63: 'The Conference deplores the existence of parallel Anglican jurisdictions in Europe and in other areas, and recommends that the Lambeth Consultative Body (or its successor) should give early attention to the problems involved. The Conference recommends that, in any such area where there exists a Church with which we are in full communion, that Church should participate in the consultations'.

[57] LC 1878, Recommendation 1.

[58] LC 1867, Res. 1.

[59] LC 1930, Res. 47: 'The Conference calls upon all members of the Anglican Communion to promote the cause of union by fostering and deepening in all possible ways the fellowship of the Anglican Communion itself, so that by mutual understanding and appreciation all may come to a fuller apprehension of the truth as it is in Jesus, and more perfectly make manifest to the world the unity of the Spirit in and through the diversity of his gifts'.

laws of churches, however, there is little evidence of interprovincial law which expressly governs the relations of a particular church with other churches along the lines of the principles contained in the Lambeth resolutions. First, the Lambeth duty of respect is very rarely expressed in formal law.[60] Secondly, the prohibition against parallel episcopal jurisdictions occasionally surfaces in actual law; the canon law of ECUSA, for example, provides that '[i]t shall be lawful . . . to organize a Congregation in any foreign land' but 'not within the jurisdiction of any Missionary Bishop of this Church nor within any Diocese, Province, or Regional Church of the Anglican Communion'; moreover, '[t]he Presiding Bishop may . . . by written commission . . . assign to a Bishop or Bishops of this Church, or of a Church in communion with this Church, the care of, and responsibility for, one or more of such Congregations and the Clergy officiating therein'.[61]

Thirdly, and by way of contrast, the Lambeth prohibition against the exercise of ministry in another diocese without episcopal consent consistently appears in the laws of most churches. The subject is treated in some detail in English ecclesiastical law. An overseas bishop in a church in communion with the Church of England, or a bishop consecrated in a church not in communion with it but whose orders are recognized and accepted by the Church of England, cannot perform episcopal functions in any English diocese without the request of the diocesan bishop and the consent and licence of the provincial archbishop.[62] However, according to English ecclesiastical quasi-legislation, female bishops of Anglican churches overseas are not permitted to exercise episcopal ministry in the Church of England as their ministry is not accepted – but they are owed respect and courtesy.[63] Under English ecclesiastical law, overseas ministers (and persons ordained episcopally in a church not in communion with the Church of England but whose orders are recognized and accepted by the church) may minister only with archiepiscopal consent given in writing and for a specified time; the minister then has the same rights and lia-

[60] See exceptionally West Indies, Cans. 8: episcopal declaration: I 'will respect and maintain the spiritual rights and privileges of all Churches in the Anglican Communion'.

[61] ECUSA, Cans. I.15.1, 7.

[62] England, Overseas and Other Clergy (Ministry and Ordination) Measure 1967; see also e.g. ECUSA, Const. Art. III: 'Bishops may be consecrated for foreign lands upon due application therefrom, with the approbation of a majority of the Bishops of this Church entitled to vote in the House of Bishops, certified to the Presiding Bishop'.

[63] England: in a statement to General Synod in 1989, the Archbishop of Canterbury (also speaking on behalf of the Archbishop of York) explained: 'it seems clear enough that the Church of England does not canonically accept the ministry of . . . women . . . bishops of other Churches, unless and until the ecclesiastical law is changed specifically to allow this or to allow the Church of England itself to ordain women to the [order] of . . . bishop' (reproduced in *Ecclesiastical Law Journal*, 1(5) (1989), 9).

bilities as English clergy. In addition, these may minister only with the permission of the diocesan bishop, and with the consent of the appropriate Church of England clergy in whose cure of souls the person is to officiate.[64] In most churches, clergy from other churches in the Anglican Communion must produce Letters of Orders,[65] Letters Dimissory,[66] or some form of recommendation,[67] to the bishop of the diocese before they are permitted to minister in the diocese they visit. The laws of some churches require also submission of evidence of orders to the local member of clergy,[68] and others limit the permission to prescribed times.[69] Very rarely do laws of a church describe the effect in other Anglican churches of a sanction imposed as a result of disciplinary proceedings within that church,[70] though occasionally laws provide for the disciplining of visiting Anglican clergy. In Scottish canon law '[t]he Bishop of any diocese shall have power to inhibit . . . any Bishop or any Priest or Deacon from outwith the diocese, from preaching or performing any ecclesiastical function

[64] England, Overseas and Other Clergy (Ministry and Ordination) Measure 1967; a minister having cure of souls must consent unless the law provides that no such permission is needed (such as the ministry of confession when a person is in danger of death: Can. B29(4)); s. 1(6): disciplinary proceedings may be taken (under the Ecclesiastical Jurisdiction Measure 1963) against an overseas minister for officiating in the absence of such consents.

[65] Philippines, Cans. III.16.13: a member of the clergy of another church in communion with the Philippine church or from another province of the Anglican Communion must, to officiate, submit Letters of Orders, which must be certified as valid by the appropriate ecclesiastical authority.

[66] Brazil, Cans. III.9: ministers from other Anglican provinces or from other churches in communion with the Brazilian church may minister in a diocese only on presentation of Letters Dimissory from their own bishop. For temporary ministry written permission is needed.

[67] Scotland, Can. 15.4: 'No cleric of any other Church or province shall be appointed to any temporary charge in this Church unless that cleric is able to produce to the Bishop of the diocese concerned a recommendation from the Bishop of the diocese in which that cleric last served'.

[68] ECUSA, Cans. III.12: clergy ordained by bishops of other churches in communion with ECUSA may officiate in a congregation after exhibiting Letters of Orders to the member of clergy in charge or, if there is none, to the vestry; before taking charge of a congregation Letters Dimissory must be exhibited to the diocesan bishop.

[69] Scotland, Can. 15.5: 'No Rector or Priest-in-charge shall allow any cleric not already instituted or licensed or holding written permission to officiate in this Church to conduct services within the charge . . . .for more than two Sundays in any one year without previously informing the Bishop of the diocese; and no cleric from another diocese shall officiate for more than five consecutive Sundays in any one year without permission in writing under the hand and seal of the Bishop of the diocese'; Southern Africa, Can. 33.2: if any person satisfies the incumbent or churchwardens that he is a cleric of the church 'or of some other Church of the Anglican Communion', he may be permitted by the incumbent or churchwardens to officiate for one Sunday 'but for no more without the permission of the Bishop'.

[70] New Zealand, Cans. D.II.1: a minister ordained in another church may be deposed but the deposition has no effect outside the church in New Zealand.

within the diocese'. If the inhibited person disregards the inhibition, 'the Bishop inhibiting shall report the action to that cleric's ecclesiastical superior, and shall also report the inhibition, with the grounds of the same, to the next Episcopal Synod'. Any cleric 'knowingly disregarding such inhibition by allowing the inhibited person to officiate, shall be liable to admonition, and if the admonition be disregarded, the Bishop may take proceedings against that cleric in Synod'.[71] Fourthly, the Lambeth responsibility for churches to communicate information about new episcopal appointments is common in actual laws.[72] Finally, the Lambeth duty for churches to co-operate surfaces from time to time,[73] as does the duty to maintain fellowship.[74] Provisions enabling a provincial church to join with another Anglican province are common,[75] and many churches, whilst retaining their individual autonomy, have combined to form regional councils designed to effect co-ordinated action.[76]

ECUMENICAL LAW

Whereas the law of inter-Anglican relations is somewhat sparse, the laws of individual churches dealing with relations between the Anglican

[71] Scotland, Can. 15.6, 7.

[72] See e.g. Central Africa, Can. 3.5: 'The Dean of the Province shall in due course announce the name of the Archbishop so elected or appointed to the Bishops of the Province and to all Metropolitans'; Can. 7.7: confirmation of the election of a bishop must be transmitted 'to the Archbishop of Canterbury, and other Metropolitans'.

[73] Korea, Fundamental Declaration of Faith and Rites: 'We believe that for the unity of Christ's Church we must enter into co-operation with all churches on the basis of our faith and practice as a member Church of the Anglican Communion'.

[74] South India, Const. II.2: 'The Church of South India desires to regulate all its actions by the principle that it should maintain fellowship with all those branches of the Church of Christ with which the Churches from which it has been formed have severally enjoyed such fellowship'.

[75] South East Asia, Declarations, 6: 'If at any time the Church of the Province desires to be constitutionally joined with another Province of the Anglican Communion . . . it may do so, subject to the provisions of these Declarations'; Central Africa, Fundamental Declarations, VI: 'If at any time . . . the Church . . . desires to be constitutionally joined with another Province or other Provinces of the Anglican Communion, nothing contained in these Declarations or this Constitution shall prevent the Province from accepting and subscribing such constitutional provisions concerning Faith, Order and Worship and government as it may think fit to accept in order to achieve the proposed constitutional union'.

[76] LC 1978, Res. 12; LC 1988, Res. 18; there are now five regional councils: Anglican Council of North America and the Caribbean (ACNAC 1969 brings together representatives of the Anglican churches in Canada, the West Indies, Cuba and ECUSA); Regional Episcopal Association of Northern South America (ARIENSA 1973: a regional association of the dioceses of Colombia, Ecuador and Venezuela; its aim is to form an autonomous province); Conference of the Anglican Provinces of Africa (1977); Council of the Churches of East Asia (1954); South Pacific Anglican Council (the Provinces of Melanesia and Papua New Guinea and the diocese of Polynesia).

church in question and other non-Anglican churches have undergone radical development in recent years, principally as a result of decisions of the Lambeth Conference. This section explores elements of this incipient ecumenical law.

The Legal Regulation of Ecumenism

The Lambeth Conference has introduced some ground rules about ecumenical development. Where there is agreement between an Anglican Church and some other church or churches, 'to seek unity in a way which includes agreement on apostolic faith and order', and where that agreement has found expression in a covenant to unite or in some other appropriate form, 'a Church of the Anglican Communion should be free to allow reciprocal acts of intercommunion under the general direction of the bishop'. Each church is 'to determine when the negotiations for union in which it is engaged have reached the stage which allows intercommunion'.[77] Actual laws of churches provide that, in this state, each communion recognizes the catholicity and independence of the other and they agree to admit members of the other communion 'to participate in the sacraments'; at the same time, however, 'inter-communion does not require the acceptance of all doctrinal opinion, sacramental devotion or liturgical practice characteristic of the other, but implies that each believes the other to hold all the essentials of the faith'.[78] In several churches in the Communion a set of basic ecumenical duties is incorporated into the law of the church: to maintain fellowship,[79] or mutual understanding;[80] to seek unity,[81] or to restore unity between

[77] LC 1968, Res. 47.

[78] See e.g. New Zealand, GS Standing Res. 1952: as to the Old Catholic Church; ibid., GS Standing Res. 1974: the church has 'unrestricted *communio in sacris*' with the Church of South India; the same formula appears in Wales, Can. of 1937.

[79] South India, Const. II.2: the church 'should continually seek to widen and strengthen this fellowship and to work towards the goal of full union in one body of all parts of the Church of Christ'; New Zealand, GS Standing Res. 1992: the General Synod reaffirms its adherence to the Act of Commitment 1967 and encourages 'joint worship and ecumenical co-operation, especially in the areas of evangelism, social service and social transformation'.

[80] Jerusalem and the Middle East, Const. Art. 5(ii): Central Synod and the dioceses should seek 'to establish and maintain relations of Christian charity, fellowship, mutual understanding and co-operation in the service of God with all other Christian Churches in the hope of the Unity of all Christian people according to the Will of God'; ibid., 5(iii): Central Synod 'welcomes [and] endeavours to promote responsible dialogue with men of other faiths and religious traditions'.

[81] Southern Africa, Resolution of Permanent Force of the Provincial Synod, 1 (1973): the Synod accepts the Declaration of Intention to seek 'the Union of the Church of the Province of South Africa, the United Congregational Church of Southern Africa, the Methodist Church of South Africa, the Presbyterian Church of Southern Africa, the Bantu Presbyterian Church and the Tsonga Presbyterian Church'; 'We believe that it is God's will that His Church should be visibly one, and that the Holy Spirit is moving us

churches.[82] Occasionally, these aims are particularized in the form of a special canonical obligation to enter agreements with other churches in order to effect intercommunion.[83] In other churches, the law imposes a duty to heal divisions.[84] Paradoxically, however, the laws of very many churches list amongst their ecclesiastical offences schism, the 'acceptance of membership in a religious body not in communion with the Church of this Province'.[85]

From the Anglican perspective, whether ecumenical relations may be had with another church depends on its legal recognition by the Anglican church in question. Churches employ a range of devices governing legal recognition: in some churches it is determined by the central church assembly,[86] in others legal recognition rests with the episcopate, either in a metropolitical authority,[87] or with the bishops of the church acting col-

---

to seek this union'; 'We undertake: to seek agreement on a common form of ministry of Word and Sacraments'; 'to admit to the Lord's Table communicant members of all our Churches as an immediate and visible sign of our common quest'; 'to work for increasing co-operation in all areas of Church life'; and 'to signify our solemn acceptance of this pledge by participating, throughout our Churches, in services of commitment to the search for Union'.

[82] Korea, Fundamental Declaration of Faith and Rites: 'we look for the restoration of the Catholic faith and principles of unity of the early Church before the Great Schism'; '[w]e will strive for the unity of Christ's Church in this land'.

[83] Portugal, Can. X: this imposes a duty to engage in ecumenical dialogue to restore visible unity, as well as a duty to establish concordats for reciprocity; X.2: this contains terms which must be embodied in concordats: mutual recognition of catholicity and independence; admission of members to the sacraments; permission for bishops, priests and deacons to minister in each other's churches; common theological investigation; and the inclusion of the statement that intercommunion does not include belief in all doctrines etc (see n. 78); the concordats must be approved by the Archbishop of Canterbury.

[84] England, Can. A8: 'Forasmuch as the Church of England has for a long time past been distressed by separations and schisms among Christian men, so that the unity for which our Lord prayed is impaired and the witness to his gospel is grievously hindered, it is the duty of clergy and people to do their utmost not only to avoid occasions of strife but also to seek in penitence and brotherly charity to heal such divisions'.

[85] Southern Africa, Can. 37.1(e); see also Wales, II.11,14; III.7, 9; IV.13; VI.2; XI.5, 13: these provide that membership of a 'religious body not in communion with the Church in Wales', is a disqualification from holding office in the church: for a critical study of these and other anti-ecumenical provisions, see A. Lewis, 'The case for constitutional renewal in the Church in Wales', N. Doe (ed.), *Essays in Canon Law* (Cardiff, 1992), 175; see Ch. 7 for similar definitions appearing in the laws of other Anglican churches.

[86] New Zealand, Cans. G.XIII.6: the church recognizes as being in full communion with itself '[t]he Church of England and all other Churches of the Anglican Communion, and such other Churches as shall be recognised by General Synod from time to time as being in full communion'; Melanesia, Standing Res. 1979, 7: the church 'accepts the relationship of full Communion' with churches listed in the resolution.

[87] Diocese of Europe, Const. 50(c): 'If any question arises whether a Church is in communion with the Church of England, it shall be conclusively determined for the purposes of this Constitution by the Archbishops of Canterbury and York'.

lectively.[88] Scottish canon law operates a system of legal recognition based on a mixture of these: according to Canon 15 the church 'recognises as in full communion with itself the Churches of the Anglican Communion, the other Churches which are listed in the Schedule to this Canon', as well as 'such other Churches as shall be added from time to time to this Schedule by the Episcopal Synod with the prior consent of the General Synod'. Moreover, in Scotland, 'should any Church listed in the Schedule to this Canon take such action as shall have rendered itself, in the opinion of the Episcopal Synod, in a state of impaired communion with this Church', the Episcopal Synod (subject to the consent of General Synod) is empowered 'to determine its removal from the said Schedule'.[89]

Whilst the laws of some churches impose on assemblies at the lowest church levels duties to promote the ecumenical life of the local church,[90] today the trend is to manage ecumenical affairs centrally, at national, regional or provincial level, through the establishment of ecumenical commissions. Such bodies do not exist in all churches, but the canon law of several requires their establishment. In ECUSA, the General Convention has a national standing commission on ecumenical relations, consisting of eighteen members (six bishops, six presbyters or deacons, and six lay persons). The commission has three functions: 'to develop a comprehensive and coordinated policy and strategy on relations between this Church and other Churches'; to make recommendations to General Convention concerning 'interchurch cooperation and unity'; and to carry out 'such instructions on ecumenical matters as may be given it from time to time by the General Convention'. It must nominate for appointment by the Presiding Bishop persons 'to serve on the governing bodies of ecumenical organizations to which this Church belongs by action of the General Convention and to participate in major conferences as convened by such organizations'.[91] The laws of other churches governing their own ecumenical bodies are much the same as those in ECUSA: this is the case in

---

[88] Central Africa, Res. of Provincial Synod 1972: 'in order to define which Churches are "approved" . . . the Bishops of the province shall compile and maintain a list of the Churches within the Province which are approved as holding the Apostolic Faith as contained in the Scriptures and summarised in the Apostles' and Nicene Creeds'.

[89] Scotland, Can. 15.1: in addition to the churches of the Anglican Communion, 'the Scottish Episcopal Church recognizes as in full communion with itself The Old Catholic Churches in communion with the Metropolitan See of Utrecht; The Church of North India, The Church of Pakistan, The Mar Thoma Church of Malabar, The Church of Bangladesh, The Church of South India, The Church of Norway, The Church of Sweden and The Evangelical Lutheran Church of Estonia'.

[90] See e.g. Wales, Const. VI.22(2)(a): the functions of the parochial church council shall include 'promotion of the whole mission of the Church, pastoral, evangelistic, social and ecumenical, in the parish'; see generally Ch. 2.

[91] ECUSA, Cans. I.1(2)(n)(3).

the Philippines,[92] in the West Indies,[93] and in New Zealand where the differences as to function are very insignificant. The canonical responsibilities of the provincial ecumenical council of New Zealand, consisting of the primate or his nominee and representatives of the dioceses, are: to promote the principle of 'Unity by Stages'; to advise on all aspects of the church's Act of Commitment to unity in 1967; to appoint Anglican representatives as may be required for ecumenical organizations and conferences; to have a responsibility for relationships with ecumenical organizations overseas; and to represent to the Anglican Consultative Council ecumenical matters of concern to the Church. The council must report on its activities to each ordinary meeting of the General Synod.[94]

The Legal Union of Churches

Quasi-legislation of the Lambeth Conference provides two rudimentary principles governing constitutional union between an Anglican church and another church. One regulates contemplation of union, the other its administration. First, union may be proposed by an Anglican church only if the other church is one with which the Anglican Communion could eventually be in full communion.[95] Secondly, when the whole ministry of the united church is under episcopal oversight, even if a non-episcopally ordained visiting minister celebrates Holy Communion in the united church, this must not be regarded 'as a bar to relations of full communion between the United Church and the Churches of the Anglican Communion'. However, in the united church 'due constitutional provisions are [to be] made to safeguard the conscience of worshippers' in such circumstances. Furthermore, each member church of the Communion must not forbid the ministry of episcopally ordained clergy of united churches to minister in that church. Finally, the united church may be invited to membership of the Lambeth Conference.[96] The constitutional

---

[92] See e.g. Philippines, Cans. I.2.2(b): the Provincial Synod's commission on evangelism and ecumenical relations must act similarly with respect to 'Asia-regional and global ecumenical bodies'.

[93] West Indies, Can. 33: the provincial standing commission on ecumenism consists of not more than eight members and its duty is 'to develop a comprehensive policy and strategy on relations between the Church of the Province of the West Indies and other Churches, and in particular to explore the possibility of closer relationships with the Dioceses of the Virgin Islands, Haiti and Bermuda'; it must make recommendations to the Provincial Synod concerning 'interchurch cooperation and unity', and 'carry out such instructions on ecumenical matters as may be given to it from time to time by the Synod'; the commission may nominate persons to the Synod for appointment to serve on the governing bodies of ecumenical organizations to which the province is affiliated and to participate in conferences convened by such organizations.

[94] New Zealand, Cans. B.XVIII.   [95] LC 1948, Res. 56; for withdrawal, see n. 4.

[96] LC 1958, Res. 21; LC 1978, Res. 32; and LC 1988, Res. 12.

union of churches is a subject rarely treated by the formal laws of individual churches in the Anglican Communion. Union is addressed in the laws of the national Church of England, the provincial Church of Kenya and, not surprisingly, in the United Churches of India. Each church employs contrasting procedural rules, but in all three the competence to effect union is reserved to the central church assembly. According to English ecclesiastical law, only the General Synod is empowered to create 'a scheme for constitutional union or a permanent and substantial change of relationship between the Church of England and another Christian body'. Its competence may be exercised only in relation to another church 'being a body a substantial number of whose members reside in Great Britain'. The scheme must not be finally approved by the General Synod unless, at a stage determined by the Archbishops, the scheme itself or the substance of the proposals embodied in it, has been approved by 'a majority of the dioceses at meetings of their Diocesan Synods'. If the archbishops consider that this provision should apply to a scheme which affects the Church of England and another Christian body but does not fall within the terms of the provision, 'they may direct that the Article shall apply to that scheme'.[97]

In Kenyan canon law negotiations for 'a scheme of union' between the province, or any of its dioceses, and 'any other Christian body', may be proposed only by the bishops collectively. The negotiations cannot proceed, however, without the consent of a simple majority of each house of the Provincial Synod. The Synod then appoints delegates representing the church and at every meeting of Synod these must submit a progress report. At any time the Provincial Synod may issue instructions to the delegates, passed by way of resolution by a simple majority of the whole Synod. Once negotiations are completed, the procedure for the adoption of a scheme of union with other churches in Kenya is as follows: a resolution of general approval of the scheme must be presented to the Provincial Synod by the Bishops' Meeting and passed by a two-thirds majority in each house – the resolution is dealt with as one involving faith or order; the proposed scheme must be communicated to the Anglican Consultative Council with a request for its opinion or advice which must be considered by the Provincial Synod before a final decision is taken. The proposed scheme of union, together with the resolution of general approval and the Council's advice, must be referred to all Diocesan Synods; it must be passed by at least two-thirds of the dioceses before final adoption by the Provincial Synod by means of a simple majority in each house and by a three-quarters majority of the members of the whole Synod voting together. Any diocese which has received permission to join a scheme of

---

[97] England, Synodical Government Measure 1969, Sched. 2. Art. 8; laws on union usually deal with constitutional union between Anglican churches: see n. 75.

union continues to be bound by the constitution, canons and rules of the Kenyan provincial church 'until such time as it becomes a constituent part of a united Church'.[98]

According to the constitution of the United Church of South India, at any time the Synod or its executive committee may appoint a committee 'to discuss with the representatives of other Churches in Joint Committee the possibility of wider Union'. The committee's report is submitted to the executive committees of all diocesan councils and to all diocesan bishops sitting separately – their comments and reports are transmitted, in turn, to the Synod executive committee. If, in the opinion of a majority of members of the executive committee, any proposal of the joint committee involves 'a matter of major principle on which the judgment of the Church is required, the question shall be referred to the Synod at its next meeting and all Dioceses shall be officially informed of this action', in order to consider the matter. The Synod takes the final decision on a scheme of union. It must be passed by a three-quarters majority of members present and voting and, in substantially the same terms, by not less than two-thirds of all diocesan councils. Following this it is resubmitted to the Synod for confirmation by a three-quarters majority vote – it then becomes an Act of the Church. The scheme must contain provisions whereby properties held upon trust for the uniting churches 'shall from the date of union be held in trust for the United Church' of South India. A further condition of admission is that members of the uniting church are 'willing to abide by the rules and customs of the Church'. No member of the church of South India who is unwilling 'to accept a decision to enter a wider Union . . . is entitled to claim continuing membership in the Church of South India'.[99]

Ecumenical Concordats

Short of constitutional union, relations between Anglican churches and other churches may be determined by means of a *concordat*,[100] an *agree-*

---

[98] Kenya, Can. II: the canon is entitled 'Of union with other Christians'.

[99] South India, Const. XV; see also North India, Const. II.IV.IV.35: the Synod 'shall have power to enter into negotiations with other Churches with a view to wider union and to do all that is necessary to bring such wider union to consummation'.

[100] For example, the Concordat of Full Communion 1961, between the Mar Thoma Church and (the former) Anglican Church of India, Pakistan, Burma and Ceylon; the Mar Thoma Syrian Church of Malabar is now in full communion with the United Churches in India and Pakistan: whilst it has affirmed its desire to preserve its eastern orthodox traditions, several Anglican churches have full communion with it (see e.g. Scotland, Can. 15.1, Sched); the Concordat of Full Communion 1961 (ECUSA and the Lusitanian Church, which was integrated as a full member (as an extra-provincial diocese) of the Anglican Communion in 1980); see also Spanish Reformed Episcopal Church, Const. IV: the church 'is integrated in the Anglican Communion and is a member of full right in the same'; for a recent failure to create a concordat, see ECUSA: the

ment,[101] a *covenant*,[102] or other arrangement the terms of which, to be operative within the participating Anglican church, must subsequently be
embodied in its canon law or other binding internal instrument.[103] For
example, formal conversations between on the one hand the Anglican
churches in the United Kingdom and in Ireland and, on the other hand, the
Nordic and Baltic Lutheran Churches resulted, in the Porvoo Common
Statements in 1993 recommending the establishment of a relationship of
full communion including interchangeable ministries and collegial consultation. The Church in Wales, for instance, has since created canon law
to implement the Porvoo Declaration. The Welsh canon fulfils three functions and effects. The first is to represent the agreed declaration in the form
of general principles. All the churches are acknowledged as belonging 'to
the One, Holy, Catholic and Apostolic Church of Jesus Christ and truly
participating in the apostolic mission of the whole people of God'. As such
it is recognized that in each church 'the Word of God is authentically
preached', 'the sacraments of baptism and the eucharist are duly administered', and the apostolic faith is genuinely confessed. Moreover, each
church affirms that its ordained ministries 'are given by God as instruments of his grace and as possessing not only the inward call of the Spirit,
but also God's commission through his body, the Church'. Finally, the
general principles confirm that each church operates a system of personal,
collegial and communal oversight (*episcope*), in which 'the episcopal office
is valued and maintained . . . as a visible sign expressing and serving the
Church's unity and continuity in apostolic life, mission and ministry'. The
second purpose of the canon is to implement the practical terms of the ecumenical agreement. Framed as duties and rights, the codified agreement is

Evangelical Lutheran Church has rejected the Concordat of Agreement proposing to
effect full communion with ECUSA, the General Convention of which had passed the
proposal (see *Church Times*, 22 August 1997: the stumbling block was the proposed concordat's terms dealing with the 'historic episcopate').

[101] The Bonn Agreement 1931 between representatives of the Old Catholic Churches
and the churches of the Anglican Communion established full communion under
which 'Each Communion recognises the catholicity and independence of the other and
maintains its own . . . [and] agrees to admit members of the other Communion to participate in the Sacraments'.

[102] See e.g. Wales, Can. of 1974, 'For covenanting between the Church in Wales and
certain Baptist Churches for Union in Wales'; 'the Church in Wales solemnly covenants'
with designated churches provided nothing in the covenant 'shall affect . . . the faith,
discipline, articles, doctrinal statements, rites, ceremonies or formularies of the Church
in Wales'.

[103] See e.g. the Mesissen Declaration approved by the General Synod of the Church
of England in 1990 and promulgated as an Act of Synod 1991: this provides for that
church and the Evangelical Church in Germany (a communion with 25 member
churches) to enjoy a closer fellowship but without interchangeable ministries; by it the
churches are committed to work towards full visible unity; the member churches are
now churches to which Cans. B43 and B44 apply (see below).

designed to enable the sharing of resources. With respect to spiritual resources, each church is obliged to welcome one another's members to receive sacramental and other pastoral ministrations and 'to regard baptized members of all our churches as members of our own'. With respect to ministry, each church must welcome persons episcopally ordained to the office of bishop, priest or deacon, to serve in any of the participating churches. Reordination may not be required. However, service may take place only by invitation and in accordance with the regulations of the host church. In relation to episcopal ministry, bishops from each church may be invited to participate in the laying on of hands at the ordination of bishops. The third function of the canon is programmatic: to impose obligations for future development. At the level of government, the agreement obliges the participating churches 'to establish appropriate forms of collegial and conciliar consultation on significant matters of faith and order, life and work'. It also obliges the participants to co-ordinate the implementation of the ecumenical agreement. Concerning ministry, the churches are committed to work towards a common understanding of the diaconate. With respect to education, the churches must strive 'to facilitate learning and exchange of ideas and information in theological and pastoral matters'.[104] In short, in this canon the Church in Wales has now bound itself to a system of duties, imposed upon itself, and rights, exercisable by members and ministers of the other churches. The canon itself has, of course, no duty-imposing effect upon the other parties to the agreement upon which the canon is based. Only the implementation of that agreement in the internal laws of the participating churches will give rise to its enforceability in those churches.

Local Ecumenical Projects

The national, regional, or provincial laws of very few churches regulate directly ecumenical relations at the lowest ecclesiastical levels.[105] Canon law in England and Wales is exceptional. There are points of contact between these two systems – but the Welsh scheme would seem to put far greater control in the hands of the bishop. In England, a diocesan bishop may enter an agreement with the appropriate authority of another church

---

[104] Wales, Can. of 28 September 1995: the parties to the agreement are: the Church in Wales, Church of England, Episcopal Church of Scotland, Church of Ireland, Estonian Evangelical-Lutheran Church, Evangelical-Lutheran Church of Finland, Evangelical-Lutheran Church of Iceland, Evangelical-Lutheran Church of Latvia, Evangelical-Lutheran Church of Lithuania, Church of Norway, and the Church of Sweden.

[105] See e.g. New Zealand, Cans. B.V.2.8: it is lawful for a Diocesan Synod to authorize its standing committee to enter agreements for co-operative ventures with other Christian churches and such agreements shall be based on 'guidelines' approved by the General Synod.

for participation in a local ecumenical project; in Wales the bishop may authorize the establishment of such a project 'by written declaration'. Whilst the Welsh canon contains no definition of a local ecumenical project, in England it is 'a scheme under which Churches of more than one denomination agree, in relation to an area or institution specified in the scheme, to co-operate in accordance with the provisions of the scheme in matters affecting the ministry, congregational life or buildings of the Churches which are participating in the scheme'.[106] In England, the bishop may enter an agreement only with the consent of the incumbent, 75 per cent of those present and voting at the parochial church council, and the diocesan pastoral committee (after consultation with the relevant Deanery Synod); in Wales, the bishop must obtain the consent of the bench of bishops, the diocesan conference, the parochial church council, and the incumbent. In both England and Wales, the bishop may terminate the agreement after consultation with the appropriate authority of the participating church. Under English canon law, once a project is entered, the bishop must make an instrument in writing authorizing liturgical acts which Church of England clergy may perform in other churches, and those acts which ministers of other churches may perform in places of worship of the Church of England: for example, ministers of participating churches may baptize in Church of England places of worship in accordance with a rite of the participating church; and an Anglican priest or a non-Anglican minister may be authorized to preside at a service of Holy Communion in accordance with a rite of a participating church. The bishop must be satisfied that the participating church's rites do not depart from the doctrine of the Church of England. In England, agreements may be entered only with churches designated by the archbishops. Like England, under Welsh canon law a project may be entered only with a church which is in communion with the Church in Wales or which holds the Trinitarian faith and administers the sacraments of baptism and Eucharist.[107] Ministers of the Church in Wales must be licensed by the bishop to officiate under the project, and duly accredited ministers or members of a participating church must have the written permission of the bishop to officiate regularly in places of worship of the Church in Wales. In both churches the bishop must ensure that public worship according to the rites of the church will be maintained on prescribed days. Three particular rules in the Welsh canon which do not appear in the English equivalent are: that the bench of bishops may make regulations permitting ministers of a participating

---

[106] Church of England (Ecumenical Relations) Measure 1988, s. 6.

[107] England, Can. B44; Church of England (Ecumenical Relations) Measure 1988, s. 5: these provisions apply to a church designated by the two archbishops acting jointly which 'subscribes to the doctrine of the Holy Trinity and administers the Sacraments of Holy Baptism and Holy Communion'.

church to attend, speak and vote at the parochial church council; that an episcopal licence or written permission may be revoked in writing by the bishop at any time; and that the minister of the other church must agree in writing to be bound by the directions of the bishop.[108]

The Recognition and Sharing of Ministries

Two models are used to enable ministers of other churches to officiate in churches of the Anglican Communion. One controls admission of ministers into the ordained ministry of the Anglican church. The other allows the sharing of ministry by means of direct executive episcopal approval rather than by means of formal agreements. With respect to the first, in several churches a legal precondition to the exercise of ministry in an Anglican church by a minister of another Christian church is recognition of orders by the bishop in whose diocese that person is to minister.[109] Contrasting systems are to be found in ECUSA and the church in North India. The canon law of ECUSA on this subject is highly complex. A bishop may permit any minister of a church in communion with ECUSA to minister in that church. A special procedure applies to a person who has been 'ordained or licensed . . . by other than a Bishop in the Historic Succession to minister in a Christian body not in communion with this Church'. Such a person is eligible for an accelerated process of ordination once they obtain the status of a confirmed adult communicant in good standing in a congregation of ECUSA. In the case of a priest or deacon ordained in a church in the historic succession but not in communion with ECUSA, that person must similarly acquire the status of a confirmed adult communicant in good standing in a congregation of ECUSA. Once this status is held, the bishop may: *receive* (with the consent of the diocesan standing committee) the person into the church in the Orders to which that person has already been ordained; *confirm* and 'make the person a Deacon' and later 'ordain as Priest' if not already ordained as priest; *ordain* as deacon and later ordain conditionally (having baptized and confirmed the person conditionally if necessary) as priest 'if ordained by a bishop whose authority to convey such orders has not been recognized' by ECUSA.[110]

In the United Church of North India, an ordained minister of another church who wishes to join the united church to serve in its ordained min-

[108] Wales, Can. of 1991.

[109] Brazil, Cans. III.8: 'If any minister wishes to have his orders recognized by this church he must request recognition from the diocesan bishop'; this applies to those coming from another church not in communion with the Anglican church in Brazil who have been ordained by a bishop in apostolic succession; see also Spain, Can. 27.

[110] ECUSA, Cans. I.16.2; III.10, 11; see also Mexico, Cans. III.25, 26; and Puerto Rico, Cans. III.12, 13.

istry must apply in writing to the bishop of the diocese. The application must be accompanied by documentary confirmation of ordination, status in their previous church, service experience, age and academic qualifications. The bishop may interview the applicant and, if willing to proceed, refers the application to the diocesan ministerial and personnel committee which, in turn, makes a recommendation to the executive committee of the diocesan council. At this stage, if accepted, different rules apply to different classes of candidate. First, ministers of the Church of South India, Pakistan, Bangladesh and the Malankara Mar Thoma Syrian Church may be received as ordained ministers and authorized to minister by the bishop, provided they accept the constitution, faith and discipline of the church. Secondly, if the person is an ordained minister of a church in communion with the Church of North India, he may be admitted into its membership and ordained ministry by 'the unification of their ministry', effected according to a special form of service. Thirdly, an ordained minister of a church not in communion with the Church of North India may undergo preparation for unification of their ministry provided four conditions are satisfied: that their motives are acceptable; that they were in 'good standing' in their original church; that the former church was Trinitarian and that its doctrine is recognized by the Church of North India; and that the church had 'an established procedure ... whereby ministers are selected, trained and ordained in a service with prayer and the laying on of hands by a minister who is authorized to do so'. However, even if a person does not fulfil these conditions, the bishop has an overriding discretion to admit them to unification – '[e]ach case may be dealt with on its own merits'.[111]

The second model appearing in Anglican canon law, which enables ministers of other churches to serve in an Anglican church, is that of direct authorization to do so from the diocesan bishop. This system is widespread. Process usually begins with an invitation. Ordinarily, this is issued by the local Anglican minister,[112] and sometimes the consent of the local church assembly is required before the invitation may be extended.[113] The

---

[111] North India, Const. III.VII.1–3.

[112] Puerto Rico, Cans. III.17: a minister of another church, with episcopal permission may minister by invitation to assist in the office of holy matrimony and read the gospel.

[113] Ireland, Const. IX.10: a minister or preacher of a church not in full communion with the Church of Ireland (as specified by the House of Bishops) may: deliver an address at any service; read Morning or Evening Prayer (but not Holy Communion) or such parts as the ordinary decides either jointly with or in the absence of a Church of Ireland minister; this may occur only with the permission of the ordinary (without prejudice 'to the normal maintenance of the recognised rules of church order') who must be satisfied that such a course is acceptable to the incumbent and churchwardens (and that 'it is not contrary to any provision of the civil law').

bishop must then approve.[114] Sometimes special provisions exist with respect to named churches,[115] and occasionally invited ministers are required to subscribe to the doctrine, worship and discipline of the host Anglican church.[116] Laws prescribe carefully the acts which may be performed by invited clergy: the giving of addresses,[117] the conduct of Morning and Evening Prayer,[118] celebration of Holy Communion, either alone or with the Anglican minister,[119] and the conducting of weddings and funerals.[120] Scottish canon law is particularly comprehensive on this subject. It confers a power on the bishop to permit only clergy of churches listed under the canons to minister in congregations. However, the bishop may permit episcopally ordained clergy of churches not listed under the canon to give an address if 'the College of Bishops has previously determined that the relation of this Church to the Church in question makes such action desirable'. Before the bishop gives any permission, the Anglican cleric must be satisfied that the person has been episcopally ordained. Whilst ministering, the person must neither act nor speak 'in a manner contrary to the doctrine and discipline of this Church'. In addition, Scottish bishops may permit, on the application from their clergy, or

[114] New Zealand, Cans. G.XIII.6: 'A Bishop may permit any Bishop, Priest or Deacon from a Church in full communion with this Church . . . to officiate in any church, parish or congregation for one or more services upon being satisfied that the person is duly ordained'; any bishop, priest or deacon of a church in full communion is eligible to be licensed or issued with a permission to officiate or to hold office as a bishop.

[115] New Zealand, Cans. G.XIII.7: when a priest or deacon ordained by a bishop of the Roman Catholic Church or other churches in communion with the See of Rome or a church recognized by the General Synod applies to a bishop to hold office, the applicant must produce: Letters of Orders; testimony of character and quality; and a declaration of baptism and membership; the applicant must subscribe the declaration (Const. C.15) and 'shall renounce all recourse to any other ecclesiastical jurisdiction'.

[116] ECUSA, Const. Art. VIII: those ordained by a bishop of a church not in communion with ECUSA, must not officiate without subscription to the doctrine, discipline and liturgy of the church; see also Mexico, Const. Art. VI.3; Puerto Rico, Cans. III.12, 13.

[117] Australia, Diocese of Sydney, *The 7th Handbook*, 8.28 and Resolution of the Archbishop-in-Council 1923: an ordained minister of another denomination may be invited to preach in a church if the minister of the parochial unit applies in writing to the assistant bishop; the application must be specific and for a stated occasion or occasions; the minister must not issue an invitation until the application has been approved; and the minister must inform the churchwardens at least one week before making the application.

[118] ECUSA, Cans. III.19: the bishop may permit clergy to invite ministers of other churches to assist in Prayer Book offices, holy matrimony or burial, or to read Morning or Evening Prayer; the bishop may also permit clergy of another church to preach or, in 'ecumenical settings', to assist in the administration of the sacraments and to permit 'godly persons' who are not clergy of ECUSA to make addresses on special occasions.

[119] Southern Africa, Can. 33.3: 'Any clergyman . . . may, with the permission of the Bishop of the Diocese, unite in the Administration of the Sacraments, or in the conduct of Divine Service, with other ministers not appointed to minister in this Church'.

[120] See n. 112.

a Rector or Priest-in-charge of any church within the diocese, any lay person in communion with the Scottish Episcopal Church 'to address the congregation in that church or to conduct any service which does not require the ministrations of a Priest'. Similarly, the bishop may permit, on request of their clergy, any minister (whether episcopally ordained or not) of a Trinitarian Church outside the Anglican Communion 'to assist at a wedding, funeral or memorial service or at a service or occasion of an ecumenical character in a church within the diocese in such manner as the College of Bishops shall direct'. Finally, Scottish clergy have a right to 'invite representatives of other Communions to give an address or assist at a service, provided that the Bishop of the Diocese consents to the invitation being given'.[121]

Of all churches in the Anglican Communion, only the canon law of Kenya seems to deal with the exchange of lay workers between the church of the province and other churches.[122] The standing committee of the Provincial Synod is obliged to draw up annually a list of posts open to non-Kenyan workers and to communicate the list to churches in full communion with the province. After consultation between the worker's own church and the bishop of the diocese in which the worker is to serve, the person on appointment must agree to accept the doctrine, worship and discipline of the Kenyan church. Salaries, allowances and the general welfare of the worker are the responsibility of the provincial church under the terms of an agreement with the worker's own church. For any alleged breach of the agreement, recourse is made to the diocesan bishop who must consult with the other church. In the event that no agreement is reached, the archbishop must notify the other diocesan bishops of the province, that the services of the worker are available, and arrange for his appointment elsewhere. Similarly, if a bishop no longer wishes to retain the services of a worker in the diocese, the archbishop in consultation with the worker's own church is obliged to arrange for his appointment elsewhere.[123]

---

[121] Scotland, Cans. 15, 16.

[122] For members of other churches being allowed to attend Anglican assemblies, see e.g. New Zealand, Cans. B.XXI.3: a member of another Christian church recognized by General Synod standing resolution 'duly chosen to represent a cooperating parish or cooperative venture in the house of laity of any diocesan synod' has a right to speak and to vote if 16 years of age or more; however, such a person may not do so with regard to the alteration of formularies, the nomination of a bishop, amending the constitution, or any other matter pursuant to the Church of England Empowering Act 1928.

[123] Kenya, Can. III: 'No Christian from another Church shall be appointed to the service of the Church of the province until he or she has agreed to accept the principles of doctrine and worship as set forth in this Constitution, and has also agreed to be bound by the Canons, Rules, Standing Orders and the principles of Christian discipline set forth in this Constitution'.

Admission and Reception

Ecumenical law in the form of rules enabling the admission of lay members of other churches into the membership of Anglican churches is well-developed throughout the Communion. Two contrasting approaches are to be found in England and Australia: in the former reception rules are liberal, and in the latter they are restricted to communicant members of other churches. For English canon law, reception occurs in six ways. When a person has not been baptized (or the validity of a claimed baptism is in question), the person must be baptized or conditionally baptized and this, following instruction, constitutes reception. Those baptized but not episcopally confirmed may be received after instruction either by confirmation or by a priest with appropriate prayers. Those episcopally confirmed must be instructed and, with the bishop's permission, received according to a form of reception approved by General Synod. The person received promises 'to live as a loyal member of the Church of England'.[124] In Australia, national canons authorize 'the use of a service for the reception into communicant membership of this Church of baptised persons who were formerly communicant members of other churches'. The canons apply only to persons who were members of churches not in full communion with the Australian church which nevertheless hold 'the apostolic faith'. When a baptized communicant member of such a church, desires to become a communicant member of the Anglican church, an application must be made to the priest who, being assured of the desire, must after due preparation present that person to the bishop at the time of confirmation or some other time. The bishop may receive and welcome that person into communicant membership of the church by imposition of hands with prayer. A canonical service must be used for the reception. The person received then enjoys 'the same status in this Church as a person who has been confirmed in accordance with the rites of this Church'. The reception must be recorded in the registers of the church. The canon affects the order and good government of the church within a diocese and does not come into force in any diocese unless and until the diocese adopts it by ordinance.[125] Some Australian dioceses have not adopted the restrictions

---

[124] England, Can. B28; see also New Zealand, GS Standing Res. 1990: 'baptised members of other Christian Churches may be welcomed in a suitable manner at any service of public worship'; see also ECUSA, Cans. I.17.1: 'All persons who have received the Sacrament of Holy Baptism with water in the name of the Father, and of the Son, and of the Holy Spirit, whether in this Church or in another Church' are members of ECUSA provided they satisfy the additional qualifications contained in Can. I.15.1(b)–(d).

[125] Australia, Cans. 1 1985 and 14 1995.

contemplated in this canon but instead mirror the more liberal English approach.[126]

A related but less well-developed body of law found in a small number of churches is that regulating the admission of congregations of other churches. The relevant canon law of ECUSA applies to 'a congregation of Christian people, holding the Christian faith as set forth in the Catholic creeds and recognizing the Scriptures as containing all things necessary to salvation, but using a rite other than that set forth by this Church'. When such a congregation desires affiliation with ECUSA, while retaining the use of its own rite, it must make an application with the consent of the diocesan bishop to the presiding bishop for 'status' as an affiliated congregation.[127] By way of contrast, in North India the admission of congregations of other churches is determined by the standing committee of the diocesan assembly. When an independent congregation desires to join the church, an application must be made to the bishop of the diocese in which it is located. The application must be accompanied by an affidavit sworn and signed by the office-bearers of the congregation; it must be accompanied by the minutes of the meeting of that congregation's governing body at which the resolution to join was passed. The application is considered by the executive committee of the diocesan council and, if approved, the congregation is received in a service of reception. The minister is then unified and authorized to minister. Members of the congregation must sign a declaration of assent to the constitution of the Church of North India to which the congregation must transfer its real property.[128]

Admission to Holy Communion

Two resolutions of the Lambeth Conference 1968 deal with the admission of members of other churches to Holy Communion in the Anglican church, and the admission of Anglicans to Holy Communion celebrated in other churches. The first resolution provides that, 'in order to meet special pastoral needs of God's people, under the direction of the bishop, Christians duly baptized in the name of the Holy Trinity and qualified to receive Holy Communion in their own Churches, may be welcomed at the

---

[126] Australia, Diocese of Sydney, *The 7th Handbook*, 8.30: 'Any person desiring to be received into the Anglican Church of Australia, who has not been baptised (or the validity of whose baptism can be held in question), must be instructed and baptised or conditionally baptised according to the directions in the 1662 Prayer Book'; a short form of service has been authorized; '[t]he form of reception may be used for baptised but unconfirmed persons at any time before confirmation, and must be used for all persons already episcopally confirmed who are to be received into or restored to the Anglican Church of Australia'; '[t]he reception should be done by an assistant bishop, representing the wider church, and if possible this should take place during a confirmation'.

[127] ECUSA, Cans. I.16.1.   [128] North India, Const. III.VIII.

Lord's Table in the Anglican Communion'. This resolution does not envis-
age, it would seem, a right of members of other churches to receive communion in an Anglican church – rather, their admission is discretionary.
The second resolution states that 'it is the general practice of the Church
that Anglican communicants receive Holy Communion at the hands of
ordained ministers of their own Church or of Churches in communion
therewith'. However, 'under the general direction of the bishop', in order
to meet special pastoral need, Anglican communicants are 'free to attend
the Eucharist in other Churches holding the apostolic faith as contained in
the Scriptures and summarised in the Apostles' and Nicene Creeds'. They
may receive the sacrament, 'as conscience dictates', only 'when they know
they are welcome to do so'.[129] Unlike the first resolution, this would seem
to recognize a right, in the form of a liberty, to approach another church
for the sacrament. The laws of many churches have implemented by adoption the spirit of the Lambeth resolutions; some mirror almost exactly their
terms. In Central Africa, members have no automatic right of admission:
episcopal consent must be obtained. To meet 'special pastoral needs'
bishops may grant general or specific permissions: (1) for priests to admit
to Holy Communion baptized communicant members of approved
churches; and (2) 'for (Anglican) Communicants of the Province to attend
the Eucharist of approved Churches and to receive Holy Communion
when they know that they are welcome to do so'. In Central Africa,
Anglicans may seek the Eucharist in another church only in prescribed circumstances, namely: '[w]hen they are cut off from the ministrations of
their own Church'; in schools, colleges and institutions; '[a]t gatherings
specifically arranged for the promotion of Christian unity, or for a special
project of close Christian co-operation'; and '[i]n family situations and
relationships where members of different Churches would naturally be
drawn to common worship'.[130]

---

[129] LC 1968, Ress. 45, 46.

[130] Central Africa, Res. of the Provincial Synod 1972: 'The Bishop of each Diocese, in
consultation with his Diocesan Synod, may admit to the Holy Communion baptised
and communicant members of other Christian Churches approved by the Bishops of
the Province, provided that such persons are in good standing in their own Churches,
and also any baptised person in danger of death'; Res. 1966–69: the bishop 'shall be
guided by the following considerations': if a person is cut off 'from the regular ministrations of his own church', he may be welcomed on the application of a parish priest
and '[i]f he continues in this position for a considerable length of time, he should be
encouraged to become a full member of the Anglican Church'; in schools, colleges and
institutions a person may be admitted 'on application by the priest to the Bishop, provided that he is a baptised and communicant member of his own Church, in good
standing'; the bishop may permit admission of baptized communicant members of
other churches at gatherings specifically arranged for the promotion of Christian union;
'[t]o meet special pastoral needs of God's people, where a person, being a baptized,
communicant member of his own Church, is married to or is a close relative of a

By way of contrast, English canon law confers a right of direct admission without the additional requirement of episcopal approval: '[t]here shall be admitted to the Holy Communion . . . baptised persons who are communicant members of other Churches which subscribe to the doctrine of the Holy Trinity, and who are in good standing in their own Church'. However, if such a person regularly receives Holy Communion over a long period which appears likely to continue indefinitely, the minister must 'set before him the normal requirements . . . for communicant status'. Where any minister is in doubt as to the application of this provision, the matter must be referred to the bishop and the minister must 'follow his guidance thereon'.[131] A parallel arrangement is to be found in Australian canon law, though here there is no automatic 'right' to admission; the rules deal with 'eligibility' for admission: 'a person who has been baptized in the name of the Holy Trinity and is a communicant member of another church which professes the apostolic faith is eligible to be admitted to the Holy Communion'; the remainder of the canonical provision, which may be adopted by dioceses, is in exactly the same terms as the English canon as a prerequisite to admission.[132] In other churches, the person is required to make affirmations of belief.[133] The English and Australian requirement that the individual must have communicant status in their own church is

regular communicant, such person, on application by the Priest to the Bishop, may be admitted to Communion'; see also Central Africa, Diocese of Mashonaland, *Pastoral Regulations* 1978, 5: baptism in listed churches is recognized by the Episcopal Synod 1973 as valid for the purposes of admission to holy communion; they include: Roman Catholic Church, Orthodox Church, Methodist Churches, Presbyterian Churches, Lutheran Churches, Baptist Church, Church of the Nazarene.

[131] England, Can. B15A.

[132] Australia, Can. 14 1973: where a priest ordinarily responsible for a congregation becomes aware that a person who is 'a customary member of the congregation and is eligible to be admitted', and has received Communion in this church over 'a long period which appears likely to continue indefinitely, the priest shall bring to the notice of the person the ordinary requirements of this Church for persons desiring to be admitted regularly at the Holy Communion and ask him to comply with those requirements'; when a cleric is in doubt as to the application of these provisions 'he may refer the matter to the bishop of the diocese for his guidance thereon'.

[133] West Indies, *Liturgical Texts* 1989, 47: this deals with the admission of baptized communicants of other churches into the communicant membership of the church – the bishop is the minister of this rite: 'When there is a delay the person who desires to be admitted may be allowed to receive Holy Communion before formal admission'; the candidate must: affirm belief in the Trinitarian God and acceptance of the Christian faith as contained in the Apostles' Creed; acknowledge 'the Church of the Province of the West Indies to be a true part of the one, holy, catholic and apostolic church'; accept the ministry of bishops, priests and deacons and the dominical basis of the sacraments of baptism and Holy Communion; the candidate must also promise to be 'a loyal member of the Church . . . accepting its discipline as well as its teaching' and to share faithfully in its 'worship, work and witness'; see also Southern Africa, *Prayer Book* 1989, 399 for the same formula.

not to be found in some other churches: according to the canon law of the church in New Zealand, for example, baptism is the sole requirement. Moreover, Anglicans are free to receive the sacrament in another church, provided they are permitted to under the terms of the discipline of that church.[134] As well as these developments in shared ministry and sacramental life, several churches have also introduced laws allowing the sharing of church property.[135]

CONCLUSIONS

The Anglican Communion is one in which there is no formal universal law applicable to all member churches. Each church is, in legal terms, autonomous. Juridically, relations between churches are rooted in a body of ecclesiastical conventions, expressed in the form of rules and principles; for many the principle of ecclesiastical autonomy itself is treated 'as if' it were a fundamental law of Anglicanism. These conventions are enunciated from time to time by the central institution of the Communion, the Lambeth Conference. This has no competence to function as a legislative synod – its competence is merely to recommend. Its resolutions do not have the force of law in the orthodox sense; to be binding they must be adopted by individual churches and incorporated by them in their own canonical systems. Its resolutions do, however, possess a strong persuasive authority, and on many occasions incorporation has occurred; depending on the language used in them, they may be understood as species of quasi-legislation. The subject of inter-Anglican relations is seldom treated in the laws of particular churches, though there is some

---

[134] New Zealand, Cans. G.IX.1(a), (b): for 'the recovery of unity in faith and order within the whole Church of Christ', '[a]ll Christians duly baptised in the name of the Holy Trinity are welcome to receive the sacrament of Holy Communion in the Anglican Church' in New Zealand; 'Baptised Anglicans are free to attend the Eucharist in other Christian Churches and to receive the Sacrament as conscience dictates when they know they are welcome to do so'; see also Can. G.IX.1(c): 'With the approval of the bishop having appropriate episcopal jurisdiction or oversight', 'an ordained minister of another Christian Church may be invited to preside at the celebration of an ecumenical eucharist in any church or other place of worship'; Melanesia, Standing Res. 1989, 18: if parents belonging to another denomination bring their child for baptism, 'it should be baptised'.

[135] See e.g. Ireland, Const. IX.11: the ordinary may permit a cathedral, a church or chapel to be used by a minister of a Christian denomination (recognized as such by the House of Bishops) for worship by members of that other denomination in accordance with its rites, liturgy and customs; the ordinary must not permit this unless satisfied that: the dean and a majority of the chapter agree, or the incumbent and churchwardens consent; or with a proprietary chapel the trustees consent; this cannot be done if such use is contrary to the terms of a trust; for England and Wales, see the secular Sharing of Church Buildings Act 1969.

evidence to suggest that churches require ministers from fellow churches to officiate in the host church only with episcopal approval. The law of ecumenism, the relations between Anglican and other Christian churches is rather different, and recent years have witnessed, mainly as a result of resolutions of the Lambeth Conference, a distinct increase in the ecumenical laws of individual churches in the Communion. In a small number the law imposes a duty on the church to seek unity. Ecumenical unions, or, short of that, ecumenical concordats and other forms of agreement, are arrangements canonically made at the national, regional or provincial levels enabling communion, the sharing of ministry and sacramental life, between Anglican churches and other Christian churches. Few churches have formal canonical provision for ecumenical relations at the lowest ecclesiastical level of the parish. However, at this level, a growing body of Anglican canon law facilitates the sharing of ministry, under prescribed canonical limits, and the law of most churches expressly provides for the admission of members of other churches by means of reception, though not all formal laws contain arrangements for admission to Holy Communion.

General Conclusions

It is considered axiomatic today that the law in many ways reflects, in a concrete and formal way, ideas which churches have individually and collectively about their own identity, purpose, standards and organization. Consequently, a study of the law, as a repository of ecclesiological ideas, of individual churches in the Anglican Communion affords a unique opportunity to elucidate the nature of the Communion itself and of Anglicanism generally. The introduction to this book opened with two claims by Wayne Hankey: on the one hand, there is a diversity in the canon laws of Anglican churches and strict legal uniformity in the Anglican Communion is neither to be expected nor to be found; on the other hand, there are common legal traditions and patterns and the Communion has a unity in fundamental canon law. This final section draws together some reflections on the evidence – from constitutions, canons, liturgical rubrics, diocesan legislation and (some) decisions of church courts of individual churches – to test and to bear out the broad thrust of Wayne Hankey's hypothesis. Needless to say, in order to come to general conclusions about overall legal unity in the Anglican Communion, it is necessary first to draw particular conclusions about the discrete subject areas of ecclesiastical life: government, ministry, doctrine, liturgy, ritual and property. Indeed, that a proposition of general unity is possible at all is dependent upon whether the treatment of individual subjects is characterized by legal diversity and a lack of uniformity or by common juridical patterns. Similarly, an assertion that there is a fundamental canon law may be made only when agreed criteria are found to give it definition.

Formulating a concept of fundamental canon law is bedevilled by a variety of difficulties. There is, objectively, no material *corpus* of binding Anglican canon law applicable globally to all churches in the Communion – no body in the Communion is currently competent to create it; each church is its own autonomous legislator. Certainly, the canon law of each church, located as it is in concrete sources, is susceptible to workable definition: it is a set of formal rules created by that church to order and to facilitate the various areas of its own public life and mission. In contrast, a fundamental canon law of the Communion is by nature a more abstract and diffuse entity. One obvious approach is to formulate a definition based on the deduction of common principles from the individual laws of member churches. It is in the coincidence of actual particular laws that any fundamental canon law is to be found. However, the deduction of shared principles is of itself, in turn, a difficult task. The higher the level of generality with which a principle is expressed, the greater the likelihood that the principle will lack any practical meaning. Principles must therefore contain a minimal material content which connects with the life and experience of the church. A particular problem relates to the criteria to be used to determine when a principle exists. A global principle exists when there is unanimity as between the laws of churches on a given subject. And very often implementation, in the laws of churches, of a resolution of the Lambeth Conference supplies the unifying principle. The proposition that a principle exists is more problematic, needless to say, when churches do not possess unanimously the same general rule on a particular subject. For practical purposes, however, when a majority of churches share a principle, for many this will justify sufficiently the assertion that such and such is a general principle of Anglican canon law. It is often the case that the majority of churches share a general principle, but the exceptions to it, or the conditions that must be satisfied in its application, vary from church to church. Moreover, in other circumstances, the assertion of a principle must be qualified: that a bare majority of churches, or a specific group of churches, operates this or that principle. Yet, with this majoritarian approach, when only a small number of churches shares a rule, a general principle may not be asserted. All that may be claimed is that a principle operates for a particular group of churches. The silence of law creates a further difficulty: sometimes the principle must be expressed negatively; when laws do not prohibit conduct, for example, an implicit principle of freedom may emerge. Finally, the fact that rules of churches are worded differently does not, of course, mean that there is no shared principle: even when the rules of one group of churches are expressed more narrowly or widely than those of other churches, still there may be a common principle uniting these rules. It is in these diverse senses that principles of Anglican canon law may be constructed.

The first set of unifying principles, in which the fundamental canon law may be found, relates to ecclesiastical government. That members of the Anglican Communion are canonical churches, churches whose public lives (at least in part) are facilitated and ordered by law, is a common fact. Each claims, in formal legal statements, membership of the one, holy, catholic and apostolic church. Churches may not share a common experience in terms of their status and territorial organization – there are regional, national, provincial, united, and extra-provincial diocesan churches – but they are united by a general principle that the final competence to make law for an individual church, whatever its status or territorial organization, rests with a central assembly representative of the bishops, clergy and laity of the church. This is a general principle of Anglican canon law – it is only in the conditions, under which law-making power may be exercised, that diversity is found. At the same time, however, for most churches amendment of the national, regional or provincial constitution is effected by referral of proposed amendments for consultation or consent by the assembly of the diocese. Indeed, that diocesan assemblies are competent to legislate for the diocese may, on an application of the majoritarian approach, be another fundamental constitutional principle of Anglican canon law. Churches are increasingly becoming united in the practice of government by ecclesiastical quasi-legislation, informal administrative rules expressed in the form of 'policies' and 'guidelines'.

A high degree of legal unity is to be found in the institutional organization of churches. It is a general principle of Anglican canon law that government is synodical. Whilst individual churches may be organized on different territorial bases, each province is organized on the basis of dioceses, and each diocese on the basis of smaller ecclesiastical units, by whatever title they may be styled, parishes, incumbencies or pastorates. Each ecclesiastical unit has its own governing assembly representative of both ordained ministers and laity. It is a common experience that the functions of each assembly are prescribed by law, and there is considerable coincidence between rules dealing with the subject-matter jurisdictions of these assemblies. In national, regional and provincial churches, whilst the general direction of ecclesiastical life is moulded by the laws and policies of the central church assembly, administration is carried on by a host of committees, commissions and other bodies. For most, the autonomy of the diocese is protected by laws forbidding interference in diocesan affairs by national, provincial or regional assemblies. Subsidiarity would seem to be an influential principle in the shaping of Anglican constitutional law. Rules about the resolution of ecclesiastical conflict disclose rather more ambiguous evidence in the search for unity. The laws of most churches confer quasi-judicial powers on a wide range of ecclesiastical authorities, principally the archbishops and bishops, but very few churches operate a formal system of hierarchical recourse to challenge administrative action. From the formal law, hierarchical recourse would seem not to be a general principle of Anglican canon law. On the other hand, the ancient institution of visitation is to be found in the laws of the vast majority of churches; in some it is a metropolitical or episcopal duty, in others a right; in few is archidiaconal visitation known to law. Only a small handful of churches have formal laws dealing expressly with the problem of the breakdown of pastoral relations. By way of contrast, all churches are united by similar hierarchical court or tribunal systems. In some these have jurisdiction over both clergy and the laity, but in others this is not the case. A system of ecclesiastical offences is employed in all churches, but generally offences are expressed with a high degree of generality. It is a general principle of Anglican canon law that disciplinary processes must give to the accused rights to be heard, to representation, to silence and to appeal; and in most churches the power to impose sentences is reserved to the bishop. It is not a general principle of Anglican canon law that judicial decisions are creative of binding law; few churches operate a formal system of binding precedent.

A second set of unifying principles is to be found in the laws of ministry. All churches in the Communion assert commitment to the threefold ministry of bishops, priests and deacons. For those churches having them, primates are a focus for unity and leadership, but their jurisdiction over other bishops is limited. The chief episcopal office in a province is that of metropolitan, charged with oversight particularly over inferior episcopal offices. It is a general principle of Anglican canon law that diocesan bishops are elected, and laws provide for the participation of the laity in the electoral process. Churches are united by the common legal tradition that bishops have general oversight of the governing, teaching and liturgical life of the church. As all churches operate elaborate rules regulating retirement and resignation, removal of bishops is a matter for the collective action of the bishops of the individual church. It is a general principle of Anglican canon law that coadjutor, suffragan and other assistant bishops are subordinate to the diocesan bishop. Again, most churches assign a corporate function to synods of bishops – it is in their jurisdiction that rules vary from church to church. The question of suitability of candidates for ordination as deacons and priests resides with the bishop. Diversity exists, however, concerning conditions for eligibility: sometimes the divorced and those in sexually active homophile relationships are barred from consideration. That ordination must be episcopal is a global requirement. Churches are also united in the modes of appointment of clergy to ministerial posts: lay people either participate directly in the process or else they are consulted, but the decision to appoint is generally in the keeping of the bishop. Under Anglican canon law clergy must be authorized by the bishop, most usually by licence, before they may minister in any ecclesiastical unit in the diocese. There is widespread consistency in ministerial functions and it is a general principle of Anglican canon law that clergy owe a duty of canonical obedience to their bishops. The silence of laws in most churches as to the precise grounds for revocation of episcopal licences suggests that arbitrariness is a possible characteristic of Anglican canon law in this area. Discrimination in the membership and government of the church is prohibited by Anglican canon law, though the laws of churches vary as to the precise meaning of membership of individual churches: baptism, at least, is an agreed qualification. The evidence would suggest that it is not possible to construct a general principle of Anglican canon law about the duties and rights of ordinary lay members of the church; formal laws very rarely treat the subject. The laws of churches are united by their silence on this subject. By way of contrast, the laws of churches provide a wide range of offices which are open to qualified lay people: provincial offices, administrative and judicial, are mirrored in the dioceses, and at the lowest ecclesiastical level, laws enable the exercise by the laity of liturgical, pastoral and administrative ministries; the ancient office of churchwarden has been particularly durable in this regard.

The subjects of doctrine and liturgy provide a third fruitful area from which to deduce principles of Anglican canon law. Whilst laws vary concerning structures for evangelism – some have central commissions devoted to it, others do not – a common experience for Anglican churches is that they are not confessional churches whose laws define in detail their beliefs. However, churches are united positively in that their laws agree about the sources of doctrine: scripture, the creeds, the dominical sacraments and, for a large number, the Thirty-Nine Articles. They are united in that the development of doctrine is a matter for the central church assembly, but in several the law expressly forbids the alteration of fundamental church doctrine. Subscription to ecclesiastical doctrine is a shared requirement of canonical systems, particularly as a prerequisite to ordination and to tenure of posts reserved to clergy. It is not a general principle of Anglican canon law that lay persons must subscribe to ecclesiastical doctrine – diversity is supplied only in those churches which exceptionally have rules requiring lay subscription. All churches operate doctrinal offences and in many the resolution of doctrinal controversy is reserved to episcopal assemblies. The concept of common prayer is at the root of the public liturgical life of churches, and most churches adopt legally the spirit of the Book of Common Prayer 1662. The right of formulating liturgical texts belongs to the central church assembly though services may be authorized at lower levels of the church: by metropolitans and by diocesan bishops, but not by individual congregations. It is a general principle of Anglican canon law that services must be consistent with the doctrine of the church. In most churches, however, the concept of uniformity to a single use has been replaced by that of conformity to a multiplicity of authorized liturgies. Churches are united by the concept of flexibility which today would seem to be at the heart of liturgical jurisprudence; the recommendatory rubric is now the norm. Moreover, serious ministerial failures to administer the lawfully approved services of churches is expressly listed amongst the ecclesiastical offences of very few churches.

A fourth subject from which unity or diversity may be tested is that concerning the ritual lives of churches. All churches have rites for the valid celebration of baptism, confirmation, the Holy Communion or Eucharist, and marriage. Diversity arises because not all churches have formal law dealing with admission to or exclusion from these rites. The traditional sequence of baptism, confirmation and Holy Communion is maintained in most churches having law on these subjects. In a small minority, however, both canonical provisions and ecclesiastical quasi-legislation allow for admission of the unconfirmed to Holy Communion. Yet the rules of these churches do not thereby disclose evidence of a fundamental disunity in the Communion. The churches in which such rules exist still adhere to the traditional sequence as the normal pattern – diversity here, then, is found merely in exceptions to a general principle of Anglican canon law. One of the achievements of Anglican canon law is the recognition of rights to baptism, confirmation and Holy Communion. Nevertheless, the enjoyment of these rights is conditional. No minister may refuse baptism – but delay is generally permitted for the purposes of instruction. Equally, it is a general principle of Anglican canon law that the bishop may authorize exclusion of individuals from Holy Communion if this is likely to cause scandal to the church. Diversity is found in relation to the procedures governing exclusion. It is a general principle of Anglican canon law that a Christian marriage is effected by an exchange of consents of two baptized persons who must have been instructed in the essentials of marriage prior to its solemniza-tion. Most churches are also united, therefore, in that lack of baptism, in one or both parties, is a lawful ground for refusal to solemnize marriages. Diversity exists with respect to the relaxation of this rule, usually by epis-copal consent. Whilst as a general principle marriage is characterized by permanence, most churches permit 'remarriage' in church following a civil dissolution – it is the mode by which permission is obtained that produces diversity: permission pursuant to episcopal consent or ministe-rial consultation with the bishop. The use of ecclesiastical declarations of nullity following civil annulment is not extensive. It is a general principle of Anglican canon law that remarried divorced persons are not to be excluded from Holy Communion. Whilst confession is available in most churches, laws are usually silent as to the disclosure of information obtained in confession. That Anglican canon law forbids violation of the seal of the confessional cannot be asserted from the evidence of the for-mal laws of churches – rather, the prohibition is unwritten. Similarly, the absence in most churches of formal rules denying funeral rites to the unbaptized, to suicides and to excommunicates suggests a unity between churches in the form of liberty to administer funeral rites for these classes.

It is with respect to property that the laws of Anglican churches are most complex and detailed. Operative shared principles may be expressed only with a high degree of generality. An overriding principle which emerges from formal laws is that ecclesiastical authorities are stewards of church property. Churches are united in that oversight of property belongs to the central church assembly, but that ownership and management at the lower levels of the church are vested in local ecclesiastical authorities acting as trustees. Church buildings cannot be used for profane purposes and their care and maintenance is the responsibility of the local church with general control being reserved to the bishop. Diversity is found, once again, only in procedural law governing the mode by which oversight is effected. Few churches impose express duties on church members to contribute to the funds of the church, and the concept of the tithe has generally been discarded. However, from the majoritarian perspective it is a general principle of Anglican canon law that parishes and their equivalents must contribute to the funds of the diocese, and that the diocese must contribute to the finances of the province for the purpose, *inter alia*, of funding ministry in the church. Diversity is to be found in the conditions applied to the administration of these common duties to contribute – such as the consequences following non-payment. It would seem to be a principle of Anglican canon law that ordained clergy have a right to financial maintenance and to a pension – arrangements enabling access to these are distributed extensively in actual church laws.

The concept of a fundamental canon law, deduced from actual laws, is perhaps weakest with respect to the relations between the member churches of the Anglican Communion. In this field, the general principles of Anglican canon law are not deduced from coincidence between the actual laws of individual churches. Generally, there are no laws. Instead, these general principles are to be found in global ecclesiastical conventions. Two of the most important of these, needless to say, are the principles of communion and autonomy. So powerful is the conventional principle of the jurisdictional autonomy of each member church that it is treated for practical purposes 'as if' it were law – it may be classed, therefore, as a part of fundamental Anglican canon law. Some shared principles may, however, be deduced from actual laws. Whilst rules require episcopal approval in the host church for the exercise of ordained ministry, the recognition of ministry by female bishops remains problematic as does the recognition of remarriages of divorced persons (for example for the purposes of candidature for ordination). By way of contrast, individual churches are beginning to enact a large and growing body of law governing their relations with other Christian churches. Churches are rapidly becoming united in their incipient ecumenical laws, and in some churches the law imposes a duty to seek unity. Ecumenical unions or, short of these, ecumenical concordats and other forms of agreement enable communion in the form of shared ministry and sacrament. This is certainly the case at national, regional or provincial level, but few churches have laws enabling ecumenical developments at the lowest ecclesiastical levels.

Whilst a fundamental canon law *in abstracto* may be deduced from the coincidences of actual laws of individual churches, Anglican jurisprudence may also be found in the resolutions of the Lambeth Conference. The Conference, like the Anglican Consultative Council, has no legislative competence to create binding laws for churches of the Communion – but its resolutions enjoy a strong persuasive authority and may best be conceived as a form of ecclesiastical quasi-legislation. One of the most striking characteristics of the canonical systems of individual churches in the Communion has been their implementation and incorporation of the terms of Lambeth Conference resolutions. Churches are united legally, therefore, by the common adoption of principles enunciated in resolutions: the requirement of synodical government; of the participation of the laity in ecclesiastical life; the terms of metropolitical jurisdiction; the election of bishops; the requirement of episcopal authorization for ministry; the need to provide offices for the fulfilment of lay ministry; the terms of baptismal, eucharistic and matrimonial discipline; the responsibility upon churches to be financially self-supporting; the obligation to provide clergy pensions; and structures used to shape the emerging ecumenical laws. With each of these instances, the processes of adoption and implementation in the actual laws of individual churches themselves supply a legal unity. In so many ways the resolutions of the Lambeth Conferences contain or express the fundamental canon law of the Communion. In this context, whilst there is ample evidence to show conformity between the laws of churches and the current law of the mother church, the Church of England, further study is required to establish the precise extent of historic continuity between English canon law and the laws of individual churches in the Communion.

Finally, Anglican churches are united on the legal level by virtue of their relations with the states in which they exist. On the one hand, the legal positions of churches are sometimes very different: some are established or quasi-established, others disestablished or non-established. However, a common experience for most is that, under secular law, they exist as voluntary associations bound together by the secular doctrine of consensual compact. Equally, all churches are united by the legal reality, flowing from the wider secular environment in which they live, that their internal government and laws are subject to the laws of the state, with which they must not be in conflict. That state courts exercise a supervisory jurisdiction over church courts is also a shared experience for several churches. Moreover, in many areas, the law of the church follows the law of the state: in representative government, in administrative accountability, in judicial proceedings and the applicability of the principles of natural justice, in validity of marriage, and in trusteeship in the area of church property. It is this rich mine of juridic forms – the substantive and procedural laws of individual churches, the standards set by the laws of states, the agreed global ecclesiastical conventions of communion and autonomy, the jurisprudence expressed in the resolutions of the Lambeth Conference, and the abstract fundamental canon law whose principles are deduced from the coincidence of actual laws – that constitutes canon law in the Anglican Communion.

Bibliography

PRIMARY SOURCES

Australia: *The Anglican Church of Australia: Constitution, Canons and Rules of the General Synod* (1995)
— *An Australian Prayer Book* (1978)
— *A Prayer Book for Australia* (1995)
Brazil: Episcopal Anglican Church of Brazil, *Igreja Episcopal Anglicana do Brasil: Constituciao* (1994)
— *Igreja Episcopal Anglicana do Brasil: Canones Gerais* (1994)
— *Livro de Oracao Comum* (1987)
Burundi: Church of the Province of Burundi, *Constitution* (1991)
Canada: Anglican Church of Canada, *Handbook of the General Synod of the Anglican Church of Canada* (1996)
— *Book of Common Prayer* (1962)
— *The Book of Alternative Services* (1985)
Central Africa: Church of the Province of Central Africa, *Constitution and Canons* (1996)
Chile: Diocese of Chile, Anglican Church of the Southern Cone of America, *Estatutos de la Corporacion Anglicana de Chile* (1995) (this includes the Canons)
Connor (Ireland), Diocese of: *Diocesan Regulations* (1990)
Cork, Cloyne and Ross (Ireland), United Dioceses of: *Rules and Regulations of the Diocesan Synod* (1989)
Dornakal (South India), Diocese of: *Constitutions of Committees under the Diocesan Council* (1977)
Down and Dromore (Ireland), Diocese of: *Diocesan Regulations* (1988)
Egypt (Jerusalem and the Middle East), Diocese of: *Constitution* (1982)
England: Church of England, *Canons of the Church of England* (1964–1997)
— *Book of Common Prayer* (1662)
— *Alternative Service Book* (1980)
Europe (England), Diocese of: *Constitution* (1995)
Gambia and Guinea (West Africa), Diocese of: *Constitution* (1982)
Indian Ocean: Church of the Province of the Indian Ocean, *Constitution and Canons* (1973–1994)
Ireland: *The Constitution of the Church of Ireland* (1988–1996)
— *Book of Common Prayer* (1960)
— *Alternative Prayer Book* (1984)
Japan: Holy Catholic Church in Japan (Nippon Sei Ko Kai), *Constitution and Canons* (1971–1994)
— *The Eucharistic Liturgy* (1971)
Jerusalem: *Constitution of the Central Synod of the Episcopal Church in Jerusalem and the Middle East* (1976–1980)

Kenya: Church of the Province of Kenya, *Constitution* (1979)

Korea: *The Constitution and Canons of the Anglican Church of Korea* (1992)

Lake Malani and Southern Malani (Central Africa), Diocese of: *Diocesan Acts* (1980)

Mashonaland (Central Africa), Diocese of: *Pastoral Regulations* (1978)

Melanesia: Church of the Province of Melanesia, *Constitution and Canons* (1992)

Melbourne (Australia), Diocese of: *An Anglican Pastoral Handbook*, C. Sherlock (ed.) (Canberra, 1988)

Mexico: Anglican Church of Mexico, *Constitucion del Sinodo General de la Iglesia Anglicana de Mexico* (1996)
— *Canones del Sinodo General de la Iglesia Anglicana de Mexico* (1996)

Mississippi (ECUSA), Diocese of: *Constitution and Canons*, in *The Journal of the One Hundred and Sixty-Eighth Annual Council* (1995)

Nandyal (South India), Diocese of: *The Constitution of the Nandyal Diocesan Council* (1990)

New Zealand: Anglican Church in Aotearoa, New Zealand and Polynesia, *Constitution and Code of Canons* (1995)
— *A New Zealand Prayer Book* (1989)

Nigeria: Church of the Province of Nigeria, *Constitution* (1979)
— *The Liturgy of the Church in Nigeria (Anglican Communion): The Order for Holy Communion or the Eucharist* (1983)

North India: United Church of North India, *Constitution and Bye-Laws* (1986)

Papua New Guinea: Anglican Church of (the Province of) Papua New Guinea, *Provincial Constitution and Provincial Canons* (1996)
— *Anglican Prayer Book* (1991)

Philippines: Episcopal Church in the (Province of the) Philippines, *Constitution and Canons* (1996)
— *Social Concerns Resolutions and Statements of the Philippine Episcopal Church: 1962–1988* (1988)
— *Holy Mass for Trial Use* (1987)

Port Moresby (Papua New Guinea), Diocese of: *The Diocesan Constitution and Canons* (1996)

Portugal: Lusitanian Church (Portuguese Episcopal Church), *Igreja Lusitana, Catolica, Apostolica, Evangelica, Canones* (1980)

Puerto Rico: *La Constitucion y Los Canones de La Iglesia Episcopal Puertorriqueña* (1996)

Rupert's Land (Canada), Ecclesiastical Province of: *The Constitution and Canons of the Ecclesiastical Province of Rupert's Land: Anglican Church of Canada* (1994)

Rwanda: Church of the Province of Rwanda, *Draft Constitution* (1996)

Scotland: Scottish Episcopal Church, *Code of Canons* (1996)
— *Digest of Resolutions of General Synod* (1997)

South East Asia: Church of the Province of South East Asia, *Constitution* and *Regulations* (1997)

South India: *The Constitution of the Church of South India* (1992)

Southern Africa: Church of the Province of Southern Africa, *Constitution and Canons* (1994) (this includes *Acts* and *Resolutions* of the Provincial Synod up to 1992)
— *An Anglican Prayer Book* (1989)

Southern Cone: Anglican Church of the Southern Cone of America, *Constitution and Canons* (1981)
— *Libro de Oracion Comun y Manual de la Iglesia Anglicana* (1973)
Spain: Spanish Reformed Episcopal Church, *Bases Fundamentales de Denominacion, Doctrina, Personalidad, Gobienro y Disciplina y Canones Complementarios de las Mismas de la Iglesia Española Reformada Episcopal* (1993)
Sudan: *The Constitution of the Province of the Episcopal Church of the Sudan* (1976: as amended, 1983)
Sydney (Australia), Diocese of: *The 7th Handbook* (1994)
Tanzania: Church of the Province of Tanzania, *Katiba na Kanuni* (1970)
Temotu (Melanesia), Diocese of: *Canons and Standing Resolutions* (1995)
Uganda: Church of the Province of Uganda, *Provincial Constitution* (1972: as amended, 1994)
USA: *Constitutions and Canons for the Government of the Protestant Episcopal Church in the United States of America* (1994)
— *Book of Common Prayer* (1979)
Venezuela: Extra-Provincial Diocese of Venezuela, *Constitucion y Canones de la Iglesia Anglicana en Venezuela* (1995)
Wales: *The Constitution of the Church in Wales* (1920–1997) 2 Volumes
— *The Book of Common Prayer* (1984)
West Africa: Church of the Province of West Africa, *Constitution and Canons* (1989)
West Indies: *Constitution and Canons of the Church of the Province of the West Indies* (1991)
— *Liturgical Texts* (1989)
Western New York (ECUSA), Diocese of: *The Constitution, Canons and Directory*, in *Journal of the One Hundred and Fifty-Eighth Annual Convention* (1995)
Zaire: Church of the Province of Zaire, *Constitution* (1992)

REPORTS AND CONSULTATION DOCUMENTS

All are Called: Toward a Theology of the Laity (London, 1985)
Canon Law in Australia, Report of the Canon Law Commission (Alexandria, NSW, undated but probably c. 1977)
Cure of Souls, Report of a Working Party set up by the Archbishop of Wales (1995)
Dispensation in Practice and Theory with special reference to Anglican Churches (London, 1992)
Episcopal Ministry, Report of the Archbishops' Commission on the Episcopate (London, 1990)
Intercommunion Today, Report of the Archbishops' Commission on Intercommunion (London, 1968)
Issues in Human Sexuality, Statement by the House of Bishops of General Synod of the Church of England (London, 1991)
Senior Church Appointments, Report of the Working Party established by the Standing Committee of the General Synod of the Church of England (London, 1992)

Subscription and Assent to the 39 Articles, A Report of the Archbishops of York and Canterbury Commission on Christian Doctrine (London, 1968)

The Canon Law of the Church of England, Report of the Archbishops' Commission on Canon Law (London, 1947)

The Nature of Christian Belief, Statement and Exposition by the House of Bishops of the General Synod of the Church of England (London, 1986)

Under Authority, the Report of the General Synod Working Party reviewing Clergy Discipline and the working of the Ecclesiastical Courts (London, 1996)

BOOKS AND ARTICLES

Addleshaw, G. W. O., 'The law and constitution of the church overseas', in E. R. Morgan and R. Lloyd (eds.), *The Mission of the Anglican Communion* (London, 1948)

Beaudoin, G-A., and Meades, E. (eds.), *The Canadian Charter of Rights and Freedoms* (3rd edn., Ontario, 1995)

Behrens, J., *Confirmation: Sacrament of Grace* (Leominster, 1995)

Border, R., *Church and State in Australia: 1788–1872* (London, 1962)

Bray, G., *The Historic Anglican Canons* (Woodbridge, 1998)

Briden, T., and Hanson, B. (eds.), *Moore's Introduction to English Canon Law* (3rd edn., London, 1992)

Brodin, E., 'The employment status of ministers of religion', *Industrial Law Journal*, 25 (1996), 211

Burrows, J., 'Judicial review and the Church of England', LL M dissertation, University of Wales (Cardiff, 1997)

Bursell, R. D. H., 'What is the place of custom in English canon law?', *Ecclesiastical Law Journal*, 1(4) (1989), 12

—— 'The seal of the confessional', *Ecclesiastical Law Journal*, 1(7) (1990), 84

—— 'The parson's freehold', *Ecclesiastical Law Journal*, 2(10) (1992), 259

—— *Liturgy, Order and the Law* (Oxford, 1996)

Cameron, G. K., 'The Church in Wales, the canons of 1604 and the doctrine of custom', LL M dissertation, University of Wales (Cardiff, 1997)

Casey, J., 'Church and state in Ireland', in G. Robbers (ed.), *State and Church in the European Union* (Baden-Baden, 1996), 147

Charles, R., 'Church schools and the law', LL M dissertation, University of Wales (Cardiff, 1997)

Clarke, H. L., *Constitutional Church Government in the Dominions beyond the Seas and in other parts of the Anglican Communion* (London, 1924)

Coleman, E. (ed.), *Resolutions of the Twelve Lambeth Conferences 1867–1988* (Toronto, 1992)

Coningsby, T., 'Chancellor, Vicar-General and Official Principal – a bundle of offices', *Ecclesiastical Law Journal*, 2(10) (1990–92), 273

Culver, T. S., 'Canon B16: excommunication in the Church of England', LL M dissertation, University of Wales (Cardiff, 1996)

Cuming, G. J., *A History of Anglican Liturgy* (2nd edn., London, 1982)

Davey, M., 'General Synod of the Church of Ireland: 1995', *Ecclesiastical Law Journal*, 3(17) (1995), 434

Dawley, P. M., *The Episcopal Church and Its Work* (Revised edn., New York, 1961)

Deane, J. L. B., *Church of Ireland Handbook* (Dublin, 1982)

Dix, G., *The Theology of Confirmation in Relation to Baptism* (London, 1946)

Doe, N., *Fundamental Authority in Late Medieval English Law* (Cambridge, 1990)

—— (ed.), *Essays in Canon Law: A Study of the Law of the Church in Wales* (Cardiff, 1992)

—— 'Canonical doctrines of judicial precedent: a comparative study', *Studia Canonica*, 54 (1994), 205

—— 'The use and legality of ecclesiastical quasi-legislation: *imperium* or *dominium*?', unpublished paper, 8 March 1996

—— *The Legal Framework of the Church of England: A Critical Study in a Comparative Context* (Oxford, 1996)

—— 'L'ordination des femmes dans les Eglises Anglicanes du Royaume Uni', *Revue de Droit Canonique*, 46 (1996), 59

Draper, J. (ed.), *Communion and Episcopacy: Essays to Mark the Centenary of the Chicago-Lambeth Quadrilateral* (Oxford, 1988)

Elliott, D. W., 'Blasphemy and other expressions of offensive opinion', *Ecclesiastical Law Journal*, 3(13) (1993), 70

— 'An evidential privilege for priest-penitent communications', *Ecclesiastical Law Journal*, 3(16) (1995), 272

Elton, G. R., *The Tudor Constitution: Documents and Commentary* (2nd edn., Cambridge, 1982)

Ervin, S., *Some Deficiencies in the Canon Law of the American Episcopal Church* (New York, 1951)

—— *An Introduction to Anglican Polity* (Pennsylvania, 1964)

—— *The Polity of the Church of Ireland* (Pennsylvania, 1965)

—— *The Polity of the Church of the Province of South Africa* (Pennsylvania, 1965)

—— *The Political and Ecclesiastical History of the Anglican Church in Canada* (Pennsylvania, 1967)

—— *The Development of the Synodical System in the Anglican Church of Canada* (Pennsylvania, 1969)

Evans, G. R., and Wright, J. R. (eds.), *The Anglican Tradition: A Handbook of Sources* (London, 1991)

Forman, C. W., *The Island Churches of the South Pacific* (New York, 1982)

Garbett, C. F., *Church and State in England* (London, 1950)

Gibbs, M. E., *The Anglican Church in India 1600–1970* (Delhi, 1972)

Gray, G. F. S., *The Anglican Communion* (London, 1958)

Grimes, C. J., *Towards an Indian Church* (London, 1946)

Guild, I., 'Synodical government in the Scottish Episcopal Church', *Ecclesiastical Law Journal*, 4(18) (1996), 493

Gumbley, K. F. W., 'Church legislation in the Isle of Man', *Ecclesiastical Law Journal*, 3(15) (1994), 240

Gunn, T. J., *A Standard for Repair: The Establishment Clause, Equality and Natural Rights* (New York, 1992)

Halsbury, *Laws of England*, Volume 14, *Ecclesiastical Law* (4th edn., London, 1975)

Hankey, W., 'Canon law', in S. W. Sykes and J. Booty (eds.), *The Study of Anglicanism* (London, 1988), 200

Hanks, P. J., *Constitutional Law in Australia* (London, 1991)

Hansen, H. B., *Mission, Church and State in a Colonial Setting: Uganda* (London, 1984)

Hastings, A., *The Church in Africa: 1450–1950* (Oxford, 1994)

Helmholz, R. H., *Roman Canon Law in Reformation England* (Cambridge, 1990)

Helminski, F., A letter concerning the seal of confession in the Episcopal Church in the USA, *Ecclesiastical Law Journal*, 4(20) (1997), 691

Hemmerick, W. J., 'The ordination of women – the Canadian experience', *Ecclesiastical Law Journal*, 2(8) (1991), 177

Hill, M., *Ecclesiastical Law* (London, 1995)

Hinchliff, P., *The South African Liturgy* (Oxford, 1959)

Hoffman, M., *A Treatise on the Law of the Protestant Episcopal Church in the United States* (New York, 1850)

Hogan, G. W., 'Law and religion: church-state relations in Ireland', *American Journal of Comparative Law*, 47 (1987), 35

Holeton, D. R., 'Christian initiation in some Anglican provinces', *Studia Liturgica*, 12 (1977), 129

—— 'Initiation', in S. W. Sykes and J. Booty (eds.), *The Study of Anglicanism* (London, 1988), 261

Iban, I. C., 'State and church in Spain', in G. Robbers (ed.), *State and Church in the European Union* (Baden-Baden, 1996), 93

Ive, A., *The Church of England in South Africa: A Study of Its History, Principles and Status* (Cape Town, 1966)

Jagger, P. J., *Christian Initiation: 1552–1969* (London, 1970)

James, D. G., 'The office of assistant bishop and the canon law of the Church in Wales', LL M dissertation, University of Wales (Cardiff, 1994)

Jasper, R. C. D., *The Development of Anglican Liturgy: 1662–1980* (London, 1989)

Jessep, O., and Luluaki, J., *Principles of Family Law in Papua New Guinea* (PNG, 1994)

Johanson, B., *Church and State in South Africa* (Johannesburg, 1973)

Kemp, E., 'Legal implications of Lambeth', *Ecclesiastical Law Journal*, 1(5) (1989), 15

Leeder, L., *Ecclesiastical Law Handbook* (London, 1997)

Lempriere, P. A., *A Compendium of the Canon Law of the Episcopal Church in Scotland* (Edinburgh, 1903)

Lewis, A., 'The case for constitutional renewal in the Church in Wales', in N. Doe (ed.), *Essays in Canon Law* (Cardiff, 1992), 175

Lewis, E., *Prayer Book Revision in the Church in Wales* (Penarth, 1958)

Luluaki, J. Y., 'When is rape not rape: the marital rape exceptions rule under the Papua New Guinea Criminal Code and related issues', *Melanesian Law Journal*, 22 (1994), 59

Lyon, J. N., 'Privileged communications – penitent and priest', *Criminal Law Quarterly* (Toronto), 7 (1964–5), 327

McGavin, A., 'The distribution of legislative power within the Scottish Episcopal Church', LL M dissertation, University of Wales (Cardiff, 1997)

McHenry, B., 'The General Synod of the Church of Ireland', *Ecclesiastical Law Journal*, 3(14) (1994), 192

Marshall, P. V., *Prayer Book Parallels: Anglican Liturgy in America*, 2 Volumes (New York, 1989)

Martos, J., *Doors to the Sacred* (London, 1981)

Mason, A. J., *The Relation of Confirmation to Baptism* (London, 1891)

Morrell, W. P., *The Anglican Church in New Zealand* (Dunedin, 1973)

Newsom, G. H., and Newsom, G. L., *Faculty Jurisdiction of the Church of England* (2nd edn., London, 1993)

Nokes, D., 'Professional privilege', *Law Quarterly Review*, 66 (1950), 88

Nowlan, K. B., 'Disestablishment: 1800–1869', in M. Harley (ed.), *Irish Anglicanism: 1869–1969* (Dublin, 1970), 1

Nwogugu, E. I., 'The validity of church marriages in Nigeria', *Nigerian Law Journal*, 8 (1974), 142

Ogilvie, M. H., 'What is a church by law established?', *Osgoode Hall Law Journal*, 28 (1990), 179

—— *Religious Institutions and the Law in Canada* (Toronto, 1996)

—— 'Canadian civil court intervention in the exercise of ecclesiastical jurisdiction', *Studia Canonica*, 31 (1997), 49

Omoyajawo, A., *The Anglican Church in Nigeria: 1842–1992* (Lagos, 1994)

Osterbye, P., *The Church in Israel* (Lund, Sweden, 1970)

Owen, J., 'Nullity of marriage in the Church of England and in the Roman Catholic Church', LL M dissertation, University of Wales (Cardiff, 1995)

Phillimore, R., *The Ecclesiastical Law of the Church of England*, 2 Volumes (2nd edn., London, 1895)

Quick, O. C., *The Christian Sacraments* (London, 1927)

Sadurski, W., 'On legal definitions of "religion"', *Australia Law Journal*, 63 (1989), 834

—— (ed.), *Law and Religion* (Aldershot, 1992)

Salter, T. J. E., 'Costume, custom and canon law in the Church of England', LL M dissertation, University of Wales (Cardiff, 1997)

Seervai, H. M., *Constitutional Law of India* (Bombay, 1983)

Simpson, T., 'The sacraments and personal faith', in J. Wilkinson (ed.), *Catholic Anglicans Today* (London, 1969), 113

Smethurst, A. F., Wilson, H. R., and Riley, H. (eds.), *Acts of the Convocations of Canterbury and York* (London, 1961)

Smith, P., 'Points of law and practice concerning ecclesiastical visitation', *Ecclesiastical Law Journal*, 2(9) (1991), 189

Sparkes, P., 'Exclusive burial rights', *Ecclesiastical Law Journal*, 2(8) (1991), 133

Stancliffe, D., 'Baptism and fonts', *Ecclesiastical Law Journal*, 3(14) (1994), 141

Stephenson, A. M. G., *Anglicans and the Lambeth Conferences* (London, 1978)

Stevenson, K., and Spinks, B. (eds.), *The Identity of Anglican Worship* (London, 1991)

Sykes, S. W. (ed.), *Authority in the Anglican Communion: Essays Presented to Bishop John Howe* (Toronto, 1987)

—— 'Episcopacy, communion and collegiality', in J. Draper (ed.), *Communion and Episcopacy* (Oxford, 1988), 35

Sykes, S. W., and Booty, J. (eds.), *The Study of Anglicanism* (London, 1988)

—— *Unashamed Anglicanism* (London, 1995)

Thomas, P., 'A family affair: the pattern of constitutional authority in the Anglican Communion', in S. W. Sykes (ed.), *Authority in the Anglican Communion* (Toronto, 1987), 119

Thompsett, F. H., 'The laity', in S. W. Sykes and J. Booty (eds.), *The Study of Anglicanism* (London, 1988), 245

Tribe, L., *American Constitutional Law* (2nd edn., New York, 1988)

Twumasi, P. K., *Criminal Law in Ghana* (Tema, Ghana, 1985)

Vyver, J. D. van der, 'Religion', in W. A. Joubert and T. J. Scott (eds.), *The Law of South Africa* (Durban/Pretoria, 1986), vol. 23, 175–202

Vyver, J. D. van der, and Witte, J. (eds.), *Religious Human Rights in Global Perspective*, 2 Volumes (The Hague, 1996)

Wand, J. W. C. (ed.), *The Anglican Communion: A Survey* (Oxford, 1948)

Wantland, W., 'The seal of confession and the Episcopal Church in the USA', *Ecclesiastical Law Journal*, 4(19) (1996), 580

Watkin, T. G., 'The vestiges of establishment: the ecclesiastical and canon law of the Church in Wales', *Ecclesiastical Law Journal*, 2(7) (1990), 110

—— 'Disestablishment, self-determination and the constitutional development of the Church in Wales', in N. Doe (ed.), *Essays in Canon Law: A Study of the Law of the Church in Wales* (Cardiff, 1992), 25

—— 'Consensus and the constitution', *Ecclesiastical Law Journal*, 3(15) (1994), 232

White, E. A., *American Church Law* (New York, 1898)

White, E. A., and Dykman, J. A. (ed.), *Annotated Constitution and Canons of the Episcopal Church in the USA* (2nd edn., New York, 1954) (Supplement, 1991)

Zollmann, C., *American Civil Church Law* (Columbia, 1917)

Index

Note that for every mention of a church in the text there is a page reference; footnote references to churches are included only when these carry material from their laws; and, therefore, occasional references to churches in the footnotes are excluded.